Antarctica

a lonely planet travel survival kit

Jeff Rubin

Antarctica

1st edition

Published by
Lonely Planet Publications
Head Office: PO Box 617, Hawthorn, Vic 3122, Australia
Branches: 155 Filbert St, Suite 251, Oakland, CA 94607, USA
10 Barley Mow Passage, Chiswick, London W4 4PH, UK
71 bis rue du Cardinal Lemoine, 75005 Paris, France

Printed by
Colorcraft Ltd, Hong Kong

Photographs by
Wayne Bernhardson, Don McIntyre, Kevin Schafer
K Hanasyde, Mark Norman, Sally Troy
Kieran Jacka, Jeff Rubin, Greg Wiles

British Antarctic Survey representing:
C Duck, P Prince

Hedgehog House representing:
Gourdon Court, Stephan Lundgren
Don Hadden, Colin Monteath
Jim Henderson, Tui de Roy

Front cover: emperor penguins, Galen Rowell
Title page: icebreaker *Kapitan Khlebnikov* near Balleny Islands, Jeff Rubin

Published
November 1996

National Library of Australia Cataloguing in Publication Data

Rubin, Jeff, 1963-.
Antarctica.

1st ed.
Includes index.
ISBN 0 86442 415 9.

1. Antarctica – Description and travel.
I. Title. (Series: Lonely Planet travel survival kit).

919.8904

Jeff Rubin
Born and raised in Michigan, Jeff Rubin has always loved cold climes. After graduation from Kalamazoo College, he moved to Western Australia and worked as a newspaper reporter, general laborer, jackaroo on a cattle station in the Kimberleys and, eventually, Sydney correspondent for Time magazine's Australian edition. He first visited Antarctica in 1987, while writing a story about Australia's Antarctic science program – a trip that stretched to nearly three months when the ship that was to take him home became trapped in pack ice and could not reach Davis station, where Jeff was staying. Since then, he has returned to Antarctica three times. Now a reporter for Time magazine in New York City, Jeff lives in Brooklyn with his wife Stephanie Wiles and their Maine coon cat Max.

STEPHANIE WILES

From the Author
This book is dedicated to the memory of William Edgett Smith, a dear friend who changed my life.

I would like to thank the following people who have been especially helpful to me while writing this book: Peter Boyer; Gary Burns; Robert Burton; Stewart Campbell; Paul Chaplin; John Charles; Fauno Cordes; Paul Dalrymple; Tom Danziger; Phil Doole; David Friscic; Guy Guthridge; Robert Headland; Jennifer Hersh & David Seideman; Bernadette Hince; Mark Hindell; Tomas Hollick; Vina M Hoover; Jo Jacka; Sally Jacka; Andrew Jackson; Nadene Kennedy; Phil Law; Graham Lewis; Eric Leyes; Dr Des Lugg; Tony & Sue Maiden; Rita Mathews; Dr Herbert McCoy; Lani McCoy; Don & Margie McIntyre; Colin McNulty; Nick Mooney; Ray Morris; Ron Naveen; the Neely Family: Jack, Margaret, Laura, Caroline, Elizabeth & Andrew; Baden Norris; Tom O'Connor; John Pickard; Jérôme & Sally Poncet; Quark Expeditions and Denise Landau, Florette Lyew and Lisa Reiss; Ricardo Ramos; Robert 'Rawhide' Reader; Katarina Salen; Darrel Schoeling and IAATO; Patrick Shaw; Brian Shoemaker; Ruth Siple; David & Elizabeth Tomlinson; Gretchen Wesselhoeft; and Michael Whitehead.

I would also like to thank my parents, Howard and Carolyn Rubin, for their continuous support, encouragement and help. Most of all I would like to thank my terrific wife, Stephanie Wiles, for making everything better, easier and a lot more fun.

From the Publisher
Much of the information in the Antarctic Gateways chapter and the Falkland Islands section of the Southern Ocean & Subantarctic Islands chapter was drawn from Lonely Planet's *South Africa, Lesotho & Swaziland – a travel survival kit; New Zealand – a travel survival kit; Tasmania – Australia guide; Chile – a travel survival kit; and Argentina, Uruguay & Paraguay – a travel survival kit.*

This book was produced at Lonely Planet's US office. Tom Downs headed the editorial effort, with help from Carolyn Hubbard, Caroline Liou, Michelle Gagné and Sandra Lopen Barker. Maps were drawn by Chris Salcedo and Alex Guilbert. The book and cover were designed by

Hugh D'Andrade. Illustrations were drawn by Hayden Foell and Rini Keagy, while the watercolors in the Wildlife Guide and the historical portraits were created by Hugh. Scott Summers coordinated production of the book. Thanks to Sally Jacka of Lonely Planet's Melbourne office for her contributions. Thanks also to all those authors and in-house staff who worked on the LP titles that make up the bulk of information in the Antarctic Gateways chapter and the Falkland Islands section.

Warning & Request

Things change - prices go up, schedules change, good places go bad and bad places go bankrupt - nothing stays the same. So, if you find things better or worse, recently opened or long since closed, please tell us and help make the next edition even more accurate and useful.

We value all of the feedback we receive from travelers. Julie Young coordinates a small team who read and acknowledge every letter, postcard and email, and ensure that every morsel of information finds its way to the appropriate authors, editors and publishers. Everyone who writes to us will find their name in the next edition of the appropriate guide and will also receive a free subscription to our quarterly newsletter, *Planet Talk*. The very best contributions will be rewarded with a free Lonely Planet guide.

Excerpts from your correspondence may appear in updates (which we add to the end pages of reprints); new editions of this guide; in our newsletter, *Planet Talk*; or in the Postcards section of our Website – so please let us know if you don't want your letter published or your name acknowledged.

Contents

Map Legend

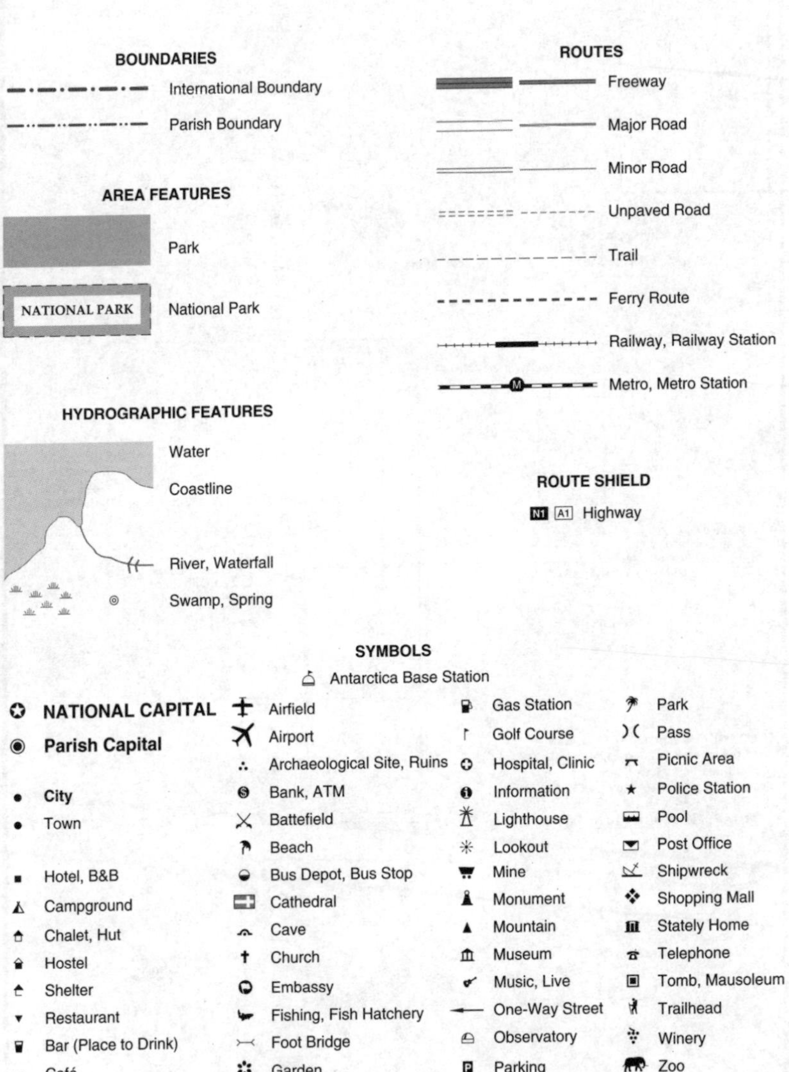

Note: not all symbols displayed above appear in this book.

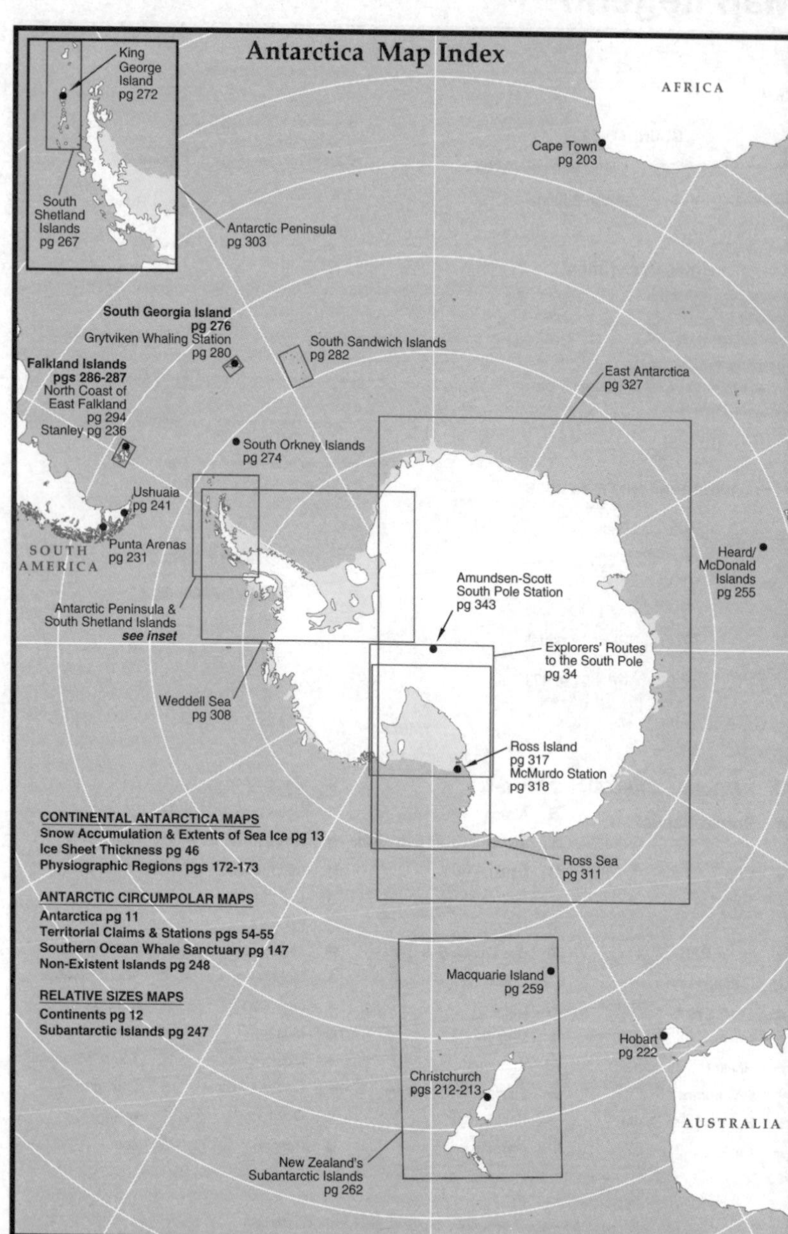
Antarctica Map Index
AFRICA
Cape Town pg 203
King George Island pg 272
South Shetland Islands pg 267
Antarctic Peninsula pg 303
South Georgia Island pg 276
Grytviken Whaling Station pg 280
South Sandwich Islands pg 282
Falkland Islands pgs 286-287
North Coast of East Falkland pg 294
Stanley pg 236
East Antarctica pg 327
South Orkney Islands pg 274
Ushuaia pg 241
Punta Arenas pg 231
SOUTH AMERICA
Heard/ McDonald Islands pg 255
Amundsen-Scott South Pole Station pg 343
Antarctic Peninsula & South Shetland Islands see inset
Explorers' Routes to the South Pole pg 34
Weddell Sea pg 308
Ross Island pg 317
McMurdo Station pg 318
Ross Sea pg 311
CONTINENTAL ANTARCTICA MAPS
Snow Accumulation & Extents of Sea Ice pg 13
Ice Sheet Thickness pg 46
Physiographic Regions pgs 172-173
ANTARCTIC CIRCUMPOLAR MAPS
Antarctica pg 11
Territorial Claims & Stations pgs 54-55
Southern Ocean Whale Sanctuary pg 147
Non-Existent Islands pg 248
RELATIVE SIZES MAPS
Continents pg 12
Subantarctic Islands pg 247
Macquarie Island pg 259
Hobart pg 222
Christchurch pgs 212-213
AUSTRALIA
New Zealand's Subantarctic Islands pg 262

Introduction

Antarctica is one of the most beautiful places on earth. Its gigantic icebergs and ice shelves are found nowhere else on the globe. Its vast mountain ranges and the enormous emptiness of the polar plateau boggle the mind.

Antarctica is still very difficult to reach. The most isolated continent, it must be earned, either through a long, often uncomfortable ship voyage or an expensive airplane flight. Weather and ice – not clocks or calendars – set the schedule, and Antarctic tour companies always emphasize that their itineraries are completely at the mercy of the continent's changing moods.

Little wonder. Antarctica's wind speeds top 320 km/h, its temperatures plunge as low as –89°C, and its average precipitation is comparable to that of the driest deserts. These superlatives merely confirm that Antarctica is a spectacular wilderness, a wilderness of landscapes reduced to a pure haiku of ice, rock, water and sky, filled with wildlife still unafraid of humans.

But Antarctica is a wilderness in a far greater sense than the mere fact that it has no indigenous people and even today remains all but unpopulated. Antarctica is also a wilderness of the mind. Traveling there is like visiting no other country. At times in Antarctica, the activities of the rest of humanity seem utterly insignificant; your ship or camp or research station becomes a world unto itself. Indeed, the personnel handbook issued by one national government funding research in Antarctica talks about 'when you return to the world.'

No one owns Antarctica, and no one ever should. The place is too big to belong to any single nation. The international treaty that governs Antarctica works so unprecedentedly well not merely because it has been carefully crafted by consensus, but also because Antarctica's real value lies in no animal, mineral or vegetable riches that can be extracted from it. The continent's true wealth, the nations of the world appear to agree, lies in the continuation of its unique status as a free, open, unmilitarized land of international cooperation, scientific research and unsullied beauty.

The first tourists to reach the Antarctic continent did not arrive until 1957, when a Pan American flight from Christchurch landed briefly at McMurdo Sound. Its lucky passengers bought the chance to see a tiny portion of the frozen 14.25 million sq km continent that until then had been the sole domain of sealers, whalers, explorers, scientists and soldiers—nearly all of them men. Antarctic tourism only really got underway in 1966 when Lars-Eric Lindblad began offering well-heeled visitors a chance to see The Ice on an annual basis.

Some people come to Antarctica simply to 'bag' their seventh continent, or to check off one more destination on their roster of obscure places. But it is also true that most Antarctic cruises contain a high percentage of repeat visitors. Antarctica, as one tour leader puts it, is 'highly addictive.'

Tourism to Antarctica has increased tremendously during the past decade. The collapse of the Soviet Union has forced cash-strapped research institutes to lease their ships in order to earn hard currency. And as word of mouth has spread news of the continent's beauty, demand has risen steeply. Today, the variety of Antarctic travel itineraries, activities and prices is wider than ever before, making the present the perfect time to head south . . . to the Far South.

Antarctica's growth industry has turned out to be tourism, not mining or oil drilling, as many people once feared. Tourists come to Antarctica to experience a clean white continent unlike any other. Provided that their visits are properly managed, these tourists just might, paradoxically, turn out to be one of the best assurances that this vast wilderness remains (nearly) as pure as the driven snow. Let us hope!

Facts about Antarctica

FORMATION OF THE CONTINENT

Around 200 million years ago, Antarctica was joined with Australia, Africa, South America, India and New Zealand in the supercontinent Gondwanaland. Ten million years later, Gondwanaland began the enormously slow process of breaking into the pieces we recognize today, and the continents, subcontinent and islands began moving into their present positions. By about 70 million years ago, the continents were becoming widely separated, the Drake Passage opened, and Antarctica made its final detachment from another continent. By about 45 million years ago, Antarctica had settled into its present polar position and began to cool dramatically.

German naturalist Alexander von Humboldt, noticing the shapes of the continents bordering the Atlantic, was the first to suggest (c1800) that they might once have been joined. In 1851, British botanist Joseph Hooker wrote to Charles Darwin about similarities he noticed among plants in New Zealand, Tasmania, Iles Kerguelen and the Falkland Islands. At about the same time, French geologist Antonio Snider-Pellegrini, noticing identical fossil remains in both Europe and North America, theorized that the continents must have been joined. He, too, fit two pieces of the supercontinent puzzle together, proposing the childishly simple idea that Africa's west coast once abutted South America's east coast.

Austrian Eduard Suess, in 1885, was the first to propose that there had been a southern supercontinent. Suess gave it the name Gondwanaland, derived from Gondwana, the historic region in central India (occupied by the Gond people) where fossil strata similar to that of other widely removed continents – and thus supporting the supercontinent theory – was found. In 1908 American Frank Taylor suggested that mountain ranges had been formed by the collision of drifting continents.

German Alfred Wegener came up with the first fully articulated theory of continental drift in 1912, which envisioned a supercontinent he called Pangaea ('all lands'). For his hypothesis, Wegener quickly received the combined scorn of the world scientific community. Mainly this was because no one could conceive of continents being able to move, and the idea of the oceans receding or land-bridges vanishing seemed equally implausible.

Later scientists – mainly working in the Southern Hemisphere – followed Wegener's work, and in 1937 South African geologist Alexander Du Toit refined the idea of Pangaea to include two continents, Gondwanaland (sometimes called Gondwana) to the south, and another called Laurasia to the north. Australian geologist S Warren Carey found evidence that the fit between the continents was even better along the offshore continental shelves, but he believed that was explained by an expanding-Earth model, in which the planet's diameter was slowly increasing.

In the 1950s and '60s exploration of the sea floor provided new data and new ideas, leading to the theory of plate tectonics. Geologist HH Hess postulated that the sea floors are spreading away from the mid-ocean ridges, thus providing the mechanism to drift the continental land masses as Wegener's theory and geologic data had suggested.

Among the fossil evidence found in Antarctica that clearly supports the supercontinent theory is a deciduous conifer *Glossopteris*, a fern *Dicroidium* and a terrestrial reptile *Lystrosaurus*. All of these species lived on Gondwanaland and their fossil remains have been found in rocks of the same age in such widely separated locales as India, South America, Australia, Africa and Antarctica. Because

AFRICA
Cape Town
ATLANTIC OCEAN
Tristan da Cunha Group
Gough Island
Prime Meridian
0° 00'
30° 00' S
40° 00' S
50° 00' S
60° 00' S
70° 00' S
30° 00' W
Bouvetøya
Prince Edward Islands
South Georgia Island
South Sandwich Islands
Shag Rocks
SOUTHERN OCEAN
Antarctic Circle
Iles Crozet
60° 00' E
Stanley
Falkland Islands
South Orkney Islands
Iles Kerguelen
Ushuaia
South Shetland Islands
Punta Arenas
Weddell Sea
Mc Donald Islands
Heard Island
Ile Amsterdam
Ile Saint-Paul
SOUTH AMERICA
ANTARCTICA
South Pole
East Antarctica
West Antarctica
90° 00' W
90° 00' E
Peter I Øy
SOUTHERN OCEAN
INDIAN OCEAN
Ross Sea
120° 00' W
120° 00' E
Scott Island
Balleny Islands
Approximate Position of the Antarctic Convergence
60° 00' S
Macquarie Island
Campbell Islands
Auckland Islands
Tasmania
Hobart
Antipodes Islands
Snares Islands
Stewart Island
Bounty Islands
Chatham Islands
Christchurch
AUSTRALIA
New Zealand
PACIFIC OCEAN
150° 00' W
180° 00'
30° 00' S
150° 00' E

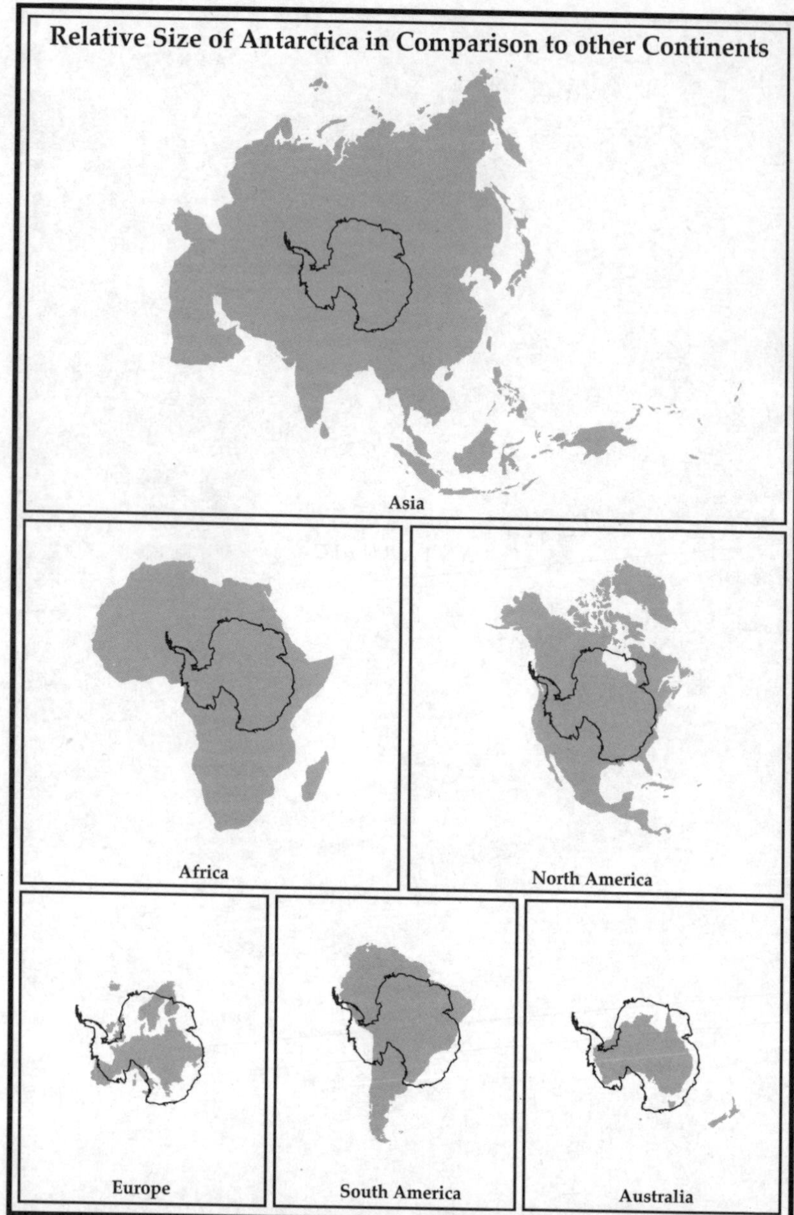
Relative Size of Antarctica in Comparison to other Continents
Asia
Africa
North America
Europe
South America
Australia

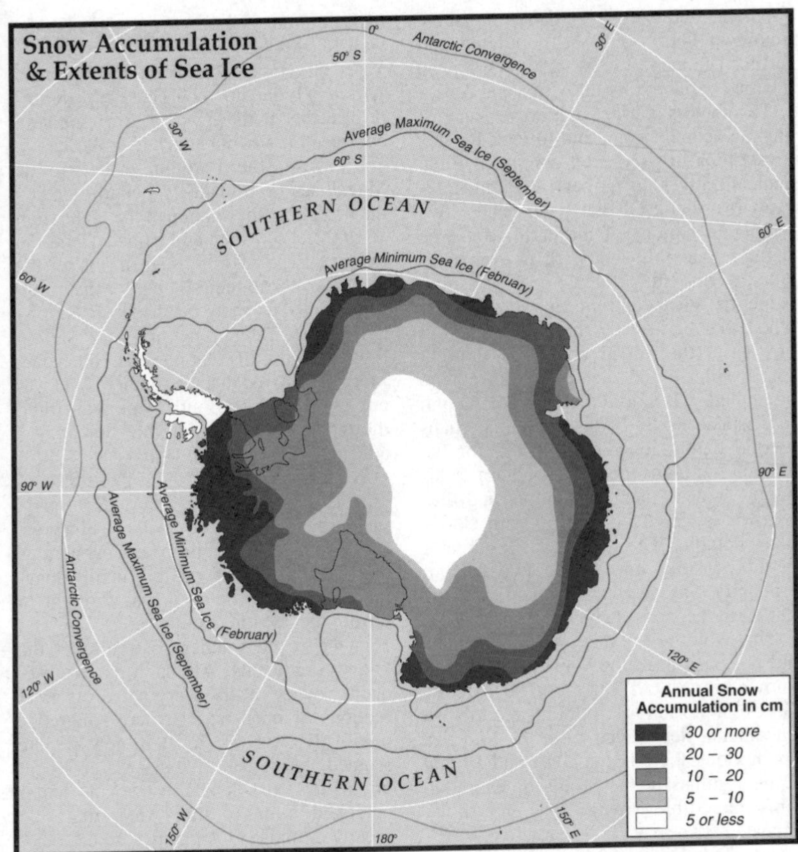

Glossopteris' seeds and *Dicroidium*'s spores could not have been blown – and *Lystrosaurus* could not have swum – across the oceans that separate these continents, their fossilized remains offer certain proof that the continents were once united.

HISTORY & EXPLORATION

Ancient History

Antarctica, unlike any of the other continents, was postulated to exist long before it was discovered, The ancient Greeks, beginning with Pythagoras in about 530 BC, believed the earth to be round, an idea Aristotle supported and refined further, suggesting that the symmetry of a sphere demanded that the earth's inhabited northern region should be balanced by an equally inhabited – or, at the very least, inhabitable – southern region. Indeed, without it, the top-heavy globe might tumble over. This idea of earthly balance gave rise to the name we give the southern continent today, Antarktos, or 'opposite Arktos,' the constellation in the northern sky. The Egyptian Ptolemy agreed that geographical equilibrium required an unknown southern continent, but he believed that the unknown land would be populated and fertile. The map he drew c150 AD showed a large continent linking Africa and Asia.

Two factors conspired, however, against anyone actually going out to look for this mysterious undiscovered continent. First, ancient thinkers as far back as Parmenides (460 BC) believed that between the two temperate regions of the earth would be found a zone of fire and perhaps even monsters. This may have been wisdom somehow gleaned from an early traveler who had experienced a tropical summer. In any case, this torrid zone was thought impassable – and deadly to those who attempted it. If mortal fear was not enough to dissuade would-be discoverers, perhaps eternal damnation did the trick, for the Church found the idea of a southern continent – with its own population, and thus its own separate relationship with God – unacceptable. The idea that the Creator could possibly have made two sets of humanity was deemed heretical, and the flat-earth theory was given full backing.

That is not to say that intrepid voyagers did not push back the boundaries of their known worlds. As early as 700 BC, the Greek historian Herodotus records, a Phoenician fleet sailed from the Red Sea south along the African coast and around Cape Agulhas to the Straits of Gibraltar. This incredible voyage was not to be repeated for nearly 2000 years. In 650 AD, according to Rarotongan legend, a Polynesian navigator named Ui-te-Rangiora sailed so far south that he reached a place where the sea was frozen. These voyages were neither repeated nor widely known, however, and it was not until late in the 15th century that further progress was made on the question of Antarctica.

The Explorers

The Portuguese made the first important penetrations south, beginning with a naval voyage in 1487-88 led by Bartholomeu Días de Novaes and João Infante, who sailed around the southern tip of Africa, Cape Agulhas, as far as present-day Mozambique. Their voyage opened the way to another naval expedition, led by Vasco da Gama, to discover the way around Africa to India, in 1497. These expeditions proved that if there was a great southern continent, it was not attached to Africa.

Likewise, the Portuguese Fernão de Magalhães (Ferdinand Magellan), leading the first circumnavigation of the globe from 1519-22, discovered and named Tierra del Fuego ('Land of Fire,' named not for the ancients' 'torrid regions,' but for the campfires spotted on shore that had been built by the native Yahgan people). By sailing through the straits that now bear his name, Magellan proved that the southern land was not connected to South America either, though it remained possible that it was attached to Tierra del Fuego.

What is remarkable about these discoveries is that their makers were *disproving*, rather than proving, the existence of a great southern land. Antarctica was a mysterious place whose extent was originally imagined to be enormous: it was thought to cover the whole Southern Ocean and connect to the southern extremes of the known continents. Although each subsequent voyage of discovery pared off great sections of open ocean where Antarctica obviously was *not* located, few people seemed able to conceive that the continent might not exist at all; instead the belief persisted strongly that Antarctica – a greatly diminished Antarctica, to be sure – must lie just a little further south. But the Southern Ocean's terrifying storms and impenetrable pack ice conspired to keep the continent's white face shrouded from inquiring eyes for centuries more.

Terra Australis – the term was first used by Flemish mapmaker Oronce Finé in 1531 – continued to exert its southerly attraction, however. Englishman Francis Drake, sailing in *Pelican* (later named *Golden Hind)*, made the second circumnavigation of the globe from 1577-80. Drake discovered the passage that now is named for him, definitively proving that no great southern continent was contiguous with either South America or Tierra del

Fuego. As the subantarctic and Southern Ocean archipelagoes were found in succession – the Falklands, the South Sandwich Islands, South Georgia, Bouvetøya, Iles Kerguelen – some were initially thought to be northerly projections of *Terra Australis*, but each eventually proved merely insular. Dutchman Abel Janszoon Tasman's voyages charting parts of Tasmania and New Zealand in 1623-25 and again in 1644 also sparked hope, at first, that they might be part of the great missing continent, but these hopes too soon died away.

Cook Yorkshireman James Cook (1728-1779), once apprenticed to a shopkeeper, was the widest-ranging explorer who ever lived. He circumnavigated the globe three times and discovered more territory than any human in history. At the age of 40, he undertook the first of his three great voyages of discovery, and between 1768 and 1771, he found New Zealand and the whole east coast of Australia, claiming them for Britain; on his third voyage, from 1776 to 1779, he explored the Arctic coasts of North America and Siberia before being killed by natives in Hawaii in 1779. Not the least of Cook's accomplishments was his virtual defeat of the dreaded disease scurvy among his crews, thanks to such provisions as sauerkraut, salted cabbage and 'Mermalade of Carrots.'

Cook's Antarctic discoveries came on his second voyage, beginning in 1772, aboard HMS *Resolution* and HMS *Adventure*. Like HMS *Endeavour*, Cook's previous ship, these vessels were colliers from the north country of England. Part of Cook's genius lay in persuading the Royal Navy of the value of these ships that he had come to know in his earliest seagoing days as a deckhand on the coal run from Yorkshire to London: he knew that these shallow-drafted barques could explore close inshore without risk of running aground. With them on his second voyage, he sailed 109,500 km and penetrated further south than anyone before. He crossed the Antarctic Circle on January 17, 1773, becoming the first person to do so, and crossed it twice again without ever sighting land, despite pushing to a record 71°10'S. On his third pass through the pack ice, Cook landed on South Georgia, which he called the Isle of Georgia, and discovered the South Sandwich Islands.

Despite his remarkable first circumnavigation of Antarctica – which he did without losing a single man – Cook failed to find the southern continent itself. It's almost more remarkable that he *didn't* find Antarctica, given that he made it so much further south than anyone before him, but Cook simply had poor luck: In the longitudes where he managed to penetrate furthest south, the coast of Antarctica itself also swerved southwards. 'The disappointment I now met with,' Cook wrote upon leaving the frozen southern seas for the last time,

Capt James Cook circumnavigated Antarctica but failed to sight land

'did not affect me much; for to judge of the bulk by the sample it [the continent] would not be worth the discovery.' If there were any remaining doubt how he felt about the prospects of a still-undiscovered Antarctica, Cook later underscored this opinion: 'Should anyone possess the resolution and fortitude to elucidate this point by pushing yet further south than I have done, I shall not envy him the fame of his discovery, but I make bold to declare that the world will derive no benefit from it.'

So convincing were those pessimistic sentiments recorded in his journal that Cook discouraged other explorers from seeking the great southern continent for decades after him. But he also recorded his observations of large numbers of seals and whales in the southern waters – and others, more commercially minded than the Royal Navy – had taken notice.

The sealers, motivated not by discovery but by profit, came from Britain, the Cape Colony (now part of South Africa), France, New South Wales (in present-day Australia), New Zealand, Tasmania and the United States. These voyages far outnumbered expeditions that can be called strictly scientific – there were about 44 times as many sealing voyages made – and nearly a third of the subantarctic and Southern Ocean islands were discovered by sealers. But they considered their discoveries proprietary information, and kept them to themselves as much as possible (though drunken sailors in harborside taverns were not always able to restrain themselves from boasting about new-found sealing grounds). So it remained for kings and czars and governments to send out expeditions to explore and chart new territory, in hopes of extending their sovereignty over ever-greater empires.

Bellingshausen Russian Fabian von Bellingshausen (1778-1852), a captain in the Imperial Navy, led the first Russian circumnavigation of the globe in 1803-06. In 1819, Czar Alexander I called Bellingshausen to St Petersburg and dispatched him on a voyage of discovery into the Southern Ocean, a dream assignment for Bellingshausen, who had long admired Cook's voyages. With his flagship *Vostok* ('East'), a newly launched corvette with copper-sheathed hulls, and the older, sluggish *Mirnyy* ('Peaceful'), which constantly slowed the expedition, Bellingshausen sailed from Kronstadt, an island off St Petersburg, in July 1819. Unique to his expedition was the shipboard sauna he constructed as a hygienic measure for his men and their clothing; heated cannonballs inside a tent on deck supplied the healthful steam for bathing and washing.

They crossed the Antarctic Circle on January 26, 1820, and the next day, Bellingshausen became the first person to sight the Antarctic continent. Through a heavy curtain of falling snow, at the position of 69°21'S, 2°14'W, he saw 'an icefield covered with small hillocks.' The trouble was, he did not realize the importance of his discovery; he merely noted the weather conditions and his position in the ship's log before continuing on. The two ships sailed further east, pushing further south than anyone had previously done. Eventually they tacked north to escape the encroaching winter, spending four months in the South Pacific. Turning south once more, they crossed the Circle six more times, eventually probing as far south as 69°53'S, where they discovered Peter I Øy, the southernmost land known at that time. They also found a second piece of ice-free land below the Circle, which Bellingshausen called Alexander Coast after the czar. It is now known to be an island joined to the Antarctic Peninsula by an ice shelf.

Returning north through the South Shetland Islands, Bellingshausen met American sealing captain Nathaniel Brown Palmer, in the sloop *Hero*, who claimed to know well the coast that Bellingshausen had just explored. A legend created by Palmer's biographer, sealing captain Edmund Fanning, claims that Bellingshausen was so impressed by Palmer's claims of knowledge that he named the new territory after Palmer, but the meticulous Bellingshausen never noted this alleged act in his diaries or charts, and the story appears now to be a fantasy.

Despite Bellingshausen's discoveries – and his duplication of his hero Cook's circumnavigation of Antarctica – he returned to Russia only to find that the reaction to his voyage was massively underwhelming. It took nearly 120 years and the start of the Cold War before his accomplishments were fully appreciated – by a Soviet Union newly anxious to assert its right to authority in the Antarctic.

Weddell Scotsman James Weddell (1787-1834), the son of an upholsterer who became a Master in the Royal Navy, rejoined the merchant service in 1819 and took command of the brig *Jane* on a sealing expedition to the recently discovered South Shetlands. Although the voyage was a financial failure, he independently discovered the South Orkney Islands, which had just been sighted by American sealer Nathaniel Brown Palmer and British sealer George Powell, who were working together. In 1822, Weddell persuaded *Jane*'s owners to send him on another voyage, and this time accompanied by the cutter *Beaufoy*, he sailed again from England in September. It was a hard passage for both ships, small and fragile in the huge rollers of the Southern Ocean. The sailors' unenviable jobs were made somewhat more bearable by their daily ration of rum: three wine-glassesfull per day.

By the end of January 1823, the two vessels had reached the eastern end of the South Orkney chain, and a landing was made at Saddle Island. Weddell himself went ashore and the skins of six members of a new species of seal were collected; today this animal is known as the Weddell seal. But by early February, Weddell had given up on finding a harvestable population of fur seals, so he changed course, heading south once more, into a sea normally covered in impenetrable ice as far north as 60°S.

Constant gales soaked the crew, but on February 16, when the 70th parallel was reached, the weather took a remarkable turn for the better. The breeze backed to the northeast and *Jane* and *Beaufoy* began a fine run south. Well aware of the remarkable conditions he was encountering, Weddell made the following notation in capital letters in his log on February 18: 'NOT A PARTICLE OF ICE OF ANY DESCRIPTION WAS TO BE SEEN.'

By February 20, they had reached an amazing 74°15'S – a new southing record, 344 km further south than Cook. Weddell, however, was worried. The season was getting on, and despite the open water that lay ahead to the south, he ordered a retreat. But first, a gun was fired in celebration and the sea named to honor the sovereign, King George IV (the name was changed in the next century to honor Weddell's discovery). The ships' crews, disconsolate at not pursuing further progress, were no doubt cheered by the extra ration of rum allotted to them.

Dumont d'Urville Long before Frenchman Jules-Sébastien-César Dumont d'Urville (1790-1842) sailed for Antarctica, he had earned a footnote in history for himself. In 1820, while doing a survey of the Eastern Mediterranean, d'Urville heard about a remarkable statue that had recently been excavated on the island of Milos. Struck by its rare beauty, he urged the French government to buy the statue, something it agreed to do 'whatever it might cost.' Today, that purchase – the Venus de Milo – stands in the Louvre in Paris.

Already a veteran of two circumnavigations of the globe (and fluent in English, German, Greek, Hebrew, Italian and Spanish), d'Urville sailed from Toulon in 1838 with *Astrolabe* and *Zélée*, which, like Bellingshausen's ships, were clad in copper for protection from the ice. Though d'Urville hoped to reach the South Magnetic Pole – magnetism was then one of science's hottest riddles – his orders from King Louis Philippe were simply to proceed as far south in the Weddell Sea as possible. Indeed, the men were promised a bonus of 100 gold francs if they reached 75°S and another 20 francs for each

Earliest Antarctic Landings

Antarctica's definite – rather than speculative – history is very short, and there is confusion in some accounts regarding the details of the continent's first sighting, earliest landing and first wintering.

The earliest crossing of the Antarctic Circle was made during the circumnavigation of the continent by Capt James Cook on January 17, 1773, but Cook saw no land. There are uncorroborated reports of early sightings, but these are very doubtful. It is far more likely that a dirty iceberg was observed during poor weather and reported as land. The first corroborated sighting was made by a Russian expedition led by Fabian Bellingshausen aboard *Vostok* (East) accompanied by Mikhail Lazarev aboard *Mirnyy* (Peace). This expedition circumnavigated in high southern latitudes and extended some of Capt Cook's work. On January 27, 1820, two coastal areas in Kronprinsesse Martha Kyst and Prinsesse Ragnhild Kyst were mapped at about 69°35'S, 02°23'W. These were parts of the ice shelf and, although not reported then as such, they were the first part of the mainland to be seen as well as the first land south of the Antarctic Circle confirmed. Three days later, Edward Bransfield discovered Trinity Peninsula, and many US and British sealers working from the newly discovered South Shetland Islands saw, and some mapped, this part of the continent.

The South Shetland Islands were discovered in February 1819 and a large number of sealers exploited it from the following austral summer. This began what was, in effect, a three year 'gold rush' which ended with the seals near to extinction. There is evidence that during the 1820-21 austral summer, two sealing masters working from the islands independently landed on the Antarctic Peninsula – thus becoming the first on the continent. These were John Davis, aboard *Cecilia* from Nantucket, on February 7, 1821, and John McFarlane, aboard *Dragon* from London, at an unknown date in that season. Few details are known of these landings because no fur seals were found, thus they were of little interest to those involved. These are the only recorded landings (their order

additional degree gained toward the Pole. But the ice in the Weddell Sea extended much further north – indeed this was its normal configuration – and much to his frustration, d'Urville was unable to penetrate to anywhere near the point that Weddell did. At the end of February, they discovered (or rediscovered, since sealers had probably already landed there) Louis Philippe Land and Joinville Island at the northern tip of the Antarctic Peninsula. By this time, scurvy plagued his ships, and on the return to Tierra del Fuego, one of the sailors died of the dread disease.

After a year spent making ethnological voyages in the Pacific, during which 23 men died of an outbreak of dysentery and fever, d'Urville headed south again in January 1840. On the 19th, they spotted what they felt certain was land, confirmed the next day by a clearer sighting. Unable to go ashore because of the massive ice cliffs, they sailed west before coming upon a group of islets just a few hundred meters offshore. A group was landed, a few chips of granite hacked off as proof that they had found *terra firma*, and the discovery claimed in the name of France. An officer who had anticipated success brought forth a bottle of Bordeaux and a toast was raised to the King.

Alone among the early explorers, d'Urville honored his wife by naming the new-found territory for her. Terre Adélie was dedicated to 'the devoted companion who has three times consented to a painful separation in order to allow me to accomplish my plans for distant exploration.' Heading east in search of the Magnetic Pole, d'Urville's lookouts were astonished one afternoon to see emerge from the fog an American man-of-war, running before

is equivocal) from more than 60 sealing vessels from Britain and the United States which worked at the South Shetland Islands and searched the region for seals during that season. Just two more continental landings by sealers are known during the rest of the century, one on the Antarctic Peninsula and the other in the vicinity of Cape Adare. It is likely that several other landings were made, but because of the absence of seals they were regarded with little interest and weren't recorded. During the sealing period, about 1780 to 1892, over 1100 sealing ships visited Antarctic regions, compared to barely 25 exploratory vessels – thus discoveries, especially of the islands, were inevitable.

An oft-quoted, but spurious, claim to a first Antarctic landing dates from 1895. A Norwegian sealing and whaling exploration, led by Henryk Bull, aboard *Antarctic* commanded by Leonard Kristensen, reached Cape Adare and landed on January 24. The assistant biologist, Carsten Borchgrevink, claimed to have been the first ashore and thus to be the 'first on the Antarctic continent.' The Captain also claimed to have been first and thus to be 'the first man who ever put foot on South Victoria Land.' Alexander Tunzleman (a boy recruited in Stewart Island) may, however, have preceded both: he claimed to have got off first to steady the boat for the captain to disembark. The expedition leader, Henryk Bull, indicated no precedence stating only 'The sensation of being the first men who had set foot on the real Antarctic mainland was both strange and pleasurable . . . ' They dispute an empty claim – for there had been at least five earlier landings by sealers. In their defense, however, earlier landings may not have been known to them.

Borchgrevink has, however, a firm claim to fame as the leader of the first expedition to winter on Antarctica, in 1899. Traveling aboard *Southern Cross*, this expedition landed on Ridley Beach near Cape Adare and built two huts which still stand today. ■

–**Robert Headland**, archivist and curator at the Scott Polar Research Institute in Cambridge, England

the wind straight towards them. The ship was *Porpoise*, part of Charles Wilkes' United States Exploring Expedition, but thanks to a misunderstanding, the two ships did not stop to exchange communication. Each side later blamed the other for raising sail and blowing past. Returning to France to great acclaim after a 38-month voyage, d'Urville and his men were rewarded by the French government with 15,000 francs to be divided by the expedition's 130 surviving members.

Smith & Bransfield Though once credited with being first to sight Antarctica, it is now agreed that Edward Bransfield (c1795-1852) had been beaten by Bellingshausen to that honor by three days.

After English merchant captain William Smith announced his discovery of the South Shetlands in 1819, the Royal Navy chartered Smith's ship *Williams* to undertake a survey of the islands. Bransfield was put in command, with Smith as pilot, and they sailed south from Valparaiso, Chile. Two months were spent charting the coastlines of what they called New South Britain; a landing was made at George Bay on King George I to claim the group for – surprise – George IV, the British sovereign.

Continuing south, Bransfield sighted the Antarctic Peninsula on January 30, 1820, calling it Trinity Land. One of his midshipman, quoted in the *Literary Gazette and Journal of Belle Lettres*, called it 'a prospect the most gloomy that can be imagined . . . the only cheer the sight afforded was in the idea that this might be the long-sought Southern Continent.' They charted the islands along it for another 20 days before being stopped by the Weddell Sea pack ice and turning north.

Palmer American sealer Nathaniel Brown Palmer (1799-1877), the son of a shipyard owner, left his home of Stonington, CT, at the age of 14 to go to sea. On his second sealing voyage to the South Shetlands in 1820, commanding the sloop *Hero*, Palmer sailed south with a small fleet of other sealers. Upon arrival in the South Shetlands, the need for a more secure anchorage for the five ships drove Palmer to push south ahead of the others. He dropped anchor inside the caldera of Deception Island, and on November 16, from a high lookout there, he caught sight of Trinity Island to the southeast and probably the Antarctic Peninsula beyond. The next day, Palmer sailed to investigate, but due to heavy ice thought it imprudent to try to land. In later years, Palmer claimed that he had found the Antarctic continent, calling his discovery Palmer Land. But even if he did spot Antarctica on that occasion, his sighting came ten months after Bellingshausen's (January 27) and Bransfield's (January 30) in that same year.

Nevertheless, Palmer has a clear Antarctic discovery to his credit: a year later, while commanding the sloop *James Monroe*, Palmer was searching for seals in the South Shetlands with a British captain, George Powell of *Dove*. Finding no seals, they steered east, and on December 7, 1821, they discovered a large island of a new group, the South Orkneys. Finding no seals, Palmer had no further interest in the island, but Powell went ashore and claimed it for the British crown, calling it Coronation Island.

Biscoe Another Briton, John Biscoe (1794-1843), joined the Royal Navy at 18 and fought in the 1812 war against the United States. Dispatched by the London firm of Enderby Brothers in July 1830, he made only the third circumnavigation of Antarctica, sailing in the brig *Tula*, accompanied by George Avery in the cutter *Lively*. The ships sighted what they called Enderby Land on February 24, 1831, and confirmed the discovery three days later, the first sighting of the Antarctic continent in the Indian Ocean sector. Biscoe also experienced a personal revelation at the same time, and like all who see it, was struck by the ethereal beauty of the aurora australis, which, he recorded in the ship's log, 'at times [appeared] not many yards above us.' Oncoming winter forced the ships to head north to Hobart, but scurvy so ravaged *Tula's* crew that only Biscoe, three men and a boy were able to work. Aboard *Lively*, which had become separated from *Tula*, all but three of the crew died of scurvy or other diseases.

Sailing again with both ships in October 1831, on what after all was supposed to be a commercial voyage, Biscoe spent three months searching for whales or seals off New Zealand. Finding none, he headed south once more, and discovered Adelaide Island (which he named for the consort of King William IV) on February 16, 1832. Biscoe discovered land again (now thought to be present-day Anvers Island) on February 21, and claimed the territory for King William IV. Still seeking seals or some other valuable cargo to bring home, he was forced to sail for England after *Tula* damaged her rudder. (En route home, *Lively* was wrecked in the Falklands.) Although he returned to London in January 1833 with empty holds and one ship missing, Biscoe was fortunate to have extremely open-minded bosses, and instead of being reprimanded or fired, he received the highest award of the newly-established Royal Geographical Society.

After Biscoe's return, the stretch of coast he discovered was named Graham Land, for James RG Graham, First Lord of the Admiralty. Although this was in fact a southern portion of the Antarctic Peninsula, which had already been sighted by Bransfield, Smith and Palmer, the name eventually came to be applied to the entire Antarctic Peninsula on British maps, while the name Palmer Land was used by American chartmakers. (This difference continued until 1964, when the US and the UK agreed to use the name Antarctic Peninsula for the entire northward-reaching extension of the Antarctic continent, with the northern part to be called Graham Land and the southern, Palmer Land.)

The British discoveries in the Antarctic Peninsula region had not escaped the attention of the US government, however, and after nearly a decade of being urged to do so, the US Congress voted to send men and ships south to explore the region.

Wilkes By the time American Lt Charles Wilkes (1798-1877) was offered command of the United States Exploring Expedition in 1838, the position had already been declined by a number of senior officers. Perhaps these men knew something that Wilkes didn't, for this inauspicious beginning foretold great hardship for the expedition. In the words of polar historian Laurence P Kirwan, it was 'the most ill-prepared, the most controversial, and probably the unhappiest expedition which ever sailed the Antarctic seas.'

For a start, the six ships selected were poor choices: three of them, *Vincennes*, *Peacock* and *Porpoise*, were naval warships whose gun ports let heavy seas pour into the ships; *Sea Gull* and *Flying Fish*, former New York pilot boats, were odd choices for Antarctic exploration; and the sluggish storeship *Relief* rounded out the sorry fleet. As might be expected of an expedition planned by committee, the US Ex Ex, as it became known, had a distinct lack of focus. Antarctica was to be only one area of its endeavor, and a minor one at that: Wilkes was also directed to explore the whole of the Pacific, from Chile to Australia to the northwest coast of North America. Meanwhile, a jealous Navy Department did all it could to exclude civilian scientists from the expedition, though Wilkes did manage to take with him the artist Titian Ramsey Peale. One unsuccessful applicant for a scientific position was the novelist Nathaniel Hawthorne.

By the time the Expedition sailed on August 18, 1838, a depressed Wilkes confided to his private diary that he felt himself to be 'one doomed to destruction.' The fleet sailed down the east coast of South America to Orange Harbour, near the tip of Tierra del Fuego, where Wilkes divided the fleet in three. He directed *Peacock* and *Flying Fish* to sail southwest to try to better Cook's southing record; *Vincennes* and *Relief* he ordered to survey the coast of Tierra del Fuego. Placing himself aboard *Porpoise*, he set off south with *Sea Gull* to see how far he could penetrate the pack ice. The ships soon lost contact with one another, each undergoing its own trials. Gales ripped sails and tangled rigging; boats were crushed by ice; men were injured and frozen. Wilkes himself, in the flagship, narrowly missed running aground on Elephant Island in fog. *Sea Gull* and crew were lost off Chile. But *Peacock* and *Flying Fish* managed to cross the 70th parallel, little more than a degree away from beating Cook's record.

Diminished by two, *Relief* having been sent home as unsuitable for ice work, the Expedition reconvened in Sydney in November 1839 after surveying in the South Pacific. After a month's recuperation, the four ships sailed south again on December 26, with Wilkes commanding *Vincennes*. Also on board: the first recorded canine visitor to the Antarctic, a dog acquired in Sydney and named after that port. Again the ships were quickly separated, and in late February *Flying Fish* gave up its search for the others and returned to New Zealand alone. The other three vessels managed to rendezvous, however, and on January 16, 1840 – three days before Dumont d'Urville made his discovery – they sighted land in the region of 154°30'E, putting a boat ashore three days later to confirm it. Separating again, *Vincennes* continued west, sighting and charting discoveries until reaching the present-day Shackleton Ice Shelf, which Wilkes named Termination Land. The massive ice shelf, which today extends nearly 290 km out to sea, convinced him that it was time to head home, which he did on February 21.

Having followed the Antarctic coast for nearly 2000 km, Wilkes, upon his return to Sydney, announced the discovery of an Antarctic continent. Although he was the first to do so, his only reward upon his homecoming in New York was a court-martial. Petty jealousy from some of his officers, coupled with his harsh shipboard discipline, entangled Wilkes in a messy trial in a Naval Court of Inquiry held at the Brooklyn Navy Yard. Two long months later, all of the charges against him – save one – were dismissed. Found guilty of ordering a too-severe punishment on some thieving seamen, Wilkes was officially reprimanded by the Secretary of the Navy. The US Congress, however, handed Wilkes his most bitter defeat, authorizing publication of just 100 copies of the expedition's official report. Today, the five-volume *Narrative* is one of the rarest – and most valuable – polar books.

Ross Scotsman James Clark Ross (1800-1862), considered one of the most dashing men of his time, had all of the advantages for Antarctic exploration that Wilkes lacked. After joining the Royal Navy at the tender age of 11 or 12, Ross went on to a career filled with Arctic discovery. Between 1818 and 1836, he spent eight winters and 15 summers in the Arctic, and in 1831, as second-in-command of a voyage led by his uncle, John Ross, he located the North Magnetic Pole. In 1839, he was asked to lead a national expedition to explore the south, and if possible, to locate the South Magnetic Pole. The contrast between his commission and Wilkes' could not have been greater. With his government firmly behind the effort, both philosophically and financially, Ross was given excellent ships, officers and provisions; the sailors on the expedition were volunteers on double pay.

Setting sail in September 1839 in *Erebus* and *Terror*, shallow-drafted three-masted barques that had been specially strengthened for ice navigation, the expedition stopped in Hobart on its way south. There, the Governor of Van Diemen's Land (Tasmania) was John Franklin, himself a veteran Arctic explorer who would later and tragically sail Arctic waters again – in the very same *Erebus* and *Terror* – before disappearing and triggering the greatest polar search in history.

In Hobart, Ross heard troubling news: Both Wilkes and Dumont d'Urville were exploring the area in which he intended to search for the magnetic pole. In the same whining tone that Robert Scott would later use upon hearing that Roald Amundsen (or Ernest Shackleton, for that matter) was heading to 'his' territory, Ross expressed his unhappiness that the Americans and the French would even consider sailing into 'his' area. The petulant Ross also refused to acknowledge a generous gesture made by Wilkes, who had left for him a chart tracing his track and discoveries, but took the useful data with him – and later used it to denounce Wilkes. Meanwhile, Ross reacted quickly, changing his plans to a more easterly longitude for the push south.

Good fortune was to be on his side, though the elements made Ross earn it. Sailing south along the 170°E meridian, he pushed through pack ice for four days, trusting that his reinforced ships would be able to go where none had before. On January 9, 1841, he broke through to open water, becoming the first to reach what we know today as the Ross Ice Shelf. The next day, Ross sighted land, a completely unexpected development. A boat was landed two days later on an islet named Possession Island and the new territory claimed in the name of Queen Victoria.

Exciting though the discovery was, Ross' goal was the South Magnetic Pole, which had been calculated to lie both north and west of his current position. To follow the coast south and eastward would appear to be the 'wrong' way to get there, but to sail west would mean following in the tracks of Wilkes and Dumont d'Urville, something equally unappealing. Ross may have been thinking of the islands and channels of the Arctic he knew so well; perhaps sailing south and eastward would reveal a passage back toward the expected pole. So he stayed his course, discovering High (now called Ross) Island, and naming its two mountains – Erebus, the steaming volcano, and Terror, its easterly sister – for his ships.

Lying in Ross' path, however, was a formidable obstacle, one which so overwhelmed him that he called it simply the 'Victoria Barrier,' an enormous wall of shimmering ice towering up to 60m above the sea that Ross described as 'a mighty and wonderful object far beyond anything we could have thought or conceived.' But this mass, today known as the Ross Ice Shelf, also frustrated Ross: 'We might with equal chance of success try to sail through the cliffs of Dover.' The two ships, tiny by comparison, cruised along the Barrier for 450 km, the sailors in awe of its unchanging face, which was oblivious to even the most gigantic wave crashing against it. After reaching a new southing record of 78°9'30"S on January 22, 1841, Ross braced the yards round and headed for Hobart.

Sailing south again in November 1841, Ross this time aimed for the eastern extremity of the Barrier. New Year's Day found *Erebus* and *Terror* moored beside a large ice floe, on which the crews held 'a grand fancy ball,' complete with carved-ice thrones for the captains and a refreshment bar cut into the ice. Then, after surviving a horrifying storm amongst ice fragments, 'hard as floating rocks of granite,' which nearly destroyed both ships' rudders, they again reached the Barrier. It appeared to join a range of mountains, but winter's onset forced a retreat. Ross' third season was equally disappointing: trying to best Weddell's southing record in Weddell's namesake sea, Ross found conditions similar to those previously encountered by everyone but Weddell and was forced to head home after reaching 71°30'S. The expedition returned home on September 2, 1843, after nearly four and a half years away. When Ross married later that year, his bride's father set one condition: he must promise to end his exploring days, a pledge Ross made and faithfully kept.

After Ross' important discoveries, Antarctica remained isolated and ignored at the bottom of the world. Ironically, this was due in part to his old ships, *Erebus* and *Terror*, which John Franklin had taken to the Arctic in 1845 to try to navigate the Northwest Passage. When Franklin failed to return, Britain's naval resources were diverted for more than a decade in the search for some sign of him.

Larsen Norwegian Carl Anton Larsen (1860-1924) went to sea at age 14, and at age 25 became captain of his first whaling ship. Larsen's first brush with polar fame came when he sailed on *Jason* on the same voyage that the ship carried Fridtjof Nansen to Greenland for his famous east-to-west crossing in 1888. Whaling entrepreneur Christian Christiansen dispatched Larsen aboard *Jason* in 1892 to search for whales in the Antarctic. In 1893, having found fur and elephant seals but no whales of species he could catch, Larsen returned home. He went south again independently later that year, this time with three ships: *Jason*, *Hertha* and *Castor*. The expedition explored both coasts of the northern end of the Antarctic Peninsula, and made the first use of skis in Antarctica. Larsen also discovered petrified wood on Seymour Island, east of the tip of the Antarctic Peninsula. Larsen went on to captain Otto Nordenskjöld's ship *Antarctic* (see below) in 1901, and to set up the whaling station at Grytviken on South Georgia in 1904.

Bull Norwegian-born Henryk John Bull (1844-1930) traveled to Australia in 1885 and set himself up in business. Convinced that a fortune could be made by reviving the Antarctic whaling trade, but unable to convince any Australians of that, Bull returned to Norway in 1893. There he persuaded Svend Foyn, the wealthy inventor of the exploding harpoon gun, to back an expedition to assess the Ross Sea's potential as a whaling ground. Whales in the Northern Hemisphere had been hunted to commercial extinction, and though petroleum products had to some degree replaced whale oil, baleen (whale bone) was as prized as ever for women's fashions.

Sailing from Norway in 1893 in a refitted

whaling steamer, *Antarctic*, Bull's expedition encountered many misfortunes in their hunt for whales, of which they saw few, and a £3,000 profit made from sealing in Iles Kerguelen evaporated when the ship ran aground at Campbell Island. Putting in for repairs at Melbourne, the ship picked up a young Norwegian naturalist, Carsten E Borchgrevink (see below), who signed on as an assistant biologist. On January 18, 1895, *Antarctic* landed on the Possession Islands, where Borchgrevink discovered lichens, the first time vegetation had been found south of the Antarctic Circle.

Six days later, a party from *Antarctic* went ashore at Cape Adare, claimed to be the first landing ever made on the continent outside the Peninsula. Although Borchgrevink himself claimed to have leapt out of the landing boat as it neared the shore in order to ensure himself a place in history – and made a widely reproduced drawing showing himself in the act – two others in the landing party disagreed upon just who first placed his foot on the frozen shore, and their differences were eventually aired in the correspondence columns of the *Times* of London. In any case, the landing was only one of several disputed 'first landings' on the continent (see the sidebar on 'First Landings'). Penguins, rock specimens, seaweed and more lichens were collected, and though the voyage was not commercially successful, it helped to revive interest in Antarctica. Bull himself continued sealing and whaling, and at the age of 62, he was shipwrecked and marooned on the Iles Crozet for two months.

De Gerlache Belgian Adrien Victor Joseph de Gerlache de Gomery (1866-1934), a lieutenant in the Royal Belgian Navy, persuaded the Brussels Geographical Society to finance a scientific expedition to Antarctica. Sailing in a refitted three-masted whaling ship (with an auxiliary engine) that he purchased in Norway and rechristened *Belgica*, de Gerlache left Antwerp in 1897 with a decidedly international crew. The Belgian Antarctic Expedition included a Romanian zoologist, a Russian meteorologist, a Polish geologist (Henryk Arctowski, for whom the Polish research base on King George Island is named) and a Norwegian who offered to join the expedition as first mate, without pay – Roald Amundsen. As the ship's surgeon, de Gerlache signed an American, Frederick A Cook, who joined *Belgica* in Rio de Janiero.

The expedition got a very late start sailing south, leaving Punta Arenas on December 14. Some now speculate that this tardy departure was a deliberate attempt by de Gerlache to ensure that *Belgica* would be beset in the ice and thus be forced to remain in the Antarctic for the winter. But others have correctly pointed out that Antarctic pack ice was known to be at its most navigable late in the summer. By early February, the expedition had discovered and mapped the strait which now bears de Gerlache's name on the west side of the Antarctic Peninsula, as well as the islands on the west side of that strait: Brabant, Liège, Anvers and Wiencke (the last named for a sailor who had fallen overboard and drowned). They also charted the Danco Coast of the Peninsula, along the east side of the strait, named for the ship's magnetician, who died during the expedition.

Photography was first used in Antarctica on this expedition, and Cook recorded that 'as the ship steamed rapidly along, spreading out one panorama after another of a new world, the noise of the camera was as regular and successive as the tap of a stock ticker.'

On February 15, 1898, *Belgica* crossed the Antarctic Circle, and by March 1, already deep into the heavy pack, she reached 71°31'S. The next day began a long imprisonment in the ice. In fact, the ship would not be freed for a full 377 days – and then only by enormous effort and a great deal of luck. During this, the first time men had wintered south of 60°S, the expedition underwent great hardships: the midwinter darkness toyed with men's sanity, and the lack of vitamin C threatened scurvy.

Frederick Cook, who had been on the North Greenland Expedition with Robert E

Peary in 1891, and returned to Greenland twice more in the next three years, likely saved the ship. He urged de Gerlache to set an example by eating fresh seal and penguin meat, which the men universally detested, to prevent scurvy. He organized elaborate betting games to take the crew's mind off their desperate circumstances and encouraged them to think of their own amusements. One popular event, held on Belgian King Leopold's birthday, was a 'Grand Concourse of Beautiful Women,' in which 464 illustrations of beauties 'representing all kinds of poses and dress and undress' were selected from a Paris journal and judged according to 21 characteristics, including 'rosy complexion,' 'underclothes,' 'most beautiful face' and 'sloping, alabaster shoulders.' It was hoped that the winners would agree to appear before the committee to receive their prizes, once the committee returned to civilization.

That they *would* return was by no means certain, however. By January 1899, Cook suggested that they attempt to liberate themselves by hand-sawing a canal 600m long from a *polynya*, or stretch of open water, back to the ship, pushing the ice pieces that they cut from the canal out into the open water. They all worked like dogs for a month, and when they were within 30m of the ship, a wind shift tightened the pack ice and their hard-won canal closed up within an hour. Two weeks later, the ice moved again, this time opening their path, and they steamed into the polynya, only to be forced to wait another month until they could go on to the open sea. *Belgica* finally reached Punta Arenas on March 28, 1899.

The primary achievement of the Belgian Antarctic Expedition – surviving the first Antarctic night – proved that bases could next be set up on the continent itself, enabling a full-time program of exploration. That knowledge would be crucial for the next phase of Antarctic discovery. Adrien de Gerlache remained involved in Antarctic affairs. In 1903, he joined Charcot's *Français* expedition (see below), but resigned in Buenos Aires. He later tried a business venture he called 'polar safaris,' taking tourists to East Greenland and Spitsbergen, but the enterprise collapsed in its initial phase, and de Gerlache sold the ship he had bought, a 300-ton barquentine called *Polaris*, to Ernest Shackleton, who renamed it *Endurance*. De Gerlache's son, Gaston de Gerlache, joined the Belgian Antarctic Expedition of 1957-59.

Borchgrevink Carsten Egeberg Borchgrevink (1864-1934), the son of a Norwegian father and an English mother, got his start in Antarctic exploration shipping out with Bull on *Antarctic* (see above) in 1894. His landing at Cape Adare convinced Borchgrevink that men could survive an Antarctic winter ashore, so he decided to organize his own expedition, with the goal of being the first to accomplish it.

After failing to raise any money for his expedition in Australia, Borchgrevink visited Britain, where he met with rejection after rejection – until 1897, when he convinced a wealthy magazine publisher, Sir George Newnes, to sponsor the expedition, to the tune of £40,000. Borchgrevink's stunning success infuriated the British exploration establishment, headed by the Royal Geographical Society, because it was preparing to mount its own voyage of Antarctic discovery. Even more galling to the establishment was the fact that Borchgrevink's 'British' Antarctic Expedition of 1898-90 was British in name only; just three (two Englishmen and one Australian) of the 31 men were not Norwegians. The expedition ship, *Southern Cross*, a converted Norwegian whaler equipped with powerful engines, sailed under the Union Jack only at the insistence of its magnanimous sponsor.

Southern Cross departed London on August 22, 1898, and arrived at Cape Adare on February 17, 1899. Two weeks later, after two simple wooden huts were erected on Ridley Beach, which Borchgrevink named for his mother, *Southern Cross* departed to winter in New Zealand. The 10 men left behind were some of the most solitary in history, having the entire Antarctic continent all to themselves.

They had plenty of canine companionship, however, for Borchgrevink had brought 90 sledge dogs with him, the first dogs used in Antarctic work. The expedition also pioneered the use of kayaks for sea travel, and was also the first to bring to Antarctica the Primus stove, a lightweight, portable pressure stove invented in Sweden six years before. Although the kayak never took off as an important mode of Antarctic transport, the Primus stove was carried by nearly every expedition that followed Borchgrevink, and it is still in use today. Unfortunately, the expedition marked another first – the first human death on Antarctica – when Norwegian zoologist Nicolai Hansen died on October 14, 1899, and was buried on the ridge above Cape Adare. Aside from Hansen's death, there were other accidents – including a nearly disastrous fire and a narrow escape from asphyxiation by coal fumes – but the expedition escaped the dietary and psychological dangers experienced by the *Belgica*'s crew during their long Antarctic night. By the time the ship returned on January 28, 1900, to pick up the expedition, it had proved a critical fact: men could survive Antarctica's fierce, dark winter ashore, using a wooden hut as a base for travels along the coasts and inland towards the Pole.

Despite these accomplishments – and others, including the excellent maps of the Ross Sea area produced by the expedition's English surveyor and magnetician, William Colbeck of the Royal Navy, that would prove invaluable to later explorers, Borchgrevink's return to England was all but unheralded. The exploration establishment was still embittered by his fundraising success – and absorbed by Robert F Scott's impending expedition. Not until 1930 did the Royal Geographical Society see fit to award Borchgrevink its Patron's Medal. He died in Norway four years later.

Drygalski University of Berlin geography Professor Erich Dagobert von Drygalski (1865-1949), leader of a four-year expedition to Greenland, was given command of the German South Polar Expedition in 1898. Three years later, Drygalski and 31 other men sailed from Kiel on August 11, 1901, aboard *Gauss*, a three-masted schooner fitted with auxiliary engines. Drygalski named the ship after the famed German mathematician, Johann Karl Friedrich Gauss, who had calculated the position of the South Magnetic Pole, the accuracy of which James Clark Ross had set out to test.

Stopping en route at Cape Town and the Iles Kerguelen (where they picked up 40 dogs), the expedition sighted land on February 21, 1902, in the region of 90°E, a territory which Drygalski named Kaiser Wilhelm II Land (now called Wilhelm II Land). On the same day, the ship got caught in the ice, soon becoming, in Drygalski's words, 'a toy of the elements.'

With *Gauss* caught in the west-drifting pack, the men settled into a routine of scientific work by day and card games, lectures, beer and music by night. With snow drifted up over the ship, its warm, humid interior was infused with a very German *gemütlichkeit*, or coziness. A sledging party journeyed 80 km to the Antarctic coast, discovering a low hill they named Gaussberg after their ship. On March 29, 1902, Drygalski ascended in a large, tethered hydrogen balloon to 480m and used a telephone to report his observations down to the ship. This was the second use of aviation in Antarctic history, after Scott's tethered flight during the *Discovery* expedition (see below). The men also recorded penguin sounds with an early phonograph, and undertook two more sledging trips to Gaussberg, on the last of which Drygalski and his companions nearly became lost in the trackless white wasteland of snow-covered sea ice.

Being beset during the winter was one thing, but when spring and then summer arrived, the men began to feel desperate, especially after sawing, drilling and even dynamiting the five- to six-meter-thick ice did nothing to free the ship. *Gauss*' captain suggested that they toss message-filled bottles into the sea – and launch others by balloon – in hopes that a rescue party might find them. In the end, they were liberated thanks to a basic principle of physics that was luckily observed by Dryglaski himself during a walk on the ice. He remarked that cinders from the ship's smokestack had caused the ice on which they had landed to melt, the ashes' darker color absorbing the sun's heat. Devising an ingenious method of escape, he ordered his men to lay a trail of coal ash, supplemented by rotting food and other garbage, across the 600m of ice that separated *Gauss* from open water.

The trick worked as hoped, and soon there was a two-meter-deep channel filled with water. Two months passed, however, before the bottom of the canal cracked open, on February 8, 1903, and the ship was freed. The expedition then spent seven weeks trying to chart the Kaiser Wilhelm II coast, but constantly shifting sea ice threatened to trap *Gauss* once more, and Drygalski reluctantly ordered the ship north on March 31. After reaching Cape Town, he wired Berlin for permission to return to the Antarctic the following season. But the Kaiser, apparently disappointed that more new territory was not discovered and claimed for the Fatherland, refused the request. Despite that disappointment, Drygalski then spent nearly three decades writing up the expedition's reports, which occupy 20 full volumes.

Nordenskjöld Swedish geologist Nils Otto Gustav Nordenskjöld (1869-1928) had previously led expeditions to both the Yukon and Tierra del Fuego, and his uncle, the North Polar explorer Nils AE Nordenskjöld, made the first transit of the Northeast Passage around Siberia. So he was well-suited for the task that was assigned to him in 1900: the formation and leadership of the Swedish South Polar Expedition, which would be the first to winter in the Antarctic Peninsula region.

Sailing in *Antarctic*, the stout former whaler used by Henryk Bull in 1893-95, the expedition left from Gothenburg on October 16, 1901. At *Antarctic*'s helm was Capt Carl Anton Larsen, the Norwegian who had already discovered Oscar II Land during a previous expedition in 1892-94 (see above), and who would later set up Antarctica's first whaling station at Grytviken on South Georgia. By late January 1902 *Antarctic* was exploring the western side of the Peninsula, making several important new geographical discoveries in the area (among them, the fact that the Orleans Strait connected with the Gerlache Strait, and not with the Weddell Sea, as had been believed) before sailing back to the tip of the Peninsula. There, they crossed between the Peninsula and off-lying Joinville Island, naming the strait for their ship, *Antarctic*.

Next, the expedition attempted to penetrate south into the Weddell Sea, but its infamous ice stopped them, and instead Nordenskjöld and five men set up a winter base on Snow Hill Island, off the east coast of the Antarctic Peninsula, in February 1902. *Antarctic*, meanwhile, sailed for the Falklands to winter there. Poor weather confined the shore party to its small hut for most of the winter, but in December Nordenskjöld was able to sledge to Seymour Island, directly north of Snow Hill, where he made some striking fossil discoveries, including the bones of a giant penguin, bolstering earlier fossil finds made by Capt Larsen on the island in 1893.

But December is mid-summer in Antarctica, and the men were getting distinctly nervous about their ship, which should have arrived by then. In fact, their fears were entirely justified, though they were not to learn why for many months to come. After wintering in Patagonia and South Georgia, *Antarctic* had returned south, again surveying the western side of the Peninsula. Trying unsuccessfully to cross through her namesake strait to reach the Peninsula's east coast – and the men at Snow Hill Island – *Antarctic* stopped at Hope Bay on the Peninsula's tip to drop off three men, who would try to hike the 320 km to Snow Hill. The ship then sailed around Joinville Island and headed south, soon becoming caught in the pack ice, whose relentless grip held and inexorably crushed it. The end, on February 12, 1903, was recorded thus by one of the men, Carl Skottsberg: 'Now the name disappears from sight. Now the water is up to the rail, and, with a rattle, the sea and bits of ice rush in over her deck. That sound I can never forget, however long I may live . . . the streamer, with the name *Antarctic*, disappears in the waves. The bowsprit – the last mast-top – She is gone!' The ship sank 40 km east of tiny Paulet Island, and the men sledged for 14 days to reach it.

The three men left at Hope Bay, meanwhile, found their way to Snow Hill Island blocked by open water, so they settled down to wait for *Antarctic* to return for them, according to a pre-arranged plan. The Swedish Antarctic Expedition was now split into three groups, two of them living in very rough conditions, with no group aware of the others' fates. How they all managed to survive is one of the greatest examples of good fortune in all of Antarctic history.

The Hope Bay trio, after eking out the winter in a primitive hut and living primarily on seal meat, set out again for Snow Hill Island on September 29. By a lucky coincidence, Nordenskjöld and another man were dog-sledging north at the same time on a research journey, and on October 12, the two groups met. Nordenskjöld was so struck by the Hope Bay men's remarkable appearance – they were completely soot-blackened, and wearing odd masks they had fashioned to prevent snow-blindness – that he wondered if they were from some previously unknown race of men. Nordenskjöld's companion, Ole Jonassen, even wondered if an unholstered revolver might be a necessary precaution in facing these disconcerting apparitions. But they quickly established the identities of their fellow expeditioners, renaming the point of their rendezvous 'Cape Well Met.'

Antarctic's crew, meanwhile, wintered on Paulet Island. They built a stone hut, killed 1100 Adélie penguins for food before the birds left for the winter, and awaited a fearfully uncertain fate. On June 7, just before Midwinter, one of the party who had been sick for weeks, Ole Wennersgaard, died. On October 31, Larsen led a group of five others in an open boat to search for the trio landed at Hope Bay. Finding a note the three had left at their hut, Larsen decided he would have to follow by sea the route that the Hope Bay men were taking to Snow Hill Island.

Even as Larsen's group rowed their boat south, outside help was on its way to Snow Hill Island. Since nothing had been heard of the Swedish expedition three search parties were dispatched. Argentina sent a naval ship, *Uruguay*, to search for it in 1903. On November 8, *Uruguay*'s crew found two of the men from Snow Hill Island camped at Seymour Island, and after waking them, joined them in the short trek to Snow Hill – arriving, by incredible fortune, only a few hours ahead of Larsen and his group. After a joyful reunion, all that was left to do (on November 11) was to pick up the remaining *Antarctic* crew members back on Paulet Island, who, ironically, had just finished collecting 6000 penguin eggs, their first surplus food supply.

Although Nordenskjöld's expedition is remembered primarily for its survival against nearly overwhelming odds, it also performed the most important research in Antarctica undertaken up to its time.

Scott's *Discovery* Expedition Even as Nordenskjöld's men were struggling for survival, British explorer Capt Robert Falcon Scott (1868-1912) was working from a base established on Ross Island. The son of an upper-middle-class brewer, Scott had joined the Royal Navy's training ship, *Britannia*, as a cadet at the ripe age of 13, and advanced through the ranks, being promoted to commander in June 1900. A month later, he was named leader of the British National Antarctic Expedition, which the country's exploration establishment had been planning since the mid-1880s. It was this expedition that Borchgrevink stole a march on by securing his large grant from Sir George Newnes in 1897.

When Scott's well-financed expedition sailed from England on August 6, 1901, in *Discovery*, a specially built wooden steam barque, it was the best equipped scientific expedition to Antarctica to that date. After stopping in New Zealand for refitting and reprovisioning, the expedition got off to an inauspicious start when a seaman fell from the top of the mainmast to his death. By January 3, 1902, *Discovery* crossed the Antarctic Circle, and six days later stopped briefly at Cape Adare. Penetrating the Ross Sea, Scott cruised along the Ross Ice Shelf, discovering King Edward VII Land on the shelf's eastern margin. He also made the first flight in Antarctica, on February 4, 1902, in a tethered balloon called *Eva*. Rising to a height of 240m, Scott viewed the undulating surface of the Ross Ice Shelf rising toward the polar plateau. Camera-toting expedition member Ernest Shackleton went up next, establishing himself as Antarctica's first aerial photographer.

By mid-February 1902, Scott's men had established winter quarters at Hut Point on Ross Island. Although a hut was built ashore, *Discovery*, frozen into the sea ice, served as the expedition's accommodation, with officers and men strictly separated into wardroom and messdeck, as befitted the quasi-naval expedition that it was. The shore building was reserved for scientific work and recreation, such as theatrical performances, when it was called 'the Royal Terror Theatre.' But life in McMurdo Sound was not all research-and-games: During a violent snowstorm on a sledge trip, a young sailor named George Vincent slipped over a precipice to his death. Otherwise, winter passed fairly quietly, their accommodation made cheerier by another Antarctic first – electric lights (powered by a windmill). With Shackleton as editor, the expedition also published Antarctica's first magazine, a monthly called the *South Polar Times*, as well as one issue of a more-ribald alternative, *The Blizzard*, whose title page featured a figure holding a bottle, captioned 'Never mind the blizzard, I'm all right.'

With spring, the expedition's real work began. To the cheers of all of *Discovery*'s men, Scott set out for the South Pole on November 2, 1902, with his scientific officer Dr Edward A Wilson, Shackleton, 19 dogs and five supply sledges hitched up in train formation. Despite initial optimism and a large depot of food laid by an advance party, the trio soon struck harsh reality, Antarctica-style. They had never tried skiing or sled dog-driving, and their inexperience produced predictably poor results.

Through sheer willpower, they reached 82°16.5'S before turning back. Actually, Scott and Wilson reached that point, Shackleton having been ordered to remain behind to look after the dogs. This may or may not have been an intentional slight on the part of Scott (though certainly it was petty), but Shackleton smarted at the gesture.

For all of them, the trip home was miserable. The remaining dogs by now were nearly worthless, and soon were hitched *behind* the sledge, which the men pulled themselves. On at least one occasion, a dog was carried on the sledge. As dogs weakened, they were shot and fed to the others. The men, meanwhile, were also breaking down. Shackleton especially was suffering from scurvy, and suffering badly – but reports in some accounts of the trip, which state that he had to be carried on the sledge, are false.

Two weeks before the southern party's return home on February 3, the relief ship *Morning* had arrived in McMurdo Sound. *Morning*'s captain, William Colbeck, had been the surveyor on Borchgrevink's *Southern Cross* expedition. Colbeck and Scott decided that with *Discovery* still frozen into the ice, *Morning* should not wait to return home, and with the prospect strong that he would have to remain another winter, Scott sent home eight men, including Shackleton, who went only upon being ordered to do so. The following summer, after Scott led a sledging party in southern Victoria Land, *Morning* returned, in company with *Terra Nova*, sent by the

British government. The two vessels bore a disturbing order: if *Discovery* could not be freed within six weeks, it would have to be abandoned. After weeks of cutting and blasting with explosives, Scott was nearly ready to give up, but nature relented, and the ice gave way almost completely. One final blast, on February 16, 1904, released *Discovery* for the long journey home.

Bruce Scotsman William Spiers Bruce (1867-1921), the physician son of a surgeon, joined a whaling voyage to the Antarctic from Dundee aboard *Balaena* in 1892, as surgeon and naturalist, and would have joined Bull's *Antarctic* expedition in 1894-95, but was unable to reach Melbourne in time to meet the ship. Bruce also later made many trips to the Arctic. In 1901, he declined the offer of a position on Scott's expedition because he was in the midst of planning his own, the Scottish National Antarctic Expedition.

Sailing from Troon on November 2, 1902, in *Scotia*, a renamed Norwegian steam whaler with extremely elegant lines, the expedition pushed south into the Weddell Sea. But by 70°S, *Scotia* was beset, and after freeing itself, the ship headed north to winter on Laurie Island in the South Orkneys. There, the expedition set up a meteorological station, hand-built of stone and called Omond House, on April 1, 1903. Mid-Winter's Day (June 22) 1903 was celebrated with a barrel of Guinness porter, a brew made more potent by the freezing of its water, unintentionally yielding pure alcohol! At the conclusion of the first season, *Scotia* sailed to Port Stanley and Buenos Aires. Bruce asked the British government to continue staffing Omond House, but his request was refused. Instead, the Oficina Meteorológica Argentina agreed to assume responsibility for the station, a duty the Argentine government maintains to the present day, making the station (now called Orcadas) the oldest continuously-operated scientific base in the Antarctic.

Pushing south again in January 1903, Bruce was able to penetrate the Weddell Sea to 74°S. There he discovered Coats Land, named for the expedition's rich patrons, Andrew and James Coats of Paisley, Scotland. *Scotia* followed the coast for 240 km, but always the fast ice kept the ship two or three frustrating kilometers offshore, and no landing could be made. The Scottish expedition, however, could claim an important milestone: moving pictures were made in the Antarctic for the first time. There was another pioneering achievement: A remarkable series of photographs, documenting the first known use of bagpipes in the Far South, shows an emperor penguin, head thrown back and beak agape, being serenaded by a kilted piper. Although an observer noted 'only sleepy indifference,' some of the photos show that the bird had to be tied by a line to prevent its escape.

Though Bruce later became a world authority on Spitsbergen in the Arctic, he must have retained an especial love for the Antarctic: upon his death in 1921, his ashes were carried south and poured into the Southern Ocean.

Charcot French physician Charcot (1867-1936) inherited 400,000 gold francs and a Fragonard painting, *La Pacha*, from his father, a famous neurologist whose work influenced that of Viennese psychologist Sigmund Freud. Charcot used this entire fortune to finance the construction of a three-masted schooner, *Français*, and to outfit it with laboratory equipment. His original intention had been to sail north to the Arctic, but when word arrived that Nordenskjöld's Swedish expedition was missing in Antarctica, Charcot decided to go south. Meanwhile, French citizens rallied to the cause of the French Antarctic Expedition, contributing another 450,000 francs.

Français sailed from Le Havre on August 15, 1903 – to immediate tragedy. Just minutes off the quay, a hawser parted, striking and killing a sailor; the expedition was delayed by 12 days, before departing without further incident. Belgian explorer de Gerlache (see above) accompanied the expedition as far as Buenos Aires, where he told Charcot that he missed his new fiancéee too much to go any further. Also in Buenos Aires, the expedition learned that the Argentine ship *Uruguay* had already rescued Nordenskjöld and his men, so Charcot decided instead to investigate the western coast of the Antarctic Peninsula. He deliberately chose to avoid the Ross Sea, with its potential for international rivalry, an act for which the territorial Robert Scott later called Charcot 'the gentleman of the Pole.'

By February 19, 1904, Charcot had discovered Port Lockroy on Wiencke Island. Continuing on, he decided to winter at a sheltered bay on the north coast of Booth Island, a place he named Port Charcot. The bay was so small that the men were able to stretch a hawser across its mouth to keep out ice that might otherwise crush their ship. The winter passed with various amusements (including reading and discussing old newspapers) and sledging expeditions to nearby islands, and was marred only by the death of the ship's pet pig, Toby, who ate a bucketfull of fish – along with the hooks that had caught them.

After the spring breakup, the expedition sailed north, running into trouble on January 15, 1903, when *Français* struck a rock. Despite attempts at plugging the hole and valiant, round-the-clock pumping by the men, the ship continued to flood. Temporary repairs effected at Port Lockroy enabled the expedition to continue to Tierra del Fuego and then Buenos Aires, where Charcot sold *Français* to the Argentine government. Then he headed home to a hero's welcome from all of France – except his wife, a granddaughter of Victor Hugo, who divorced him for desertion.

Four years later, Charcot returned to Antarctica, this time as head of an expedition sponsored by the French government, which granted him 600,000 francs. On August 15, 1908, he again sailed from Le Havre, this time in the newly-built and amusingly-named *Pourquoi Pas?* ('Why Not?'), which he had once christened his toy boats as a child. Among those aboard was Charcot's second wife, Meg, who sailed as far as Punta Arenas. (Wary of repeating his failed first marriage, Charcot had secured a prenuptial agreement from her that she would not oppose his explorations.)

After a stop at the Deception Island whaling station, where Dr Charcot saved a man from a hideous death by amputating his gangrenous hand, *Pourquoi Pas?* departed on Christmas Day 1908, and continued the survey work on the west side of the Peninsula that Charcot had begun with *Français*. As on his previous voyage, unfortunately, Charcot struck a rock, damaging *Pourquoi Pas?*, whose pumps were able to manage the water pouring into the seam. The expedition pushed on, discovering and naming the Fallières Coast, circling Adelaide Island and proving its insularity, and discovering Marguerite Bay, naming it for Meg. Most useful for this survey work was a small, iron-prowed motorboat carried on *Pourquoi Pas?*; the ship also boasted electric lighting and a 1500-volume library.

Those amenities proved valuable during the winter of 1909, when the expedition wintered at Petermann Island, with *Pourquoi Pas?* frozen into the ice at a bay they called Port Circumcision. The men set up a shore station, with huts for meteorological, seismic, magnetic and tidal research, and passed the long dark winter with reading, lectures, meetings of the 'Antarctic Sporting Club' and recitations from a novel being written by one of the officers.

At winter's end, they returned north to restock their coal supply at Deception Island – where a whaling-company diver inspected the ship's damaged hull and warned against further exploration. This advice Charcot ignored, heading south one final time. On January 11, 1910, he made his most personally treasured discovery, sighting an uncharted headland at 70°S, 76°W. This he called Charcot Land (since proven to be an island) – not after himself, but after his esteemed father. Twenty-six years later, Charcot and *Pourquoi Pas?* were again sailing in treacherous waters, this time off

Iceland, when a gale arose and claimed captain, ship and all but one of 43 crew.

Shackleton's *Nimrod* Expedition Irishman Ernest Henry Shackleton (1874-1922), the second of 10 children born to a doctor and his Quaker wife, had been badly stung by his breakdown on the return from Scott's furthest south in 1902. Indeed, Shackleton lived by his family motto: *Fortitudine Vincimus* (By Fortitude We Conquer). Even as he was being sent home as an invalid by Scott, Shackleton resolved that he would one day return to Antarctica – and return he did, in 1908. An indefatigable worker with a charming and forceful personality, Shackleton inspired fierce loyalty and admiration from his men, who called him 'The Boss.'

Following his return from the *Discovery* expedition, Shackleton had married and fathered the first of his three children, while at the same time holding a succession of jobs: magazine journalist, secretary of the Scottish Royal Geographical Society, (unsuccessful) candidate for Parliament, and finally, public relations man for a big Glasgow steelworks. The works' owner, William Beardmore, took a liking to Shackleton, and agreed to sponsor an Antarctic expedition.

The British Antarctic Expedition sailed from Lyttleton, New Zealand, on New Year's Day 1908, in *Nimrod*, a three-masted sealing ship with 40 years' experience in the Arctic. To conserve coal, the ship was towed 2700 km to the ice edge by *Koonya*, the first steel ship to cross the Antarctic Circle. Although Shackleton had originally intended to use *Discovery*'s old base at Ross Island, Scott wrote to him describing his own plans for another Antarctic expedition and asking him to establish his shore base elsewhere, a show of territoriality that seems remarkably presumptuous today. Shackleton agreed to seek his own headquarters, but when he arrived at the Ross Ice Shelf in January 1908, he was dismayed to find that the inlet where *Discovery* had launched its balloon just six years before, the Bay of Whales, had disappeared. Evidently the great ice shelf had calved, and if so, it would be very risky to try to set up a base on top of it. But *Nimrod* was unable to push further east, due to dangerous pack ice, so Shackleton was very reluctantly forced to use Ross Island as his base – breaking his promise to Scott.

Unforgiving ice blocked his path to Hut Point, however, and Shackleton was compelled to build his hut at Cape Royds, on Ross Island, more than 30 km further from the polar goal. Although he repeated Scott's mistake in not bringing dogs, Shackleton did not agree with Scott's romantic but misguided notion that man-hauling was 'more noble and splendid' than dog-driving. Instead, he brought with him ponies from Siberia, which were unsuited to the task demanded of them. The ponies did manage to pull loads a considerable distance across the Ross Ice Shelf, but could not offer the stamina or versatility of dogs.

With three companions – Jameson Adams, Eric Marshall and Frank Wild – Shackleton pioneered the route up to the polar plateau (which he claimed, and named, for King Edward VII) via the Beardmore Glacier, which he named for the expedition's patron. By January 9, 1909, the foursome had trudged on foot to within 156 km (though later sources figure it was more like 180 km – but who's counting?) of the Pole before being forced by dangerously dwindling supplies of food to turn and run for home. It was the hardest decision of Shackleton's life, and he told his wife Emily later: 'I thought you'd rather have a live donkey than a dead lion.' Still, they had achieved a remarkable run, beating Scott's furthest south by 589 km, discovering almost 800 km of new mountain range, and showing the way to anyone who would attempt the Pole after them. They also found coal and fossils at Mt Buckley at the top of the Beardmore Glacier.

The expedition marked other accomplishments as well. Six men, led by Professor TW Edgeworth David, ascended Mt Erebus for the first time, reaching the rim

MARK NORMAN

Academic Shokalski navigates the Ross Sea

COLIN MONTEATH (HEDGEHOG HOUSE)

Climber on Brunhilde Peak, Asgard Range

COLIN MONTEATH (HEDGEHOG HOUSE)

Relaxing on deck

COLIN MONTEATH (HEDGEHOG HOUSE)

Tourists bathe in thermally heated water, Pendulum Cove, Deception Island

of the volcano's crater on March 10, 1908, after a five-day climb. While the polar party was out, three of the expedition's members – Douglas Mawson, Alistair Mackay, with Professor David again leading – hiked nearly 1600 km to the South Magnetic Pole, reaching it on January 16, 1909, the first time it had been visited. (Today the pole is offshore in the Dumont d'Urville Sea, and Antarctic tour ships routinely sail over it.) The *Nimrod* expedition saw the Antarctic's first motor car, an Arrol Johnston, tested at Cape Royds (it was no good in snow, but proved useful for transporting loads across the sea ice) and produced about 100 copies of *Aurora Australis*, the first – and still only – book published in Antarctica.

Amundsen Norwegian Roald Engebreth Gravning Amundsen (1872-1928) was already a veteran explorer by the time he sailed in 1910 from Christiana (modern-day Oslo) on his way to what only he and a few others knew was the Antarctic. Amundsen had been with the first group to winter ashore in Antarctica, the *Belgica* expedition (see above), and had accomplished the first navigation of the Northwest Passage, a goal sought by mariners for centuries, in 1903-06. Amundsen spent three winters in the Arctic, learning much that would later prove invaluable from the native Eskimos about polar clothing, travel and dog-handling.

The Arctic had always been Amundsen's first interest, and he had long dreamed of reaching the North Pole. Indeed, he was well into the planning for an expedition to freeze his ship into the ice and drift with the current across the Pole when news reached him that American Robert E Peary had claimed to have reached 90°N on April 6, 1909. Amundsen quickly – and secretly – decided to turn his ambitions 180°.

Fram, Amundsen's aptly named ship (it means 'Forward') that had been used by Norwegian explorer Fridtjof Nansen on his unsuccessful attempt to reach the North Pole, sailed from Norway on June 6, 1911. *Fram* had a diesel engine, allowing quick start-up (as opposed to a coal-fired steam engine), as well as a rounded hull so that she would rise up out of pressing ice floes rather than being nipped as a standard hull would. In order not to let his rival Robert Scott know of his plans, Amundsen kept quiet about his plans – he revealed them to just three members of the expedition – until he reached Madeira. There he told his stunned men, and soon after, sent his infamous telegram to Scott in Melbourne: 'Beg leave to inform you *Fram* proceeding Antarctic Amundsen.'

Amundsen did not share Shackleton's fear of a dangerously calving Ross Ice Shelf. Instead, he established his base, Framheim ('home of *Fram*'), right on the shelf at the Bay of Whales, where Scott

First to the Pole: Roald Amundsen

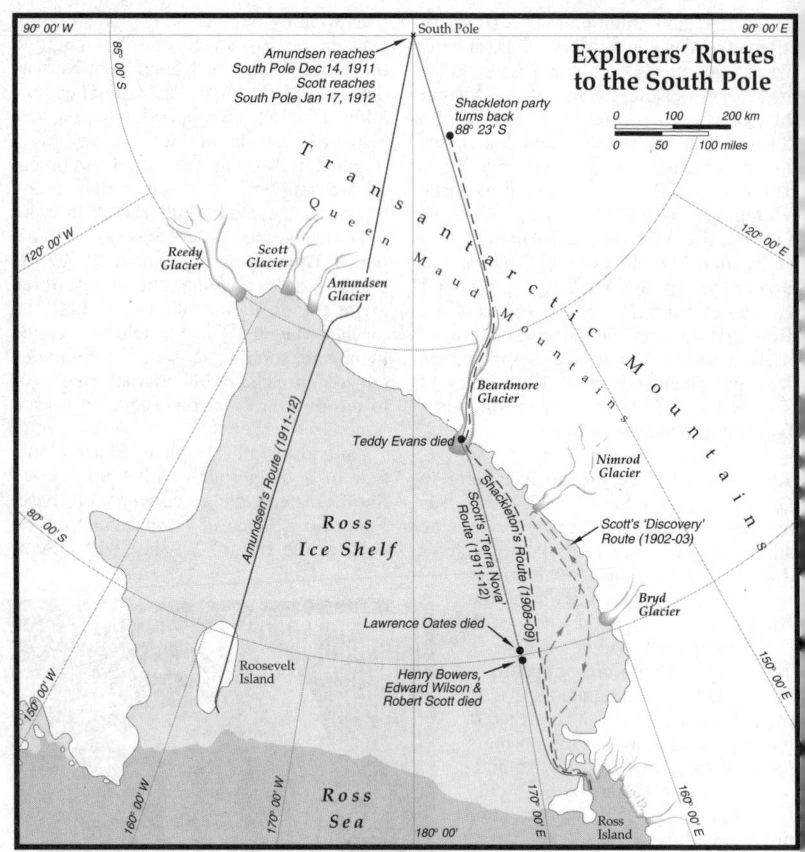

had previously made Antarctica's first balloon flight. There, in a small wooden prefab hut, nine men spent the winter. Outside, some of the 15 identical 16-man tents served as store sheds – and some as dog-houses for the expedition's 97 North Greenland dogs. From Framheim, Amundsen had the advantage of starting 100 km closer to the Pole, but he also had to pioneer a route up to the polar plateau from the Ross Ice Shelf. Scott, following Shackleton's lead, could take the charted course up the Beardmore Glacier.

Setting out from Framheim on October 19, 1911, Amundsen and his four companions had four sledges, each pulled by 13 Greenland dogs. Dogs and skis made the difference for them. As Norwegians, they were well-trained in the use of skis, and during his years in the Arctic Amundsen had developed excellent dog-driving skills. He also planned meticulously, took three or four backups of every critical item, and laid 10 extremely well-marked depots as far as 82°S, which, all together, contained 3400 kg of stores and food.

The five men – Amundsen, Olav Bjaaland, Helmer Hanssen, Sverre Hassel and

Oscar Wisting – reached the South Pole on December 14, 1911, camping there for three days at what they called *Polheim*. Amundsen claimed the polar plateau for Norway, calling it King Haakon VII Land, and wrote a note to Scott in the black tent he left behind. Then, they turned for home.

'On January 25, at 4 am,' Amundsen laconically recorded in his diary, 'we reached our good little house again, with two sledges and eleven dogs; men and animals all hale and hearty.' Despite his near-flawless success, Amundsen's achievement was overshadowed by several factors. In some ways, he had made the polar journey look *too* easy. There was also the view taken by some that Amundsen's surprise assault on the Pole had forestallen Scott, as though the British explorer had the 'right' to reach the Pole first (though Amundsen, in fact, preceded him to the Antarctic). Finally, the tragic drama of Scott's expedition was much more the stuff of legend than was Amundsen's cool triumph of technical skill.

Scott's *Terra Nova* Expedition When Amundsen's startling cable reached him, Scott became deeply distressed, though he worked hard not to show it. He had first watched Shackleton come close to snatching what he regarded as his prize, and now a dangerous new threat had arisen.

Sailing from New Zealand on November 29, 1910, in *Terra Nova*, the old Scottish whaler that had been one of the two relief ships sent at the end of the *Discovery* expedition, Scott's British Antarctic Expedition got off to a rough start. Just three days after weighing anchor, *Terra Nova* was hit by a screaming gale that lasted 36 hours and nearly sank the ship. Arriving at Ross Island in January 1911, Scott found that ice blocked the way to his old *Discovery* hut on Hut Point, so he established winter quarters at Cape Evans, also on Ross Island, which

PHOTO COURTESY THE SCOTT POLAR ARCHIVES

When Scott reached the Pole, Amundsen's tent and the Norwegian flag informed him that he wasn't the first to arrive.

he named after his second in command, ERGR 'Teddy' Evans. As soon as the hut was built, Scott commenced an ambitious program of depot-laying. He also introduced a useful innovation to Antarctica: A telephone line was established between Cape Evans and Hut Point. Mules, ponies, motor-sledges and dogs were employed to set up the supply caches, but once again, when these methods failed, the expedition resorted to the old British standby, man-hauling.

The next spring, on October 24, Scott dispatched a party with two motor-sledges, and eight days later followed with a larger group of men and 10 ponies. Various teams relayed the supplies and laid depots until, on January 4, 1912, the final support party turned back. For the final push to the Pole, Scott had chosen his companion on his previous furthest south, Edward Wilson, along with Lawrence Oates, Edgar Evans and Henry Bowers, who was added only the night before. (Another tactical error, since the food, tent and skis had been planned for four-men teams.)

What happened next is the most famous Antarctic story of all: the five arrived at the South Pole on January 17, 1912, to find that Amundsen had beaten them by 33 days. Nothing tells the tale better than Scott's diary itself, unless it is one of the many biographies that deconstruct what has since grown to be a hoary legend. Their return home was a haunting, desperate run of barely sighted depots, slow starvation and incredible cold. A delirious Evans died on February 17; a month later, Oates was in such bad shape that he prayed not to wake upon retiring. The next morning, deeply disappointed to find himself still among the living, Oates walked out of the tent during a raging blizzard, telling his companions simply, 'I am just going outside and may be some time.' Or so they say; we'll never know for certain.

Over at Commonwealth Bay, Douglas Mawson (see below) recorded the final blizzard that pinned down Scott and his two remaining companions in their tent from March 21 onwards. Scott's last entry was dated March 29.

Despite the deadly failure of the polar party, Scott's last expedition accomplished a great deal of important science. (In fact, the push for research had itself contributed to Scott's polar party's destruction, since the men dragged a sledge which carried, among other items, 16 kg of geological samples.) The infamous three-man midwinter trek to Cape Crozier, which Apsley Cherry-Garrard chronicled so eloquently in *The Worst Journey in the World*, braved 24-hour darkness and temperatures as low as -59°C – so cold that the men's teeth cracked in their mouths and they were 'beginning to think of death as a friend,' as Cherry-Garrard wrote – all so that they could be the first to collect emperor penguin embryos. A separate Northern Party, led by Victor Campbell, discovered Oates Land (named for Lawrence Oates) and spent a winter of terrible privation in a snowcave at Terra Nova Bay on the western shore of the Ross Sea. And the six-man party led by geologist Griffith Taylor explored the mysterious, otherworldly Dry Valleys, which Scott had found on the *Discovery* expedition.

Shirase Coming from a country with no tradition of exploration, Nobu Shirase (1861-1946), a lieutenant in the Japanese Navy, was a surprise. Despite the Japanese public's indifference and outright scorn to his fundraising efforts, Shirase managed to organize an Antarctic expedition in 1910. Sailing from Tokyo on December 1 aboard *Kainan Maru* ('Southern Pioneer'), the expedition reached Victoria Land in March 1911. Unable to land, however, it returned to winter in Sydney, where Shirase and his countrymen received a cold welcome from many Australians, though one well-to-do resident of suburban Vaucluse allowed the expedition to set up camp in his garden.

By mid-January 1912, *Kainan Maru* was back in the Ross Sea, where it met up with Amundsen's expedition at the Bay of Whales on the Ross Ice Shelf. Amundsen – and Scott, too – had by this time already reached the Pole, though Shirase, of course, could not know it. Despite being far behind, Shirase and six of his men formed a 'dash patrol' and in a symbolic gesture, headed south with dogs and sledges. First, however, they somehow had to claw their way to the top of the Ross Ice Shelf, which towered nearly 90m over the sea where *Kainan Maru* stood offshore. The patrol pushed 260 km to a furthest south of 80°5'S, which it reached on January 28, 1912. There, Shirase claimed all the area of the Ross Ice Shelf within sight as the 'Yamoto Yukihara,' or 'Yamato Snow Plain.' This claim has never been taken seriously (even by Japan), understandably so, given that Amundsen had already traveled through it on his way south to the Pole. Nevertheless, the expedition was welcomed as heroes when they returned to Yokohama on June 20, 1912.

Filchner With the Pole won, Bavarian army lieutenant Wilhelm Filchner (1877-1957) decided to tackle another problem of Antarctic discovery, namely, the question of whether the Weddell and Ross seas were joined by a channel, as some geographers posited. Educated at the Prussian Military Academy and already a veteran of a pioneering horseback journey through the Pamirs and another expedition to Tibet, Filchner hoped to make a crossing of the continent, starting from the Weddell Sea, in an attempt to solve this puzzle. But he was unable to raise the large amount of money such a two-ship expedition would require, so he decided merely to push as far south as he could into the Weddell Sea.

Sailing from Bremerhaven on May 4, 1911, in a Norwegian ship renamed *Deutschland*, the Second German South Polar Expedition called in at Buenos Aires on the way south. There, Filchner met aboard *Fram* with Amundsen, who was on his triumphant return home from the Pole. By mid-December, *Deutschland* had reached the Weddell Sea pack ice. After 10 days of pushing through narrow leads and breaking through floes, the ship had penetrated to the Weddell's southern coast, William Bruce's Coats Land. Sailing west along this coast, Filchner reached new territory, which he called 'Prinz Regent Luitpold Land' (now Luitpold Coast). He also discovered a vast ice shelf, naming it 'Kaiser Wilhelm Barrier,' for his emperor (who later insisted that it be renamed the Filchner Ice Shelf). Filchner then tried to establish a winter base ('Stationseisberg') on the ice shelf, but these plans had to be hastily abandoned when a huge section of the shelf – carrying the expedition's nearly completed hut – calved into the sea.

All of this work took time, however, and the Antarctic winter closed in before *Deutschland* could escape to lower latitudes; the ship was beset and drifted for nine months. In contrast to the hardships experienced by other overwintering expeditions – notably the *Belgica* – the Germans had a fairly uneventful winter, with both ship and crew managing well. Filchner even led a three-man party on a dangerous midwinter dog-sledging trip over some 65 km of sea ice to the charted location of 'New South Greenland,' which American sealer Benjamin Morrell claimed to have sighted in 1823. Finding nothing but frozen ocean, Filchner proved the non-existence of Morrell's 'discovery.' Successfully navigating back to the ship was a great feat, since their instruments were nearly destroyed by the -34°C cold – and *Deutschland* had drifted nearly 65 km with the current-driven pack ice.

On November 26, 1912, the decaying ice released the ship, which sailed on to South Georgia and home. Back in Germany, armed with his newly won knowledge of the Weddell Sea coast, Filchner again tried to raise interest in a crossing of Antarctica, from the Weddell to the Ross Sea. But Germany's attention, on the eve of WWI, was turned elsewhere.

Shackleton's *Endurance* Expedition Despite having lost his sought-after prize – but having saved his life and those of his companions – on his *Nimrod* expedition, Ernest Shackleton had also set his aim on an Antarctic crossing. And the threat of a

Despite three attempts, Ernest Shackleton never reached the Pole.

German expedition attempting the same journey helped Shackleton to raise funds, as nationalistic Britons sent in contributions to the planned 'first crossing of the last continent.' His plan was simple but ambitious. Shackleton would sail in *Endurance* to the Weddell Sea coast, establish a base, and then trek across the continent via the South Pole. At the top of the Beardmore Glacier, the crossing party would be met by another group, which would be landed at Ross Island by another ship, *Aurora*, sailing from Hobart.

Even as *Endurance* prepared to sail, the firestorm that had been ignited by the assassination of Archduke Franz Ferdinand and his wife on June 28, 1914, was engulfing Europe. Britain declared war on Germany on August 4, and Shackleton immediately offered *Endurance* and her crew for service. Winston Churchill, then First Lord of the Admiralty, wired his thanks, but the expedition was told to proceed. *Endurance* sailed from Plymouth on August 8 'to carry on our white warfare,' as Shackleton put it. After calling in at Madeira, Buenos Aires and South Georgia, the expedition pushed into the Weddell Sea pack and soon found itself squeezing through leads that were ever narrower.

By January 19, 1915, *Endurance* was caught. The events that followed have grown to near-legend, becoming nearly as famous as the story of Scott's last expedition. The ship, inexorably crushed by the grinding ice floes, finally sank on November 21. Shackleton and his men lived on the pack ice for five months before they managed to sail three small boats to Elephant Island in the South Shetlands. Since Elephant Island was uninhabited, however, Shackleton and five others were forced to sail another 1300 km across the open sea in one of the boats, the six-meter *James Caird*, which the ship's carpenter had decked over with spare timbers, to seek help from the whalers at South Georgia. After 16 exhausting days at sea, they landed at South Georgia, completing one of the greatest feats of navigation in history.

But their landfall was at King Haakon Bay, on South Georgia's uninhabited southwest coast, and the whaling stations were on the island's northeast side. Although no one had previously penetrated further than a kilometer or so from the coast, Shackleton had no choice but to try to cross the island. He and two of the six men who had sailed *James Caird* with him, Tom Crean and Frank Worsley, hiked for 36 hours continuously over the 1800m mountains and crevassed glaciers to reach the whaling station at Stromness Harbour; as they neared the station, impassable ice cliffs forced them to lower themselves down an icy, nine-meter waterfall. Upon their arrival at the whaling station, on May 20, 1916, their long beards, matted hair, ragged clothes – and fierce body odor, no doubt – caused the first three people they met to flee in disgust. At the home of the station manager, where they bathed and were fed and clothed, Shackleton asked, 'When was the war over?' 'The war is not over,' the manager answered. 'Millions are being killed. Europe is mad. The world is mad.' That night a whaler was dispatched to King Haakon Bay to pick up the three men left behind there. After three failed rescue attempts over the next four months, Shackleton enlisted the help of *Yelcho*, a steamer lent by the Chilean government, and was finally able to pick up all 22 men stranded at Elephant Island on August 30.

Still, Shackleton's troubles were not over, for the Ross Sea party had encountered its own difficulties. *Aurora* had intended to winter at Ross Island, but a blizzard had blown the ship from its moorings, stranding 10 men at Cape Evans, who spent a miserable winter with minimal supplies. *Aurora* was beset for 10 months, finally getting free on March 14, 1916. Shackleton joined up with the ship in New Zealand, and, after an extensive refitting, *Aurora* was able to relieve the marooned Cape Evans party on January 10, 1917. The war, meanwhile, would rage for 23 more bloody months.

Mawson Australian geologist Douglas Mawson (1882-1958) had been asked by Robert Scott to accompany *Terra Nova*, but he declined the invitation in favor of heading up his own expedition. Already a veteran of Shackleton's *Nimrod* expedition (see above), Mawson wanted to explore new territory west of Cape Adare. With the Australian government granting him more than half the expedition's cost, Mawson escaped some of the financing worries that plagued many other explorers.

The Australasian Antarctic Expedition (AAE) sailed from Hobart on December 2, 1911, in *Aurora*, an old sealer with years of experience in the Arctic and the relief of Shackleton's Ross Sea party to its credit. At the helm was Capt John King Davis, and on board was the first airplane taken to the Antarctic, a Vickers REP monoplane that had crashed during a test flight before the expedition left Australia. Mawson brought the wingless aircraft with him anyway, hoping to use it as an 'air tractor,' but it failed at this task too when its engine seized while towing a heavy load.

Aurora arrived at the ice edge in January 1912, then headed west and followed the coast to new territories, which Mawson called King George V Land and claimed for the British crown. At Cape Denison on Commonwealth Bay, Mawson set up his base, unaware that the roaring katabatics – gravity-driven winds – made the spot one of the windiest places on earth. Mawson later memorably called it 'the home of the blizzard.' Another party of eight men, led by Frank Wild, also a veteran of Shackleton's *Nimrod* expedition, was landed at the Shackleton Ice Shelf, 2400 km west of Cape Denison. Battling wind speeds that occasionally reached more than 320 km/h at Commonwealth Bay, the AAE managed to systematically explore King George V Land, as well as neighboring Terre Adélie, during the austral summer of 1912-13. On one of these sledging trips, the first Antarctic meteorite was found. The expedition also made the first radio contact between Antarctica and another continent, on September 25, 1912, using a wireless relay at the five-man station the expedition established on Macquarie Island.

Despite those accomplishments and the comprehensive research done by the AAE, however, it is remembered primarily for the ordeal that its leader endured on a deadly dog-sledging journey. With two companions, BES Ninnis, a British soldier, and Xavier Mertz, a Swiss mountaineer and ski champion, Mawson left Cape Denison on November 10, 1912, with the goal of exploring far to the east of the expedition's base. By December 14, after crossing two heavily crevassed glaciers (later named for Mertz and Ninnis), the party had reached a point 500 km from their base. That afternoon, Ninnis disappeared down an apparently bottomless crevasse with his team of dogs – and most of the party's food, all of its dog food and its tent. Wrote Mawson later: 'It seemed so incredible that we half expected, on turning round, to find him standing there.'

Thus began a harrowing trek home. Battling hunger, cold, fatigue and vitamin A poisoning from the dog livers they were forced to eat, Mawson and Mertz struggled on. After Mertz died on January 7, when they were still more than 160 km out, Mawson sawed their remaining sledge in half with a pocket knife to lighten his load. By now his body was literally falling apart: hair coming out, toenails loosened and even the thick soles of his feet sloughing off. Somehow he managed to arrive back at Cape Evans – just in time to see *Aurora* on the horizon, sailing away.

Six men had remained behind at the hut, hoping against hope that the missing party might return. Though they radioed the ship, heavy seas prevented *Aurora* from reaching Cape Denison, and they were forced to spend another winter, arriving back in Australia in late February, 1914. In 1929-31, Mawson returned to Antarctica, leading the two summer voyages of the British, Australian and New Zealand Antarctic Research Expedition (BANZARE) to the west of Commonwealth Bay, where they discovered MacRobertson Land.

Wilkins In 1928, Australian George Hubert Wilkins (1888-1958), a Balkan War combat photographer and veteran of two Antarctic expeditions, including Shackleton's final voyage on *Quest*, decided that the time was right to attempt a flight in Antarctica. He had already flown 4000 km across the Arctic Ocean earlier in the year, the first pilot to cross the region, and now Wilkins took the same pilot (Carl Ben Eielson) and the same plane (now called *Los Angeles)* south to tackle The Ice.

With his Arctic success guaranteeing him a well-funded expedition – including a lucrative $25,000 news rights contract with American press baron William Randolph Hearst, Wilkins hitched a ride on a whaling ship, *Hektoria*, that called in at Deception Island. He also brought with him a back-up pilot, Joe Crosson, and another copy of the wood-framed Lockheed Vega monoplane, which he christened *San Francisco*. These planes were revolutionary for their time, having no wires or exposed controls to offer extra wind resistance.

Wilkins had equipped the Vegas with pontoons to enable them to take off from the protected waters of Deception's Port Foster, but on test runs he encountered a uniquely Antarctic obstacle: hundreds of albatrosses, which were attracted to the expanse of open water that was created when the ship broke the harbor ice. So Wilkins and his men – aided by crews from the nearby whaling station – were forced to clear a rough runway on shore. Rough it was: running 800m up a hill, down across ditches, up another hill, and down to the harbor. If a plane hadn't gotten up enough speed to take off by then, it would plunge into the water. On November 16, 1928, Wilkins and Ben Eielson took off from Deception in *Los Angeles*, flying for just 20 minutes before the weather closed in. Still, it was a useful shakedown – and it made history as the first powered flight in Antarctica.

A little more than a month later, Wilkins and Ben Eielson were ready to tackle a longer flight. Although they had hoped to fly from the Peninsula to the Ross Sea, bad weather made that option impractical. But on December 20, after taking off again from Deception, they flew for 11 hours across the Peninsula and along its eastern side, covering 2100 km and reaching a furthest south of 71°20'S. Eight years before, as a member of the British Imperial Expedition to Graham Land, Wilkins had been frustrated by 'the slow, blind struggles' to make progress over the difficult terrain. 'This time,' he exulted, 'I had a tremendous sensation of power and freedom – I felt liberated . . . for the first time in history, new land was being discovered from the air.' Important though the flight was, Wilkins was deceived by the appearance of the Peninsula from the air and wrongly concluded that it must be an archipelago.

Wilkins returned to the Antarctic the next summer, making more flights and new discoveries. All told, he mapped some 200,000 sq km of new territory, proving beyond any doubt the efficacy of the airplane in Antarctic work. Wilkins later supported Lincoln Ellsworth (see below) with his flights over Antarctica.

Byrd Wilkins scared American flier Richard Evelyn Byrd (1888-1957). A graduate of the US Naval Academy at Annapolis, Byrd had in 1926 claimed to be the first man to fly over the North Pole (a boast that recently has all but been disproved based on studies of his own diary from the flight). In 1927, he was narrowly beaten by Charles Lindbergh in the era's greatest race: solo across the Atlantic. With only a probable fraud and a second-place finish behind him, Byrd was now obsessed with achieving what only he knew would be his first genuine aviation milestone: first to fly over the South Pole.

Crowned with his own Arctic 'success' (few then knew that it was, in fact, a failure), Byrd raised nearly a million dollars from such eminent sponsors as Charles Lindbergh ($1000), the National Geographic Society and the *New York Times*, which paid $60,000 for exclusive rights and the privilege of sending its own reporter, Russell Owen, on the expedition. Byrd's United States Antarctic Expedition was the best-funded private expedition to Antarctica in history, and it sailed from Hoboken, New Jersey, in August 1928, in the square-rigged ship *City of New York* with not one, but three separate aircraft. 'Accompanied by business managers, physicians, cameramen, dog trainers, scientists, aviators, newspapermen,' *Time* magazine wrote of the departing expedition, 'the size and diversity of its personnel suggests a circus.'

The expedition's base, 'Little America,' was established at the Bay of Whales on the Ross Ice Shelf in January 1929. Byrd quickly set up a flying program with his three planes – the big aluminum Ford trimotor, *Floyd Bennett*, named for his North Pole pilot who had died of pneumonia earlier in the year, the smaller single-engined Fairchild, *Stars and Stripes*, and a single-engined Fokker Universal, named *The Virginian* for his home state.

In March, the expedition suffered Antarctica's first plane crash, but luckily no one was in *The Virginian*. A five-man party had been flown south to survey the Rockefeller Mountains (named for an expedition sponsor) when a blizzard blasted them for 12 days. Although the Fokker was tied down, so furious was the wind that when the pilot sat in the plane to make a radio call back to Little America, the airspeed indicator read 140 km/h. A few mornings later, the men woke to find that the plane had 'slipped the surly bonds of earth' and flown itself 800m to an inevitable crash; Byrd and the others eventually rescued them.

With winter's onset, the two remaining planes were cached in snow shelters and the men settled down to an under-snow routine of research, repair work, radio training, and recreation that included watching some of the expedition's 75 movies, specially selected for their non-provocative story lines. On August 24 the sun rose again, and preparations for the big flight were begun. By November a fuel depot had been set up at the foot of the Axel Heiberg glacier (the same one Amundsen had used) leading up to the polar plateau, since *Floyd Bennett*'s fuel tanks were not large enough to accommodate the fuel needed to get to 90°S and back.

On November 28, an expedition field party working in the Queen Maud Mountains far to the south radioed to Little America that the weather was clear. Four men – Byrd as navigator; Bernt Balchen, chief pilot; Harold June, second pilot and radio operator; and Ashley McKinley, photo surveyor – climbed into the big Ford tri-motor. Flying up the Liv Glacier, an icy on-ramp to the polar plateau, the plane was unable to climb due to the cold, thin air, forcing the men to ditch their 110 kg of emergency rations. Balchen, an experienced Arctic pilot, gained a little more altitude by throwing the plane into a hard turn toward the towering rock face on his right and catching a tiny updraft amidst the rush of air flowing down the glacier.

From there, it was simply a four-hour drone to the Pole, praying that *Floyd Bennett*'s engines would continue to beat out their powerful rhythm. They did, and at 1:14 am, on November 29, 1929, the men reached the earth's southern axis. 'For a few seconds we stood over the spot where Amundsen had stood December 14, 1911, and where Scott had also stood,' Byrd wrote. 'There was nothing now to mark that scene; only a white desolation and solitude disturbed by the sound of our engines.'

Byrd returned to the US as a national hero, feted with tickertape parades, a promotion to Rear Admiral, and a special gold medal struck in his honor. He went on to lead four more Antarctic expeditions including the second USAE of 1933-35 (in which he nearly asphyxiated himself with carbon monoxide while living alone at a tiny weather station called 'Advance Base') and the massive US Government exercise known as Operation Highjump (see below). But this was his finest hour.

Ellsworth American Lincoln Ellsworth (1880-1951), the scion of a wealthy Pennsylvania coal-mining family, had whetted his appetite for polar exploration in 1926, when he made the first flight across the North Pole with Roald Amundsen and Umberto Nobile in the airship *Norge*, three days after Byrd's (now-dismissed) claimed attainment of the Pole.

In 1931, Ellsworth began what would become a long and productive association with Hubert Wilkins (see above) – with the goal of crossing Antarctica by air. For the first of their four expeditions together, Ellsworth bought a Northrop Gamma monoplane, which he named *Polar Star*, and a stout-timbered Norwegian fishing vessel, which he named *Wyatt Earp*, after his hero, the gun-slinging marshal of the Old West, whose wedding ring Ellsworth wore and whose gun and holster he carried with him everywhere. For his pilot, Ellsworth chose Bernt Balchen, chief pilot on Byrd's expedition.

The first Ellsworth Antarctic Expedition in 1933-34 ended after just one short flight from skis in the frozen-over Bay of Whales. The plane was left overnight on an ice floe, and a massive breakup early that morning left the aircraft dangling by its wingtips from two separate pieces of the floe. The expedition was forced to retreat north, where the millionaire's money soon had the plane repaired.

In late 1934, Ellsworth was back in the Antarctic, with a new flight plan: The expedition would fly from Wilkins' old base at Deception Island to the Ross Sea via the Weddell Sea. But the season's first try was another disaster, when an engine seized up after its heavy preserving lubricant was not drained before starting. The expedition was again forced to retreat north, to pick up a spare part that Ellsworth had flown in from the factory to a southern South American port. The next flight was equally frustrating: Balchen turned the plane around after little more than an hour, citing heavy weather to the south, though Ellsworth saw only a small squall. While he retained respect for Balchen, Ellsworth did not hire him again.

The third expedition, in 1935, was lucky for Ellsworth, but only on the season's third attempt. After two false starts – a leaky fuel gauge and a threatening storm – with a new pilot, English-born Canadian pilot Herbert Hollick-Kenyon, *Polar Star* finally took off from Dundee Island at the tip of the Antarctic Peninsula on November 22, 1935, headed for the Bay of Whales on the Ross Ice Shelf. As the pair flew south, sighting and naming the Eternity and Sentinel ranges, Ellsworth was overcome with realization that his years of effort were finally paying off: 'Suddenly I felt supremely happy for my share in the opportunity to unveil the last continent in human history.'

Though the 3700-km flight was intended to last just 14 hours, even with landings to refuel, poor weather stretched the actual trip to two weeks, during which time the pair established four separate camps. Unfortunately, their radio went dead during that period, prompting fear that they had perished. Even on the last leg of the flight, problems plagued them: *Polar Star* ran out of fuel 25 km from the Bay of Whales on the Ross Ice Shelf, and they spent eight days on foot to reach it. Australia, meanwhile, urged on by Douglas Mawson and John King Davis, dispatched a 'rescue' attempt, although Wilkins and *Wyatt Earp* had already made detailed plans to pick up Ellsworth and Hollick-Kenyon at the Bay of Whales after their flight. The Australians met the explorers at Byrd's former base, Little America II, where the explorers had been living comfortably for nearly a month. Heavy ice, meanwhile, slowed *Wyatt Earp*, which arrived four days later. After returning to a heroes' welcome in the US, Ellsworth made one final expedition to Antarctica with his faithful friend Hubert Wilkins in 1938. He then retired from exploration for good.

The Modern Era

Wilkins' flight was one of the last large private expeditions made to Antarctica. WWII severely interrupted the plans of many explorers, and after the war the cost of mounting a major expedition pushed nearly everyone but national governments out of the game. In 1943, the British began the permanent occupation of Antarctica, with its establishment of 'Base A' at Port Lockroy on Weinecke Island.

Operations 'Highjump' & 'Windmill' In 1946, the United States launched Operation 'Highjump,' the largest Antarctic expedition ever mounted. Officially called the US Navy Antarctic Developments Project, the expedition was primarily a training exercise that gave US forces experience in polar operations, which would have been especially valuable had the Cold War, then developing with the Soviet Union, flared into an all-out Arctic fight. Highjump sent 4700 men, 33 aircraft, 13 ships and 10 Caterpillar tractors to the continent, and used helicopters and icebreakers for the first time in the Antarctic. Tens of thousands of aerial photographs were taken along nearly three-quarters of the continent's coast (though their usefulness for mapmaking was limited by a lack of ground surveys). A smaller, follow-up expedition the next year (later nicknamed Operation 'Windmill' for its extensive use of helicopters) surveyed major features sighted by Highjump.

ANARE In February 1954, Phillip Garth Law and the Australian National Antarctic Research Expeditions (ANARE) set up Mawson station in East Antarctica. (See Law's sidebar on ANARE's early years, in the East Antarctica chapter.) Named for Douglas Mawson, this was the first permanent scientific station set up on the continent, and the only one outside of the Peninsula. Today, Mawson is one of Australia's three continental stations.

International Geophysical Year (IGY) A growing interest in earth and atmospheric sciences during the late 1940s prompted the declaration of the International Geophysical Year. The IGY, which ran from July 1, 1957, to December 31, 1958, was timed to coincide with a peak level of sunspot activity. Although its objective was to study outer space and the whole earth, with 66 countries participating from locations all around the planet, the IGY left its greatest legacy in the Antarctic.

Twelve countries – Argentina, Australia, Belgium, Chile, France, Japan, New Zealand, Norway, South Africa, the UK, the US and the USSR – established more than 40 stations on the Antarctic continent and another 20 on the subantarctic islands. Among these were the US base at the South Pole, created through a massive 84-flight airdrop of 725 metric tons of building materials, and the Soviet base ('Vostok') at the Geomagnetic Pole. Many countries also operated tractor traverses across great sections of the continental interior, and the British Commonwealth Transantarctic Expedition, led by Vivian Fuchs, was the first to make an overland crossing of the continent (see also the Private Adventures in Antarctica chapter). The international cooperation promoted by the IGY led to the creation of the

'Oh My God, It's Female!'

That was all I heard as I climbed a rope to the ceiling of the aircraft hangar at McMurdo. 'How the hell does he know from that angle?' was my first thought. 'I'm wearing the same trousers as everyone else.' I'd been at McMurdo for almost three weeks and thought I had run the gauntlet of male mumblings, fumblings and assaults. After all, here I was with my peers – scientists from all over the world – learning to prusik (the mountaineering word for climbing a rope) in a survival skills course.

I was also learning, however, that as a woman in Antarctica I needed to master another, entirely different set of survival skills. The Antarctic had always been a men's club. When I first arrived, I got the distinct feeling that the men thought we women were there just to have a look, much as you used to be allowed to peek in on the exclusive men's club in the big cities. I arrived in 1978, just four years after the first woman had wintered at McMurdo. We were still treated as strange animals – but the opinions about exactly how we should be handled differed as much as the individual men on the station. There were 650 men on base, and their treatment of the 42 women ranged from abject deference to out-and-out solicitation, from respect to contempt.

Being a biologist, I found that the men fell into three natural categories. The Predators were the big nuisance. They would lie in wait at every turn. I could go nowhere – except the women's toilet – without encountering a Predator waiting to pounce. The best thing to do was hook up with someone, which I discovered stopped most of the Predators the way it does among wolf packs. (The strongest male wolf gets to the female first and all the others wait around in a circle without interfering until he's finished. How far above the animals or below the angels are we?)

That brings me to the Scavengers. They served a most useful purpose in scavenging the pieces left after the gauntlet of the Predators. The Scavengers were considerate enough to stay away and wait for a signal from you – so, after several dinners in the mess hall sitting next to what I thought were the most attractive of the men, I hooked up with one. He accompanied me most places, and this kept the Predators at bay.

The Herbivores were a different matter. They apparently would have nothing to do with the flesh. In fact, they usually gathered in groups at any function, including meals. They would not even look at you. Conversation with a female was evidently a no-no, and even a curt nod of the head or a sly glance was too much. They did not want to be bothered with females and since we were in such short supply, maybe they didn't have such a bad idea. Out of sight, out of mind – with no subsequent longings or problems. Don't stir or heat, and it won't boil!

Within this framework, we all had a great time. We shared the work, the troubles and the fun as good companions. And there was lots of work: from 6 am to 10:30 pm every day except Sunday, when we had brunch instead of breakfast and went to chapel afterwards. Then, of course, back to work. ■

–Dr Rita Mathews, retired biologist, frequently lectures on polar cruise ships.

Antarctic Treaty (see Government & Politics, below).

Women in Antarctica Women were largely excluded from the work done in Antarctica until very recently. Norwegian Caroline Mikkelsen, the first woman to set foot on the Antarctic continent, landed at the Vestfold Hills with her whaling captain husband Klarius on February 20, 1935, but it was nearly 40 years before women had a significant presence on The Ice.

In fact, the Antarctic programs operated by various national governments had an official ban on women for decades. This sexism was justified by rationalizations about physical strength and the difficulty of providing separate toilet facilities. The real difficulty, in all likelihood, would have been experienced by the women left at home by male Antarctic expeditioners, who doubtless felt pressure from those women to prevent other females from going south. Indeed, many people say that the sexual tensions that build in Antarctica's isolation *are* exacerbated by mixed company.

The first women wintered on Antarctica in 1947, when Edith Ronne and Jennie Darlington spent a year with their husbands on Stonington Island in the Antarctic Peninsula region during the Ronne Antarctic Research Expedition. The women had planned to accompany the expedition just as far as Valparaiso, Chile, and only at the last minute was leader Finne Ronne able to convince his wife to stay with the expedition to help write its newspaper dispatches. Jennie Darlington, who was asked to remain as well, became pregnant during the expedition and nearly gave birth to the first native Antarctican. She later wrote *My Antarctic Honeymoon* (see Books in Facts for the Visitor), about the expedition's trying personal relationships.

The first women to see the South Pole were two stewardesses, Patricia Hepinstall and Ruth Kelly, aboard the first commercial flight in Antarctica, a PanAm stratocruiser that departed Christchurch and landed at McMurdo on October 15, 1957.

In 1956, Russian marine geologist Marie V Klenova worked for part of the austral summer at the Russian station Mirnyy, and in 1968-69, four Argentine women did hydrographic research in the Antarctic Peninsula region.

In 1969 the US finally allowed women to participate in the national Antarctic program for the first time. A four-woman group of geologists and a husband-and-wife team worked on The Ice that year, and New Zealand also sent a woman biologist to Antarctica. On November 11, 1969, the first women to reach the Pole arrived by US Navy aircraft; they spent a few hours there before flying back to McMurdo.

In 1974, American biologist Mary Alice McWhinnie, who had spent nearly a decade doing research in Antarctic seas aboard the research vessel *Eltanin*, became the chief scientist at McMurdo station. McWhinnie and her colleague, Sister Mary Odile Cahoon, a teaching nun from Minnesota, wintered at McMurdo that year, the first women to do so. Sister Mary later said, in Barbara Land's excellent book, *The New Explorers: Women in Antarctica*, that the US Navy and the National Science Foundation 'felt more comfortable having a couple of maiden aunts test the situation.' The first woman to winter at the South Pole, physician Michele Eileen Raney, was the station's lone female during the winter of 1979.

Artist Nel Law was the first Australian woman to set foot in Antarctica, accompanying her husband Phillip Law there in 1960-61. It was another 15 years before the first Australian women were allowed to work in Antarctica, and the first Australian woman (Louise Holliday) wintered only in 1981, at Davis Station.

The first woman leader of an Antarctic station was Australia's Diana Patterson, who was the officer-in-charge at Mawson station in 1989.

In December 1990, Germany's Georg von Neumayer station was staffed by the first all-female group to winter on Antarctica. Eight women spent 14 months at the

Glaciology

The Antarctic Ice Sheet The Antarctic ice sheet has an area of about 13.3 million sq kms (1.7 times the size of Australia, 1.4 times the size of the USA or 1.3 times the size of Europe). It is thicker than four km in some locations and on average is about 2.7 km thick – giving a total ice volume of about 32.4 million cubic kms.

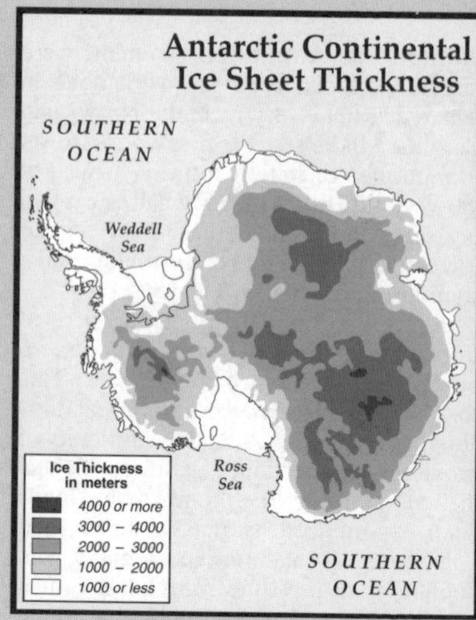

This enormous amount of ice has formed through the accumulation of snow over millions of years. The amount of snow deposited in any one year is relatively very low – Antarctica is a desert, and it is the driest continent on Earth. Because the snow has deposited over so many years without melting, the ice sheet provides a natural archive that glaciologists and climatologists study for evidence of past environments and of climatic changes.

As snow is deposited year after year in the interior of the ice sheet, it consolidates to form ice. The ice flows (due to pressure created by its own weight) from the high interior towards the Antarctic coast, where large slabs break off the ice sheet to form icebergs.

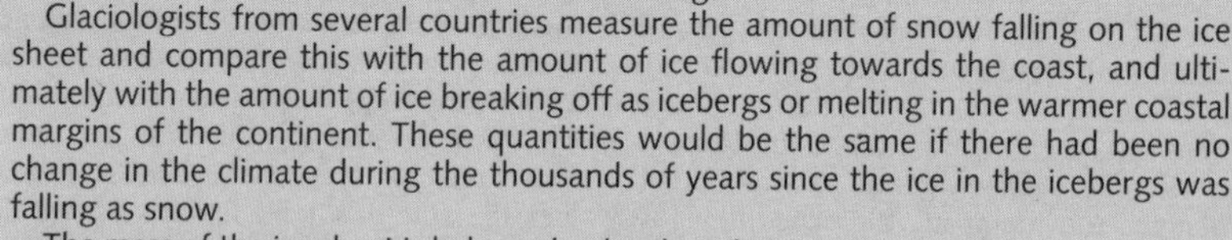

Glaciologists from several countries measure the amount of snow falling on the ice sheet and compare this with the amount of ice flowing towards the coast, and ultimately with the amount of ice breaking off as icebergs or melting in the warmer coastal margins of the continent. These quantities would be the same if there had been no change in the climate during the thousands of years since the ice in the icebergs was falling as snow.

The mass of the ice sheet is balanced only when the amount of ice coming in is equal to the amount flowing out, a condition called steady state. A positive mass budget – meaning more snow is falling than is flowing out to the coast – suggests that there has been a climate change in which more snow is falling now than did some time (maybe thousands of years) in the past. A negative mass budget suggests that less snow is falling now than in the past.

To calculate the mass budget of a particular section of the Antarctic ice sheet, glaciologists make measurements of ice surface height and thickness, then determine the rate of snow accumulation and the speed of the ice as it moves towards the coast. By flying over the ice sheet, or by traversing it with oversnow tractor trains, glaciologists are able to utilize satellite surveying techniques to measure ice surface height. Ice thickness is measured using downward-looking radars. Global positioning satellites accurately measure the position of markers in the ice sheet, which over time reveals the speed of the ice flow.

Although such measurements have been made over much of the Antarctic ice sheet, it is not feasible to directly measure the whole ice sheet. But remote sensing from satellites is used to provide observations of large areas and long time intervals, and computer modeling studies are carried out to estimate the mass budget of different areas of the ice sheet and of the whole Antarctic ice sheet.

Drilling into the Past As snow is deposited on the surface of the Antarctic ice sheet, different chemicals and gasses that have dissolved and mixed in the snow and in the atmosphere become trapped in the ice. By drilling through the ice sheet and analyzing the ice and air trapped in the bubbles, glaciologists access an archive of past climate change.

The oxygen isotope ratio (or 'delta value') of melted ice samples is related to the temperature when the ice was deposited as snow. Thus, a climate history can be built up by measuring delta value from the surface of the ice sheet down. At Russia's Vostok station in central Antarctica, an ice core has been drilled to a depth of more than three km. The ice at the bottom of this core is about 250,000 years old, and the delta values show several glacial cycles; that is, several ice ages and warmer interglacial periods.

Air pockets between snow grains on the surface of the ice sheet become bubbles under high pressure deep down in the ice. These bubbles contain tiny samples of the atmosphere from earlier times. Analysis of the air trapped in the bubbles allows glaciologists to examine how the concentrations of different gasses in the atmosphere have changed over time.

While some ice cores, like the one drilled at Vostok, give us a climate history extending back hundreds of thousands of years, they cannot be dated accurately. Others, however, drilled at locations where the snow accumulation is relatively high, can provide very accurate dating. This is because several samples can be analyzed for each year of snow accumulation if the annual snow layer is thick enough. However, these ice cores do not extend back in time as far as the deeper, low accumulation cores, so the shallower, high snow accumulation ice cores provide very accurately dated climate and environmental data, but only for the past few thousand years.

Because the delta value is related to temperature when the snow was deposited, it has an annual cycle: it is colder in winter, warmer in summer. The chemical compound hydrogen peroxide, which is dissolved in the ice, also shows an annual cycle. Hydrogen peroxide is formed in the atmosphere naturally by a chemical reaction that requires ultraviolet light. In Antarctica, where the sun is above the horizon for 24 hours per day at midsummer, yet below the horizon at midwinter, there is a large variation in ultraviolet light throughout the year and thus a marked annual cycle of hydrogen peroxide in the ice cores. Once the annual cycles in the ice core have been detected, the core is dated very easily by counting the number of cycles.

There is a third technique (completely independent of the above annual cycles) for dating an ice core. Sulfate is a chemical which is blasted into the atmosphere from time to time by erupting volcanoes. The sulfate is then distributed around the globe in the atmosphere, and dissolved in the rain and snow. By measuring sulfate concentration in the ice cores, glaciologists can 'see' past volcanic eruptions. By collaborating with volcanologists, they can then determine which sulfate signals in the ice correspond with which volcanic eruption and, more importantly, when that eruption occurred. ■

–Dr Jo Jacka, glaciologist, Antarctic Cooperative Research Centre and the Australian Antarctic Division

station, nine of them in complete isolation. The group's physician, Monica Puskeppeleit, was the station leader. For more on women in Antarctica, see the sidebar 'Oh My God, It's Female!'

GEOGRAPHY

Viewed on a map, Antarctica somewhat resembles a giant stingray, with its tail snaking up toward South America's Tierra del Fuego and its head swimming into the Indian Ocean. Discounting the 'tail,' the continent is roughly circular, with a diameter of about 4500 km and an area of about 14.2 million sq km. It is the fifth-largest continent, ahead of Australia and Europe. It is also the most arid and – with an average elevation of 2250m – the highest continent. Surrounded by the Southern Ocean, Antarctica is the most isolated continent as well.

Antarctica is divided into two parts by the massive range of the Transantarctic Mountains, which run for about 2900 km. The two parts are East Antarctica (sometimes referred to as 'Greater Antarctica') and West Antarctica (sometimes called 'Lesser Antarctica'), with the directions deriving from 0° Longitude. The continent's highest point is 4897m Vinson Massif.

The Antarctic Peninsula separates the two great embayments into the continent, the Weddell and Ross Seas. Each of these seas has its own ice shelf – the Ronne Ice Shelf and the Ross Ice Shelf, respectively – which are extensions of the great Antarctic ice sheet. The Ross Ice Shelf, roughly the size of France, is the world's largest ice shelf; the largest glacier in Antarctica is the Lambert Glacier, which flows onto the Amery Ice Shelf in East Antarctica.

Although many sources describe Antarctica as being 98% covered by ice, analysis of the most recent satellite imaging of the continent shows that, in fact, ice covers 99.6% of Antarctica. Antarctica's ice sheets contain 90% of the world's ice – 30 million cubic km – which contains nearly 70% of the world's fresh water. This ice is up to 4775m thick, and in some places, its enormous weight has depressed the underlying landmass by nearly 1600m. (Antarctica's continental shelf is about three times deeper than that of any other continent.) In the unlikely event of the Antarctic ice sheet melting, the world's oceans would rise by up to 70m, and West Antarctica would become an archipelago of small, mountainous islands (much like Indonesia), while East Antarctica would be a continental landmass about the size of Australia.

In September, Antarctica's late winter, the size of the continent effectively doubles with the freezing of the sea ice, which can extend more than 1000 km from the coast.

The Antarctic Convergence is a temperature and salinity boundary of the Southern Ocean. North of this seasonally and longitudinally varying line, the summer surface seawater temperature is about 7.8°C, while south of it the temperature drops to 3.9°C. In winter, the temperature drops from 2.8°C north of the Convergence to 1.1°C south of it. The Convergence is an area of great biological importance, for the mixing of the cooler southern seas with the warmer northern waters acts as a great mixing agent, bringing a great upwelling of nutrients to the surface. See the Icebergs sidebar in the Antarctic Peninsula chapter.

GEOLOGY

The rocks of East Antarctica are at least three billion years old, placing them among the oldest on earth. In fact, the oldest terrestrial rock yet discovered was found in Enderby Land (roughly between 40° and 60°E) by Australian geologist Lance Black in 1986. Zircon dating put the sample at 3.93 billion years old. West Antarctica, meanwhile, is relatively new: only 700 million years old. See the Antarctic Science chapter and the sidebar Glaciology.

CLIMATE

The Antarctic is synonymous with cold, thanks to its polar location, its high elevation, its lack of a protective, water vapor-filled atmosphere, and its permanent ice cover, which reflects about 80% of the sun's radiation back into space. Interestingly, the South Pole is not the coldest part

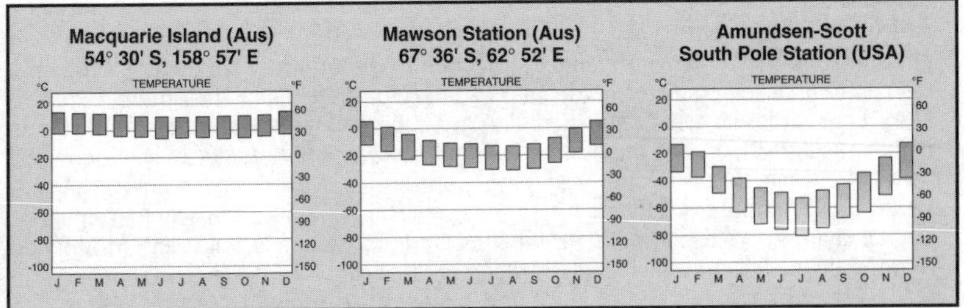

of the continent. The lowest temperature ever recorded on Earth's surface was measured at -89.6°C at Russia's Vostok station on July 21, 1983. Mean temperatures in the Antarctic interior range from -40°C to -70°C during the coldest month, and from -15°C to -35°C during the warmest month. On the coast, temperatures are considerably warmer: -15°C to -32°C in the winter, and from +5°C to -5°C in the summer, with the Antarctic Peninsula experiencing the highest temperatures year round.

The interior of Antarctica, despite its ice cap, is the world's driest desert, since the extreme cold freezes water vapor out of the air; annual snowfall on the polar plateau is equivalent to less than five cm of rain.

Antarctica experiences the strongest winds on the planet: the katabatic winds caused by denser, colder air rushing down off the polar plateau to the coast. These can achieve velocities of up to 320 km/h. The winds on the polar plateau, by contrast, are usually very light, with the highest monthly mean velocity at the Pole not greater than 30 km/h.

Blizzards are a typical Antarctic phenomenon in which very little, if any, snow actually falls. Instead, the snow is picked up and blown along the surface by the wind, resulting in blinding conditions in which objects less than a meter away may be invisible. Obviously such conditions are extremely dangerous, and several people have perished just meters from safety when they could not find their way back to shelter.

Whiteouts are another peculiar Antarctic condition, in which there are no shadows or contrasts between objects. A uniformly grey or white sky over a snow-covered surface can yield these whiteouts, which cause a loss of depth perception – for both humans and birds.

ECOLOGY & ENVIRONMENT

Antarctica, with its extremely harsh climatic conditions, has a fairly sensitive ecology. Visitors must respect that sensitivity to ensure that no damage is done – and also to avoid fines of up to $10,000 (US citizens) or even imprisonment (British citizens)! Once it is ratified, the Antarctic Treaty system's Protocol on Environmental Protection will be legally binding on all visitors (who are nationals of its signatory countries) to Antarctica, whether they are on governmental or private visits. See the Environmental Issues chapter.

Although tourism to Antarctica is occasionally criticized as being harmful to the Antarctic environment, in truth the impact made by tourists is absolutely minimal when compared to that of scientific activities on the continent. Using the unit of a 'person-day' (that is, one person spending 24 hours on the Antarctic continent or a subantarctic island), tourists accounted for about 0.5% of all person-days logged in Antarctica during the 1995-96 season. Ship-based tourists leave behind almost no trace of their stay (hopefully!), and those few who spend the night on the continent are not supposed to leave behind any evidence of their having done so.

Some scientists like to raise the point that cumulative visits to the same place (by tourists, for example) may have long-term effects not yet understood. In fact, there are

Antarctic Site Inventory

The 1991 Protocol on Environmental Protection to the Antarctic Treaty (the 'Protocol') is an exciting development (see sidebars Guidance for Visitors and The Antarctic Treaty). The Treaty parties have long grappled with Antarctic environmental issues, and this new regime of assessments and monitoring is aimed at protecting Antarctica's environmental riches over time. But assessments and monitoring will have little utility unless they are supported by rigorously collected data that allows a fair analysis of whether environmental changes are occurring at visitor sites, and unfortunately, sufficient information is presently unavailable. Such analysis is complicated, as visitors' impact will depend on many variables, such as the physical and biological features of the sites visited, the frequency and timing of visits, the number of visitors, and what visitors do while on site.

The Antarctic Site Inventory project, which began field work in 1994, intends to fill this void. The Inventory has begun assembling a database to assist the Treaty Parties in determining how best to minimize any potential adverse impacts from tourism or other activities. At key times during the course of the Antarctic spring and summer field season, the project places two-person field teams aboard expedition ships and other platforms (most notably, the British ice patrol ship HMS *Endurance)* to collect three kinds of information. The first, Basic Site Information, includes descriptions of key physical and topographical characteristics; the latitude and longitude; the locations of floral assemblages (lichens, mosses and grasses), haul-out sites and wallow areas of Antarctic seals, discrete groups of breeding penguins and flying birds, penguin molting areas and guano-melt streams; glacial-melt streams; and how the site is accessed and exited.

The second category, Variable Site Information, includes specific data concerning weather and other environmental conditions (sea ice extent, cloud cover, snow cover, temperature, wind direction and speed); particular biological variables relating to penguins and flying birds (numbers of adults or individual animals, active nests, numbers and ages of chicks); and the nature and extent of any visitor impacts that may be observed (footprints or paths through moss beds, cigarette butts, film canisters and other litter). It is important for the project's field teams to visit sites during the peak of

several places on Antarctica that do get remarkably high tourist traffic (see chart, Most Visited Sites, in Antarctic Peninsula chapter). Many of these locations, however, are being studied (see the sidebar above). Yet scientific stations – permanent facilities – represent the largest possible number of cumulative visits to a single site. As any visitor to one can attest, it is clear that by far the most serious environmental impacts in Antarctica occur at scientific stations, where personnel eat, sleep, work, drive, fly and eliminate on shore every day for years on end.

By the time their ship reaches the continent, many tourists are better-versed in environmental concerns in Antarctica than some members of certain national Antarctic science programs.

FLORA

Plant species are actually more numerous than first impressions of Antarctica would lead you to believe, but they are far smaller and more inconspicuous than plants in other latitudes. Some 350 species of lichens, 100 species of mosses, and hundreds of species of algae, including 20 species of snow algae – which form colorful patches of pink, red, yellow or green on areas of permanent snow – live in Antarctica. Some remarkable species of lichens and algae can even live *inside* rocks, inhabiting the spaces between individual grains of the rock. But there are no trees or shrubs in Antarctica and just two species of indigenous vascular plants: a grass *(Deschampsia antarctica)* and a pearlwort *(Colobanthus quitensis)*. The subantarctic islands, of course, have much more diverse

penguin egg-laying, when the best nest counts are obtained, and then, about five to six weeks later, when chick numbers are at their peak; because the numbers of chicks produced per active nest indicates the productivity of a particular colony.

At each site, investigators attempt to select and establish control colonies (those that are seldom disturbed) and experimental colonies (frequently disturbed) to census. The intent is to regularly repeat censuses both near and far from landing beaches where visitors access a particular location, to allow comparisons over time between frequently and infrequently visited areas. As standard practice, investigators count all seals at the landing beaches of all survey sites visited, and all southern elephant seal wallows that are found.

The third information category is Maps and Photodocumentation. The project intends to produce accurate up-to-date maps of each site, showing the major physical features of the site, locations of the principal colonies and assemblages of fauna and flora, and points that offer clear vantage for photographing penguin colonies, seal haul-out sites, floral associations and other features. In the first two field seasons, 1994-96, Inventory investigators made 157 survey visits to 47 different locations, including 27 of the 29 most frequently visited (by tourists) locations on the Antarctic Peninsula.

These sites are the ones likely to generate the most attention – and possibly concern about potential adverse environmental effects – under the Protocol. At these 47 sites, 299 locations have been established for conducting repetitive, in-season and season-to-season, censuses of penguins, flying birds, and seals; and 60 of these 299 locations have been selected and established as potential 'control sites' to allow comparisons between visited colonies and non-visited colonies over time.

The Antarctic Site Inventory's database should assist the Treaty parties in fulfilling the environmental assessment and monitoring requirements of the Protocol and lead to a better understanding of the environmental impacts of tourists – and all visitors to Antarctica. ■

–**Ron Naveen**, principal investigator of the Antarctic Site Inventory project

floras, with South Georgia alone boasting at least 50 species of vascular plants.

FAUNA

Antarctica's native land animals are all invertebrates, with nearly all terrestrial macrofauna belonging to the phylum *Arthropoda*, including mites, lice, springtails, midges and fleas, many of which are parasites of seals and birds. The largest animal that permanently dwells on land in Antarctica is a wingless midge *(Belgica antarctica)* that grows to just over a centimeter long.

Approximately 45 species of birds breed south of the Antarctic Convergence, including seven of the 17 living species of penguins. Just a few bird species breed in Antarctica, among them emperor, Adélie and gentoo penguins, the snow petrel, the Antarctic petrel and the South Polar skua.

The Southern Ocean, by contrast to Antarctica's relative barrenness, is an environment teeming with life. With the tiny, shrimplike krill *(Euphasia)* as the basis of its food chain, the Southern Ocean supports a wealth of fish, seal, whale and seabird species.

For more information regarding Antarctic fauna, refer to the color Wildlife Guide.

When viewing Antarctic wildlife, it is important to keep your distance. For one thing, the Guidelines for Visitors to the Antarctic require it – as often does your safety. But there's another reason to keep back: your photos will not turn out as well if you press in close: the animals are more likely to move, blurring your picture. Your

The Antarctic Treaty: A Unique Agreement for a Unique Place

Imagine a world where there has never been war, where the environment is fully protected, where research has priority. This is the land the Antarctic Treaty parties call a natural reserve, devoted to peace and science.

The Antarctic Treaty is a landmark agreement through which countries active in Antarctica consult on the uses of the whole continent. The Treaty, which applies to the area south of 60°S, is surprisingly short but remarkably effective. (For the full text of the Treaty, see Appendix.) In its 12 articles, the Treaty:

- stipulates that Antarctica should forever be used exclusively for peaceful purposes and not become the scene or object of international discord
- prohibits nuclear explosions, the disposal of nuclear waste and measures of a military nature
- guarantees freedom of science and promotes the exchange of scientists and research results
- allows on-site inspection by foreign observers to ensure the observance of the Treaty
- removes the potential for sovereignty disputes between Treaty parties.

The Treaty was negotiated by the 12 nations present in Antarctica during the International Geophysical Year (IGY) (1957-58). They wanted to maintain the cooperation that characterized the IGY, when science proceeded unhindered. Such cooperation was particularly important in the context of the Cold War, then causing international tensions elsewhere. Since entering into force on June 23, 1961, the Treaty has been recognized as one of the most successful international agreements ever negotiated. Problematic differences over territorial claims are effectively set aside and as a disarmament regime the Treaty has been outstandingly successful. Treaty parties remain firmly committed to a system still effective in protecting their essential Antarctic interests.

Membership continues to grow. There are (as of May 1996) 43 parties to the Treaty Twenty-six of them are Consultative Parties on the basis of either being original signatories or by conducting substantial research in Antarctica. The parties meet annually to discuss issues as diverse as scientific cooperation, measures to protect the environment, management of tourism and preservation of historic sites – and they are committed to taking decisions by consensus.

presence changes the animals' behavior, so the further back you keep, the more natural the animal will act. While wildlife may not seem to be concerned about your presence, this can be a false impression – animals may in fact be under considerable stress. A single thoughtless gesture can cause the loss of a bird egg or chick, or the crushing of a seal pup by a frightened adult.

SPECIES CONSERVATION

International measures adopted in 1964 provide overall protection for *all* animal and plant species in Antarctica. No animal or plant in Antarctica may be collected or killed without a license, except in an emergency as food. For details about international measures to further protect Antarctic wildlife, see the Environmental Issues chapter, and for information regarding the status of individual species, refer to the color Wildlife Guide.

PROTECTED AREAS

Since no nation indisputably owns any part of Antarctica, there are no national parks.

Protection of the Environment Protecting Antarctica's unique ecosystem is a priority of the Treaty system. Specific environment measures include:

The **Agreed Measures for the Conservation of Antarctic Fauna and Flora** (1964) protect native animals and birds. In addition, areas of outstanding ecological interest may be set aside as Specially Protected Areas. Sites of Special Scientific Interest were later added to protect significant scientific values.

The **Convention for the Conservation of Antarctic Seals** (1978) provides a means to regulate commercial sealing activities, in the unlikely event that they should ever be resumed. Three species of seal are totally protected and catch limits are set for others.

The **Convention on the Conservation of Antarctic Marine Living Resources** (1980) was adopted in response to fears that unregulated fishing for krill, at the center of the Antarctic food chain, might threaten the marine ecosystem. It ensures that the Southern Ocean's living resources are treated as a single ecosystem. Measures under CCAMLR identify protected species, set catch limits, identify fishing regions, define closed seasons, regulate fishing methods and establish fisheries inspection.

The **Protocol on Environmental Protection to the Antarctic Treaty** (1991) was negotiated following the failure of the Antarctic minerals convention in 1989. Also known as the Madrid Protocol, it arose out of proposals for a comprehensive regime that would guarantee protection of the environment. The Protocol integrates a number of existing measures in a single legally binding form. Among its provisions, the Protocol:

- designates Antarctica as a 'natural reserve, devoted to peace and science'
- establishes environmental principles for the conduct of all activities
- prohibits mining
- subjects all activities to prior assessment of their environmental impacts.

Annexes to the Protocol detail measures relating to environmental impact assessment, conservation of Antarctic fauna and flora, waste disposal, marine pollution and management of protected areas. The Protocol will enter into force when it is ratified by the 26 Consultative Parties to the Antarctic Treaty. All Treaty parties have agreed to comply with the Protocol, pending its formal entry into force. ■

–**Andrew Jackson**, Acting Assistant Director of the Australian Antarctic Division's Policy and Planning Branch

But the Antarctic Treaty System does offer protection to different kinds of areas.

Specially Protected Areas (SPAs) are designed to preserve unique ecological systems. Sites of Special Scientific Interest (SSSIs) protect areas where research is either underway or planned.

Tourists – and all other unauthorized people – must stay out of both SPAs and SSSIs. While many of these areas are not marked by any signs or markers, tour leaders should know these areas and it is their responsibility to ensure that their passengers do not stray into them. Pay attention to your cruise staff so that you are aware of any SPAs or SSSIs on your visits ashore.

EXPLOITATION

Antarctica's exploration was tied directly to the exploitation of its marine mammals, specifically seals and whales. Throughout the 19th century, the discovery of new sealing grounds on subantarctic islands was in each case immediately followed by the near-extinction of the local population (see

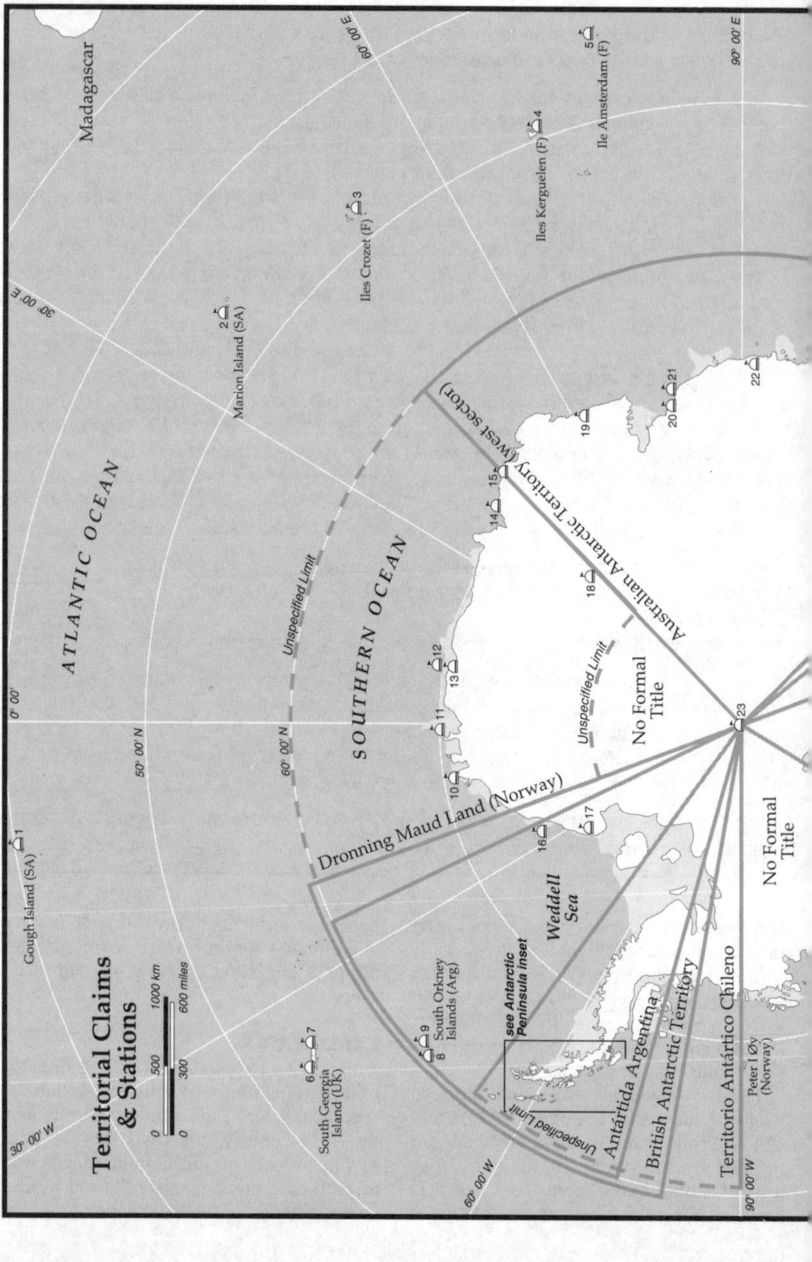

Territorial Claims & Stations

0 500 1000 km
0 300 600 miles

ATLANTIC OCEAN
SOUTHERN OCEAN
Weddell Sea
Madagascar
Gough Island (SA) 1
Marion Island (SA) 2
Iles Crozet (F) 3
Iles Kerguelen (F) 4
Ile Amsterdam (F) 5
South Georgia Island (UK) 6 7
South Orkney Islands (Arg) 8 9
10 11 12 13 14 15 16 17 18 19 20 21 22 23
Peter I Øy (Norway)
see Antarctic Peninsula inset
Unspecified Limit
Unspecified Limit
Unspecified Limit
Dronning Maud Land (Norway)
Australian Antarctic Territory (West sector)
No Formal Title
No Formal Title
Antártida Argentina
British Antarctic Territory
Territorio Antártico Chileno
30° 00' W
0° 00'
30° 00' E
60° 00' E
90° 00' E
60° 00' W
90° 00' W
50° 00' N
60° 00' N

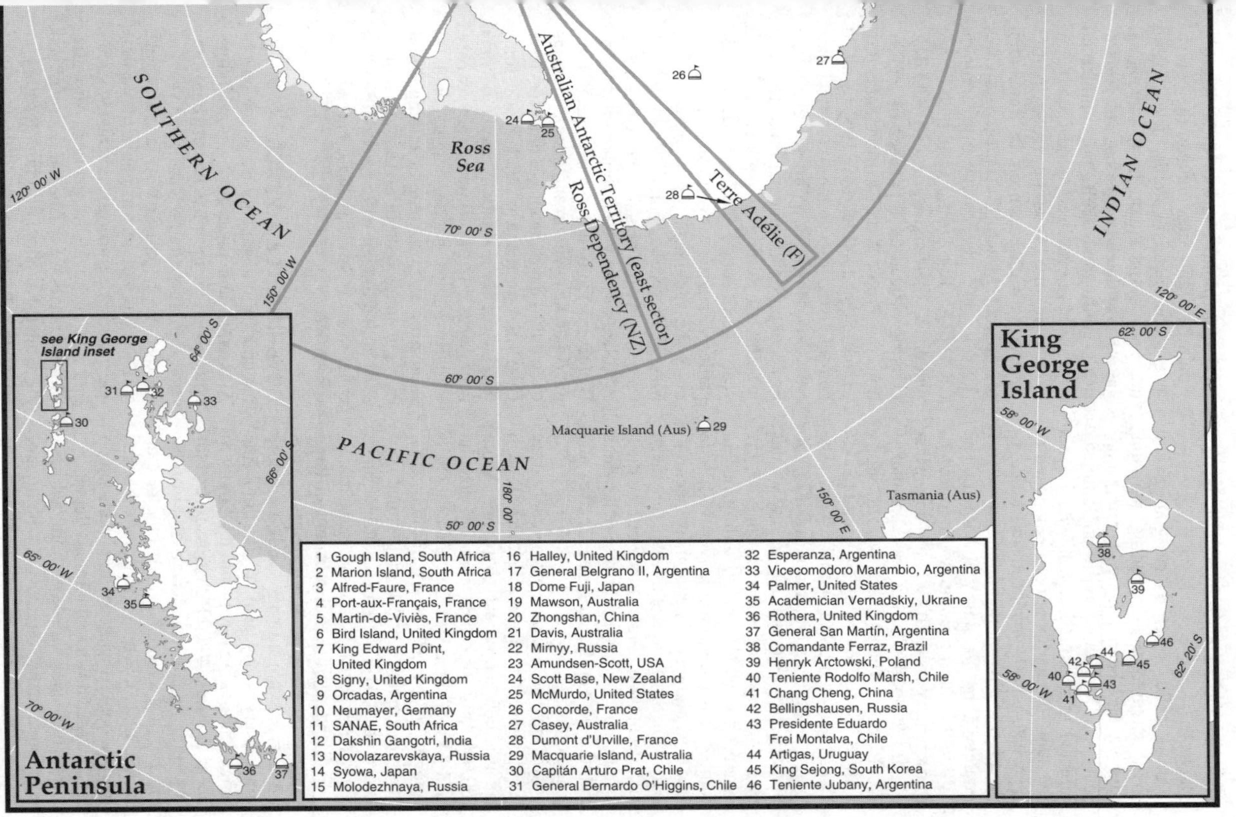
SOUTHERN OCEAN
120° 00' W
150° 00' W
Ross Sea
Australian Antarctic Territory (east sector)
Ross Dependency (NZ)
Terre Adélie (F)
INDIAN OCEAN
120° 00' E
70° 00' S
60° 00' S
50° 00' S
180° 00'
150° 00' E
PACIFIC OCEAN
Macquarie Island (Aus)
Tasmania (Aus)
Antarctic Peninsula
see King George Island inset
64° 00' S
66° 00' S
65° 00' W
70° 00' W
King George Island
62° 00' S
62° 20' S
58° 00' W
1 Gough Island, South Africa
2 Marion Island, South Africa
3 Alfred-Faure, France
4 Port-aux-Français, France
5 Martin-de-Viviès, France
6 Bird Island, United Kingdom
7 King Edward Point, United Kingdom
8 Signy, United Kingdom
9 Orcadas, Argentina
10 Neumayer, Germany
11 SANAE, South Africa
12 Dakshin Gangotri, India
13 Novolazarevskaya, Russia
14 Syowa, Japan
15 Molodezhnaya, Russia
16 Halley, United Kingdom
17 General Belgrano II, Argentina
18 Dome Fuji, Japan
19 Mawson, Australia
20 Zhongshan, China
21 Davis, Australia
22 Mirnyy, Russia
23 Amundsen-Scott, USA
24 Scott Base, New Zealand
25 McMurdo, United States
26 Concorde, France
27 Casey, Australia
28 Dumont d'Urville, France
29 Macquarie Island, Australia
30 Capitán Arturo Prat, Chile
31 General Bernardo O'Higgins, Chile
32 Esperanza, Argentina
33 Vicecomodoro Marambio, Argentina
34 Palmer, United States
35 Academician Vernadskiy, Ukraine
36 Rothera, United Kingdom
37 General San Martín, Argentina
38 Comandante Ferraz, Brazil
39 Henryk Arctowski, Poland
40 Teniente Rodolfo Marsh, Chile
41 Chang Cheng, China
42 Bellingshausen, Russia
43 Presidente Eduardo Frei Montalva, Chile
44 Artigas, Uruguay
45 King Sejong, South Korea
46 Teniente Jubany, Argentina

Southern Ocean & Subantarctic Islands chapter).

Until 1870, when Norwegian Svend Foyn patented the exploding harpoon, whaling had been practiced from small boats, as Herman Melville so famously depicted in *Moby Dick*. But with Foyn's invention, the harpoon, once embedded in the whale's flesh, exploded and killed it. No more being pulled along in a tiny whaleboat by an angry leviathan. The Antarctic whaling boom soon followed. During the years from 1904 to 1966, when whaling at South Georgia ceased, a total of 41,515 blue whales were caught, along with 87,555 fins, 26,754 humpbacks, 15,128 seis and 3716 sperm whales. The total slaughter: an astounding 175,250 animals. Little wonder that so few whales exist today: Some species, such as the mighty blue whale, are so diminished in number that individuals may have a hard time even finding another of their species to mate with. Still, about 300 whales are taken each year now by Japan – they sell the meat to help fund their scientific research, which includes data collected on age, calves and gestation.

Krill have been fished commercially since 1974, primarily by Japan and Russia, though Japan is now the primary harvester. About 100,000 tons are caught annually, and the total harvest since krill were first caught is thought to be about six million tons. Brochures marketing krill suggest that consumers mask krill's strong flavor by using a pungent spice such as soy sauce or garlic.

Fish and squid are also caught in large numbers, and around South Georgia, crabs are taken. An unfortunate – and completely unnecessary – 'bycatch' of the long-line fishermen looking for tuna in the Southern Ocean are some 40,000 albatrosses (including 8000 female wandering albatrosses, which feed at a more northerly latitude than do the males), which are drowned when they are hooked while stealing bait, which gets dragged down to enormous depths.

Iron ore, coal and other minerals have been found in the Antarctic, but their quantities – and qualities – are unknown. At present, exploiting any of these deposits would be highly uneconomic, the equivalent, in one scientist's words, of 'mining on the moon.' And although oil and natural gas are postulated to exist beneath Antarctica's continental shelf, no commercial deposits have ever been found.

In 1988, the Antarctic Treaty parties agreed to a Convention on the Regulation of Antarctic Mineral Resources Activities (known by the awkward acronym CRAMRA). But Australia and then France repudiated their signatures of CRAMRA, favoring instead another piece of legislation, the Protocol on Environmental Protection. Signed in Madrid in 1991 by all 26 consultative parties to the Antarctic Treaty (see Government & Politics, below), the Protocol on Environmental Protection will prohibit all mining in Antarctica for 50 years once it comes into force. All of the 26 parties still must pass national legislation to ratify the agreement – also known as the Madrid Protocol – before it is effective. (See the Environmental Issues chapter.)

Although many believe that the Madrid Protocol is the best possible protection for the Antarctic environment, others think that it would have been better to have CRAMRA in place instead, ready for a time when its regulations might become necessary. In the future, they worry, resource-hungry nations might decide to reverse any ban on Antarctic mining, and if no regulations controlling Antarctic mining exist at that time, it will be very difficult to enact laws as strict as those agreed to in CRAMRA.

GOVERNMENT & POLITICS

No country indisputably owns any part of Antarctica, and since there are no indigenous people there, it has no native government to run its affairs. During the years of its discovery, parts of Antarctica were being 'claimed' in the name of various queens, kings, emperors, potentates, dictators and presidents. Argentina, Australia, Chile, France, New Zealand, Norway and the United Kingdom all claim territory in Antarctica. As long as very little was going on in Antarctica, no one cared too terribly much about these claims of sovereignty. It is also important to note that many world powers – the US and Russia, for example – have made no formal territorial claims on Antarctica – but have carefully preserved their right to do so in the future. See the Territorial Claims and Stations map.

In the wake of the International Geophysical Year (see History, above), scientists and diplomats decided to codify the spirit of international cooperation shown during the IGY. This incredible and unprecedented document, called the Antarctic Treaty, has governed the continent since 1961. Although countries such as Malaysia have complained that the Antarctic Treaty member nations constitute an elite 'club' and should be replaced by a United Nations-ruled Antarctica, in fact the Treaty members represent about 80% of the world's population. Also, the Treaty is in fact open to any nation that wishes to accede to it, and any country performing significant scientific research there can become a 'consultative party,' or full voting member.

Despite the Treaty's 'freezing' of territorial claims, various methods have been employed by different countries in order to try to establish or reinforce their 'sovereignty' over large sections of Antarctic real estate. Chief among these have been flagpoles, plaques and even large representations of national flags painted on the sides of buildings. Conflicting claimants used to remove offending physical representations of 'sovereignty' placed there by rivals, and pointedly, though politely, return them via diplomatic channels. Antarctic historian Robert Headland imagines that a typical scene might have involved an ambassador being called in by a rival head of state, who would have said something like: 'We found this in *our* territory recently and wondered if you might like it back . . . '

Only a few times in Antarctic history has this careful diplomacy nearly disintegrated into 'political relations . . . by other means,' as Clausewitz famously euphemized war. The first such incident occurred in 1952 at Hope Bay on the Trinity Peninsula, when British expeditioners arriving to re-establish a base that had burned down earlier were greeted with a decidedly unfriendly welcome from their Argentine neighbors, who fired machine-guns at them (over their heads, fortunately). The governor of the Falkland Islands responded by dispatching two gunboats to reassert British sovereignty, and the commander of the Argentine station was recalled. In 1953, the British found that the Argentines and Chileans had gotten together and each built a hut on an airstrip used by Britain at Deception Island. Royal Marines arrived to oust the Argentines and Chileans from 'British territory,' and several Argentines were brought to Grytviken in South Georgia and deported to Argentina. Finally, in 1975, the British ship HMS *Shackleton* was fired on by an Argentine navy ship, which demanded that it proceed to Ushuaia, a demand *Shackleton* ignored, sailing to Stanley instead.

Acts of war – or even of physical destruction – are actually extremely rare in Antarctica. More common are subtle, even somewhat pathetic, attempts made by countries to bolster their territorial claims – and usually completely ignored by their rivals. As part of its effort to 'colonize' Antarctica, for example, Argentina has frequently sent women and children to its Esperanza station at Hope Bay on the Antarctic Peninsula. One such woman, Silvia Morello de Palma, was married to Army Captain Jorge de Palma, Esperanza's station leader, and on January 7, 1978, she gave birth to Emilio Marcos de Palma, the first 'native-born' Antarctican.

Other methods used by governments to assert territorial 'sovereignty' include the issuance of special Antarctic stamps, which, being prized by philatelists, offer the added benefit of generating a profit at the same time. The leaders of national bases in Antarctica are often given titles reflecting a governmental or administrative role over their slice of The Ice: justice of the peace, for example, or local administrator. Some countries go so far as to 'naturalize' foreign citizens at their Antarctic

GUIDANCE FOR VISITORS TO THE ANTARCTIC

Activities in the Antarctic are governed by the Antarctic Treaty of 1959 and associated agreements, referred to collectively as the Antarctic Treaty system. The Treaty established Antarctica as a zone of peace and science.

In 1991, the Antarctic Treaty Consultative Parties adopted the Protocol on Environmental Protection to the Antarctic Treaty, which designates the Antarctic as a natural reserve. The Protocol sets out environmental principles, procedures and obligations for the comprehensive protection of the Antarctic environment, and its dependent and associated ecosystems. The Consultative Parties have agreed that, pending its entry into force, as far as possible and in accordance with their legal system, the provisions of the Protocol should be applied as appropriate.

The Environmental Protocol applies to tourism and non-governmental activities as well as governmental activities in the Antarctic Treaty Area. It is intended to ensure that these activities do not have adverse impacts on the Antarctic environment, or on its scientific and aesthetic values.

This *Guidance for Visitors to the Antarctic* is intended to ensure that all visitors are aware of, and are therefore able to comply with, the Treaty and the Protocol. Visitors are, of course, bound by national laws and regulations applicable to activities in the Antarctic.

Respect Protected Areas

A variety of areas in the Antarctic have been afforded special protection because of their particular ecological, scientific, historic or other values. Entry into certain areas may be prohibited except in accordance with a permit issued by an appropriate national authority. Activities in or near designated historic sites and monuments and certain other areas may be subject to special restrictions.

- Know the locations of areas that have been afforded special protection and any restrictions regarding entry and activities that can be carried out in and near them.
- Observe applicable restrictions.
- Do not damage, remove or destroy historic sites or monuments, or any artifacts associated with them.

Respect Scientific Research

- Do not interfere with scientific research, facilities or equipment.
- Obtain permission before visiting Antarctic science and logistic support facilities; confirm arrangements 24 to 72 hours before arriving; and comply strictly with the rules regarding such visits.
- Do not interfere with, or remove, scientific equipment or marker posts, and do not disturb experimental study sites, field camps or supplies.

Be Safe

Be prepared for severe and changeable weather. Ensure that your equipment and clothing meet Antarctic standards. Remember that the Antarctic environment is inhospitable, unpredictable and potentially dangerous.

- Know your capabilities, the dangers posed by the Antarctic environment, and act accordingly. Plan activities with safety in mind at all times.

- Keep a safe distance from all wildlife, both on land and at sea.
- Take note of, and act on, the advice and instructions from your leaders; do not stray from your group.
- Do not walk onto glaciers or large snow fields without proper equipment and experience; there is a real danger of falling into hidden crevasses.
- Do not expect a rescue service; self-sufficiency is increased and risks reduced by sound planning, quality equipment and trained personnel.
- Do not enter emergency refuges (except in emergencies). If you use equipment or food from a refuge, inform the nearest research station or national authority once the emergency is over.
- Respect any smoking restrictions, particularly around buildings, and take great care to safeguard against the danger of fire. This is a real hazard in the dry environment of Antarctica.

Protect Antarctic Wildlife

Taking or harmful interference with Antarctic wildlife is prohibited except in accordance with a permit issued by a national authority.

- Do not feed, touch or handle birds or seals, or approach or photograph them in ways that cause them to alter their behavior. Special care is needed when animals are breeding or molting.
- Do not damage plants, for example by walking, driving or landing on extensive moss beds or lichen-covered scree slopes.
- Do not use guns or explosives. Keep noise to the minimum to avoid frightening wildlife.
- Do not bring non-native plants or animals into the Antarctic (eg, pet dogs and cats, house plants).
- Do not use aircraft, vessels, small boats, or other means of transportation in ways that disturb wildlife, either at sea or on land.

Keep Antarctica Pristine

Antarctica remains relatively pristine, and has not yet been subjected to large scale human perturbations. It is the largest wilderness area on earth. Please keep it that way.

- Do not dispose of litter or garbage on land. Open burning is prohibited.
- Do not disturb or pollute lakes or streams. Any materials discarded at sea must be disposed of properly.
- Do not paint or engrave names or graffiti on rocks or buildings.
- Do not collect or take away biological or geological specimens or man-made artifacts as a souvenir, including rocks, bones, eggs, fossils or parts or contents of buildings.
- Do not deface or vandalize buildings, whether occupied, abandoned or unoccupied, or emergency refuges. ■

stations. Britain charges its citizens a special 'British Antarctic Territory' tax, which goes to the colonial government of the territory and is used for activities such as producing publications or restoring old research stations as historic sites. The territory is governed by a British Government-appointed commissioner, so its residents must endure 'taxation without representation,' something that got Britain in trouble with another of its colonies long ago! Interestingly, the commissioner makes no effort to collect taxes from other residents of British Antarctic Territory, including the nationals of at least eight other nations that maintain stations there.

The US has found a practical way to put other countries at a distinct disadvantage in the Antarctic 'competition.' It bans the licensing to anyone but the American military of LC-130s, the ski-equipped Hercules cargo planes that are so useful in resupplying its continental stations at McMurdo and the South Pole. The powerful aircraft would be just as useful in the Arctic as well, so the US Government considers their use a security issue, but the restriction also neatly hampers other nations' Antarctic efforts.

POPULATION & PEOPLE

Antarctica has never had a native population. Even today, its harsh environment assures that all residents are temporary. The continent's winter population is around 1200 people; about one-third are scientists and the rest are support personnel. During the 1996 austral winter, 44 stations – operated by 18 countries – were open in Antarctic regions recording meteorological data and involved in other scientific research. In summer, the population increases seven-fold.

SOCIETY & CONDUCT

Antarctica's social rules are fairly straightforward: simply remember that anytime you are inside a shelter, even one as simple as a hut or tent, you are a guest in someone else's home. You should treat it accordingly. Antarctic bases, especially smaller ones, can be somewhat fragile societies, each with its own national character. Discretion is always advised.

All residents of Antarctic bases must take some time away from their work or otherwise adjust their schedule when tourists visit. Often, they are trying to maintain a delicate balance between a desire to be hospitable to visitors and an enormous time pressure to complete their scientific work before the season ends.

Never enter any building unless specifically invited to do so. You might interfere with scientific work, or you might simply invade someone else's privacy, an all-too-rare commodity at most Antarctic stations. Also, take off your shoes or boots whenever you enter a station building, especially accommodations, living quarters or dining area. Cleaning up mud or guano dragged in by 90 pairs of tourist boots can be a real drag, and might make bases reluctant to allow visitors in the future. Be a polite guest!

Another rule to remember: *Never* ask to use the station toilet. For one thing, you are coming from a well-equipped ship – it's environmentally inexcusable to leave your waste on Antarctica when other alternatives exist. Secondly, although it appears to be a small favor to ask, imagine multiplying the task of emptying or cleaning the toilet by several dozen, and you can understand what a major hassle tourists can be for station staff. Just make sure to go before you leave the ship!

Facts for the Visitor

PLANNING

When to Go

No tourists visit Antarctica during the winter, when the pack ice extends its icy mantle for a thousand kilometers around the continent, barricading it against all ship traffic. In any case, few people would pay thousands of dollars to experience the Antarctic winter's nearly 24 hours of darkness each day and its extreme cold – the thermometer can plummet to -50°C. At that dramatic temperature, boiling water thrown into the air freezes instantly into a cloud of snow.

So the Antarctic tour season is short – about 5½ months long, with each month offering its own highlights. October and November is early summer: The spring pack ice is breaking up, and birds – especially penguins – are courting and mating. December and January, when penguins are hatching eggs and feeding chicks, are the height of the austral summer, bringing warmer temperatures and up to 20 hours of daylight. In the late summer months of February and March, whale sighting is best, penguin chicks are beginning to fledge and adult penguins are ashore molting.

There are other factors to consider: Cruises later in the season may be less crowded, that is, not filled to capacity, so there may not be as much waiting around for Zodiacs (inflatable, motorized boats), guided station tours, etc. However, the later you wait to go, the greater the risk that much of the wildlife will already be gone to sea. For those wishing to see the historic huts of Ross Island, the best bet is to go as late in the season as possible, because even with an icebreaker, it may be impossible to penetrate the pack ice that far south earlier in the season.

Some ships visit Antarctica 10 or more times in a single season. On such ships, many staff members and lecturers are noticeably – and understandably – 'burned-out' by the end of the season. By that stage, it's 'If it's Thursday, this must be Cuverville,' and they deliver their lectures and then hightail it for their cabins, anxious to escape from the 'pax.'

What Kind of Trip

The vast majority of tourists visit Antarctica by ship. This is both practical – hotel, restaurant and sightseeing vehicle are all combined in one unit – and environmentally sound, since no tourism infrastructure is located ashore, competing for the already scarce areas of ice-free rock. This bare rock is needed by birds and seals for breeding grounds and by national Antarctic programs for their stations.

Not everyone is content to restrict themselves to the coast, however, and tourists can visit the continent's vast interior, parts of which are still largely unexplored. At present there is just one company offering visits to the interior mountains, ice sheets and even the South Pole itself (see Getting There & Away). Naturally, the complicated logistics of these visits make them very expensive.

Questions to Ask Your Tour Operator

What kind of ship is it? Is it ice-strengthened and designed for safe polar travel? Or is it an unstrengthened cruise ship that just happens to be routed south to The Ice for a cruise or two? Note also that while an icebreaker is able to push its way through far thicker ice than a merely ice-strengthened vessel, its shallower draft will also cause it to roll more in heavy seas, causing discomfort for those prone to motion sickness.

What – *exactly* – is included in the quoted 'price' of the trip? Find out whether 'port taxes' and other additional charges are included; some companies leave these charges out in order to make their advertised prices appear more competitive, but they can add as much as US$595 to your cost. What about airfare? Some tour operators include this in their prices, but most do not. Price, however, should be only one factor in your decision.

How many days will you actually spend in Antarctica? Some tour operators, for instance, include as many as three nights in South America as part of a 14-day 'Antarctica' program. How long is the voyage? Cruises to the Peninsula from South America are generally more popular because they require the least amount of time (about two days each way, as opposed to three or four, each way, for non-Peninsula destinations) at sea, which many people find uncomfortable or boring. But there are many attractions in the other parts of Antarctica that make the longer voyages worthwhile.

How many other passengers will be on board? Some ships are much more crowded than others – the smallest ships accommodate just 38 passengers, while the largest carry more than 10 times that. In general, the smaller the passenger complement, the better. Fewer than 100 passengers per cruise is best, and any ship carrying more than 150 passengers to Antarctica is simply ridiculous. This is not simply a matter of having two or more seatings in the dining room. Lectures become standing-room-only affairs, and landings ashore become assembly lines. The rules governing visits to the historic hut sites in the Ross Sea area, for example, allow no more than 40 people ashore at one time, and at one of them, no more than three passengers are allowed inside at once. Most scientific stations are reluctant to welcome more than 80 passengers in a single visit.

Although all members of IAATO (the International Association of Antarctica Tour Operators) pledge themselves to put no more than 100 people ashore at any site at the same time, this IAATO bylaw is based on the honor system, and even member companies sometimes violate it when it suits them. With a smaller ship, you will not have such crowding. There is a different atmosphere aboard larger ships, too: You don't feel as much like you are on an expedition as you are on a Caribbean or Mediterranean cruise, with all of the luxury amenities that image calls to mind – glitzy nightclubs, marble bathtubs, six-course dinners, chocolates on your pillow each night.

What are the other passengers like? Some special interest groups especially bird watchers or alumni groups, sometimes buy a large proportion of a ship's cabins for one or two cruises. Occasionally, a tour operator may try to sell the remaining cabins to unsuspecting people with different interests (or alma maters). These divergent agendas can cause tensions on a voyage. Also, where do most of the other passengers come from? Although meeting people from other countries is one of travel's chief joys and opportunities, language can be a problem on some cruises. While most Antarctic cruise passengers speak English, many do not, and if there is a large group of non-English speakers aboard, lectures and briefings may be cut short or skipped, meaning that some passengers miss important information.

Who are the lecturers aboard? The quality and enthusiasm of the lecture staff vary widely from ship to ship – and even from cruise to cruise. Ask to see the résumés of the lecturers for the cruise you have chosen. The better cruise companies arrange this well in advance of sailing. Most importantly, ask about each lecturer's previous experience in lecturing aboard cruise ships, especially *polar* cruise ships. Many eminent scientists are poor lecturers. Delivering a top-quality talk is a special skill, blending knowledge, entertainment and good humor. Is there a dedicated lecture hall aboard? On some ships, lectures appear to be an afterthought, with slide projectors and screens set up in the dining room or a drafty equipment room. What is the capacity of the lecture theater? Are there seats for all passengers, or is it 'standing room only' for latecomers?

What are the credentials of the physician on board? Some cruise lines use the doctor of the ship's crew, while others have a special doctor for the cruise. You may feel more comfortable having a doctor whose first language is English.

Does the ship carry helicopters? These can be invaluable for getting to places otherwise inaccessible (say by Zodiacs) and with their aerial reconnaissance capabilities, they can also help prevent the ship from getting stuck in ice and wasting valuable time. Helicopters can, of course, also be used for evacuation in the case of a medical emergency if the ship is close enough to an inhabited area. There's one disadvantage to helicopters, however: It is difficult to move large groups of people with them, since many models carried on Antarctic cruise ships can accommodate only six to eight passengers at a time.

Is the tour operator an IAATO member? This self-regulating industry group has banded together to promote responsible travel to Antarctica and can pressure its members to maintain high standards in ship, staff and passenger behavior in the delicate Antarctic ecosystem. (For more information, see Useful Organizations in this chapter.)

How experienced are the Expedition Leader and the Assistant Expedition Leader? (To heighten customers' sense of adventure, Antarctic tour operators refrain from calling these people 'tour leaders' or 'cruise directors.') Since the Expedition Leader and the ship's captain make all on-the-spot decisions about landings and itinerary choices, this is an important element of your cruise. Inexperienced leaders may be overly ambitious in their planning or fail to conduct as many landings as might otherwise be possible.

Maps

Although most map stores do not carry a large selection of Antarctic maps, good shops can usually order maps or navigation charts for you, or put you in touch with a national mapping agency, from which maps can be ordered.

In the United States, the US Geological Survey has topographic, geologic and reconnaissance maps of portions of Antarctica at various scales. *An Index to Topographic Maps – Antarctica* is available from the Distribution Branch, US Geological Survey, Box 25286, Federal Center, Building 41, Denver, CO 80225 USA (☎ 1-800-872-6277). One particularly nice map is the USGS' 'Satellite Image Map of Antarctica' (number I-2284 in the Miscellaneous Investigations Series), which shows that the continent is far from being a monochromatic mass of white. For aeronautic and hydrographic charts, contact the National Ocean and Atmospheric Administration's Distribution Division, National Ocean Service, Riverdale, MD 20737-1199 USA (☎ 1-301-436-6990). One particularly good map they sell is a large and detailed map of the continent on a 1:5,000,000 scale (code number GNC 26). The Smithsonian Oceanographic Sorting Center, Washington, DC 20560 USA (☎ 1-301-238-3797) offers another very good map of Antarctica on the same scale. For an index of hydrographic charts of Antarctic coastal waters, contact the Defense Mapping Agency, Office of Distribution Services, Washington, DC 20315 USA (☎ 1-301-227-2495).

The British Admiralty charts of Antarctica are also excellent. They can be purchased from many firms; one of the best is Kelvin Hughes, Charts Department, 145 Minories, London, EC3N 1NH, UK (☎ 44-171-709-9076; fax 44-171-481-1298). All charts are £13.30 each with a postage and packing cost of £3.50 per order.

A catalog of Australian mapping of the Antarctic is available from the Australian Surveying and Land Information Group (AUSLIG). The mailing address is AUSMAP Sales, PO Box 2, Belconnen,

Australian Capital Territory, 2606 Australia (☎ 61-6-2014-201; fax 61-6-2014-377).

One of the best atlases of Antarctic maps was produced, not surprisingly, by the US Central Intelligence Agency. The oversize paperback, entitled simply *Polar Regions Atlas*, was published in Washington, DC, in 1981. There's no spy stuff, just a comprehensive, chart-filled look at both the Arctic and the Antarctic, with an eye on the resources of each region. It's out of print, but can be found in the catalogs of Antarctic book dealers (see Books below).

Besides the excellent topographic maps and navigation charts available, three 'tourist' maps of Antarctica have also been produced. *Australian Geographic* magazine published an excellent, well-annotated map of Antarctica (scale 1:11,000,000) in 1994. It is available for A$5.50 plus postage and handling from *Australian Geographic*, PO Box 321, Terrey Hills, New South Wales 2084 Australia (☎ 61-2-450-2300; fax 61-2-986-3517). Another, the Antarctica Info Map, was produced by the International Antarctic Centre in Christchurch (see Antarctic Gateways chapter) in conjunction with New Zealand's Department of Survey and Land Information. One side offers a large and detailed map of the continent (with an inset of Ross Island), while the other gives basic information on Gondwana, the ozone hole, exploration, ice, plants and animals, geology and the Antarctic Treaty. The third (and much inferior) map is the English-Spanish 'ecomapa' of the Antarctic Peninsula produced by Zagier & Urruty publications of Buenos Aires and Miami, Florida, and sold at the Antarctica Office of the Tourism Board of Tierra del Fuego in Ushuaia (see the Antarctic Gateways chapter) as well as at the Ushuaia airport. Although the 'ecomap' has some handsome illustrations of whales and penguins, its detailed maps of the Peninsula are labeled almost exclusively in Spanish, despite its claim of being bilingual.

The newly-updated 'Antarctic Habitat' poster map produced by the Antarctica Project (see Useful Organizations in this chapter) is large (63 by 102 cm) and attractively illustrated, showing the major Antarctic and subantarctic breeding sites for penguins, whales, seals and seabirds, and accompanied by descriptive text, all for US$15.

What to Bring

Along the coast, Antarctic summers are less cold than you might imagine, and anyone who has lived through a reasonably tough winter in the northern part of the Northern Hemisphere should be fine without running out and buying hundreds of dollars of expensive clothing. Dressing for the cold is best accomplished by wearing several layers of lighter clothing rather than a single extremely heavy sweater, coat or pair of pants, since air is trapped and warmed between these layers. A windproof and waterproof jacket is preferable to a heavy, bulky coat as an outer layer.

In fact, for shipboard wear – which is very casual – a pair of jeans and a sweatshirt or sweater will be most comfortable, since the ship's interior is, of course, heated to room temperature. The ship's bridge, a favorite spot for passengers while underway, is also heated, and often includes a door to an outside deck, to which passengers can make quick trips for photos. Remember, you'll be sailing from a Southern Hemisphere port in the summertime, so your days before and after the cruise will require summer wear.

For footwear, the single most important item to bring for landings should be a pair of knee-high waterproof rubber boots (ie, Wellingtons). For shipboard wear, a comfortable pair of sneakers or even sandals will suit perfectly. Hiking boots can be useful for long walking trips ashore on subantarctic or Southern Ocean islands, but they may be more weight and trouble than they are worth.

The following is a suggested packing list for a two-week Antarctic cruise. This list assumes a certain number of repeated wearings and perhaps one laundering en route: waterproof pants and jacket; two or three pairs wool pants or jeans; two wool

MARK NORMAN
Pack ice

KIERAN JACKA
Ice crystals hanging from an iceberg

JEFF RUBIN
Old ice

JEFF RUBIN
Tabular iceberg with striations

JEFF RUBIN
Fractured iceberg

JEFF RUBIN
Ice edge, East Antarctica

COLIN MONTEATH (HEDGEHOG HOUSE)

Storm cloud and iceberg, Paradise Harbor, Antarctic Peninsula

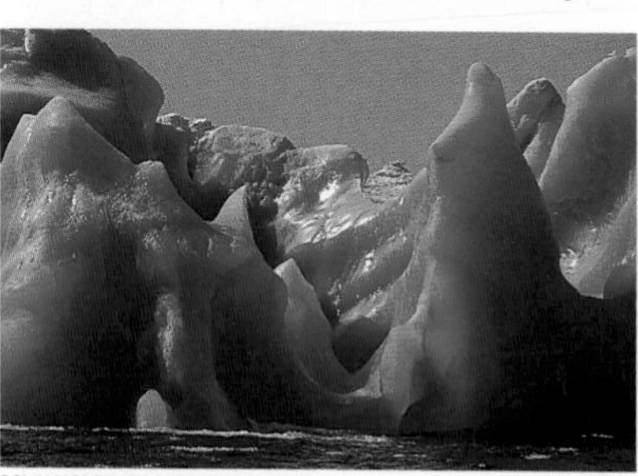

COLIN MONTEATH (HEDGEHOG HOUSE)

Old blue iceberg, Scotia Sea

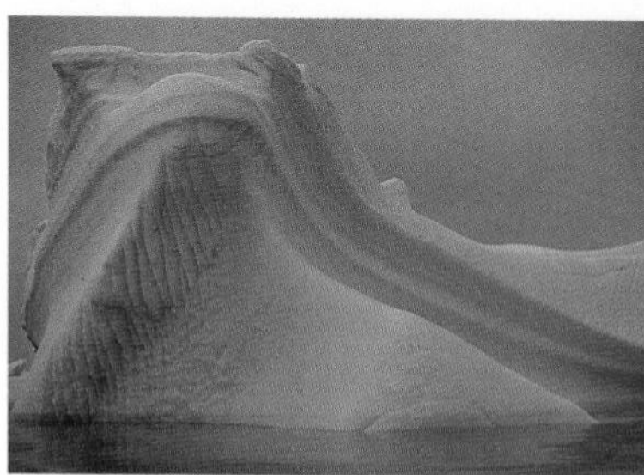

JEFF RUBIN

Overturned iceberg

JEFF RUBIN

Heavily crevassed ice

JEFF RUBIN

Ross Ice Shelf

sweaters or polar-fleece pullovers; three or four flannel or wool shirts; two pairs long underwear pants; three or four pairs thick wool socks; five pairs cotton socks to wear underneath wool socks; three or four cotton turtleneck shirts; warm, waterproof, ski-style gloves (invest in good ones!); silk gloves to wear beneath ski gloves; and a thick wool or even fur hat. High-tech synthetic fabrics are readily available and are in many ways superior to wool and cotton. Polartec, famously made from recycled plastic bottles, is especially good: it's lightweight and fast-drying. Brightly-colored Polartec pullovers are *de rigueur* aboard ship and are favored by expedition staff. Also very good, especially for underwear, are such fabrics as Capilene and polypropylene, which wick perspiration away from the skin and are easily washed and dried overnight in a sink.

Other essentials include: UV-filtering sunglasses – absolutely necessary, with sun reflecting off ice, snow and water; a nice dress for women and sport jacket & tie for men (for Captain's welcome dinner and farewell dinners); lip balm and sunscreen, for the southern summer sun can burn (remember the thinning of the ozone layer!), as well as moisturizing lotion, since the extremely low humidity of Antarctic air dries and even cracks skin; shampoo and conditioner, which most Antarctic cruise lines do not supply; and, of course, camera equipment – almost nobody visits Antarctica without it, even the most jaded ship staff member!

Among the optional items are: a small backpack or fanny pack for carrying items ashore; a bathing suit (for shipboard pools and saunas, and the Deception Island thermal springs); binoculars; flashlight (can be especially useful inside dark historic huts); extra eyeglasses or contact lenses; aspirin; seasickness pills (though the ship's doctor will also have a supply); travel alarm clock. Avid exercisers may wish to bring workout gear, though shipboard gyms and exercise equipment tends to be limited to fairly basic weightlifting barbells tucked away on a lower deck.

HIGHLIGHTS

In many ways, the whole of the Antarctic, with its stark and rarely seen beauty and abundant wildlife, is the highlight of a voyage to the continent, but there are some extra-special places within its realm. The narrow passage of the **Lemaire Channel**, with its reflected mountains plunging straight into the sea, is particularly spectacular. The **Dry Valleys**, with their otherworldly beauty and sculpted ventifacts, are unlike anywhere else on earth. The **historic huts of the Ross Sea region** are eerie, ghost-filled time capsules. The **aurora australis'** ethereal shimmering curtains of green, red, pink and orange are mysterious and awe-inspiring. A huge chinstrap penguin rookery at **Zavodovski Island** in the South Sandwich Islands, home to about one million birds, is one of the largest penguin colonies in the world. **Paradise Harbor** is one of the Antarctic's most heavily visited areas, and for good reason: Zodiac cruising among its icebergs and glacier-and-mountain reflections is wondrous. The **Ross Ice Shelf** glistens in the summer sun like exquisitely bright white Carrara marble. **Deception Island's** natural harbor is entered through the sea-breached wall of a volcanic crater, and the thermally heated waters at Pendulum Cove are warm enough to bathe in!

TOURIST OFFICES

The only Antarctic tourist office is a small, not terribly useful one in Ushuaia, the Antarctic Office of the Tierra del Fuego Institute of Tourism, at Avenida Maipu 505 (☎ 54-901-23340, 54-901-21423; fax 54-901-30694). Although the staff are helpful, they are not in the business of recommending tours; instead, they collect information about the growing number of tourists who pass through Ushuaia on the way to The Ice. They do sell an 'ecomapa' of the Antarctic Peninsula, postcards and a small selection of other Antarctic-related trinkets. They also have a small display of relics left behind in the Antarctic by Nordenskjöld's expedition.

Antarctic Museums

Although there are no permanent museums in Antarctica, many of the scientific stations maintain at least a small 'cabinet of curiosities' for visitors to view. The Antarctic Treaty, meanwhile, has designated 72 'historic sites and monuments.' A proportion of these mark sites of genuine international importance (though many important sites remain unmarked), while many others, including statues of recent national leaders, are of quite dubious interest.

The following museums display Antarctic material. Many other museums have smaller exhibits, and temporary exhibitions on Antarctica circulate frequently.

Argentina Ushuaia has a small Antarctic display in the prefectural museum (see Ushuaia in the Gateways chapter). There is also a small display of Antarctic artifacts in the Tierra del Fuego Tourism Institute's Antarctic Office across from the public pier where Antarctic cruise ships tie up.

Australia The Antarctic Division has a permanent display at its headquarters at Kingston, south of Hobart (see Hobart in the Gateways chapter). The Queen Victoria Museum in Launceston, the Power House Museum in Sydney and the Victorian National Museum in Melbourne all have small Antarctic displays.

Falkland Islands The Stanley Museum documents the association between the islands and the Antarctic Peninsula (see Stanley in the Gateways chapter).

Germany The sealer *Grönland* is docked at Bremerhaven, and includes a display about her 1872 Antarctic voyage.

Japan The icebreaker *Fuji* has a permanent exhibition aboard; she is moored near Osaka. The Nobu Shirase Museum near Konoura includes much material on Shirase's Antarctic expedition of 1910-12.

For information about the companies that offer tours of Antarctica, contact IAATO (see Useful Organizations section).

VISAS & DOCUMENTS

Passports & Visas

Since no one owns Antarctica, there are no visas required to visit it. However, even people traveling from their home country directly to Antarctica and back need their passports, for Antarctica's notoriously difficult weather and ice often force changes in itineraries, and you could easily find your ship returning to a different port – and country – than originally planned, though that is unlikely.

If your passport is within a few months of expiring, you will need to get a new one, as many countries will not issue you a visa if your passport has fewer than six months validity remaining on it. Also be sure that it has a few blank pages remaining for exit and entry stamps and visas.

When you come aboard your Antarctic ship, the expedition staff will most likely collect your passport and keep it until you disembark. This is to enable ship staff to handle all passports as a group, for instance, if you visit an Antarctic research station and they plan to stamp your passport with the station's stamp. (This is for 'vanity' purposes only, and you may request that your passport not be stamped if you wish.)

Visas are often required for the country of departure for your Antarctic cruise. Check with the tour operator or your travel agent for the specific details. But don't get sucked into the expensive 'visa services' offered by some cruise lines. These can cost up to US$30 each for a visa that is often free for the asking from the issuing country.

New Zealand Christchurch has two major centers: the Canterbury Museum and the International Antarctic Centre at the airport (for each, see Christchurch in the Gateways chapter). The Southland Museum in Invercargill includes an interesting display on New Zealand's subantarctic islands. In Auckland, Kelly Tarlton's Antarctic Encounter includes a replica of Scott's Cape Evans hut, an Antarctic aquarium and displays on the history of Antarctica.

Russia St Petersburg is home to the Arctic and Antarctic Museum, located in a former church at Ul Marata 24A.

Norway Sandefjord and Tønsberg each have excellent whaling museums with much Antarctic material (they are particularly strong on South Georgia). Oslo has the famous polar ship *Fram*, used by Amundsen, and there is some additional Amundsen material in the Ski Museum.

United Kingdom The Scott Polar Research Institute in Cambridge, England, is a major polar center, with a public museum that presents many artifacts from the expeditions of Scott and Shackleton as well as from more recent research activities. Scott's ship *Discovery* is moored in Dundee, Scotland.

United States Portland, Oregon, is home to the Hero Foundation, which maintains the ship *Hero*, which worked along the Antarctic Peninsula for 20 years. The many New England whaling and sealing museums often have Antarctic material, particularly where it refers to the early sealing industry. New York City's American Museum of Natural History includes a large, but often-overlooked display, of material on Lincoln Ellsworth. ■

– **Robert Headland**, archivist and curator of the Scott Polar Research Institute in Cambridge, England

Photocopies

Losing your passport is very bad news, since getting a new one takes time and money that you could be spending doing something else. It's a good idea to carry a driver's license, ID card, birth certificate or some form of photo identification to make replacement of a lost passport a little easier. Having an old, expired passport can be very useful. It also helps to have a separate record of your passport number and issue date, as well as a photocopy of the identification pages. While you're compiling that information, add the serial numbers of your traveler's checks, details of health insurance, and about US$100 cash for emergencies.

Travel Insurance

Most tour operators recommend travel insurance to 'insure' you against their trip-cancellation penalties, which in most cases are quite severe. For relatively early cancellations, penalties vary widely among the tour operators, but typically, if you cancel any later than 60 days before sailing, you forfeit 100% of the cruise price. With the cost of a cruise sometimes totaling upwards of US$10,000, this can be a very expensive change in plans. On the other hand, the travel insurance for a US$13,000 cruise will set you back nearly US$1000, so if you are nearly certain that you will be able to go on the trip, then you are better off without the insurance.

CUSTOMS

Some countries allow travelers to the Antarctic to purchase goods duty-free, since technically you leave all national territory by going to Antarctica. Make sure to save any duty-free receipts, however, since Customs officials may board your ship upon return to port. Even if the tour operator tells you that Customs does not plan to do an inspection after the voyage, bureaucrats can always change their mind while you are away.

Remember also that citizens of some countries, including Australia and the US, are subject to national laws that prohibit taking any animal, mineral or plant 'souvenirs' from Antarctica, and the Antarctic Treaty's Protocol on Environmental Protection will also prohibit such taking by anyone when it comes into force Customs agents inspecting your bags upon return from The Ice may seize such items – and impose heavy fines for violating these laws. At its headquarters in Hobart, the Australian Antarctic Division has a display of seals' teeth confiscated from the luggage of tourists returning from Antarctica. Don't souvenir: It's against the ethic of what Antarctica is about – and if that argument doesn't convince you, just remember that it's not worth the risk of getting caught.

MONEY

Costs

Most Antarctic tour brochures carefully spell out what is not included in the price of the cruise, although some tour operators try to make their trips appear cheaper by separating the port taxes from the price (which can add nearly US$600 to the price of the cruise). More typically, however, the additional costs of a cruise are charges for optional items including alcohol, laundry service, faxes or satellite phone calls, tips, souvenirs, extra helicopter time and massages.

Cash, Traveler's Checks & Credit Cards

Each ship runs its shipboard economy in a slightly different manner, but generally a 'chit system' is used, whereby passengers merely sign for items like drinks, laundry services and souvenirs. Often, no prices are even listed for items in the shop or at the bar, which can be hazardous for spendthrifts, since the day of reckoning always comes. On the penultimate day of the voyage, the ship's purser or hotel manager distributes bills. These can usually be settled either with cash, traveler's checks or credit cards (some ships take an imprint of your credit card early in the trip so that you merely have to sign off on your accumulated charges at the end of the voyage). Most ships, regardless of country of origin, accept only US dollars for cash transactions, so it pays to check with your cruise company ahead of time.

At most bases, regardless of their nationality, tourists are expected to pay in either the national currency or in US dollars. But others may be more flexible. The shop at New Zealand's accommodating Scott Base, for example, accepts NZ and US dollars, as well as Visa, Mastercard and American Express.

Tipping

Tipping is not included in the cruise fare and so is an additional (though optional) cost. While tipping is always at your discretion, it is considered an appropriate supplement to crew and staff wages for their (one hopes) excellent service. Most tour operators distribute an information sheet near the end of the voyage offering tipping guidelines, which are just that: guidelines only and not in any way requirements. Generally US$10 a day from each passenger is considered appropriate. Depending on the tour company, this sum may be divided evenly among all the cruise staff (including chefs, sous chefs, bartenders and cabin attendants) as well as the ship's crew, from the captain on down to the lowliest deck hand. Other companies choose to divide the tipping groups into two categories, distinguishing the staff from the crew. Sometimes expedition leaders and lecturers are included in the tip pool, although often they are not. Of course, if you wish to reward particularly good service from an individual (bartender, cabin attendant, lecturer, etc), the best way is the most direct: Simply slip them an envelope with your cash gratuity enclosed. Personal gifts can also be a nice gesture for showing appreciation. Depending on the tour company, gratuities may be paid by credit card, traveler's checks or cash, or any combination of these. You should check with your cruise operator in advance.

POST & COMMUNICATIONS

Postal Rates & Sending Mail

In general, you should only send letters or postcards from Antarctica for the novelty value of doing so, since service is understandably very, very slow (typically, three or four months). Many Antarctic stations send tourists' mail back to the program's home country to send it on to the recipient, while others send the mail from the relief ship's first port of call on the voyage home. Many stations (US ones in particular) do not handle tourist mail, although arrangements are sometimes made so that tour ship staff can stamp postcards and letters with a station stamp. The current rate for a postcard from Antarctica is usually US$1 each, probably because this is a nice round number requiring no change. For that you will get a (sometimes surprising) postmark, and – if you send one to yourself – a happy reminder of your trip, right around the time your memory of it is starting to fade.

Telephone & Fax

Sure, modern satellite technology makes it possible to call your mom back home while you're cruising along the front of the Ross Ice Shelf – but it will cost you. Ship communications (fax, telephone and, in some cases, electronic mail) use the INMARSAT (International Maritime Satellite), which provides reliable connections. However, there is often a significant time lag (two or three seconds) from transmission to reception, so until you get the rhythm of the delay, you will find yourself speaking over your answering party. All this can be a bit frustrating, as the meter is running at a rate of anywhere from US$12 a minute on up. (Much of this charge is in fact pure profit for the ship, since the normal charges for INMARSAT are less than US$5 per minute.)

Some ships offer INMARSAT service in individual cabins, while others require passengers to visit the ship's radio room to make or receive calls. Receiving calls, by the way, is relatively easy, since the ship's radio officer can simply page a requested passenger. Unless the ship is making landings ashore at that time, the passenger will be found by intercom. Typically, the radio officer will ask the outside caller to ring back in five minutes, allowing the receiving party enough time to get to the radio room to await the incoming call, thereby saving five minutes of expensive dead time.

Remember to calculate carefully the time difference between your ship and the recipient of your call, who will surely better appreciate your kindness if they are not awakened at 3 am to hear about the enchanting antics of the penguins you just saw. Again, the ship's radio officer can help you to accurately determine this.

BOOKS

Some of the most interesting Antarctic books that follow are out of print. To find them, you can either haunt secondhand bookshops, or, if you prefer things the easy way, try contacting one of the following specialists, who will most likely be happy to send you a catalog. Unfortunately, interest in collecting Antarctic titles has increased greatly over the past two decades, creating competition that drives up book prices, but many of the titles below are still available through one or more of these specialists:

Antipodean Books
PO Box 189, Cold Springs, NY 10516 USA
(☎ 1-914-424-3867; fax 1-914-424-3617).

Arnold Books
11 New Regent St, Christchurch,
New Zealand (☎ 64-3-365-7188).

Astrolabe Books
81 Salamanca Place,
Hobart, Tasmania, Australia
(☎ / fax: 61-02-23-8644);
mailing address: PO Box 475, Sandy Bay,
TAS 7005 Australia.

Blue Dragon Book Shop
293 East Main St, Ashland, OR 97520 USA
(☎ 1-541-482-2142).

Bluntisham Books
Oak House, East St, Bluntisham,
Cambridgeshire, England PE17 3LS
(☎ 44-487-840-449).

Chessler Books
PO Box 399, 26030 Highway 74,
Kittredge, CO 80457 USA
(☎ 1-303-670-0093; fax 1-303-670-9727).
Specializes in books on mountaineering, but also has out-of-print polar books.

Colin Bull's Polar Books
Box 4675, Rolling Bay, WA 98061 USA
(☎ 1-206-842-9660).

Gaston Renard
51 Sackville St, Collingwood,
Victoria, Australia 3066
(☎ 61-3-417-1044; fax 61-3-417-3025);
mailing address: GPO Box 5235BB,
Melbourne 3001, Australia.

High Latitude Books
PO Box 11254,
Bainbridge Island, WA 98110 USA
(☎ 1-206-842-0202; fax: 1-206-842-6101).

Patrick Walcot
60 Sunnybank Rd, Sutton Coldfield,
West Midlands, England, B73 5RJ
(☎ 44-21-382-6381; fax 44-21-386-1251).

Parmer Books
7644 Forrestal Rd,
San Diego, CA 92120-2203 USA
(☎ 1-619-287-0693; fax 1-619-287-6135).

Terra Incognita Books
244 West 74th St,
New York, NY 10023 USA
(☎ 1-212-686-0268 or 1-212-362-2849).
Mail and phone orders only.

Top of the World Polar Books
20 Westview Circle,
Williston, VT 05495 USA
(☎ /fax 1-802-878-8737).
Despite the name, includes Antarctic titles.

West Side Book Shop
113 West Liberty,
Ann Arbor, MI 48104 USA
(☎ 1-313-995-1891).

Geographica
718 Broadway, No 9-C,
New York, NY 10003 USA
(☎ 1-212-677-8015; fax 1-212-529-8684).
Provides a reader's guide to current Antarctic books, as well as some maps and posters. Ask about the discounted 'Essential Antarctica' package for US$99. Mail and telephone orders only.

Lonely Planet

Lonely Planet publishes guides covering every country in the world, including each of the countries that has an Antarctic Gateway: *Australia* (see also the *Tasmania* state guide); *Argentina, Uruguay & Paraguay* (including the Falkland Islands); *Chile & Easter Island*; *New Zealand*; and *South Africa, Lesotho & Swaziland*. Also look for *Cape Town City Guide*. When accompanying younger travelers, you should also look at Lonely Planet's *Travel with Children*.

Guidebooks

Antarctic guidebooks to the present have been extremely thin. Diana Galimberti's *Antarctica: An Introductory Guide* (Miami Beach: Zagier & Urruty Publications, 1991) is just what it says it is: a good first look at the continent, but it has no photos and only rudimentary maps. Marco Polo's 96-page *Antarktis* (Ostfildern, Germany: Mairs Geographischer Verlag/Hachette, 1993), written by Diana Galimberti and Rolf Erdorf, is a great little pocket-size guide – if you can read German. If you don't, the photos and maps are still interesting, but you'll probably get quite frustrated at not being able to read it.

If you are interested in the historic explorers' huts, David L Harrowfield's excellent *Icy Heritage: Historic Sites of the Ross Sea Region* (Christchurch: Antarctic Heritage Trust, 1995) is absolutely indispensable. Harrowfield, who has been helping to restore the huts since 1977, has put together fascinating and detailed accounts of 34 historic places, from major attractions like Shackleton's Hut to more obscure supply depots and message posts of early 20th-century explorers.

Adventure

Many of the numerous adventurers who have skied, walked or mushed dogsleds across sections of Antarctica, or sailed around it, have written memoirs of their trips. New Zealand yachtsman-physician David Lewis describes circumnavigating Antarctica singlehandedly in his 10-meter sloop *Ice Bird* in his book of the same name (New York: Norton, 1976). In *Icebound in Antarctica* (New York: Norton, 1987), he tells of research done in *Explorer* along the Ingrid Christensen Coast west of Australia's Davis station.

Britain's Sir Ranulph Fiennes accomplishes the first pole-to-pole circumnavigation of the globe in *To the Ends of the Earth: The Transglobe Expedition* (New York: Arbor House, 1983). Not content with one pass at the South Pole, Sir Ran was back in Antarctica again in 1992 to ski across the continent with Dr Mike Stroud. Fiennes' *Mind Over Matter* (New York: Delacorte Press, 1993) and Stroud's *Shadows on the Wasteland* (Woodstock, NY: Overlook Press, 1994) offer interesting, complementary views of their two-man, unsupported race against starvation and cold.

Britons Roger Mear and Robert Swan's book *In the Footsteps of Scott* (London: Jonathan Cape, 1987) chronicles their recreation of the British explorer's polar journey with a third companion, Gareth Wood; where Scott's party met disappointment, Mear and Swan found frosty disapproval from the Americans at Amundsen-Scott station – and a rescue forced on them by Washington.

Austrian Reinhold Messner, the world's greatest mountain climber, crossed the continent on skis with Arved Fuchs in 1989-90. His *Antarctica: Both Heaven and Hell* (Seattle: The Mountaineers, 1991) offers a unique perspective of adventure in Antarctica. American Will Steger and a five-man international team mushed dog sleds across the continent, a story told in *Crossing Antarctica* (New York: Knopf, 1982) written with Jon Bowermaster.

The most disgusting title for any Antarctic book ever published has to be Jerry Corr's *The Snotsicle Traverse* (East Lansing, MI: Frandorson Publications, 1993) about a ski trip he made with two fellow adventurers from the South Pole to the Ross Ice Shelf. Joseph E Murphy and his friends went in the opposite direction in *South to the Pole by Ski* (St Paul, MN: Marlor Press, 1990).

General

Unquestionably the single best book on the subject, Readers Digest's *Antarctica: The Extraordinary History of Man's Conquest of the Frozen Continent* (Sydney: Readers Digest, 1990) is packed with photos, charts and facts. It's only available in hardcover and is a bit bulky for travel, but if you only bring one book (besides the one now in your hands, of course!) with you, it should probably be the one. It is also the one book most often stocked by shipboard shops on Antarctic cruises. Two other very good general works about Antarctica are *The Greenpeace Book of Antarctica* (New York: Doubleday, 1988) by John May and *The Australian Geographic Book of Antarctica* (Terrey Hills, NSW: Australian Geographic, 1993) by Keith Scott. Louise Crossley's *Explore Antarctica* (Melbourne: Cambridge University Press, 1995) appears to be written primarily for students, with lots of charts and graphics, but it's a valuable reference for readers of any age.

Of the many photographic books produced about the most photogenic continent of all, two stand out far above the others. The best, *Wild Ice* (Washington, DC: Smithsonian Institution Press, 1990), includes the work of four photographers – Ron Naveen, Colin Monteath (author of this book's chapter Private Adventures in Antarctica), Tui de Roy and Mark Jones – who between them have made more than 70 voyages to Antarctica. Their extremely beautiful photos are the best of a rich harvest. Eliot Porter's *Antarctica* (New York: Arch Cape Press, 1978) shows the unusual views shot by the noted lensman, who visited The Ice at age 73.

John Stewart's two-volume *Antarctica: An Encyclopedia* (Jefferson, NC: McFarland & Co, 1990) is a comprehensive reference with thousands of entries but, unfortunately, no illustrations.

In the geography/natural history essay category, Michael Parfit's *South Light* (New York: Macmillan, 1985), David G Campbell's *The Crystal Desert* (Boston: Houghton Mifflin Co, 1992) and Bill Green's *Water, Ice & Stone* (New York:

Tekeli-Li – The Lure of Antarctic Fiction

Antarctic fiction began in 1605 with the publication of a Utopian story, *Mundes Alter et Idem* ('Another World and Yet the Same'), by Bishop Joseph Hall of England, in which a traveler to Antarctica finds that it is inhabited by gluttons, drunkards and eccentrics. The genre has remained in vogue for almost 400 years, and such celebrated writers as Samuel Taylor Coleridge, James Fenimore Cooper, Rudyard Kipling, Edgar Allen Poe and Jules Verne all wrote about the Antarctic.

Coleridge, of course, wrote the most famous polar poem, *The Rime of the Ancient Mariner* (1798), in which an Antarctic ship is cursed when a sailor kills an albatross. In Cooper's fantasy, *The Monikins* (1835), a British baronet rescues four South Polar Monikins (simian-like beings) and returns them to their home. Another novel by Cooper, *The Sea Lions* (1849), draws on his personal experience as a major owner of a Sag Harbor whaling ship to tell the story of two rival schooners searching for a mysterious sealing ground in the Antarctic. Kipling's *The Jungle Book* (1893) includes the story of Kotick, the white seal, who visits several subantarctic islands.

Poe's novella *The Narrative of Arthur Gordon Pym* (1837) is the most influential Antarctic story. It so inspired Verne that he wrote a sequel, *Le Sphinx des Glaces*, in 1897. Other authors who took up Poe's storyline were Charles Romyn Dake in *A Strange Discovery* (1899), Steven Utley and Howard Waldrop in the short story 'Black as the Pit, From Pole to Pole,' (in *The Year's Finest Fantasy*, 1978) and Rudy Rucker in *The Hollow Earth* (1990). Echoing from Pym through all these works is the eerie cry *Tekeli-li*, the call of the white birds in the South Polar region. (Poe also wrote another story about a whirlpool at the South Pole, the shorter and more mysterious 'Ms Found in a Bottle' of 1833.)

Adventure Stories Antarctic fiction generally reflects the public knowledge of the continent at the time it was written. The last part of the 19th century was notable for the great number of British and American boy's adventure stories. Antarctica was the symbol of mystery that lured these young men. There were, however, several good adult stories, including George Griffith's *Olga Romanoff or the Syren of the Skies* (1894), in which Kerguelen Island is used as a submarine and aircraft base. In 1906, Emilio Salgari imagined a bicycle team pedaling from the Antarctic Peninsula to the South Pole, in *Au Pole Sud A Bicyclette*.

20th-Century Classics Writers of the 20th century gave us three established classics and another one that should be included. First, we were thrilled by the unspeakable horrors of HP Lovecraft's Palaeogean Megalopolis in *At the Mountains of Madness* (1931)? Then John Campbell's 'Who Goes There?' (collected in *They Came From Outer Space)* frightened us with an alien that changes its configuration at will while terrorizing an Antarctic station – inspiring two movies, 1951's *The Thing from Another World* and its 1982 remake, *The Thing*. Réné Barjavel's *La Nuit des Temps* (1968), published in English as *The Ice People*, about a thawed 900,000-year-old woman, was a bestseller. To that list, add Edison Marshall's *Dian of the Lost Land*, written in 1935 in response to the theory of continental drift. It describes tribes of Cro-Magnons and Neanderthals living in a warm Antarctica, which had been connected to South America and Africa at the end of the Pleistocene.

As the era of technology developed, more books were written about terrorism and war. Eco-terrorists try to blow up a Russian whaling factory ship in John Gordon Davis' *Leviathan* (1976), and an oil cartel-backed group seizes control of Antarctica in DC Poyer's *White Continent* (1980). Marion Morris' *The Icemen* (1988) envisions a remnant group of Nazis taking over an Argentine Antarctic station. Nuclear winter closes in on *The Last Whales* (1989) by Lloyd Abbey, while in *The Last Ship* (1989), by William Brinkley, a group of Russians and Americans aboard the submarine *Pushkin* arrive at McMurdo just after a global nuclear war and discover enough rations to survive 12 years. One of Hammond Innes' several Antarctic novels, *Isvik* (1991), revolves around an icebound ship implicated in the disappearance of a group from Argentina. In David Smith's *Freeze Frame* (1992), Frenchmen develop a secret uranium mine at Dumont d'Urville.

Natural catastrophe is another common theme. In Godfrey Sweven's *Limanora, the Island of Progress* (1903), volcanic activity destroys part of Antarctica, while in the title story of Valery Brussof's *The Republic of the Southern Cross and Other Stories* (1977), an epidemic wipes out most of Antarctica's human population. A 33,000-cubic-kilometer portion of the ice cap breaks away in James Follett's *Ice* (1977), while in Richard Moran's *Cold Sea Rising* (1986), an undersea volcanic plume severs the Ross Ice Shelf and sends it on a northerly drift. Solar flares cause a surge of the icecap in Crawford Killian's *Icequake* (1979), and Antarctica is about to heat up after nuclear war tilts the earth's axis in David Graham's *Down to a Sunless Sea* (1981).

Antarctic air disasters make up a distinct subgenre. Paralee Sweeten Sutton's *White City* (1949) describes a young couple lost in a small plane. They discover an old Antarctic civilization whose members communicate by thought transference. In David Burke's *Monday at McMurdo* (1967), a flight carrying a US Congressman crashes on a glacier and has to be rescued by a US Navy detachment. Not surprisingly, the Air New Zealand crash on Mt Erebus in 1979 inspired several fictional stories, including John Gordon Davis' *Seize the Wind* (1985), in which an Australian DC-10 filled with sightseers crashes on the Beardmore Glacier. Charles Neider used his personal experience of surviving a helicopter crash to write *Overflight* (1986), in which a DC-10 tourist flight slams into Erebus.

Ship-based Antarctic tourism has not been overlooked by the fiction writers. Most of the stories, however, deal with less-than-desirable vacations. Who would care to be a passenger on *Sinbad*, a cruise ship trapped in the Lemaire Channel, after (another) sudden tilt of the earth's axis, in Edwin Woodard and Heather Woodard Bischoff's *Storehouses of the Snow* (1980)? Or aboard *Golden Adventurer*, which runs aground in Wilbur Smith's *Hungry As the Sea* (1978)? Or a teenager stranded on an iceberg during a cruise on the appropriately named *Argosy*, in Madeleine L'Engle's *Troubling a Star* (1994)? How about surviving a powerful sonic bombardment only to discover that your ship has abandoned you on Seymour Island, in Clive Cussler's *Shock Wave* (1996)?

Take heart! You can always recover on Ross Island in the summer home built by an East Hollywood chef in Crispin Kitto's novel *The Antarctica Cookbook* (1984).

Mysteries Agatha Christie weaves a good yarn about a geophysicist who returns from the Antarctic to discover that he was the alibi for a late murder suspect, in *Ordeal by Innocence* (1958). Thomas Keneally tells a chilling tale about the killing of a newsman during the dark Antarctic winter in *Victim of the Aurora* (1977). The 'first' Antarctic murder is solved by a policeman from Florida working as a substitute research assistant for his son in Emmy Lou Schenk's 'Ice Cave' (in *Alfred Hitchcock Mystery Magazine*, August 1987). In Bob Reiss' *Purgatory Road* (1996), the members of a small Antarctic station are plagued by spies, madness and murder. ■

– **Fauno Cordes**, the world's foremost authority on Antarctic fiction

Crown, 1995) are all excellent, but Stephen J Pyne's *The Ice: A Journey to Antarctica* (Iowa City: University of Iowa Press, 1986) may be the best of the genre.

National scientific programs in Antarctica are well covered. Australia's research in Antarctica is chronicled in at least three books: Philip Law and John Bechervaise's *ANARE: Australia's Antarctic Outposts* (Melbourne: Oxford University Press, 1957); RA Swan's *Australia in the Antarctic* (Parkville, Victoria: Melbourne University Press, 1961); and Elizabeth Chipman's *Australians in the Frozen South* (West Melbourne: Thomas Nelson, 1978). Canada's under-recognized Antarctic work is documented in Dean Beeby's book *In a Crystal Land: Canadian Explorers in Antarctica* (Toronto: University of Toronto Press, 1994).

Unquestionably the most poetically titled Antarctic book, Sir Vivian Fuchs' *Of Ice and Men* (London: Anthony Nelson, 1982), describes Antarctic exploration, British government-style, specifically the work of the British Antarctic Survey (BAS) from 1943 to '73. Wags now sometimes honor Sir Vivian's title by referring to BAS as 'Office and Men.'

Women's role in Antarctic research is covered in just two books, Barbara Land's *The New Explorers: Women in Antarctica* (New York: Dodd, Mead, 1981) and Elizabeth Chipman's *Women on the Ice* (Carlton, Victoria: Melbourne University Press, 1986). Jennie Darlington offers a unique perspective of personality conflicts during a mid-century American expedition to The Ice in *My Antarctic Honeymoon* (London: Frederick Muller, 1957).

History

Robert K Headland's *Chronological List of Antarctic Expeditions and Related Historical Events* (Cambridge: Cambridge University Press, 1993) is an invaluable resource for all authors, including this one, who write about Antarctic history. An updated version is due to be published in 1997.

Nearly every one of the explorers wrote a firsthand account of his expedition, and many of them have been reprinted in the past 20 years. These accounts include books by Amundsen *(The South Pole)*; Borchgrevink *(First on the Antarctic Continent)*; Byrd *(Alone*; *Discovery*; *Little America*; *Skyward)*; Frederick Cook *(Through the First Antarctic Night)*; Mawson *(The Home of the Blizzard)*; Nordenskjöld *(Antarctica)*; Scott *(The Voyage of the Discovery*; *Scott's Last Expedition)*; and Shackleton *(Heart of the Antarctic*; *South)*. Beau Riffenburgh, editor of the journal *Polar Record*, has examined the role that newspapers played in 'creating' explorers, both Arctic and Antarctic, in *The Myth of the Explorer* (Oxford: Oxford University Press, 1994).

Apsley Cherry-Garrard's *The Worst Journey in the World* (London: Constable, 1922) is regarded by many as the single best Antarctic book ever written, and it has been republished several times in recent years. His highly readable account of Scott's *Terra Nova* expedition details the incredible suffering endured on the hellish midwinter man-haul to the emperor penguin rookery at Cape Crozier, as well as the discovery of the ill-fated polar party the spring after they perished.

Several good general histories of Antarctica have been published. LP Kirwan, who wrote *The White Road* (London: Hollis and Carter, 1959), never visited Antarctica, but spoke with many of the 20th-century explorers who mapped the continent. His book is authoritative and highly readable. David Mountfield's *A History of Polar Exploration* (New York: Dial, 1974), like Kirwin's book, includes information on both ends of the earth, and is extremely well illustrated. GE Fogg's *The Explorations of Antarctica* (London: Cassell, 1990) includes interesting paintings by David Smith. Two other, more scholarly works about US exploration of the continent include Philip I Mitterling's *America in the Antarctic to 1840* (Urbana: University of Illinois Press, 1959) and Kenneth J Bertrand's *Americans in Antarctica, 1775-1948* (Burlington, VT: American Geographical Society, 1971).

An early, though hard to find book, G Barnett Smith's *The Romance of the South Pole* (London: Thomas Nelson, 1902), describes early expeditions by Cook, Weddell, Ross, Wilkes, Nares and Bruce – and is illustrated with fine engravings. Oddly reflecting the limited knowledge about Antarctica of the time, it features a parade of polar bears marching across the cover.

Antarctic aviation, from the early balloon trials performed by Scott to the US Navy's ski-equipped Hercules flights, is covered in David Burke's excellent *Moments of Terror* (Kensington, Australia: New South Wales University Press, 1994) which is information-packed and filled with wonderful rare photographs.

Biography

Many good biographies of Antarctic explorers have been written, and only some of them can be described here. Most famous – or infamous – of the recent titles is Roland Huntford's *Scott and Amundsen* (London: Hodder and Stoughton, 1979), which argues (not without reason) that Scott's 'tragedy' was due to incompetence, but his anti-Scott bias is so strong that one cannot help wondering what drives it. His *Shackleton* (New York: Fawcett Columbine, 1985) is a well-researched and more balanced biography of the most heroic Antarctic explorer. Huntford also wrote a book showcasing a rare trove of lantern slides used by Amundsen for his lectures, found by one of his descendants in a Norwegian attic in 1986, *The Amundsen Photographs* (New York: Atlantic Monthly Press, 1987). James and Margery Fisher's *Shackleton and the Antarctic* (Boston: Houghton Mifflin, 1958) is a thorough biography, sympathetically written, with a unique appendix covering Shackleton's poetry and prose. Lowell Thomas' biography of his friend, *Sir Hubert Wilkins* (New York: McGraw-Hill, 1961), gives a detailed look at the Australian's many adventures. Finally, Lars-Eric Lindblad's *Passport to Anywhere* (New York: Times Books, 1983) is a ghostwritten autobiography of the free spirit who pioneered mass-market Antarctic tourism in 1965-66.

The Rarest of Rare

The first – and only – book ever published in Antarctica is Ernest Shackleton's *Aurora Australis*, hand-printed in 1908-09 by four of his men at Cape Royds on Ross Island, bound in a leather spine and covered with boards taken from provision crates. Thus the various editions, of which only 75 to 100 were ever made, are known as the 'Butter' edition or the 'Bottled Fruit' copy or the 'Irish Stew' edition. The book was intended as a souvenir for expedition members and as a gift for expedition patrons. Today, many are in institutional libraries. Only one or two copies come up for sale each decade; the current asking price is about US$25,000 to US$30,000. Fortunately, *Aurora Australis* was also reprinted by Bay Books of Kensington, Australia, in 1988, enabling average folks to get an inkling of what this rare beauty looks – and reads – like. It's a very interesting treat, offering a behind-the-scenes look at the expedition.

Controversial American Lieutenant Charles Wilkes' report on the United States Exploring Expedition was limited by the US Congress to just 100 copies, making the five-volume *Narrative* published in 1844 one of the rarest Antarctic books, although it is not strictly about Antarctica. The complete set of the expedition's reports, comprising 26 volumes including many volumes of plates, was published over a 30-year period. If a complete set were to find its way to the market today – a very unlikely possibility – one knowledgeable dealer estimates that it would fetch a cool US$200,000.

Wildlife

There are many excellent books about Antarctic wildlife, but few are portable enough to drag down to the continent with you. Tony Soper's small book *Antarctica: A Guide to the Wildlife* (Old Saybrook, CT: Globe Pequot Press, 1994) is an exception, and its handsome drawings by Dafila Scott (granddaughter of Robert F Scott) offer a different perspective than the usual photographs. Sanford Moss' *Natural History of the Antarctic Peninsula* (New York: Columbia University Press, 1988) has no color illustrations but includes much good biological data. Among the large volumes, Eric Hosking's *Antarctic Wildlife* (Beckenham, Kent: Croom Helm, 1982) is primarily a photographic book, but the text by Bryan Sage is informative. Bernard Stonehouse's *Animals of the Antarctic* (New York: Holt, Rinehart & Winston, 1972) is dated, but the photos are quite good; his *North Pole, South Pole* (London: Multimedia Books, 1990) is more current, but deals with both the Arctic and the Antarctic.

The beautiful and detailed sketches and watercolors of Edward Wilson, chief scientific officer on both of Scott's expeditions, are used as illustrations for *Birds of the Antarctic* (Poole, Dorset: Blandford Press, 1967). Two other excellent bird guides to the Antarctic and the Southern Ocean are David F Parmalee's *Antarctic Birds* (Minneapolis: University of Minnesota Press, 1992) and George E Watson's *Birds of the Antarctic and Sub-Antarctic* (Washington, DC: American Geophysical Union, 1975), still considered a classic. Pauline Reilly's *Penguins of the World* (South Melbourne: Oxford University Press Australia, 1994) is a serious guide to the birds, with only a few color illustrations (many black-and-white ones, however), and includes good data on feeding, breeding, distribution and population.

Whales of the World, by Lyall Watson (London: Hutchinson & Co, 1981), is a detailed and scholarly look at its subject, with many excellent photographs and illustrations. A heavy 302-page hardcover, it is not highly portable.

Science

There are several good books about Antarctic science. David Walton, author of this book's chapter Antarctic Science, has edited an excellent book with the same title, *Antarctic Science* (Cambridge: Cambridge University Press, 1987). GE Fogg's *A History of Antarctic Science* (Cambridge: Cambridge University Press, 1992) is also very comprehensive. Richard S Lewis' *A Continent for Science* (New York: Viking Press, 1966) is dated now, but it is very readable and has many excellent photographs. AJW Taylor's *Antarctic Psychology* (Wellington: Science Information Publishing Centre, 1987) tends toward the scholarly, but contains an interesting discussion of the psychological research and testing done in Antarctica, including the exams used in selecting personnel for Antarctic stations.

Politics

Tomes on Antarctic politics tend to veer dangerously toward the scholarly and the legalistic and thus sometimes can be a good cure for insomnia. Among the better (more reader-friendly) books on the subject are Keith Suter's *Antarctica: Private Property or Public Heritage?* (Leichardt, NSW: Pluto Press Australia, 1991) and Deborah Shapley's *The Seventh Continent: Antarctica in a Resource Age* (Washington, DC: Resources for the Future, 1985). Although both are a bit out-of-date, both offer good backgrounds to the current issues.

Children's Books

During the past five years there has been an explosion of children's books about Antarctica, especially Antarctic wildlife. Jonathan Chester's *A for Antarctica* (Hunters Hill, Australia: Margaret Hamilton Books, 1994) is a photographic alphabet book with a polar twist for very young children. Mark Cawardine's *Whales, Dolphins and Porpoises* (London: Dorling Kindersley, 1992) is a children's version of the excellent cetacean guide for adults by the same author, aimed at elementary- and middle-school students. Alastair Fothergill's *Life in the Freezer* (London: BBC Children's Books, 1994) is another elementary- and middle-school children's version of an adult guide to Antarctic wildlife; both versions are associated with the excellent video series by the British Broadcasting Corporation. Laurence Pringle's *Antarctica, the Last*

Unspoiled Continent (New York: Simon & Schuster, 1992) is a survey of Antarctic plants and animals for middle-school children. Barbara Taylor's *Arctic and Antarctic* (London: Dorling Kindersley, 1995) compares the regions; it's part of the excellent Eyewitness Guides series for elementary- and middle-school children. Trish Hart's aptly named *There Are No Polar Bears Down There* (Sydney: Nelson Australia, 1994) includes handsome illustrations.

Jenny Woods' *Icebergs* (New York: Penguin Books, 1990) provides solid factual information for elementary- and middle-school children about Antarctica's most beautiful feature.

There are also many titles covering Antarctic exploration and research. Ian Cameron's *Exploring Antarctica* (Burnt Mill, Harlow, Essex: Longman, 1984) is another children's version of an adult book; this one is part of the Royal Geographical Society's Exploring Series for elementary- and middle-school students. Leo Flaherty's *Roald Amundsen and the Quest for the South Pole* (New York: Chelsea House, 1992) is part of the World Explorers series, which also includes *Lt Charles Wilkes and the US Exploring Expedition*; both are for middle-school children.

Two authors offer fictional fun. Geoffrey T Williams' *The Last Frontier: Antarctica* (Los Angeles: Price, Stern, Sloan, 1992) is an adventure story for elementary- and middle-school children, while Helen Cowcher's *Antarctica* (New York: Farrar, Straus & Giroux, 1990) is a story about penguins for elementary-school children.

For additional ideas, contact The Antarctica Project (see Useful Organizations in this chapter), which publishes excellent 'Antarctica Resource Lists' of suggested reading for elementary, middle- and high-school students.

CD-ROM

There are two CD-ROMs about Antarctica currently available, and both are very good, especially as educational tools, though even this advanced multimedia technology can't compete with simply being there.

First on the market was Aoraki Corp's *Antarctica* (1994), produced in conjunction with the International Antarctic Centre of Christchurch. It costs $US29.99 and is distributed in North America by Cambrix Publishing, 6269 Variel Ave, Suite B, Woodland Hills, CA 91367 USA (☎ 1-818-992-8484; in the US: 1-800-992-8781; fax 1-818-992-8781).

Virtual Antarctica (1996), produced in partnership with Antarctic tour operator Mountain Travel-Sobek and WorldTravel Partners, features the excellent photography of Jonathan Chester (see Books, above). It is available for $US24.95 from Peak Media Inc, 1211 Cornwall Ave, Bellingham, WA 98225 USA (☎ 1-360-733-6010; in the US: 1-800-453-5322; fax 1-360-733-7818; email: orders@peak-media.com; world wide web: http://www.peak-media.com).

ONLINE SERVICES

There are several internet sites of interest to Antarcticophiles. The addresses are given in the table below. One of the best is the Gateway to Antarctica, created by New Zealand's International Center for Antarctic Information and Research. Besides information about Antarctic wildlife, science, history, politics and tourism, it includes a near-comprehensive list of links to other Antarctic sites. This is your best starting point for online exploration of Antarctica.

The Australian Antarctic Division's website gives a look at Australia's Antarctic program, with such highlights as hourly

Online Addresses

Alfred Wegener Institute
http://www.awi-bremerhaven.de/

Antarctic Heritage Trust
http://icair.iac.org.nz/reports/aht/aht.html

Antarctica Sun Times
http://www.asa.org/nsfa/ast.htm

Antarctic Support Associates
http://www.asa.org

Australian Antarctic Division
http://www.antdiv.gov.au/

Australian Surveying and Land Information Group
http://www.auslig.gov.au
email: mapsales@auslig.gov.au

Belgian Antarctic Research Program
http://www.belspo.be:80:/antar/

British Antarctic Survey
http://www.nerc-bas.ac.uk

CIA's Antarctica page
http://www.odci.gov/cia/publications/95fact/ay.html

Gateway to Antarctica
http://www.icair.iac.org.nz:/

Information about Japan's Antarctic program
gopher://stis.nsf.gov:70/00/SBE/intdocs/int9403

Italian Antarctic Program
http://pnracas01.casaccia.enea.it/

National Science Foundation
http://www.nsf.gov/od/opp/start.htm

The New South Polar Times
http://205.174.118.254/nspt/home.htm

South African National Antarctic Program
http://www.puk.ac.za/fskdocs/omg/omg_antE.html

'virtual tour' of McMurdo
http://astro.uchicago.edu/cara/vtour/mcmurdo/ ■

updated video views of Mawson station, a map showing the location of Australia's research ship *Aurora Australis*, and stacks of information on Australian Antarctic science, stations and history.

The US program is represented both by the National Science Foundation home page and the site developed by the US Antarctic Programs' private logistics contractor, Antarctic Support Associates. Both sites offer an inside look at life on an American Antarctic station as well as the research undertaken there.

Many of the other national programs operating in Antarctica are also represented on the Web, including the Australian Antarctic Division, the Belgian Antarctic Research Program, the British Antarctic Survey the Italian Antarctic Program, the South African National Antarctic Program, and Germany's polar research center, the Alfred Wegener Institute. Information about Japan's Antarctic program can be found in a document produced by the US government.

The CIA's page devoted to Antarctica is outdated, but contains the little-known fact that Antarctica's international digraph is AY.

The New South Polar Times is an on-line newspaper produced by the staff of the US Amundsen-Scott South Pole Station. Also check out the US Navy-published *Antarctica Sun Times* newspaper, and reports produced by Antarctic Heritage Trust (see Useful Organizations below).

FILMS & VIDEOS

Starting with motion pictures recorded by William Spiers Bruce on the Scottish National Antarctic Expedition of 1902-04, the Antarctic boasts a rich, if spare, legacy of films. Two recently restored movies of early expeditions offer an inside look at Antarctic exploration. 'Camera-artist' Herbert Ponting's *90° South: With Scott to the Antarctic* (1933) was restored by the British Film Institute's National Film Archive. Ponting's tribute to his lost companions is deeply moving, but the first half of the film is far more interesting, with superb cinematography of wildlife and the expedition's daily activities, all narrated by Ponting. Watch for the politically incorrect penguin chase, as well as the expedition's amazing jumping cat. Joseph Rucker and Willard Van der Veer's *With Byrd at the South Pole: The Story of Little America* (1930), a record of Richard Byrd's flight to the Pole in 1929, actually won the Academy Award for Best Cinematography in 1930. The film begins with a remarkably stilted introduction by Byrd himself, but the images that follow are spectacular. The gung-ho narration is corny ('Oh, for a chance to slap those plucky devils on the back!' goes a typical line) but amusing. Watch for the politically incorrect penguin outfitted with a black bow tie, as well as Byrd's mascot dog 'Igloo.' Both of these movies are distributed by Milestone Film & Video (275 West 96th St, Suite 28-C, New York, NY 10025; ☎ 1-212-865-7449; fax 1-212-222-8952). Another popular classic is Charles Frend's *Scott of the Antarctic* (1948). This melodramatic British film, perhaps not surprisingly, takes a near-worshipful view of Capt Robert Scott, played by John Mills.

While not strictly about Antarctica, Irving Johnson's film of his 1929 voyage around Cape Horn in the square-rigger *Peking* gives an eyewitness view of the Southern Ocean's ferocity – as well as life aboard a 19th-century wooden sailing ship. Though he shot the film in 1929, Johnson narrated it a half-century later. By then he was a captain with a lifetime of ocean-going experience, and his matter-of-fact descriptions add to the realism of the spectacular footage. *Around Cape Horn* (1929) is a production of Mystic Seaport Museum (47 Greenmanville Ave, Mystic, CT, USA 06355-9947; ☎ 1-860-572-5386; fax 1-860-572-5324).

Ironically, a movie that is somehow more genuinely heart-rending than *Scott of the Antarctic* chronicles the fate not of men on a British expedition, but of sledge dogs on a Japanese expedition in 1958: Koreyoshi Kurahara's *Antarctica* (1984). The eerie soundtrack of the same name, by Vangelis, is highly regarded among Antarctic audiophiles.

Another Japanese film, Harushi Kadokama's gloriously awful nuclear-holocaust thriller, *Virus* (1980), partially filmed on location in Antarctica, has achieved cult status aboard some Antarctic tour ships for its sheer over-the-top absurdity. After a deadly germ wipes out the earth's entire human population, 858 men – and eight very nervous women – struggle to survive in Antarctica.

Two other sci-fi movies – *The Thing from Another World* (1951) and its remake, *The Thing* (1982) – star an extraterrestrial that terrorizes polar research stations. Among serious sci-fi buffs, the earlier *Thing*, directed by Howard Hawks, is widely regarded as one of the best science-fiction films ever made, but it is set in the Arctic, not the Antarctic. The much-too-gory remake, however, is a bona fide Antarctic movie.

A naval expedition sent to explore Antarctica discovers a tropical region filled with clunky-looking dinosaurs in *The Land Unknown* (1957), while an investigation among Antarctic whalers turns deadly in *Hell Below Zero* (1953).

There's even a dopey Antarctic comedy, *Quick Before It Melts* (1965), in which a magazine reporter, sent to cover a naval expedition to the Little America base in Antarctica, tries to engineer the defection of a Russian scientist in order to obtain a 'scoop.'

IMAX's *Antarctica* (1991) offers magnificent scenery but leaves many people cold. First-timers may be blown away by the spectacular images, but some Antarctic connoisseurs feel disappointed that the unique medium – outside of some terrific underwater shots of penguins and seals – wasn't more effectively exploited. The Swiss Hans-Ulrich Schlumpf's *Der Kongress der Pinguine* ('The Congress of the Penguins') of 1994 stars penguins in a bizarre, 91-minute morality tale of alleged environmental destruction in Antarctica and at South Georgia. It's definitely weird, but worth the effort of finding it.

In recent years, TV documentary series about Antarctica – and especially its wildlife – have proliferated, and many of them are available on video. The best wildlife documentary among them may well be David Attenborough's *Life in the Freezer* series produced by the BBC; among its amazing underwater footage are some rare views of a leopard seal devouring a penguin, which it toys with just as a cat does with a mouse. *The Last Place on Earth* is a made-for-TV series that tells the story of Amundsen's and Scott's race to reach the South Pole in seven parts over 6½ hours. Made in 1985 by Central Independent Television and based on Roland Huntford's book of the same name, it takes some annoying narrative liberties – and even appears ridiculous in places, ie Scott cries at the South Pole after seeing Amundsen's tent – but overall it is well made and interesting. Both *Life in the Freezer* and *The Last Place on Earth* are often shown on Antarctic cruise ships. Television New Zealand's 'Wild South' series (PO Box 474, Dunedin, NZ, ☎ 64-3-479-9979; fax 64-3-479-9917) is truly excellent, in particular, *The Longest Night*, which chronicles the lives of a small group of men and women spending the winter at Scott Base – watch for the courageous winter skinny-dippers! Another gem among the dozen Antarctic titles in the 'Wild South' series is *Solid Water, Liquid Rock*, offering a unique look at Mt Erebus, from its undersea foundation to its lava-showering summit.

MAGAZINES & JOURNALS

Although there are no general-interest magazines devoted strictly to Antarctica, some popular titles like *Australian Geographic*, Germany's *Geo* and the US's *National Geographic* all run occasional feature stories on the southern continent. Even the glossy, gossipy *Paris Match* has carried an article about a French expedition to The Ice!

The quarterly *Polar Record*, published by Cambridge University Press, is very scholarly, mainly containing academic research papers, but it also includes reports on Antarctic logistics, books, history and other matters of general interest about Antarctica. Subscriptions cost £44 per year, and are available from Cambridge University Press, Edinburgh Building, Shaftesbury Rd, Cambridge, England CB2 2RU, UK (☎ 44-1223-312-393; fax 44-1223-315-052).

ANARE News, 'Australia's Antarctic Magazine,' gives a detailed look inside the Australian National Antarctic Research Expeditions (ANARE). A handsome glossy, it is published quarterly and is available from the Australian Antarctic Division, Department of the Environment, Kingston, Tasmania 7050 Australia (☎ 61-3-6232-3209; fax 61-3-6232-3288).

The *Antarctic Journal of the United States* is a quarterly newsletter describing US research and activities on The Ice. There is also a fifth issue comprising an annual review of the US Antarctic Program. The *Antarctic Journal* is available for $13 per year ($16.25 for foreign subscriptions) by writing to: New Orders, Superintendent of Documents, PO Box 371954, Pittsburgh, PA, 15250-7954 USA. Orders can also be faxed to 1-202-512-2233. Visa and Mastercard are accepted.

The Antarctican Society newsletter, written in inimitable style by Paul Dalrymple, is a lively compendium of information about American activities on the continent as well as a good deal of news about the way things once were in Antarctica (see Useful Organizations).

The Polar Times, published by the American Polar Society (PO Box 692 Reedsport, OR 97467 USA; ☎ 1-503-759-3589; fax 1-503-759-3403), is mainly a collection of news clippings about Antarctica from US newspapers, along with articles written by members. The Montreal Antarctic Society publishes a quarterly newsletter, *The Seventh Continent*, with a view toward Canadian work in Antarctica. *Aurora*, published by Australia's ANARE Club, gives another view of Australian Antarctic activities, while the New Zealand Antarctic Society's quarterly, *Antarctic*, is justifiably famous for its unique coverage of activities by all countries operating in Antarctica.

Heritage Hearsay, published by the Antarctic Heritage Trust, includes information about the restoration of Antarctic historic sites. (For information on all of these societies, see Useful Organizations below.)

The Antarctic Century, a well-written and very knowledgeable newsletter published by Oceanites (see Useful Organizations), is filled with current news about both Antarctic politics and research, and contains handsome B&W photographs by its editor, Ron Naveen.

Expedition News is a monthly review of significant expeditions and adventures, many of them in Antarctica. It is available either by email or by regular mail for US$36 per year from Blumenfeld and Associates, 397 Post Rd, Suite 202, Darien, CT 06820 USA (☎ 1-203-656-3300, email: BlumAssoc@aol.com).

The six-page *Antarctic Sun Times* is published weekly during summer at McMurdo tation by US Navy personnel. It includes a popular 'Around the Continent' section as well as articles about station life and Antarctic history. The shipping news includes announcements about the scheduled arrival of both tourist cruise ships and station resupply vessels. Outside of Antarctica you can get this via the internet (see Online Services in the chapter), but if your ship calls into McMurdo, one of the ship's staff may be given a stack of the actual newspapers to bring back for the shipboard library. The paper gives an interesting, 'inside' look at life in Antarctica's biggest town.

PHOTOGRAPHY & VIDEO

Nearly all types of cameras are suitable for Antarctica. Pocket-size autofocus cameras, with their built-in flash units, are perfect for recording shipboard life and the dark interiors of historic huts, whose windows are often boarded over to protect against drifting snow. For most other situations, single-lens reflex (SLR) cameras, with their higher-quality and changeable lenses, produce sharper images. Disposable cameras – especially the panoramic types – can be useful for shots where you don't want to risk damaging a more expensive camera – ie, when shooting from aboard a salt spray-soaked Zodiac or in a blinding snowstorm. Don't be tempted to think that B&W film will do justice to Antarctica's phenomenal beauty, unless you are aiming for an artistic or historical look, and then bring it only *in addition to* color film.

Remember to bring a good case to protect your camera from salt spray, rain, snow and dust. Helicopters, with their powerful downblasts full of grit and gravel, can ruin a valuable lens in seconds. In a pinch, a plastic bag will work, but you run the risk of a strong gust ripping it away from you to pollute either Antarctica or the sea. A camera bag with shoulder strap offers protection and leaves hands free for ascending and descending steep gangways to the ship.

Movie & Video

Many of the principles detailed above and in Ron Naveen's sidebar, hold true for movie and video photography, but shooting movies or video in Antarctica requires some additional special handling. The light meters on video cameras especially can be fooled by the bright polar light; framing your composition so that less sky is visible should help to alleviate overexposure. Video and movie camera operators should also try to limit the amount of automatic panning, zooming and fading they do, despite the sophisticated capabilities of many cameras on the market today. Not only will limiting the camera's movement prevent dizziness for those who eventually view the footage, it will also save precious battery time, which cold will shorten by as much as 50% or more. In fact, where possible, it is desirable to shut off the autofocus and/or automatic zoom features on the camera entirely to save battery time.

Try to ensure that your shots run for at least 10 or 15 seconds before you change subjects; otherwise, your work will seem jerky and too much like a music video (unless, of course, that's the effect you intend). It is best to shoot your footage and then pause or stop the camera before setting up the next shot. Also, be mindful of

Taking Photos in the Antarctic

Equipment Antarctic photography is made considerably easier by today's modern, computer-chip-driven cameras. It is very difficult not to come home with great shots, if just a few simple rules are followed:

Take lots of color slide or color print film – perhaps twice as much as you might ordinarily carry. Slower speed film (ASA 64, 100 and 125) is usually quite adequate because of the high reflectivity of light during the austral summer. And slower speed film produces much snappier results because it is finer-grained than the ASA 200 and 400 speed films. A few higher speed rolls may be useful on the very cloudy, murky days that do occur, or to assist your efforts to capture fast-flying seabirds on film.

Wide-angle lenses (24–28mm) and 70- or 80–200mm zoom lenses are extraordinarily useful. The wide angles allow you to capture all of the breathtaking scenery you'll encounter, and the zoom allows you some alternatives for framing and capturing shots of the many penguins, seals and flying birds you'll see – and at relatively close distances. Antarctic animals are, generally speaking, quite relaxed about human visitors. You'll encounter numerous situations where you, the photographer, have plenty of time to frame your picture and take excellent shots. Longer lenses, 300mm and 400mm, are very bulky, but useful when trying to capture distant seabirds at sea.

Don't hesitate to rely on your camera's built-in, sophisticated metering systems. The matrix metering systems in new cameras do a great job of sorting through light imbalances.

Technique Antarctic scenery and animals are so spectacular that it's quite natural to worry whether one's trophy shots will actually come out, but by observing the following suggestions, you should experience no difficulty.

Take a millisecond before each shot to ask: Is there too much white or black in the viewfinder? Remember that the camera's meter wants to turn everything to what is called '18% gray,' which is like photographically mixing together the black and

others when filming; don't get so involved in looking through your viewfinder (or narrating your shot aloud to your camera's microphone) that you step on an animal or intrude on a fellow visitor's photography.

Restrictions

Politeness dictates that whenever you are inside a scientific station, you ask the residents about taking photographs or video before you do so. The station is their home, and you should treat it that way.

Photographing Wildlife

The apparent tameness of Antarctic animals may be deceiving, and even animals that appear to be unconcerned about humans nearby may in fact be under considerable stress. People approaching as far away as 30m from a penguin rookery have been shown to increase the birds' heart rates significantly. And for as long as three days after people visit, penguins may deviate from their usual path when approaching or leaving a colony.

Always remember to keep the required distances from animals: five meters from penguins, seabirds and seals – except fur seals, which should not be approached closer than 15m. Never block an animal's path to the sea or its young. When approaching animals, remember to stay low, and don't move suddenly or speak loudly. When you are finished photographing, back out quietly, the same way you moved in. If an animal starts to move, you're too close. If an animal changes its behavior, you're too close. The further you stay from an animal,

white on a checkerboard. If your intended shot has too much white (snow or ice), the picture will come out gray unless you 'open up' at least one stop and add a little extra exposure. This is done by reducing the shutter speed to the next slowest speed, using the next larger aperture (f-stop), or by turning your camera's exposure compensation dial to +1. Conversely, if there's too much dark color in the viewfinder (black hillsides, volcanic ash) you need to 'stop down' by at least one stop to prevent the black from being turned into a gray wash. This is done by increasing the shutter speed to the next fastest speed, using the next smallest aperture (f-stop), or by turning your camera's exposure compensation dial to -1. There may be up to a three-stop difference between a proper exposure and a stark white or stark black subject; thus, you might even extend your exposure adjustment to +2 or -2, but the recommendation is not to go all the way to +3 or -3 because the definition in your intended subject is likely to be lost. When you really want to make sure you've nailed a particularly wonderful composition, consider bracketing, which means taking a few shots at different exposures: With close-to-average shots, follow your camera's recommendation, then shoot down one stop (-1) and open up one stop (+1); with shots having much white, follow your camera's recommendation, then open up by one (+1) and two (+2) stops.

A UV filter on the end of your lens keeps it from being scratched and cuts off the blue cast that might creep into your shots. Polarizing filters cut through glare in the water and darken skies, and can lead to nice shots; but they also cost about two stops of light, meaning that you'll have to use a slower shutter speed or wider aperture to get your shot.

Finally, don't forget to bring lots of batteries. The ship you're on probably won't have what you need, and if it does, the stock is likely to be outdated. ■

– **Ron Naveen**, author of *Wild Ice: Antarctic Journeys* and Chief Operating Officer of the Oceanites Foundation

the more natural its behavior will be. For this reason, many biologists and naturalists prefer to view wildlife through binoculars or telephoto lenses even when ashore, rather than moving in close.

It is much better to get animals to come to you, which they often will do if you merely sit down, stay quiet and be a bit patient.

TIME

Time is all but irrelevant to the visitor to the Antarctic, since the tourist season occurs during summer, when daylight lasts as long as 20 hours a day. Most Antarctic ships maintain their clocks at the same time as their port of departure (if they return to the same port), or else slowly adjust it to the port of disembarkation as they cross the Southern Ocean on the return voyage. Life aboard ship is often ruled by landing opportunities, as meals are delayed or advanced according to possibilities for getting ashore.

Most Antarctic stations are run on a time similar to that of their home countries or logistics bases, so that communications are coordinated. But others are adjusted slightly to account for their geographic location. Australia's Antarctic stations, for instance, are managed from headquarters in Hobart. But when it is noon in Hobart, it is 9 am at Casey station, 8 am at Davis station and 7 am at Mawson station. Scientists working in the field generally develop their own time schedules, often working in midnight 'day'-light and sleeping late into the 'morning.'

Your main concern with time will be to make sure that when you telephone someone in the 'civilized world,' you make sure that you're not waking them up. The ship's radio officers should be able to help you calculate the time difference (see Post & Communications).

ELECTRICITY

Each ship has its own type of electricity, based on its country of origin, so you should check with the tour operator before buying converters, etc. Many of the ships are from Russia, and use 220 volts, 50 hertz, with electrical outlet sockets accommodating the standard European two round-pin plug.

LAUNDRY

Every Antarctic tourist ship has a laundry, and service is generally excellent. You simply leave your laundry in a bag in your cabin, and the attendant picks it up and returns it for you. Being on a per-item basis, shipboard laundry prices are not cheap, but they're also not so expensive as to discourage occasional use. Shipboard laundries can actually deliver very good value, since they allow you not to pack – and carry – so many clothes from home. Service is usually within two days.

Hand-laundering items like socks (polypropylene sock liners are especially fast-drying) will allow you to pack less and still not become a social outcast. Rolling washed items in a towel and squeezing before hanging them to dry will help ensure dry clothes in the morning.

HEALTH

Antarctica is largely a clean, healthy, disease-free place, but medical attention, obviously, is limited. While the ship's doctor stands ready to treat any problems that arise *en voyage*, the doctor is not available for general consultation or treatment of previous illnesses or ailments. Care in what you eat and drink is the most important health rule; stomach upsets are the most likely travel health problem, but the majority of these upsets will be relatively minor. Tap water is fine to drink aboard all Antarctic tour ships.

Travel Health Guides

There are a number of books on travel health: *Travelers' Health*, by Dr Richard Dawood (Oxford University Press, 1995), is comprehensive, easy to read, authoritative and highly recommended, although it's rather large to lug around. *Travel with Children*, by Maureen Wheeler (Lonely Planet Publications, 1995), includes basic advice on travel health for younger children.

Predeparture Preparations

Health Insurance A travel insurance policy to cover theft, loss and medical problems is a good idea. There are a wide variety of policies and your travel agent will have recommendations. Some policies offer lower and higher medical expenses options, but the higher one is chiefly for countries like the US which have extremely high medical costs. Check the small print: Some policies specifically exclude 'dangerous activities' which can include scuba diving and hiking. You might want to check if they include travel to Antarctica in that activity! Check if the policy covers an emergency flight home. If you have to stretch out, you will need two seats, and somebody has to pay for them!

Medical Kit A small, straightforward medical kit is a wise thing to carry. A possible list includes:

- Aspirin or other pain reliever – for pain or fever.
- Antihistamine (such as Benadryl) – useful as a decongestant for colds, allergies, or to help prevent sea sickness.
- Kaolin preparation (Pepto-Bismol), Imodium or Lomotil – for stomach upsets.
- Rehydration mixture – for treatment of severe diarrhea, particularly important if traveling with children.
- Antiseptic, Mercurochrome and antibiotic powder – for cuts and grazes.
- Bandages (Band-aids) – for minor injuries.
- Scissors, tweezers and a thermometer (note that mercury thermometers are prohibited by airlines).

Health Preparations Make sure you're healthy before you start traveling. It is also a good idea to schedule a dentist appointment before your trip to make sure your teeth are OK.

If you wear glasses take a spare pair and your prescription. Losing or breaking your glasses can be a real problem, since there's obviously no way to get a new set while you're in Antarctica.

If you require a particular medication take an adequate supply, as it likewise will not be available. It's a wise idea to have the prescription with you to show that you are using the medication legally – it's surprising how often over-the-counter drugs from one country are illegal without a prescription, or even banned in another.

Immunizations You don't need any vaccinations to visit Antarctica. It's always a good idea to keep your tetanus immunization up-to-date no matter where you are – boosters are necessary every 10 years and protection is highly recommended – but even this is not strictly required.

Sunburn

In Antarctica, you can get sunburned surprisingly quickly, even on overcast days. The sun is particularly dangerous here, because the sun reflects off of snow, ice and the sea. Use a sunscreen. Calamine lotion is good for mild sunburn.

Snow Blindness

Antarctica's reflecting sunlight produces a powerful glare, so sunglasses are essential in Antarctica. Be sure to buy UV-filtering sunglasses. Cheap sunglasses can be very harmful, since their dark lenses cause your pupils to dilate even more, while offering no protection from harmful ultraviolet. Your best bet are glacier glasses, which include leather side flaps to prevent light from entering from the sides. Snow blindness is an extremely painful – though relatively rare – inflammation that results in headaches and a temporary loss of sight.

Hypothermia

Too much cold can be dangerous, particularly if it leads to hypothermia. Although shore visits are not conducted in severe weather, and most are not long enough for you to become hypothermic, it is still possible. Hypothermia occurs when the body loses heat faster than it can produce it, and the core temperature of the body falls. It is surprisingly easy to progress from very cold to dangerously cold due to a combination of wind, wet clothing, fatigue and hunger, even if the air temperature is above freezing. It is best to dress in layers; silk, wool and some of the new artificial fibers are all good insulating materials. A hat is important, as a lot of heat is lost through the head. A strong waterproof outer layer is essential, since keeping dry is vital.

Symptoms of hypothermia are exhaustion, numb skin (particularly fingers and toes), shivering, slurred speech, irrational or violent behavior, lethargy, stumbling, dizzy spells, muscle cramps and violent bursts of energy. Irrationality may take the form of sufferers claiming they are warm and trying to take off their clothes.

To treat hypothermia, first get the patient out of the wind and/or rain, remove his/her clothing if it's wet and replace it with dry, warm clothing. Give the patient hot liquids – not alcohol – and some high-calorie, easily digestible food. This should be enough for the early stages of hypothermia, but if it has gone further it may be necessary to consult with the ship's doctor. If possible, place the sufferer in a warm (not hot) shower.

Dehydration

The extremely dry Antarctic environment can lead to mild dehydration. You should drink at least a gallon of water a day while in Antarctica. Signs of dehydration include dark-yellow urine and/or a feeling of fatigue. Coffee and tea are diuretics and as such are counterproductive when trying to combat dehydration.

Antarctic Medicine

> *The chief work of the surgeon of a polar expedition is done before the ship leaves . . . if it has been properly carried out there should be little to do during the actual journey . . . casualties are excepted for . . . they cannot be foreseen . . . ordinary sickness can be largely ruled out by careful examination . . . .*

Thus wrote Dr AH Macklin at the conclusion of Ernest Shackleton's *Quest* expedition, on which Shackleton died of a heart attack, a pre-existing condition. Macklin's words are as relevant as ever for anyone journeying to Antarctica, where health care services are limited. All persons, whether tourists, scientists or support staff, should be physically fit and free of significant disease. National operators as well as tourist groups and private expeditions have varying standards of medical screening and provision of health care services. All, however, must be self sufficient and not rely on outside assistance.

Most wintering expeditions have a rigorous screening program, and some include psychological testing. Despite this screening, doctors selected for Antarctic service must have the skills to cope with any eventuality. Since it is unrealistic to expect any doctor to have all the specialist skills necessary, pre-departure training is organized in environmental and occupational medicine, anaesthetics, surgery, laboratory techniques, radiography, dentistry, physiotherapy and medical communications so that specialist advice can be obtained from outside Antarctica. As there has been a high rate of appendicitis in Antarctica, some nations require their doctors to undergo a prophylactic appendectomy. Lay personnel are given basic first aid training and some are trained in anaesthetics and sterile operating theater techniques in order to assist the doctor should an operation be necessary.

The lack of all-weather airfields or permanently based aircraft in Antarctica, and the inability of all but a few nations to make direct intercontinental flights during most of the year, makes many stations and bases remain largely inaccessible. Most wintering groups are accompanied by one doctor (some national expeditions have two doctors; others have paramedics). This doctor works on the principle that he or she must handle any medical, surgical or dental emergency without the assistance of medical evacuation.

There is no Antarctic-specific disease or ailment. Cold injury, snow blindness and other environmental conditions are always a threat but serious cases are not common. Trauma resulting from accidents is most common, along with resultant lacerations, broken bones, burns or death.

More than 500 people have died in Antarctica since humans first went to the southern continent (half of them in the Air New Zealand crash on Mt Erebus), but the mortality in this relatively young and fit population is still low compared with more densely populated regions. Antarctica is not spared from conditions such as heart attacks, ulcers, intracranial bleeding, psychiatric conditions, carbon monoxide poisoning and infectious diseases brought from the outside world (malaria, sexually transmitted diseases, amoebiasis, polio).

Antarctic doctors must be masters of improvisation. In 1961, the physician to the Soviet expedition was forced to operate on himself for acute appendicitis. He was assisted by two co-workers, who held the retractors and a mirror. The operation was successful. In the same year, a ruptured intracranial aneurysm was operated on at an Australian station. The doctor had neither previous neurosurgical experience nor sufficient instruments, but a brain cannula and sucker were improvized using illustrations from a surgical catalogue. A neurosurgeon in Melbourne provided advice via radio telegrams for the operation, which also was successful.

The records of most expeditions highlight ingenuity: Dentures have been repaired with teeth made from a seal's tooth, and intricate equipment has frequently been repaired and fabricated. One scientist lost both glasses and contact lenses, so new ones had to be ground out of perspex in the station workshop according to a prescription provided by an eye specialist remote from Antarctica.

Primitive medical offices, however, are now being replaced. Modern offices contain a consulting room, dental and examination room, operating theater, laboratory, medical ward, storeroom and area for treatment of hypothermia. Equipment includes X-ray machines, electrocardiograph monitors and defibrillators, anaesthetic machines, pulse oximeters, electro-surgical units, dry chemistry laboratory analyzers, dental equipment, autoclave and gas sterilization and therapeutic ultrasound. The doctor's work includes all the practical tasks of laboratory tests, radiology, nursing, cleaning the surgery, sterilizing instruments and even bed-making. A wide range of pharmaceuticals is supplied, and as with the equipment, the selection is continually reviewed and upgraded.

Many doctors also perform research. Particular emphasis has been placed on research in the applied areas such as health and behavioral studies, nutrition, epidemiology, thermal adaptation, hormone adaptation, cardiovascular studies, photobiology (especially ultraviolet radiation) and diving medicine. Research into the capacity of winterers to resist infection has indicated that living for long periods in Antarctic isolation causes reduced immunity. Further studies are continuing.

International cooperation has always been excellent in the Antarctic, especially in dealing with operational problems. Although polar human biology was carried out on early Antarctic expeditions, it was ad hoc and had little continuity or coordination. The advent of the Scientific Committee on Antarctic Research (SCAR), and coordination by subsidiary groups such as the SCAR Working Group on Human Biology and Medicine, has had a great impact on research and Antarctic health care. The International Biomedical Expedition to the Antarctic 1980-81 (IBEA), the first Antarctic expedition solely for human studies, was organized by the Working Group.

Collaborative research is now taking place between Antarctic and space agencies. Much of the research has relevance beyond Antarctica. The problems faced by personnel in polar regions, including those related to isolation and living and working in confined environments, are also experienced by space crew. Mutual studies have enormous potential to enhance the performance, health and safety of people in both settings. ■

– **Dr Des Lugg**, Head of Polar Medicine at the Australian Antarctic Division

Insomnia

Sleeplessness can be a problem in the Antarctic, with its extended hours of sunlight in summer and darkness in winter. There's even a special term coined for the problem – 'Big Eye.' Caused by a disruption in the body's normal circadian rhythm, this insomnia usually cures itself after a few days. If you are feeling sleepless, you might try going up on the bridge or out on deck for a look at the scenery – you can always sleep at home.

Seasickness

The bane of many a traveler, seasickness (or, in French, the much more poetic *mal de mer)* can be one of the prices exacted by King Neptune for passage through his often-stormy Southern Ocean. One cynical suggestion for alleviating this uniquely horrible feeling is to sit down under a tree and wait for it to go away.

Eating lightly during your trip will reduce your chances of seasickness. If you are prone to seasickness, try to find a cabin that minimizes disturbance – close to midship can be slightly more comfortable. Fresh air usually helps; reading, cigarette smoke and diesel fumes don't. One remedy formerly used on ore boats in the Great Lakes of North America was to cinch a belt or a length of rope extremely tightly around one's midsection. This will not prove effective for everyone, however.

In fact, no method is effective for everyone. Many commercial motion-sickness remedies are on the market, and the ship's doctor will readily dispense one or two types – and on some ships, the pills are placed in bowls in public areas, like little candies. However, if you are concerned about seasickness, it might be a good idea to bring several types of remedies in case one is ineffective. Many of these pills can cause drowsiness, and they must be taken before heavy seas start the ship rolling – when you're feeling sick it's too late. Ginger is a natural preventative for seasickness and is available in capsule form. Other methods commonly tried include acupressure wrist bands and even special recorded music.

WOMEN TRAVELERS

Women traveling to Antarctica will most likely experience nothing different from male visitors. In fact, on most Antarctic cruise ships, there is a slight majority of women (since they outlive men, and most Antarctic tourists are older). While women are still in the minority at most Antarctic bases, they are no longer rare, and the days are gone when the sight of an attractive young female visitor brought the immediate and persistent attention of the male members of a research station.

One unique adaptation enables women to accomplish a necessary function more easily in the harsh Antarctic environment. The SaniFem, or 'sanitary funnel,' is sometimes used by women expeditioners at Antarctic stations to relieve themselves out in the field without exposure to the wind and weather. The anatomically contoured funnel (known colloquially as the 'pissphone' or 'whizzomatic') is slipped into the underwear while getting dressed, and when the need arises, the wearer can simply unzip her trousers and proceed like a man. The same does not apply to tourists, however: Both men and women tourists have no excuse for not taking care of all toilet functions on board ship.

It probably goes without saying, but women should pack an adequate supply of tampons and pain medication, since supplies of these will be extremely limited – or, more probably, nonexistent – aboard ship.

DISABLED TRAVELERS

The physical challenges of shipboard life, Zodiac boats and icy landing sites can make Antarctica a difficult and dangerous place for able-bodied as well as disabled travelers. However, it may be possible for a disabled tourist to make special arrangements with a tour operator, especially if an able-bodied traveler accompanies him/her. Although Antarctica is spectacular enough simply when viewed from the deck of a ship, helicopters can also be employed to make otherwise-inaccessible sites within reach, so a ship equipped with helicopters can offer advantages (as does a ship with elevators). Even wheelchair-bound visitors have been able to enjoy Zodiac rides on calm days, thanks to willing cruise staff members who have carried wheelchairs down the gangway. Check with the individual tour operators to see how flexible they are and how well-equipped the ship is to handle wheelchairs.

Some travel agencies specialize in helping disabled clients fulfill their adventures. One company that has helped clients to book Antarctic cruises is Flying Wheels Travel of Owatonna, MN, USA (☎ 1-507-451-5005). Ask for Edna Cook.

SENIOR TRAVELERS

The majority of passengers on many if not most Antarctic cruises are senior citizens, since they often have more time and money to spend on travel than younger people do. Indeed, there's absolutely no reason why advanced age should present insurmountable difficulties for visiting Antarctica. Norman Vaughan, who first set foot on the continent in 1928 with American aviator Richard E Byrd, reached the summit of the 10,300-foot mountain in Antarctica that Byrd named for him – three days before his 89th birthday in 1994. Vaughan's personal motto: 'The only death you die is the death you die every day by not living.'

On the other hand, you don't necessarily want to die in Antarctica, either. Some of the more strenuous walks may be beyond the ability of the older traveler. Know your limits. Good advice for people of all ages is just enjoy what you can do, and don't overexert yourself. Antarctica's beauty – and fascinating wildlife – are often best experienced simply by standing still or even sitting down. Too many people of all ages rush around while ashore, snapping photos and marching from one end of a landing site to another. Slow down and enjoy.

TRAVEL WITH CHILDREN

Children are still relatively rare visitors to Antarctica, which is a shame. For example, fewer than half a dozen children have visited the US McMurdo station in its entire 40-year history (and four of those visited only in 1996)! However, more affordable fares and more interested parents are bringing more children to The Ice – a positive situation for everyone involved.

Antarctica's amazing landscapes and abundant wildlife are especially exciting for children. But if your kids are the kind who can't go for more than an hour without playing with a Game-Boy, then leave them at home: They won't be able to handle the long sea time, which is difficult enough even for phlegmatic adults. If you do decide to go and it is financially possible, try to get a suite so that children have enough room to spread out and play with toys and books on the floor. Also, check to see if an in-cabin video player is available, since children can screen their favorite videos as well as educational tapes about Antarctica. You should probably count on there being no other children aboard the ship for your kids to play with.

Unfortunately, you should also be prepared to encounter resentment from other passengers – especially older travelers – until they see that your children can behave in a civilized manner (if they can!). 'No one talks to you for the first three days,' said a perfectly behaved subteenaged young lady on a recent voyage. People will even sometimes tell parents later in the trip that they weren't happy to see the children aboard the ship – at first. But often, kids soon find themselves becoming the object of grandparent-like attention from other travelers, especially in the dining room, where seating is usually open and unreserved.

Children traveling to Antarctica (just like grown-ups) will get more out of the experience if they are prepared for it. Watching videos and reading books about Antarctica (see Children's Books section in this chapter) before sailing can help to build excitement and knowledge. Giving children 'assignments' to learn about particular Antarctic topics while on the voyage – and encouraging them to ask the ship's lecture staff to help them with research – can enrich their learning experience. Remember to bring plenty of materials such as drawing paper, pencils, crayons, markers, scissors, Scotch tape and glue for arts & crafts projects.

USEFUL ORGANIZATIONS

There are several organizations that concern themselves with Antarctica, especially its environment and human history.

American Polar Society In 1934 this society was founded as a forum for people involved or interested in the polar exploration and research. Annual membership dues are US$10 (US$12 for foreign memberships) and members receive *The Polar Times* twice a year. Contact Brian Shoemaker, the Society's Secretary at PO Box 692 Reedsport, OR 97467 USA (☎ 1-503-759-3589; fax 1-503-759-3403; email: iceman@presys.com).

ANARE Club The club has various categories of membership for those who have served with the Australian National Antarctic Research Expeditions (ANARE), including a category called 'subscriber,' (annual dues: A$30) which entitles one to receive the Club's magazine *Aurora*, published four times a year. Contact the Club's Secretary, Dick Saxton, at GPO Box 2534 W, Melbourne 3001 Australia.

Antarctic Heritage Trust This organization coordinates the preservation and protection of the historic sites of the Ross Sea region. Contrary to popular belief, the sites and their relics are not permanently preserved by the Antarctic climate, but in fact are being deteriorated by time and the elements. The Trust has established a database of all the artifacts in the Ross Sea huts and has also done extensive repair and protection work on the huts themselves. All tourist visits to the huts are chaperoned by designated representatives of the Antarctic Heritage Trust. Membership in the Trust, which was established in 1987, costs NZ$20 for New Zealand residents and NZ$25 for people living overseas; the difference is mainly due to the costs of mailing out the Trust's newsletter, *Heritage Hearsay*, which is published two or three times a year. The Trust also published David Harrowfield's excellent book, *Icy Heritage: Historic Sites of the Ross Sea Region*. AHT's address is: PO Box 14-091, Christchurch Airport, New Zealand (☎ 64-3-358-0200; fax 64-3-358-0211). The Trust has a British sister organization, called the **United Kingdom Antarctic Heritage Trust**, which is beginning to develop a protection program for such historic non-Ross Sea sites as the former British base at Port Lockroy on Weinecke Island, established in 1944. UKAHT's address is: c/o Capt Pat McLaren, RN, UK AHT, The Blue House, East Marden, Chichester, W Sussex, PO18 9JE, UK (☎ 44-1243-535-256).

Antarctica Project This organization is the only environmental organization in the world devoted exclusively to protecting Antarctica. It is also a co-founder and supporter of the Antarctic and Southern Ocean Coalition (ASOC), which has more than 200 member conservation organizations in nearly 50 countries. The group lobbies national governments on behalf of conservation issues, and attends Antarctic Treaty System meetings as a certified Non-Governmental Observer (NGO). Regular membership is US$30 per year (tax deductible in the US), and contributing members receive four newsletters per year covering Antarctic environmental issues. As part of its mission to educate the public about the continent, the Antarctica Project publishes three valuable 'Antarctica Resource Lists' for elementary-, middle-, and high-school students. Each list suggests appropriate books, films, CD-ROMs, study aids, teacher packets and magazines for the different age levels. The Antarctica Project's address is: PO Box 76920, Washington, DC 20013 USA (☎ 1-202-544-0236; fax 1-202-544-8483).

Antarctican Society This society was organized to unite 'persons interested in Antarctica to facilitate friendly and informal exchanges of information and views on Antarctica, and encourage interest in . . . the increasing importance of Antarctica.'

ceremony on some convenient sea ice – with the ship's captain presiding. However, it would be wise to check the validity of such weddings upon returning home to be sure that they are legally recognized.

SPECIAL EVENTS

Antarctica's biggest endemic holiday is Midwinter's Day, June 22, when the long polar night is half over. The day is traditionally celebrated with a feast, games, songs and even theatrical performances. The last day of the sun and the return of the sun are also, understandably, very important dates on the Antarctic calendar, but they occur at different dates depending on the latitude. Tourists are unlikely to experience any of these holidays, since they occur during the winter, but Christmas and New Year's Eve are celebrated in unique Antarctic style and with enthusiasm aboard ship.

ACTIVITIES

By and large, tourist activity in Antarctica is limited to trooping around ashore during Zodiac landings from the ship. Fat-walleted visitors can fly into the continent's interior with Adventure Network International (see Getting There & Away) for mountain climbing, skiing, camping and trekking.

In 1996-97, for the first time, scuba diving is being offered as an option on Antarctic cruises for advanced divers, and short camping and mountain-climbing trips have also recently become available for cruise passengers (see Getting There & Away). Mountaineers foresee Antarctica becoming one of the great climbing meccas in the 21st century.

In 1995, just over a hundred runners participated in an Antarctic marathon (42 km) over a double-loop course at King George Island in the South Shetlands, arranged by Marathon Tours & Travel of Charlestown, MA. The run was dubbed 'The Last Marathon' by its promoters – and indeed, the poorly managed race almost was the last lap for several of its participants. It began at the Uruguayan base of Artigas and passed through Russian, Chilean and Chinese stations, with many dangerously unsupervised hazards along the way: a crevasse-serrated glacier, a freezing meltwater stream and a five-km-long boulder field. Some runners became delirious with hypothermia, others got lost in fog on top of the glacier, and one even plunged into a crevasse up to his chest. In short, it is remarkable that no one was killed. The marathon rightly drew heavy criticism as a totally inappropriate activity for Antarctica, but Marathon Tours planned another for February 1997.

WORK

Unless you are a scientist (and even then), landing a job with one of the national scientific programs in Antarctica is very difficult. The days are long past when charismatic expedition leaders hand-picked their men (and only men) based on personal intuition and old friendships. Now anyone landing a job in Antarctica has to submit to a battery of physical and psychological tests – and most importantly, must possess advanced skills in one or probably several areas. The length of service varies from three to 24 months.

National programs almost without exception hire only citizens of their own country. For this reason, you should write to your home country's national Antarctic program (see below for some addresses) to inquire about employment possibilities. While scientists are usually sent to Antarctica as the result of specific research proposals approved by peer review, support personnel are selected and hired by the national programs themselves, or, in the case of the US, the largest employer in Antarctica, by a private contractor.

Antarctic Support Associates
: recruits about 600 people per year (this may change if the US Congress decides to cut back funding for the US Antarctic Program) to fill job categories at US Antarctic stations ranging from chefs, clerks, carpenters, electronics technicians and hair stylists to physicians, pipe fitters and welders. Pay and benefits are explained upon successful application. ASA, 61 Inverness Drive East, Suite 300, Englewood, CO, 80112 USA (☎ 1-800-688-8606).

Australian Antarctic Division
Channel Highway, Kingston,
Tasmania 7050 Australia
(☎ 61-3-6232-3209; fax 61-3-6232-3288).

British Antarctic Survey
High Cross, Madingley Rd, Cambridge,
England CB3 0ET, UK
(☎ 44-1223-61188).

French Institute for Polar Research and
Technology (Institut Français pour la
Recherche et la Technologie Polaires),
Technopôle Brest-Iroise
BP 75 – 29280 Plouzané, France
(☎ 33-98-05-65-00; fax 33-98-05-65-55).

Japanese National Institute for Polar Research
Ministry of Education, Science and Culture,
3-2-2 Kasumiga-seki,
Chiyoda-kyu, Tokyo 100, Japan
(☎ 81-3-3581-4211; fax 81-3-3591-8072).

New Zealand Antarctic Programme
International Antarctic Centre,
Orchard Rd, PO Box 14-091,
Christchurch, New Zealand
(☎ 64-3-358-0200; fax 64-3358-0211).

South African National Antarctic Programme
Dept of Environmental Affairs and Tourism,
Private Bag X447, Pretoria 0001,
South Africa
(☎ 27-12-310-3560).

ACCOMMODATIONS

Nearly all Antarctic tourism involves ship-based visits, although a couple of tour operators offer camping on the continent (a polar-rated sleeping bag is highly recommended!).

FOOD

Although the food on Antarctic cruises varies somewhat from ship to ship (predictably, the variation is in pretty direct proportion to the price of the cruise), none is truly outstanding. None is truly awful either, though vegetarians might find it rough going at times. On longer cruises especially, fresh fruits and vegetables are eventually exhausted, with no chance of reprovisioning until the ship returns north. Gourmet cooking, however, is simply not the emphasis in Antarctic tourism. If five-star gourmet dining is critical to your enjoyment of a vacation, you might be better off taking *QEII* across the North Atlantic. Otherwise, query the tour operator for specific details about the 'European chef aboard' so boastfully described in the brochure – what exactly are his/her credentials? It would be unusual to learn that the

Life Aboard a Polar Ship

Voyages to polar seas are different from other sorts of travel, and even seasoned 'cruisers' may need to make some adjustments. Some people find shipboard life difficult to handle at first, feeling a bit claustrophobic. This slight claustrophobia can be heightened in Antarctica, since the cruise ships are small and relatively spartan compared to the lavish floating 'palaces' that ply the Caribbean, Mediterranean and other seas. It's also completely normal to feel lethargic and sluggish during the several days of sailing required to cross the Southern Ocean to reach Antarctica.

Typically, a printed bulletin listing the day's planned activities is distributed the night before to let you know what's ahead. It helps to attend the educational lectures and video screenings that are given, in part, to relieve the monotony of long ocean crossings. Inquiring passengers will find activities to occupy themselves – seabird watching, iceberg spotting, visits to the bridge or engine room, diary writing, reading, etc – but even these can feel stale after three or four days. Don't worry: Antarctica is worth the wait.

International law requires that every ship hold a lifeboat drill within 24 hours of sailing. These drills are quite serious and are mandatory for all passengers. Each cabin should contain a sign or card telling which lifeboat station the occupants should use. There will also be a life vest for each person in the cabin; these are usually equipped with a whistle, reflective patches and a battery-powered beacon light that starts flashing automatically upon contact with saltwater. The universal signal to proceed to lifeboat stations is seven short blasts on the ship's bell or horn, followed by a long blast. This signal may be repeated several times for the lifeboat drill. Since there is only one such drill held during each voyage, if you ever hear the signal a second time during your voyage, it is the *real thing*. You should go immediately to your cabin to pick up your life vest and warm clothing and then straight to your lifeboat station to await directions by the crew.

Extra care is needed when moving about any ship, but passengers on Antarctic cruises especially should keep in mind the rule of 'one hand for the ship,' always keeping one hand free to grab a railing or other support should the ship roll suddenly. You may notice that even some berths on the ship (usually those running fore-and-aft) are equipped with airline-style seat belts for use when seas get a bit heavy. Take care not just when climbing steep ladders and stairwells, but even when in wide-open 'flat' areas such as the bridge, dining room or lecture hall, where a sudden slam into a chair or table could result in a broken arm or leg. Although the rolling motion of a ship on the open ocean tends to be fairly regular and predictable, a vessel pushing through ice can lurch suddenly, pitching an unaware passenger onto his/her nose. Closet and bathroom doors likewise can become dangerous swinging projectiles in high seas, and you should also take care not to accidentally put your fingers into door jambs as a fractured finger can easily result if the door closes suddenly. Decks can be slippery with rain, snow or oil, and you can easily trip on raised door sills, stanchions and other shipboard tackle.

Personal gear like cameras or video equipment should be securely stowed in the cabin. The best place to put such valuables is either on the floor or closet-bottom, especially before you retire for the night, since the first you may be aware of a storm is when you hear the sound of your Leica shattering as it flies off the desk.

Most Antarctic tourist ships generally maintain an 'open bridge,' welcoming passengers to the area from which the officers navigate and steer the ship. (During tricky navigation – and whenever the pilot is aboard or the ship is in port – the bridge will be closed.) Etiquette demands that no food or drink be brought to the bridge, especially alcohol, and going barefoot on the bridge is also not appreciated. Keep your voice down; excessive noise interferes with communication between the navigator and helmsman. Of course, it's always unwise to touch any radar or other equipment without being specifically invited to do so by an officer of the watch. One further warning: Sailors are a superstitious lot, and whistling anywhere on a ship is considered extremely bad luck. Tradition says it means that the person is calling up the wind and a storm will result. ■

chef has gone to a prestigious cooking school (or even, sometimes, to any cooking school at all).

At least once during the cruise, you will probably experience the de rigueur 'Antarctic barbecue,' in which grills are set up out on deck or even down on the fast ice and everyone bundles up for hamburgers, hot dogs and other such fare. It's a bit clichéd but fun nevertheless and a change from the dining room.

If you have your own favorite 'national' foods – peanut butter, Vegemite, Marmite, Promite, orange marmalade, miso soup – you might want to bring them with you for a welcome bit of home.

DRINKS

Drinks are widely available in Antarctica, and it would be fair to say that alcohol is available almost everywhere on the continent that you find humans, with the possible exception of a remote field camp or two (though even many field camps have some 'medicinal' hooch around somewhere). Champagne is a popular tourist drink, especially when it is the center of such Antarctic cruise set pieces as Champagne On The Ross Ice Shelf, Champagne On The Sea Ice, etc. You should also have little trouble finding some glacier ice for your whiskey; many Antarcticans enjoy sipping their Scotch on *very* old rocks!

One of the few 'native' Antarctic drinks is a concoction called the Antarctic Old Fashion, which was apparently invented by the crew at the US Little America V research base from 1956 to 1958, and perfected at Camp Michigan on the Ross Ice Shelf. Here's the recipe, as described by James 'Gentleman Jim' Zumberge in the Antarctican Society newsletter (reprinted by permission):

> This is a long way around to telling the recipe (formula is a better word) for an Antarctic Old Fashion. It is impossible to make a simple Antarctic Old Fashion. All the research at Little America V was based on a batch quantity. Here are the ingredients: one fifth of Old Methusala (100 proof Navy 'bourbon') and seven packages of multi-flavored Life Savers. Pour the Old Methusala into another container and fill the empty bottle half full with freshly melted snow. Then force the Life Savers, one by one, into the mouth of the Methusala bottle and shake until all are dissolved. (Here it should be noted that painstaking research on the formula by the originators revealed that the final product was vastly improved if only two of the red Life Savers were used. All of our Camp Michigan Antarctic Old Fashions were made accordingly.) The final step in the process is to pour the Old Methusala, stir well, and serve over Antarctic glacier ice. No fruit or other garbage is needed since those flavors are all embodied in the mixture.

Zumberge also recalled the utility of 60 ml bottles of Navy brandy in coping with the cold: 'Our usual practice [was to drink] half before getting into our sleeping bags and the other half the next morning when rising. Because we slept in unheated tents, an ounce of brandy gave one the feeling of warmth before crawling into a cold sack, and in the morning it gave you the courage to get out.'

THINGS TO BUY

Antarctic souvenirs, once relatively rare, now run the full range: cheesy sweatshirts, baseball caps, coffee mugs, refrigerator magnets, cheap ceramic 'sculptures' and postcards all the way up to high-quality coffee-table books of photographs (see Books, above) and maps (see Maps, above). Prices vary widely, but generally you should expect to pay a premium for these souvenirs. Remember that the items for sale at Antarctic bases have had to come a long way to reach the store shelf. The revenues from the station's sales often go toward recreation for base members – or, more rarely, to support the scientific program itself. The items in shipboard shops, meanwhile, are usually sold via 'chit,' so they sometimes don't even display a price tag, on the principle that you'll just sign your credit-card slip at the end of the voyage. Often the shipboard shop is run by a separate company from the cruise itself, and their overhead can be quite high.

Among the many handsome posters of Antarctica, which are too numerous to list here, a few stand out both for beauty and educational value: the 'Antarctic Habitat' poster produced by the Antarctica Project (see Useful Organizations). This large (64 by 102 cm) and attractively illustrated poster shows the major Antarctic and subantarctic breeding sites for penguins, whales, seals and seabirds, accompanied by descriptive text. Two handsome posters featuring the work of photographer Jonathon Chester, 'Penguins of Antarctica' and 'Penguins of the World,' are each 58 by 89 cm and cost US$9.95 a piece, or US$15 the pair. To order, contact Celestial Arts, PO Box 7123, Berkeley, CA 94707 USA (☎ 1-510-559-1600; in US only: 1-800-841-2665; fax 1-510-559-1629).

The most unusual of the various clothing items with an Antarctic theme are the splendid, brightly colored tights featuring royal penguins, sold at the International Antarctic Center. The best T-shirt slogan I've seen is one that says simply, 'Ski South Pole: 2 miles of base, ½ inch of powder.' It is not widely available.

A unique gift for any Antarcticophile (even yourself!) would be a limited-edition photographic print made from the original glass plates painstakingly exposed by Australian photographer Frank Hurley during Ernest Shackleton's British Trans-Antarctic Expedition of 1914-17. Hurley took some 500 photographs, and after *Endurance* was trapped in the pack ice and crushed, he dove into the flooded and slowly sinking ship to retrieve them. When Shackleton asked him to winnow the heavy glass negatives down to a manageable number, Shackleton smashed all but 120 of them so that he would never regret having left them behind. Thirty five of the surviving negatives, which are now in the possession of Britain's Royal Geographical Society, were each used to make 400 prints, including shots of *Endurance* caught in the ice. Each image measures 30 by 40 cm, on paper measuring 40 by 50 cm. Prices range from US$220 to US$305 each (within the European Union, add 17.5% VAT) and shipping charges are extra. Contact: Atlas Limited Editions, 2 Dunstable Mews, London W1N 1RQ UK (☎ 44-171-486-4195; fax 44-171-487-5036).

Philatelic items including first-day-of-issue souvenir covers of Antarctic stamps – and often, the stamps themselves – are popular items sold at Antarctic stations. They are suitably embossed or stamped with the station's name and, perhaps, the date of your visit. These are usually beautifully illustrated miniature artworks, and have the advantage of being highly portable. Be prepared to pay, however: One popular station at King George Island was recently charging US$20 for a single envelope covered with postmarked Antarctic stamps from six countries.

Antarctic calendars are perennially popular. Appropriately for a continent of such sweeping splendor, they come in several sizes. The smallest (30 by 21 cm) is the United States Antarctic Program's offering. The photo reproduction quality is quite poor, but it lists bits of Antarctic historical trivia on many dates each month. The January page is inscribed 'With the Compliments of the Season,' but the calendar sells for about US$8 at McMurdo. Slightly larger (23 by 33 cm) is the beautiful calendar produced by Colin and Betty Monteath's Hedgehog House New Zealand (398 Barrington St, PO Box 33-152, Christchurch, New Zealand; ☎ /fax 64-3-332-8970). This beauty, which features unusual photographs of icebergs, wildlife and scenery, costs NZ$15; overseas economy post orders are NZ$17. The biggest of them all is the handsome calendar produced by Verlag Dr Rudolf Georgi – Woldemar Klein (Postfach 407, 52005 Aachen, Germany; ☎ 49-241-477-9121; fax 49-241-477-9160). This calendar's massive size (49 by 45 cm) shows off its stunning images quite well. For penguin lovers, there's the Bruno P Zehnder's Penguin Calendar, a collection of penguin pics taken by the Swiss photographer, who is so obsessed by his subject that he had his middle name changed to 'Penguin.' The calendar is available directly from Zehnder, whose address is Grand Central Station Box 4570, New York, NY 10163-4570 USA.

Getting There & Away

Choosing your trip is a very individual matter, but there are several general things you should know. First, see the Planning section in the Facts for the Visitor chapter, along with the section on 'Questions to Ask Your Tour Operator.' Second, use the information below as a guide *only*. Obviously, particulars – especially prices – change, so be sure to call several tour operators for their free brochures. New ones are usually printed up by February or March each year, although it may be later. Read through the brochures carefully, and compare the options. Don't be afraid to ask the tour operator as many questions as you can think of. As one tour brochure puts it, you are making an 'investment' in your Antarctic cruise – although with some of the prices charged, it's more likely that you might have had to *liquidate* a few investments!

SEA

Cruises

One of the most important factors in the large increase in Antarctic tourist numbers during the late 1980s and early '90s was the collapse of the Soviet Union. Economic hard times increased the Soviet scientific academies' hunger for hard currency, enabling Western companies to lease many ice-strengthened or even ice-breaking research ships for favorable rates. This helps to explain why so many of the tour vessels visiting the Antarctic today are Russian-flagged ships. Note that the same ship may have different passenger capacities for different cruises, based on the varying staff accommodation requirements on each cruise.

The following companies offer cruises to the Antarctic. Those marked with an asterisk (*) are members of IAATO, the International Association of Antarctica Tour Operators (see Useful Organizations in the Facts for the Visitor chapter).

Abercrombie & Kent* A&K operates *Explorer*, the ice-strengthened vessel commissioned by Antarctic tourism pioneer Lars-Eric Lindblad and originally known as *Lindblad Explorer*. The 100-passenger ship has sailed to Antarctica for each of the past 26 years, and was refurbished in 1992, with twin cabins all offering outside views, two lower berths, and private shower and toilet facilities.

A&K offers voyages to Antarctica, one of which goes to the 'Lost Islands of the South Atlantic,' including the rarely visited Tristan da Cunha and Gough Island. Two 14-day cruises (10 nights aboard ship) sail from Ushuaia to the Antarctic Peninsula; prices begin at US$5385 for a single berth in a double cabin. A 16-day trip (12 nights aboard) also visits the Peninsula from Ushuaia, with single berths in double cabins beginning at US$6385. A 14-day trip (10 nights aboard ship) to the Peninsula and the Falkland Islands from Stanley to Ushuaia begins at US$5385 for a single berth in a double cabin, while two 15-day voyages (11 nights aboard) to the same areas costs US$5885 for a similar berth, and a 17-day voyage (13 nights aboard) is US$6885 for a similar berth. Two 19-day (15 nights aboard) voyages visit Antarctica, the Falklands and South Georgia, with prices beginning at US$8015 for a single berth in a double cabin. The 35-day 'Lost Islands' cruise departs from the Canary Islands, visiting the Cape Verde Islands, Ascension Island, St Helena, Tristan da Cunha, Nightingale Island and Gough Island, with disembarkation in Stanley. The price is a relative bargain, with single berths in double cabins beginning at US$3990.

In conjunction with Quark Expeditions, A&K also offers passage on the first tourist circumnavigation of Antarctica, aboard *Kapitan Khlebnikov*. Abercrombie & Kent's address is: 1520 Kensington Rd,

Oak Brook, IL 60521-2141 USA (☎ 1-708-954-2944; in North America 1-800-323-7308; fax 1-708-954-3324).

Adventure Associates This company offers trips aboard the 164-passenger *Bremen* to Macquarie Island, the Balleny Islands, Cape Adare, the Ross Sea, Campbell Island and the Auckland Islands. The 25-day cruises (23 nights aboard) depart from and return to Hobart. Prices begin at US$8890 for a single berth in a double cabin, and a limited number of triple-share cabins for three people booking and traveling together is available, in which case the third person pays US$4445.

Adventure Associates also offers a 31-day voyage to Iles Kerguelen, Heard Island and rarely-visited East Antarctica, on the icebreaker *Kapitan Khlebnikov.*

Adventure Associates also arranges fly/cruise trips from Australia to South America and on to Antarctica aboard other tour operators' ships. Adventure Associates' address is: 197 Oxford St (PO Box 612), Bondi Junction, NSW 2022 Australia (☎ 61-2-389-7466; in Australia 1-800-222-141; fax 61-2-369-1853).

GMMS Polar Journeys* Having expanded from its original role arranging mountain-climbing expeditions, GMMS now offers the chance to camp ashore overnight in Antarctica, the only company to offer this opportunity. Previously this option had only been available to those who visited Antarctica via aircraft (see Air, below).

Some of the GMMS voyages are aboard the 38-passenger *Professor Molchanov*. The 12-day (11 nights) 'Climbers and Photographers' trip sails roundtrip from Ushuaia, with prices beginning at US$4250 per person in a double cabin with communal bathroom facilities. Two nights' camping is planned in two different locations. People wishing to camp ashore must bring sleeping bags and foam mats. Climbers must supply their own boots, crampons, ice axe and harness. Three 11-day voyages, sailing from Ushuaia to the Antarctic Peninsula, will include a one-night camping option. Prices begin at US$3800 for a single berth in a double cabin with communal bathroom.

GMMS also plans one 19-day (18 nights aboard) voyage to the Falklands, South Georgia and the Antarctic Peninsula in the 80-passenger *Akademik Ioffe*. Prices for the cruise roundtrip from Ushuaia begin at US$5490 for a single berth in a double cabin with communal bathroom facilities.

GMMS has also started to plan Antarctic scuba diving trips. Divers must have 50 logged dives and must bring their own gear. GMMS' address is: 441 Kent St, Sydney, NSW, 2000 Australia (☎ 61-2-264-3366; fax 61-2-261-1974).

Hanseatic Tours GmbH* Hanseatic operates two ice-reinforced (rated 1A1) vessels, the 180-passenger *Hanseatic* built in 1991 and the 164-passenger *Bremen* (formerly *Frontier Spirit)* built in 1990. The luxurious accommodations include cabins and suites with two lower berths, closed-circuit television, marble bathrooms, hair dryers, in-cabin satellite telephones, refrigerators and 24-hour room service. Certain cabins and suites also feature their own private veranda; private butler service is available for deluxe suites and staterooms.

The 21-day (20 nights aboard) 'Christmas and New Year's in Antarctica Adventure' sails from Puerto Montt, Chile, and returns to Ushuaia. The voyage visits the Chilean fjords, the Falkland Islands, South Georgia (Christmas in Grytviken Church), the South Orkneys and Elephant Island, Paulet Island and the Antarctic Peninsula. Prices begin at US$7970 for a single berth in a double cabin and include airfare from Santiago and to Buenos Aires.

Three voyages of the 11-day (10 nights aboard) 'Antarctica Adventure' sail roundtrip from Ushuaia, visiting the Antarctic Peninsula. Prices begin at US$4605 for a single berth in a double cabin and include airfare from Buenos Aires and back.

Hanseatic Tours GmbH's address is: Nagelsweg 55, 20097 Hamburg, Germany

(☎ 49-40-23-91-12-53; fax 49-40-23-21-10). In the US, Hanseatic markets its cruises through Radisson Seven Seas Cruises, 600 Corporate Drive, Suite 410, Fort Lauderdale, FL 33334 (☎ 1-305-776-6123; in North America: 1-800-477-7500; fax 1-305-772-3763).

Marine Expeditions* This company operates six ships: *Akademik Sergey Vavilov* (80 passengers), *Livonia* (38 passengers), *Akademik Golitsin* (38 passengers), *Professor Multanovsky* (46) passengers, *Akademik Ioffe* (80 passengers) and *Alla Tarasova* (118 passengers). All cabins and suites have outside views. Marine offers more than 40 programs, all of which involve several nights' stay in South America, and all of which sail to the Antarctic from Ushuaia. Most of Marine's offerings are 14-day programs which include the Antarctic Peninsula and the South Shetlands and involve eight nights aboard the ship; prices begin at US$2890 for a single berth in a four-person ('quad') cabin, and US$4390 per person in a double. Marine also offers several other options, including eight sailings of the 'Extended Antarctica' program (16 days; 10 nights aboard); prices begin at US$3490 per person in a quad, US$5590 per person in a double. Four programs

Zodiacs

Without Zodiacs, Antarctic tourism would be much more difficult and much less pleasurable. Popularized by French oceanographer Jacques Cousteau, Zodiacs are small, inflatable boats powered by outboard engines. Their shallow draft makes them ideal for cruising among icebergs and icefloes and for landing in otherwise inaccessible areas. They are made of a synthetic, rubberlike material forming a pontoon in a roughly wishbone shape, with a wooden transom on the back holding the engine. The deck (floor) is made of sections of aluminum. Zodiacs are very safe and stable in the water and are designed to stay afloat even if one or more of their six separate air-filled compartments are punctured. Zodiacs come in a variety of different sizes, but on most trips you can expect to share your boat with about nine to 14 other passengers, a driver and possibly another cruise staff member.

Smoking anywhere near Zodiacs is prohibited – and dangerous – since the fuel tanks are exposed. Safety vests must be worn during Zodiac trips, and wet weather jackets and pants are also critical, because even in fine weather, the boat's flying spray will give a good shower. For this reason, personal items should be carried in a waterproof backpack (or in a waterproof bag inside the backpack); you can also tuck cameras, binoculars, or bags inside your foul-weather jacket or parka to keep them dry. And remember, there are no toilets ashore, so go before you leave the ship.

To ensure that no one gets left behind in Antarctica, tours maintain a system of keeping track of passengers' whereabouts. On some ships, a staff member checks your name off of a list when you leave the ship, and again when you leave the shore. On others, you are responsible for turning over a colored tag on a large notice board inside the ship, indicating your departure from and return to the ship.

Entering and exiting Zodiacs are probably the most hazardous aspects of a visit to Antarctica for the tourist – but with a little care there is no need for anyone to get hurt. Passengers descend the ship's gangway to the Zodiac, which is held to the landing at the bottom of the gangway by a crew member and/or several lines. Since the Zodiac may be rising and falling with the swell, it is important to have both hands free. If you have a camera, bag, etc, the Zodiac crew will ask you to hand it to them. They will then take hold of your wrist (you should likewise seize theirs) in a hold known as the 'sailor's grip.'

include 'Antarctica and the Falklands' (19 days; 13 nights aboard); prices begin at US$4090 per person in a quad, and US$5590 in a double. The 24-day (18 nights aboard) program including 'Antarctica, the Falklands and South Georgia' costs US$5590 per person in a double. Unique to Marine, airfare from Los Angeles, Miami, Montreal, New York or Toronto is included in the price of all programs. Marine also charters one of its ships, *Akademik Ioffe*, to Elderhostel (the education vacations for travellers over 55) and another, *Livonia*, to Mountain Travel-Sobek (see below). Marine Expeditions' address is: 13 Hazelton Ave, Toronto, Ontario M5R 2E1 Canada (☎ 1-416-964-9069; in North America 1-800-263-9147; fax 1-416-964-2366).

Mountain Travel-Sobek* This company offers cruises of various lengths, all on the 38-passenger *Livonia*, and all departing from and returning to Ushuaia. With its small passenger complement, Mountain Travel-Sobek rightfully prides itself on having the highest passenger-to-staff ratio in the business. The 13-day 'Explore Antarctica' program takes in the Peninsula, with eight nights aboard ship; prices begin at US$3995 per person for a double cabin. The 19-day 'Kingdom of the Penguin'

This is much safer than a mere 'handshake' grip, since if one party accidentally lets go, the other still has a firm hold. Move slowly: step onto the pontoon of the Zodiac and then down onto the deck or floor, before moving to your seat, a spot along the pontoon. Sit facing the inside of the boat, and hold onto the ropes tied to the pontoon behind you, since the ride can be quite bumpy.

Only one passenger at a time should stand in a Zodiac, and you should never stand while the boat is moving. Ask the driver before you do, and s/he will slow the Zodiac down for you.

Exiting is equally simple. Most landings are made bow-first, and tour staff will be on hand to help you exit. Passengers sitting in the bow should swing their legs towards the *stern* of the Zodiac (naturally taking care not to kick their neighbor), then over the side and down onto the beach. Swinging your legs to the front of the Zodiac will be much more difficult since the pontoon is higher in the bow, and you may well fall back into the Zodiac, making a great photo – for someone else. If there is a large swell, landings may be made stern first. In this case, passengers in the stern disembark first. Don't try to exit over the transom, since a surging wave could knock you over or lift and drop the heavy engine or entire Zodiac onto you.

Zodiac landings are either 'wet,' meaning you have to step into a bit of water before getting to the dry beach, or 'dry,' in which case you can step directly onto a rock, jetty, dock or other piece of dry land. No matter what anyone may tell you, *all* landings in Antarctica are 'wet.' ■

visits South Georgia, the South Orkneys, the South Shetlands and the Peninsula, with 15 nights aboard; prices begin at US$6395 per person for a double. The 16-day (11 nights aboard) 'Quest for the Circle' visits the South Shetlands and the Peninsula and aims to push south of the Antarctic Circle; prices begin at US$5495 per person for a double. The 19-day (14 nights aboard) 'Footsteps of the Explorers' itinerary visits largely the same places as 'Kingdom of the Penguin,' but puts an emphasis on the historical aspects of the region; prices begin at US$5995 for a double. Mountain Travel-Sobek, one of the seven founding members of IAATO, is located at 6420 Fairmount Ave, El Cerrito, CA 94530 USA (☎ 1-510-527-8100; in North America: 1-800-227-2384; fax 1-510-525-7710; email: info@mtsobek.com; website: http://www.mtsobek.com).

Orient Lines Orient operates the 800-passenger luxury liner *Marco Polo*, although in order to comply with IAATO bylaws, it 'only' takes 400 passengers on its Antarctic cruises. Alone among the vessels regularly visiting the Far South, *Marco Polo* has a casino, piano bar and nightly entertainment, including cabaret shows; cabin amenities include televisions, hair dryers, international direct-dial telephones and, in some cases, personal refrigerators. The 15-day 'Expedition Antarctica' (13 nights aboard) visits the Antarctic Peninsula and the Falkland Islands. Ten-day 'Antarctic Peninsula' programs include eight nights aboard. The badly misnamed 'Grand Antarctic Circumnavigation' (25 days; 23 nights aboard) visits only the Peninsula and the Ross Sea. Beginning prices for a single berth in a double cabin for the cruises are: 'Expedition,' US$5025; 'Peninsula,' US$3720; and 'Grand Antarctic,' US$7298; bookings made at least 120 days before sailing are discounted 5%. Orient Lines' address is: 1510 SE 17 St, Ft Lauderdale, FL 33316 USA (☎ 1-954-527-6660; in North America: 1-800-333-7300; fax 1-954-527-6657).

Quark Expeditions* Using some of the world's most powerful icebreakers (Russian-flagged), Quark has made several pioneering tourist cruises, including the first voyage to the emperor penguin rookeries of the Weddell Sea and the first attempted circumnavigation of Greenland.

The company plans to operate the first attempted circumnavigation of Antarctica by a tourist vessel. The Russian icebreaker *Kapitan Khlebnikov*, with two helicopters aboard, is set to sail from Stanley on a 19,300-km, 66-day journey around the continent. The itinerary is daunting: Elephant Island in the South Shetlands, the Riiser-Larsen Ice Shelf in the Weddell Sea, Japan's Syowa station, Russia's Molodezhnaya station, Proclamation Island, the Auster emperor penguin rookery, Australia's Mawson station, the Kloa emperor rookery, the Flutter emperor rookery, the Amery Ice Shelf, the Amanda Bay emperor rookery, the Larsemann Hills, the Vestfold Hills, the Windmill Islands, the West and Shackleton ice shelves, the Dalton and Dibble Iceberg Tongues, Commonwealth Bay, Cape Adare, the Dry Valleys, McMurdo Sound, the Ross Ice Shelf, Peter I Øy, Petermann Island, the Lemaire Channel, Paradise Bay, Deception Island and back to Elephant Island. Don't be fooled by all those names, however. Antarctic weather, as all the brochures tell you, is notoriously unreliable, and some landings can't be made. Also, 66 days is a long time at sea (precisely 1584 hours, in fact), even with a crack staff of naturalists and lecturers to help fill the time. Prices begin at US$29,900 per person for a shared triple room and reach all the way to US$55,000 per person for a corner suite. Single occupancy rates are 1.7 times the share price, making a single corner suite worth a mind-boggling US$93,500.

Quark also offers a 31-day (29 nights aboard ship) voyage in *Kapitan Khlebnikov* from the 'Antarctic Peninsula to the Ross Sea,' with prices beginning at US$12,900 for a single berth in a triple cabin. Two 19-day voyages aboard *Akademik Ioffe* will visit the Peninsula, South Georgia and the Falklands, with prices beginning at US$4990 for a single berth in a double cabin with a communal bathroom. The 164-passenger *Bremen* visits the Ross Sea, Macquarie Island and New Zealand's subantarctic islands on a 25-day program (23 nights aboard ship) roundtrip from Hobart. Prices begin at US$8890 for a single berth in a double cabin.

Quark also offers six different 10- and 12-day voyages to the Antarctic Peninsula aboard four different vessels: the 36-passenger *Professor Khromov*, the 36-passenger *Professor Molchanov*, the 80-passenger *Akademik Ioffe* and the 118-passenger *Alla Tarasova*. Prices begin at US$3495 for a 10-day voyage aboard *Professor Khromov* or *Professor Molchanov* for a single berth in a twin cabin with a communal bathroom, at US$3390 for a 12-day voyage aboard *Akademik Ioffe* for a single berth in a twin cabin with a communal bathroom, and at US$3350 for a 12-day voyage aboard *Alla Tarasova* for a single berth in a shared triple cabin with a bathroom.

Another voyage Quark offers is a 24-day voyage to the rarely visited subantarctic island of Bouvetøya, as well as to the Falklands, South Georgia and the South Sandwich Islands, departing from Ushuaia and disembarking in Port Elizabeth. Prices were unavailable at presstime. It also plans a 30-day 'Far Side of Antarctica' trip to East Antarctica, Heard Island and Kerguelen Island, sailing from Fremantle, Australia aboard *Kapitan Khlebnikov* and disembarking in Hobart; prices begin at US$13,600 for a single berth in a triple cabin with private bathroom. Costs for a 26-day voyage roundtrip from Hobart to the Ross Sea start at US$10,490 for a single berth in a triple cabin with private bathroom.

Quark Expeditions' address is: 980 Post Rd, Darien, CT 06820 USA (☎ 1-203-656-0499; in North America: 1-800-356-5699; fax 1-203-655-6623; email: 76255.3266@compuserve.com).

Society Expeditions* This company operates the 138-passenger *World Discoverer*, which has made nearly 300 Antarctic voyages over 18 years. Society plans six

Helicopter Safety

Some ships that visit Antarctica carry helicopters, both for reconnoitering through the pack ice and, of course, for carrying passengers ashore and on sightseeing flights. This is a spectacular way to view Antarctica and to get to less-accessible places further inland such as the Dry Valleys.

The cruise staff will hold a briefing before your first helicopter flight to alert you to safety regulations. The rules are simple:

- Wear a lifejacket in case of a forced water landing.
- Listen to directions from staff regarding entry and exit from the helicopter landing area. Pilots are justifiably concerned about people accidentally wandering into the landing zone.
- Keep away from the rear of the helicopter, where the rapidly spinning (and deadly!) tail rotor can be hard to see. Always approach the helicopter from the front or side.
- Stay low when entering or exiting, because a sudden windshift could force the rotor down. For the same reason, never raise your hands or arms above your head.
- Fasten clothing, hair, jewelry and bags securely before entering the landing zone; the rotor's powerful downblast of air will blow away any loose items.
- Protect your eyes and cameras from the dust, sand and gravel blown by the rotor downblast. ■

different expeditions, including two unique trips that include Chile's South Pacific coastline, which is serrated by long fjords.

The 24-day (23 nights aboard ship) 'Antarctica and the Chilean Fjords' includes five days in the Antarctic Peninsula area and a stop at Elephant Island. The voyage embarks in Talcahuano, Chile, and disembarks in Ushuaia, with prices beginning at US$5330 for a single berth in a triple-share cabin and US$6950 for a berth in a double. Three voyages will be 15-day (14 nights aboard) programs roundtrip from Ushuaia to the Peninsula and Elephant Island, with prices beginning at US$3830 for triples and US$4990 for doubles.

The 20-day (19 nights aboard) voyage roundtrip from Stanley visits South Georgia, the South Orkneys, Antarctica and the Falklands, with prices beginning at US$5700 for triples and US$7440 for doubles. The 21-day (20 nights aboard) voyage to the Falklands, Antarctica and the Chilean Fjords departs from Stanley and returns to Puerto Montt, Chile, with prices beginning at US$5360 for triples and US$6990 for doubles.

Society Expeditions, one of the seven founding members of IAATO, is at 2001 Western Ave, Suite 300, Seattle, WA 98121 USA (☎ 1-206-728-9400; in North America: 1-800-548-8669; fax 1-206-728-2301).

Southern Heritage Expeditions* Southern Heritage offers scuba diving options on some of its trips. Southern Heritage offers six voyages on the 36-passenger, ice-reinforced *Akademik Shokalski*. 'Subantarctic Auckland Islands' is a seven-day (six nights aboard ship) roundtrip voyage from Bluff, New Zealand, with prices beginning at US$2499 per person in a double cabin. 'Subantarctic Islands Downunder' is a 16-day trip (14 nights aboard) from Bluff to the Snares Islands, Auckland Islands, Macquarie Island, Campbell Islands, Antipodes Islands, Bounty Islands and Chatham Islands, with disembarkation at Lyttelton (Christchurch); prices begin at US$5182 per person in a double. 'Wildgardens of the Subantarctic,' an 11-day trip (nine nights aboard) roundtrip from Bluff, visits Stewart Island, the Snares, the Aucklands and Campbell Island; prices start at US$3069 per person in a double. 'The World of Penguins' is a 26-day trip (24 nights aboard), sailing from Bluff to the Snares, the Aucklands, the Antipodes Islands, Commonwealth Bay in Antarctica and Macquarie Island, with disembarkation in Hobart; prices start at US$8687 per person in a double. 'South to Antarctica: The Ross Sea' is a 30-day (28 nights aboard) voyage from Hobart to Macquarie Island, the Balleny Islands, Cape Adare, Ross Island, Campbell Islands, Auckland Islands and Bluff, New Zealand. Prices start at US$9882 per person in a double room. 'In the Footsteps of Scott and Shackleton' is a 23-day roundtrip voyage from Bluff (21 nights aboard) visiting Campbell Island, the Balleny Islands, Cape Adare, Terra Nova Bay, Ross Island, Cape Hallett and the Auckland Islands. Prices begin at US$7989 per person, double accommodation.

Diving is planned for both the 'Subantarctic Auckland Islands' and the 'South to Antarctica' voyages. Diving on the Aucklands trip will cost an additional US$250, with approximately nine dives planned, including night dives and wreck dives. No decompression dives will be conducted, and all dives will be less than 39m. All divers must have a minimum of 100 logged dives and be certified as a PADI Rescue Diver or higher (equivalent qualifications accepted). Southern Heritage will provide air tanks (*Akademik Shokalski* has an air compressor on board); divers must bring their own gauges, regulator, octopus, wetsuit (for the hardy) or drysuit, mask, snorkel, fins, gloves, booties, dive knife, flashlights, cylume sticks and buoyancy-control device with whistle attached. A dive computer is highly recommended.

For the 'South to Antarctica' trip, the dive option will cost an extra US$450. Diving possibilities include under-ice diving at the Erebus Glacier Tongue in McMurdo Sound, as well as in open water and offshore of historic huts like Robert F Scott's at Cape Evans. All dives will be made from an open inflatable boat and only during perfectly calm conditions. Divers (two down at a time, each on a lifeline) will be assisted by a tender, dive master and boatman. Diving will be terminated if dangerous marine mammals (eg, killer whales) are active in the area. The same visitor rules apply as when ashore anywhere in Antarctica, meaning no artifacts or natural history specimens can be removed. Divers must be certified at least as a PADI Rescue Diver or equivalent and must have completed a diving medical examination in the past 12 months. Twin valve air cylinders, air fills, life lines, weight belts and weights will be supplied by Southern Heritage. Divers must bring their own full-length dry suit, gloves, two separate first- and second-stage regulators, cylinder contents gauge, depth gauge, watch, fins, mask, snorkel and knife. Because the sea temperature will be -2°C all equipment should be mechanical and drysuits should be completely checked out. Divers should have completed two dives using all of the above equipment within two months of the voyage.

Southern Heritage also plans a trip to the rarely visited islands of the South Indian Ocean. The 29-day trip sails from Fremantle, Australia, to Ile Amsterdam, Ile St Paul, Iles Kerguelen and Heard Island, returning to Hobart. Prices begin at about US$11,000 per person in a double cabin. Southern Heritage Expeditions' address is: PO Box 20-219, Bishopdale, Christchurch, New Zealand (☎ 64-03-314-4393; fax 64-03-359-3311; email: hertexp@ibm.net).

Travel Dynamics* For the past 25 years, this company has operated small ships on educational voyages to Antarctica for non-profit and alumni organizations; the marketing arm of Travel Dynamics is known as Classical Cruises. It remains a member of IAATO, of which it is one of the seven founding members. Travel Dynamics' address is: 132 East 70th St, New York, NY 10021 USA (☎ 1-212-517-7555; in North America 1-800-257-5767; fax 1-212-517-0077).

WildWings* This company has operated bird and wildlife tours to Antarctica since 1991 and acts as an agent for other Antarctic tour operators. Voyages aboard the 400-passenger *Marco Polo* are led by bird expert Dick Filby and cetacean authority Mark Carwardine. An 18-day program visits the Antarctic Peninsula and the Falklands; prices begin at £3465 for a single berth in an inside twin cabin and from £4015 for a single berth in an outside twin cabin. A 27-day program visits the Antarctic Peninsula, the Bellingshausen and Amundsen seas and McMurdo station and the Ross Sea (ice conditions permitting); prices begin at £4935 for a single berth in an inside twin cabin and from £5865 for a single berth in an outside twin cabin. WildWings' address is: International House, Bank Road, Bristol, Avon BS15 2LX, UK (☎ 44-117-984-8040; fax 44-117-967-4444).

Zegrahm Expeditions* Zegrahm offers cruises on four different vessels. The 28-day 'Ultimate Antarctica' (24 nights aboard) on the 120-passenger *Kapitan Khlebnikov* departs from Ushuaia, visiting Elephant Island, the South Orkneys, the Norwegian-claimed sector, the Riiser-Larsen, Brunt and Filchner ice shelves, the South Sandwich Islands and South Georgia, with disembarkation in Stanley; prices begin at US$11,990 for a single berth in a double cabin. All of *Kapitan Khlebnikov*'s cabins have private toilet and shower facilities. The 15-day 'Antarctica' program (11 nights aboard) on the 92-passenger *Alla Tarasova* visits the Peninsula and the South Shetlands on a roundtrip voyage from Ushuaia; prices begin at US$4350 for a single berth in a double cabin. The 20-day 'Circumnavigation of South Georgia and the Falkland Islands' (16 nights aboard) on the 98-passenger *Explorer* sails on a roundtrip

Southern Ocean Yachting

Yachts have visited the Antarctic since 1966, when Bill Tilman, aboard *Mischief*, called in at Deception Island. Since then, over 150 yacht voyages have been made south to The Ice, in vessels ranging from luxurious 30-m motor-sailors with professional crews and the latest in electronic wizardry, to more modest 10-m cruising yachts equally well prepared and crewed by husband and wife teams. These yachts and their crews and passengers go to Antarctica primarily to experience the beauty of the White Continent. Some are on expeditionary, sporting or scientific missions, while others carry small numbers of tourists. All share a common awe for Antarctica.

In recent years, an average of around 15 yachts visit the Antarctic Peninsula each summer, a remarkably small number, given the popularity of cruising. The widespread use of radar, Global Positioning System navigation devices, radio, satellite communications and weather fax – together with the availability of strong, reliable hull materials and improved navigation charts – may tempt some sailors to rely less on experience and skill and increasingly on modern technology. It is far easier to sail to the Antarctic today than it was 30 years ago – but the rules remain the same.

Whatever the size of the yacht and its budget and goals, there are a few essential points to remember when preparing for a cruise to the Antarctic. The first is autonomy: You must make sure to carry enough of everything – food, fuel, clothing and spare parts – to be completely self-sufficient for the duration of your cruise. A reliable engine, a cabin heater, a hull strong enough to withstand collision with ice and rocks and a generously dimensioned anchor and chain – together with an experienced crew – will increase the odds for a trouble-free cruise. It is also very important to be certain that you are physically and mentally capable of coping with several weeks of isolation under often strenuous conditions.

Familiarize yourself and your crew with the latest Antarctic Treaty regulations for visitors. This applies especially to the international guidelines designed to protect the Antarctic wildlife and its environment. (See the sidebar about the Antarctic Treaty in the Facts about Antarctica chapter.)

When planning your itinerary, bear in mind that there are a number of protected areas which may not be entered, and that most stations maintain long-term scientific research programs on adjacent islands or ice-free areas, to which access is restricted. Visits to stations require advance notice so that they can be scheduled around the station's work program and resupplying. If simply anchoring in the vicinity of a station, courtesy requires that you contact the station manager by VHF radio to inform him or her of your intentions while in the area.

Typically, a voyage to Antarctica commences in Tierra del Fuego, at the southern tip of South America. This is the shortest ocean crossing south, taking around four days, depending on the weather and the size of the yacht. Provisions and fuel are loaded in Ushuaia – which, thanks to its international airport, has become the center of a small but thriving yacht charter industry. Formal clearance for Antarctica is carried out at Puerto Williams, 50 km east of Ushuaia along the Beagle Channel, by the Chilean Navy, who follow the movements of yachts with administrative zeal and friendly interest.

Actual departure time may depend on the succession of low-pressure systems coming in from the west and funneling through Drake Passage. A deep front and its usual attendant gale-force winds can transform the crossing from an exhilarating three-day cruise into six days of headwinds, huge seas and much discomfort. Yachts with weather fax plan their departure accordingly, seeking shelter among the islands near Cape Horn while waiting for fronts to pass through.

Once at sea, life on board quickly settles into a routine of watch-keeping, with crew members sharing the cold hours on deck, keeping a constant watch for fishing boats, freighters and, of course, icebergs. Although most yachts are equipped with self-steering gear, which obviates the need for a helmsman, crew and passengers alike benefit from spending time outside each day. Astern, the wake spins out a voyager's tale to the ocean and its seabirds as the yacht heads south at six or seven knots, covering 300 km or more every 24 hours.

During a four-week voyage to the Antarctic, a yacht will probably experience several extremes of cruising, and there may well be moments when it is essential that the yacht, her crew and equipment are all fully functioning and unhesitatingly ready to improvise from one crisis to the next. Cruising the Southern Ocean is as much a feat of mental strength as it is of practical and physical preparation.

There is nothing quite like an ocean passage in the southern latitudes: It can be cold, uncomfortable and frightening. Yet the miseries of yesterday are quickly forgotten after a few hours of fair winds, sailing along at eight knots in a white-crested sea, with a cape petrel keeping pace at the stern rail.

On a clear day the white peaks of Brabant and Anvers islands are visible more than 80 km away. Tucked between them are the Melchior Islands, a popular landfall for yachts, with seaward approaches clear of dangers. There is also an excellent anchorage within the island group, which is only a few hours sail from one of the most beautiful – and most visited – areas of the Antarctic: the Gerlache Strait, with its 100 km of sheltered waterways, its bays, coves, islands and glaciers, dominated by the mainland plateau and mountain peaks, which rise 1800m above the sea. Although much of the coastline is ice, snow and sheer cliffs, there are a number of low, rocky headlands and islands that provide ideal nesting sites for a variety of seabirds, including great numbers of penguins.

Exploring this coastline by boat is a constant challenge, but it has its daily rewards. Working with incomplete – and in some cases, inaccurate – marine charts means that constant vigilance is required when close inshore, as the danger of uncharted rocks is very real.

There are a handful of all-weather anchorages – among them, Dorian Cove at Port Lockroy, the Argentine Islands, and Pléneau Island, while Cuverville, Enterprise, Booth Island and Paradise Harbor offer temporary shelter in certain conditions. Thus, a day's cruising can be planned around reaching safe anchorage by nightfall – and hopefully before the worst of a gale arrives.

Sea ice is rarely a problem in this area during the height of austral summer. There is little risk of becoming beset if extensive fields of sea ice are avoided and a careful eye is kept on the weather. A healthy respect for bergs and pack ice is essential, however, particularly in areas where current and wind could jeopardize a yacht's attempts to reach the safety of open water.

But there will be moments when the sea and the sky could not be more tranquil, when the high plateaux of the Antarctic Peninsula reflect in waters of perfect silence and utter stillness, peaks aglow in evening gold tinged with pink and lilac. From a nearby Adélie colony comes a distant clamor of hungry chicks and harassed parents, with the occasional raucous call of a passing skua. To glimpse the Antarctic on such a day is incomparable. ■

–Sally Poncet, co-author of *Southern Ocean Cruising*

voyage from Stanley to South Georgia, with landings planned both at South Georgia and on many of the Falklands' western islands. Prices start at US$5990 for a single berth in a shared cabin. The 21-day 'Antarctica, South Georgia and the Falkland Islands' (17 nights aboard) trip on the 130-passenger *World Discoverer* visits the named places as well as the South Shetlands and the South Orkneys; prices begin at US$8000 for a single berth in a shared cabin. In conjunction with Quark Expeditions, Zegrahm also offers passage on the first tourist circumnavigation of Antarctica, aboard *Kapitan Khlebnikov*.

A 37-day 'Antarctica: The Far Side' (33 nights aboard) on *Kapitan Khlebnikov*, sails from Port Elizabeth, South Africa, to Fremantle, Australia, with stops at the seldom-visited subantarctic islands of Marion, Crozet, Kerguelen and Heard. Prices begin at US$18,850 for a single berth in a double cabin. The 'Antarctica, South Georgia and the Falkland Islands' program costs approximately US$8390 to US$11,990.

'Antarctica 2000' will sail on December 17, 1999, and return January 4, 2000. Rates had not been announced at presstime.

Zegrahm is one of the seven founding members of IAATO and is located at 1414 Dexter Ave, Suite 327, Seattle, WA 98109 USA (☎ 206-285-4000; in North America: 1-800-628-8747; fax 206-285-5037; email: zegrahm@accessone.com).

Yacht Voyages

A tiny but growing handful of visitors reach the Antarctic aboard private vessels. All are sailboats (though obviously they are equipped with auxiliary engines), and some have even wintered in sheltered anchorages like Yankee Harbor at Greenwich Island or near Palmer Station on the Antarctic Peninsula. In three decades of Antarctic cruising, there have been about 150 yacht voyages to The Ice. For some reason, this type of travel particularly appeals to French people, and they have formed the majority of yacht visitors to Antarctica.

Although the national Antarctic programs cannot regulate such yacht tourism, since Antarctica is open to everyone, research stations are no longer instantly hospitable when a yacht turns up on their doorstep. Where once they welcomed the rare visitors from the outside, these days traffic is so heavy at most stations that advance notice of several weeks or even months is normally required for a station tour, though there are some exceptions, mainly among the smaller countries operating in Antarctica.

Sailing a yacht to Antarctica is obviously not something one undertakes lightly. It would also be foolish to attempt the enterprise without taking one – or, preferably, both – of the following: *Sailing Directions (Planning Guide & Enroute) for Antarctica*, 2nd Edition, 1992, published by the US Defense Mapping Agency's Hydrographic/Topographic Center (DMA stock number SDPUB200), and *The Antarctic Pilot*, 4th Edition (1974), along with supplement No 11-1993, published in 1993, both by Britain's Hydrographer of the Navy. Anyone considering a yacht voyage to Antarctica would also do well to read Sally and Jérôme Poncet's excellent 60-page guide, *Southern Ocean Cruising*. (See the sidebar Southern Ocean Yachting, by Sally Poncet.)

For those who do not own a yacht, or prefer to have someone else do the skippering, there are a handful of yachts that take fare-paying passengers. Passengers aboard these yachts are generally expected to lend a hand with the sailing and watch-keeping. Seven such yachts are managed by Eric Leyes of Croisieres Australes, L'Abbaye 35770 Vern S/Seiche, France (☎ 33-99-62-76-63; fax 33-99-00-48-46). The 28-day (29 nights aboard) voyages sail from and return to Ushuaia and cost 37,000 French francs per person. The 42-day (43 nights on board) trip to South Georgia sails from and returns to either Ushuaia or Stanley and costs 47,000FF per person.

Croisieres Australes' member yachts include the 16-m *Kotick I* (four to five participants), the 12-m *Kekilistrion* (three to four participants); the 12-m *Ksar* (four to five participants), the 18-m *Croix St Paul* (eight participants), the 21-m *Fernande* (10 participants), the 14-m *Le Boulard* (four to five participants), and the 20-m *Valhalla* (seven participants).

Another agency that handles a much smaller number of Antarctic voyaging yachts is Grand Nord Grand Large, 15 rue Cardinal Lemoine, Paris, 75005 France (☎ 33-1-40-46-05-14; fax 33-1-43-26-73-20).

Two other yachts also sail to the Antarctic regularly, though they primarily charter themselves out to private expeditions and commercial groups like film crews: *Pelagic*, owned by Skip Novak of Ocean Voyages Inc, 92 Satchell Lande, Hamble, S03 5HL UK (☎ 44-1703-454-120; fax 44-1703-456-405), and *Damien II*, owned by Sally and Jérôme Poncet, Beaver Island, c/o PO Stanley, Falkland Islands via UK (☎ 500-42316; fax 500-22659).

Resupply Vessels

'Hitching' a ride, for a fee, aboard a Chilean or Argentine military ship resupplying a scientific base was possible in the 1980s. Although the Argentine navy has largely stopped the practice since the *Bahía Paraíso* oil-spill disaster of 1989, it still may be possible to get a berth aboard a Chilean vessel, since passenger fares provide an attractive addition to revenue. This type of cruise to Antarctica would not offer the educational lecture and slide programs found on commercial cruises, however, and non-Spanish speakers would find themselves at a severe disadvantage.

AIR

Although three countries operate airstrips in Antarctica – the Argentines at Vicecomodoro Marambio station on Seymour Island, the British at Rothera station on Adelaide Island and the Chileans at Teniente Marsh station on King George Island – none of the airfields provide any facilities for private or commercial planes, neither landing rights, fuel or accommodation. All private flights to one of these fields require advance permission, which is very difficult, if not impossible, to secure. Antarctic aviation can also be extremely dangerous: More than 50 wrecked aircraft litter the Antarctic ice.

The first Antarctic tourist flight occurred on December 22, 1956, when a LAN Chile DC-6B flew from Chacabuco, Chile, over the South Shetlands and the Antarctic Peninsula with 66 passengers. Regular flights to the continent, however, did not begin until February 1977, when Air New Zealand and Australia's Qantas began regular schedules.

Those overflights came to an abrupt halt soon after all 257 people aboard Air New Zealand flight 901 died when their DC-10 slammed into 3795-m Mt Erebus on Ross Island on November 28, 1979. Peter Mahon's book *Verdict on Erebus* is a thorough examination of the disaster; Mahon was New Zealand's Royal Commissioner of Inquiry for the crash. Three more flights were made before the overflight programs were discontinued. During the two seasons that the airlines offered them, however, approximately 10,000 people saw the continent from the air.

Flightseeing

Qantas resumed Antarctic overflights in 1994, and the new program quickly proved just as popular as had the earlier overflights. For those who can't afford the cost of an Antarctic cruise – or who don't want to take the week or more it takes to visit The Ice – flightseeing is a good alternative. You travel in relative comfort (the plane never touches down in Antarctica) and you get a good glimpse of the continent's spectacular glaciers, mountains and icebergs.

For safety, no smoking is allowed during the flights, and no cargo is carried in the hold. The Boeing 747-400 aircraft do not descend below 3050m – or 610m above the highest terrain within 185 km, whichever is higher. While over Antarctica, the jet engines are operated at less than a third of full throttle, giving a slower airspeed as well as reducing noise and exhaust. All of Qantas' Antarctic pilots are Management Captains, with at least 25 years' flying experience.

Croydon Travel, of Melbourne, lobbied Qantas for several years to get it to resume the overflights, and it is acting as the primary booking agency for the flights. For flights from Melbourne, Sydney and possibly one from Perth no passport is required, since the roughly 12-hour flights are considered 'domestic' Australian travel. Lunch and dinner are served inflight. Just as on ship cruises to the Antarctic, there are onboard lecturers, as well as Antarctic-themed videos. Another interesting aspect of the flight is provided by a nose-mounted video camera, which shows the view beneath the plane, projected onto the movie screen. This is especially interesting during takeoff and landing. Once over Antarctica, the pilots fly 'figure eights' over points of interest so that both sides of the plane can get a good view. And the beauty of traveling 800 km/h is that if one part of Antarctica is clouded over, you simply fly on to a part of the continent that is clear.

There are five fare categories: 1st class,

Vinson Massif

Antarctica's highest mountain is Vinson Massif (4897m) in the Sentinel Range, discovered only in 1958 by US Navy aircraft. It is named for Congressman Carl G Vinson of Georgia, who influenced the US government to support Antarctic exploration during the period from 1935 to 1961. Thanks to the mountaineering hajj of the 'Seven Summits' (scaling the highest peak on each continent), Vinson is also Antarctica's most climbed mountain.

Four members of a private US expedition, led by Nicholas B Clinch, made the first ascent, on December 17, 1966. Over the next few days, the summits of Antarctica's second-, third- and fourth-highest peaks, neighboring Tyree (4845m), Shinn (4801m) and Gårdner (4686m), were also reached. You can read all about it in the June 1967 issue of *National Geographic* magazine (vol 131, no 6). Interestingly, this early expedition, sponsored by the American Alpine Club, received not only cooperation but outright vital help from the US government, being flown by the Navy through Christchurch and McMurdo. This friendly policy was soon reversed 180°, with the US and other governments doing all they could to discourage and even oppose private expeditions to Antarctica (see also the Private Expeditions chapter).

Adventure Network International has guided over 200 climbers to Vinson's summit since 1985. You must be in top physical shape to attempt the climb, since you will need to carry a load of 27 kg at high altitude. You also need several years' alpine experience on peaks above 4300 m. ANI must review your climbing résumé before it will accept your participation in one of its guided attempts on Vinson. An ANI brochure states: 'Technically, Vinson is not a difficult climb . . . However, climbers should be experienced and in good physical condition to cope with the stresses of altitude and low temperature.' Although it varies with fitness, experience and weather, the time required to reach the summit ranges from two to 14 days. One successful summiteer calls Vinson 'similar in difficulty, weather and altitude' to the West Buttress of Alaska's Mount McKinley. Neighboring Mt Tyree, only 52m lower, is regarded as the continent's most challenging peak, but dozens of other Antarctic mountains remain virgin. ■

A$2999; business, A$2499; economy premium (not over a wing), A$1499; economy standard (over a wing), A$1099; and economy center, A$799. All seats except economy center are required to rotate seating, which generally is accomplished without too much fuss – after all, the flights spend three to four hours over The Ice. No center seats are sold in the 1st class or business cabins. Although some passengers have reported that economy center (non-rotation) passengers seem to get a chance to see out the window as much as anyone else, it might be a false economy not to spend the extra A$300.

Croydon Travel's address is 34 Main St, Croydon, Victoria 3136 Australia (☎ 61-3-9725-8555; in Australia: 1-800-633-499; fax 61-3-9723-9560).

The Interior by Air

Adventure Network International, also known as Antarctic Airways, is the first and only private company offering flights to the Antarctic interior. ANI began operating in Antarctica during the 1985-86 season, with one De Havilland Twin Otter aircraft. Its fleet now includes two ski-equipped Twin Otters; one bright-orange, ski-equipped Cessna 185 dubbed the 'Polar Pumpkin;' and a Hercules C-130 (without skis, as only the US military is certified to fly ski-equipped LC-130s). ANI has carried more than 700 passengers on nearly 100 roundtrip flights to Antarctica (covering nearly 1.3 million km), and the company has supported every private expedition to the Antarctic interior since 1985 (including mountain climbing, skiing and man-hauling expeditions). ANI is also one of the seven founding members of IAATO.

With the Hercules, ANI flies passengers six hours south from Punta Arenas, Chile, to its camp at Patriot Hills, between the Ellsworth Mountains and the Ronne Ice Shelf. Discovered in 1986 by one of ANI's cofounders, Giles Kershaw, along with British polar researcher Charles Swithinbank, the Patriot Hills area offers a natural blue-ice runway, one of the few places in the continent's interior where wheeled aircraft can land. From Patriot Hills, ANI flies ski-equipped Twin Otters to the South Pole, Vinson Massif (see the sidebar), an emperor penguin colony at the Dawson-Lambton Glacier in the Weddell Sea, the mountains of Dronning Maud Land and just about anywhere else deep-pocketed customers would like to go.

Trips to Vinson Massif last an average of 12 to 14 days and costs US$25,750 from Punta Arenas. South Pole trips last approximately 10 days and costs US$21,000 from Punta Arenas. Ten to 12-day trips to the emperor rookery cost US$21,000, with several days' camping at the rookery, and a single two-week trip to both the emperor rookery and the South Pole costs US$39,000. Two climbing trips to the Transantarctic Mountains, each lasting about three weeks, cost US$28,500, while two Ellsworth Mountains Ski Safaris, which vary in length, begin at US$12,500. Three trips to the 'Heart of Antarctica' (US$10,750) vary in length, but emphasize opportunities to camp and to learn celestial navigation.

Passengers generally spend a few days at Patriot Hills to get acclimated to Antarctica's altitude and cold. Weather may delay takeoff on the six-hour, 1100-km flight to the Pole, but Patriot Hills is a reasonably comfortable place to wait out a blizzard. The only private semi-permanent camp in Antarctica, it offers accommodations for 50 guests in large insulated tents (bring your own polar-rated sleeping bag). Cooking and kitchen facilities (which turn out such delicate meals as smoked salmon, chocolate mousse and Welsh rarebit, accompanied by fresh fruit, vegetables and wine flown in from Chile) are in another tent, while staff sleep in several others. There's even a 'library tent.' Primitive hot-water showers are also available, though most guests prefer sponge-baths, and a fully trained physician is part of the camp staff. There is a good chance that you will be sharing the camp with world-class mountain climbers preparing to tackle a nearby summit. Among the more interesting recreational activities available at Patriot Hills are snow-mobiling, hiking or zipping along on skis over the smooth, flat ice while being towed by a wind-borne 'Skygrazer' kite!

Adventure Network is based at Canon House, 27 London End, Beaconsfield, Buckinghamshire HP92HN, UK (☎ 44-1494-671-808; fax 44-1494-671-725) or, from October until the end of January only, at 935 Arauco, Punta Arenas, Chile (☎ 56-61-247-735; fax 56-61-226-167).

Wildlife Guide

By Dr John Cooper

Dr John Cooper has undertaken ecological, physiological and taxonomic research on African, subantarctic and Antarctic seabirds over a 25-year period at the University of Cape Town. His interests include the conservation management of Southern Islands. He is Chair of the Scientific Committee on Antarctic Research Bird Biology Subcommittee and Vice-Chair of the Subantarctic Islands for the World Conservation Union Antarctic Advisory Committee. He is currently Marine Advisor to the South African Minister of Water Affairs and Tourism.

Humpback Whale

Humpbacks *(Megaptera novaeangliae)* may be recognized by their enormous flippers, which can reach a third of their total body length. They are normally black, but undersides of flippers and flukes have varying amounts of white and can be used as aids for individual recognition. Maximum lengths recorded are 17.5m for a male and 19m for a female.

COLIN MONTEATH (HEDGEHOG HOUSE)

Humpbacks and tourists

Humpback whales occur in all oceans. They migrate seasonally from their Southern Ocean summer feeding grounds towards the equator, where they breed during the southern winter, generally in shallow waters close to land. Humpbacks are highly vocal on their breeding grounds: Songs that can last up to 20 minutes are thought to be mainly produced by adult males to advertise their presence. Diet in the Southern Ocean consists mainly of Antarctic krill *(Euphausia superba)*: More than a ton a day may be taken.

Humpbacks were grossly over-exploited by whalers in the past. They are now fully protected (since 1963 in the Southern Hemisphere).

Southern Right Whale

Whalers named the slow-moving, inshore-visiting *Balaena glacialis* 'right' because it could be relatively easily rowed down and harpooned (and then it obligingly stayed afloat to yield its long baleen plates and much oil). Southern rights go up to 16m in length and can attain 74 metric tons. The whitish callosities on the jaws and forehead can be used to identify individuals throughout their life.

Southern right whales occur in the southern oceans between 20°S and 50°S, and have been recorded around the more northerly of the southern islands. The species is seasonally common (May to September) and easily seen from the shore in bays on the southern coast of South Africa, where calving and mating occur.

Southern right whales are lucky not to be extinct: They were over-exploited to 'commercial extinction' as early as the mid-19th century, although full protection came only in 1935. Numbers are now slowly recovering at a rate of 7% a year, based on South African long-term studies. Watching southern rights court within 100m of the shore is an experience not to be forgotten.

Sperm Whale

The sperm whale *(Physeter macrocephalus)* is an unmistakable species, of *Moby Dick* fame, with its enormous head and narrow tooth-filled jaws. At sea, the low 'bushy' forward-directed blow and small fleshy dorsal fin are important identifying features. Male sperm whales can reach 19m in length, and females attain 12m.

Sperm whales occur in all the world's oceans, but rarely in shallow seas. Most sperm whales south of 40°S are adult males. Schools (20 to 25 individuals) are made up of females and their young, and are joined by males during the breeding season in October to December. A four-meter long calf is born after a gestation period of 15 to 16 months. Diet is of mid- to deep-water squid, some of which reach 200 kg: veritable krakens of the deep, caught in absolute darkness at depths of nearly three km.

Sperm whales were much exploited in the past: for their oil, ambergris and teeth. Nowadays, the species is fully protected in the Southern Ocean and it can only be hoped its numbers will build up to pre-exploitation numbers.

Killer Whale

Killer whales *(Orcinus orca)* are the largest of the dolphin family. Also known as orcas, their black and white markings and tall dorsal fins (especially in the adult male) are distinctive. Males reach nine meters in length, females nearly eight meters. Large specimens can weigh nearly nine tons.

Orcas occur in all seas, but are more abundant in colder waters. They occur in schools or pods of up to 50 individuals. Pods have their own 'dialect' of discrete calls and are presumably made up of closely related animals. Maturity is reached from 12 years of age in females and 14 years in males. Orcas are predatory animals that feed on squid, fish, birds and marine mammals. King penguins at Marion Island have been seen to be swallowed whole by resident killer whales. Orcas will also tip up small ice floes to get at resting seals.

There are still many killer whales in the Southern Ocean, and they have not been caught commercially since 1979-80 when Soviet whalers killed 916 of them. Catching orcas for captive display is an emotive issue, but can hardly be said to be of conservation significance based on the small numbers taken, so there is no reason to believe that this splendid animal will not continue to grace southern seas.

Sei Whale

Sei whales *(Balaenoptera borealis)* are the third-largest species to be found in the Southern Ocean. Average size on maturity is 14.5m in males and 15.5m in females. A 16.4m female was weighed at 37.75 metric tons. The blow is similar to that of the fin whale but not so high. Sei whales can achieve 30 knots over short distances.

The species can be found in all oceans, but only the larger individuals have been recorded south of the Antarctic Convergence. Sei whales occur in small schools of three to eight animals. Some sexual segregation seems to occur, based on harpooners' records. The calf is 4.5m long at birth and is weaned after six months when it has grown to a length of about eight meters. In the Southern Hemisphere, sei whales feed on copepods and euphausiids, with the former thought to be the more important. Their finely fringed baleen plates help them feed on such small prey.

Like humpback, blue and fin whales, seis were over-exploited through greed to the point of 'commercial extinction': Over 20,000 were harpooned in the 1964-65 season, immediately after which the population collapsed. Completely protected since 1979, let us hope that the species may one day recover.

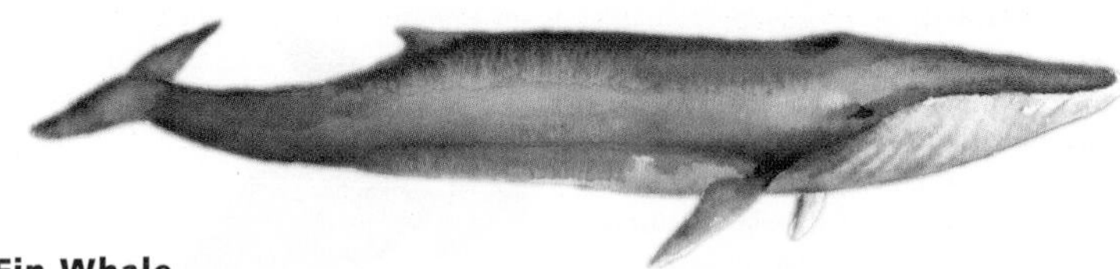

Fin Whale

Female fin whales *(Baleanoptera physalus)* attain 27m in length and males 25m. They are the second largest whales, after the blue. Unusually, the anterior part of the animal is asymmetrically colored: The left mandible is bluish-grey, the right mandible is white. The reason for this peculiar patterning is unclear but may be related to the species feeding in a tilted position. Fins are the fastest swimmers of the baleen whales: Maximum speed may be 20 knots.

Fin whales occur in all oceans. In Antarctic waters fins have a circumpolar distribution in summer, moving to lower latitudes in winter. Calves are born at about 6.5m in length in temperate or subtropical waters. Principal food in southern seas is euphausiid crustaceans. Like all other baleen whales, animals may not feed at all in winter, relying on their accumulated blubber for energy.

Fin whales formed the largest part of whalers' catches after WWII, when a maximum 28,761 were taken in 1960-61. Whaling reduced the population from an estimated 400,000 to about 84,000. The species has been totally protected since 1976. Like all the baleen whales, protection only came after 'commercial extinction.' Recovery rates are likely to be slow in this long-lived species. (The fin's longevity was exemplified when one whaler's identifying mark was recovered after 37 years.)

Blue Whale

Blue whales *(Balaenoptera musculus)* are the largest animals that have ever lived. A female landed at South Georgia reached 33.5m in length. A 27.6m female caught by a Soviet whaling fleet in 1947 weighed 190 metric tons. Characteristics include the animal's huge size and habit of showing its flukes on diving (other baleen whales do not).

Blue whales occur in all oceans. In the southern summer they frequent the fringes of the ice shelf, moving to subtropical waters in winter. The larger individuals occur the farthest south. Blue whales are usually solitary or occur in pairs. Sexual maturity is reached at about five years of age in females. Diet in southern waters is predominantly Antarctic krill *(Euphausia superba)*: As much as 4.5 metric tons may be consumed in one day, filtered out by the 250 – 400 pairs of baleen plates.

The blue whale population of the Southern Hemisphere is thought to have once numbered 200,000 animals. Commercial whaling from the 1930s severely reduced their numbers and the species became fully protected on a global scale in 1965. Nevertheless, recovery has not been fast, and the current populations are thought to be only 1% of original numbers.

Minke Whale

The minke whale *(Balaenoptera acutorostrata)* is the smallest of the great baleen whales, although with a maximum length of 10m and a weight up to eight metric tons it is still a very large animal. They are fast swimmers and will approach slow-moving and stationary vessels. The blow reaches two meters.

Minke whales are circumpolar in distribution in summer, with highest densities seen at the pack ice edge. In winter most animals move to lower latitudes. Sexes and age classes are often segregated, with the largest animals – usually females – occurring the farthest south. Pairing and calving takes place in the southern winter. Diet consists mainly of krill and copepods.

Minkes are by far the most abundant baleen whales in the Southern Ocean, with a population of possibly half a million. They were not targeted by whalers because of their relatively small size and thus escaped the slaughter of the first half of the 20th century. However, a few hundred are currently (and controversially) taken by Japanese whalers each year, ostensibly for scientific purposes, although their meat is sold for human consumption in Japan to 'allay costs.'

Antarctic & Subantarctic Fur Seals

Fur seals can be found on most of the circumpolar southern islands – in large numbers at some of them. Vagrants have reached the southern continents. The Antarctic fur seal *(Arctocephalus gazella)* occurs farther south than its close and slightly smaller relative, the subantarctic fur seal *(A tropicalis)*, with which it sometimes hybridizes. Female Antarctic fur seals are grey to brownish with creamy throats and chests. Adult males are silvery-grey with a mane of longer hair.

SALLY TROY

Antarctic fur seal pup

Subantarctic females are greyish with orange throats and chests. The males are buff to black with cream to orange throats and chests, and they have a 'top-knot' that helps distinguish them from male Antarctics. Fur seals show sexual dimorphism in size: Males, at over 200 kg, far outweigh females, at up to 55 kg.

Fur seals breed in harems, and males can be formidable opponents to rivals and human visitors alike: Quite a few scientists bear the scars of injudicious approach. Pupping takes place in December. Diet consists of squid, fish and crustaceans, such as krill.

Fur seals are now showing a remarkable recovery in numbers from over-exploitation for their coats early in the 19th century – so much so that at some localities they are displacing breeding albatrosses and killing vegetation, leading to conservation dilemmas. Perhaps some form of carefully controlled exploitation will one day be allowed, but this is certain to be controversial.

Southern Elephant Seal

The southern elephant seal *(Mirounga leonina)* is the world's largest seal: Males attain 3.5 metric tons and five meters in length and females can weigh up to 900 kg and measure three meters in length. The animal has a circumpolor distribution, occurring on most of the southern islands and also on the Antarctic Peninsula.

JEFF RUBIN

Moulting female elephant seal

WAYNE BERNHARDSON

Bull elephant seal

Breeding follows a seasonal pattern: Males spend the winter at sea and first haul out in August, followed by the females. Fighting then follows among the males to see who will be 'beachmaster.' Pups grow incredibly quickly, quadrupling their mass (the females' milk is 50% fat) by the time they are weaned at 22 days of age. Their diet is predominantly squid, caught during very deep (below one km!) and long dives, separated by remarkably short periods at the sea surface.

Elephant seals were heavily exploited ashore (especially males) for their oil during the 19th and early 20th centuries. Although this fortunately no longer occurs, numbers are decreasing at some of the southern Indian Ocean islands and so the species is being studied in an attempt to explain this alarming trend, which may be linked to climatic change affecting food supplies.

Crabeater Seal

Crabeaters *(Lobodon carcinophagus)* actually eat krill, not crab as their name suggests. They are slim seals reaching about 2.7m (females) and three meters (males). Their distribution is circumpolar, preferring 30–70% pack ice. Although considered to be the world's most abundant seal (by one estimate, they number 30 million), the species' habit of occurring in small family groups suggests smaller numbers when compared with the teeming breeding beaches occupied by fur seals.

MARK NORMAN

MARK NORMAN

Not much is known about breeding in crabeaters, which occurs among the pack ice during the austral spring. Like southern elephant seals, pups grow very quickly and are weaned within two to three weeks. Crabeaters have teeth that form a sieve to strain out Antarctic krill, their almost exclusive diet.

Very little is known about this abundant animal (for example, copulation has never been observed), as pack ice is a difficult place for scientists to study these seals. The species seems to be safe and under no conservation threat.

Female crabeater seal with pup (above), angry crabeater seal (left)

Leopard Seal

Adult male leopard seals *(Hydrurga leptonyx)* reach a length of three meters and weigh up to 300 kg. Females are larger, at four meters and 450 kg. Leopard seals have a large head with a huge gape, making them fearsome predators. Leopards are found among the pack ice in summer and on the more southerly subantarctic islands in winter.

STEPHAN LUNDGREN (HEDGEHOG HOUSE)

Leopard seal

Little is known about their breeding behavior: Pups are born on the ice during summer. Except during the breeding season, the species is a solitary one. Their diet includes penguins and seals.

There is much folklore about the dangers of leopard seals, perhaps mostly untrue. However, given their size and formidable jaws, caution is recommended.

Weddell Seal

Weddell seals *(Leptonychotes weddellii)* are fat animals, not streamlined like crabeater and leopard seals. They reach three meters in length and a mass of 400 kg, with females being a little larger than males. Weddell seals have a circumpolar distribution, living farther south than any other mammal (other than Antarctic explorers!). Fast shelf ice is their main home year round, but the species has been recorded in pack ice.

Pups are born in colonies in September and October, on fast ice near cracks and holes that allow their mothers access to the water. Excessive tooth wear occurs as animals use their incisors and canines to scrape away at the ice to keep their breathing holes open. Weddells are the best studied of the four Antarctic seals, because they can be more easily approached over fast ice than can the pack-ice species. Studies have shown Weddells can dive to 60m and stay under water for over an hour. Their diet consists of fish, squid and crustaceans.

Weddells are the archetypical Antarctic seal, and along with the Adélie penguin are fixed in the public consciousness as animals of the far south.

JEFF RUBIN

JEFF RUBIN

Weddell seals

Emperor Penguin

The emperor penguin *(Aptenodytes forsteri)* is the world's largest penguin, although some fossil penguins were even larger. It stands over a meter high and can weigh up to 40 kg. The emperor can only be confused with its close relative, the subantarctic king penguin, which is smaller and more brightly marked. The chick is silvery-grey with white face mask and blackish head.

About 42 breeding localities are known, concentrated in the Weddell Sea and Dronning Maud Land, Enderby and Princess Elizabeth Lands, and the Ross Sea. At-sea distribution does not extend north of the Antarctic Polar Front, except for vagrants. The total known population is a little under 200,000 breeding pairs.

KEVIN SCHAFER

Emperor penguin and chick

The emperor penguin is the only Antarctic bird that breeds in winter. A single egg is incubated on the feet of the male. Birds huddle in the winter cold to reduce heat loss. Incubation averages 66 days, and chicks become independent during November to January. Diet includes fish such as the Antarctic silver fish *(Pleurogramma antarcticum)*, krill and squid. Breeding birds may travel long distances across the ice to find open water to feed. Prey is captured by pursuit-diving, often to amazing depths and lengths: The records stand at 535m and 22 minutes, by far the deepest and longest dives for any bird.

Emperor penguins are not globally threatened, although human disturbance has been implicated at the Pointe Géologie colony in Terre Adélie, which decreased in size from 6000 pairs to 2000 pairs between 1952 and 1987.

JEFF RUBIN

Tourists photographing an emperor penguin colony

King Penguin

The king penguin *(Aptenodytes patagonicus)* is the world's second largest penguin, standing 20 cm shorter than the closely related emperor, but is much lighter at nine to 15 kg. The downy chick is uniform dark brown (and was once described as the 'woolly penguin': a species of its own!). It breeds on seven subantarctic island groups, with a breeding population estimated to be between a million and 1.5 million pairs.

MARK NORMAN

King penguin

Breeding occurs in often very large colonies close to the shore on rocky terrain. A single egg is incubated during summer on the feet of both parents, each taking turns. The egg takes 55 days to hatch. Incubating birds can shuffle along slowly with their eggs – to avoid lumbering southern elephant seals, for instance. Chicks are reared right through the winter (huddling in creches to keep warm) and only fledge the following summer, making annual breeding impossible. Scientists have worked hard to unravel the species' breeding interval: Is it every second year or two years in three? Diet includes fish and squid, caught by deep dives during daylight hours.

King penguins have been exploited in the past, but thankfully their numbers have subsequently increased at several breeding localities and the species' conservation status seems secure.

Adélie Penguin

The Adélie *(Pygoscelis adeliae)* is the archetypical penguin, named after French explorer Dumont d'Urville's wife. They are purely black and white, with a distinctive white eye ring. Like all penguins, the sexes are similarly marked, although females are smaller. The downy chick is uniformly brown. Breeding occurs all around the Antarctic continent and Peninsula and at some of the more southerly subantarctic islands. There are about 2.5 million breeding pairs known

GORDON COURT (HEDGEHOG HOUSE)

Adélie penguins

for 177 localities, although there are very likely new colonies to discover in little-explored sections of the Antarctic coastline.

Breeding occurs during summer in large colonies. Comical-looking chases of adults by chicks ensure that meals are not fed to chicks that give up chases first. Diet is mainly Antarctic and ice krill *(Euphausia superba* and *E crystallarophias)*. Deep dives for prey (reaching depths of nearly 150m) may be undertaken, but usually dives are much shallower. In winter, Adélies stay at sea, resting on pack ice and icebergs in groups.

Adélie penguins are well studied. Their breeding success, numbers and diets are monitored as part of international studies conducted under the auspices of the Convention for the Conservation of Antarctic Marine Living Resources (CCAMLR). Some colonies near Antarctic stations have decreased in size, a change thought to be due to human disturbance. Elsewhere, colonies have grown in size, so the species is not in danger.

Chinstrap Penguin

Chinstraps *(Pygoscelis antarctica)* are superficially similar to Adélies, being black and white, but they have a distinctive black line connecting the black cap to below the chin – hence the name. Breeding occurs around the Antarctic Peninsula and on islands south of the Antarctic Polar Front. With an estimated 7.5 million pairs, the chinstrap penguin is the second-most abundant Antarctic/subantarctic penguin, after the macaroni penguin. Five million of these are found on the little-visited South Sandwich Islands.

KEVIN SCHAFER

Chinstrap penguin

Two eggs are laid in November or December and chicks fledge in late February and early March. Pursuit dives for prey – almost entirely krill – are usually less then 100m deep. Chinstraps forage among the pack ice, although vagrants may be seen in the open sea.

Whereas population changes have been detected among colonies on the Antarctic Peninsula studied by a number of nations (as part of CCAMLR), the species' numbers overall seem stable. There is a pressing need for accurate surveys of the huge South Sandwich populations: The five-million-pair estimate has been described in scientific literature as being 'very imprecise' (a polite euphemism for a wild guess).

Gentoo Penguin

An orange bill and a white flash behind its eye distinguish the black and white gentoos *(Pygoscelis papua)* from the slightly smaller Adélie and chinstrap species. Breeding distribution is circumpolar on subantarctic islands and on the Antarctic Peninsula. There are estimated to be about 300,000 breeding pairs of gentoo penguins. Large populations occur at South Georgia (100,000 pairs), Falkland Islands (70,000 pairs) and Iles Kerguelen (30,000 pairs).

WAYNE BERNHARDSON

Gentoo penguins

At the more northerly subantarctic islands gentoos breed in winter, laying two eggs as early as July. On the more southerly islands and the Antarctic Peninsula laying occurs from October to December. Pursuit dives for prey can go deeper than 100m, reaching the bottom in inshore waters, but most dives are probably shallower. Diet includes crustaceans (mainly euphausiids), fish (mainly lantern fish, myctophidae) and squid.

Gentoo penguin populations are mainly stable and no long-term trends are discernable overall, although year-to-year fluctuations can be large.

Macaroni Penguin

Orange tassels meeting between the eyes distinguish the macaroni penguin *(Eudyptes chrysolophus)* from the slightly smaller (and lighter billed) rockhopper penguin. 'Maccies' breed on subantarctic islands near the Antarctic Polar Front from South America eastwards to Heard Island and off the Antarctic Peninsula. This is the most abundant of the subantarctic/Antarctic penguins, with a minimum breeding population of 11.8 million pairs. Major concentrations are to be found at South Georgia (5.4 million pairs), Iles Crozet (2.2 million), Iles Kergeulen (1.8 million) and Heard and McDonald Islands (two million).

Macaroni penguins are summer breeders. Breeding colonies, which can be immense, are deserted in winter. Two eggs are laid, the first smaller than the second (extremely unusual for birds) . The first-laid ('A') egg is usually kicked out of the nest soon after the 'B' egg is laid and only one egg ever hatches. This odd system has prompted many studies.

WAYNE BERNHARDSON

Macaroni penguin (left) talking to a rockhopper penguin (right)

Macaroni penguins feed on lantern (Myctophidae) fish and euphausiid crustaceans, caught by pursuit diving.

Like the pygoscelid penguins, maccies are monitored for CCAMLR purposes. The species is not of any special conservation concern, but more accurate censuses are required at the major breeding localities – easier said than done in a million-strong colony.

Rockhopper Penguin

'Rockies' *(Eudyptes chrysocome)* are smaller than macaroni penguins and have yellow tassels that do not meet between the eyes. Although there is as yet no consensus, three subspecies have been recognized. Rockhopper penguins are subantarctic and southern cool temperate island breeders, to be found as far north as Tristan da Cunha. There are an estimated 3.7 million pairs of rockies. The largest population (one million pairs) is to be found at the Falkland Islands.

K HANDASYDE

Rockhopper penguin

Rockhopper penguins breed in summer, laying two dimorphic eggs. The smaller first-laid 'A' egg is often lost during incubation and does not always hatch if retained. Breeding colonies are smaller than those of macaroni penguins, and the birds are able to breed among tumbled boulders on exposed shores, where their hopping and swimming abilities are required to enter and emerge from the sea and to reach their nest sites. The species pursuit dives for lantern fish and small euphausiid crustaceans.

Rockhopper penguins have decreased alarmingly at islands south of New Zealand, and perhaps at some other localities as well. Disease, introduced rats and sea temperature rises have all been suggested as reasons. Still, with a well-scattered population in the millions, the rockhopper penguin is not at any risk of extinction.

Royal Penguin

Royal penguins *(Eudyptes schlegeli)* are found only at subantarctic Macquarie Island. Essentially, they look like white-faced macaronis, although some dark-faces do occur. The 1984-85 (most recent) census found 848,700 breeding pairs, which is now regarded to be an underestimation of the species' numbers.

MARK NORMAN

Royal penguin

Two eggs are laid in often huge coastal colonies in October. As usual in *Eudyptes* penguins, the smaller, first-laid 'A' egg is ejected from the nest and does not usually hatch; the reason for this is still unclear despite a number of studies. Chicks fledge in late January or early February and colonies are deserted by May, after adults complete their moult ashore. Diet consists mainly of small euphausiid crustaceans and lantern fish of the family myctophidae, caught by pursuit-diving.

Royal penguins have been well studied in recent years, and much is now known about their foraging ecology and breeding biology. There appear to be no serious conservation threats to the species. Years ago they were exploited for their oil, but protest against this led to Macquarie Island being made the first subantarctic island nature reserve.

Amsterdam Albatross

Confined to Ile Amsterdam in the South Indian Ocean with a tiny population of less than a hundred birds and only 13 pairs breeding in 1995, the Amsterdam albatross *(Diomedea amsterdamensis)* was only described as a separate species in 1983. It is the rarest Southern Ocean seabird – indeed, one of the world's rarest birds. Looking for one at sea is thus likely to be a forlorn task. Good news is that ornithologists think its numbers are slowly increasing, now that feral cattle have been removed from its breeding habitat 600m up on the island's central plateau.

Wandering Albatross

The wandering albatross *(Diomedea exulans)* is a bird of superlatives – for many travelers, it is *the* bird of the Southern Ocean. To see one glide past your vantage place on a ship, just a few meters away as it watches you with its soft brown eyes, is to experience a thrill not for 'lesser mortals.' The species is distinguished by its huge size (wing span up to 3.5m) from the smaller 'mollymawk' albatrosses, but telling it at sea from the closely related (but less widespread) royal and Amsterdam albatrosses is not easy and needs recourse to a specialized field guide or friendly marine ornithologist. In fact, recent genetic studies propose splitting the wanderer into four species.

Latest population estimates are 21,000 annual breeding pairs at 10 island groups in the Southern Ocean. But the bird's more than year-long breeding season means it breeds (if successful) only every second year, so the total breeding population is nearly twice this figure. At several localities populations have decreased because the bird is at serious risk from being caught on tuna longlines; an ignoble death by drowning for such a splendid animal. All is not lost, however, because much research is currently being undertaken into ways of reducing this mortality, and some populations have stabilized, perhaps as a result.

Diet is mainly squid and fish caught, it is thought, by predation at night and scavenging by day. Wanderers can cover vast tracts of the Southern Ocean, flying up to several thousand kilometers on a single foraging trip, as satellite tracking has very recently revealed, so they are aptly named!

COLIN MONTEATH (HEDGEHOG HOUSE)

Wandering albatrosses

Royal Albatross

The royal albatross *Diomedea epomophora* is one of the three 'great' albatrosses of the Southern Ocean, primarily recognized by its huge size and its combination, when adult, of an all-white tail with black upper wings. It breeds on islands off New Zealand (Chathams, Campbell and Aucklands), with a small population on Taiaroa Head near Dunedin on the mainland of New Zealand's South Island. This must be the most accessible breeding locality of a southern albatross and it is a famous tourist attraction. Total annual breeding population is about 11,000 pairs, but biennial breeding means there are about twice this number of breeders. As with the wandering and Amsterdam albatrosses, the very long breeding season means royals, if successful, can only breed every second year. There are two subspecies, considered by some ornithologists to be worthy of specific status, but interbreeding has occurred at Taiaroa Head.

MARK NORMAN

Royal albatross

Diet is squid, fish and crustaceans, caught at the sea surface. Like wanderers, royals are caught by tuna longlines. Recent regulations and new practices (such as only setting lines at night, and using 'tori poles' with attached streamers to scare birds away from baited hooks) will hopefully protect this splendid bird.

Blackbrowed Albatross

The blackbrowed albatross *(Diomedea melanophris)* is one of the smaller 'mollymawks,' but with a 2.5m wingspan and a mass up to five kg, it is still a big bird. This albatross can be identified at a distance by its underwing pattern featuring a wide dark leading edge. At close range, the adult bird's yellow bill with orange-red tip and dark line through the eye makes identification easy.

The species is widespread in southern seas, and numbers may be seen accompanying fishing trawlers off Australasia, southern Africa and South America. Breeding occurs at nine island groups, spread from South Georgia to the Antipodes Islands, as well as at Cape Horn. There are many blackbrows – probably more than half a million breeding pairs – so with nonbreeding birds the species' population will be over two million. An annual breeder, the bird builds cone nests out of mud and vegetation, laying a single egg. The blackbrow breeds

WAYNE BERNHARDSON

Blackbrowed albatrosses

colonially, often in vast numbers: Beauchene Island, off the Falklands, has a colony estimated at 135,000 pairs in 1991.

Blackbrows' diet consists of squid, fish and crustaceans, caught at the sea surface or by shallow dives. Interactions with fisheries, especially Asian tuna longliners, are a cause for concern, but the species is still abundant and new measures being adopted in the fishery should help with its conservation.

Shy Albatross

The shy albatross *(Diomedea cauta)* is the largest of the southern mollymawks, with wing span of up to 2.6m. Its distinguishing features are its humped-back appearance in flight, dark upperwings which are not as black as other mollymawks' and a narrow dark leading edge to the underwing in both adults and juveniles. The shy's name is a misnomer, because it will follow and approach ships. Shy albatrosses breed on islands south of New Zealand and around Tasmania, with a very small population of about four pairs recently found breeding on the Iles Crozet. However, the species has a widespread at-sea distribution and can be seen anywhere in the Southern Ocean in the Roaring Forties and Furious Fifties. Total estimated population is of the order of a million birds, including juveniles. The largest breeding colonies are on the Bounty and Auckland Islands.

A single egg is laid, in a mud and vegetation nest in colonies on cliffs. The shy albatross eats fish, squid and crustaceans. Interactions with fisheries are a serious cause for concern, but some colonies have increased in size this century as exploitation of the birds' feathers and eggs has ceased.

Yellownosed Albatross

The yellownosed albatross *(Diomedea chlororhychos)* is the smallest of the southern mollymawks, weighing up to three kg. Viewed up close, the black bill with its striking orange streak on the upper mandible is a distinguishing feature. Yellownoses breed on the northerly islands of the Southern Ocean: the Tristan da Cunha group, the French subantarctic islands and Prince Edward Island. The Atlantic and Indian Ocean populations are subspecifically distinct, and may even be separate species: the Atlantic birds have noticeably greyer heads.

P PRINCE (BAS)

Yellownosed albatross

The total species' population is about 100,000 breeding pairs. At sea, yellownosed albatrosses can be seen in the South Atlantic and Indian, but not Pacific Oceans. Birds breed annually, laying a single egg in summer on mud and vegetation nests. At some localities, such as Tristan da Cunha, they nest in a widely scattered pattern among dense fern vegetation. Elsewhere, such as at Prince Edward Island, they nest on cliff ledges in a mixed colony with greyheaded albatrosses.

The species' diet is similar to the other mollymawks, with fish predominating at Iles Crozet. The bird scavenges on trawler discards off southern Africa, where a number of banding recoveries have been made, showing the birds originate from the

Tristan group and Gough Island. The species was exploited for its eggs and flesh by the Tristan Islanders in the past, but is now fully protected. Interaction with fisheries are a cause for concern.

Greyheaded Albatross

The greyheaded *(Diomedea chrysostoma)* is a typical mollymawk albatross. The greyish head, broad dark leading edge to the underwing and orange stripes on both upper and lower mandibles identify this species. A more southerly breeding species than the yellownosed albatross, with colonies on South Georgia, the Prince Edwards, Iles Crozet and Kerguelen, Campbell and Macquarie, the greyheaded albatross has a circumpolar breeding distribution. The most recent population estimate is 106,000 breeding pairs, which can be doubled since the bird normally breeds only every second year, the only mollymawk to do so.

JIM HENDERSON (HEDGEHOG HOUSE)

Greyheaded albatross

Greyheads breed in colonies on cliff ledges, sometimes along side blackbrowed or yellownosed albatrosses. Like all albatrosses, greyheads lay only one egg, and both parents share incubation and chick-feeding in turns.

Diet has been studied at three breeding localities and consist of fish, cephalopods and crustaceans, including Antarctic krill *Euphausia superba* off South Georgia. Fishery interactions remain the most serious conservation problem.

Sooty & Lightmantled Sooty Albatrosses

The two species of sooty albatrosses can be distinguished at sea with care. The sooty albatross *(Phoebetria fusca)* is uniformly chocolate brown, whereas the lightmantled sooty albatross *(P palpebrata)* has a contrasting pale back. When viewed close-up (impossible at sea unless the bird flies right alongside your vessel), the sooty has a yellow stripe 'sulcus' along its lower mandible, whereas the lightmantle has a blue one. Their long, pointed tails and narrow wings make these two species easily distinguished at sea from giant petrels, which have broader, shorter wings. Their flight is most graceful and many a happy hour can be spent watching them fly behind and alongside vessels traversing the Southern Ocean.

COLIN MONTEATH (HEDGEHOG HOUSE)

Lightmantled sooty albatross

Both species have circumpolar at-sea distributions, but lightmantles tend to occur farther south, reaching the edge of the pack ice. This is mirrored by their breeding distribution, with the sooty albatross generally breeding farther to the north, such as in the Tristan group. In contrast, only lightmantles breed at South Georgia. Both species occur on subantarctic islands in the Indian Ocean, making for interesting comparative studies of breeding biology and feeding ecology. Both are cliff nesters, in small colonies. Their paired courtship flights and haunting calls around misty cliffs make up one of the quintessential experiences for visitors to the southern islands.

Annual breeding populations are about 16,000 pairs for sooties and 23,000 pairs for lightmantles. Diet includes squid, fish and crustaceans, but also small seabirds such as prions and diving petrels. Exactly how these last are caught remains unknown, but the species' agile flight and dark coloration suggests predation at night. Sooty albatrosses used to be heavily exploited in the Tristan group by the inhabitants, but fortunately no more. *Phoebetria* albatrosses do not seem to get caught on longlines like the great albatrosses and mollymawks, so their populations are secure. This is a blessing, because they are very special birds, admired by all who are fortunate enough to see them.

Giant Petrels

Giant petrels are the largest of the petrel family, which goes to make up the order of tubenose or procellariiform seabirds, along with albatrosses, storm petrels and diving petrels. The crucial feature used to distinguish the northern giant petrel *(Macronectes halli* from the closely related southern giant petrel *(M giganteus)* is the color of the bill tip: greenish in northerns, reddish-brown in southerns. This characteristic is not always easy to spot at sea. Some southerns are all white, except for the odd dark feather. This color phase does not occur in northerns, helping with specific identification. White-phase southerns are more common at southerly breeding sites, and are absent at the northerly ones, such as Gough and Marion Islands.

COLIN MONTEATH (HEDGEHOG HOUSE)

Southern giant petrel

Giant petrels can be seen in all parts of the Southern Ocean, with southerns occurring farther south – indeed some breed on the Antarctic Peninsula and in Terre Adélie. At the New Zealand subantarctic islands, only northerns occur, whereas the birds that breed at the most northerly island, Gough, are southerns and not northerns as might be expected. Genetic studies should lead to a clearer understanding of these patterns. There are an estimated 12,000 breeding pairs of northern giant petrels and 36,000 pairs of southern giant petrels.

Southerns breed in colonies, northerns singly or in scattered groups. Genetic isolation is helped by northerns commencing breeding earlier than southerns. Both species are annual breeders.

Unlike albatrosses, giant petrels forage on both land and sea. On land they kill birds as large as king penguins, and scavenge in seal colonies. At sea, they feed on fish, squid and crustaceans, and scavenge on dead cetaceans and seabirds. Watching blood-stained giant petrels squalling and fighting over a seal carcass is not for the faint-hearted, but the birds have a raffish charm that appeals to some!

Giant petrels are caught by tuna longliners in the Southern Ocean, but it is hoped that improved fishing techniques will help keep their populations secure.

Antarctic Fulmar

A medium-sized petrel (800g, 1.2m wingspan), the Antarctic fulmar *(Fulmarus glacialoides)* is readily identified by its pale grey plumage with white head and black flight feathers. The bill is pink with a dark tip and the dark eye is a distinguishing feature. Antarctic fulmars are a southerly species with a circumpolar distribution at sea, commonly found on pack ice fringes. They breed in large colonies on the islands around the Antarctic Peninsula, such as the South Orkneys and South Sandwich Islands, as well as along the Antarctic coastline. There are no good population estimates as yet, but the bird is abundant, and there is no evidence of any large population changes.

Antarctic fulmars breed on rock ledges on coastal cliffs, often in large and dense colonies from December to April. Diet includes Antarctic krill and other crustaceans, fish and squid, as well as carrion. Food is caught by surface-seizing and occasionally shallow dives.

Antarctic Petrel

The Antarctic petrel *(Thalassoica antarctica)* is a boldly marked dark brown and white petrel, a little smaller than the Antarctic fulmar. It is bigger but less speckled than a cape petrel, which is also dark brown and white. This species breeds only on the Antarctic continent, but not many colonies are known, and more may still be found. One colony, at Svarthamaren in Dronning Maud Land, supports about a quarter of a million pairs and is the largest known. There is no good estimate for the breeding population, since many colonies have never been properly surveyed.

MARK NORMAN

Antarctic petrel

The Antarctic Petrel breeds in dense colonies on cliffs and steep rocky slopes, some of them 100 km or more from the open sea on inland nunataks and mountain ranges. Eggs are laid in November after the adults arrive at their nest sites the previous month; chicks fledge in March. The rest of the year the colonies are deserted while the birds stay at sea among and just north of the pack ice. Diet is made up of Antarctic krill, fish such as *Pleuragramma antarcticum* and small squid taken by surface-seizing, dipping and shallow diving.

Snow Petrel

Snow petrels *(Pagodroma nivea)* are unmistakable: With their all white plumage, black bill and small black eyes, they are truly creatures of the ice. Their flight is more fluttering than most petrels. Snow petrels breed on the Antarctic continent and Peninsula, and also at Bouvetøya on rocky slopes and in crevices among boulders on nunataks and sea cliffs. Their at-sea distribution does not extend far to the north; snow petrels are very much birds of the pack-ice zone, where they roost on icebergs.

The single egg is laid in late November or early December and chicks fledge in March or April. The species is nervous at the nest and will desert its egg if overly disturbed. This is in contrast to most of the petrel family, which are not too concerned about the presence of humans.

Diet is primarily krill, fish and squid, caught mainly by surface-dipping while on the wing. Birds regurgitate their stomach oil as a defence mechanism. Deposits of this substance, called 'mumiyo,' have built up around nest sites over thousands of years and can be radio-carbon dated to obtain an idea of colony ages. The oldest known dates back an astounding 34,000 years. No conservation problems are known for the snow petrel.

STEPHAN LUNDGREN (HEDGEHOG HOUSE)

Snow petrel

Cape Petrel

The cape petrel *(Daption capense)* is a dark brown/ black and white petrel smaller than the Antarctic petrel. Its speckled appearance has earned its other common name, pintado, which means 'painted' in Spanish. Interestingly its generic name *Daption* is an anagram of pintado and has no meaning otherwise. Some ornithologists think 'pintado' a far better name than the dull 'cape.'

MARK NORMAN

Cape petrel

The cape petrel has a circumpolar at-sea distribution, which extends much farther north than does the Antarctic petrel. In fact, a cape can be quite common off the southern continents, especially in winter, where it is an assiduous ship-follower. It also has a wide breeding range: from the Antarctic continent to the more southerly subantarctic islands where it breeds on cliff ledges. As a ship-follower, it eats just about anything edible thrown overboard. In the days of whaling, it was seen in vast noisy numbers around the shore factories of South Georgia. There is no good information on population trends and there seem to be no conservation problems of note.

Greatwinged Petrel

The greatwinged petrel *(Pterodroma macroptera)* is an all dark-brown gadfly petrel found in the Roaring Forties. Separating it from the slightly smaller Kerguelen petrel is tricky and requires guidance from an expert or a good field guide. In New Zealand, a clearly differentiated subspecies is known as the greyfaced petrel. Greatwings breed on the subantarctic islands of the South Indian Ocean, and also on islands around southern Australia and New Zealand.

The species is a winter breeder, laying its single egg in burrows it excavates in vegetated peat slopes in May to July, with chicks fledging in November and December, just when the summer-breeding burrowing petrels are getting started. Like most burrowing petrels, greatwings arrive at their burrows after dark, to reduce their chances of being caught by predatory subantarctic skuas. Breeding in winter may thus be an advantage, since most skuas leave the islands then to overwinter at sea.

Greatwinged petrels' diet is primarily squid caught at night. The species is numerous and not globally threatened. At some islands, however, introduced cats have played havoc, reducing populations and causing breeding success to approach zero, as at Marion Island in the 1970s and 1980s. Happily, Marion Island is now cat-free after a long and expensive eradication program, and the greatwings are breeding successfully again.

Whiteheaded Petrel

A distinctive burrowing petrel of the subantarctic region, the whiteheaded petrel *(Pterodroma lessonii)* has a pale body and tail, dark wings and a white head with a dark eye. It can be picked up at great distances at sea, from its white appearance, which is helpful to bird watchers, since it seems to be unattracted to ships. Whiteheadeds have a circumpolar distribution at sea in the 40 to 60°S latitudes. The species breeds on Iles Crozet and Kerguelen, Macquarie, the Aucklands and the Antipodes.

Breeding occurs in summer, the single egg being laid in excavated burrows in the soft peat of tussock grassland. Diet is not well known, but includes squid, crustaceans and lantern fish, caught by surface-seizing.

The species is not rare and the total population probably numbers in the low hundred thousands. As is the case with many burrowing petrels of the subantarctic islands, introduced cats have reduced populations, especially at Macquarie Island. Australia has instituted a cat-eradication program at Macquarie, so let us hope, in due course, for a success story similar to the revival of the greatwinged petrels on now cat-free Marion Island.

Atlantic Petrel

The Atlantic petrel *(Pterodroma incerta)* is one of the largest gadfly petrels, recognized by its white breast and belly, clearly demarcated from the rest of its uniformly brown plumage. The species breeds only on the Tristan da Cunha-Gough group and its at-sea distribution hardly extends out of the Atlantic Ocean.

Practically nothing is known of its population size, but it must be in the low tens of thousands at least. The species breeds in excavated burrows in winter, with chicks being fed on Gough Island in October. The Atlantic petrels' diet on Gough Island is mainly squid.

In the past, the species – like other burrowing petrels occurring on the island – was exploited for meat and eggs by the Tristan Islanders. Fortunately, it is now legally protected throughout the Tristan group, so it faces no serious conservation problems.

Softplumaged Petrel

The softplumaged petrel *(Pterodroma mollis)* is a dark-brown and white, medium-sized gadfly petrel. In flight the back and upperwings carry a dark 'M' shape.

Softplumes occur at sea from South American waters eastwards to New Zealand, mainly in subantarctic latitudes, but they are absent from the South Pacific. The species breeds on the Tristan-Gough Islands, the Prince Edwards, Iles Crozet and Kerguelen and the Antipodes. There are no sensible estimates of total population size since burrowing petrels are notoriously difficult to count, but the species is abundant at many breeding localities and commonly seen at sea within its normal range.

Diet is primarily squid, caught by surface-seizing thought to occur mostly at night. Exploitation at Tristan da Cunha has halted and the recent removal of feral cats from Marion Island should lead to a recovery in time. Cat eradication at other breeding islands where they occur (such as Iles Crozet and Kerguelen) would improve the species' conservation status further.

Kerguelen Petrel

P PRINCE (BAS)
Kerguelen petrel

Kerguelen petrels *(Lugensa brevirostris)* are uniformly dark brown, except for their silvery underwings. Their smaller size and proportionally large head distinguishes them from the greatwinged petrel. Kerguelen petrels' distinctive and fast soaring flight is also helpful in identification at sea.

The species breeds on the Tristan-Gough Islands in the south Atlantic Ocean and on the Prince Edwards and Iles Crozet and Kerguelen in the South Indian Ocean. At-sea distribution is circumpolar, with irregular irruptions, linked to adverse weather conditions, bringing sometimes large numbers of birds to the waters off southern Africa and Australasia. Such birds are often then 'wrecked,' and may be found washed dead up on beaches.

Kergies' diet consists mainly of squid, fish and crustaceans, caught by surface-seizing at night. The species breeds in burrows in summer. There are probably several hundred thousand birds so it is in no danger of extinction, but eradication of introduced cats and rats at its breeding islands will help this bird's conservation status.

Blue Petrel

P PRINCE (BAS)
Blue petrel

The small (65-cm wing span) blue petrel *(Halobaena caerulea)* superficially resembles a prion, but look for the white – not black – terminal band to the tail. The species has a prominent dark 'M' shape on its upper wings and back. It breeds at the Diego Ramirez Islands off Cape Horn, South Georgia, the Prince Edwards, Iles Crozet and Kerguelen, Heard and Macquarie. Its at-sea distribution is circumpolar, from far south to the southern parts of the South American, African and Australian continents (where irregular irruptions following bad weather may bring large numbers to be 'wrecked' on shorelines).

The species is abundant, breeding in large, dense colonies in thick tussock, which it fertilizes. One estimate puts the total population as 'several million' – hardly very accurate, but it gives an idea! No information is available on population trends, except that breeding success has improved with the removal of feral cats from Marion Island. The South Africans are to be congratulated for this eradication program, which is probably the greatest conservation success at any subantarctic island since the exploitation of royal penguins for their oil was halted at Macquarie Island many years ago.

The blue petrels' diet is primarily small crustaceans, such as krill and amphipods.

Prions

Prions *(Pachyptila spp)* are small grey-blue and white birds. They can be distinguished from blue petrels by their black terminal band to the upper tail. All have a distinctive 'M' shape on their upperparts. Their taxonomy is still a matter for debate: There may be as many as six species, which vary subtly in their markings and also by the width of their bills. Broadbilled prions *(P vittata)*, affectionately known as 'Donald Ducks' in some quarters, have the broadest bills, with lamellae for straining out food, analogous to the baleen plates of the great whales. The fairy prion *(P turtur)* and thinbilled prion *(P belcheri)* have narrow bills. At-sea identification of species can stump the very best experts in all but excellent (and close-up) viewing conditions.

C DUCK (BAS)

Fairy prion

Breeding takes place at many southern islands, with one or two species occurring together. Prions may burrow, or breed in crevices among boulders and at the base of cliffs in scree slopes. Prions will be seen in all areas of the Southern Ocean north of the pack ice to continental waters, often in large to very large flocks.

The birds' diet varies with species and bill width, as does its method of foraging, but small crustaceans, especially amphipods, taken by filtering or surface-seizing, are the main prey. Like most burrowing petrels of the southern islands, prions have suffered from predation by cats and rats. Removal of these 'alien killers' should eventually lead to population recoveries.

Grey Petrel

Grey petrels *(Procellaria cinerea)* breed at the Tristan-Gough Islands, the South Indian subantarctic islands and the Campbell and Antipodes. At-sea distribution is circumpolar, extending south past 60°S and north to continental coasts. Little is known of numbers, because like all burrowing petrels, grey petrels are incredibly difficult to count accurately.

Grey petrels are winter breeders, laying their single egg in burrows in peat or in rock crevices in March, and fledging their chicks in October. Diet is poorly known, but at Iles Crozet, it is mainly squid and fish.

Introduced cats have severely diminished some populations, such as at Marion Island, where the grey petrel is now a rarity. Rats also take chicks at Iles Crozet and Campbell Island. Eradication of cats and rats from breeding sites is required for this species – and for a number of other burrowing petrels – to ensure a healthy conservation status.

Whitechinned Petrel

The whitechinned petrel *(Procellaria aequinoctialis)* is the largest burrowing petrel, with a wing span reaching nearly 1.5m. The clearly marked spectacled form *conspicillata* may be a distinct species. Whitechinned petrels are bigger than the all-dark gadfly petrel species, such as greatwinged and Kerguelen, and the wings are held unbent in a 'stiff' manner, making them look like small giant petrels as they follow ships.

The species breeds at the Falkland Islands, South Georgia, Prince Edwards, Iles Crozet and Kerguelen and on New Zealands' subantarctic islands. At-sea distribution is circumpolar, with a wide latitudinal range. The whitechinned petrel is a summer-breeding bird, and its burrows are recognizable by their large size and the presence of a pool of muddy water at their entrance.

C DUCK (BAS)

Whitechinned petrel

Whitechinneds' diet is well known: It consists of fish, squid and crustaceans, with the proportions varying at different localities. On the fishing grounds off South Africa's west coast, birds scavenge on discards left by trawlers.

Introduced cats have reduced breeding success (and probably numbers) at islands where they occur. Their eradication at Marion will help secure the whitechinned petrel's future, although birds being caught on longline hooks is also a problem.

Great Shearwater

The great shearwater *(Puffinus gravis)* is handsomely marked: Its black cap and white band at the base of the upper tail are very noticeable. Great shearwaters breed only in the Tristan-Gough group of islands and they are not seen to any great extent outside the Atlantic (except off the east coast of South Africa). The species is a trans-equatorial migrant and it is better known from its winter quarters in the North Atlantic than at its Southern Hemisphere breeding grounds, where it still awaits detailed study.

The Tristan-Gough population is huge, and may number more than five million breeding pairs. The population appears stable, although the species has been brought to very low numbers by past exploitation and habitat loss on Tristan da Cunha, and eggs and chicks (for their fat) are still legally taken by the Tristan Islanders on nearby Nightingale Island.

The species is a summer breeder, laying its single large egg in short burrows among tussock and under trees. Great shearwaters often forage by plunge-diving and so can exploit more of the ocean than the essentially surface-seizing gadfly petrels. Conservation issues that have been studied include ingestion of plastic particles and levels of pesticides.

Little Shearwater

The small (wingspan up to 27 cm) black and white little shearwater *Puffinus assimilis* is recognizable by its low flight that alternates glides with a few rapid wing beats. The little shearwater is often seen in small groups of two to three birds or so, usually close to breeding localities. It has a circumpolar at-sea distribution in the Southern Ocean. Breeding takes place on the more northerly islands of the Tristan-Gough group, Ile St Paul and on islands around Australia and New Zealand.

Little shearwaters are summer breeders, in burrows, among tussock and in rock crevices. Diet includes fish and squid, caught both by pursuit-plunging and surface-diving.

More studies are needed on this little-known seabird. The effects of introduced cats and rats at some breeding localities needs to be assessed, and cat- and rat-eradication programs need to be initiated on some islands.

Sooty Shearwater

The sooty shearwater *(Puffinus griseus)* is all brown. Its distinctive swift flight, long, narrow wings and habit of occurring in large to huge flocks distinguish this species from the noticeably larger whitechinned petrel and the more solitary gadfly petrels.

DON HADDEN (HEDGEHOG HOUSE)

Sooty shearwater

Sooty shearwaters have a circumpolar at-sea distribution. The birds' range crosses the Equator in both the Atlantic and Pacific Oceans, and extends south to the pack ice fringe. Breeding occurs in often vast colonies on islands off New Zealand and South America. In temperate waters, wrecks are common in bad weather as the birds undergo their trans-equatorial migrations. The single egg is laid in burrows in November, chicks departing in April or May. Diet consists of fish (such as anchovies), squid and crustaceans, with proportions of prey varying with place and time.

Sooty shearwaters face several pressures: Exploitation continues in New Zealand as part of traditional rights and customs, with perhaps a quarter of a million young taken annually by Maoris. Birds are also drowned in the North Pacific in gill nets and on some islands predatory species have been introduced. But with one estimate putting the Snares' population alone at 2.75 million breeding pairs, there is no reason to be concerned about this species' conservation status.

Wilson's Storm Petrel

Storm petrels are the smallest and lightest seabirds in the world. The Wilson's storm petrel *(Oceanites oceanicus)* weighs only 35 to 45g. 'Willies' have a circumpolar distribution and cross into the Northern Hemisphere in the Atlantic, Indian and Pacific Oceans. This species breeds on the more southerly subantarctic islands, such as South Georgia, and on the Antarctic Peninsula and continent, as well as on islands near Cape Horn and in the Falkland Islands. It has been regarded as the world's most abundant seabird: There are certainly several million of them.

The Wilson's storm petrel lays its single egg in December in burrows and rock crevices in cliffs, rocky slopes and scree banks. Diet is mainly planktonic crustaceans, including copepods, krill and amphipods, as well as small squid and fish. It feeds while on the wing, skimming and pattering with its feet over the sea surface. It is a regular ship follower and associates with whales.

Greybacked Storm Petrel

The small greybacked storm petrel *(Garrodia nereis)* is distinctively marked with white underparts, dark brown head and back and a grey rump. Greybacks have a disjunct at-sea distribution in the Southern Ocean, with three centers near breeding localities in the South Atlantic, South Indian Ocean and south of Australasia.

There are no accurate censuses, but the species probably numbers in the tens of thousands of pairs. It is a summer breeder, laying in December. Nests are to be found in coastal grassland among tussocks and in hollows among rocks. The species' diet has been little studied, but at Iles Crozet it was formed almost exclusively of immature and planktonic *Lepas* barnacle larvae. The species feeds by pattering over the sea surface, as well as by dipping and shallow-plunging.

Whitefaced Storm Petrel

The whitefaced storm petrel *(Pelagodroma marina)* has a distinctively marked head with a white line above the eye (the supercilium). The projecting feet on very long legs have yellow webs. The species breeds on islands around Australia and New Zealand as well as at the Tristan-Gough group in the South Atlantic and across the Equator in the North Atlantic. The species must number in the low millions.

Whitefaces breed in summer, laying in November and fledging in February. Eggs are laid in burrows in colonies. Their diet is formed of planktonic crustaceans and small fish and squid, caught by pattering and dipping, probably at night. Birds sometimes get their legs entangled with free-living trematode larvae, which later can cause birds to become snared in vegetation at their nest sites. An estimated 200,000 were found dead from this in the Chatham Islands off New Zealand in 1970.

Blackbellied & Whitebellied Storm Petrels

Blackbellied *(Fregetta tropica)* and whitebellied *(F grallaria)* storm petrels are medium-sized storm petrels Closely related, they are separated by the presence or absence of a black line down the center of an otherwise white underbody.

Whitebellied storm petrels breed on the more northerly islands of the Southern Ocean, such as Tristan and Gough, whereas blackbellies breed on the more southerly ones, such as South Georgia and Iles Crozet and Kerguelen.

Both are summer breeders, nesting in burrows in loose colonies. Diet, based on a study of blackbellied storm petrels at Iles Crozet, includes free-living barnacle larvae, amphipods and small euphausiids, with fish occasionally taken. Foraging is by pattering and dipping.

Diving Petrels

Diving petrels are small seabirds with stubby wings that seem to whir like wind-up toys as they fly fast and low above the sea surface. Two species of diving petrel, the South Georgian *(Pelecanoides georgicus)* and the common diving petrel *(P urinatrix)*, are difficult to tell apart, even in the hand, and most ornithologists do not even attempt to distinguish between the two species at sea.

Diving petrels are not seen at great distances from their breeding sites. South Georgians breed at South Georgia, and on islands in the South Indian Ocean and off New Zealand. Common diving petrels breed at a number of southern islands, from South Georgia to Tristan da Cunha and south of New Zealand. Nobody knows how many diving petrels there are, but their populations are estimated in the millions.

Both species are summer breeders. The birds breed in burrows in bare ground or in vegetated peat. Diet consists of planktonic crustaceans, such as krill, copepods and amphipods, as well as small fish and squid. Prey is caught underwater by pursuit-diving, the birds using their half-open wings to fly through the water like diminutive auks of the Northern Hemisphere.

As with practically all the burrowing petrels, introduced cats and rats have severely reduced some populations. Both species of diving petrel seem to be extinct at South Africa's Marion Island, for example, most likely due to predation by the now-extinct feral cat population.

Cormorants or Shags

There is yet no clear agreement on how many species of cormorants *(Phalacrocorax spp)* inhabit the southern islands and the Antarctic Peninsula – there could be as many as seven or as few as two, depending on what taxonomic levels the different populations are differentiated. All are reasonably similar.

K HANDASYDE

Imperial shag

Cormorants are inshore-feeding birds and will not normally be seen out of sight of land. Their presence besides a ship in the mist is a sure sign of approaching land, which must have been a comfort to the sailing vessels of the past. Breeding occurs on the Antarctic Peninsula, on all the subantarctic islands and on the islands south of New Zealand. Interestingly, the more northerly islands of Tristan da Cunha, Gough, St Paul and Amsterdam do not have resident cormorant populations.

Cormorants are summer breeders. Nests in colonies are made of seaweed and terrestrial vegetation on cliff tops and ledges directly above the sea. Up to three eggs are laid, and the young hatch naked, which is unique for a southern seabird. Diet is mainly of benthic fish, caught by deep and long dives from the sea surface.

The different populations do not seem to be under any threat, but some are so small (a few hundred pairs) that their conservation status needs monitoring. Development of new fisheries, for example, could have adverse effects.

Sheathbills

Sheathbills are odd birds in a number of ways. They are not seabirds (for example, their feet are not webbed) but are in their own family, allied to waders. They cannot be mistaken for anything else as they strut and squabble around penguin colonies. The greater, American, snowy or pink-faced sheathbill *(Chionis alba)* occurs at South Georgia, the South Shetlands, South Orkneys and on the Antarctic Peninsula. It migrates north to South America and the Falkland Islands

COLIN MONTEATH (HEDGEHOG HOUSE)

Sheathbills

in winter. Lesser or blackfaced sheathbills *(C minor)* are somewhat smaller, with noticeably shorter wings, and are strict residents of the four subantarctic island groups of the South Indian Ocean, each with its own subspecies.

Sheathbills make their nests in crevices in summer, often near penguin colonies, from where they scavenge widely on eggs, spilled food being fed to chicks, and carcasses killed by giant petrels. They also feed on intertidal life and on invertebrates in the peat.

At Marion Island, the lesser sheathbill population has decreased in the last two decades. This may be due to competition for terrestrial invertebrates with an increasing house mouse population, but research is needed to see if the species is at any real risk. Elsewhere, no conservation problems have been described.

Kelp Gull

The kelp, or Dominican gull *(Larus dominicanus)*, is the only gull of the Southern Ocean. Kelp gulls occur on the Antarctic Peninsula and at most subantarctic islands, where they are resident year round, generally in small numbers.

JEFF RUBIN

Kelp gulls & female elephant seals

Summer breeders, like most southern seabirds, kelp gulls lay up to three mottled eggs (usually two) in an open nest lined with vegetation. Chicks can leave the nest soon after hatching, but are still fed by their parents until after they can fly. Diet includes scavenging from giant petrel kills and in penguin colonies, terrestrial invertebrates such as earthworms and moth larvae and intertidal shellfish such as limpets.

No conservation problems are known for this species, which also breeds in southern Africa, Australasia and South America.

Terns

Several species of terns *(Sterna spp)* may be seen in the Southern Ocean. The Antarctic *(S vittata)* and Kerguelen *(S virgata)* terns are breeding residents of a number of southern islands, the former being more widespread and occurring on the Antarctic Peninsula as well. Away from land, terns seen at sea are most likely to be Arctic terns *(S paradisaea)*, which are migrants from the Northern Hemisphere. All three species are similarly sized, long-winged grey and white birds. Arctic

TUI DE ROY (HEDGEHOG HOUSE)

Tern

terns in nonbreeding plumage have dark bills. The two breeding species are red billed and have conspicuous black caps. Distinguishing Antarctic from Kerguelen terns, however, can confound even the experts at times. Kerguelen terns are probably resident on the few islands where they occur, whereas Antarctic terns migrate, several thousand of them reaching South African waters to spend the winter.

Antarctic and Kergeulen terns breed in summer, laying mottled eggs in open nests in loose colonies. Diet is mainly small fish caught at the surface or by shallow dives within sight of land, often within the kelp bed zone.

Skuas

Skuas are large, heavily built gull-like birds. South Polar skuas *(Catharacta maccormicki)* are smaller than subantarctic skuas *(C antarctica)* and have a paler plumage. Their flight is heavy with relatively little gliding and much flapping.

MARK NORMAN

Subantarctic skua

Subantarctic skuas breed on most of the southern islands, while South Polars occur on the Antarctic continent. On the Antarctic Peninsula, both species occur and hybrid pairs have been recorded. The South Polar skua has the distinction of being the world's most southerly bird: At least two have turned up at the South Pole. In winter, both species of skuas leave their breeding localities and spend time at sea, occasionally even reaching the Northern Hemisphere.

Both species breed in summer, generally laying two mottled eggs in open nests on the ground. Breeding birds are strictly territorial and will quickly chase off intruders.

Skuas number in the thousands and seem to be at no particular conservation risk, although it has been postulated that decreases in burrowing petrel numbers (important prey) could have led to declines in Subantarctic skua populations at islands with cats. This is hard to prove, due to the lack of pre-cat censuses. South Polar skuas prey upon penguins and other colonial seabirds but also feed at sea on Antarctic krill.

Fishes of the Southern Ocean

The Southern Ocean supports over 270 species of fish. Several are interesting because of their ability to survive in sub-zero waters without freezing: They actually have 'antifreeze' glycopeptides in their blood. Members of the family Channichthidae, the ice fishes, have no haemaglobin and are 'white-blooded,' such as the mackerel icefish *(Champsocephalus gunnari)*.

Some finfish are now the target of commercial fisheries. As a consequence of initially uncontrolled fishing, several species are now 'commercially extinct,' such as the marbled notothon *(Notothenia rossii)* and the mackerel icefish. Fisheries have targeted new species, which in turn have been over-exploited. Fortunately, CCAMLR now attempts to control the fisheries with a system of annual quotas and inspections. One of the most recent fisheries is long-lining for Patagonian toothfish *(Dissostichus eleganoides)*, which has caused some mortality to seabirds that become hooked as lines are set, especially in the vicinity of South Georgia and Iles Kerguelen. This problem has led to the adoption by CCAMLR of a number of measures (such as only setting lines in the hours of darkness) in an attempt to reduce such mortality.

Antarctic Krill

Antarctic krill (*Euphausia superba)* is a small six-cm long planktonic crustacean that occurs in what at times are enormous swarms south of the Antarctic Polar Front (or Antarctic Convergence). Krill is sifted out of the water by the baleen whales, but also eaten by many species of southern seabirds (especially penguins), squid, fish and the crabeater seal, which has specially adapted teeth for this purpose. Indeed, without krill the ecosystem of the Southern Ocean would no doubt collapse, leading to huge losses in predator populations. Antarctic krill (there is also a smaller species, the ice krill *E crystallarophias)* has been the target of a fishery for a number of years. Krill is difficult to process for human consumption. Catches peaked in the early 1980s at over half a million tons a summer season, but have subsequently dropped to much lower levels. Quotas are now set by CCAMLR, which also encourages research on krill and its predators.

Terrestrial Invertebrates

The subantarctic islands and the Antarctic continent are populated with very specialized terrestrial invertebrates. On the islands, the often strong winds make flight maladaptive (too risky to be blown out to sea), so some flies and moths have become flightless. On the continent, tiny free-living mites inhabit the exposed soil and somehow survive the extreme cold and also the dryness, since liquid water is at a premium.

Inadvertently introduced invertebrates can become a problem on the islands. Slugs, snails, earthworms, spiders and aphids have all arrived, some changing the ecosystem balance in subtle ways – as has the cabbage moth *(Plutella xylostella)*, which has attacked the Kerguelen cabbage on Marion Island.

On the Antarctic continent, which supports no native terrestrial vertebrate life at all, studies have concentrated on the microbiota: ciliates, rotifers, tardigrades (also charmingly called 'water bears') and free-living nematodes. Most of these need a microscope to be visible, but their unseen presence does bring life to the apparently sterile nunataks and mountains of the continent.

Terrestrial Plants

The terrestrial plants of the subantarctic islands and the Antarctic continent are very different. The high rainfall and long hours of summer light allow the islands to support an at-times lush vegetation, epitomized by tussock grassland, fertilized by thousands of burrowing petrels. The continent, in contrast, supports only mosses, lichens and algae, except for two flowering plants, one a grass *(Deschampsia antarctica)*, the other a cushion plant *(Colobanthus quitensis)*, that have a foothold on the comparatively milder Antarctic Peninsula. Interestingly, global warming leading to climate amelioration in the far south is given as a reason for the observed spread of this grass.

The true subantarctic islands have many vascular ('higher') plants, but no woody species, so native trees are absent. The more northerly cool temperate islands, such as Tristan da Cunha and Gough, do support a few native tree species. One of the most intriguing plants of the South Indian Ocean islands is the Kerguelen cabbage *(Pringlea antiscorbutica)*. As its scientific name suggests, it was used by shipwrecked 19th century sealers to ward off scurvy. The early accounts differed in their opinion of its tastiness (and how to cook it), but it can be imagined that necessity came first.

Marine Plants

The intertidal and subtidal areas of the southern islands support the giant kelps, such as *Durvillea antarctica*, which forms thick bands around many of the islands that protects their shores from rough seas. The kelp 'forests' offer an environment that supports fish, shellfish, octopus and crustaceans, which in turn are food for inshore-foraging birds such as cormorants and terns.

Kelps have a phenomenal rate of growth, constantly replacing fronds as they are worn away by the action of the waves. Some plants are broken free under stormy conditions and washed ashore, where they contribute to a new environment by fertilizing shore vegetation and providing soft 'beds' for resting elephant seals!

Other types of marine plants make up the phytoplankton, tiny single-celled plants, which are at the bottom of the open-ocean food chain. There are even ice algae, which stain pack ice pink or brown. Algal blooms can occur at sea, when the sheer density of phytoplankton colors the sea.

Environmental Issues

By Dr Maj De Poorter

Dr Maj De Poorter began working with Greenpeace in 1984, and has participated in five expeditions (three as leader) to Antarctica since 1986. She has also developed all of the group's environmental impact statements to date. She has attended Antarctic Treaty consultative meetings, meetings of the Convention of the Conservation of Antarctic Marine Living Resources (CCAMLR) and meetings of Scientific Committee for Antarctic Research (SCAR) groups as an NGO observer. She has also personally inspected more than 35 scientific bases throughout Antarctica. Dr De Poorter is a senior advisor to the Antarctic and Southern Ocean Coalition (ASOC) and to Greenpeace.

Antarctica is often called 'the last paradise on Earth.' That may be a clichéd description, but it's also a good one. Where else can snow glow with so much deep pink warmth? Where else can silence be so pervasive, accentuated only by a distant penguin squawk? Where else will a penguin be so curious as to waddle up to pick your shoelace, or a seal be so unafraid that it barely even lifts its head to look at you before snoozing on?

As in that other Paradise, it was the human species that brought discord. Antarctica has a history of human folly to rival that of human intrepidness and endeavor on the continent.

The contemporary era – with science as the main activity and governments as the main players – has also brought more modern and enlightened views about environmental protection, including an appreciation of Antarctica's intrinsic wilderness values. However, this modern outlook has not been reached without active pressure from the public.

In addition, modern technology has also brought with it new problems and new threats to the Antarctic environment – including fishing, tourism and the potential for deep-sea mining. Some of these developments await satisfactory solutions.

Antarctica is also impacted by human activities and pollution from other, often-distant parts of the globe. Radioactive fallout from atmospheric nuclear tests have been traced in snow cores, and birds and seals have been found to have pesticides and other man-made chemicals in their tissues. However, with the exception of the effects from global warming and the 'ozone hole,' which also have their root causes half a world away, this chapter will focus on impacts created in the Antarctic itself.

PAST HUMAN IMPACTS ON MARINE LIVING RESOURCES

Sealers were the first to follow the explorers – and in many cases they actually *preceded* them. For instance, the South Shetland Islands were discovered in 1819, and in the 1820-21 season, more than 50 British and American sealing vessels arrived, and their returns reportedly exceeded 42,000 skins. By 1823-24, the fur sealing was over, owing to virtual extinction of the populations. Imagine, for a moment, the present day fur seal colony at Bird Island, and then imagine the level of butchery it must have taken to wipe out such teeming life in a mere four summers. The sad pattern started with seals and then repeated itself with whales and finally fish.

The first Antarctic whaling station was established in 1904 by a Norwegian company, which took 195 whales in its first season. Another exploitation explosion followed: In 1912-13 there were six land stations, 21 factory ships and 62 catcher boats, killing and processing 10,760 whales; by 1930-31, the seasonal kill had increased to 40,000, and, with exception of the war years, it continued at this level for the next 20 years. Targeted species had to be switched as one after another they were driven into near oblivion. Of the large whales, only the minke whale is still abundant. The other species – including the humpback whales seen frolicking in the Gerlache Strait – have been reduced to a small percentage of their original number.

Next to be exploited, in the 1970s, were fish (finfish, as they are called, to distinguish them from shellfish): Commercially interesting species (Antarctic cods and ice fish) in the South Georgia area were 'vacuumed up' with great enthusiasm, mostly by the Soviet Union's fishing fleet. Commercial extinction followed from which these species have never recovered.

At the same time, world interest turned to krill, when it was postulated that millions of tons might be harvested each year, solving the world's famines. Unfortunately, the optimistic estimates of huge sustainable catches were based on a lack of knowledge. For example, the small-sized krill present in wintertime were not juveniles (which would have pointed towards high productivity) but adults, shrinking to reduce their need for food! Krill-fishing took off before this was discovered and krill would probably have been added to the infamous list of mismanagement, but for the natural restriction to its use for human consumption: Fluoride from the krill's carapace starts to move into the meat after the catch, making it unsuitable for human consumption unless it has been processed very quickly, which technologically is very difficult. The bulk of the 200,000 to 500,000 tons caught each year is therefore used as fertilizer or food for fish or cattle – quite an irony after the high hopes that it might solve the world's hunger problems!

PRESENT MANAGEMENT OF LIVING RESOURCES

Seals

The Agreed Measures (1964) protects seals on land and ice shelves, where they can only be killed for scientific purposes, provided a permit has been obtained. This will be superceded by one of the annexes of the Protocol on Environmental Protection, to the same effect. The Convention for the Conservation of Antarctic Seals (CCAS) extends protection to the sea as well as to sea ice and pack ice. It prohibits commercial culling of fur, elephant and Ross seals and establishes closed areas and closed seasons for the other species.

As recently as the 1986-87 season, a total of 4804 seals, mostly crabeaters, were killed by a Soviet expedition near the Balleny Islands. A certain amount of research was done on teeth from these catches, but environmental groups questioned what kind of 'science' could be the motivation for the kill. In reply, one of the Russians' official explanations was that many schools wanted to have a seal specimen for educational purposes. The fact that no significant catches have taken place since then could indeed be due to the mindboggling possibility that every school that wanted one now has its own stuffed seal. More likely, however, it is thanks to the large scars from orca or leopard seal attacks on many crabeater seals, which cause the crabeater skins to fall apart along these scars, making them commercially worthless. Talk about being saved by the enemy!

However, CCAS still contains catch limits for crabeater (175,000), leopard (12,000) and Weddell seals (5000). In theory, commercial sealing could occur at any time, but the public outcry it would generate makes this unlikely.

Whales

The International Whaling Commission (IWC) was established in 1946 to regulate the 'orderly development of the whaling industry' worldwide. It agreed to a moratorium on all commercial catches that came into force in 1986, but that agreement has come under pressure from whaling nations lately. Additionally, in May 1994 the IWC established the Southern Ocean Whaling Sanctuary, protecting the primary feeding grounds of the majority of great whales, and providing an opportunity for depleted species to recover. The sanctuary does not allow commercial whaling, even if the worldwide moratorium were to be lifted again. However, 'science' is used as a loophole, with Japan continuing to kill 300 to 400 minke whales a year in the Southern Ocean, calling it 'research,' even though the program has not been endorsed by the IWC Scientific Committee and the meat still ends up in restaurants.

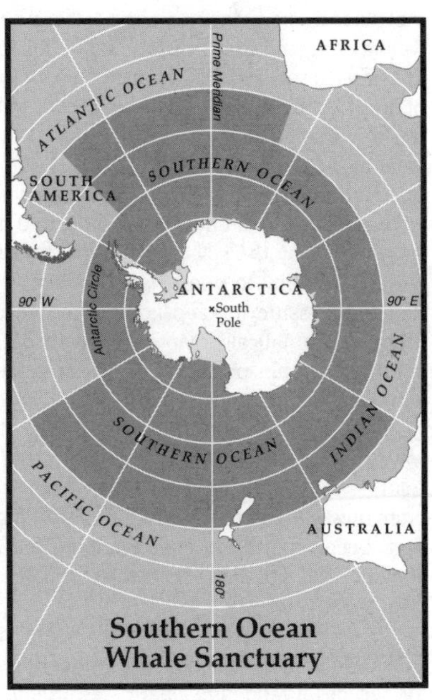

Southern Ocean Whale Sanctuary

Finfish, Krill & Squid

The Convention for the Conservation was brought into effect in April 1982. CCAMLR represented a major breakthrough in marine conservation because, instead of considering each species separately, decisions on harvesting have to take into account the effect on other species (eg, predators). Its area of application is the area south of the Antarctic Convergence, an area much larger than the Antarctic Treaty area, which makes more sense ecologically.

The principles of CCAMLR are: (1) prevention in decrease in the size of any harvested population to levels below those which ensure stable recruitment (a fisheries term meaning the new animals that are born each year); (2) maintenance of ecological relationships between harvested, dependent and related species, and the restoration of depleted species to the level at which recruitment is stable; (3) prevention of changes or minimization of the risks of changes in the marine ecosystem which are not potentially reversible over two or three decades. CCAMLR is one of the most ecologically enlightened international fisheries agreements to date.

Unfortunately, CCAMLR came too late to save many finfish species that had already gone into commercial extinction during the 1970s. Initially, too, CCAMLR could not make much headway towards establishing its innovative principles at all: consensus decision-making was used by fishing nations to block any regulations they didn't like. Moreover, the fishing nations tended not to provide sufficient fishing data, and then insisted that in the absence of such data, there was no scientific basis to set catch limits. Since then, however, the tide has turned and the burden of proof has been reversed: fishing tends to be limited unless there are scientific data to show that catches can be increased. Inspection and scientific observer schemes have also been put in place. This evolution has been due in part to the pressure of environmental non-governmental organizations (NGOs), in part to the increased environmental awareness worldwide, and, to be honest, it has been facilitated to a large extent by the collapse of the former Soviet Union. The change from a communist economy to one where the fleets had to pay market prices for fuel meant that the pressure to keep going after what had long been uneconomical catches dropped dramatically. Moreover, with détente, there was much less need for a Southern Ocean 'presence' of Soviet vessels (some of the fishing vessels bristled with an amazing array of unusual radio antennae).

However, at present, many issues of environmental concern remain unresolved by CCAMLR. Massive illegal catches of Patagonian toothfish in the South Georgia area (estimated to equal if not surpass the legal harvest), for example, dramatically increases the risk of overfishing. Mostly Chilean and Argentine vessels have been reported in contravention, but Russian and Korean ones have too. In addition, the situation has created a flare-up of political tension in this region of disputed sovereignty.

Another contemporary issue is the killing of albatrosses and petrels in the CCAMLR longline fisheries. The wandering albatross has been declining in numbers for decades. Wandering albatrosses, true to their name, roam the oceans, and birds banded at South Georgia have been killed as far away as the Brazilian fishing grounds. The birds drown after they get hooked on the longlines when diving for the bait on them. Most casualties occur outside the CCAMLR area, but birds also are killed by the South Georgia longline fleets. CCAMLR has acted to address this problem in its own area, for instance by requiring the use of streamers to scare birds off and by taking measures to ensure that the baited hooks sink faster. In addition,

CCAMLR has shifted the remaining mortality away from albatrosses by prohibiting longlining during daylight hours. However, as a result of this change, mortality has been shifted at least partially towards the more nocturnal petrels instead, which, environmentalists point out, is no solution.

MINERALS EXPLOITATION

Thoughout the 1980s, Antarctic Treaty nations held closed-door negotiations for an Antarctic Minerals regime. According to some, it would provide at least some protection when the 'inevitable' mining and minerals exploitation began. But to environmentalists, it meant that the wrong question was being asked: Rather than 'How should we mine?' they felt the question should be 'Should we touch Antarctic minerals at all?' Convinced that world opinion would answer that question with a resounding 'No,' the NGO community set out to make sure that the world at large knew about the negotiations and about the threat of mining to the environment, peace and science. Petitions were circulated (and millions of signatures collected) and secret documents from the governmental meetings were leaked and distributed. The public movement against the minerals exploitation in Antarctica built up and gained momentum. In spite of this, governments signed the Convention for the Regulation in 1988.

It was never ratified, though: the Exxon *Valdez* accident in Alaska, and the resulting images of oiled birds, sea otters and beaches on every night's TV news, followed in January 1989 by the sinking of the *Bahia Paraiso*, which spilled refined fuel in the Antarctic itself, brought home to decision makers what environmentalists had been stressing all along: accidents would happen and the results would be devastating. Shortly after, the Belgian Parliament, against its government's position, passed a national law prohibiting Belgian nationals from taking part in Antarctic minerals activities. Then, the French and the Australian governments decided not to ratify CRAMRA, stopping it from ever coming into force. The Protocol on Environmental Protection, including a ban on mining, was negotiated and signed instead. The ban will continue indefinitely; in 50 years' time, the criteria required to lift it become less stringent, but if no action is taken, the ban goes on. It is expected to come into force in 1997, a clear – and rare! – example of people power overturning government plans.

GLOBAL CHANGES AFFECTING ANTARCTICA

Possibly the most spectacular discoveries in Antarctica have been those regarding the global effects of pollution, and the dramatic and disastrous effects that may follow. The issues of ozone depletion and global climate change are of relevance to everyone (not to mention plants and animals).

Ozone Depletion

Since its discovery in 1985, the spring ozone 'hole' over the Antarctic continent has continued to grow. The stratospheric ozone depletion is caused by various human produced chemicals such as CFCs and halons, mostly created in the Northern Hemisphere, half a world away from the Antarctic. This depletion is significant because stratospheric ozone restricts the amount of ultraviolet-B radiation reaching the surface of the earth. The hole allows substantially higher levels of ultraviolet-B to reach the Antarctic continent and the waters of the Southern Ocean in spring and early summer, coinciding with the peak of biological activity in the region. These increased ultraviolet levels threaten the plankton at the base of the Antarctic marine ecosystem, upon which all life – from fish to seabirds, penguins, seals and great whales – ultimately depends. Antarctic research has shown that there is already a 6% to 12% reduction in marine primary productivity during the period of the 'hole,' and there are indications that the composition of planktonic communities may also be altered. In addition, Antarctic animals and the sparse terrestrial vegetation of the continent may be directly damaged by increased ultraviolet-B, or the even more worrying appearance of a band of shorter wavelength ultraviolet-C, which is by far the most damaging form of this radiation. Nobody knows yet to what degree Antarctic life can adapt to withstand this increasing stress.

Global Climate Change

The world's top climate scientists (members of the Intergovernmental Panel on Climate Change, or IPCC) suggest that global warming, resulting from the production of 'greenhouse gases' like carbon dioxide, will be greatest in the polar regions. Recent British data show a sustained atmospheric temperature increase of around 2.5°C since the 1940s in the Antarctic Peninsula region. This is 10 times faster than the global average warming over the last century.

Also consistent with the predictions of global climate change is the fact that vast areas of ice shelves have been rapidly disintegrating. In February 1995, an iceberg the size of Luxembourg calved off the Larsen Ice shelf in the Antarctic Peninsula, and at the same time, a large tongue of ice connecting the mainland with James Ross Island also disappeared, together with a section of the northern part of the Larsen Ice shelf. While the formation of icebergs is a regular occurrence in Antarctica, this iceberg was unusual in that it had not been foreseen and was accompanied by large scale disintegration of the ice shelf, including a 60-km long crack.

Some researchers suspect that winter sea ice is contracting, and this is postulated to result in fewer associated sea algae. The extent of sea ice is known to influence penguin breeding success, and contracting of the sea ice cover is postulated by some to have affected Adélie penguins in the Antarctic Peninsula area in a negative way.

To make matters worse, ozone depletion over the Antarctic might exacerbate climate change even further, by allowing greenhouse gases to persist longer in the troposphere, and by killing off plants and phytoplankton that remove carbon dioxide from the atmosphere. Disturbances caused by ozone depletion and/or global warming may therefore have major disruptive effects on the Southern Ocean ecosystems. The vast continent, set aside for its environmental and scientific value, can still be lost due to human disturbance!

What effect would the melting Antarctic ice have on the rest of the world? In 1990, the IPCC calculated that warming in Antarctica would actually reduce sea level rise because the increase in snowfall was expected to be bigger than the increase in melting. Now, scientific opinion has changed, and it is thought that Antarctica's ice sheet will contribute to sea level rise. A rise of 30 or 50 cm, for instance, would spell the disappearance of entire Polynesian island-states. An alarming possibility is that the additional loss of West Antarctica's ice sheet (grounded ice that is thought to be unstable) could contribute to a sea level rise of up to six meters.

ENVIRONMENTAL IMPACTS OF SCIENCE

There is no doubt that much Antarctic science is of global importance, while other subjects are more local in focus but nevertheless of intense interest. One does not have to be a scientist to be intrigued by polar summers with 24 hours of daylight, by ice cores several thousands of meters deep revealing the earth's past climate, by fish with anti-freezing agents in their blood, or by emperor penguins fasting for several months in winter, while incubating a single egg on their feet.

Most humans on the Antarctic continent and islands are involved in some scientific endeavor: research or related logistic operations. However, political motivations have always played a role in a nation's decision to establish scientific stations in Antarctica, from the seven nations with territorial claims and the US' establishment of a station at the South Pole itself (cleverly acquiring a presence in every claimed portion) to the rush of Antarctic scientific bases being established during the 1980s – coinciding with the negotiations for mineral exploitation. Scientific activity, genuine or pretended, gives a country Consultative Party status in the Antarctic Treaty System, putting it 'inside' the decision-making circle.

There has been criticism about the apparent lack of environmental awareness at scientific bases. This is not an argument to stop science, but to ensure that science – and all other Antarctic activities – is carried out in such a way that the ecological, wilderness and aesthetic values are protected, along with the continent's value for future science. A clean Antarctic has great scientific value; a contaminated one doesn't.

The bases and some field activities have undoubtedly had their share in creating negative environmental impacts. Hallett station, for example, was established in 1956-57 as a joint US and New Zealand station. The site chosen, on the edge of the Ross Sea, was in the middle of a penguin rookery. So, to make room for it, more than 6000 birds were 'relocated.' Penguins that tried to return to their former nesting site were kept out with barricades of fuel drums.

The US' McMurdo station on Ross Island installed a nuclear reactor in 1961. The reactor was shut down in 1972 and shipped back to the US – along with 101 large drums of earth made radioactive by 'normal discharge of effluent.' Later another 11,000 cubic meters of soil were removed, and the site, still visible as the 'bite' taken out of Observation Hill, was not released for unrestricted use again until May 1979. The seafloor offshore from McMurdo station holds one of the most extraordinary collections of inorganic rubbish, and toxic waste (including PCBs) pollutes its sediments.

Meanwhile, the Fildes Peninsula on King George Island, recommended as a Specially Protected Area (SPA) by the 1966 Antarctic Treaty Consultative Party meeting because of the biological value of its melt lakes, was largely turned into a construction site by both the USSR and Chile in 1968 and '69, respectively, when those two countries decided to build stations there. The area's protected status had to be abandoned because its biological value had already been diminished. China and Uruguay added bases later, within walking distance from each other, and the melt lakes have been used both for drinking water sources and, ironically, for rubbish tips. Today, only a very small Site of Special Scientific Interest (SSSI) remains protected on the Fildes Peninsula – and it protects fossils, not the lakes!

Other scientist-imposed damage on the Antarctic environment includes Argentina's Marambio station, which for decades threw thousands of empty, full or partially filled barrels containing fuel, chemical wastes and ordinary rubbish over a bank where they blanketed a vast slope to the sea, leaking into soil and streams. At Australia's Casey station, a visiting scientist in 1986 found that an SSSI had been partially bulldozed, and that cement from nearby construction was killing mosses and lichens. More famously, in 1982-83, France started the construction of a hardrock airstrip at its Dumont d'Urville station, thereby destroying the habitat of thousands of birds, including cape pigeons, snow petrels, Wilson's storm petrels and Adélie penguins, which, ironically, were named by French explorer (and station namesake) Jules-Sébastien-César Dumont d'Urville for his wife. Explosives used to construct the airstrip also killed many birds with rock shrapnel.

Even in the 1980s, many standard practices in the rest of the world had not yet caught up with Antarctica. Environmental impact assessments, for instance, were commonplace in many parts of the world, but not in Antarctica, the most pristine place on earth.

Waste disposal by open burning or by putting large pieces of discarded equipment on the sea ice until it melted would not have been acceptable at home in many Antarctic Treaty countries. 'So why in Antarctica?' NGOs asked. Military personnel, logistical restraints and financial considerations had probably all contributed to the situation in the past, but possibly one of the main reasons for the careless behavior was that there were no independent eyes and ears to see 'down there.'

In the 1980s that changed. Tourists on ships were the first independent visitors. They also were the first to comment: Abandoned Hallett station, for instance, was cleaned up after tourists complained about the mess. Then came expeditions by NGOs like Greenpeace, which took pictures, wrote reports, brought independent journalists, and generally poked their noses where no one had done so before. And the results showed. Station personnel, after initial suspiciousness, actually welcomed these environmental 'inspections' from Greenpeace, because it created pressure on the politicians at home to provide the bases with resources to operate in a more environmentally sound manner, something that the personnel on The Ice quite often had wanted to do, but had not been able to convince headquarters of the need.

What has been the result? Hallett station (which was abandoned after two decades) has been cleaned up, and the penguins have reclaimed their territory. McMurdo is now running in a much more environmentally acceptable way: They now recycle, return wastes to the US and no longer burn, incinerate or 'ice stage' rubbish (though NGOs still question the need for the base to be so big and point to the irreversible changes in landscape and soils). Bases on the Fildes Peninsula have emptied the lakes of rubbish (though it appears that some merely bulldozed the rubbish under soil and loose rock). They are also collecting and storing wastes for return to the country of origin. Marambio is not adding further drums to its hillside collection and is reportedly studying ways to clean up the old ones. The Australians had a big cleanup of their stations and old rubbish dumps and initiated stringent training of personnel. The French airstrip created so much controversy that 'mitigative measures' were put in place, at least preventing birds from being blown up during the dynamiting, and establishing artificial breeding burrows for petrels (which may or may not be successful – the jury is still out). In spite of widespread protest, the construction continued however, until January 1994, when a tidal wave caused by a calving iceberg resulted in such destruction that the use of the runway was abandoned after all (a case of natural justice, according to some).

In general, many government programs now have waste management programs, environmental awareness training for all staff, and environmental officers. They have cleaned up several old sites and abandoned buildings, and they have, in some cases, begun to make environmental audits of the impacts of their programs.

The major international change in attitude, though, was the abandonment of CRAMRA and the 1991 signing of the Protocol on Environmental Protection instead. The Protocol designates Antarctica a special conservation area, dedicated to peace and science. Its main principle (Article 3) states that the protection of the Antarctic environment and dependent and associated ecosystems, and the intrinsic values of Antarctica (including wilderness, aesthetic and scientific values) shall be fundamental considerations in the planning and conduct of all activities in the Antarctic Treaty Area. The Protocol also contains provisions on Environmental Impact Assessments (EIA), monitoring of environmental impacts, Protection of Flora and Fauna, Waste Disposal, Avoidance of Marine Pollution, and Protected Areas. Although the Protocol is not yet legally in force, all of the Antarctic Treaty Consultative Parties have pledged to abide by it just as though it were, and it is anticipated that by 1997 all of the Consultative Parties will have ratified it, so the Protocol will be legally binding.

While attitudes towards the environment have changed dramatically in the last decade, this does not mean that all the problems have been solved. Some of the further changes that the environmental community would like to see are: proper EIA procedures applied even more consistently to Antarctic activities; increased public participation in government and decision making on matters concerning the Antarctic environment (in some countries it still is nearly unheard of); increased environmental monitoring; development of management in such a way that cumulative impacts are dealt with; increased cooperation (both scientific and logistic), which would reduce the need for construction (The Netherlands showed the way by obtaining Consultative Party status, based on its research program, without having built its own Antarctic base); speedy negotiations for environmental financial liability; and further cleaning up of abandoned bases.

Also, changes are sought on a practical level: increased use of alternative energy (sun and wind); no disposal of raw or merely macerated sewage; and phasing out of incineration, with all wastes being returned to the country of origin.

While proper implementation will require adequate funding, environmentalists and scientists agree that these resources should be made available without cutting science budgets.

ENVIRONMENTAL IMPACTS OF TOURISM

Antarctica is an increasingly popular tourist destination. In fact, the number of tourists visiting the Antarctic each season greatly exceeds the number of scientists and support personnel on the continent. While the number of person-days is higher for scientists than tourists, the majority of tourist mainly visit areas of wildlife concentrations, which increases the risk for impacts. Large numbers of people making frequent visits to a few popular sites also increases the risk for cumulative impacts.

Some damage from tourism is obvious: Graffiti certainly does not benefit the historic relics on Deception Island, for instance. A more serious possibility is the introduction of alien (or non-native) organisms to Antarctica. Cockroaches and houseplants have been found on board tourist ships. On subantarctic islands especially, these species could create ecological havoc if they were to 'escape' into the environment. In East Antarctica's Larsemann Hills, non-native grasses have been found surviving after their inadvertent introduction by scientific personnel. Incidents of such accidental introduction are reported more and more frequently and are a growing concern.

An older example of environmental impact is Cape Royds, the southernmost Adélie penguin colony and home of Shackleton's Hut. Between 1956 and 1975, the number of penguins at Cape Royds declined sharply because of the steady flow of base personnel and VIPs and their accompanying helicopter traffic. The site was declared an SSSI, access to the actual breeding colony was restricted, and the penguin numbers have recovered.

On the other hand, recent results from a long-term study in the vicinity of the US' Palmer station in the Antarctic Peninsula region that compared changes in the population sizes of Adélie penguins at Torgerson Island (visited regularly) and Litchfield Island (a protected area) suggest that environmental variability rather than human disturbance had been the key factor in forcing changes in the penguin populations studied. However, one or two studies cannot – and should not – be extrapolated to other sites, other populations, other species or other local circumstances. Many more long-term, scientifically structured research programs are needed. In general, the absence of data does not equal the absence of deleterious effect. In other words, even if no damaging effect has been shown, it does not mean that there is no impact at all. It could simply mean that either the damage was not noticed, that only under specific circumstances is there no damage, or that not enough research has been done yet. Tourism in particular, with its many repeated visits to breeding colonies, carries with it many questions about its impact on populations.

We do know about specific cases in which human presence in the Antarctic has an impact. The classic example is a footprint in a moss bed, still visible a decade or two after it was made. Less obvious is the impact on 'invisible' wildlife, like the algae species living inside rocks or flora underneath snow that may get trampled, or the damage done to ancient geological formations simply by walking over them (in the Dry Valleys, for example). Animals, too, can be affected even when they do not show it in their behavior, or at least not in a way that humans can easily notice. German researchers, for instance, found that heart rates of incubating Adélie penguins increased markedly when they were approached by a human still 30m away, even though birds did not show any visible behavioral response.

Other effects of human presence can be very unexpected: The same German researchers found that a solitary human being, standing at a 20m distance from penguins 'commuting' on a well used 'pathway' to the sea, caused the birds to deviate from their path by 70m, even hours after the person had gone. In one case, the single observer caused an estimated 11,934 birds to deviate during 10 hours (resulting in an extra 835 penguin km walked). Not surprisingly, the disturbance from helicopters was even more pronounced.

Does it matter? The assumption has to be it does. Energy expenditure can be a crucial factor in breeding success, and whereas one disturbance may not matter, the combined effect of several disturbances could very well be detrimental.

This research concluded with a recommendation that nesting birds should not be approached closer than 30m unless absolutely necessary, that penguins walking between the colony and the sea should not be approached closer than 100m by humans on foot, that aircraft should use the same paths each time, and that very noisy aircraft (Puma helicopters, for instance) should not approach colonies closer than 1000m horizontally and 200m vertically.

In the past, Antarctic Treaty System (ATS) regulations included 'safe' distances to approach wildlife, but the 1991 Special Consultative Meeting decided to abandon these, because they were probably too liberal, and because it was very hard to reach agreement on what they should be. Where tour companies have rules about approaching wildlife, the recommended distances tend to be based on the former ATS regulations and allow far closer approaches than the distances suggested by the German research. Of course, the above study was only performed on one species (Adélies), and on a limited number of birds. But, who should carry the risk caused by our ignorance about the exact effects of human beings on wildlife? Should the risk be that animals are disturbed? Or that people may be unduly restricted and miss a particular photo opportunity? The precautionary approach demands the latter option.

One problem, very specific to the tourist industry, is the number of different operators involved, all with their own commercial interests to protect. However, if tourism is to continue, it will have to comply properly with the Protocol on Environmental Protection. As a start, under the Protocol all operators will have to make environmental impact assessments (EIAs) for planned activities (only a few do at present). Then, operators will have to produce joint EIAs, sitting down with each other, prior to each season, to work out how their activities are going to affect each other and the environment, and how to limit the combined impact. One shore visit by one vessel to a particular colony may have a negligible impact, but what about several ships a day, several days in row? In practice, this will almost certainly require limits on where to visit, and on the number of ships or people allowed into a particular region or site during a particular season.

Land-based tourism, including the building of hotels and hardrock airstrips, is opposed by all environmental NGOs, on the basis that the environmental impact cannot be justified. Some environmental groups are opposed to all tourism in Antarctica, but many environmental NGOs, including Greenpeace, the Worldwide Fund for Nature (WWF) and the Antarctic and Southern Ocean Coalition (ASOC) are not opposed to most ship-based, yacht-based or small adventure tourism groups per se, provided their environmental management is, as a minimum, in accordance with the Protocol. However, if joint EIA procedures, and adequate research on tourism's impacts, continue to remain the exception rather than the rule, it would not be surprising if environmental concerns focus increasingly on all commercial tourism as a problem activity. The tour industry's attitude towards the Antarctic environment will determine its fate.

YOUR OWN PRESENCE

Before undertaking a trip to the Antarctic, you should ask yourself: Would I be just as happy going somewhere else or watching a documentary? Or is visiting Antarctica truly a dream come true?

While you are on The Ice, there are further aspects to consider. As a minimum, stick to the guidelines that you are given by your operator – but don't hesitate to apply your own, more stringent rules, especially about approaching wildlife. Don't be afraid to speak up if there are aspects that you particularly like or dislike about the tour operator, ship or voyage, or about your fellow passengers' environmental attitude – *at the time, not later*. If you have comments, tell the captain, the expedition leader, the organizing company, IAATO, environmental watchdog organizations and your department or ministry of foreign affairs. Remember, your comments don't have to be limited to the tour you were on. If you feel positive or negative about anything else you witnessed, whether it was by commercial or government programs, tell people about it: Antarctica is still a remote place, and its native inhabitants cannot speak for themselves. You can – and must – do it for them.

Any human presence in the Antarctic has an environmental impact. Depending on the activity, the impact will be small or large, direct, secondary or cumulative. There are cases where the impact can be justified, and there are cases where it cannot. If you are visiting Antarctica, you have a responsibility to treat this subject seriously.

Antarctic Science

by Dr David Walton

Dr David Walton first became interested in the Antarctic while a teenager. After a first degree in botany from Edinburgh University, he began work in 1967 with the British Antarctic Survey, studying subantarctic plants. He still works for BAS and is now responsible for all terrestrial and freshwater research as well as the conservation and environmental management done by the UK in the Antarctic. Dr Walton also chairs the international Antarctic scientific committee on environmental affairs and conservation and represents the interests of Antarctic science at Antarctic Treaty Meetings. He is the author of more than 80 scientific papers, the editor of several books and the editor in chief of the international journal *Antarctic Science*.

INTRODUCTION

From Exploration to Science

Capt James Cook, a veteran explorer and world tourist with a vengeance, was not impressed by Antarctica in 1775. He had been looking for a fabled continent rich in resources that he could claim as an ideal extension to the British Empire. Instead, he found foul weather and endless ice. Cook, who qualified his failure to reach the continent of Antarctica by stating that the world would not 'be profited' by the discovery, would have been suprised to see, 220 years later, just how important Antarctica has become for science. But how could he have known about the importance of the Antarctic ice sheet to world climate and sea level, the special features of the high atmosphere that produce the southern lights, the remarkable food chains in the Southern Ocean, or the key role played by Antarctica in the origin of all the southern continents?

Antarctica is no longer an unknown wasteland of little value or concern. During the 20th century – particularly in the last 40 years – Antarctica has come to play a central role in many scientific disciplines. Coordinated international scientific projects stem from the International Geophysical Year (IGY) in 1957-58. The original 12 countries from the IGY have welcomed 14 additional countries to Antarctic research, developing a web of ever more complex international programs and logistics.

Why Do Science in Antarctica?

Antarctic science is expensive science. All of it is supported by government funding that could easily be spent on other things. So why do science in Antarctica? The answer is slightly different for each discipline, but all have three principles in common: Only undertake the kind of science in Antarctica that cannot be done elsewhere in the world; only undertake the highest quality science; and if possible make sure it contributes to solving a global problem. Despite the remoteness of Antarctica, some of the research is immediately relevant to the more populated areas of the world. The most obvious example is the study of the increase in ultraviolet radiation – but there are others, such as world sea level and satellite communications.

The breadth of science in Antarctica has steadily expanded. Starting with meteorology over 50 years ago, there has been a steady growth of interests to include virtually all areas of science. Research now covers topics ranging from the physiology of fish to the effects of the sun on the atmosphere, from the origin of the continental rocks to the food of penguins, from the pollution record in deep ice cores to the growth of aquatic mosses in ice-covered lakes, from the melting of the ice cap to the psychology of small groups living in the Antarctic winter.

Two important features for all science in Antarctica are (1) that the research findings are freely available to everyone and (2) that many of the projects are internationally coordinated and supported. This coordination has been organized since 1957 through a non-governmental scientific body, the Scientific Committee for Antarctic Research (SCAR). Each year, every country active in Antarctic science makes a report on its projects to SCAR, and every two years SCAR organizes a two-week international meeting to report on progress and plan for the future. Such a strong commitment to international cooperation is the true measure of the practical implementation of the Antarctic Treaty in 'a continent for science.'

The extent and quality of science undertaken by any nation in Antarctica depends not only on the excellence of the scientists themselves but also on the logistic facilities provided. The largest investment has been made by the United States, in research facilities at McMurdo, Palmer and the South Pole. In many fields, state-of-the-art science can now be carried out in Antarctica. For example, the quality of the laboratory facilities and technical support in the Crary Laboratory at McMurdo means that scientists can conduct molecular biology investigations there in the same way they would in a university laboratory in the US. The installation of research aquaria at McMurdo, Palmer, Jubany, Rothera and Terra Nova Bay stations has been as important to marine biologists as the expansion of automatic weather stations on the polar plateau has been to climatologists. On most stations there is the combination of routine, universal observations that contribute to world databases, along with specific Antarctic research, which uses the unique characteristics of Antarctica to answer questions about the continent itself.

When visiting scientific stations or field camps in Antarctica, you will only be able to gain a glimpse of the complex facilities required to support modern science. Many of the most exciting developments are too remote to be easily accessible to tourists, yet you should see and hear enough from those scientists that you do meet to capture something of the excitement and importance of Antarctic science.

LIVING ON A SCIENTIFIC STATION

There is a wide range of sophistication among the various stations. Some are little more than storage containers or primitive huts, providing only the most basic protection for short visits. Others are the height of modern convenience, with private rooms, showers and a range of sports facilities. Some have email facilities available to all, while others have limited communications. Each one in its own way reflects the culture of the nation that established it – visiting Antarctic research stations is seeing a distillation of national characteristics!

Many of the scientists and support staff are there only for the summer, or part of it. They come from a wide range of backgrounds, but there are major differences in the way each country organizes its programs. The UK, Germany, Russia and Japan all have major polar research institutes that provide most of the scientists and the support staff. Other countries such as the US, Italy, New Zealand, Sweden, Argentina, Chile and Brazil draw most of their scientists from universities, and contract the support systems either from civilian or military operators. Australia and Norway have a hybrid system, with a research institute that runs the logistics and provides a limited number of scientists, while the remainder come from universities. Two countries, the Netherlands and Belgium, possess neither stations nor ships, but instead buy places for their scientists on the expeditions organized by other countries.

While some scientists using the airlink to McMurdo or Rothera spend as little as a month in Antarctica, personnel at British and Russian stations may spend up to 2½ years there without a break. Wintering in a small community, completely cut off from the rest of the world, is a profound experience for many people and often produces life-long friendships.

For a long time, Antarctic stations were seen as a male preserve, a historical hangover from the days of Amundsen, Scott and Byrd. All that has changed, with women assuming increasingly important roles at all levels in the organization of stations, including base commander and the leadership of scientfic teams. Most stations are still predominantly staffed by men, especially where the support staff are supplied by the military, but women have comprised nearly half the population of McMurdo in recent years.

For those who are in Antarctica for a long period, especially over winter, a variety of activities occupies their time. Quite apart from the work programs, there are opportunities to develop hobbies, learn new skills (have you ever wanted to operate a radio or overhaul a generator?), and learn to ski and travel over snow. Midwinter is a special occasion for all overwintering staff, when social life and parties take precedence over work. The sun is below the horizon and the stations

Field camp lodging – these prefab huts are known as 'apples.'

have been cut off from the rest of the world for months. Some stations even continue the tradition started by Scott and Shackleton of preparing a Midwinter book, with poems, paintings and photographs contributed by the station members.

For many, going to Antarctica is an opportunity to visit what is perhaps the least disturbed part of the world, to take part in their own adventure, to go where few have gone before. For others, it is the interest in the science, the unique features of Antarctica and its surrounding seas that make for special scientific opportunities. And for some, it is probably the extra pay that they get while in Antarctica. Regardless of their reasons, they all experience the same magic of Antarctica that draws you.

THE SOUTHERN OCEAN

The stormy waters of the Southern Ocean encircle Antarctica in a continuous ring of mainly eastward-flowing water. This water comprises 10% of the world's oceans; as well as connecting the Atlantic, Pacific and Indian Oceans, it also isolates the continent from warmer waters. The Antarctic Circumpolar Current is an enormously powerful force with an average rate of flow four times greater than that of the Gulf Stream. Where it flows through the constricted area of the Drake Passage, between the tip of South America and the Antarctic Peninsula, the current is especially strong.

The region where the cold Antarctic water meets with the warmer waters of the northern oceans is called the Polar Front. This zone has moved back and forth as world climate has changed, and marine sediments around some of the subantarctic islands provide information about these historical changes. At present, one of our major interests in the Southern Ocean arises from its influence on global climate.

The seas south of the Polar Front contain the coldest and densest water in the world. This water, called Antarctic Bottom Water, is formed as seawater sinks to the ocean floor when ice shelves melt. It then moves northwards along the ocean floor and up into the Northern Hemisphere, where it both reduces the temperature of these seas to less than 2°C and adds oxygen. This cooling effect on tropical and temperate seas is a very important feature of the heat balance of the world, and the pattern and strength of these north-flowing bottom currents is the subject of considerable research. Several countries have put current meters on the sea floor around Antarctica to provide data on these deep water movements. This is part of a major international program called the World Ocean Current Experiment (WOCE), which is attempting to measure current patterns for all the world oceans in order to improve the existing computer models that provide key information for predicting climate change. It is even possible to collect samples of deep water from the northern oceans and, by analyzing their salt content, trace their origin back to Antarctica.

Within the circumpolar current moving eastwards, there are other smaller but important water movements. Especially important for biologists is the East Wind Drift, a current flowing westwards close to the continent. It mixes with the water coming out of the Weddell Sea and flows north to mix with the larger circumpolar current in the Scotia Sea. It is this tremendous mixing of water types and the disruption to water flow caused by the islands in the Scotia Sea that makes it such an awful place for poor sailors but a fascinating place for marine scientists!

In the late 19th century, oceanographers realized that tides were different in different oceans. While it was relatively easy to measure tides in temperate and tropical waters, it has always been more difficult in icy waters because the ice destroys the gauges. However, there is now a network of robust gauges installed at various Antarctic stations, often reporting its data via satellite. This provides useful information on how the world ocean level is changing, which is of great interest to those living in coastal communities all over the world. We know that there are three circumstances that would result in sea level changes: expansion of the volume of the world's oceans as they warm up; melting of valley glaciers; and changes in Antarctica and Greenland icesheets. Existing data already suggest that the mean world sea level has risen by 10 cm in the last hundred years. In this period, the Antarctic ice sheet is believed to have remained roughly stable. Sea level looks as though it will go on rising at one or two millimeters per year without any extra contribution from the Antarctic. Any minor melting of the Antarctic ice cap will significantly affect the rate of rise, with potentially disastrous results for some communities.

ANTARCTIC MARINE LIFE

The most impressive aspects of Antarctica are the scenery and the wildlife. As you sail south through the Polar Front, where the cold Antarctic water wells up to meet the warmer temperate waters, you may sail through the fog banks into a world dominated by sea and ice. Albatross and petrels wheel around the ship, whales and seals surface alongside, and sometimes vast patches of pink krill stain the sea. The waters of the Southern Ocean might be too cold for humans, but the low temperature allows more oxygen to dissolve in the sea, which is very advantageous for marine life. This, together with the upwelling of deep currents which bring nutrients up from the sea bed to feed the microscopic algae at the surface, is the key feature of all life in the Southern Ocean.

In this marine food chain, the microscopic green algae (plankton) provide the food for the krill, while they in turn are eaten by fish, whales, seals and birds. There are some other diet preferences – for example, leopard seals eat penguins, sperm whales eat squid, and seals eat fish – but despite this, the food web remains remarkably simple when compared with other oceans.

For a biologist, there are many fascinating problems in Antarctica. On land, there are relatively few species of plants, and almost all of them are mosses, lichens or algae. In the sea, on the other hand, there is a tremendous diversity of organisms living on the seabed (benthic species), but a limited and very closely interrelated range of fish living in the water column (pelagic species). There are relatively few species of birds, but some species, such as Adélie penguins, are tremendously abundant. Many of the birds are very long-lived, some have unusual breeding patterns, while the penguins have turned flightlessness into a way of life. There is a great deal of research being carried out on seals, birds and terrestrial plants, but the major part of current research is devoted to the marine ecosystem. To undertake such research requires expensive infrastructure: icebreaking research vessels, scuba-diving facilities, as well as laboratories at research stations and access to satellite data. Not all countries can afford this, which has helped to promote international research cruises, like those successfully undertaken by the German vessel *Polarstern*, in which the costs of research are shared among several countries.

The importance of being able to work anywhere in the Southern Ocean has prompted several countries to make huge investments in modern research vessels capable of operating in heavy ice. Some examples that you might see around the Antarctic include the US's *Nathaniel B Palmer*, Britain's *James Clark Ross*, Australia's *Aurora Australis*, Germany's *Polarstern*, Japan's *Shirase* and Russia's *Akademik Federov*.

Warmblooded Animals

Birds Antarctic birds are spectacular – in size, numbers and habits. Many are very tame, making them accessible subjects for scientific research. Their total dependence on the sea for food, the bizarre breeding habits of some species, and their unusual ecological adaptations are of great interest to ornithologists. Research on Antarctic penguins was begun on Scott's first expedition, which studied the breeding habits and behavior of the Adélie and emperor penguins. Among the birds, penguins have remained the favorite research group, and as a result we probably know more about the Adélie penguin than about many of the birds in temperate latitudes. The other group of particular interest are the albatrosses. These are long-lived birds nesting on the subantarctic islands rather than the continent.

The initial requirements for researching penguins and albatrosses are to record their breeding behavior, rates of growth and diet. All the species return to the same nesting sites each year, so it is easy to mark individual birds with numbered leg rings when they are chicks and follow them through their life. Analysis of stomach contents of adults when they return to feed their chicks soon gave information on diet, while daily weighing of the chicks with a spring balance provided chick growth rates. More complex questions were soon framed: Where were the adults getting the food, when did they find it, how much energy did they use searching for it?

Since the adult birds spend most of their lives away from land, their activities cannot be directly observed. Modern technology, however, has supplied the answer with new electronic devices that can be attached to the birds. Now a tiny satellite transmitter on the bird's back can report on its position, while a small tube on its leg collects data on the depth and timing of its dives for food. Modern advances in electronics mean that even the oxygen consumption required for swimming or flying can now be measured automatically. Back at the colony, the chick sits on an electronic replica nest, which weighs it automatically every 10 minutes, avoiding the disturbance of the bird that manual weighing used to produce. From this data, the weight of each meal and the growth of the chick can be calculated very accurately. The latest nests are so sensitive that they even detect rain by the increase in the chick's weight!

The increasing numbers of banded birds has allowed the calculation of when birds first breed and the success of individuals in raising chicks, and the identification of the origin of birds found dead. Annual monitoring of the breeding success of penguins is undertaken at a number of sites around the Antarctic as a check on the effects of fishing on the marine ecosystem; the assumption is that if too many fish or krill are caught, there will not be enough to feed the chicks. This monitoring program is a key contribution to the work of the Convention for the Conservation, and it relies on imput from many countries, including Chile, the US, the UK and Argentina. It is the job of CCAMLR to set the levels of the fish catches for the Southern Ocean and to make sure that the size of these catches does not damage the populations of birds and seals.

Seals Of the 31 species of seals, six are found in the Antarctic, with another three species on the subantarctic islands. Only the fur seal and the elephant seal have been commercially exploited. There is probably no other group of animals that has attracted such a wide and detailed range of national and international legislation. Even in the Antarctic, there is a special Convention for the Conservation of Antarctic Seals, and two species – the fur seal and the Ross seal – are the only animals given special protection under the Antarctic Treaty. Such large animals at the top of the marine food chain pose some exciting research questions. While the original impetus for research came from a need to control exploitation, the emphasis has now changed to establishing seals' role in the food chain and understanding their life cycle for conservation purposes.

Recent research has largely focused on elephant, fur and Weddell seals, but there is increasing interest in crabeater seals, probably the most numerous seals in the world. Elephant seals spend most of their lives at sea. While their mating behavior on land has been well described, until recently we knew nothing of their lives at sea. Again, the use of satellite transmitters and other electronic equipment has provided remarkable data. Tracking elephant seals from South Georgia has shown that they may swim far south to the Antarctic Peninsula, following underwater canyons. While at sea, they spend almost 90% of the time submerged, making dives of 15 to 45 minutes' duration, with one exceptional dive being recorded as lasting two hours. These dives usually take them to depths of 25m to 450m, but some animals frequently dive to more than 975m. How seals manage this is the subject of considerable physiological research at present, mainly by British scientists at South Georgia and American scientists (working on Weddell seals) at McMurdo.

Rather more difficult to determine is the diet of each seal. The latest research is concentrating on analyzing the feces to identify prey from hard parts such as fish bones, which pass through the gut, or by using unique biochemical marker compounds associated with particular prey types. There are long-term studies on seal populations by British, US, Australian and French scientists to determine if the populations are increasing or declining. For those species that breed on land, the numbers of pups can be counted, and for some studies individual animals are marked with flipper tags. For those like crabeaters that breed on ice, even pup-counting is difficult. If there really are 16 million crabeater seals in the Antarctic, how can they be counted accurately? Efforts continue, using helicopters and icebreakers to allow scientists to get into the pack ice when the maximum number of animals are likely to be visible.

The application of the latest techniques in molecular biology now extends to the Antarctic. To be certain how large each breeding population is, it is necessary to analyze the animals' DNA. This fingerprinting of individuals is now being taken even further to see if it is possible to determine reproductive success for those species that mate on ice or in the water.

Sampling the blubber and milk of seals has shown a slow but steady accumulation of pesticides and other organic poisons, toxic compounds transported south from the industries and agriculture of the Northern Hemisphere. As yet, we do not know what the longterm effects of these will be on seals.

Whales The most productive research period on whales coincided with commercial whaling, and the data collected was used by the International Whaling Commission to set quotas. Since commercial whaling was banned, almost all whale research in the Antarctic has ceased. While there are still occasional attempts to survey areas in order to estimate population numbers, whale research is undertaken at present in more congenial areas such as Baja California. The Japanese and the Norwegians are still able to take a few small whales, usually minkes, each year under a rule that allows limited collection for scientific purposes, although many countries object to this.

Coldblooded Animals

Fish The first fish from Antarctica were collected in 1840 during Sir James Clark Ross' expedition. Since then, a great deal of research has been undertaken to establish both the diversity, the life histories and the extent of the fish stocks. There has been an active fishery in the Southern Ocean since the Soviet Union began fishing there in the mid-1960s. The fishery is now the subject of international regulation by the Convention for the Conservation of Antarctic Marine Living Resources (CCAMLR). In order to provide the management of the fishery, continuing research is required.

About 200 species of fish have been recorded south of the Polar Front. The main deep water species are not restricted to the Antarctic, whereas the coastal species are. Although this latter group has representatives from 15 families, over 60% of the species and over 90% of the individuals belong to just four families. This makes Antarctic fish very different from those of other oceans.

Most of the research, not suprisingly, has concentrated on the two most abundant groups: the Antarctic cod (Nototheniidae) and the ice fish (Channichthyidae). Initial interest focused on the evolution of the groups, their ability to survive in icy waters, their reproduction and growth rates and their population age structure. These last areas of research also interested commercial fisherman, who would like to learn how to find the fish and catch them efficiently.

The studies on Antarctic fishes' freezing resistance have been pioneered largely by American scientists, who have shown that the fish blood contains protein-based antifreezes that prevent ice crystals from forming within their tissues. This reaction is one of great commercial interest, relating to the way in which freezing changes the texture of food – ice cream manufacturers have taken particular notice.

Other scientists from France, Italy, New Zealand and the US have been interested in the physiology of the ice fish. These fish have no hemoglobin in their blood to carry oxygen, so scientists have tried to learn what mechanisms have evolved to take its place. We now know that the oxygen is carried in the blood plasma, but this has only 10% of the carrying capacity of normal (hemoglobin-containing) fish blood. The ice fish, however, have several adapatations to make up for this: They have more blood, a larger heart, larger blood vessels and more gill surface area, and they can even exchange oxygen through their tails.

All Antarctic fish grow slowly, with most coastal species taking five to seven years before they can breed. This is of great importance when deciding how many fish can be caught. Unfortunately, when fishing started in the Southern Ocean, this was not recognized and too many fish were caught, endangering the survival of some species. Current research is concerned with making more accurate estimates of growth and the size of populations, while in some of the less well-researched species, more fundamental work is being done on diet and reproduction.

Squid Little is known about the biology of most species of squid. They can move very quickly in the water, and with their excellent vision they are difficult to catch. Much of our knowledge has come from squid found inside the stomachs of fish, birds, seals and whales. Now there are several research projects at present attempting to collect basic data on the most common species by fishing for them. Subjects of particular importance are when and where squid breed, what they eat, and how many there are of each species.

Squid seem to be able to grow much faster than Antarctic fish and vary greatly in their adult size, measuring from only an inch long to as long as 20m (encounters with giant squid feature in some of the early accounts of whaling). Birds like wandering albatrosses and emperor penguins eat the smaller squid, while the larger ones have been found inside seals and whales. Most squid appear to be cannibals. They have several defense mechanisms, the best known being the black 'ink' squirted out to blind or confuse predators.

In some countries, squid are a highly prized food. They have become another commercially important group in the Southern Ocean fisheries, with many fishing boats coming from Japan and Taiwan. Unfortunately, many squid species have only a one-year life cycle, making them sensitive to overfishing. Although most of the studies so far have been on the squid stocks around the Falkland Islands, there is every reason to suppose that there are significant quantities of squid further south. As yet, however, there is too little data to ascertain this.

Krill The tiny animals in the sea that graze on the phytoplankton are called zooplankton. In Antarctic waters, the zooplankton is dominated by one group of pink-colored shrimp – *Euphausia* – which are called by the Norwegian name krill. Krill occur in swarms that are often dense enough to color the sea. You may also find them washed up on beaches as a pink tide. They are the single most important food source in the Southern Ocean for whales, seals and birds (especially penguins).

There are literally hundreds of research papers reporting on every aspect of the life cycle and biology of krill. Many of these are concerned with how to find krill, how to estimate the size of a krill swarm using acoustics, and how best to process krill for various uses. Though relatively easy to catch once the swarm has been identified, krill have proved to be costly to process and difficult to market. It is essential to catch them in small amounts to stop them from being crushed; this requirement greatly increases the fishery costs. Krill also possess some of the most powerful protein-digesting enzymes ever found, which means that they must be processed very rapidly or their tissues begin to break down, turning black and mushy. They become unfit for human consumption after three hours on the deck and unfit for cattle feed after 10 hours. At an early stage, it was also discovered that krill possess high levels of fluorine in their outer shell, making them toxic for humans and animals unless the shell is completely removed. The Russians and the Japanese, who dominate this type of fishing, have perfected equipment for peeling krill and then rapidly processing it so that frozen blocks of krill meat can be produced for human consumption or for krill paste as a high-protein additive for pig or cattle feed. At present, up to 400,000 tons are caught commercially each year, mostly in the South Atlantic. The original estimates of the available stock of krill were very large, and some hoped it would provide a cheap, protein-rich food for the world's famine-plagued regions. The catching and processing costs have made krill a First World rather than a Third World food.

While krill haven't solved world hunger problems, the interest in krill research continues unabated, and there are ongoing research projects from South Africa, Australia, the US, the UK, Chile, Korea, Brazil and Germany. We still need to know more about krill populations within the pack ice in winter, how much of the Southern Ocean algae is eaten by krill, how long krill live (they are difficult to age) and how much krill there actually is in the entire Southern Ocean. Even krill behavior is inadequately described, although there has been some success recently using video cameras powered off the side of a ship into the middle of a krill swarm. Slowly but surely, we are unravelling the complex role that krill plays in the various parts of the Southern Ocean.

Algae The productivity of all Antarctic ecosystems rests on the photosynthesis of the microscopic algae (phytoplankton) floating in the upper layers of the Southern Ocean. The upwelling of cold, nutrient-rich water provides ideal conditions for the growth of these planktonic species. Over 100 species of algae make up the major part of the phytoplankton, whose role is to provide grazing for the animals in the food chain.

When a ship is breaking its way through sea ice, the floes often turn over and show brownish bands or discoloration underneath. This is a film of ice algae, grazed during the winter by krill, and a major part of the annual productivity of the ocean.

The phytoplankton contain chlorophyll, which can be detected by satellite instruments. Recent research, using satellite data on chlorophyll to map the distribution and density of phytoplankton around Antarctica during the summer, shows that the highest concentration of phytoplankton coincide with high concentrations of nutrients, especially iron. The phytoplankton takes up carbon from carbon dioxide dissolved in the water, and, when it dies, takes the carbon down into the sediments. It can therefore be seen as a 'sink' for carbon. Given the present interest in the role of increasing levels of carbon dioxide in global warming, this has prompted considerable research on how much carbon can be taken out of the atmosphere by the phytoplankton and what, if anything, can be done to increase the rate. Some scientists have even suggested that iron is in such short supply that we should consider stimulating carbon uptake by dumping iron in the ocean. So far, experiments have not demonstrated that this would work.

Of equal concern for global warming is the relationship between phytoplankton and a compound called dimethyl sulphide (DMS). This compound is believed to form aerosols when it leaves the sea, and these aerosol droplets promote cloud formation. The subsequent increase in cloudiness increases the amount of radiation reflected back into space and this in turn leads to atmospheric cooling. This mechanism would therefore act to slow down global warming produced by increased greenhouse gas concentrations. As yet, we know too little about the whole DMS cycle, but what we do know suggests that the Southern Ocean may play a very important role in DMS production.

The increase in springtime ultraviolet levels has stimulated continued research on its effects on phytoplankton. Analysis by Australians of historical data from sediments suggests that there has been no significant change, yet experimental studies by Americans have shown that some species are very sensitive to ultraviolet and that diatoms in particular are able to protect themselves by making protective pigments.

The inshore areas of Antarctica have a good covering of seaweeds (macroalgae), below the level at which the scouring effects of winter ice would remove them. Suprisingly little research has been undertaken on these species, with most of the recent work being done by Dutch and German scientists. Even less data is available about the giant kelp, a seaweed found around the bays of the subantarctic islands and the Falkland Islands. The large brown strap-like fronds of the biggest kelp, *Macrocystis pyrifera*, is known to grow at a rate of 30cm per day during the summer, despite the low temperature of the water.

Seafloor communities The seafloor in the Antarctic is rich in plants and animals as diverse and exciting in its way as a tropical coral reef, but still little known. These communities are called the benthos, and they comprise the true indigenous flora and fauna of the continent, formed of animals and plants that have adapted to life in a cold ocean over tens of millions of years.

While the major studies of the sea floor have been undertaken from ships, an important part of the research is conducted from a limited number of shore stations equipped with aquaria and diving facilities. The principal efforts in this area are being made by US scientists at Palmer and McMurdo, German and Argentine scientists at Jubany, British scientists previously at Signy and now at Rothera, Italian scientists at Terra Nova Bay, together with ship-based contributions from China and Spain.

There is still a great deal to learn about the benthos, but we already know that it is rich in species, many of which are limited to the cold waters south of the Antarctic Convergence (Polar Front). Almost every time a deep-sea sample is brought up, it includes some species new to science, or one that has been collected only a single time before. Our knowledge of the deep oceans everywhere is limited and the seas around Antarctica are no exception.

The annual formation of sea ice has a strong effect on much of the benthos, whose food supply consists mainly of algal cells falling to the bottom as they die. In winter, there are no algae, only ice at the surface, so the organisms must learn to live for long periods with little food or to use a much wider range of foods than that used by benthos in other oceans. Not suprisingly, this means that they grow slowly and usually reproduce slowly.

Current research experiments increasingly take place on board ships or in controlled aquaria at stations to study life cycles of individual species, while video cameras and diving observations are providing details of the structure of the communities on both rocky and muddy bottoms. The greatest potential for research probably lies in studies of the benthos' biochemistry and physiology. Some species, such as sponges, may possess the same sorts of anti-microbial defense chemicals that warm-water sponges have been shown to possess, which may be of pharmaceutical interest. A better understanding of all these fields might also help us to deal with the effects of pollution on benthos.

ANTARCTIC TERRESTRIAL LIFE

Plants & Microbes

With only 0.5% of Antarctica free of permanent snow and ice, there is not a very large area for plant communities. In addition, any new species spreading to Antarctica has not only to cross the Southern Ocean but to hit one of the snow-free patches in order to have any chance of surviving. Under these circumstances, it is quite surprising that Antarctica is home to at least 200 species of lichens, over 100 species of mosses and liverworts, more than 30 species of macrofungi, two species of flowering plants and many species of algae. The relationships between these plants and those on the surrounding continents have interested botanists for almost 150 years, and it is only now, after a great deal of specimen-collecting and detailed taxonomic study, that the relationships are finally becoming clear. Within the next few years, definitive guides to both lichen and mosses will be published, based on work by Norwegian, Polish and British botanists. These will not only show the distribution of species in and around the Antarctic, but will also provide some data on whether all the species spread to the continent after the last glaciation or whether some survived on isolated mountain peaks. Meanwhile, there is continuing research by Australia, New Zealand, the Netherlands, Germany, Spain and Britain on how these lichens and mosses survive the extreme cold and desiccation of the Antarctic winter.

Research over a period of more than 20 years by American scientists has unravelled the details of one of the most unusual plant habitats on Earth. In areas formed from large-grained sandstone rock, most obviously in Victoria Land, the outer skin of the rocks has been colonized by plants. These plants live within the rock, growing between the sand grains and forming separate layers of algae, fungus and lichen. Acids excreted by the plants eventually dissolve the rock and the outer skin breaks off, leaving an obvious dark mark where the algal cells remain. Just enough light penetrates the rock for photosynthesis to occur for a short period each year when melt water is available. The rate of growth of these plants is so slow that it is estimated that some of them must be many thousands of years old.

In some areas, especially around the Antarctic Peninsula, it is possible to see very large specimens of lichens and even banks of moss over a meter deep. Because they grow quite slowly, some of the lichens have been estimated to be more than 500 years old, while radiocarbon dates show the base of the large moss banks to be

over 5000 years old. Both are extremely vulnerable to disturbance.

Antarctica's two flowering plants are restricted to the islands to the west and north of the Antarctic Peninsula. These species have been and continue to be the subject of considerable study. At present there are two active research projects, from the UK and the US. The British project is concerned with establishing how the plants survive very low temperatures, while the American project is studying their sensitivity to increased ultraviolet radiation.

It has been obvious for a long time that microbial communities are important in Antarctica. In the last 20 years, scientists from New Zealand, the UK, Australia, Belgium and the US have taken increasing interest in these communities and the features of their physiology that allow them to survive in such inhospitable habitats. Glacier margins are retreating in several places in Antarctica, revealing bare rock and soil. This is what happened at the end of the last ice age in the temperate regions, yet we know little about the initial colonization by microbes that eventually developed into the grasslands and forests of today. Using new technologies, it is possible to investigate the earliest stages of colonization of these areas and to develop a better understanding of how complex communities develop.

Considerable research effort is going into a joint program between several countries (Italy, Argentina, Australia, New Zealand, the UK and the US) to study what is being carried to Antarctica by the winds, how these new species establish themselves and what the effects of increased ultraviolet radiation are on survival in terrestrial communities. This sort of continent-wide program is only possible through international collaboration.

Invertebrates

The largest native land animal on the Antarctic continent is a tiny midge less than two cm long. In fact, Antarctic insects are all very small and not very diverse. With no beetles, spiders, or biting flies, Antarctica is the ideal place for those who do not like insects! You will have to look hard to find any insects, but you might see a springtail jumping among vegetation or find a group of tiny mites huddled under a stone. Despite their size, these insects, and the slightly larger ones on the sub-antarctic islands, are the subject of research by British, French, American, Italian and South African scientists. The insects successfully survive extremes of cold, lack of water and oxygen, and high salt levels in the soil. How do they do it?

Research has centered on identifying some key features of these insects' survival abilities. Many of them are able to make special anitfreezes in their bodies which allow them to survive temperatures as low as -28°C. When frozen into ice in winter, some species can put their metabolism into a special state to survive the lack of oxygen, and they show a remarkable ability to survive dessication without long-term damage to their cells. The lack of species diversity makes these invertebrate communities among the simplest anywhere in the world, and as such they provide ideal models for developing a better understanding of how ecosystems work.

The Life of Lakes & Streams

Most people do not expect to see lakes and streams in Antarctica. Yet there are many ponds and lakes scattered around the ice-free areas, with the highest concentration in the Vestfold Hills and Bunger Hills. The water bodies range from Don Juan Pond, which contains the saltiest solution on Earth (and does not freeze even at -55°C), to small lakes that have almost no nutrients in them at all. The lakes are ice-covered for most or all of the year and have very limited flora and fauna. There are no fish – the most developed animal is a small shrimp and the most complex plant is an aquatic moss. Most of the lakes are dominated by microbial communities.

Again, it is the simplicity of the systems that initially attracted scientists, especially as they could choose a lake with just the right chemical characteristics for their studies. Much of the work has concentrated on the lakes in the Taylor and Wright Valleys (mainly by American, Japanese and New Zealand scientists), at the Vestfold Hills (Australian), at the Bunger Hills (Russian) and at Signy Island (British). Some of the saline water bodies are effectively sterile, with just a few bacteria living in them. In other cases, nutrients from the surrounding catchment have allowed a steady development of the aquatic ecosystem. Lake Vanda in the Wright Valley has been intensively investigated for many years. This lake consists of two ecosystems: The top 45 cm (beneath four-meter-thick ice) is nutrient-poor freshwater; below that is saline water four times as salty as seawater, with a lake-bottom temperature of +25°C. The two layers support quite different microbial communities.

In the more nutrient-rich lakes, and in those where there is significant melt-water running into the lake from the surrounding area, there are new research opportunities. The sediment at the bottom of a lake contains a record of how the lake has changed over a period perhaps as long as 10,000 years. In light of the present interest in documenting historical characteristics of global change, these lake sediments are a valuable history of the recent regional climate in Antarctica.

GEOLOGY, GEOMORPHOLOGY & PALEONTOLOGY

Even though less than 1% of the rock is accessible for direct examination, geologists are very interested in the Antarctic continent. Antarctica forms one of the seven major rock plates that cover the surface of the globe. The margins of the plate are constantly changing and offer one of the best observational laboratories anywhere in the world for studying the movements of the Earth's crust. It also contains one of the best climatic archives of the past, with terrestrial sediments covering the last 200,000 years, marine sediments millions of years and even older areas of ancient continental rocks. Antarctic fossils tell us a great deal about the evolution of some important groups of organisms. There also are several active volcanoes amidst the ice.

Minerals

Is the Antarctic ice sheet lying over vast deposits of precious metals or ores? Do the Weddell and Ross Seas have huge basins of gas and oil below them? Such ideas were the focus of a great deal of diplomatic activity in the 1980s, as governments struggled to agree how exploitation could be controlled. All in vain, as it turned out, since the Antarctic Treaty's Protocol on Environmental Protection has established an absolute prohibition on any mining activities for at least 50 years. Even more interesting were the estimates of the fabulous wealth of the Antarctic, since almost all of the projections were based on little scientific evidence.

In fact, there are no strong data to show that hydrocarbon basins exist in the Antarctic. The geological maps that indicate mineral outcrops simply show where mineral deposits have been identified, but none are of economic value. Antarctic minerals are still being investigated by geologists, who now are working to determine how the minerals were formed and what they can tell us about geological processes, rather than their economic value.

Fossils

The existence of coal beds and plant fossils in the Transantarctic Mountains was reported by both Shackleton and Scott, clearly indicating that the Antarctic was not always covered with ice. Since Shackleton and Scott's time, much more fossil evidence of the preglacial periods has been uncovered. Paleontology has been undertaken by geologists of many countries, with those from New Zealand, Australia, the UK, the US, Poland, Chile and Argentina making especially important contributions. Fossils provide several types of information: They provide evidence of the connections between the parts of Gondwanaland; they give indirect information about the changes in Antarctic climate over many millions of years; and they give insight into the evolution of present Antarctic species. Fossil wood is widely preserved as petrified wood, sometimes in pieces as long as 20m. The trunks and leaf impressions show that about 80 million years ago the climate was temperate, and distinct annual growth rings show that it was also seasonal. In some places, ferns and other woodland species are preserved in great detail.

There are many deposits containing fossil plants and fossil pollen, but fossils of land animals are much less common. Material that appears to be from carnivorous dinosaurs about 200 million years old has been found in the Transantarctic Mountains and parts of Cretaceous plant-eating dinosaurs about 75 million years old have been unearthed on Ross Island off the east coast of the Antarctic Peninsula, but no complete fossils have been recovered. Marine deposits containing molluscs, many other types of marine invertebrates, and fish provide a great deal of information on the evolution of these groups in the Southern Ocean.

In fossil sequences in various parts of the world, there are sudden, major changes in the species recorded at what is called the Cretaceous/Tertiary boundary. All sorts of theories have been put forward to explain this event, since it appears that it caused mass extinctions. The most topical theory is that a huge meteorite collided with Earth, producing such massive climate changes that many species could not survive. The evidence for this is thought to be the occurence of a high level of the

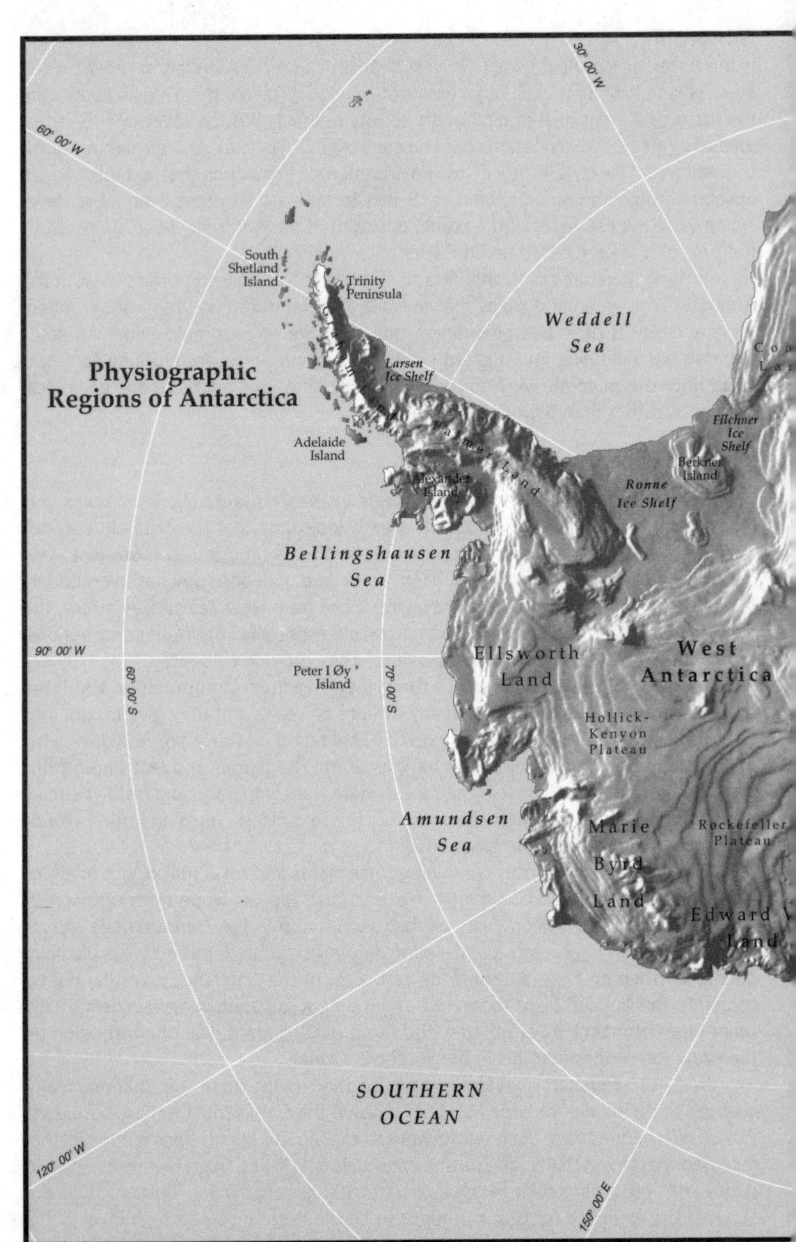
Physiographic
Regions of Antarctica
30° 00' W
60° 00' W
South
Shetland
Island
Trinity
Peninsula
Weddell
Sea
Larsen
Ice Shelf
Graham Land
Palmer Land
Filchner
Ice
Shelf
Berkner
Island
Adelaide
Island
Alexander
Island
Ronne
Ice Shelf
Bellingshausen
Sea
90° 00' W
Ellsworth
Land
West
Antarctica
Peter I Øy
Island
60° 00' S
70° 00' S
Hollick-
Kenyon
Plateau
Amundsen
Sea
Marie
Byrd
Land
Rockefeller
Plateau
SOUTHERN
OCEAN
120° 00' W
150° 00' E

0° 00'
Haakon VII Sea
30° 00' E
SOUTHERN OCEAN
Dronning Maud Land
Enderby Land
60° 00' E
Kemp Land
MacRobertson Land
Lambert Glacier
Amery Ice Shelf
Vestfold Hills
Princess Elizabeth Land
East Antarctica
West Ice Shelf
× Geographic South Pole
90° 00' E
Wilhelm II Land
Davis Sea
Queen Mary Land
Queen Maud Mountains
Shackleton Ice Shelf
Bunger Hills
Ross Ice Shelf
Wilkes Land
Ross Island
Dry Valleys
Terre Adélie
Victoria Land
120° 00' E
George V Land
Oates Land
Cape Adare
× South Magnetic Pole
150° 00' E
Dumont d'Urville Sea
180° 00' E

rare element iridium, which can be found associated with particular layers in sedimentary rocks. Seymour Island off the east coast of the Antarctic Peninsula is one of the best sites in the world for studying the Cretaceous/Tertiary boundary.

Antarctic Landforms

The study of landforms is called geomorphology. In the Antarctic, geomorphologists have mainly been concerned with the effects of the ice sheet on the underlying rock, as well as the study of the moraines left at the end of glaciers, the remains of old beaches left when the sea level fell, and the formation of patterned ground.

Glaciers have an important effect on the rock underneath them. As the ice flows slowly down towards the sea, it gradually grinds up the rock and produces a suspension of fine yellowish or white particles that flow out of the glacier front with the meltwater. This is called 'glacial flour' and runs off into the sea to form sediments. On their way down the valleys, the glaciers may also pick up boulders and weathered rock from the valley sides or outcrops. These, together with glacial flour, are often deposited at the end of the glacier as it melts and retreats, forming mounds called moraines. Where there is a seasonal cycle of melt and retreat of the glacier snout, a series of annual moraines may form, providing clear evidence of the rate of retreat.

Sea level goes up and down with changes in ice cover. There are relics of previous sea levels all around Antarctica: old beaches of shingle, sand and shells that mark the height of previous wave action. Some of these shells have been dated and give an indication of the timing of major changes in the extent of the ice sheet over the last 5000 years.

Patterned ground is found in polar and mountain regions all over the world. These are the polygons, circles, stripes and sometimes even hummocks that can be seen throughout the Antarctic, formed by alternate freezing and thawing of water in the soil which produces lateral sorting of coarse and fine particles. A stone polygon, with its border of large rocks and center of fine particles, is believed to result from the process of frost heave. This usually happens at night when ice crystals form in the soil and push up the large rocks. When the sun melts the crystals the following morning, the rocks roll down to one side. This, repeated many times over many years, produces the polygons. In extremely dry areas such as the Dry Valleys a related process, called ice wedging, produces similar features.

Soils

With less than 1% of Antarctica free of snow and ice, and with very little vegetation, how can there be any soils? Soils are mixtures of weathered rock particles, salts and organic matter (dead plant material). Antarctic soils are, for the most part, almost without organic matter, very dry and with a high salt content. They are primitive soils, and as such have been the subject of detailed research mainly by New Zealand scientists in Victoria Land, although there have been studies elsewhere by the British on Signy Island, and by several countries on the subantarctic islands.

On the continent all the soils contain permafrost, which means they are permanently frozen just below the surface. The breakdown of the rocks into soil particles is due to damage caused by ice crystals, formed when films of water freeze inside cracks, and to chemical breakdown of the rock by the high salt concentrations. Scientists working on the soils in the Dry Valleys have been able to show that some of them are at least five million years old, thus giving a possible date for the retreat of ice from these valleys.

On some of the islands around the Antarctic Peninsula, there are other unusual soils. These are made from accumulations of dead moss and in some places may be nearly 1.5m thick. Because of the permafrost, the dead moss cannot decay, so these peat banks simply keep getting thicker. It is possible to date the bottom of the banks by radiocarbon analyses, and these give dates up to 7000 years. On the subantarctic islands, with a much warmer climate, the soils have no permafrost and are better developed, resembling those found in more temperate mountain areas. There is still a great deal to investigate about Antarctic soils, including their origins and the microbial processes occuring in them.

Meteorites

Meteorites are a major source of information about the early history of our solar system. Most of our knowledge about meteorites comes from analysis of those collected in Antarctica, which acts as a huge meteorite collector and preserver. The first Antarctic meteorite was found by Australians in 1912, but serious collecting did not begin until 1969. Since then, more than 10,000 have been discovered, mainly by Japanese and American scientists. The meteorites are generally found in the 'blue ice' areas of Antarctica, which are expanses of old ice held back by mountains and kept free of snow by constant winds. These areas of stagnant ice allow the meteorites to gradually rise to the surface. The Allan Hills region and the Yamato Mountains have been the most prolific areas so far. Among the large number of meteorites already found, there are some that appear to be parts of the moon and others that appear to have come from other planets in the solar system. Most are thought to be roughly the same age as the Earth.

ICE ON LAND & SEA

The Ice Sheet

Antarctica both drives the weather and responds to long-term changes at a global level. The continent's large mass of snow and ice contains around 85% of all the freshwater in the world and acts as a cold sink for the whole of the Southern Hemisphere, generating the endless series of storms that circle Antarctica. The Antarctic ice sheet is constantly changing, with snow falling and icebergs breaking off. Because the ice sheet is such an important feature we cannot be complacent about its state. Small changes in its volume might have a catastrophic effect on global sea levels. We need to be able to detect small changes in a very large total volume to provide adequate warning of any such rise.

Many years of effort by many countries have gone into attempting to determine the volume of the ice sheet. The principal method is to record the top and bottom of the ice sheet using airborne radar, and there are now maps showing the topography of the underlying rocks, which allow a rough calculation of total volume. The errors, however, are still considerable and are due both to difficulties in deciding the exact thickness of the ice from radar echoes and in mapping the changes in thickness frequently enough at a continental level. All this will soon change when new satellite instruments come into use.

Underneath the ice sheet, which is more than four km thick in places, lies the rock of Antarctica. Geothermal heat from the core of the Earth raises the temperature of the base of the ice sheet and melts enough ice to form freshwater lakes in some basins. Glaciologists have identified 79 of these under-ice lakes all over East Antarctica. The largest lake – Lake Vostok – is comparable in area to Lake Ontario and may be up to 500m deep, with sediment on its bottom. Because they are cut off from the sea, and because they are melted down from ice possibly hundreds of thousands of years old, the lakes may contain important information about previous climates. They might even contain ancient microbes with special features no longer present in today's world. At present, however, nobody knows what is in these under-ice lakes, since the technical problem of how to sample the water without contaminating the lake has not yet been solved.

Researching the History of Our Climate

Snow may simply be frozen water to most people, but to a glaciologist it is a treasure trove of information. When snow falls, it brings with it valuable details about the state of the atmosphere at the time the snowflake was formed. As it is slowly compressed and recrystallized by the snow of later years, it forms a historical record of times past. The present interest in global change makes any information on our past climates valuable for modelling purposes, so a great effort has been made collecting ice cores from some of the oldest and deepest parts of the ice sheet.

Drilling is a difficult and highly skilled activity that extends over several years. The ice sheet is always moving, so the drill hole is continually being bent and squeezed shut. The major cores have been obtained by the Russians, the French and the Americans. At present, preparations are being made for drilling by the Japanese, and further plans include joint drilling by the Italians and the French. The deepest core so far has come from the Russian Vostok station and is 3300m long, with an estimated age of 420,000 years at the bottom.

Study of the ice cores can reveal patterns of mean air temperature, evidence of major volcanic eruptions and, by analysis of the air trapped in ice bubbles, data on the composition of the atmosphere. To make these useful, it is necessary to date the levels in the core. No single method works, so glaciologists have to use a combination of techniques, including counting annual layers, dating the decay rates of natural isotopes, and modelling the changes in ice flow with age.

Since there is still disagreement about the effects of the present increase in carbon dioxide, the historical record from the ice cores is of considerable importance. The data so far indicate that levels of carbon dioxide were reduced throughout the last Ice Age and increased sharply as the ice melted, with a 30% increase in just a few thousand years. The carbon dioxide level remained stable for the next 10,000 years before beginning to increase again about 200 years ago.

Analysis of the ice cores' microparticles will show if they come from dust storms associated with more arid conditions, or from volcanic eruptions. Analysis of the salt types and concentrations can even indicate which volcano erupted.

JEFF RUBIN

Davis station

JEFF RUBIN

Hagglunds tracked vehicle, Davis station

JEFF RUBIN

An 'apple' hut, extended into a 'zucchini' hut

KIERAN JACKA

Magazines from the 'Wilkes Hilton' at the abandoned Wilkes station

COLIN MONTEATH (HEDGEHOG HOUSE)

Shackleton's hut, Ross Island

MARK NORMAN

Mawson's hut, Commonweath Bay

MARK NORMAN

Mawson's hut, Commonweath Bay

The Record of Global Pollution

Since industrial development began, there have been increasing amounts of pollutants escaping into the atmosphere. Over the last 200 years, the emissions of toxic heavy metals have increased dramatically, as has the acidity level in rain in the Northern Hemisphere. Nuclear tests and accidents have released radioactive fallout that has also spread worldwide. Antarctica is remote from all of these sources, but all of the pollutants can be found in snow and ice cores. The continent thus provides a global baseline against which we can measure the damage inflicted on the rest of the planet.

Research has shown that while lead levels in Greenland snow have increased 100-fold in the last 200 years, there has been little change in Antarctica. Data for other toxic metals, such as cadmium, zinc and mercury, are not yet complete enough to indicate any trends. The nuclear fallout shows clearly as datable events in the cores, but there is no evidence of sulfur dioxide that, as 'acid rain,' has caused so much damage in the Northern Hemisphere. The ice cores also have considerable potential for providing baseline data for other compounds, especially organic compounds.

Floating Ice Shelves

Along the Antarctic seacoast there are massive floating ice shelves; the largest are in the Ross and Weddell seas. At the edge of the shelf, massive icebergs break off and drift north, slowly melting as they reach warmer water. Satellite data now allow glaciologists to monitor not only when a giant berg breaks off, but also its slow progress away from the continent. Antarctic icebergs are much larger than any produced in the Arctic, where there are no major ice shelves. Research on the Antarctic ice shelves concentrates on measuring flow rates to see how quickly ice is moving off the continent, and how rapidly the shelf ice thins from the melting of its underside. The long-term objective is to provide a computer model that will allow the loss of ice to the Southern Ocean to be accurately predicted.

Sea Ice

Antarctic sea ice cover varies from a minimum of four million sq km in February to a maximum of 20 million sq km in September. This huge seasonal change has enormous repercussions, since the ice changes the exchange of heat, moisture and momentum between the sea and the air, and all of the marine ecosystem has to adapt to lower temperatures and a lack of light under the ice. Developing models of the way in which sea ice affects energy transfers between sea and air is a major concern of several countries, including Finland, the US and the UK.

The ice cover, even in September, is not complete, however. Satellite pictures show that areas of open water, called polynyas, occur in the same places deep in the pack ice each year. We know little about these polynyas, as only the strongest icebreakers can reach them. It seems likely that they play an important role for seals and whales in the winter, providing a breathing space hundreds of kilometers from the open sea.

At present, the sea ice is considered one of the most important research areas for many countries, for several reasons. The big General Circulation Models, which attempt to predict the magnitude of global warming, show important discrepancies in their predictions for the Antarctic. To improve the predictions, we need much better data on sea ice, and much of this is now being obtained by special instruments mounted on satellites. These instruments also allow us to determine ice movement and ice type deep within the pack ice, and help to provide ever more accurate estimates of the area covered by the ice. But to make sure the satellite data are verified, there is a need for research inside the pack ice. In 1992, a very successful drifting ice camp was established by the Russians and the Americans in the eastern Weddell Sea to study features of the summer sea ice. Several countries are showing an increased interest in drifting buoys, which will give more information about ice movement within the pack ice, as well as meteorological and oceanographical data, without endangering a ship.

There is also a major SCAR research program in the sea ice – Coastal and Shelf Ecology of the Antarctic Sea Ice Zone (CS-EASIZ). This brings together biologists, physicists, chemists and oceanographers in an attempt to understand this rapidly changing and fragile habitat. This is a big program, designed to run for 10 years, with contributions from most Antarctic countries. The scientists will be looking at six key questions: What role does ice play in the coastal marine ecosystem? How do Antarctic communities differ from those in other oceans? What factors determine the patterns of production and nutrient cycling in these ecosystems? How are the organisms adapted to low temperatures? What is the interaction between land and sea in the coastal zone? How are these coastal communities impacted by human activities?

WEATHER FORECASTING

All the countries surrounding Antarctica have great interest in the meteorology of the continent. The weather systems that constantly circle Antarctica drive storms across the Southern Ocean and beyond, while the seasonal formation and melting of sea ice has a major effect on the weather throughout the Southern Hemisphere. Since before the IGY, all stations in the Antarctic have tried to collect daily meteorological observations and broadcast them to surrounding countries to help in weather forecasting. This is coordinated through the World Meteorological Organization to make sure the data are included in all the necessary national forecasting programs. At most stations, you will see a small white meteorological screen housing standard instruments.

But stations were not sited on the basis of where it would be useful to collect meteorological data, and for a long time there were huge holes in the data maps for Antarctic weather. Now those holes are being filled, as more and more automatic weather stations are carefully positioned. The majority of these weather stations are American, but they are put into place and maintained by the cooperative efforts of several other nations.

ATMOSPHERIC SCIENCE

Antarctica might seem an odd place to go if you want to study the atmosphere. Indeed, many people have little idea why it is important to study the atmosphere at all. It is certainly the most difficult field of Antarctic science to explain to the layman, at least in part because, unlike biology or geology, there are few important effects that can be seen, heard or felt without the aid of complicated instruments. For present purposes, the atmosphere can be thought of as three layers: The lowest, the troposphere, is the inhabited layer and has the most gases; the second, the stratosphere, starts at about 10 km above the earth's surface and has very few gas molecules; the third layer, the ionosphere, begins at about 39 km up and stretches out into space.

Atmospheric science is an expensive and active field of research. Global warming and ozone destruction have made the study of atmospheric gases a major discipline, and the Antarctic has an important role to play in this research. There are also unique features of the invisible magnetic fields that surround the Earth that can be most easily investigated in Antarctica.

Atmospheric Chemistry & Ozone Depletion

Probably the most famous science project ever undertaken in Antarctica is the monitoring of stratospheric ozone at Halley, a British station in the Weddell Sea. A paper published in the international scientific journal *Nature* in 1985 provided such alarming evidence of the increasing rate of ozone destruction that it resulted in a worldwide agreement to ban the principal culprits, chlorofluorocarbons (CFCs) – and it also stimulated a massive increase in research on polar chemistry.

One of the direct results of this research was the discovery that CFCs are not the only chemicals involved in ozone destruction. The destruction was found to be localized in stratospheric clouds formed from nitric acid and water. Discovering the other chemical reactions involved has been a major concern of many countries, both in the Antarctic and in laboratories elsewhere. While the chemicals involved are now fairly well agreed upon, there is still further work necessary to understand all of the reactions involved. This is especially important to try and ensure that whatever chemicals take the place of CFCs in air conditioning systems and fridges do not produce further ozone destruction.

A variety of approaches are now being used to make sure ozone data are as accurate as possible. Satellites stare down on the continent, reporting the levels of ozone as seen from above. Looking up from the ground, many countries use Dobson or Brewer spectrophotometers to monitor stratospheric ozone. Upward-pointing laser systems used by Japanese scientists can also detect the formation of the stratospheric clouds in which ozone destruction occurs. There are even direct measurements of ozone obtained by launching hydrogen- or helium-filled ballons with detectors on them.

For quite some time, the way in which ozone destruction took place in the clouds was unknown, as the detailed structure of the cloud particles carrying the nitric acid remained only theoretical. Then balloons were sent up, carrying a sampler that could not only catch the microscopic particles but photograph them and transmit the images back to a ground station.

Now we have a much clearer picture of the whole complex cycle. During the Antarctic winter, a strong westerly circulation is established, which acts as a vortex, cutting the Antarctic stratosphere off from the rest of the atmosphere. Inside this vortex, the atmosphere cools to temperatures as low as -79°C and thin clouds are formed from aerosols, altering the chemical balance between the chlorine derived from the breakdown of the CFCs and other gases in the stratosphere. During this period, it is dark, and it is not until the sun returns in spring that enough energy comes back to the atmosphere to begin the chemical reactions in which the chlorine, together with other chemicals, destroys the ozone. It is because the conditions for the reaction normally occur above the Antarctic that ozone destruction occurs mainly there, rather than in the Arctic, where no polar vortex forms.

Greenhouse Gases & Global Warming

Carbon dioxide is a key component of the atmosphere. It is produced by almost all animals when they breathe and it is taken up by plants during photosynthesis. Along with certain other gases, it has the important property of absorbing heat radiation from the surface of the Earth, thus preventing it from being lost to space and causing the planet to cool. For this reason, carbon dioxide is called a 'greenhouse gas.' The presence of carbon dioxide and water vapor in the Earth's atmosphere makes the planet warm enough for life. Of course, too much of the greenhouse gases can cause too much heating of the atmosphere, or 'global warming.' Burning of fossil fuels produces a mixture of gases of which the principal one is carbon dioxide.

Agriculture, especially cattle raising and rice growing, produces a greenhouse gas called methane. Thus, if you want to measure changes in these gases at a global level, you need a site far away from industry and with as few animals and plants as possible. For this reason, the US chose the South Pole for global carbon dioxide measurements in 1956. This series of measurements is still running and is perhaps one of the most important monitoring activities in the world.

More recently, it has been realized that levels of other gases (which may also be involved in global warming) are also rising, and these have been added to the analyses at the South Pole. The measurements from the Pole provide the baseline for global changes in these greenhouse gases and are extremely important in deciding what needs to be agreed upon internationally to reduce global warming. Decisions on the continued unrestricted use of cars, the burning of coal and gas, and the production of waste gases by factories worldwide will all be influenced in large part by projections based on this data. The sampling has now been extended to a large number of other sites all over the world, providing independent checks on the rate of change.

GEOMAGNETISM

Everyone knows that the Earth has a magnetic field around it, and the experiments you may remember from school clearly showed that magnetic lines bend around the ends of a magnet. This is also what happens with Earth's magnetic field, so that, at each end of the world, there is a magnetic pole as well as a geographic pole. For physicists interested in what happens to this huge magnetic field, Antarctica is a special place.

The magnetic field is invisible, but it is of considerable importance to us. The sun produces a continuous stream of electrically charged, high-energy particles that stream out into space. This flow is picturesquely termed the 'solar wind,' and when it comes into contact with other particles or enters a magnetic field, its energy becomes channelled and discharged. The only visible signs of this are the spectacular displays of aurora that can be seen at both poles. Those in the south, called the aurora australis, form vast, multicolored, waving patterns across the sky as the particles from the sun collide with gas particles in the ionosphere.

A less-visible but much more important sign of the solar wind is interference with communications. Radio, TV and telephones and a variety of navigation systems are all dependent either on bouncing radio waves off charged particles at particular levels in the atmosphere, or on relaying messages via satellites. The crackling and fading or even complete failure of these signals means that there have been changes in the outer part of the atmosphere, caused by the solar wind, that block the signals. Since we rely heavily on perfect communications, we need as good an understanding of this phenomenon as possible.

The peculiar structure of the magnetic field over Antarctica makes it the best place in the world to investigate how the sun's activities affect the ionosphere and to try and model these effects so that they can be predicted. To do this, the UK, Japan and South Africa are attempting to set up three overlapping radar systems located at their respective bases, Halley, Syowa and SANAE. The radars are similar to military systems used to look over the horizon to detect incoming missiles. These, however, will be used for peaceful purposes, utilizing the overlap between the beams to create a three-dimensional picture of the ionosphere above the pole. Building and maintaining these complicated radars with their huge aerial arrays is a difficult and costly exercise.

ANTARCTIC ASTRONOMY

In many parts of the world, life is becoming increasingly difficult for astronomers. Growing pollution, including light pollution, makes studying the stars a problem. To get over these problems, astronomers have taken their telescopes to the tops of mountains on remote islands. This has helped, but a major problem remains: the atmosphere contains too much water, making it difficult to see certain types of stars. Telescopes mounted on satellites do not have this problem, but they are horrifyingly expensive. Antarctica provides the next best thing – at a much lower cost.

Some stars produce only infrared radiation, which we think of as invisible warmth. The amount of this radiation that reaches Earth is infinitesimally small and, since water vapor absorbs infrared, even more is lost as it passes through the atmosphere. To detect infrared stars, you need to go to a place with a very thin and dry atmosphere, where there is as little heat from the ground as possible. Antarctica is the best place on earth for this type of astronomy, and at present the infrared telescopes at the South Pole and Terra Nova Bay are providing a great deal of new information on these previously invisible stars.

Another branch of astronomy has also been enthusiastically developed in the Antarctic. Research on the way in which the sun affects the Earth has been going on for centuries. For a long time, it has been known that the sun pulsates, producing plumes of gas that shoot out into space. These events are obviously related to what is happening inside the sun, but it has been difficult to find a way of discovering what exactly this is. Now a new branch of astronomy called helioseismography is making some progress. Using a special telescope, astronomers monitor the fluctuations in the size of the sun and its relationship to surface changes. Eventually, there will be enough data to extract the frequencies of various types of pulsing, but this is a difficult job since the frequencies produce about 10 million resonations! One scientist has likened the work to 'trying to record the New York Philharmonic from the other side of a concrete wall, while a guy is using a jack hammer on the wall and someone is playing with the volume control; from an analysis of the measured frequencies, you then attempt to determine which instruments are being played!'

Searching for the Origins of the Universe

Antarctica is also playing its part in unraveling the mysteries of where the universe came from. It turns out to be the perfect place to study the cosmic microwave background radiation that is believed to be the remaining echo of the Big Bang. The very dry, cold conditions are ideal for US and Swedish scientists to make measurements that should show whether there is a spatial structure to the radiation as predicted by some theories of the evolution of the universe.

MEDICAL RESEARCH IN ANTARCTICA

Antarctic stations are among the most remote places on earth. In winter, their isolation is comparable to that of a space station. The climate outside is extreme and major medical facilities are a very long way away. All the countries operating in Antarctica obviously need to make sure that everyone going there is healthy. They must also make whatever arrangements they can to provide medical facilities on the continent.

Many people expect medical research in Antarctica to be about cold resistance, but while there is a continuing interest in this topic, it is not as important as others. After all, everyone tries hard to stay either in heated buildings or dressed in special clothing to ensure that they keep warm! The real opportunities in Antarctic medical research are the seasonal changes in the climate and the isolation experienced by the station personnel during winter. The way in which hormone patterns change during the winter darkness, how the isolation from outside infection affects the persistence of microbes on and in the human body, and the psychology of isolated small groups are all of great interest (see the aside Antarctic Medicine, in Facts for the Visitor).

Health Care

The length of time that people spend working in Antarctica varies greatly, both with individual projects and also between countries. Some nations (Italy and Spain, for instance) staff their stations only during the summer, so that the maximum period of duty is around four months. Others have year-round research programs, with some staff spending from one year (Australia) to two and a half years (the UK) in Antarctica.

All staff of Antarctic stations must undergo stringent health checks before they are allowed to go south, and the requirements are even higher for anyone who will be scuba diving in Antarctica. However, each country undertakes the health checks in a different way, largely influenced by cultural attitudes towards health care. For example, some countries undertake psychological testing (Australia, New Zealand, and France), while others require a wide range of chemical and physiological tests (Italy). India is currently investigating the value of yoga in promoting good health at its Antarctic stations. With increasing movement of scientists between national programs, and the formation of large international teams, this could lead to considerable confusion, so the national programs are trying to agree on a standard minimum health check acceptable to all.

Most stations have doctors or paramedics, and a few (McMurdo, Presidente Frei) have mini-hospitals to provide immediate care. All the doctors receive extra training before going to Antarctica. For more information on medicine, see the sidebar on Antarctic Medicine, in Facts for the Visitor.

Telemedicine

Several countries have now established remote advice systems to hospitals elsewhere. This telemedicine is of increasing importance in providing high-quality medical advice to ships, remote communities and even astronauts. Much of the research on which it is based has been developed or proved in Antarctica. The idea is to connect the doctor or paramedic in Antarctica with a specialist elsewhere and to provide the specialist with as much data as possible to aid diagnosis and treatment. To do this, doctors can digitize ECG data, X-rays, photographs and even videos and send them back by satellite.

Other developments include staging mock consultations to improve the ability of paramedics to gather the right information, and detailed analyses of the types of medical care required to improve the initial health checks and briefings for doctors.

Endocrinology

It has been known for a long time that the hormone melatonin is closely associated with regulating body rhythms. Shift workers and long-distance air travelers have difficulty in resynchronizing their sleeping patterns. The pattern of melatonin secretion becomes disturbed and must be adjusted before the normal pattern of sleeping can be reestablished. Obviously, a method for correcting jet lag or sleep disturbance is of great social and industrial importance. The long Antarctic night removes the normal trigger, bright sunlight, that phases melatonin secretion. Research has therefore concentrated on using bright light to supress melatonin secretion and on using melatonin tablets to increase the hormone. So far, results have been mixed, with some people showing a rapid response to these treatments and others showing no response at all. More recently, there has been increasing interest in looking at hormones produced by the thyroid gland and their relationship to the immune responses produced by the white blood cells.

Epidemiology

Work in Antarctica should tell us more about the ways in which our bodies operate. With a carefully selected workforce, it is not suprising that the statistics show Antarctica to be quite a healthy place to live. However, living a long way away from sources of infection appears to lower natural immunity, and there are many recorded cases of the rapid spread among an over-wintering population of colds or flu introduced by people on the first ship or aircraft to arrive at the end of winter.

This isolation can be turned to scientific advantage, however. In normal societies, it is difficult to study the detailed pattern of how a disease spreads between people. To do this scientifically, it is essential to reduce the opportunities for new sources of infection to enter the experimental group. Apart from hermits and members of closed religious orders, there are few people who are willing to live completely cut off from society for long periods to ensure this! Antarctic stations during winter, however, provide such an opportunity. Using the latest molecular biology techniques, it is possible, on a small station, to characterize every strain of a particular microbe. At the start of the winter, every person has a personal profile made of his or her microbe strains. By monitoring these, it is possible to see which strains become dominant, which are passed on and to whom, and which disappear completely. The most recent development of this research has been to use the rate of evolution of Antarctic microbe strains as a baseline measurement against which to assess natural change in microbial populations in Europe and North America.

The Psychology of Small Groups

Remote groups have a particular fascination for psychologists. Add to this both a hostile environment and an opportunity to assess changes by testing people before and after the Antarctic experience, and you have an ideal opportunity to develop an understanding of personality characteristics and human interactions. The most detailed and long-running studies in this field have been those done by French, New Zealand and American scientists, although several other countries have undertaken specific projects. In general, the psychologists are trying to assess three features of behavior: how well a person performs his/her job, how emotionally stable a person remains through the stresses and isolation of the winter, and how well a person integrates in a group. A wide range of tests have been used, and the conclusions have been incorporated into the screening programs for selecting recruits in many countries.

Until recently, however, there has been no attempt to standardize the testing to see how different national cultures affect the response of individuals. Now, a project run from Canada will do just that, with a questionnaire translated into several languages, so that the experience of quite different cultures, for example the Japanese and the Argentines, can be compared scientifically.

THE FUTURE OF ANTARCTIC SCIENCE

With so many countries now active in Antarctic science, there is the real possibility of being able to tackle problems on a much larger scale than any one country could manage on its own. To do this effectively, indeed to ensure that all research is effective, there is a growing need for better cooperation and coordination. The contributions made to this by both SCAR and the Council of Managers of National Antarctic Programs (COMNAP) are critical to success.

Some major new international programs are already underway. In astronomy, there is great interest in constructing some large telescopes at the South Pole for international use. Meanwhile, a program on the sea ice is bringing together biologists, chemists, glaciologists and oceanographers to investigate the processes that take place within the ice as it grows and decays. Geophysicists are pooling their data to provide a more inclusive picture of the geology of the ocean floor, while an international team of geologists is drilling a deep core at Cape Roberts in the Ross Sea not far from Ross Island to investigate the history of continental glaciation.

In all these efforts, there is a genuine attempt to utilize the special features of Antarctica to answer our scientific questions. Using the latest tools, we can now map the Antarctic more accurately than ever before to help scientists assess the changing continent. With geographical information systems, we can synthesize widely differing types of data to gain better understanding of how glaciology interacts with meteorology and geology.

At the same time, scientists are working to protect the continent for the future. In the past, many people treated Antarctica, like the oceans, as an inexhaustible dump for anything unwanted. We have learned that such practices are not healthy, that better mainenance is essential for the good of the planet. These days, Antarctic science is conducted under the rigorous requirements of the Antarctic Treaty's Protocol on Environmental Protection, and great efforts are made to ensure that as little ecological damage as possible is done and that all wastes are removed. When you see an Antarctic station, remember that its impact is local, its inhabitants are trying hard to be more responsible than most of us are back home, and that the research being done there is likely to benefit us and our children in years to come. Antarctic science may be a long way from your back yard, but it is important and relevant science – for now and for the future.

Private Expeditions

By Colin Monteath

Colin Monteath has had 21 seasons in Antarctica since 1973, including 10 years with the New Zealand Antarctic Programme. Since 1983, he has been a freelance photographer and writer, specializing in polar and mountain regions, and with his wife Betty he runs the Hedgehog House New Zealand photo library. Colin has climbed many new routes on Antarctic peaks and has been involved in seaborne tourism since 1983.

INTRODUCTION

Joseph Banks, the botanist on James Cook's first voyage of discovery to the southern latitudes in 1769-71, was perhaps the first person to express a desire to stand at the geographic South Pole. 'O, how Glorious would it be,' Banks said, 'to set my heel upon the Pole! and turn myself 360 degrees in a second!'

The drive to reach the South Pole rapidly grew into an obsession for a number of explorers, as the myth of the great southern continent *Terra Australis Incognita* was dispelled – or at least vastly diminished – by Cook's second voyage in 1772-75 and as the coastline of the Antarctic continent was gradually delineated by exploratory voyages throughout the 1800s.

Norwegian Roald Amundsen inspired the world with his exhibition of efficient expedition organization and use of skis and dogs while becoming the first to reach the Pole in 1911. Amundsen's triumph, however, did not stifle the desire to cross the forbidding Polar Plateau and stand briefly at 90°S. Just as the first ascent of Everest in 1953 proved that the mountain could be climbed and opened the gate for a continuous stream of mountaineers to attempt the peak, Amundsen's success spawned other attempts.

A passion for the Pole runs deep in our psyche. Today, it has reached fever pitch, now that many of the psychological and bureaucratic barriers in gaining access to Antarctica have been overcome. Traverses to the interior of the continent have become commonplace over the last decade as private air transportation to the Antarctic has become routine.

Antarctica is geographically well endowed for adventure. Not only are its flat ice sheets suitable for skiing and hauling sledges, but the continent is studded with some of the world's great mountain ranges. While not as high as Andean or Himalayan peaks, Antarctic summits have an allure of their own, enhanced as they are by remoteness and extreme cold. Antarctica will certainly be one of the most important mountaineering meccas of the next century.

THE EVOLUTION OF PRIVATE EXPEDITIONS

Much of the exploration and science in Antarctica during the early 1900s would not have happened without private initiative and sponsorship under the leadership of famous figures from the heroic era, such as Mawson, Shackleton, Amundsen, Gerlache and Nordenskjöld. As far back as the 1820s, explorers such as Weddell, Smith, Bransfield, Biscoe and Palmer played a vital exploratory role resulting from the commercial incentive of the sealing industry. During the late 1920s and early '30s, wealthy and influential private aviators such as American Lincoln Ellsworth and Australian Hubert Wilkins provided the drive and daring to make the first long-distance flights in Antarctica. Likewise, American Richard Byrd's two expeditions in 1928 and 1933 at his Little America base on the Ross Ice Shelf were essentially private affairs.

More modest private expeditions on the Antarctic Peninsula in the 1930s and '40s played a significant role in piecing together Antarctica's geographical puzzle. Australian John Rymill led the 1934 British Graham Land Expedition, while American Finn Ronne in 1946 led an unhappy though productive team from his base on Stonington Island. Both Rymill and Ronne made skillful use of aircraft and sledging parties, and among Ronne's team were the first two women to winter in Antarctica.

In the 1950s, private expeditions took a backseat to the buildup for the International Geophysical Year, or IGY, when a coordinated, multi-nation drive established government science bases around Antarctica (and in the Arctic, too).

Commonwealth Trans-Antarctic Expedition

Associated with the IGY was the Commonwealth Trans-Antarctic Expedition, inspired and led by Englishman Vivian Fuchs. On his way to complete Shackleton's dream of crossing Antarctica from the Weddell Sea coast to the Ross Sea, Fuchs reached the South Pole with heavy tracked vehicles on January 19, 1958, after a winter at Shackleton Base on the Weddell Coast. With Fuchs was a dog team, the first to reach the Pole since Amundsen. Preceding Fuchs' arrival at the Pole by two weeks was Edmund Hillary's team of New Zealanders. They had driven modified farm tractors to lay fuel depots from Scott Base on Ross Island, New Zealand's newly established IGY station.

Although the Commonwealth Trans-Antarctic Expedition was partly government sponsored and partly privately sponsored, it was never planned that Hillary would go past his last depot and push on for the Pole. His action considerably angered the Ross Sea Committee, which was the New Zealand organizer of Fuchs' support team. Perhaps this discord foretold of future misunderstanding and distrust between government departments (which rapidly asserted their control over access to Antarctica) and strong-willed individuals with proven field experience and an adventurous spirit.

First Ascent of Vinson Massif

The origins of modern Antarctic mountaineering came even later. Although Ellsworth saw the northern part of the Ellsworth Mountains during his transantarctic flight in

1935, he did not see the highest peak in the range, Vinson Massif. Remarkably, Vinson – the highest peak on the continent – was not even sighted until US Navy pilots made a reconnaissance flight in association with the IGY in 1957.

In 1966, after three years of lobbying by the American Alpine Club, the US National Science Foundation agreed to support a US mountaineering expedition which had as its prime objective the summitting of Vinson. This granting of semi-official status to well-known American alpinists with a considerable track record in the Himalaya was, in part, designed to forestall the efforts of another American, Woodrow Wilson Sayre, who was also trying to reach Vinson Massif.

This was perhaps expedient as Sayre's aircraft logistics seemed questionable and the US government probably worried that it would be involved in a costly rescue mission if Sayre actually made it to the continent. Sayre had already fallen from grace in 1962, when he created a diplomatic incident after his small team of climbers crossed illegally from Nepal into Chinese-occupied Tibet to make a clandestine attempt on Mt Everest. Four years later, Sayre teamed up with American Max Conrad but failed to reach Antarctica when their aircraft 'developed unspecified difficulties in Buenos Aires,' as the journal *Antarctic* reported. (In 1970, at the age of 77, Conrad did reach Antarctica. Flying a Piper Aztec from New Zealand to McMurdo Station, he made the first solo flight to land at the South Pole. However, on his subsequent take off for South America, he crashed, ending the expedition.)

The American Alpine Club team, led by Nicholas Clinch, was flown from New Zealand to McMurdo and on to the Sentinel Range in the Ellsworth Mountains, using US Navy ski-equipped Hercules. With the first ascent of Vinson behind them, a climb of little technical consequence, the expedition went on a climbing spree of other major summits, notably Mts Tyree (which may well be Antarctica's most difficult peak), Gardner and Shinn.

In 1967, another group received valuable government assistance. The New Zealand Antarctic Expedition, inspired by Edmund Hillary, was flown by the US Navy from McMurdo Sound in a ski-equipped Hercules, which landed on the sea-ice at Cape Hallett. The expedition made the first ascent of the elegant 3300m Mt Herschel in North Victoria Land. For New Zealand climbers to gain US Navy support was unprecedented; it would not have happened without Hillary's influence on senior New Zealand government officials. Even so, the New Zealand team was obliged to take surveyors and geologists with them to add a veneer of 'respectable' science.

After the American Alpine Club expedition and the New Zealand Antarctic Expedition, it was clear to US and New Zealand officials that providing official support to private teams had created two awkward precedents. These precedents were likely to spark an avalanche of requests for transport and backup logistics from mountaineers and adventurers all over the world.

The US Government became the most obvious target for requests of support, thanks to its extensive network of fuel depots around the continent, principally at McMurdo, Byrd, Siple and South Pole stations, and its long range ski-equipped Hercules aircraft and icebreaking ships. Many applicants thought they should receive assistance as a matter of right, yet they had little idea of just how stretched the Americans were themselves in servicing a complicated science program so far from home. The cost of fuel alone became astronomical after it had been transported by sea from the US to New Zealand and on to McMurdo, before being flown to inland Antarctic bases. To support private expeditions with aircraft or ships, even in a meager way, would require cancellation of pre-planned science programs. It also became evident that some of the aspiring expeditions simply didn't have a proven track record of expedition planning and independent travel in other remote regions. Understandably, the US Government feared that if these teams were given official support, then a percentage of them would require rescue, which would again divert scarce resources away from their primary mission of science.

The US and New Zealand governments drafted a joint policy on private expeditions which effectively ruled out any assistance to private teams in the future. It was much simpler to give all applicants the 'cold shoulder' and ignore or brush off the protests from the growing band of adventurers who were rapidly realizing the recreational potential of Antarctica. A well-planned New Zealand team hoping to climb Mt Minto, the highest peak in North Victoria Land, was the first victim of this policy in 1969. While the US-New Zealand policy of non-cooperation was understandable, its interpretation and application soon became overly bureaucratic and unnecessarily obstructive, and resentment towards government 'ownership' of Antarctica grew.

Embarrassingly for US Antarctic administrators, the rug was pulled from under their own policy several times when senior American politicians insisted that their pilot friends attempting 'record-breaking' jaunts across Antarctica receive all-important refueling at McMurdo. In 1971, for example, Elgin Long, who'd already flown solo over the North Pole, flew solo in his twin-engined Piper Navaho from Chile to McMurdo via the South Pole to become the first person to fly solo over both poles. In 1983, pilot Brooke Knapp, whose husband was an associate of US President Ronald Reagan, received similar support at McMurdo after a flight from New Zealand with a crew of three. Knapp then flew over the Pole to South America, claiming no less than 41 aviation records during her speedy round-the-world flight.

BRITISH JOINT-SERVICES EXPEDITIONS

With the US-New Zealand policy in place, no private expeditions made traverses to the interior of Antarctica during the 1960s and much of the '70s. Instead, the British government allowed several 'Joint Services' expeditions to hold 'adventure training' exercises, which made use of Royal Navy transport to reach remote islands such as South Georgia. Several British teams have repeated Shackleton's epic crossing of South Georgia following his boat journey from Elephant Island in 1916. The first crossing was under the command of Malcolm Burley in 1964. In 1970, Burley led a British military group which landed on Elephant Island and carried out survey and ornithological work. One member of the team, Chris Furse, returned to Elephant Island in 1976 with 15 others to climb its rugged peaks and experiment with sea-kayak transport in the ice-choked waters. Furse, with another large military team of mountaineers, returned to the Antarctic in 1983-85 to winter over in tents and snow caves on Brabant Island off the Antarctic Peninsula.

MAJOR PRIVATE TRAVERSES

During the 1960s and '70s, many government expeditions criss-crossed the Polar Plateau with large tractor trains supporting glacialogical or geophysical research.

Antarctica by this stage had also been well mapped and documented by aerial photography. As such, the private traverse parties that have reached Antarctica since 1979 can in no way be called explorers. Far from denigrating these journeys, they should be seen as a highly valid form of recreation in their own right – superb tests of spirit and endurance, as well as of many types of new lightweight equipment. As a result of their responsibilities to sponsors, these expeditions have also provided a means to educate schoolchildren and the public of the need to look after the polar regions.

Transglobe Expedition

The British Transglobe Expedition of 1979-82 did what all of the polar pundits of the day said couldn't be done: complete a crossing of Antarctica using open skidoos pulling small wooden sledges. Determined to circumnavigate the globe following the Prime Meridian (0°), Ginnie and Ran Fiennes led a small team to the South African side of Antarctica. They commissioned a ship to transport all their own equipment to the continent, and pick the expedition up from Ross Island after the crossing. For resupply on the Polar Plateau, the expedition had a ski-equipped Twin Otter, flown by veteran polar pilot Giles Kershaw. The Transglobe team wintered on the edge of the continent in a prefabricated cardboard hut before setting out for the interior the following spring. Later, when at the South Pole, Kershaw flew the Otter back to the South African base to help in a major rescue – an important example of private adventurers helping government personnel in trouble. Despite concerted efforts by the US, British and New Zealand governments to block Transglobe, Ran Fiennes and team members Ollie Shepard and Charlie Burton completed the second crossing of Antarctica in only 67 days, reaching the New Zealand Scott Base in January 1981. Fiennes and Burton went on to cross the Arctic Ocean, becoming the first people to reach both poles by surface means. The Transglobe Expedition proved that, given the determination and ingenuity to bring together a massive pyramid of resources, a small private team could safely undertake a major traverse in Antarctica.

In the Footsteps of Scott

Determined to retrace Robert F Scott's 1911-12 journey to the South Pole via the Beardmore Glacier, Englishmen Robert Swan and Roger Mear and Canadian Gareth Wood set out from an overwinter base beside Scott's Cape Evans hut in October 1985. Seventy days later, the trio manhauled their fiberglass sledges up to the US Amundsen-Scott South Pole station. They received a rather 'frosty' official reception – in tune with the poor relations the expedition had experienced with US leaders at McMurdo. This overreaction to private teams has often proved highly embarrassing to junior government support personnel who naturally wish to extend warm-hearted hospitality to anyone who stumbles in out of the wilderness to reach their lonely outpost.

Just moments after reaching the Pole, the Footsteps of Scott team received the news that their support vessel, the old trawler *Southern Quest*, had been crushed by pack ice and sunk off Beaufort Island in the Ross Sea. The expedition's aircraft, a modified Cessna 185 flown by Giles Kershaw, had already been off-loaded and was on standby near Ross Island to retrieve the trio from the Pole. US helicopters recovered the ship's crew to McMurdo, sparking heated debate on both sides. Kershaw reluctantly agreed not to fly to the Pole as long as the US didn't call the retrieval of Swan's group a 'rescue.'

Most of *Southern Quest*'s crew were flown back to New Zealand by US Hercules. However, a team of three stayed for a second winter at Cape Evans to look after the Cessna and with the view of removing the entire base the following summer. The Footsteps of Scott hut was eventually incorporated into Greenpeace's Cape Evans base and subsequently removed from Antarctica when the Greenpeace base closed. The trio were picked up at Cape Evans in the spring of 1986 by a Twin Otter again piloted by Giles Kershaw, a remarkable 9600-km roundtrip flight from Punta Arenas.

The US government charged Swan's expedition US$80,000 for the expedition's 'rescue' from Ross Island and repatriation to New Zealand. Relations between governments and private expeditions had reached an all-time low.

Norwegian 90° South Expedition

The next private expedition to Antarctica was led by Norwegian glaciologist Monica Kristensen. 'Was it difficult,' she was asked, 'to be a woman and lead a group of men?' Kristensen responded that she had no experience of being anything other than a woman.

The expedition attempted to retrace Amundsen's route to the Pole using dog teams. Sailing from New Zealand in November with her own ship, *Aurora*, to transport dogs and equipment, she positioned the vessel near a flat-topped iceberg in the Ross Sea. A Greenland Air Twin Otter then took off from southern New Zealand and, at the limit of its fuel, landed on the tabular berg. Refueled from *Aurora*, the plane took off and flew to the Bay of Whales on the Ross Ice Shelf. From here the aircraft positioned depots across the Ross Ice Shelf and at the head of the Axel Heiberg glacier, Amundsen's gateway through the Transantarctic Mountains.

Kristensen and her three male companions then drove 22 huskies all the way to the Polar Plateau. Slowed down by heavy glaciology gear and having missed one of the depots, the team turned back several hundred kilometers short of the Pole. Not wishing to winter on the continent, Kristensen knew the timing of her decision to turn back was crucial: She needed to arrive back early enough so that *Aurora* would not be trapped by sea-ice forming in the fall.

In 1993, Kristensen returned to the Antarctic, this time on the Weddell Sea side, for another private expedition that combined science, adventure and the dream of locating Amundsen's black tent buried beneath the South Polar snow. This expedition was criticized for poor glacier-travel techniques, and one man died in a crevasse accident, sparking a rescue mission by mountaineers from US and New Zealand bases on Ross Island.

ADVENTURE NETWORK INTERNATIONAL

It is important to interrupt the chronology of overland traverses to the Pole at this point, because all expeditions after the Norwegian 90° South Expedition – not wishing to overwinter or outfit their own ship – have chosen to use aircraft to reach Antarctica.

Mountain climbers led the way. The attraction of Vinson Massif and other remote peaks spurred mountaineers to overcome the barriers of aircraft logistics and government bureaucracy to reach Antarctica's inland Ellsworth Mountains.

In 1983, American businessmen Frank Wells and Dick Bass wanted to climb Vinson Massif in their quest to ascend the highest peak on each of the seven continents. With pilot Giles Kershaw and mountaineers Chris Bonington and Rick Ridgeway, Bass and Wells flew to Antarctica in an 'experimental' ski-equipped tri-turbo DC-3. Their climb of Vinson, only its third ascent, was the forerunner of dozens of ascents that have now taken place each summer over the past decade.

The tri-turbo operation was risky, with no backup should the plane become grounded. Canadian Pat Morrow – on his own Seven Summits odyssey in 1984 – failed to reach Vinson with the tri-turbo on his first attempt, after developing engine trouble at Adelaide Island while near Britain's Rothera station. Morrow remained determined to reach Vinson. Pulling together major sponsorship and a landmark deal with the Chilean air force to airdrop aircraft fuel for the expedition, Morrow, along with fellow Canadian guide Martyn Williams and pilot Giles Kershaw, flew to Vinson in a ski-equipped Twin Otter in November 1985. This was the birth of Adventure Network International, which henceforth took paying passengers on other adventures in Antarctica. (See Getting There & Away for more on ANI.)

By 1986, Giles Kershaw was experimenting with a wheeled DC-4, which could be flown in a single 10-hour flight from Punta Arenas, Chile, to land on natural areas of wind-polished ice. This allowed ANI to set up a base camp at Patriot Hills, near the Ellsworth Mountains. With the DC-4, and eventually a DC-6, hauling clients and reserves of fuel from South America, expeditions could then be serviced from the Patriot Hills camp with two Twin Otters. Since 1993, ANI has chartered a South African wheeled Hercules for the Punta Arenas-Patriots Hills flight. This large aircraft has an increased payload; being pressurized, it can fly above bad weather, thereby offering a more predictable flight schedule.

Using its own chartered ship or Quark Expedition's Russian icebreakers to position Twin Otter fuel depots on both sides of the continent, ANI has gradually developed the capability to safely reach even the remotest locations in Antarctica. This has allowed climbers to begin dreaming of vast new mountain playgrounds in the Transantarctic Mountains and in the Queen Maud Mountains. (The mountains on the coast of Queen Maud Land were climbed in 1993 on a private Norwegian expedition led by Ivar Tollefsen. This expedition used a Russian government ship to reach Antarctica and achieved by far the hardest mountaineering yet done in Antarctica.)

In 1988, ANI director Martyn Williams led a commercial expedition from the edge of the Ronne Ice Shelf to the South Pole. This was an especially-remarkable piece of guiding, since one of the clients had never been on skis before. The expedition included the first two women to ski overland to the Pole, Tori Murden and Shirley Metz. The group flew back to Patriot Hills, now a commonplace way to end a traverse to the Pole.

Fuchs-Messner Ski Traverse

The austral summer of 1989-90 was a big season in the Antarctic for private expeditions, as both the third and fourth crossings of the continent took place. The third was made by Austro-Italian mountaineer Reinhold Messner, the most celebrated climber in the history of the sport, and German Arved Fuchs (no relation to Vivian Fuchs). The pair teamed up to ski across Antarctica, using depots laid by ANI aircraft.

Although Messner was the first person to ascend all 14 8000m peaks in the Himalaya, he had not previously been to the polar regions. Fuchs was a good choice of partner and navigator, since he had just returned from the North Pole. Towing heavily laden plastic sledges, Fuchs and Messner reached the South Pole on New Years Eve, 1989. Fuchs thus achieved the distinction of skiing to both geographic poles within 12 months.

The pair continued on across the continent, striking out for Ross Island on January 3, 1990, and reaching Ross Island on February 12 – a total of 92 days since departing the Weddell Sea coast. With no resupply flight on the second half of the trip, they pared everything to a minimum; not even radios were carried. When the wind allowed, parachutes were used to help pull the sledges. The best day with parachutes saw one degree of latitude (60 nautical miles, or about 111 km) clatter under their skis.

Messner and Fuchs had arranged a pickup from the Ross Sea coast by a tourist ship scheduled to visit the region. If this rendezvous had failed, they could have elected to summon a costly ANI flight from Patriot Hills. As it turned out, the pair sailed for New Zealand on board an Italian government resupply vessel. Despite external political pressure not to do so, the Italians were probably pleased to assist Messner, who was almost a cult figure at home in Italy.

International Trans-Antarctic Expedition

The fourth crossing of Antarctica turned out to be a truly marathon journey, spanning seven months from July (midwinter) 1989 to March 1990. The international team of six from Japan, UK, China, Soviet Union, France and the United States, led by Jean-Louis Etienne and Will Steger, planned to drive dog teams across the continent. For preparation, the expedition made a 2400-km south to north traverse of the Greenland ice cap.

In Antarctica, the expedition chose to traverse the longest possible axis: down the continent's spine along the Antarctic Peninsula to the South Pole, then via Vostok to Mirnyy. In all, the trek covered a punishing 6400 km. Making use of seven depots laid the year before along the Peninsula by an ANI Twin Otter, the expedition sledged into the US base at the South Pole on December 11, 1989, after 137 days and 3187 km.

Unlike the last dog team to reach the Pole in 1958 (with the Commonwealth Trans-Antarctic Expedition), which was flown out, Steger's American huskies were still only halfway through their journey: 3212 km lay between them at 90°S and Mirnyy. Somewhere in between, across the 'zone of inaccessibility,' was the Soviet Vostok station and a rendezvous with supplies they could not afford to miss. By providing aircraft fuel at the South Pole, the Soviets made it possible for an ANI Twin Otter to bring in supplies at the crucial mid-point of the expedition as well as to place two depots between the Pole and Vostok. After nearly losing Japanese team member Keizo Funatsu in a frightful blizzard, the dog teams and their weary drivers finally reached Mirnyy on March 3. From New Zealand, Reinhold Messner sent the expedition a message: 'Congratulations on completing one of the great polar journeys of all time. Let us both now fight for a World Park Antarctica.'

Sjur & Simen Mordre

The fifth crossing of Antarctica, in 1990-91, was carried out with efficiency and élan. The Norwegian Mordre brothers, Sjur and Simen, both expert Nordic skiers, used a dog team in their journey to the Pole from the Weddell Sea. An ANI Twin Otter then flew the dogs back to Patriot Hills while the brothers, together with a photographer, skied on towards Ross Island. Pulling sledges and making use of parachutes where possible, the trio used Amundsen's route from the Polar Plateau down the steep Axel Heiberg glacier to the Ross Ice Shelf. They reached the Ross Sea coast after a 105-day crossing and were picked up on schedule by the tour ship *World Discoverer*.

Ran Fiennes & Mike Stroud

The planned sixth crossing of Antarctica didn't quite make it. Englishman Ran Fiennes returned to Antarctica in 1992, this time with Footsteps of Scott veteran and physician Mike Stroud. The pair planned to manhaul sledges from the Weddell to the Ross Sea coasts, with no aircraft support or pre-laid depots: a 2500-km journey. That they made it some 2100 km to the southern edge of the Ross Ice Shelf before requesting evacuation by ANI aircraft was a feat of considerable endurance.

Erling Kagge

At the same time that Fiennes and Stroud were walking to the Pole, Norwegian skier Erling Kagge was skiing solo to the Pole. Although some of the media – inaccurately – tried to represent this as a replay of the 'race' between Amundsen and Scott, Kagge never intended to make a complete traverse. He reached the Pole with little fuss after 49 days and flew back out to Patriot Hills.

Ann Bancroft

In contrast to the media attention given to Fiennes, Stroud and Kagge, the American Women's Expedition received little notice in the international press. This group, led by Ann Bancroft, successfully reached the South Pole in January 1993. Although the expedition originally planned to make a complete crossing of the continent, the members decided against pushing on past the Pole, primarily due to sickness in the team. Bancroft became the first woman to travel overland to both poles, having reached the North Pole in 1986 on an expedition led by Will Steger.

Other Traverses

Other recent traverses to the Pole include Norwegian Liv Arnesen's solo ski trek in 1994, and the journey made by three other Norwegians (including Cato Pederson, who lost one arm and half of the other in an accident at age 14) who also skied to the Pole in 1994. Still another Norwegian, Borge Ousland, gave up an attempt at a solo crossing of Antarctica in 1995-96, but not before he reached the South Pole, thus attaining both poles on ski, solo and without depots. And the quest for the Pole goes on . . . .

MOUNTAINEERING

Australian Bicentennial Antarctic Expedition

On December 31, 1987, on the eve of Australia's bicentennial year, the yacht *Dick Smith Explorer* (renamed *Alan and Vi Thistlethwayte)* sailed from Sydney with an adventurous team on board: climbers, who under Greg Mortimer's leadership, would make the first ascent of Mt Minto, at 4163m the highest peak in North Victoria Land. The peak was only reached after manhauling 150 km inland from Cape Hallett.

Mt Vaughan Expedition

Norman Vaughan, an 87-year-old Alaskan, had been a dog driver with Richard Byrd's 1928 expedition to Antarctica. Since then, he has led a colorful life revolving around huskies and dogsled racing. In 1993, Vaughan planned to drive sled dogs across the Ross Ice Shelf and climb the 3140m virgin summit of Mt Vaughan, named after him by Byrd. His inspiring motto: 'Dream big, dare to fail.'

Vaughan's big dream was to reach the summit of 'his' mountain on December 19, 1993 – his 88th birthday. Vaughan's team took the gamble of flying people, dogs and supplies from Punta Arenas to Patriot Hills in an old rented DC-6, flown by a pilot who had worked for Adventure Network in the past. In late November, however, the plane crashed short of the ice runway at Patriot Hills in bad weather, badly injuring one of the four team members on board. Anne Kershaw, Giles' wife and director of ANI, immediately launched a Hercules aircraft stationed in Punta Arenas to evacuate the team from the continent.

After daring to fail, Vaughan was back in Antarctica in 1994, this time with ANI air support and two experienced mountaineering guides, Vernon Tejas and Gordon Wiltsie. Three days short of his 89th birthday, Vaughan and his wife Carolyn Muegge-Vaughan reached the summit of their dreams.

Dry Valley Mountaineering Expedition

Until 1990, no cruise vessel had ever been twice into the Ross Sea in a single season. Now, however, it is not uncommon for tour vessels to achieve this. On its maiden voyage, the Antarctic tour ship *Frontier Spirit* (now called *Bremen)*, dropped off a five-man expedition at Cape Royds under the leadership of Colin Monteath. With their own helicopter to transport them across McMurdo Sound, the climbers were able to ascend several peaks in the Dry Valleys. An ascent of Mt Erebus was also made with two members of the Greenpeace Cape Evans overwinter team.

South Georgia Climbs

Climbers have reached South Georgia on expeditions based from their own yachts or by gaining permission to be transported by British military vessels. Although delayed by the Falklands war, the 1984-85 New Zealand expedition to the peaks above St Andrew's Bay, led by Ian Turnbull, successfully combined science and mountaineering and made a film of its exploits. Another expedition to use military transport was a British one led by Stephen Venables in 1989, which made several first ascents including Mt Carse at the southeast end of South Georgia.

AIRBORNE ADVENTURES

One impressive venture helped pave the way for future cooperation between private expeditions and governments operating science programs in Antarctica began on November 5, 1988. ANI's Giles Kershaw acted as co-pilot for Australian aviator Dick Smith, flying a Twin Otter from Hobart to Australia's Casey station. This 14-hour flight was the first-ever direct flight from Australia to land in Australia's claimed territory in Antarctica. Such a flight in a Twin Otter was only possible thanks to six auxiliary fuel tanks, which extended its range from 1600 km to 3500 km.

Kershaw and Smith assisted the Australian government science program for two weeks, completing extended aerial surveys along the coastline to Davis and Mawson stations. They also made goodwill visits to Syowa, Molodezhnaya and Mirnyy stations, with the Japanese and Soviets extending real Antarctic hospitality. The aviators continued on to the South Pole on November 23, having flown from Casey to Ross Island to pick up two Greenpeace members who wanted to inspect the South Pole station. By November 29, they were back at Casey and ready for a flight to South America via Vostok, the South Pole, Patriot Hills and King George Island.

Giles Kershaw's calm and positive manner as a pilot and skillful knowledge of a Twin Otter's capability took the expedition across 41,448 km of Antarctica and the Southern Ocean in the space of five weeks (with a total of 171 hours in the air). Sadly, on March 5, 1990, Giles Kershaw died in a gyrocopter crash on the Antarctic Peninsula while he was assisting a film crew on another private expedition led by Mike Hoover. Antarctica lost a great ambassador.

SEABORNE ADVENTURES

As early as 1910, the British travel company Thomas Cook advertised that it planned to run a 50-day cruise from New Zealand to McMurdo Sound. It was reported that 'members of the New Zealand Parliament, a number of ladies and several gentlemen interested in scientific matters' were keen to endure the rigors of the Ross Sea in a wooden vessel, but the voyage never eventuated.

Today, tourist vessels ply Antarctic waters in large numbers every season. Some of them have acted as stepping stones for private expeditions, which have been dropped off on one cruise and then picked up at a predetermined location during a later voyage. The Australian ski kayak expedition led by Wade Fairley in 1994 spent two weeks paddling along parts of the Antarctic Peninsula, having been dropped off by a tour ship.

Wake of Shackleton

In 1993, during a tourist voyage on the Russian icebreaker *Kapitan Khlebnikov*, a replica of Shackleton's lifeboat *James Caird* was transported to Elephant Island. Led by Trevor Potts, three Englishmen and a woman then sailed the craft, which they called *Sir Ernest Shackleton*, 800 nautical miles (1480 km) to South Georgia. The 'Wake of Shackleton' team did not, however, attempt to cross the mountainous island and later became a burden on British authorities at Grytviken due to its poor planning and lack of finances.

David Lewis

In 1972, New Zealand physician David Lewis attempted a solo circumnavigation of Antarctica in his 10m *Ice Bird*. The yacht capsized twice on the 14-week voyage from Sydney to the American Palmer station on Anvers Island. After repairs and a winter's delay, Lewis sailed for Cape Town, again capsizing en route. In 1977-78, Lewis sailed to Cape Adare in the Ross Sea on the yacht *Solo* under the auspices of the Sydney-based Oceanic Research Foundation. With five others in 1982, Lewis froze the steel yacht *Dick Smith Explorer* into an anchorage near Australia's Davis base and spent the winter aboard the yacht.

Don & Margie McIntyre

Australians Don and Margie McIntyre also spent a winter in Antarctica, during 1995, after being dropped off by their yacht at Mawson's old base at Cape Denison in Commonwealth Bay (see the sidebar by the McIntyres in the East Antarctica chapter).

Project Blizzard

Led by Bill Blunt, the Australian 'Project Blizzard' expedition twice visited Mawson's hut at Commonwealth Bay. The voyages, in 1984 (aboard *Dick Smith Explorer)* and 1985 (aboard *Southern Quest)* were undertaken to make an assessment of the historic huts' condition.

Jean-Louis Etienne

Apart from James Clark Ross' *Erebus* and *Terror* in 1841, no yacht had ever been south of Victoria Land's Cape Hallett until 1993, when Frenchman Jean-Louis Etienne returned, this time on board the luxury steel yacht *Antarctica* instead of behind a dog team. Etienne's yacht-based expeditions made an ascent of Mt Erebus and shot footage for children's educational TV films on the Antarctic Peninsula.

Gerry Clark

In 1983, Gerry Clark, a 56-year-old New Zealander, set off from New Zealand in the 10m wooden yacht *Totorore* to circumnavigate Antarctica. His three-year odyssey involved some remarkable single-handed yachting combined with adventures and ornithological work achieved with crews picked up in South America. Clark had an epic of survival near Heard Island, when *Totorore* lost its mast and rigging, and he was lucky to make it to Fremantle, Western Australia.

Hughes Delignieres

The first-ever true solo winter in Antarctica was achieved in 1990 by Frenchman Hughes Delignieres on his nine-meter *Oviri*, which was frozen into a bay near Pleneau Island on the Antarctic Peninsula. (Admiral Byrd's celebrated winter alone in 1934 at Advance Base on the Ross Ice Shelf is not considered by some authorities to have been a solo, since Byrd was close to assistance by other expedition members.)

Ned Gillette

No survey of adventurous expeditions on the Southern Ocean would be complete without mentioning American Ned Gillette's four man team, which *rowed* across the

Drake Passage to Antarctica in March 1988. The men required 14 days to row their boat, *Sea Tomato,* across the 1100 km passage from Cape Horn to Nelson Island in the South Shetland Islands. Taking the easy – and sensible – route back from Antarctica, Gillette exchanged *Sea Tomato* with the Chilean Navy for a flight home.

CONCLUSION

Independent private expeditions to Antarctica are a spirited and valuable expression of human desire to travel in a great polar wilderness. Today, there is no excuse for poor planning. Expedition leaders must discuss objectives and support plans with their own government's Antarctic program administrators before departure. They have an obligation to leave Antarctica exactly as they find it: pristine. Above all, they must educate others upon their return of the dire need to treat Antarctica with the greatest of respect.

Antarctic Gateways

Every trip to Antarctica, whether by ship or plane, leaves from a Southern Hemisphere city. Many of the cruise programs include one or more nights' stay in one of these Antarctic gateways. The following information on Cape Town, Christchurch, Hobart, Punta Arenas, Stanley, and Ushuaia is adapted from material in other Lonely Planet guides.

Cape Town

Cape Town, or Kaapstad, is one of the most beautiful cities in the world. No matter how long you stay, the image of the mountains and the sea will be seared into your mind.

About 40 km from the Cape of Good Hope, near the southern tip of the vast African continent, it is one of the most geographically isolated of the world's great cities. Dominated by a 1000m high, flat-topped mountain with virtually sheer cliffs, it's surrounded by superb mountain walks, vineyards, and beaches.

Cape Town has the reputation for being the most open-minded and relaxed city in South Africa, but the scars of apartheid run deep. Perhaps it is partly because blacks are in many ways culturally integrated, but in the Western-style city center you could easily imagine the problems of South Africa are a figment of journalistic imagination.

History

San & Khoikhoi The human history of the Cape began tens of thousands of years ago with Stone Age tribes. They were followed by the San, hunter-gatherers who left no sign of their occupation beyond superb cave paintings. By the time the first Portuguese mariners arrived, however, the Cape was occupied by Khoikhoi, close relatives of the San, who were semi-nomadic sheep and cattle pastoralists.

Portuguese The Portuguese came in search of a sea route to India and that most precious of medieval commodities – spice. Bartholomeu Dias rounded the Cape in 1487 naming it Cabo da Boa Esperanca (Cape of Good Hope), but his eyes were fixed on the trade riches of the east coast of Africa and the Indies. In 1503, Antonio de Saldanha became the first European to climb Table Mountain. The Portuguese, however, were not interested in settling on the Cape. It offered little more than fresh water; attempts to trade with the Khoikhoi often ended in violence, and the coast and its fierce weather posed a terrible threat to their tiny caravels.

Dutch By the end of the 16th century, the English and Dutch were beginning to challenge the Portuguese traders. In 1647, a Dutch East Indiaman was wrecked in Table Bay, and its crew built a fort and stayed for a year before they were rescued. This crystallized the value of a permanent settlement in the minds of the directors of the Dutch East India Company (Vereenigde Oost-Indische Compagnie or VOC). They had no intention of colonizing the country but simply of establishing a secure base for ships.

Jan van Riebeeck was the man they chose to lead a small expedition in his flagship *Drommedaris*. His specific charge was to build a fort, barter with the Khoikhoi for meat, and plant a garden. He reached Table Bay on April 6, 1652, built a mud-walled fort not far from the site of the surviving stone castle, and planted gardens that have now become the Botanical or Company's Gardens. The European men of the community were mostly employees of the VOC and overwhelmingly Dutch – a tiny official elite and a majority of ill-educated soldiers and sailors, many of whom had been pressed into service. In 1685, they were joined by around 200 French Huguenots – Calvinists who fled from persecution by King Louis XIV.

The population of whites did not reach 1000 until 1745, but small numbers of free (meaning non-VOC) burghers had begun to drift away from the close grip of the company, and into other areas of Africa. These were the first of the Trekboers, and their inevitable confrontations with the Khoisan were disastrous. The indigenous people were driven from their traditional lands, decimated by introduced diseases, and destroyed by superior weapons when they fought back. The survivors were left with no option but to work for Europeans in a form of bondage little different from slavery. There was a shortage of women in the colony, so the female slaves and Khoisan survivors were exploited both for labor and sex. In time, the slaves also intermixed with the Khoisan. The offspring of these unions formed the basis for sections of today's colored population.

The VOC maintained almost complete control, but the town was thriving – providing a comfortable European lifestyle to a growing number of artisans and entrepreneurs who serviced the ships and crews. Cape Town was known as the 'Tavern of the Seas,' a riotous port used by every navigator, privateer, and merchant traveling between Europe and the East (including Australia).

British Dutch power was fading by the end of the 18th century, and in response to the Napoleonic wars, the British decided to secure the Cape. In 1806, at Bloubergstrand north of Cape Town, the British defeated the Dutch and the colony was permanently ceded to the Crown on August 13, 1814.

The slave trade was abolished in 1808, and the remaining Khoisan, who were treated as slaves, were finally given the explicit protection of the law (including the right to own land) in 1828, moves that contributed to Afrikaners' dissatisfaction and the Great Trek (1834-40).

At the same time that these apparently liberal reforms were introduced, however, the British introduced new laws that laid the basis for an exploitative labor system little different from slavery. Thousands of dispossessed blacks sought work in the colony, but it was made a crime to be in the colony without a pass, and without work. It was also a crime to leave your job. In 1854, a representative parliament was formed in Cape Town, but much to the dismay of the Dutch and English farmers to the north and east, the British government and Cape liberals insisted on a multiracial constituency (albeit with financial qualifications that excluded the vast majority of blacks and coloreds).

The discovery and exploitation of diamonds and gold in the center of South Africa in the 1870s and '80s led to rapid changes. Cape Town was soon no longer the single dominant metropolis in the country, but as a major port it was a beneficiary of mineral wealth that laid the foundations for an industrial society. The same wealth led to imperialist dreams of grandeur on the part of Cecil John Rhodes (who became the premier of the Cape Colony in 1890), who had made his millions as the head of De Beers Consolidated Mines.

In 1860, construction of the Alfred Basin in the docks commenced, finally making the port storm-proof. In 1869, however, the Suez Canal was opened, and Cape Town's role as the Tavern of the Seas began to wane. Today, the massive supertankers that are too big to use the Suez are also too big to enter Table Bay, so they are serviced by helicopter.

In 1895, Rhodes sponsored the unsuccessful Jameson Raid, which attempted to overthrow the South African Republic (Transvaal), under President Kruger and bring it into a federation under British control. Rhodes was forced to resign, but the fiasco made the 1899-1902 Anglo-Boer War almost inevitable. Cape Town avoided any direct bloodshed in the terrible conflict, but it did play a key role in landing and supplying the half-million imperial and colonial troops who fought on the British side.

After the war, the British made some efforts toward reconciliation, and moves toward the union of the separate South African provinces were instituted. The question of who would be allowed to vote was solved by allowing the provinces to retain their existing systems: Blacks and coloreds retained a limited franchise in the Cape (although only whites could become members of the national parliament, and eligible blacks and coloreds only constituted around 7% of the electorate) but did not have the vote in other provinces.

The issue of which city should become the capital was solved by the unwieldy compromise of making Cape Town the seat of the legislature, Pretoria the administrative capital, and Bloemfontein the seat of Appellate Division of the Supreme Court. The Union of South Africa came into being in 1910.

Apartheid & the Townships In 1948, in the first election after WWII, the National Party campaigned on its policy of apartheid and narrowly won. In a series of bitter court and constitutional battles, the right of the coloreds to vote in the Cape was removed, and the insane apparatus of apartheid was erected. Since the coloreds had no Homeland, the western half of the Cape Province was declared a 'colored preference area,' which meant no black could be employed there unless it could be proved there was no suitable colored person for the job. No new black housing was built. As a result, illegal squatter camps mushroomed on the sandy plains to the east of Cape Town. In response, government bulldozers flattened the shanties, and their occupants were dragged away and dumped in their Homelands. Within weeks the shanties would rise again.

In 1960, the African National Congress and the Pan African Congress organized marches against the hated pass laws, which required blacks and coloreds to carry passbooks that authorized them to be in a particular area. In response to the crisis, a warrant for the arrest of Nelson Mandela and other ANC leaders was issued. In 1964, after establishing the ANC's military wing, Mandela was captured and sentenced to life imprisonment at the infamous Robben Island prison near Cape Town. In the early 1970s, rules were sufficiently relaxed to allow Mandela to write his now-famous prison notebooks and teach politics.

Nelson Mandela was released from prison in 1990 after the ANC was delcared a legal organization. In 1991 he was elected president of the ANC and began the long negotiations which were to end minority rule. He shared the 1993 Nobel peace prize with FW De Klerk and in the first free elections the following year he was elected president of South Africa.

Orientation

On first impression, Cape Town is surprisingly small. The city center lies to the north of Table Mountain and east of Signal Hill, and the old inner-city suburbs of Tamboerskloof, Gardens, and Oranjezicht are all within walking distance of it. This area is sometimes referred to as the City Bowl. On the other side of Signal Hill, Sea Point is another older suburb densely populated with high-rise flats, apartments, hotels, restaurants and bars.

Information

Tourist Offices It's worth visiting both Captour and Satour. Captour concentrates on the peninsula, and although Satour caters for the whole country, it also has some excellent local information (including the best free map). The staff at Satour (☎ 21-6274) are extremely helpful. The desk is open daily (except Sunday) from 8 am to 4:30 pm (until 4 pm on Friday and 12:30 pm on Saturday). Captour (☎ 418-5214) has some good tourist, accommodations and restaurant guides, for R4 each. Both Captour and Satour also have offices in the Tourist Rendezvous (☎ 418-5202) complex at the railway station, which also features several other useful information desks. The Tourist Rendezvous is open from 8 am to 7 pm on weekdays, from 8:30 am to 5 pm on Saturday, and from 9 am to 5 pm on Sunday.

Foreign Consulates Most countries have their main embassy to South Africa in Pretoria, with an office or consulate in Cape

Town that becomes the official embassy during Cape Town's parliamentary sessions. The following is not a comprehensive list. If your consulate is not listed, consult the telephone directory under consulates and embassies. Many are open in the morning only.

Australia
14th Floor, BP Centre, Thibault Square (☎ 419-5425)

Belgium
Vogue House, Thibault Square (☎ 419-3410)

Canada
Reserve Bank Building, Hout St (☎ 23-5240)

France
2 Dean St, Gardens (☎ 23-1575)

Germany
825 St Martini Gardens, Queen Victoria St (☎ 24-2410)

Israel
Church Square House, Plein St (☎ 45-7207)

Japan
Standard Bank Centre, Heerengracht (☎ 25-1695)

Netherlands
100 Strand St (☎ 21-5660)

Sweden
17th Floor, Southern Life Centre, 8 Riebeeck St (☎ 25-1687)

Switzerland
9th Floor, Waldorf Building, 80 St George's Mall (☎ 26-1040)

UK
Southern Life Centre, 8 Riebeeck St (☎ 25-3670)

USA
4th Floor, Broadway Centre, Heerengracht (☎ 21-4280)

Money All prices quoted in the Cape Town section are in rand (R). Money can be changed at any commercial bank; they're open from 9 am to 3:30 pm. There are offices of American Express at the Tourist Rendezvous (☎ 418-5225), Thibault Square at the end of St George's Mall (☎ 21-5586) and at the Victoria & Alfred Waterfront (☎ 21-6021). Rennies Travel is the agent for Thomas Cook and has branches on the corner of St George's and Hout Sts (☎ 26-1789); 2 St George's St, Thibault Square near Amex (☎ 25-2370); 182 Main Rd, Sea Point (☎ 439-7529); and at the Waterfront (☎ 418-3744).

Post & Communications The General Post Office is on the corner of Darling and Parliament Sts and is open weekdays from 8 am to 4:30 pm and Saturday from 8 am to noon. It has an international phone center where you can pay cash to make a call (open from 8 am to 10:30 pm Monday to Saturday and from 9 am to 8:30 pm Sunday and public holidays). The public phones in the post office are open 24 hours, but they're often very busy. Cape Town's area code is 021.

Bookstores Exclusive Books (☎ 419-0905), at the Waterfront, has an excellent range; it's open until 9:30 pm on Saturday and from 11 am to 5 pm on Sunday. The main mass-market bookstores/news agents are CNA and Paperbacks. Both have numerous shops scattered around the city. CNA has a large shop in the Golden Acre Centre. Paperbacks has a branch at 202 Main Rd, Sea Point, and near the American Express office in Thibault Square. The latter sells some foreign newspapers (mainly British).

Film & Photography For camera repairs go to Camera Care, on Castle (Kasteel) St between Burg St and St George's Mall. Prolab, 177 Bree St (on the corner of Pepper St), will do slide processing and mounting in two hours for less than R30 for 36 exposures – and they do a good job.

Medical Services Medical services are of a high standard. Doctors are listed under Medical in the phone book, and they generally arrange for hospitalization, although in an emergency you can go directly to the casualty department of Groote Schuur Hospital (☎ 404-9111), which is at the intersection of De Waal (M3) and the Eastern Boulevard (N2) to the east of the city. Call the police (☎ 10111) to get directions to the nearest hospital. Many doctors make house

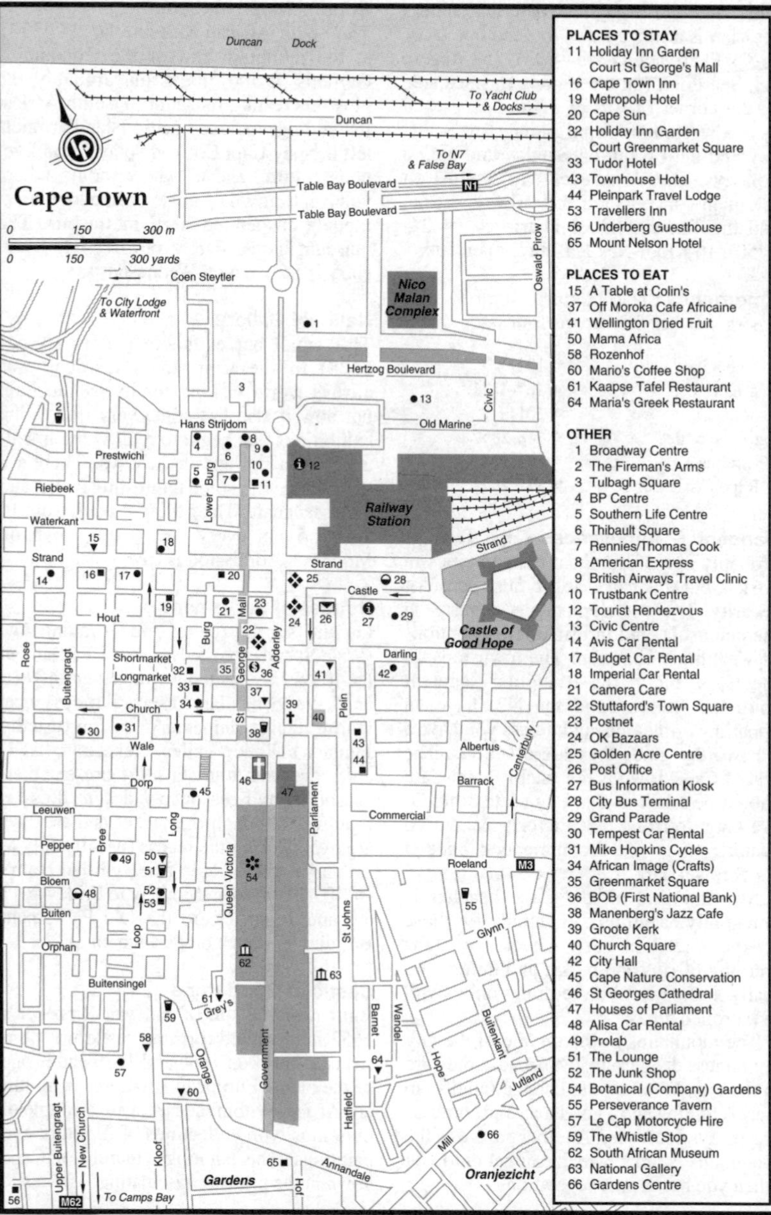
Cape Town
0 150 300 m
0 150 300 yards
Duncan Dock
To Yacht Club & Docks
Duncan
To N7 & False Bay
Table Bay Boulevard
Table Bay Boulevard
N1
Oswald Pirow
Coen Steytler
To City Lodge & Waterfront
Nico Malan Complex
Hertzog Boulevard
Civic
Old Marine
Hans Strijdom
Prestwichi
Riebeek
Lower Burg
Waterkant
Railway Station
Strand
Strand
Strand
Castle
Castle of Good Hope
Hout
Burg
St George Mall
Adderley
Darling
Rose
Buitengragt
Shortmarket
Longmarket
Church
Plein
Wale
Albertus
Canterbury
Barrack
Dorp
Leeuwen
Commercial
Parliament
Long
Bree
Pepper
Queen Victoria
Roeland
M3
Bloem
Buiten
Loop
Glynn
St Johns
Orphan
Buitensingel
Grey's
Barnet
Wandel
Buitenkant
Hope
Orange
Government
Jutland
Upper Buitengragt
New Church
Kloof
Hatfield
Mill
Annandale
Hof
Gardens
Oranjezicht
M62
To Camps Bay
PLACES TO STAY
11 Holiday Inn Garden Court St George's Mall
16 Cape Town Inn
19 Metropole Hotel
20 Cape Sun
32 Holiday Inn Garden Court Greenmarket Square
33 Tudor Hotel
43 Townhouse Hotel
44 Pleinpark Travel Lodge
53 Travellers Inn
56 Underberg Guesthouse
65 Mount Nelson Hotel
PLACES TO EAT
15 A Table at Colin's
37 Off Moroka Cafe Africaine
41 Wellington Dried Fruit
50 Mama Africa
58 Rozenhof
60 Mario's Coffee Shop
61 Kaapse Tafel Restaurant
64 Maria's Greek Restaurant
OTHER
1 Broadway Centre
2 The Fireman's Arms
3 Tulbagh Square
4 BP Centre
5 Southern Life Centre
6 Thibault Square
7 Rennies/Thomas Cook
8 American Express
9 British Airways Travel Clinic
10 Trustbank Centre
12 Tourist Rendezvous
13 Civic Centre
14 Avis Car Rental
17 Budget Car Rental
18 Imperial Car Rental
21 Camera Care
22 Stuttaford's Town Square
23 Postnet
24 OK Bazaars
25 Golden Acre Centre
26 Post Office
27 Bus Information Kiosk
28 City Bus Terminal
29 Grand Parade
30 Tempest Car Rental
31 Mike Hopkins Cycles
34 African Image (Crafts)
35 Greenmarket Square
36 BOB (First National Bank)
38 Manenberg's Jazz Cafe
39 Groote Kerk
40 Church Square
42 City Hall
45 Cape Nature Conservation
46 St Georges Cathedral
47 Houses of Parliament
48 Alisa Car Rental
49 Prolab
51 The Lounge
52 The Junk Shop
54 Botanical (Company) Gardens
55 Perseverance Tavern
57 Le Cap Motorcycle Hire
59 The Whistle Stop
62 South African Museum
63 National Gallery
66 Gardens Centre

calls, and you'll pay less than R60 unless the visit is arranged by a top-end hotel.

K's Pharmacy (☎ 434-9331), 52 Regent Rd, Sea Point (on the Camps Bay/sea side of the corner of Cassel St) is open seven days a week, until 9 pm Monday to Saturday and until 6 pm on Sunday and public holidays. There's a seven-day chemist on the main concourse in the railway station, and the Tamboerskloof Pharmacy (☎ 24-4450), 16 Kloof Nek Rd, stays open late.

Emergency The contact numbers for emergency services are as follows:

ambulance	☎ 10177
fire brigade	☎ 461-4141
police	☎ 10111
tourist police	☎ 418-2852
Lifeline	☎ 461-111
Rape Crisis Centre	☎ 47-9762

Dangers & Annoyances Cape Town is probably one of the most relaxed cities in Africa, but this can instill a false sense of security. There is tremendous poverty on the peninsula, and informal redistributions of wealth are common. The townships on the Cape Flats (the triangular segment south of Athlone and the N2) have an appalling crime rate, and unless you have a trustworthy guide they are off-limits. The rest of Cape Town is reasonably safe. Care should be taken in Sea Point late at night. Walking to/from the Victoria & Alfred Waterfront is not recommended once it starts to get dark.

Swimming at all the Cape beaches is potentially hazardous, especially for those inexperienced in surf. Check for signs warning of rips and rocks, and unless you really know what you're doing only swim in patrolled areas.

The mountains in the middle of the city are no less dangerous just because they are in the city. Weather can change rapidly, so warm clothing and a good map and compass are always necessary. Another hazard of the mountains is ticks, which can get onto you when you brush past vegetation.

South African Museum

The South African Museum (☎ 24-3330), at the mountain end of the Company's Gardens, is the oldest and arguably the most interesting museum in South Africa. Its holdings include Pacific Island artifacts left here by Capt Cook, displays of indigenous culture, and a 'whale room,' where you can hear whale noises while looking at models suspended high in the air. The museum is open daily from 10 am to 5 pm; entry is R2 (free on Wednesday).

National Gallery

This small but exquisite gallery (☎ 45-1628) in the Company's Gardens was always worth visiting for its architecture, but now it also has some very interesting exhibitions that begin to redress the imbalance from the apartheid days. There's a good shop with some interesting books and a pleasant café. The gallery is open from 10 am to 5 pm every day (from 1 pm on Monday). Admission is free.

Houses of Parliament

On the south side of Government Ave (Wale St end) are the Houses of Parliament (☎ 403-2911), which were opened in 1885 and have been enlarged several times since. During the parliamentary session (usually January to June), gallery tickets are available; overseas tourists must present their passports, and reasonably decent dress is required, although the jacket and tie days are over. During the recess (usually July to January) there are free guided tours (☎ 403-2198) from Monday to Friday at 11 am and 2 pm. Go to the Old Parliament Building entrance on Parliament St.

Castle of Good Hope

Built near the site of Jan van Riebeeck's 1652 mud-walled fort, the castle was constructed between 1666 and 1679 and is one of the oldest European structures in southern Africa. Within the castle are a couple of museums with collections of furniture and paintings. The paintings, mainly of Cape Town in the past, are fascinating. The castle opens at 10 am with the Ceremony of the Keys. Sentries change every half hour, and there is a full ceremonial Changing of the Guard at noon. There are guided tours hourly between 10 am and 3 pm. The castle closes at 4 pm. Entry (from the Grand Parade side) is R5.

Table Mountain & Cableway

The cableway is such an obvious and popular attraction you might have difficulty convincing yourself that it is worth the trouble and expense. It is. The views from the top of Table Mountain are phenomenal, and there are some excellent walks on the summit. The mountain is home to over 1400 species of flowering plants, as well as Rock Dassies, curious rodent-like creatures whose closest living relative is the elephant. If you plan to walk, make sure you're properly equipped with warm and waterproof clothing. Table Mountain is 1000m high and conditions can become treacherous quickly. There's a small restaurant and shop at the top.

The cable cars don't operate when it's dangerously windy. Call in advance (☎ 24-5148 or 24-8409) to see if they're operating. Weather permitting, they operate from 8 am to 10 pm from December 1 to April 30 and from 8:30 am to 6 pm for the rest of the year. The best visibility and conditions are likely to be first thing in the morning, or in the evening. Coming back down the mountain, make sure that you stand at the front of the car – it's exhilarating. An adult roundtrip ticket is R21, one-way is R12.

Victoria & Alfred Waterfront

The Victoria & Alfred Waterfront is packed with restaurants, bars, music venues and interesting shops. The huge Victoria Wharf complex adds shops, cinemas, a produce market, and still more restaurants and bars, but also, unfortunately, a fair splash of the antiseptic atmosphere you'll find in rich white suburbs all over South Africa. Still, the development is tremendously popular, day and night. There is an information center (☎ 418-2369) in the middle of the complex. See Organized Tours for cruises on Table Bay.

The Waterfront is *the* place to go for nightlife. Although security is strict and it is safe to walk around, there are plenty of merry men, so lone women should be a little cautious.

Kirstenbosch Botanic Gardens

The Kirstenbosch Botanic Gardens (☎ 762-1166) on Rhodes Drive, Constantia, are one of the most beautiful gardens in the world. The gardens are devoted almost exclusively to indigenous plants, including 9000 of Southern Africa's 22,000 plant species. The gardens are open year-round from 8 am, closing at 7 pm from September to March, and 6 pm from April to August; entry is R4. Visit free on Tuesday.

Atlantic Coast

The Atlantic coast of the Cape Peninsula has some of the most spectacular coastal scenery in the world. The beaches include the trendiest on the Cape, and the emphasis is on sunbathing rather than swimming. The water comes straight from the Antarctic (courtesy of the Benguela current), and swimming is nothing if not exhilarating. At **Sea Point**, Main and Regent Rds are lined with restaurants and shops. The coast itself is rocky, but there are swimming pools. Catch any Clifton, Bakoven or Camps Bay bus from the Golden Acre terminal. There are four linked beaches at **Clifton**, accessible by steps from Victoria St. They're the busiest beaches on the Cape. There are frequent buses from OK Bazaars, Adderley St, and minibus taxis from the Strand. It's a pleasant three-km walk from Sea Point and another 1.5 km to **Camps Bay**, which is often windy and not as trendy as the beaches at Clifton. But it *is* more spectacular. The **Twelve Apostles** running south from Table Mountain tumble into the sea above the broad stretch of white sand.

Organized Tours

For a quick orientation on a fine day you can't beat Topless Tours (☎ 448-2888), which runs a roofless double-decker bus. The two-hour city tour (R25) between Dock Rd in the Waterfront and the Tourist Rendezvous departs about six times a day in summer. Sealink Tours (☎ 25-4480) has tours of Cape Point (R110), Winelands (R120), Tulbagh Valley (R140), and Hermanus (R140). Other major companies with similar deals include Springbok Atlas Tours (☎ 417-6545) and Hylton Ross (☎ 438-1500), a big local company and a bit more up-market. One City Tours (☎ 387-5351, 387-5165) has an excellent three-hour township tour for R75. Tana-Baru Tours (☎ 24-0719) offers a highly recommended two-hour walk or drive through Bo-Kaap (the Malay quarter), including tea and some very tasty traditional snacks in a private home. If you're going to take any tour of this area, make it this one, rather than a white-run bus tour that treats the area like a zoo.

Cruises A trip into Table Bay should not be missed. The cheapest cruise (R8) is a quick 25-minute voyage with Hylton Ross. *Spirit of Victory* (☎ 25-4062), a new yacht built in the old style, has hour-long cruises for R25, and 90-minute cruises, with drinks, in the evening for R45. Sealink Tours (☎ 25-4480), East Pier Rd, has one-hour, R15 trips. Sealink Tour's other cruises include half-hour harbor trips (just R8).

Places to Stay – bottom end

Guesthouses *Travellers Inn* (☎ 24-9272), 208 Long St, is in one of the oldest wrought-iron-decorated buildings and was once the British Guesthouse; that name is still on the door. Singles start at R60 and doubles at R100, including a make-it-yourself breakfast. *Palm Court Holiday Lodge* (☎ 23-8721), 11 Hof St, Gardens (a block from Orange St), is a big old house with boarding house overtones; singles/doubles go for just R75/140 and three/four bedrooms are R175/200.

Places to Stay – middle

B&Bs & Guesthouses *Belmont House* (☎ 461-5417), 10 Belmont Ave, Oranjezicht, is a small but comfortable guesthouse overlooking the City Bowl, charging from R60/90.

Ambleside Guesthouse (☎ 45- 2503), 11 Forest Rd, Oranjezicht has comfortable singles/doubles and family rooms, and a fully equipped guest kitchen; doubles start at R130. The *Underberg Guesthouse* (☎ 26-2262), on the corner of Carstens St and Tamboerskloof Rd, is a restored Victorian that's not too fussy. Singles/doubles start at R160/255, including breakfast. Nearby at 10A Tamboerskloof Rd, *Table Mountain Lodge* (☎ 23-0042) is another restored house with B&B from R200/220.

Hotels *Tudor Hotel* (☎ 24-1335), Greenmarket Square, is a cozy little hotel (30 rooms); singles/doubles start at R145/190 including breakfast. The *Metropole Hotel* (☎ 23-6363), 38 Long St, is an attractive old-style hotel, with a dark, wood-panel interior; rooms start at R165/190.

The two-star *Pleinpark Travel Lodge* (☎ 45-7563), on the corner of Corporation and Barrack Sts, is a conveniently located hotel; singles/doubles start at R165/220 including breakfast. In the same league is the high-rise *Cape Town Inn* (☎ 23-5116), on the corner of Strand and Bree Sts; rooms begin at R160 for a double, with breakfast. At 16 Hof St, Gardens, the *Helmsley Hotel* (☎ 23-7200) seems a little out of place in the middle of a city – it's like an old-style country hotel, though it's a bit expensive at R190/260.

Places to Stay – top end

Staying at the *Mount Nelson Hotel* (☎ 23-1000), 76 Orange St, is like stepping back in time to the days of the British Empire. Dating from 1899, the hotel is set in seven acres of parkland; mid-season rates start around R950/1350. In complete contrast, the five-star *Cape Sun* (☎ 23-8844), Strand St, is a large, modern, classy hotel; rooms start at around R850. Less expensive but still very good is the four-star *Townhouse Hotel* (☎ 45-7050), 60 Corporation St (on the corner of Mostert St), which charges R233/250; rooms with numbers ending in six have good views of the mountain.

There are also a few members of the Holiday Inn Garden Court chain:

Greenmarket Square
    On Greenmarket Square (☎ 23-2040), R204/218
St George's Mall
    On the corner of Riebeeck St & St George's Mall (☎ 419-0808), R224/248
De Waal
    Mill St, Gardens (☎ 45-1311), R209/228

Close to both the city and the Waterfront, *City Lodge* (☎ 419-9450), on the corner of Dock Rd and Alfred St, is a big place; rooms start at R225/266 singles/doubles. The *Victoria & Alfred Hotel* (☎ 419-6677), right in the middle of the Waterfront, has everything a five-star hotel should have; singles/doubles start at R405/700.

Places to Eat

Cape Town could easily claim to be the gastronomic capital of Africa. Although you have to go looking for it, the traditional Cape cuisine – a curious cross between Dutch/European and Indonesian/Malay – is worth searching for. The seafood is top quality, and the local wines are sensational.

The two main restaurant zones are Sea Point, along Main Rd, and the Victoria & Alfred Waterfront. Most of the inner neighborhoods in the City Bowl have good places to eat as well.

The popular *St Elmo's Restaurant & Pizzeria* is a chain worth looking out for. It serves pizzas, made in wood-fired ovens, from R15 and a range of other reasonably priced dishes. Among others, it has a branch at 118 Main Rd, Sea Point.

City Center One good place to grab a snack is the so-called Fruit and Vegetable Market at the Adderley St end of the Grand Parade. There's a cheap bakery and a number of stalls that sell various Indian takeaways, including excellent samosas.

Off Moroka Café Africaine, 120 Adderley St, near Church St, is a very pleasant place to sample some African food and listen to tapes of African music. It's open daily, except Sunday, for breakfast and lunch. *The Tea Garden* in the Company's Gardens has quite a large menu. It's also open for breakfast.

Wellington Dried Fruit is a Cape Town institution. It's a long, narrow store on Darling St near Plein St, selling a huge range of dried fruit, deli items, tinned foods, and *lots* of candy. Well worth a visit even if you don't want to buy anything.

If you're looking for a pleasant and stylish place to have lunch in the city center, try *Squares*, a bright, good-value restaurant in Stuttaford's Town Square, overlooking St George's Mall. In the impressive old Martin Melck House on Strand St between Buitengracht and Bree St, *A Table at Colin's* (☎ 419-6533) is a good restaurant in a very pleasant setting. There's an art gallery upstairs. One of the dining rooms is non-smoking. Colin's is open for lunch and dinner.

The *Kaapse Tafel Restaurant* (☎ 23-1651), 90 Queen Victoria St, is a nice little restaurant that serves a variety of traditional Cape dishes.

A little further up Long St, on the corner of Pepper St, *Mama Africa* is a very stylish new bar and restaurant with interesting décor and a slightly African menu. Entrées such as roasted beef marrow bone or mussels cost between R10 and R16; main courses include steaks (including ostrich steaks) and bobotie (Malay curry served with stewed fruits and chutney), and cost around R25 to R35. There's live African music on Friday and Saturday nights.

Gardens & Tamboerskloof There's a batch of interesting places in the old Gardens and Tamboerskloof areas, southeast of the city center. You could start with a beer in the *Stag's Head Hotel* on Hope St (rowdy) or the *Perseverance Tavern* on Buitenkant (civilized) and go on to dinner at *Maria's Greek Restaurant* or the *Old Colonial*, and finish with Irish coffees at *Roxy's Coffee Bar*.

Mario's Coffee Shop, on Rheede St, has excellent and very cheap meals. It's open from 8 am to 4 pm. Not far away, the *Kloof Corner Café* (a corner store, not a café) is known for its chips (fries). If you have a sweet tooth and a caffeine addiction, check out *Zerban's Cake & Coffee Shop* on the lower level of the Gardens Centre, Mill St.

The *Perseverance Tavern* (☎ 461-2440), 83 Buitenkant (across from Rust-en-Vreugd), is an old pub, built in 1808 and licensed since 1836. On Friday nights it can be too crowded to move.

Maria's Greek Restaurant (☎ 45-2096) is a small taverna where booking is essential, which speaks for itself. It's on the corner of Barnet and Dunkley Sts and is open from 7 to 11:30 pm daily.

The *Old Colonial Restaurant* (☎ 45-4909), 39 Barnet St, is another place where you can find traditional Cape cuisine, such as matjie (marinated) herring, bredie (mutton stew with vegetables) and bobotie. You're advised to book.

Rozenhof (☎ 24-1968), 18 Kloof St, is one of the best restaurants in town, with small but interesting seasonal menus. Despite the quality it isn't too expensive for a splurge: Three courses with wine could cost under R70.

Victoria & Alfred Waterfront New restaurants and night spots are mushrooming at the Waterfront. As well as the franchised places such as *St Elmo's* and *Spur*, there are some interesting places to eat, although most are aimed squarely at tourists. An exception is the group of smaller places in the King's Warehouse, next to the Red Shed Craft Workshop. You can buy from various stalls and eat at common tables. *Ari's*, the Sea Point institution for Middle Eastern dishes, has a branch here. Also here is *Captain Bartholomeu's Seafood Restaurant*, with an adjoining fresh fish market.

The *Musselcracker Restaurant*, upstairs in the Victoria Wharf shopping center, has a seafood buffet for R50 at lunch and R59 at dinner. There's also the relaxed *Musselcracker Oyster Bar*, a good place for a drink and some seafood.

The *Green Dolphin* (☎ 21-7471), beneath the Victoria & Alfred Hotel, is a popular restaurant with excellent live jazz, nightly from 8 pm. If there's an international act in town it will probably play here. There's a cover charge of R10 (R6 if you don't have a view of the stage).

For fish & chips overlooking the water, head for *Fisherman's Choice*, where you can take out or eat in. Hake and chips cost R14.

Sea Point One of Cape Town's surprisingly few Indian restaurants is the *Little Bombay* (☎ 439-9041), 245 Main Rd. It's a Hindu-run 'pure-veg' restaurant. It's open daily for lunch and dinner.

L'Orient (☎ 439-6572), 50 Main Rd (near the corner of Marine Rd), is a good restaurant with Malaysian and Indonesian dishes. It's open for dinner daily except Monday.

San Marco (☎ 49-2758), 92 Main Rd (on the corner of St James), is a long-established and excellent formal Italian restaurant, with some of the few professional waiters in town. They let it go to their heads sometimes. It's open daily except Tuesday for dinner, plus lunch on Sunday. The gelateria in front of the restaurant has delicious takeaway gelati and other ice cream.

Ari's Souvlaki (☎ 439-6683), 150 Main Rd (on the corner of Oliver Rd), is an extremely popular Sea Point institution famous for felafels and souvlaki.

Entertainment

You can't do without the entertainment guide in the *Weekly Mail & Guardian* (R3). *The Cape Times* newspaper has the Funfinder section on Friday. *Soundwaves* is a free paper aimed at musicians and is available at many music shops. *Going Out in the Cape* is a monthly booklet listing most mainstream events; it's sold at various information offices for R3. When in doubt, the place to go is the Waterfront, which is easily accessible and has a number of possibilities all within walking distance of

JEFF RUBIN

Sign in Ushuaia, Argentina, listing Antarctic tour ships that are in port

JEFF RUBIN

Russian-flagged tour ship rolling through the Southern Ocean

JEFF RUBIN

Cape Horn, southernmost tip of South America

JEFF RUBIN

Ushuaia, main tourist departure point

each other. For any entertainment bookings, contact Computicket (☎ 21 4715), a computerized booking agency that has *every* seat for *every* theater, cinema, and sports venue on its system.

Pubs & Bars At the Waterfront, *Cantina Tequila* is currently very popular with visitors, and the *Quay 4 Bar* is still crowded. The *Fireman's Arms*, on the corner of Buitengracht and Mechau (near Somerset), is one of the few old pubs left in town and it dates from 1906. *Blue Rock*, Main Rd, Sea Point, is a smallish, coolish bar specializing in cocktails.

The *Lounge*, upstairs at 194 Long St, is a small, relaxed place, with its own iron-lace balcony, a great place for a drink on a hot night. *District Six Café*, on the corner of Sir Lowry Rd and Darling St, is similar but more down-to-earth.

The *Whistle Stop*, at the top end of Long St near the Long St Baths, is the only bar in the city area where you'll drink with ordinary people of all colors. It's open 24 hours, seven days a week, and good, cheap meals are available.

Live Music The *Green Dolphin* is a top-class jazz venue at the Waterfront, and the *Brass Bell* at the Kalk Bay station has live bands on Wednesday and Saturday nights, and Saturday and Sunday afternoons. One of the best places for a drink, a snack and live jazz is *Manenberg's Jazz Cafe*, upstairs on Adderley St on the corner of Church St. It's a pleasant place with a racially mixed clientele.

For classical music, see what's on at the *Town Hall* (☎ 462-1250), where the Cape Town Symphony has regular concerts.

Things to Buy

Crafts There are craft shops all over town, but don't forget that few items come from the Cape Town area. There are, however, some township-produced items such as recycled tin boxes and toys, which make great gifts. The Siyakatala stall in the craft market at the Waterfront sells items made by self-help groups in the townships, and the quality is as good as anywhere. In St George's Cathedral is a small shop that's worth looking at. It has some guidebooks and crafts – and you know that the profits are going to people who need them. African Image, on the corner of Church and Burg Sts, has an interesting range of new and old craft works and artifacts. Prices are very reasonable. Nearby on the Church St mall, Out of Africa is a very expensive but very good craft/antique shop. Mnandi Textiles, 90 Station St (near the corner of Lower Main Rd), Observatory, sells cloth and clothing printed with everything from ANC election posters to animal patterns.

Antiques, Collectibles & Old Books The Junk Shop, on the corner of Long and Bloem Sts, has some intriguing junk from many eras. In the same area there are several good secondhand and antiquarian bookstores. Not far away, Church St between Long and Burg Sts is a pedestrian mall where there are several antique shops; a flea market is also held there on Thursday, Friday, and Saturday (daily in summer).

Getting Around

The Airport Intercape's Airport Shuttle links the central railway station (outside Platform 24) and the DF Malan Airport. It's best to call to get the railway station departure times (☎ 934-4400, 386-4414), which are irregular – usually about one hour before flight departures, although it doesn't have services for all flights. The shuttle has a counter in the domestic terminal of the airport. The scheduled service costs R22; coming from the airport, the shuttle can usually drop you off where you want (if it's reasonably close to the city center) for another R5. If you want to be picked up for a trip outside the regular schedule it will cost about R50, depending on your pickup point. Taxis are very expensive; expect to pay more than R100.

Bus Cape Town has a pretty effective bus network centered on the Golden Acre terminal. You can get almost anywhere in the city for under R2. There's a helpful information kiosk at the Parade terminal. It's open from 7:45 am to 5:45 pm Monday to Friday and from 8 am to 1 pm on Sunday. There are a couple of inquiry numbers (☎ 934-0540, 0801-21-2111). If you are using a particular bus regularly, it's worth buying clipcards, which give you 10 trips at a discount price. When traveling short distances, most people wait at the bus stop and take either a bus or a minibus taxi, whichever arrives first.

Train The Train Information office (☎ 405-2991), in the main railway station near the old locomotive opposite Platform 23, is open Monday to Saturday from 6 am to 8 pm and on Sunday and public holidays from 7 am to 7 pm. The local trains have 1st- and 3rd-class carriages, but slightly softer seats don't justify a ticket price that is twice as expensive. It's reasonably safe to travel in 3rd class (check the current situation), but unless someone reliable tells you otherwise, don't do it during peak hours or on weekends. Probably the most important line for travelers is the Simonstad/Simon's Town line that runs through Observatory and then around the back of the mountain through upper-income white suburbs.

Taxi Taxis are expensive. There is a cab rank at the Adderley St end of the Grand Parade in the city, or phone Star Taxis (☎ 419-7777), Marine Taxi (☎ 434-0434), or Sea Point Taxis (☎ 434-4444). For a cheaper alternative around the City Bowl and as far as Camps Bay, see the Rikki section that follows.

Minibus Taxi Minibus taxis cover most of the city with an informal network of routes. They are a cheap and efficient way of getting around the city. They go virtually everywhere and can have flexible routes. Their main terminus is on the upper deck of the railway station, accessible from a walkway in the Golden Acre Centre or from stairways on Strand St. The terminus is well organized and finding the right rank is easy.

Minibus taxis cost a little less than the municipal buses. There's no way of telling which route the taxi will take except by asking the driver.

Rikki These tiny, open vans provide Asian-style transport in the City Bowl and nearby areas for low prices. Telephone Rikki's (☎ 23-4888) or just hail one on the street – you can pay a shared rate of a few rand or more if you phone for the whole van. They run between 7 am and 6 pm daily except Sunday and go as far afield as Sea Point and Camps Bay but not Observatory. Although they are cheap, Rikki's is not the quickest, as other passengers are dropped off en route.

Bike The Cape Peninsula is a great place to explore by bike, but distances can be deceptively large – it's nearly 65 km from the center to Cape Point. Bikes are not allowed on suburban trains. For a trouble-free bike contact Mike Hopkins (☎ 23-2527), 133A Bree St (near the corner of Wale St), or Day Trippers (☎ 461-4599 or 531-3274).

Christchurch

At the base of the hills of Banks Peninsula, Christchurch is often described as the most English of New Zealand's cities. It is a large, ordered city with a population of 308,200. Nestled beneath the Southern Alps, the city exists as a great South Pacific incongruity. Many statues honor persons with English names; and trams rattle past streets with oh-so-English names (Oxford, Worcester, etc). It is easy to forget that this epitome of Englishness is the capital of Te Wahipounamu, long-time ancestral home of the Ngai Tahu.

The first Europeans in Christchurch began building huts along the Avon in

1851, but it was not until March 1862 that it was incorporated as a city. The name Christchurch comes from Christ Church College at Oxford, as one of the leaders of the early settlers was educated there. The Avon River, which flows through Christchurch, is named after a stream in Ayrshire, Scotland.

Even the central square is dominated by a neogothic cathedral in the fashion of English towns. Get away from the center, out to the western suburbs such as Fendalton, Avonhead, Bryndwr, Burnside and Ilam, and you'll be struck by the tranquil atmosphere. Here are the exquisite gardens Christchurch is famous for, expanses of geraniums, chrysanthemums and carefully edged lawns where not a blade of grass is out of place.

Orientation

The Cathedral Square is very much the center of town. To find it, just look for the spire, and once there, climb to the top to get your orientation. Christchurch is a compact city and walking around is easy, although slightly complicated by the river that twists and winds through the center and crosses your path in disconcertingly varied directions. The network of one-way streets adds even more excitement if you're driving. Colombo St, running north-south through the square, is the main shopping street. You will find the post office and pay phones in the southwest corner of the square.

Information

Tourist Offices Walk down Worcester St from the Square to the Christchurch/Canterbury Visitor Centre (☎ 379-9629; fax 377-2424) by the river, on the corner of Oxford Terrace. It's open from 8:30 am to 5 pm Monday to Friday and from 8:30 am to 4 pm on weekends; it stays open later in the summer. This is the best bet for local information. Adventure Canterbury, where you can get information on all manner of outdoor pursuits, is in the same building and uses the same phone number. There are branches of the information center at both Christchurch airports, domestic (☎ 353-7774) and international (☎ 353-7783). A good free publication is the monthly *In and Around Christchurch*. Note that bus numbers refer to Canride buses unless indicated otherwise.

The Disabilities Service (☎ 366-6189), 314 Worcester St has information on accessible facilities and equipment for hire. They are open from 9 am to 5 pm Monday to Friday,

Money All prices quoted in the Christchurch section are in New Zealand dollars (NZ$).

Foreign Consulates Consulates in Christchurch include:

Denmark	☎ 389-5086
France	☎ 351-6259
Germany	☎ 379-3193
Japan	☎ 366-56800
Netherlands	☎ 366-9280
Sweden	☎ 365-0000
UK	☎ 365-5440
USA	☎ 379-004

Bookstores Christchurch has numerous bookstores. Arnold Books, 11 New Regent St, Christchurch, New Zealand (☎ 365-7188), carries the best selection of Antarctic titles. Scorpio Books, on the corner of Hereford St and Oxford Terrace has a wide range of books. Smith's Bookshop, at 133 Manchester St, is a classic secondhand bookstore – one room is devoted to books on New Zealand, including Maori culture and art, and poetry and fiction by New Zealand authors. The Epicentre in the Arts Centre, Hereford St, the place for environmental books, is open daily from 10 am to 4:30 pm.

Medical Services The Christchurch Hospital (☎ 364-0640) is on the corner of Oxford Terrace and Riccarton Ave, and there is an after-hours surgery (☎ 365-7777) at 931 Colombo St, on the corner of Bealey Ave, open from 5 pm to 8 am on weekdays and 24 hours on weekends and public holidays.

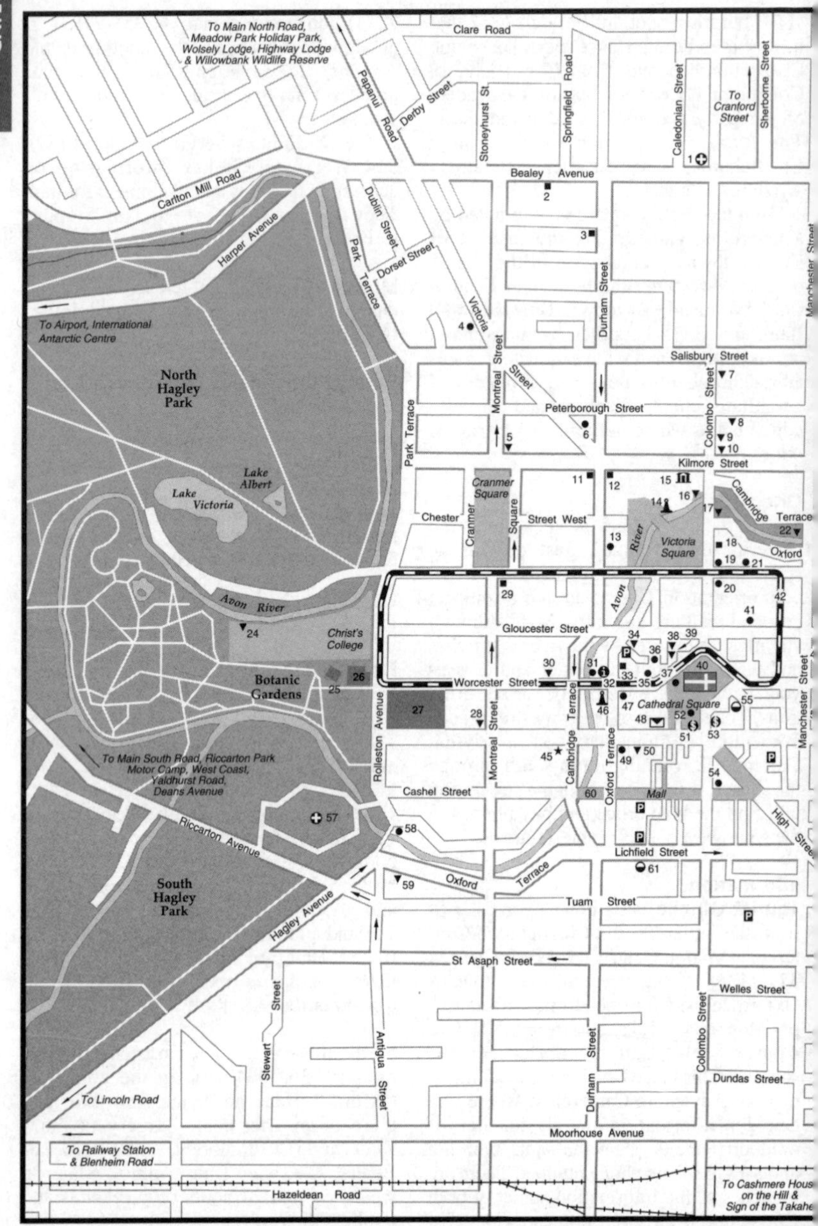
To Main North Road, Meadow Park Holiday Park, Wolsely Lodge, Highway Lodge & Willowbank Wildlife Reserve
Clare Road
Papanui Road
Derby Street
Stoneyhurst St
Springfield Road
Caledonian Street
To Cranford Street
Sherborne Street
Bealey Avenue
Carlton Mill Road
Harper Avenue
Dublin Street
Park Terrace
Dorset Street
Victoria
Durham Street
Manchester Street
To Airport, International Antarctic Centre
North Hagley Park
Salisbury Street
Montreal Street
Peterborough Street
Colombo Street
Kilmore Street
Lake Albert
Lake Victoria
Cranmer Square
Chester
Street West
Cambridge Terrace
Avon River
Victoria Square
Oxford
Christ's College
Gloucester Street
Botanic Gardens
Worcester Street
Rolleston Avenue
Cathedral Square
To Main South Road, Riccarton Park Motor Camp, West Coast, Yaldhurst Road, Deans Avenue
Oxford Terrace
Cashel Street
Mall
High Street
Riccarton Avenue
Lichfield Street
South Hagley Park
Oxford Terrace
Tuam Street
Hagley Avenue
St Asaph Street
Welles Street
Stewart Street
Antigua Street
Dundas Street
To Lincoln Road
Moorhouse Avenue
To Railway Station & Blenheim Road
Hazeldean Road
To Cashmere House on the Hill & Sign of the Takahe

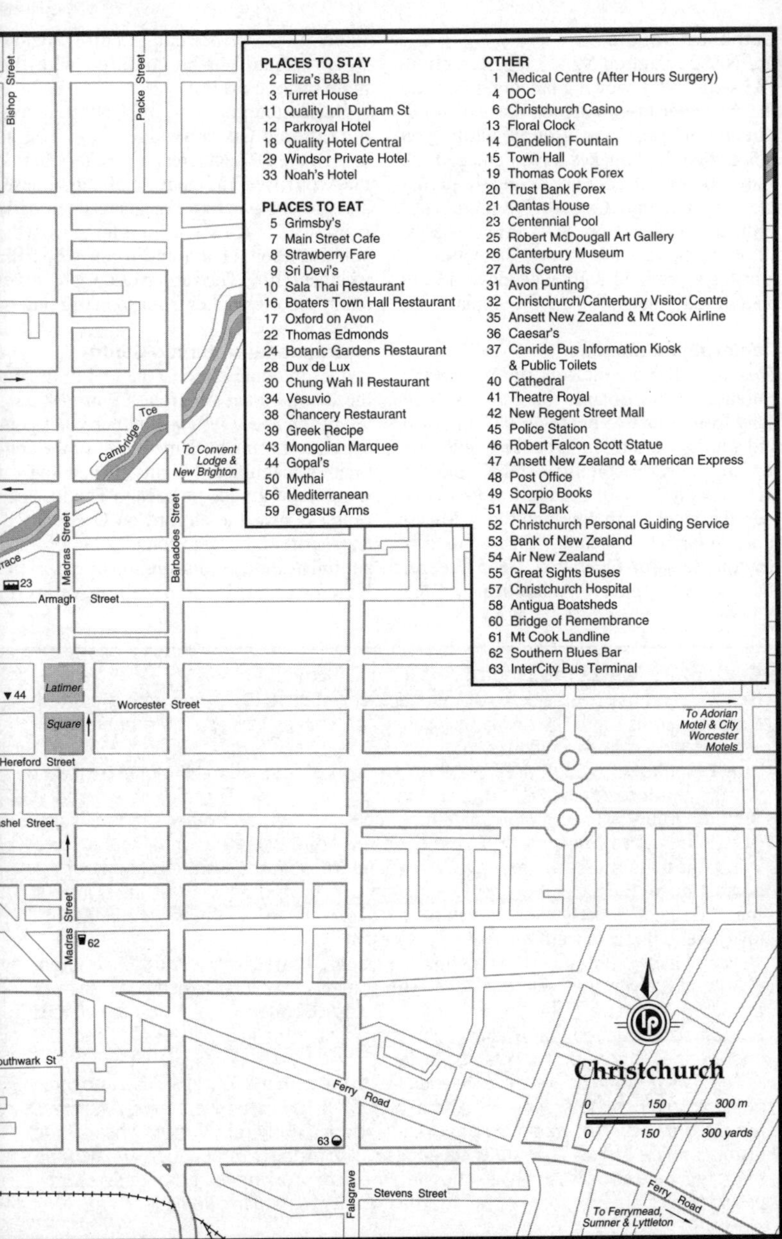
PLACES TO STAY
2 Eliza's B&B Inn
3 Turret House
11 Quality Inn Durham St
12 Parkroyal Hotel
18 Quality Hotel Central
29 Windsor Private Hotel
33 Noah's Hotel
PLACES TO EAT
5 Grimsby's
7 Main Street Cafe
8 Strawberry Fare
9 Sri Devi's
10 Sala Thai Restaurant
16 Boaters Town Hall Restaurant
17 Oxford on Avon
22 Thomas Edmonds
24 Botanic Gardens Restaurant
28 Dux de Lux
30 Chung Wah II Restaurant
34 Vesuvio
38 Chancery Restaurant
39 Greek Recipe
43 Mongolian Marquee
44 Gopal's
50 Mythai
56 Mediterranean
59 Pegasus Arms
OTHER
1 Medical Centre (After Hours Surgery)
4 DOC
6 Christchurch Casino
13 Floral Clock
14 Dandelion Fountain
15 Town Hall
19 Thomas Cook Forex
20 Trust Bank Forex
21 Qantas House
23 Centennial Pool
25 Robert McDougall Art Gallery
26 Canterbury Museum
27 Arts Centre
31 Avon Punting
32 Christchurch/Canterbury Visitor Centre
35 Ansett New Zealand & Mt Cook Airline
36 Caesar's
37 Canride Bus Information Kiosk & Public Toilets
40 Cathedral
41 Theatre Royal
42 New Regent Street Mall
45 Police Station
46 Robert Falcon Scott Statue
47 Ansett New Zealand & American Express
48 Post Office
49 Scorpio Books
51 ANZ Bank
52 Christchurch Personal Guiding Service
53 Bank of New Zealand
54 Air New Zealand
55 Great Sights Buses
57 Christchurch Hospital
58 Antigua Boatsheds
60 Bridge of Remembrance
61 Mt Cook Landline
62 Southern Blues Bar
63 InterCity Bus Terminal
Bishop Street
Packe Street
Cambridge Tce
To Convent Lodge & New Brighton
Madras Street
Barbadoes Street
Terrace
23
Armagh Street
Latimer
Square
44
Worcester Street
Hereford Street
Cashel Street
Madras Street
62
Southwark St
Ferry Road
63
Falsgrave
Stevens Street
To Adorian Motel & City Worcester Motels
Christchurch
0 150 300 m
0 150 300 yards
Ferry Road
To Ferrymead, Sumner & Lyttleton

Cathedral Square

For NZ$2 (children NZ$1), you can climb 133 steps to the viewing balconies 30m up the 63-meter-high spire of the cathedral. There you can look around while you reflect that earthquakes have damaged the spire on several occasions, once toppling the very top into Cathedral Square! The cathedral is open from 8:30 am weekdays, 11:30 am Sunday afternoon. There are free tours at 11 am and 2 pm weekdays, 11 am on Saturday, and 11:30 am on Sunday.

Canterbury Museum

This fine museum, on Rolleston Ave at the entrance to the Botanic Gardens, is open daily from 9 am to 5 pm (closed Christmas) and admission is free. Particularly interesting are the early colonist exhibits and the RH Stewart Hall of Antarctic Discovery (see the sidebar about Canterbury Museum's Antarctic collection). Christchurch is headquarters for Operation Deep Freeze, the US supply link to Antarctica (see the International Antarctic Centre, below, which should not be confused with this more historic exhibit).

Beside the museum, off Rolleston Ave, the **Botanic Gardens**, open from 7 am to sunset, are 30 hectacres of greenery beside the Avon River. The many floral-show houses and the popular fern house are open daily from 10:15 am to 4 pm. Tours leave from the café between 11 am and 4 pm when the weather is fine. The garden restaurant serves smorgasbord lunches from noon to 2 pm.

International Antarctic Centre

It doesn't come close to the real thing, but the International Antarctic Centre (☎ 358-9896, fax 353-7799) will either whet your appetite or bring back memories of the continent's magnificent sights, depending on whether or not you've been to The Ice. The center is near the airport, on Orchard Rd, and is part of the huge complex built for the administration and warehousing for the New Zealand, US and Italian Antarctic

Canterbury Museum's Hall of Antarctic Discovery

New Zealand has been linked to Antarctica since the 1840s, when both the British explorer James Clark Ross and US Navy Capt Charles Wilkes visited during their voyages to and from the continent.

In 1901, Robert F Scott used Lyttelton, the port of Christchurch, to prepare for his voyage south to Antarctica. Edward Wilson, the expedition's zoologist, worked at the Canterbury Museum while preparing albatross skins and other specimens collected during the voyage from England. Because of this association between Scott, Wilson and the museum, upon *Discovery*'s return from the Antarctic, many of the items used on the expedition were deposited with the museum. These items are still the nucleus of the collection, which now ranks as the most comprehensive assembly of genuine relics from the Antarctic's past.

Nearly every subsequent expedition – including those led by Ernest Shackleton, Scott and Richard Byrd – left artifacts with the museum; later expeditions, such as the US's Operation Deep Freeze and the British Commonwealth Trans Antarctic Expedition, continued that tradition. The result is that the gallery covers most of the important events in recent Antarctic history.

The Hall of Antarctic Discovery opened to the public in 1977. It is divided into three sections: geology, natural history and exploration. The extensive geology gallery is arranged in order of geological age and includes numerous fossils. The natural history section includes dioramas covering the life histories of penguins, whales and seals; there are also displays about huskies, the hard-working dogs that until recently provided welcome companionship for the continent's human population.

programs, which are supported by air from Christchurch.

The center has hands-on exhibits, video presentations, and the 'sights and sounds' of the vast continent. The first room you enter is the introductory 12-minute 'Antarctic experience,' which allows visitors to 'experience' an aurora, changes in weather, and a penguin rookery, with the aid of freezing air blasts, special lighting, sound effects, and holograms. The 13-minute 'Great White South' audio-visual show is very good, flashing 900-odd images of Antarctica on a huge screen using 20 slide projectors. There is also a fascinating polar aquarium displaying Antarctic fish and invertebrates such as starfish, sea anemones, sea spiders, and sponges in a 2500-liter tank kept chilled at -0.2°C, the only such public aquarium in the world. There is also a stunning blue ice cave, complete with delicate ice crystals, fabricated from plaster, foam and acrylic.

The center is open October to March from 9:30 am to 8:30 pm; and April to September from 9:30 am to 5:30 pm. Entry is NZ$10 per adult, NZ$6 per child. To get there catch a bus bound for the airport; ask for the visitor center. To return, catch an airport bus heading for the city. The center has a room for luggage storage, and there are bicycle stands. There is a well-stocked souvenir shop and the 60° South Café & Bar.

Art Gallery & Arts Centre

Behind the Canterbury Museum is the **Robert McDougall Art Gallery**. It has an extensive collection of NZ and international art and is open from 10 am to 4:30 pm daily; admission is free.

The **Arts Centre** is worth a look, even if just to see the beautiful old buildings. New Zealand has a lot of good handicraft centers producing some fine pottery, jewelry and other crafts, and Christchurch is particularly well represented. The Arts Centre has everything from handmade toys to Maori

---

The exploration gallery may well be the Hall's most popular. It includes many fascinating relics, among them a dinner plate from James Clark Ross' ship *Erebus*, a medicine chest for sledge dogs, and what is perhaps the collection's single most important item, the Polar Medal awarded to Scott in 1904, the first one ever presented.

Shackleton's expeditions are also well represented, with such artifacts as the red ensign flown from his ship *Nimrod*, tinned supplies recovered from the hut at Cape Royds, the Arroll-Johnson motor sledge his Ross Sea party took with them on the ill-fated Imperial Trans-Antarctic Expedition of 1914-16, and a surprisingly modern-looking primus stove taken on *James Caird* on its 1420-km journey from Elephant Island to South Georgia after *Endurance* was crushed in the pack ice.

Roald Amundsen, victor in the race to the South Pole, is given prime billing in a display that features the pocket knife used to sharpen a bamboo stake, which Amundsen's party drove into the ice at the Pole to proudly support the Norwegian flag.

Items from Scott's *Terra Nova* expedition include pony snowshoes, a shaft from one of the motor sledges and Wilson's microscope. Byrd's important role in Antarctic aviation is documented by a primus lamp from his Advance Base and a champagne bottle covered with the signatures of many of the men who were involved in his first flight over the Pole.

Dominating the Hall are two large pieces: a Tucker Sno-Cat oversnow vehicle, one of four used by Vivian Fuchs in the first crossing of Antarctica; and a Ferguson farm tractor, one of three employed by Edmund Hillary to reach the South Pole.

–Baden Norris, Antarctic curator at the Canterbury Museum ■

carvings, a couple of good restaurants, and a good bookstore.

Air Force Museum

This museum is exceptionally well presented. On display are a variety of aircraft used by the NZ Air Force over the years, convincingly displayed with figures and background scenery: Antarctic aircraft sit in the snow, a WWII fighter is hidden in the jungle. You can even pretend to pilot an A4 Skyhawk jet in a flight simulator. The museum is at the former Wigram air base, which is a 15-minute drive south of the city on Main South Rd. A courtesy bus runs from the visitor center in Worcester St, or it can be reached by a Hornby bus Nos 8 or 25 from Cathedral Square. It's open daily from 10 am to 5 pm. Entry is NZ$9 (children NZ$4).

Avon River

The invitingly calm and picturesque Avon River obviously requires canoes, so head to the Antigua Boatsheds by the footbridge at the southern end of Rolleston Ave. One-person canoes are NZ$4, two-person canoes are NZ$8 an hour, and paddle boats are NZ$8 a half-hour. The boat sheds are open from 9:30 am to 4 pm daily, and there's a good sandwich bar right by it.

Or you can relax and be punted along the river. Punts depart from behind the visitor center, with departures and landings also available opposite the Town Hall Restaurant and the Thomas Edmonds Restaurant. Prices range from NZ$10 to NZ$15 (children under 12 half price). The punts ply the river daily from 10 am, stopping at 6 pm from October to March, 5 pm in April and September.

Christchurch Casino

New Zealand's premier casino is located right in the heart of town on Victoria and Kilmore Sts. It is open from 11 am to 3 am Monday to Wednesday then continuously from 11 am Thursday to 3 am Monday. All the traditional methods of losing your money are provided and dress standards (ie, no jeans) apply.

Christchurch Tramway

Trams, first introduced to Christchurch in 1905, only lasted as a means of transport for 60 years. Restored green and cream trams have been reintroduced as part of a 2.5-km inner-city loop that takes in many of the city's best features and shopping areas. The trams operate every day from 8 am to 11 pm. Tickets are NZ$3 for one hour, NZ$5 for four hours, and NZ$10 for a full day (children NZ$2/3/7). It's probably quicker (and certainly cheaper) to walk! One plus is the fact that it passes through the historic precinct of **New Regent St**, where there are many examples of Spanish architecture.

Christchurch Gondola

For a cost of NZ$12 for adults (NZ$9 after 5 pm), NZ$5 for children, and NZ$25 for families, you can be whisked up from the Heathcote Valley terminal on a 4½-minute ride to a point somewhere above the Lyttelton Rd tunnel. There are great views at the top (Mt Cavendish, 930m).

The gondola runs from 10 am daily, and the free gondola bus leaves regularly from the city center and major hotels, or you can reach it on bus No 12. Once up there, you can mountain bike down with the Mountain Bike Adventure Company (☎ 329-9699) for NZ$38 or paraglide down with Nimbus Paragliding (☎ 332-2233).

National Marae

The largest marae (Maori cultural center and sacred place) in New Zealand is at 250 Pages Rd, six km northeast of the city. Nga Hau e Wha ('The Four Winds') is a multicultural facility open to all people. You get the opportunity to see the carvings, weavings, and paintings in the whare nui ('meeting house') and whare whananga ('house of learning').

Tours (☎ 388-7685) are NZ$5.50 (children NZ$3.50), and the powhiri (welcome ritual) is NZ$2.50 per head by arrangement. You can reach the marae on bus No 5. The times for tours are 9 and 11 am and 1 and 3 pm Monday to Friday, weekends by arrangement.

Wildlife Reserves

The **Orana Park Wildlife Trust** has an excellent nocturnal kiwi house and lots of other animals including tigers, rhino, camels, water buffalo and the rare scimitar-horned oryx. It's open from 10 am to 5:30 pm daily (last admission at 4:30 pm) and entry is NZ$10 per adult (children NZ$5). It's on McLeans Island Rd, Harewood, beyond the airport, and about 20 minutes from the city. There's no public bus, but tour buses and the City Circuit bus do come here.

The **Willowbank Wildlife Reserve** has exotic and local animals including a variety of domestic animals. There's also a model of a traditional Maori village and a nocturnal kiwi house. The reserve is open daily from 10 am to 10 pm and entry is NZ$8 (children NZ$3.50). The reserve is on Hussey Rd. The City Circuit bus runs there from outside the visitor center daily.

Beaches

The closest beaches to the city are North Beach (10 km, bus No 19), South Brighton beach (10 km, bus No 5), Sumner (11 km, bus No 3), Waimairi (10 km, bus No 19), and New Brighton (8 km, bus No 5).

Organized Tours

The City Circuit bus departs on the hour from the visitor center (see Getting Around in this section). Unique Tours (☎ 366-1661) operates a number of tours that are a good value. There's a 9:30 am three-hour tour of the city that costs NZ$39, and a three-hour afternoon tour of the hills, coast and harbor for NZ$44. It also has full-day tours to Akaroa (NZ$84) and to Kaikoura (NZ$187); the latter includes a whale-watch trip.

Gray Line (☎ 343-3874) has a three-hour morning highlights tour that includes Mona Vale and the Port Hills (NZ$26, children half price), an afternoon sights tour to Sumner, Lyttelton Harbour (launch cruise), and the Port Hills (NZ$32, children half price); an afternoon sights tour with the gondola ride thrown in (NZ$44, children half price).

Travel Pioneer (☎ 388-2042) has interesting trips that offer activities that other bus trips don't. Akaroa via the coastal back roads is NZ$58; Arthur's Pass and the Otira Gorge NZ$78; and Hanmer Springs via the Waipara Gorge back road is NZ$58. All trips depart at about 8:30 am and return about 6 pm.

Christchurch Sightseeing Tours (☎ 366-9660) offers half-day city tours (NZ$23) and three-hour garden tours to the city's gardens on Tuesday, Thursday, and Saturday from November to March (NZ$20).

Canterbury Leisure Tours (☎ 351-0551) has half- and full-day golfing tours (equipment, fees and transport included) for NZ$85/120.

The Christchurch Personal Guiding Service Walks (☎ 342-7691) run two-hour guided walks of the city, departing from its red and black kiosk in the southwestern section of the Square. These tours leave at 10 am and 2 pm daily from the Square (or 15 minutes earlier from the visitor center), cost NZ$8, and are most informative. Independent walkers can get a copy of the free, informative brochure *Central City Walks* and venture further from the Square.

Places To Stay

Christchurch is the major city and the only international arrival point on the South Island. As a result it has many accommodations choices. (Distances quoted are taken from Cathedral Square.)

Guesthouses & B&Bs The *Windsor Private Hotel* (☎ 366-1503), 52 Armagh St, is just a five to 10 minutes' walk from the city center. It's meticulously clean and orderly and rooms with private bath cost NZ$50/78 a single/double. Built in 1885, *Turret House* (☎ 365-3900), 435 Durham St, has been elegantly restored. The NZ$85 room charge for two includes a continental breakfast, and private bathroom. At 82 Bealey Ave is the elegantly restored *Eliza's B&B Inn* (☎ 366-8584) with bedrooms from NZ$75 to NZ$130. It has a fully licensed restaurant, a bar and provides hot chocolate at any time.

At 141 Hackthorne Rd, at the foot of the Cashmere Hills, is an elegantly restored mansion called *Cashmere House on the Hill* (☎ 332-7864). It has an acre of gardens and views of the city. Singles/doubles cost NZ$110/140.

For those who elect to stay near the beach there is *Convent Lodge* (☎ 388-3388), 97 Lonsdale St, New Brighton; singles/doubles are NZ$40/60, but they offer budget beds for NZ$14 per person.

Hotels Top-bracket Christchurch hotels include the *Christchurch City Travelodge* (☎ 379-1180) at 356 Oxford Terrace, the *Chateau on the Park* (☎ 348-8999) on the corner of Deans Ave and Kilmarnock St, the *Quality Hotel Durham* (☎ 365-4699) on the corner of Durham and Kilmore Sts, the *Quality Hotel Central* (☎ 379-5880) at 776 Colombo St, *Noah's* (☎ 379-4700) on the corner of Worcester St and Oxford Terrace, and out at the airport the *Airport Plaza* (☎ 358-3139). In these hotels doubles are from NZ$140 to NZ$160 (and up).

Right at the top of the price scale is the imaginatively designed and wonderfully situated *Parkroyal Hotel* (☎ 365-7799), corner of Durham and Kilmore Sts, where a double with great views costs nearly NZ$340.

Places To Eat

You can find whatever you want everyday and at all hours. The *Classic Canterbury Dining Out Guide* (NZ$9.95) dodges any critique of its advertisers but is a good reference for opening hours, locations and menus.

Fast Food & Cafés If you would like to sit at the base of one of Christchurch's many statues or on a bench in the square, then go to one of the many nearby takeaway food stalls that sell a variety of international cuisines. The *Greek Recipe* at 55 Cathedral Square, beside the West End Theatre, has authentic, inexpensive Greek takeaways and is open from 10 am to 10 pm every day but Sunday. Only a block from the square at 176A Manchester St, the *Mediterranean* has that eastern Mediterranean blend of Turkish/Greek/Lebanese food, including doner kebabs.

The coffee bar in the foyer of the *Town Hall* is open every day and in the evening whenever there's a concert. When visiting the Casino, try *Grand Cafe*. *Vesuvio* at 182 Oxford Terrace is another street-front café that is popular with locals. It has a small Japanese restaurant attached.

Pub Food On Colombo St by the river, the conveniently located *Oxford on Avon* has a family restaurant. It's open daily from 11 am to 10 pm. Main courses, which span the pub-food universe from family roasts to T-bone steaks, are in the NZ$8 to NZ$15 range, and there's also a cheaper children's menu. A favorite is *Nancy's at the Park*, corner of Deans Ave and Riccarton Rd, and it is good to see that it pays attention to old-fashioned NZ fare as well as innovative new dishes.

Other possibilities include the *Carlton Hotel* on the corner of Papanui Rd and Bealey Ave; the *Coachman Inn*, at 144 Gloucester St, with a theater restaurant setup; *Churchills*, an English-style pub at 441 Colombo St, Sydenham; the *Pegasus Arms*, 14 Oxford Terrace near the hospital, for a bistro lunch and a view out over the 1886 topsail cutter *Pastime*; and the *Chancery* in Chancery Lane, which features roasts and steaks at around NZ$12.

Restaurants The *Botanic Gardens Restaurant* in the wonderful Botanic Gardens is renowned for an excellent smorgasbord that costs NZ$12.50 including coffee; it's served from noon to 2 pm daily. The restaurant is open from 10 am to 4:30 pm for snacks and other light meals.

The riverside setting of the *Boaters Town Hall Restaurant* in the town hall makes it a popular place to eat. There's a weekday lunchtime buffet for NZ$20, a Sunday smorgasbord lunch or dinner for NZ$22, and a regular à la carte menu for dinner or late supper, with main courses from NZ$19 to NZ$25. Across the plaza at the ultra-modern, ultra-expensive Parkroyal Hotel, the inner courtyard is given over to a rather elegant *Victoria Street Café*, which is not as expensive as it looks – main courses, both meat and vegetarian, cost around NZ$20. The wine list is extensive.

The riverside *Thomas Edmonds* is housed in what used to be a band rotunda by the river on Cambridge Terrace. It's in a great location, and you could complement the romantic atmosphere by arriving by punt! It's reasonably priced with light main courses for lunch at around NZ$10, for dinner from NZ$20, with both meat and vegetarian selections. It's open for lunch Monday to Friday and on Sunday; in the evening from Monday to Saturday.

The restaurant areas off Colombo St offer good dining possibilities. These include the *Main Street Café*, with its smoke-free bar. Or try *Sri Devi's Marco Polo* at No 812 with an interesting mix of Indian and Southeast Asian dishes. It's open daily for lunch and dinner, with main courses from NZ$11 to NZ$15.

Café Valentino's, at 813 Colombo St, is a casual place with spacious wooden beam-and-brick décor. It serves Italian food, is open daily from noon until late, and dinner entrées are from NZ$11 to NZ$23.

Strawberry Fare at 114 Peterborough St is a restaurant famed for its desserts, such as the ubiquitous Death by Chocolate. It also serves great breakfasts including a Parisian special; meals are served from 7 am to midnight daily, except weekends when it opens at the more respectable hour of 8 am.

There are plenty of Asian restaurants including the imposing *Chung Wah II* at 63 Worcester St. At the *Mongolian Marquee*, on the corner of Manchester and Gloucester Sts, you can eat as much barbecued food as you like for the set price of NZ$22. It is open daily from 5:30 pm until late. The *Jade Garden*, 109 Cambridge Terrace, is a good choice for Cantonese and Szechuan styles.

Fans of Thai food will not be disappointed with the authentic cuisine at *Mythai*, 84 Hereford St; *Kannigai's Thai Foods*, 18A Carlton Courts in the city; and the *Sala Thai*, corner of Colombo and Kilmore Sts.

Grimsby's, opposite Cranmer Square, on the corner of Kilmore and Montreal Sts, is considered by many to be the pinnacle of dining in this town, but is definitely not in the budget category. It's open daily from 6:30 pm until late.

Vegetarian Vegetarians are well catered for in all price categories. *Gopal's* at 143 Worcester St is a Hare Krishna-run restaurant. It's open for lunch on weekdays and on Friday night.

Exceptionally good vegetarian food can be found at the *Main Street Café* at 840 Colombo St. This is a relaxed and very popular place with an open-air courtyard at the back. Imaginative main courses are from NZ$8 to NZ$14, or you could have bread and salad for NZ$5. The salads are good, and the desserts, particularly the varied selection of cheesecakes, are mouthwatering. It's open from 10 am to late daily.

Dux de Lux is another very popular place for gourmet vegetarian taste treats. It's close to the Arts Centre, on Montreal St near Hereford St. There's a green outdoor courtyard, and service is counter style, with main courses around NZ$10 for lunch or NZ$14 for dinner. It's licensed, with its own bar and brewery, and showcases live music several nights a week. Dux de Lux is open from around 10 am until midnight, every day.

Entertainment

Clubs There are several pubs with rock music at night, particularly on the weekends. Popular ones include *Dux de Lux* (see the Vegetarian section, above) and *Bush Inn*, 364 Riccarton Rd, which has a small cover charge.

An old favorite is *Bailie's* at Backpackers Inn the Square, where smoke fills the room, the Guinness is carefully decanted into pint glasses, boiled eggs and salt are left on the bar for patrons, and Irish and folk music are performed live.

There's rock all week at *The Playroom* on the corner of Cuffs and Pages Rds. *Caesars* in Chancery Arcade is a quintessential nightclub. Other nightclubs are the *Palladium* on Gloucester St, and *Warners*, in Cathedral Square, which has rock music.

The best place for aficionados of blues music is the *Southern Blues Bar*, firmly ensconced in the red-light/bathhouse enclave at the corner of Madras and Tuam Sts. Here workers mix with the city's elite. For a good old-fashioned night out that lingers well into the wee hours there is the *Jolly Poacher* opposite the Casino on Victoria St.

Classical Music & Theater Christchurch is the cultural center of the South Island. The focus is the *Town Hall* (☎ 366-8899) on Kilmore St by the riverside. This is where you are likely to see a symphony orchestra. The James Hay Theatre in the town hall and the *Theatre Royal* in Gloucester St have live performances.

Getting Around

The Airport The public bus service to the airport is operated by Canride from Cathedral Square. Buses depart about every half-hour from around 6 am to nearly 6 pm, then less frequently until the last at 9:45 pm on weekdays; they're also less frequent on Saturday and Sunday. The cost is NZ$2.40 (children NZ$1.20).

There are several door-to-door airport shuttle buses. Super Shuttle (☎ 365-5655) operates 24 hours a day, serving not only the airport (NZ$8) but also the bus and railway stations. A taxi to or from the airport will cost about NZ$14 to NZ$18 depending on the time you go, so it can work out cheaper than the shuttles with several people.

Car The major operators all have offices in Christchurch, as do many smaller local companies.

Avis
  Lichfield St (☎ 379-6133)
Avon Freedom
  corner of Tuam & Antigua Sts
  (☎ 379-3822)
Budget
  corner of Oxford Terrace & Lichfield St
  (☎ 366-0072)
Economy
  518 Wairakei Rd, Burnside (☎ 359-7410)
Hertz
  48-50 Lichfield St (☎ 366-0549)
Pegasus
  127 Peterborough St (☎ 365-1100)
Renny Rentals
  156 Tuam St. (☎ 366-6790)

Bus Most city buses are operated by Canride and run from Cathedral Square. Christchurch's bus service is good, cheap and well organized. For bus information phone Bus Info (☎ 366-8855). Fares start at 50¢ and step up 50¢ for each additional section to NZ$2.50.

The Double Decker Bus (☎ 377-1644) passes more than 100 points of interest in the city in a 90-minute circuit; the cost is NZ$22 (children NZ$10). The City Circuit bus (☎ 385-5386) has two circuits (Plains and Port), both leaving from the visitor center hourly from 9 am to 6 pm; it costs NZ$25 for eight hours of travel.

Taxi There are plenty of taxis in Christchurch, but they don't cruise. You find them on taxi ranks, or phone: Blue Star (☎ 379-9799), First Direct (☎ 377-5555), and Gold Band (☎ 379-5795).

Bicycles Bikes are ideal for Christchurch as it is nice and flat. There are cycling lanes on many roads, and Hagley Park, which encompasses the Botanical Gardens, has many cycling paths. You can pedal away on a mountain bike from Summit Cycles (☎ 355-7017) in St Albans, or the Mountain Bike Adventure Co (☎ 384-0006) in Lyttelton; both companies also conduct guided trips of the Port Hills and Banks Peninsula.

Hobart

Hobart (population 127,000) is Australia's second-oldest capital city and also the smallest and most southerly. Straddling the mouth of the Derwent River and backed by mountains that offer excellent views of the city, Hobart has managed to combine the progress and benefits of a modern city with the rich heritage of its colonial past. The beautiful Georgian buildings, the busy harbor, and the easy-going atmosphere all make Hobart one of the most enjoyable and engaging of Australia's cities.

History

The first inhabitants of the city area were members of the Aboriginal Mouheneer tribe, who lived a semi-nomadic lifestyle. The first European colony in Tasmania was founded in 1803 at Risdon Cove, but a year later Lieutenant-Colonel David Collins, governor of the new settlement in Van Diemen's Land, sailed down the Derwent River and decided that a cove about 10 km below Risdon and on the opposite shore was a better place to settle. This, the site of Tasmania's future capital city, began as a village of tents and wattle-and-daub huts with a population of 262 Europeans.

Hobart Town, as it was known until 1881, was proclaimed a city in 1842. Very important to its development was the Derwent River estuary, one of the world's finest deep-water harbors, and many merchants made their fortunes from the whaling trade, shipbuilding and the export of products like corn and merino wool.

Orientation

Hobart is sandwiched between the steep hills of Mt Wellington and the wide Derwent River. The city, clinging to the shores of the Derwent River, is about 20 km long but very narrow. Some development has spread into the hills, and you will find many streets extremely steep.

The city center is fairly small and simply laid out, and it is easy to find your way around. The streets in the city center are arranged in a grid pattern around the Elizabeth St Mall. Hobart has controlled the traffic in its narrow streets by making them one-way and, if you are driving, you should first study a map.

Salamanca Place, the famous row of Georgian warehouses, is along the waterfront, while just south of this is Battery Point, Hobart's delightful, well-preserved early colonial district. If you follow the river around from Battery Point you'll come to Sandy Bay, the site of the yacht clubs, Hobart's university, and the circular tower of Wrest Point Hotel Casino, one of Hobart's main landmarks.

The northern side of the city center is bounded by the recreation area known locally as the Domain (short for the Queen's Domain), which includes the Royal Tasmanian Botanical Gardens and the Derwent River. From here the Tasman Bridge crosses the river to the eastern suburbs and the airport. North of the Domain the suburbs continue beside the Derwent River almost all the way to Bridgewater.

Information

Tourist Offices The Tasmanian Travel & Information Centre (☎ 6230-8233) on the corner of Davey and Elizabeth Sts opens on weekdays from 8:30 am to 5:15 pm, and on weekends and public holidays from 9 am to 4 pm. You can also get tourist information from the travel section of Mures Fish Centre, Victoria Dock and from many accommodations establishments.

If you have an FM radio, you can pick up a tourist information broadcast on 88 MHz within a six-km radius of the city center.

Money All prices quoted in the Hobart section are in Australian dollars (A$). Banks are open for business from 9 am to 4 pm on Monday to Friday. ATMs can be used at any time and are available at the banks in the city center and at some of the

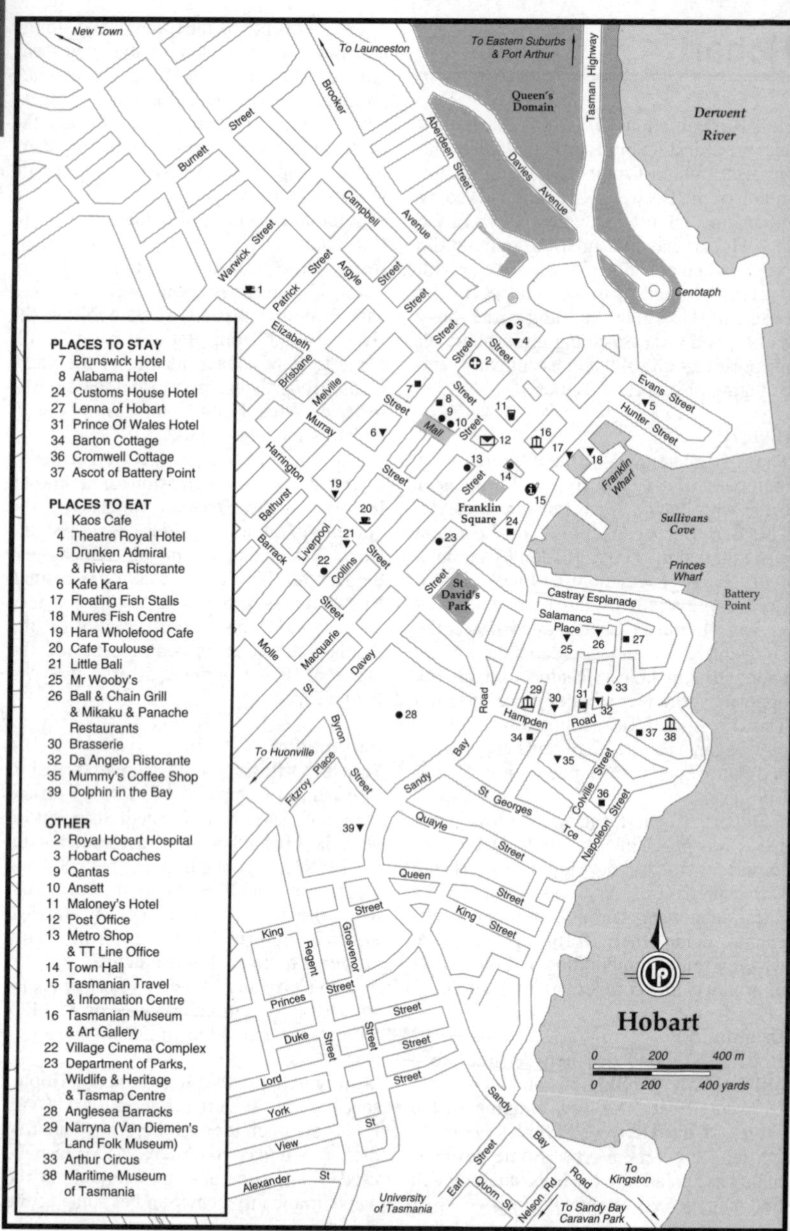
New Town
To Launceston
To Eastern Suburbs & Port Arthur
Tasman Highway
Queen's Domain
Derwent River
Brooker
Burnett
Street
Aberdeen Street
Davies Avenue
Campbell
Avenue
Warwick Street
Patrick Street
Argyle Street
Street
Cenotaph
Elizabeth
Brisbane
Melville
Murray
Harrington
Bathurst
Barrack
Liverpool
Collins
Street
Mall
Evans Street
Hunter Street
Franklin Wharf
Franklin Square
Sullivans Cove
Princes Wharf
Battery Point
St David's Park
Castray Esplanade
Salamanca Place
Molle
Macquarie
Davey
St
Byron
Road
Hampden Road
Bay
Sandy
To Huonville
Fitzroy Place
Street
St Georges Tce
Colville Street
Napoleon Street
Quayle Street
Queen Street
King Street
King
Regent
Grosvenor
Street
Princes
Street
Duke
Street
Lord
York
View
Alexander
St
Sandy Bay Road
Street
Earl
Quorn St
Nelson Rd
University of Tasmania
To Kingston
To Sandy Bay Caravan Park
Hobart
0 200 400 m
0 200 400 yards
PLACES TO STAY
7 Brunswick Hotel
8 Alabama Hotel
24 Customs House Hotel
27 Lenna of Hobart
31 Prince Of Wales Hotel
34 Barton Cottage
36 Cromwell Cottage
37 Ascot of Battery Point
PLACES TO EAT
1 Kaos Cafe
4 Theatre Royal Hotel
5 Drunken Admiral & Riviera Ristorante
6 Kafe Kara
17 Floating Fish Stalls
18 Mures Fish Centre
19 Hara Wholefood Cafe
20 Cafe Toulouse
21 Little Bali
25 Mr Wooby's
26 Ball & Chain Grill & Mikaku & Panache Restaurants
30 Brasserie
32 Da Angelo Ristorante
35 Mummy's Coffee Shop
39 Dolphin in the Bay
OTHER
2 Royal Hobart Hospital
3 Hobart Coaches
9 Qantas
10 Ansett
11 Maloney's Hotel
12 Post Office
13 Metro Shop & TT Line Office
14 Town Hall
15 Tasmanian Travel & Information Centre
16 Tasmanian Museum & Art Gallery
22 Village Cinema Complex
23 Department of Parks, Wildlife & Heritage & Tasmap Centre
28 Anglesea Barracks
29 Narryna (Van Diemen's Land Folk Museum)
33 Arthur Circus
38 Maritime Museum of Tasmania

suburban branches. All the major banks have their offices near the mall on Elizabeth St.

Post & Communications The picturesque GPO is in the center of the city, on the corner of Elizabeth and Macquarie Sts. Besides its obvious utility, the post office building has a link to Antarctic history. On March 8, 1912, Roald Amundsen – who had slipped ashore dressed as a simple Norwegian seaman from his ship *Fram*, which was anchored out in the Derwent – sent a telegram from here to the world announcing his attainment of the South Pole.

Hobart's area code is now the same as the rest of southeastern Australia: 03. All numbers for the Hobart region begin with 62, and calls within the city are classed as local. Calls from Hobart to country regions are usually at long-distance rates, even when they begin with 62. If you hear three beeps at the start of a call, then long-distance rates are being charged and you should be ready to insert more coins if you are using a pay phone. Local calls from pay phones are 40¢ for unlimited time.

Australian Antarctic Division

Located on Channel Hwy in the suburb of Kingston, the Australian Antarctic Division (☎ 6232-3209), headquarters of Australia's Antarctic program, has a large one-room museum of Antarctic materials, open 9 am to 5 pm weekdays except public holidays. The centerpiece of the display is a bright-orange Caterpillar D4 tractor used on a traverse to Russia's Vostok station at the Pole of Inaccessibility. There is also a mounted skin of an Adélie penguin you can touch, samples of Antarctic minerals, scale models of Australia's Antarctic stations, and bits of wind-scoured timber from Mawson's Hut at Commonwealth Bay. There is also a small souvenir shop.

Tasmanian Museum & Art Gallery

The excellent Tasmanian Museum & Art Gallery (☎ 6235-0777), at 5 Argyle St (enter via 40 Macquarie St), incorporates Hobart's oldest building, the Commissariat Store, built in 1808. The museum section features a collection of Antarctic and Southern Ocean artifacts, including whaling relics, as well as a Tasmanian Aboriginal display and artifacts from the state's colonial heritage. The gallery has a good collection of Tasmanian colonial art. There are interesting displays of animals, including extinct and prehistoric ones, and a large mineral collection. The bookstore beside the entrance sells a wide range of books, many of which are not available elsewhere. The museum is free and is open daily from 10 am to 5 pm.

Van Diemen's Land Folk Museum

This is the oldest folk museum in Australia. It's based in Narryna, a fine Georgian home at 103 Hampden Rd, Battery Point. Dating from the 1830s, it stands on beautiful grounds and has a large and fascinating collection of relics from Tasmania's early pioneering days. It's open on weekdays from 10 am to 5 pm and on weekends from 2 to 5 pm; admission is A$5, children A$2, or family A$10.

Maritime Museum of Tasmania

This museum, at Secheron House, Secheron Rd in Battery Point, contains an extensive collection of photos, paintings, models and relics depicting Tasmania's – and particularly Hobart's – colorful shipping history. Admission is A$2. The museum is open daily from 10 am to 4:30 pm except Christmas Day and Good Friday.

Risdon Cove Historic Site

This is the site of the first European settlement in Tasmania and is definitely worth a visit. Very little remains of the original buildings and most sites are simply foundations, but the pyramid-shaped visitor center has an excellent informative display. It's open every day from 9:30 am to 4:30 pm and is located on the eastern shore about 10 km from the city. Entry is free. To get there, take a No 68 bus from the Eastlands Shopping Centre.

Historic Buildings

One of the things that makes Hobart so unusual among Australian cities is its wealth of old and remarkably well-preserved buildings. More than 90 buildings in Hobart are classified by the National Trust and 60 of them, featuring some of Hobart's best Georgian architecture, are on Macquarie and Davey Sts. The National Trust's office is on the corner of Brisbane and Campbell Sts (☎ 6223-5200), and it has a shop at 33 Salamanca Place, open all day Monday to Friday and on Saturday morning.

Close to the city center is **St Davids Park**, which has lovely old trees and some gravestones dating from the earliest days of the colony. On Murray St is **Parliament House**, which was originally used as a customs house. Hobart's prestigious **Theatre Royal**, at 29 Campbell St, was built in 1837 and is the oldest theater in Australia.

The historic **Penitentiary Chapel & Criminal Courts** are at 28 Campbell St; the National Trust runs daily tours of the buildings between 10 am and 2 pm (admission is A$4). Groups of more than 10 can arrange a tour outside these hours (☎ 6231-0911).

In New Town, at 61 Bay Rd, **Runnymede** is a gracious colonial residence dating from the early 1830s. It was built for Robert Pitcairn, who was the first lawyer to qualify in Tasmania, and was a leading advocate for the abolition of transportation of convicts. Now managed by the National Trust, it is open daily from 10 am to 4:30 pm; admission is A$5, children A$3, or family A$10. It is closed in July and on major public holidays. To get there take bus No 15, 16 or 20 from the corner of Argyle and Macquarie Sts.

Cascade Brewery

Australia's oldest brewery, on Cascade Rd close to the city center, is still producing some of the finest beer in the country. Two-hour tours take place daily at 9:30 am and 1 pm, and bookings are essential (☎ 6224-1144); entry is A$7, children A$2. The brewery is on the southwestern edge of the city center; bus Nos 44, 46, 49 and 50 go right by it – get off at stop 18.

The Waterfront

Hobart's busy waterfront area centers around **Franklin Wharf**, close to the city center. At **Constitution Dock** there are several floating takeaway seafood stalls, and it's a treat to sit in the sun munching fresh fish & chips while watching the activity in the harbor. The docks also have some fine sit-down restaurants if you prefer something more formal. At the finish of the annual Sydney to Hobart Yacht Race, around New Years, and during the Royal Hobart Regatta in February, Constitution Dock really comes alive.

The whole wharf area is actually reclaimed land. When Hobart was first settled, Davey St ran along the edge of the sea, and the Hunter St area was originally an island that was used to safely store food and other goods. Subsequent projects filled in the shallows and provided land upon which the warehouses of Hunter St and Salamanca Place were constructed.

Salamanca Place

The row of beautiful sandstone warehouses on the harborfront at Salamanca Place is a prime example of Australian colonial architecture. Dating back to the whaling days of the 1830s, these warehouses were the center of Hobart Town's trade and commerce. Today they have been tastefully developed to house galleries, restaurants, night spots and shops. Every Saturday morning a popular 300-stall open-air **craft market** is held at Salamanca Place from 8:30 am to 3 pm in summer and 2 pm in the other seasons. Goods on sale range from the fresh vegetables grown by the Hmong community (a migrant group from Laos), flowers, clothing and artworks made by local artisans.

From Salamanca Place you can climb up the **Kelly Steps**, which are wedged between two of the warehouses about halfway along the main block of warehouses to reach Battery Point.

Battery Point

Behind Princes Wharf and Salamanca Place is the historic core of Hobart, the old port area known as Battery Point. This area was a colorful colonial maritime village, home to master mariners, shipwrights, sailors, fishers, coopers and merchants. The houses reflect their varying lifestyles, ranging from tiny one- and two-room houses such as those around Arthur Circus to large mansions. While most houses are still lived in by locals, a range of buildings are used for visitor accommodations, so you can stay here and experience the village atmosphere of this unique area.

Battery Point's pubs, churches, conjoined houses and narrow winding streets have all been lovingly preserved and are a real delight to wander around, especially when you get glimpses of the harbor between the buildings. There is so much to see here; don't miss out on **Arthur Circus** – a small circle of quaint little cottages built around a village green – or St George's Anglican Church.

Anglesea Barracks was built in Battery Point in 1811. Still used by the army, this is the oldest military establishment in Australia. There is no admission to the museum, which is usually open on weekdays from 9 am to 3:30 pm, and there are guided tours of the restored buildings and grounds on Tuesday at 11 am. At other times you are free to wander around the buildings and look at the outside.

The only way to see the area properly is to walk around, and the *Battery Point & Sullivans Cove Tourist Trail* brochure is well worth obtaining. It's available from many businesses in Battery Point or from the supplier, Avon Court, at 4 Colville St, for A$1. Alternatively, you can go on an organized walking tour on Saturday – see the Organized Tours section below.

Queens Domain

This large park contains reserves and playing grounds for cricket and athletics as well as wide areas of native grasslands. There are good views across the river and the city from many areas of the Domain; the best view is from the lookouts on top of the hill on the northern end of the park. If walking across the park, don't try to descend the northern end to New Town as deep road cuttings prevent pedestrian access.

On the eastern side, near the Tasman Bridge, are the **Royal Tasmanian Botanical Gardens**, which are open from 8 am to 4:45 pm daily; admission is free. Established by the early Governors, the gardens are very pleasant and definitely worth a visit. The massive brick walls were heated by wood fires to combat frost. Some features worth visiting are the Japanese Garden and the French Memorial Fountain.

Organized Tours

Cruises Cruise timetables are pretty changeable as they depend on tides and seasons, so it is best to book. Some cruises have advertised running times, but only operate if there are enough passengers; if you arrive to book just before it leaves, you may find the tour that day has already been canceled.

Four cruise companies operate from the Brooke St Pier and Franklin Wharf and offer a variety of cruises in and around the harbor. One of the most popular is the four-hour Cadbury's Cruise, run by the Cruise Company (☎ 6234-9294), which costs A$33 (children A$16). Leaving at 10 am on weekdays you do a slow roundtrip cruise to the Cadbury Schweppes factory in Claremont where you disembark and tour the premises.

MV *Cartela* (☎ 6223-1914) runs morning cruises for two hours for A$14, one-hour lunch cruises for A$20, one-hour afternoon-tea cruises for A$12, and 2½-hour dinner cruises for A$20. On Friday, it runs a counter-lunch cruise for a bargain at A$10.

On Saturdays only, MV *Southern Contessa* (☎ 6297-1110) operates a five-hour cruise from Hobart south to Port Huon with return by bus. Bookings are essential.

Walking Tours One of the best ways to get a feel for Hobart's colonial history is to take the Saturday morning walking tour organized by the National Trust. The tour concentrates on the historic Battery Point area and departs at 9:30 am from the wishing well in Franklin Square – no bookings necessary. The walk costs A$5, children A$2.50, and takes 2½ hours.

During October to March, twilight walks along the waterfront are run by Sullivans Cove Walking Tours, starting at 6:30 pm. You must book earlier in the day at the Information Centre (☎ 6230-8233) in Elizabeth St; the cost is A$8.50.

For a spooky experience the Hobart Ghost Tour (☎ 6273-3361) is a two-hour candlelit tour that runs at 8 pm and 9:30 pm during the warmer months. The tour visits the Penitentiary Chapel and the Criminal Courts on the corner of Brisbane and Campbell Sts and costs A$7, children A$4, or a family A$19.

Bus Tours Day and half-day bus tours in and around Hobart are operated by Tasmanian Redline Coaches (TRC; ☎ 6231-2200), Hobart Coaches (☎ 6234-4077), and Tasmanian Wilderness Travel (☎ 6234-2226). Bus tours usually run only if there are bookings.

Typical half-day tours with TRC and Hobart Coaches are trips to Bonorong Wildlife Park and Richmond (A$22), Richmond only (A$17), and the City Sights and Mt Wellington (A$20).

Full-day tour destinations with TRC and Hobart Coaches include Port Arthur (A$49), the Huon Valley (A$55), the Derwent Valley (A$47), Ross (A$25), Maria Island (A$43), Swansea (A$30) and Bruny Island (A$75).

Tasmanian Wilderness Travel runs one-day bus trips to Port Arthur (A$33), Mt Field National Park (A$60 if guided, A$27.50 if self-guided), and to Hastings Caves (A$27.50). Entry fees to caves and parks are not included.

Scenic Flights Scenic flights are offered by Par Avion (☎ 6248-5390) and Tasair (☎ 6248-5088) from Cambridge Airport, 15 km from the city. Flights start from A$60 each for 30 minutes and they operate according to demand. If you have a particular place you want to see, then book in advance. The most common planes used for scenic flights carry three or five passengers. A popular flight is into the southwest.

Places to Stay

Hobart has a wide variety of accommodations catering to all tastes and price brackets. The most popular suburb in which to stay is historic Battery Point, just south of the city and very close to the waterfront.

Hotels Hobart has a large number of old hotels built during the 19th century close to the city center. They generally offer rooms with shared bathroom. Often the hotel area downstairs is very classy while the rooms upstairs are fairly plain.

At 67 Liverpool St, near the Elizabeth St Mall, the *Brunswick Hotel* (☎ 6234-4981) is pretty central and has average rooms costing A$33/50 singles/doubles with a continental breakfast. Across the road, at 72 Liverpool St, the *Alabama Hotel* (☎ 6234-3737) is a little more comfortable and charges A$27/44 for singles/doubles. The *Astor Private Hotel* (☎ 6234-6611), 157 Macquarie St, is centrally located only two blocks from the mall, and the tariff of A$40/55 for singles/doubles includes breakfast. Just around the corner the *Freemasons Hotel* (☎ 6223-6655) on the corner of Harrington and Davey St, has rooms for A$40/50.

The best value of the middle- to upper-range hotels is *Country Comfort Hadleys Hotel* (☎ 6223-4355), at 34 Murray St. Rated as a four-star hotel, the 140-year-old building has a lot more charm than the large, new hotels and at A$83 a double is a bit cheaper for about the same standard. Once known as Hadley's Orient Hotel, this is where Roald Amundsen stayed when he went ashore to wire his triumphant message. Tarted up into a suite that is a far cry from the simple room in which he lodged, the 'Amundsen Suite' (A$188 per night) combines rooms 201 and 202, at least one of which was Amundsen's. His photograph hangs above the bed on which he allegedly laid his head.

Five-star accommodations are available at the *Hotel Grand Chancellor* (☎ 6235-4535), at 1 Davey St. Previously known as the Sheraton Hobart Hotel, this red-brick block dominates the city center and costs from A$180 a suite.

If you want to stay near the docks in Battery Point, the *Customs House Hotel* (☎ 6234-6645), at 1 Murray St, charges A$40/65 with a continental breakfast. The *Prince of Wales Hotel* (☎ 6223-6355) in Hampden Rd, Battery Point, is a little more than a kilometer from town and provides basic accommodations with private facilities for A$50/65 singles/doubles including breakfast.

For top-end accommodations, the *Salamanca Inn* (☎ 6223-3300), just behind Salamanca Place at 10 Gladstone St, has rooms from A$164 to A$188 a double. About half of the 60 suites have kitchens. If none of these appeal, there's always the wonderful *Lenna of Hobart* (☎ 6232-3900), an old mansion at 20 Runnymede St, Battery Point, which is steeped in history and luxury and charges A$140 to A$200 for a double room.

Guesthouses & B&Bs These are often in buildings of historical significance. The facilities vary widely but are often of a fairly high standard. All of the following recommendations are in Battery Point, where you pay a little bit more to stay in this popular historic area.

At 72 Hampden Rd, *Barton Cottage* (☎ 6224-1606), is a two-story building that dates back to 1837 and is classified by the National Trust. There are six rooms and B&B accommodations cost A$75/95 singles/doubles. Another similar place worth considering is *Cromwell Cottage* (☎ 6223-6734) at 6 Cromwell St. This two-story townhouse dates from the late 1880s and is in a beautiful location overlooking the Derwent River. Each of the five rooms costs A$75/95 and includes a cooked breakfast.

At 32 Mona St, *Colville Cottage* (☎ 6223-6968) has six rooms with B&B for A$77/98 singles/doubles. Further down the same street at No 8, *Tantallon Lodge* (☎ 6224-1724) has seven rooms at A$75/95.

Very close to Salamanca Place is the *Battery Point Guest House* (☎ 6224-2111 or 018-124-102) at 7 McGregor St. Hidden down a side lane, this was originally the coach house and stables for the nearby Lenna of Hobart. A cooked breakfast is included for A$85/110, and families with young children are welcome.

The only five-star-rated B&B is the *Colonial Battery Point Manor* (☎ 6224-0888), 13 Cromwell St, Battery Point. Built in 1834, it has fine views to the southeast over the Derwent River; B&B is A$120/145 for singles/doubles. Just around the corner and almost as luxurious is *Ascot of Battery Point* (☎ 6224-2434) at 6 Colville St. The rate includes a cooked breakfast and is A$90/115.

Places to Eat

Cafés & Light Meals Hobart has plenty of street cafés, such as the *Kaf Kara*, 119 Liverpool St, which has good food, real cappuccinos (not too common in Hobart), and great décor.

A good lunchtime café is *Café Toulouse*, 79 Harrington St. There's a good selection of croissants and quiches and you can get a quick, light meal for around A$8. A trendy place that serves excellent light meals is the *Kaos Café* at 273 Elizabeth St. It's open daily from noon to midnight, except Sunday when it closes at 10 pm.

If you're looking for a late-night snack, you could also try *Mummy's Coffee Shop* at 38 Waterloo Crescent, just off Hampden Rd, Battery Point. Cakes of various types are the speciality, and it's popular for after-theater snacks. It's open from 10 am to midnight Sunday to Thursday and from 10 am to 2 am Friday and Saturday.

Constitution Dock has a number of floating takeaway seafood stalls such as *Mako Quality Seafoods* and *Flippers*. Close by is *Mures Fish Centre*, where you can get excellent fish & chips and other fishy fare at the bistro on Lower Deck, or an ice cream. Another good fish & chip shop frequented by locals is the *Dolphin In The Bay* at 141 Sandy Bay Rd.

For more exotic takeaways try the tiny *Little Bali* at 84a Harrington St. The dishes are mainly Indonesian and are an excellent value for around A$5. It's open from 11 am to 3 pm weekdays and every evening from 5 to 9:30 pm. *Little Italy*, 152 Collins St, serves excellent, cheap pasta and is open from 8:30 am to 8 pm or later on weekdays. Both of these places have limited tables at which to sit.

Pub Meals For A$8 you can get a very filling meal at the *New Sydney Hotel*, 87 Bathurst St. Many other hotels serve good counter meals, and those in the A$8 to A$14 range include the *Shamrock* on the corner of Harrington and Liverpool Sts and the *Aberfeldy Hotel* on the corner of Davey and Molle Sts.

Stoppy's Waterfront Tavern, on Salamanca Place, is a little trendier and has good counter meals for around A$10 or more, and showcases bands from Thursday to Sunday nights.

Restaurants Australian restaurants are either 'licensed' (to serve alcohol) or 'BYO' (you can Bring Your Own alcohol).

The licensed *Hara Wholefood Café* (☎ 6234-1457) at 181 Liverpool St has an extensive range of mouth-watering vegetarian and vegan dishes and is open from 10 am until late evening Monday to Saturday.

Elizabeth St, in North Hobart, has a reputation for good value, and is one of the most interesting places to eat. At 321 Elizabeth St is *Ali Akbar* (☎ 6231-1770), a popular BYO Lebanese restaurant. For good Italian dishes try *Trattoria Casablanca* at 213 Elizabeth St. Open every evening until after midnight, it's popular with taxi drivers.

At Salamanca Place, *Mr Wooby's* (☎ 6234-3466), tucked away in a side lane, is a pleasant licensed eatery where you can get excellent meals; it's open until quite late. Nearby, at 87 Salamanca Place, is the licensed *Ball & Chain Grill* (☎ 6223-2655) for grilled steaks; main courses are around A$13.

At No 89 there's *Panache* (☎ 6224-2929), a licensed café/restaurant which has an outdoor eating area by the adjoining rock walls. For excellent Japanese food, try the licensed *Mikaku* (☎ 6224-0882) at 85 Salamanca Place.

At 31 Campbell St, there's the *Theatre Royal Hotel* (☎ 6234-6925), with a highly acclaimed bistro. It's right next door to the Theatre Royal, Australia's oldest functioning performing-arts theater.

In Hampden Rd, Battery Point, is the very popular *Brasserie*, which has a reputation for excellent food at moderate prices. Also in Hampden Rd, at No 47, is *Da Angelo Ristorante* (☎ 6223-7011), which serves pasta and pizza for A$8 to A$12 for main courses. Come early or book as it's often full.

On the waterfront, the licensed *Drunken Admiral* (☎ 6234-1903) at 17 Hunter St is open every evening and has good seafood and a great atmosphere. Right next door is the *Riviera Ristorante* (☎ 6234-3230), a popular Italian restaurant.

Entertainment

The *Mercury* newspaper, published daily, has information on most of Hobart's entertainment.

The *New Sydney Hotel*, 87 Bathurst St, is Hobart's Irish pub and there's live music most nights. For jazz, blues and rock & roll, *St Ives Hotel*, 86 Sandy Bay Rd, and *Travellers Rest*, 394 Sandy Bay Rd, have bands from Wednesday to Sunday nights.

You're guaranteed a good time at *Maloney's Hotel* on the corner of Macquarie and Argyle Sts; there are bands on Friday and Saturday nights and a nightclub upstairs.

There are 17 bars at the Wrest Point Hotel Casino; and some, like the *Birdcage*, need to be seen to be believed. The casino also has a disco every night with a cover charge on Friday and Saturday only.

At 375 Elizabeth St, North Hobart,

you'll find the *State Cinema* (☎ 6234-6318), which screens alternative films, while at 181 Collins St there's a large *Village* complex (☎ 6234-7288), which shows the mainstream releases.

Things to Buy

At 81 Salamanca Place is the Antarctic Connection (☎ 6224-8233), which has a wide selection of Antarctic-related items, including books, bookmarks, postcards, magnets, stamps, stuffed toys, etc. There is also an interesting selection of historic photographs for sale.

Several of Hobart's secondhand bookstores sometimes carry Antarctic titles. Astrolabe Books (☎ /fax 6223-8644), upstairs at 81 Salamanca Place, has many old and rare books, including a fine selection of Antarctic material. Both the Imperial Bookshop (☎ 6223-1663), in the Imperial Arcade at 138 Collins St, and C Pearce Hobart Bookshop (☎ 6234-9654; fax 6231-5504), at 29 Criterion St, sell new and used books, including Antarctic and subantarctic titles.

There is also a good selection of shops selling Tasmania-related items. Among the best of these is the Tasmania Shop (☎ 6231-5200), at 108 Elizabeth St, with a wide variety of handsome and unique gifts, including many made from beautifully finished Tasmanian wood.

Getting Around

The Airport The airport is in Hobart's eastern suburbs, 16 km from the city center. TRC (☎ 6231-3900) runs a pick-up and drop-off shuttle service between the city center and the airport for A$6.60.

Bus The local bus service is run by Metro. The main office (☎ 6213-2201) is at 18 Elizabeth St, opposite the GPO. Most buses leave from this area of Elizabeth St, known as the Metro City Bus Station, or from around the edges of the nearby Franklin Square.

If you're planning to bus around Hobart, it's worth buying Metro's user-friendly timetable, which only costs A$1.50. For A$2.80 (A$8 for a family), you can get a Day Rover ticket, which can be used all day at weekends and between 9 am and 4:30 pm and after 6 pm on weekdays. It cannot be used at peak hours so you do need to plan carefully.

Car There are more than 20 car rental firms in Hobart. Some of the cheaper ones include Rent-a-Bug (☎ 6231-0300) at 105 Murray St; Advance Car Rentals (☎ 6224-0822) at 277 Macquarie St; Bargain Car Rentals (☎ 6234-6959) at 189A Harrington St; and Statewide Rent-a-Car (☎ 6225-1204) at 388 Sandy Bay Rd, Sandy Bay.

Bicycle The Transit Centre Backpackers has mountain bikes for A$15 per day, or for A$70 per week. Brake Out (☎ 6234-7632) also rents bicycles from the Wrest Point Casino. If you find Hobart's hills too steep, then Brake Out provides transport to the summit of Mt Wellington (A$25) and Mt Nelson (A$21), allowing you an easy ride downhill.

Boat On weekdays the ferry MV *Emmalisa* (☎ 6223-5893) operates between Franklin Wharf and Bellerive Wharf and is a very pleasant way to cross the Derwent River. It departs Hobart at 7:30 and 8:15 am and 4:35 and 5:15 pm. From Bellerive there are services at 7:57 and 8:35 am and at 4:50 pm. A one-way ticket costs A$1.20, children 60¢. Extra services run during the warmer months and the crossing takes 15 minutes. There is no weekend service.

Punta Arenas

At the foot of the Chilean Andes on the western side of the Strait of Magellan, Patagonia's most interesting and liveliest city features many mansions and other impressive buildings dating from the wool boom of the late 19th and early 20th centuries. As the best and largest port for thousands of kilometers, Punta Arenas (population 110,000) attracts ships from the burgeoning South Atlantic fishery as well as Antarctic research and tourist vessels. Free port facilities have promoted local commerce and encouraged immigration from central Chile.

Punta Arenas has experienced a large influx of foreign visitors, compared to their relative paucity in Argentina, but the town is utterly dead on Sunday, which is a good day to explore some of the surrounding area.

History

Ona, Yahgan, Alacaluf and Tehuelche Indians, subsisting through fishing, hunting and gathering, were the area's original inhabitants. There remain very few individuals of identifiable Ona or Yahgan descent, while the Alacalufes and Tehuelches survive in much reduced numbers. In 1520, Magellan was the first European to visit the area, but early Spanish colonization attempts failed; tiny Puerto Hambre (Port Famine), on the strait south of Punta Arenas, is a reminder of these efforts. Nearby, the restored wooden bulwarks of Fuerte (Fort) Bulnes recall Chile's initial colonization in 1843, when President Manuel Bulnes ordered the army south to an area then only sparsely populated by indigenous peoples.

Founded in 1848, Punta Arenas was originally a military garrison and penal settlement that proved to be conveniently situated for ships headed to California during the Gold Rush. Compared to the initial Chilean settlement at Fuerte Bulnes, 60 km south, it had a better, more protected harbor, and superior access to wood and water. For many years, English maritime charts had called the site 'Sandy Point,' and this became its rough Spanish equivalent.

In Punta Arenas' early years, its economy depended on wild animal products, including sealskins, guanaco hides and feathers; mineral products, including coal, gold and guano; and firewood and timber. None of these was a truly major industry, and the economy did not take off until the last quarter of the 19th century, after the territorial governor authorized the purchase of 300 purebred sheep from the Falkland Islands. The success of this experiment encouraged others to invest in sheep and, by the turn of the century, there were nearly two million sheep in the territory.

In 1875, the population of Magallanes province was barely 1000, but European immigration accelerated as the wool market boomed. Among the most notable immigrants were Portuguese businessman José Nogueira; Irish doctor Thomas Fenton, who founded one of the island's largest sheep stations; and José Menéndez, an entrepreneur from Spanish Asturias who would become one of the wealthiest and most influential individuals not just in Patagonia, but in all of South America.

The opening of the Panama Canal in 1914 marked the beginning of a decline in traffic around Cape Horn, which in turn diminished the port's international importance.

Orientation

The city has spread north and south from its original center between the port and the Plaza de Armas, properly known as Plaza Muñoz Gamero. Street names change on either side of the plaza, but street addresses on the plaza itself bear the name Muñoz Gamero. Most landmarks and accommodations are within a few blocks of the plaza. Mirador La Cruz, at Fagnano and Señoret, four blocks west of the plaza, provides a good view of town and the strait. Most city streets are one-way, though grassy medians divide Av Bulnes and a few other major thoroughfares.

Information

Tourist Offices Sernatur (☎ 22-5385), the Chilean state tourist agency, is at Waldo Seguel 689, just off Plaza Muñoz Gamero. It's open weekdays 8:15 am to 5:45 pm, and has a friendly, helpful, and well-informed staff. It publishes an annually updated list of accommodations and transport, and provides a message board for foreign visitors.

The municipal Kiosko de Informaciones (☎ 22-3798) in the 700 block of Av Colón,

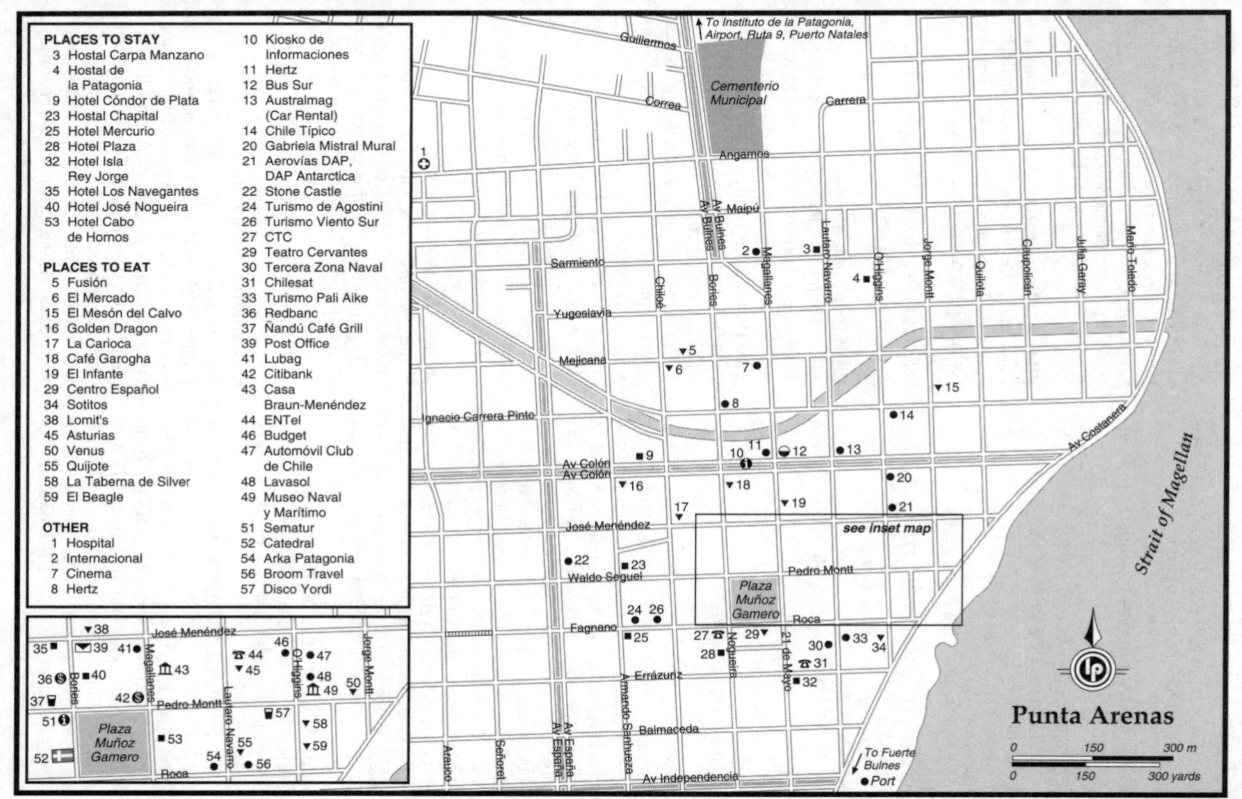
Punta Arenas
PLACES TO STAY
3 Hostal Carpa Manzano
4 Hostal de la Patagonia
9 Hotel Cóndor de Plata
23 Hostal Chapital
25 Hotel Mercurio
28 Hotel Plaza
32 Hotel Isla Rey Jorge
35 Hotel Los Navegantes
40 Hotel José Nogueira
53 Hotel Cabo de Hornos
PLACES TO EAT
5 Fusión
6 El Mercado
15 El Mesón del Calvo
16 Golden Dragon
17 La Carioca
18 Café Garogha
19 El Infante
29 Centro Español
34 Sotitos
38 Lomit's
45 Asturias
50 Venus
55 Quijote
58 La Taberna de Silver
59 El Beagle
OTHER
1 Hospital
2 Internacional
7 Cinema
8 Hertz
10 Kiosko de Informaciones
11 Hertz
12 Bus Sur
13 Australmag (Car Rental)
14 Chile Típico
20 Gabriela Mistral Mural
21 Aerovías DAP, DAP Antarctica
22 Stone Castle
24 Turismo de Agostini
26 Turismo Viento Sur
27 CTC
29 Teatro Cervantes
30 Tercera Zona Naval
31 Chilesat
33 Turismo Pali Aike
36 Redbanc
37 Ñandú Café Grill
39 Post Office
41 Lubag
42 Citibank
43 Casa Braun-Menéndez
44 ENTel
46 Budget
47 Automóvil Club de Chile
48 Lavasol
49 Museo Naval y Marítimo
51 Sematur
52 Catedral
54 Arka Patagonia
56 Broom Travel
57 Disco Yordi
To Instituto de la Patagonia, Airport, Ruta 9, Puerto Natales
Cementerio Municipal
Guillermos
Correa
Carrera
Angamos
Av Bulnes
Maipú
Sarmiento
Yugoslavia
Mejicana
Ignacio Carrera Pinto
Av Colón
José Menéndez
Waldo Seguel
Fagnano
Errázuriz
Armando Sanhueza
Balmaceda
Av Independencia
Av España
Señoret
Arauco
Chiloé
Bories
Magallanes
Lautaro Navarro
O'Higgins
Jorge Montt
Quilota
Caupolicán
Julia Garay
Mario Toledo
Av Costanera
Pedro Montt
Roca
Nogueira
21 de Mayo
Plaza Muñoz Gamero
see inset map
Strait of Magellan
To Fuerte Bulnes
Port
0 150 300 m
0 150 300 yards

between Bories and Magallanes, is open weekdays 9 am to 7 pm all year, and Saturdays 9 am to 7 pm in summer.

Foreign Consulates Consulates in Punta Arenas include:

Argentina
 21 de Mayo 1878 (☎ 26-1912)
Belgium
 Roca 817, Oficina 61 (☎ 24-1472)
Germany
 Av El Bosque 0398 (☎ 21-2866)
Italy
 21 de Mayo 1569 (☎ 24-2497)
Netherlands
 Sarmiento 780 (☎ 24-8100)
Norway
 Av Independencia 830, 2nd floor (☎ 24-1437)
Spain
 José Menéndez 910 (☎ 24-3566)
UK
 Roca 924 (☎ 24-7020)

Money All prices quoted in the Punta Arenas section are in US dollars (US$). Money changing is easiest at cambios and travel agencies along Lautaro Navarro, which are open weekdays and Saturday mornings, but not Sundays. Traveler's checks are easy to negotiate, but many hotels and restaurants also accept US dollars at a fair rate of exchange. Bus Sur, at Magallanes and Colón, will cash traveler's checks for Saturday afternoon arrivals.

Redbanc has an ATM at Bories 970, half a block north of the plaza, and there are several others in the area.

Post & Communications Correos de Chile, the central post office, is at Bories 911 near José Menéndez, a block north of the plaza.

Long-distance telephone service is good and cheap. Chile's country code is 56, and Punta Arenas' area code is 61. Chilean telephone companies provide offices from which you can call long distance. CTC has a long-distance office at Nogueira 1116, at the southwest corner of the plaza, while Chilesat has one at Errázuriz 856. ENTel also has an office at Lautaro Navarro 931.

Travel Agencies In addition to the agencies listed under Organized Tours below, also try Broom Travel (☎ 22-8312) at Roca 924 (in the same building as the British Consulate), Turismo Comapa (☎ 24-1437) at Av Independencia 840, and Turismo de Agostini (☎ 22-1676) at Fagnano 518.

Film & Photography A good, conscientious place for film developing, including slides, is Todocolor, Chiloé 1422 between Av Indepencia and Boliviana.

Medical Services The hospital is at Arauco and Angamos.

Casa Braun-Menéndez

Also known as the Palacio Mauricio Braun, this opulent mansion testifies to the wealth and power of pioneer sheep farmers in the late 19th century. Much of the house, including original furnishings, remains as it did when still occupied by the family.

The museum also has excellent historical photographs and artifacts of early European settlement. The admission fee is modest (US$1.20), but there's an extra charge for photographing the interior. Hours are Tuesday to Sunday from 11 am to 4 pm. Access to the grounds is easiest from Magallanes, but the museum entrance is at the back of the house.

Museo Naval Y Marítimo

Punta Arenas' new naval and maritime museum occupies the 2nd and 3rd floors at O'Higgins 989, at the corner of Pedro Montt. It's open weekdays from 9:30 am to 12:30 pm, Saturdays from 10 am to 1 pm, and daily except Sunday from 3 to 6 pm.

Cementerio Municipal

The walled municipal cemetery, at Av Bulnes 949, tells a great deal about the history and social structure of the region. The first families of Punta Arenas flaunted their wealth in death as in life – wool baron José Menéndez's extravagant tomb is, according to Bruce Chatwin, a scale replica of Rome's Vittorio Emmanuel monument. But the headstones among the topiary cypresses also tell the stories of Anglo, German, Scandinavian and Yugoslav immigrants who supported the wealthy families with their labor. There is also a monument to the now nearly extinct Onas. Open daily, the cemetery is about a 15-minute walk from the plaza, but you can also take any taxi colectivo from the entrance of the Casa Braun-Menéndez on Magallanes.

Instituto de la Patagonia

Part of the Universidad de Magallanes, the Patagonian Institute features an interesting collection of early farm and industrial machinery imported from Europe, a typical pioneer house and shearing shed (both reconstructed), and a wooden-wheeled trailer that served as shelter for shepherds. Visitors can wander among the outdoor exhibits at will, but ask the caretaker at the library for admission to the buildings.

The library also has a display of historical maps and a series of historical and scientific publications for sale to the public. A rather overgrown botanical garden, a small zoo, and experimental garden plots and greenhouses are also open to the public.

Admission costs US$1. Hours are weekdays 9 am to 12:30 pm and 2:30 to 6:30 pm. Weekend visits may be possible by prior arrangement. Any taxi colectivo to the Zona Franca (duty-free zone) will drop you across the street.

Penguin Colonies

Also known as the 'jackass penguin' for its characteristic braying sound, the Magellanic penguin *(Spheniscus magellanicus)* comes ashore in spring to breed and lay its eggs in sandy burrows or under shrubs a short distance inland. There are two substantial colonies near Punta Arenas: The easiest to reach is the mainland pingüinera on **Seno Otway** (Otway Sound), about an hour northwest of the city, while the larger and more interesting **Parque Nacional Los Pinguinos** is accessible only by boat to Isla Magdalena or Isla Marta in the strait. Several species of gulls and cormorants are also common, along with rheas and southern sea lions.

Magellanic penguins are naturally curious and tame, though if approached too quickly they scamper into their burrows or toboggan awkwardly across the sand back into the water. If approached too closely, they will bite, and their bills can open a cut large enough to require stitches – never stick your hand or face into a burrow. The least disruptive way to observe or photograph them is to seat yourself among the burrows and wait for their curiosity to get the better of them. Since there is no scheduled public transport to either site, it is necessary to rent a car or take a tour to visit them (see Organized Tours, below). Admission to the sites costs US$2.50 per person.

Organized Tours

Turismo Pali Aike (☎ 22-3301), Lautaro Navarro 1129, goes to the Seno Otway penguin colony (US$12), with trips running daily at 3:30 pm, to Fuerte Bulnes (US$12) daily at 10 am, and to Río Verde (US$15) on Seno Skyring; all their tours include sandwiches and soft drinks. Arka Patagonia (☎ 22-6370), Roca 886, Local 7, also runs trips for similar prices, as do Turismo Aonikenk (☎ 22-8332) at Magallanes 619 and Turismo Viento Sur (☎ 22-5167) at Fagnano 565. It's possible to take more than one tour in a day, as these companies usually offer various trips daily.

Places to Stay

Sernatur maintains a very complete list of accommodations and prices.

Probably the best midrange value is *Hostal Chapital* (☎ 24-2237), Armando Sanhueza 974, which charges US$31/39 singles/doubles with shared bath, US$37/50 with private bath. At reader-endorsed *Hostal de la Patagonia* (☎ 24-1079), O'Higgins 478, rates are US$36/40 with shared bath, US$45/53 with private bath. *Hostal Carpa Manzano* (☎ 24-2296), Lautaro Navarro 336, is also worth a try for US$48/64.

Comfortably modern *Hotel Cóndor de Plata* (☎ 24-7987), Av Colón 556, costs US$46/53 singles/doubles – a better value than others charging considerably more. *Hotel Mercurio* (☎ 22-3430), Fagnano 595, is also modern, clean and comfortable at US$49/62 with breakfast. Convenient *Hotel Plaza* (☎ 24-1300), at Nogueira 1116 one floor below Residencial París, charges US$54/68.

Perhaps the best in town, *Hotel Los Navegantes* (☎ 22-4877), José Menéndez 647, has rooms for US$103/131, while the slightly more central and refurbished *Hotel Cabo de Hornos* (☎ 22-2134), on the east side of Plaza Muñoz Gamero, charges US$129/150. The latter has a good but expensive bar, and its solarium displays a number of stuffed birds, including rockhopper and macaroni penguins, which visitors to local penguin colonies are unlikely to see.

Part of the Sara Braun mansion has become *Hotel José Nogueira* (☎ 24-8840), half a block from Plaza Muñoz Gamero at Bories 959. It costs US$114/137 singles/doubles, but selective travelers on a budget can afford a drink or a meal in its conservatory/restaurant, beneath what may well be the world's most southerly grape arbor. Another new top-end choice is *Hotel Isla Rey Jorge* (☎ 22-2681), 21 de Mayo 1243, for US$102/136.

Places to Eat

Fusión (☎ 22-4704), Mejicana 654, offers a very good fixed price lunch for US$4, if you can tolerate the appalling music. *Quijote*, Lautaro Navarro 1087, also has reasonable lunches. *La Carioca* (☎ 22-4809), José Menéndez 600, offers good sandwiches and lager beer, although its pizzas are small and expensive. A good choice for breakfast and onces ('elevens,' Chilean afternoon tea) is *Café Garogha* (☎ 24-1782), Bories 817. A portion of their 'selva negra' chocolate cake is large enough for two, as are their sandwiches. *Lomit's*, José Menéndez 722, also serves excellent sandwiches.

A local institution at Mejicana 617 (the ground-level entrance to this upstairs restaurant is inconspicuous), *El Mercado* (☎ 24-7415) prepares a spicy ostiones al pil pil (a spicy scallop dish) and a delicate but filling chupe de locos (an abalone dish); prices are generally moderate. The *Centro Español* (☎ 24-2807), above the Teatro Cervantes on the south side of Plaza Muñoz Gamero, serves delicious cóngrio (conger eel) and ostiones, among other specialties. *Golden Dragon*, a Chinese restaurant at Colón 529, is also very good.

Highly regarded *Sotitos* (☎ 24-5365), O'Higgins 1138, serves outstanding if pricey dishes like centolla (king crab), but there are also more reasonably priced items on the menu. The same holds for nearby *El Beagle* (☎ 24-3057), O'Higgins 1077. Prices are moderate at *La Taberna de Silver* (☎ 22-5533), O'Higgins 1037, but its fish dishes are often deep-fried. Another recommendation is *El Mesón del Calvo* (☎ 22-5015), specializing in lamb, at Jorge Montt 687.

Asturias (☎ 24-3763), at Lautaro Navarro 967 is worth a try at the upper end of the scale, as is *El Infante* (☎ 24-1331) at Magallanes 875. Recent readers' recommendations include *Venus* (☎ 24-1681), Pedro Montt 1046, and *Monaco* on Nogueira near the post office.

Entertainment

In recent years Chilean nightlife has become quite exuberant. *Café Garogha* has a lively crowd late into the evening, and sometimes provides live entertainment. As in any port, there are numerous bars: Try the *Ñandú Café Grill*, at Waldo Seguel 670, which also serves meals. *Disco Yordi* is on Pedro Montt between O'Higgins and Lautaro Navarro.

Two central cinemas often show North American and European films: *Teatro Cervantes* (☎ 22-3225) is on the south side of Plaza Muñoz Gamero, while the *Cinema* is at Mejicana 777.

On the outskirts of downtown on Av Bulnes are the *Club Hípico* (municipal racetrack) and the *Estadio Fiscal* (stadium), where the local soccer league club plays.

Things to Buy

Punta Arenas' Zona Franca (duty-free zone) is a good place to replace a lost or stolen camera, and to buy film and other luxury items. Fujichrome slide film, 36 exposures, costs about US$5 per roll without developing, but it is increasingly difficult to find; print film is correspondingly cheap. Taxi colectivos run frequently from downtown to the Zona Franca, which is open daily except Sunday.

Chile Típico (☎ 22-5827), Ignacio Carrera Pinto 1015, offers artisanal items in copper, bronze, lapis lazuli, and other materials.

Getting Around

The Airport Aeropuerto Presidente Carlos Ibáñez del Campo is 20 km north of town. Austral Bus runs minibuses to the airport from Hotel Cabo de Hornos, on Plaza Muñoz Gamero. DAP runs its own bus to the airport, while LanChile and Ladeco use local bus companies (US$1.25).

Bus & Colectivo Although most places of interest are within easy walking distance of downtown, public transportation is excellent to outlying sights like the Instituto de la Patagonia and the Zona Franca. Taxi colectivos, with numbered routes, are only slightly more expensive than buses (about US$0.30, a bit more late at night and on Sundays), much more comfortable and much quicker.

Car The following companies have offices in Punta Arenas:

Hertz
  Av Colón 798, Ignacio Carrera Pinto 700 (☎ 24-8742)
Budget
  O'Higgins 964 (☎ 24-1696)
Automóvil Club de Chile
  O'Higgins 931 (☎ 24-3675)
Internacional
  Sarmiento 790-B (☎ 22-8323)
Australmag
  Av Colón 900 (☎ 24-2174)
Lubag
  Magallanes 970 (☎ 24-2023)

Stanley

Stanley, the Falkland Islands' capital, is little more than a village which, by historical accident, acquired a political status totally out of proportion to its size. Because many of its houses were built from available materials – often locally quarried stone and timber from shipwrecks – it has a certain ramshackle charm, as the houses' metal cladding and brightly painted corrugated-iron roofs contrast dramatically with the surrounding moorland. Nearly all the houses have large kitchen gardens, where residents grow much of their own food and enough ornamentals to give the townscape a spot of color. The sweetish fragrance of peat fuel still permeates the town on calm evenings, even though many households now use oil, gas and electricity for cooking and heating.

For information on the rest of the Falklands, see the Southern Ocean & Subantarctic Islands chapter.

History

Stanley was founded in 1844, when the British Colonial Office ordered the removal of the seat of government from Port Louis, on Berkeley Sound, to the more sheltered harbor of Port Jackson, since renamed Stanley Harbour. Originally a tiny outpost of colonial officials, vagabond sailors, and British military pensioners, the town grew slowly as a supply and repair port for ships rounding Cape Horn en route to the California Gold Rush. Some damaged vessels were forced to limp back into port, their cargos legitimately being condemned and sold. The port acquired an unsavory reputation, as ships were scuttled under questionable circumstances, which undoubtedly discouraged growth. Only as sheep replaced cattle in the late 19th century did Stanley begin to grow more rapidly, as it became the transshipment point for wool between the outlying sheep ranches and the UK.

As the wool trade grew, so did the influence of the Falkland Islands Company, already the Islands' largest landowner. FIC soon became the town's largest employer, especially after acquiring the property of JM Dean, its only commercial rival, in the late 19th century. Over the next century, FIC's political and economic dominance was uncontested, as it ruled the town no less absolutely than the owners of the large sheep stations ruled the countryside (locally known as 'camp'). At the same time, the company's relatively high wages and good housing provided a paternalistic security, although these 'tied houses' were available only so long as the employee remained with the company.

During the 1982 war over the Falklands, the capital escaped almost unscathed despite its occupation by thousands of Argentine troops. For more about the Falklands war, see History in the Falkland Islands section of the Southern Ocean & Subantarctic Islands chapter.

Stanley remains the service center for the wool industry, but since the declaration of a fisheries protection zone around the Islands, it has become an important port for the deep-water fishing industry, and many Asian and European fishing companies have offices in town.

Orientation

On a steep hillside on the south shore of Stanley Harbor, Port William's sheltered inner harbor on East Falkland, Stanley is surrounded by water and low hills. For protection from the prevailing southwest winds, the town has sprawled east and west along the harbor rather than onto the exposed ridge of Stanley Common, to the south. Ross Road, running the length of the harbor, is the main street, but most government offices, businesses and houses are within a few blocks of each other in the compact town center. Most Stanley roads are paved, but outside town they are invariably graveled. The only good roads outside Stanley are those to Mt Pleasant airport, to Darwin/Goose Green, and from Pony's Pass to Port Louis and Volunteer Point.

Information

Tourist Offices The Falkland Islands Tourist Board (☎ 22215, 22281) at the Public Jetty distributes an excellent guide

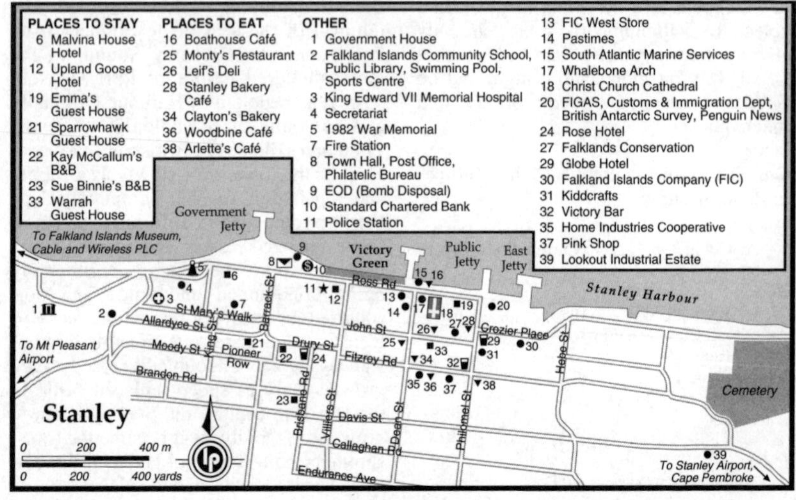

to Stanley, as well as other useful brochures, including a list of accommodations throughout the Islands. Hours are 8 am to noon and 1:15 to 4:30 pm weekdays.

The Mount Pleasant Travel Office (☎ 76691) is at 12 Facility Main Reception, at Mt Pleasant international airport.

Money All prices quoted in the Stanley section are given in British pounds (£). Standard Chartered Bank, on Ross Rd between Barrack and Villiers Sts, will change foreign currency and traveler's checks, and cash personal checks drawn on several UK banks with the appropriate guarantee card. Hours are weekdays 8:30 am to noon and 1:15 to 3 pm. Most Stanley businesses readily accept traveler's checks.

Remember that Falklands currency is valueless outside the Islands – change your local notes for sterling or US dollars before leaving.

Post & Communications The post office (☎ 27180), in Town Hall on Ross Rd at Barrack St, is open weekdays 8 am to noon and 1:15 to 4:30 pm. Hours are weekdays 9 am to noon and 1:15 to 4 pm.

Easily identified by its satellite dish, Cable and Wireless PLC (☎ 20804) operates the Falklands' phone, telegram, telex, and fax services from offices on Ross Rd near Government House. To make an overseas call from the booths in the office, purchase a magnetic card over the counter – this is cheaper than an operator-assisted call. Counter hours are 8:30 am to 5 pm weekdays, but public booths are open 24 hours.

Travel Agencies For special itineraries or assistance for groups or individuals within the Islands, contact Jacki Draycott at Stanley Services (☎ 22622, fax 22623), on Airport Rd.

Immigration The Customs & Immigration Department (☎ 27340), on Ross Rd next to Penguin News, also sells maritime charts of the Islands.

Film & Photography Falkland Printz (☎ 32185), at Mt Pleasant airport, stocks and develops both color print and slide film. In Stanley, leave your film at Pastimes, on Dean St near Ross Rd behind the FIC's West Store, for 36-hour service.

Medical Services The King Edward VII Memorial Hospital (☎ 27328 for appointments, ☎ 27410 for emergencies), a joint military-civilian facility, is probably the best in the world for a community of Stanley's size. The hospital is at the west end of St Mary's Walk. Dental services are also excellent. Since care is on a fee-for-service basis, be certain to have insurance.

Emergency The police (☎ 27222) are on Ross Rd, and Fire & Rescue (☎ 27333) is on St Mary's Walk.

Government House

Probably Stanley's most photographed landmark, rambling Government House has been home to London-appointed governors since the mid-19th century. Government House is just off Ross Rd. There's a register that guests should sign before entering the building.

Christ Church Cathedral

Completed in 1892 and undoubtedly the town's most distinguished landmark, the cathedral, on Ross Rd, is a massive brick-and-stone construction with a brightly painted corrugated-metal roof and attractive stained-glass windows. Several interior plaques honor the memory of local men who served in the British Forces in WWI and WWII. On the small square next to the cathedral, the recently restored **Whalebone Arch** commemorates the 1933 centenary of British rule in the Falklands.

1982 War Memorial

Just west of the Secretariat on Ross Rd is a wall honoring the victims of the 1982 Falklands conflict. Designed by a Falkland Islander living overseas, it was paid for by public subscription and built with volunteer labor. Somber ceremonies take place here every June 14.

Falkland Islands Museum

Ironically, the facility that houses the Falklands museum was built for the Argentine Air Force officer who was the local representative of LADE, which until 1982 operated air services between Comodoro Rivadavia and Stanley. For several years after the war, it was the residence of the Commander of British Forces Falkland Islands (BFFI), but after the garrison moved to Mt Pleasant it became the new home of the local museum (☎ 27428), on Holdfast Rd south of Ross Rd West, just beyond the 1914 Battle Memorial.

Curator John Smith is especially conversant with the Islands' maritime history; his booklet *Condemned at Stanley* relates the stories of the numerous shipwrecks that dot the harbor. Hours are Tuesday to Friday 10:30 am to noon and 2 to 4 pm, Sunday 10 am to noon. Admission costs £1.50 for adults, but is free for children.

Stanley Harbour Maritime History Trail

See the tourist office on the Public Jetty for Graham Bound's informational brochure on the various wrecks and condemned ships in Stanley Harbor. There are now informational panels near the remains of vessels like *Jhelum* (a sinking East Indiaman deserted by her crew in 1871), *Charles Cooper* (an American packet from 1866 still used for storage by the FIC), and *Lady Elizabeth* (a striking three-masted freighter that limped into Stanley after hitting a reef in 1913).

Penguin Walk & Gypsy Cove

To visit the most convenient penguin colonies, about 1½ hours' walk northeast of Stanley, go to the east end of Ross Rd beyond the cemetery and cross the bridge over the inlet known as The Canache, continuing past the wreck of *Lady Elizabeth* and Stanley airport. Gentoo penguins crowd the large sand beach at Yorke Bay north of the airport where, unfortunately, the Argentines anticipated a British frontal assault and buried countless plastic mines. While you cannot go onto the beach itself, you can get a good view of the penguins by walking along the mine field fence. Farther on, at Gypsy Cove, are Magellanic penguins, upland geese, kelp geese and many other shorebirds. There are no known mines in this area, but some may have washed up onshore.

Kidney Island

This small nature reserve north of Port William is covered with tussock grass, forming the habitat for a wide variety of wildlife, including rockhopper penguins and sea lions. Arrange visits through the Agricultural Officer (☎ 27355). Dave and Carol Eynon's South Atlantic Marine Services (☎ 21145) on Ross Rd offers boat transportation.

Places to Stay

Accommodations in Stanley are good but limited and not cheap – reservations are a good idea. Several B&Bs also offer the option of full board.

The most economical is *Kay McCallum's B&B* (☎ 21071), 14 Drury St, charging £15 per person. *Sue Binnie's B&B* (☎ 21051), 3 Brandon Rd, charges £25. As of this writing, *Sparrowhawk Guest House* (☎ 21979, fax 21980), 7 Drury St, was undergoing renovation, but it's usually one of the more economical lodgings.

Warrah Guest House (☎ 22649), a renovated 19th-century stone house at 46 John St between Dean and Philomel, charges £25 with breakfast and £44 with full board. Popular *Emma's Guest House* (☎ 21056), 36 Ross Rd near Philomel St, charges £30.50/55 singles/doubles for bed and breakfast, while rates with full board are £48/90.

Malvina House Hotel (☎ 21355), 3 Ross Rd, has Stanley's most congenial ambience, with beautiful grounds and a conservatory restaurant. Rates are £37.50 for an economy single with breakfast, £49.95 for a regular single with breakfast, and £47.25 per person for a twin or double with breakfast (£10 supplement for a single).

The tourist rate, which includes full board, is £65.50.

The venerable *Upland Goose Hotel* (☎ 21455), a mid-19th- century building at 20/22 Ross Rd, charges £39.50 per person for an economy room or £49.50 per person for a twin room with separate facilities (shared bath) and breakfast, and £59.50 per person for a twin/double with breakfast and private bath. There is a single supplement of £20 in all cases. Tourist rates, with full board, are £72.50 per person with a £40 single supplement. The Goose is the only lodging to accept Visa and Mastercard.

Places to Eat

Most of Stanley's eateries are modest and inexpensive snack bars with limited hours. Two bakeries serve bread, snacks and light meals: *Clayton's Bakery* (☎ 21273) on Dean St (open daily 7:30 am to 1:30 pm), and *Stanley Bakery Café* (☎ 22692), Waverley House on Philomel St (open weekdays 8:30 am to 3:30 pm, Saturday 9 am to 12:30 pm).

The *Boathouse Café* (☎ 21145), on Ross Rd near the cathedral, is open for lunch 10 am to 4 pm Monday, Wednesday and Friday, 10 am to 2 pm Tuesday and Thursday. *Woodbine Café* (☎ 21002), 29 Fitzroy Rd, serves fish & chips, pizza, sausage rolls and similar items. It's open Tuesday to Friday 10 am to 2 pm, Wednesday and Friday 7 to 9 pm, and Saturday 10 am to 3 pm. *Arlette's Café* (☎ 22633), Atlantic House, Fitzroy Rd, is open daily except Wednesday, 9 am to 9 pm. *Leif's Deli* (☎ 22721), 23 John St, has specialty foods and snacks; it's open weekdays 9 am to 5 pm, Saturday 9:30 am to noon and 1 to 4 pm. The varied menu at *Monty's Restaurant* on John St includes vegetarian dishes.

Most Stanley hotels also have restaurants, but meals should be booked in advance. *Emma's Guest House* has more elaborate lunches for £6.50 and dinner for £11, while *Warrah Guest House* offers lunch for £7 and dinner for £12. The *Conservatory Restaurant* at Malvina House Hotel and the *Upland Goose Hotel* both serve three-course meals and bar snacks.

Entertainment

Stanley is no mecca for nightlife but has several pubs, open Monday to Saturday 10 am to 2 pm, Monday to Thursday 5:30 to 11 pm, Friday and Saturday 5:30 to 11:30 pm, and Sunday, Good Friday and Christmas Day noon to 2 pm and 7 to 10 pm. When cruise ships are in port, they are open all day.

The most popular is the *Globe Hotel* (☎ 22703) at Crozier Place and Philomel St, which serves bar meals; try also the *Rose Hotel* (☎ 21067) on Brisbane Rd, the *Victory Bar* (☎ 21199) on Philomel St at Fitzroy Rd, and the *Stanley Arms* (☎ 22258) on John Biscoe Rd at the far west end of town. The Upland Goose Hotel's *Ship Bar* (☎ 21455) is open to the public, as is Monty's bar, *Deano's* (☎ 21292).

Many dances, with live music, and discos also take place throughout the year, usually at the town hall. Listen to the nightly FIBS announcements for dates and times. There are no cinemas, but most hotels and guesthouses have video lounges.

Things to Buy

There are a few Falklands souvenirs, but most come from the UK. The exception is locally spun and knitted woolens, some of which are outstanding. Try the Home Industries Cooperative on Fitzroy Rd, open weekdays 9:30 am to noon and 1:30 to 4:30 pm. Kiddcrafts (☎ 21301), 2A Philomel St, makes stuffed penguins and other soft toys appealing to kids.

The Pink Shop (☎ 21399), 33 Fitzroy Rd, sells gifts and souvenirs in general, Falklands and general-interest books (including a selection of Lonely Planet guides), and excellent wildlife prints by owner Tony Chater.

Postage stamps, available from the post office and from the Philatelic Bureau, are popular with collectors. The Bureau also sells stamps from South Georgia and British Antarctic Territory, and accepts Visa.

Getting Around

The Airport The Falklands have two main airports. Mt Pleasant international airport is 55 km southwest of Stanley via a good graveled road, while Stanley airport (☎ 27303), for local flights and flights from Punta Arenas, is about five km east of town. C&M Travel (☎ 21468) takes passengers to Mt Pleasant airport for £13 single; call for reservations the day before. They will also take groups to Stanley airport or meet them there.

Taxi For cabs, contact Ben's Taxi Service (☎ 21191) or Lowe's Taxis (☎ 21381), but be aware that they're expensive.

Car Since roads are so few, it's hard to justify renting a car, but Land Rovers are available from Ian Bury (☎ 21058), 63 Davis St; Ben Claxton (☎ 21437) on Ross Rd East; and the Upland Goose Hotel (☎ 21455) on Ross Rd. Drivers without local experience often get stuck in the boggy soft camp. This problem is so common even for experienced drivers that locals often carry a radio to call for help if they 'get bogged.'

Ushuaia

Over the past two decades, fast-growing Ushuaia has evolved from a village into a city of 42,000, sprawling and spreading from its original site, but the setting is still one of the most dramatic in the world, with jagged glacial peaks rising from sea level to nearly 1500 km.

Frequent air connections link Ushuaia to Buenos Aires and other parts of Patagonia, though its short runway, steep approach and frequent high winds have traditionally made landing here an adventure that timid flyers have preferred to avoid. A new 2.7-km runway will permit planes larger than 737s to land safely and Aerolíneas Argentinas' loss of a landing monopoly may soon permit long-distance competition from foreign airlines such as Ladeco, Varig and Vasp. At press time, LAPA was due to begin flights into Ushuaia.

History

The Yahgan Indians, now few in number, built the fires that inspired Europeans to give this region its name, famous throughout the world. Tierra del Fuego consists of one large island, Isla Grande de Tierra del Fuego, and many smaller ones, only a few of which are inhabited. The Strait of Magellan separates the archipelago from the South American mainland.

In 1520, when Magellan passed through the strait that now bears his name, neither he nor any other European explorer had any immediate interest in the land and its people. In search of a passage to the spice islands of Asia, early navigators feared and detested the stiff westerlies, hazardous currents, and violent seas that impeded their progress. Consequently, the Ona, Haush, Yahgan and Alacaluf peoples who populated the area faced no immediate competition for their lands and resources.

As Spain's control of its American empire dwindled, the area slowly opened to settlement by other Europeans, which led to the rapid demise of the indigenous Fuegians.

From the 1850s, Europeans attempted to catechize the Fuegians. The earliest such instance ended with the death by starvation of British missionary Allen Gardiner. Gardiner's successors, working from a base at Keppel Island in the Falklands, were more successful despite the massacre of one party by Fuegians at Isla Navarino. Thomas Bridges, a young man at Keppel, learned to speak the Yahgan language and became one of the first settlers at Ushuaia, in what is now Argentine Tierra del Fuego. His son, Lucas Bridges, born at Ushuaia in 1874, left a fascinating memoir of his experiences among the Yahgans and Onas entitled *The Uttermost Part of the Earth* (1950).

Since no other European power had

MARK NORMAN

Cruising the Ross Sea

JEFF RUBIN

Photographing elephant seals, King George Is.

JEFF RUBIN

Zodiac drivers, Deception Island

JEFF RUBIN

Outdoor 'barbie,' Davis station

MARK NORMAN

Campbell Island vegetation

MARK NORMAN

Heard Island

MARK NORMAN

Scott Island, Ross Sea

JEFF RUBIN

Taylor Valley, Dry Valleys, Victoria Land

JEFF RUBIN

Lonely Adélie penguin

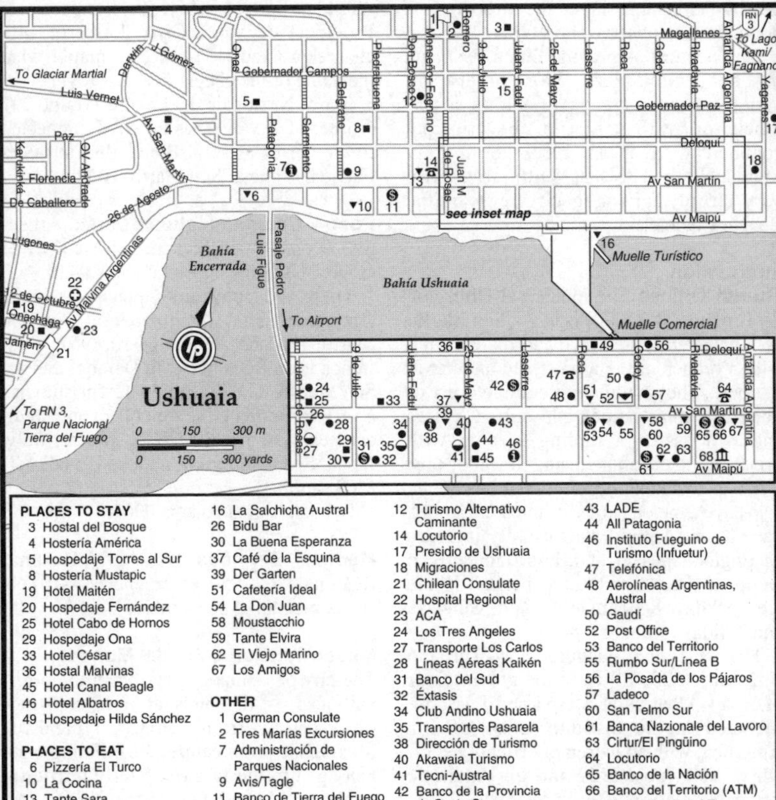

had any interest in settling the region until Britain occupied the Falklands in the 1770s, Spain too paid little attention to Tierra del Fuego, but the successor governments of Argentina and Chile felt differently.

In 1870, the British-based South American Missionary Society made Ushuaia its first permanent outpost in the Fuegian region.

Between 1884 and 1947, Argentina incarcerated many of its most notorious criminals and political prisoners here and on remote Isla de los Estados (Staten Island). Since 1950, the town has been an important naval base, supporting Argentine claims to Antarctica, and in recent years it has become an important tourist destination.

Orientation

Running along the north shore of the Beagle Channel, the Av Maipú becomes Av Malvinas Argentinas west of the cemetery and, as RN 3, continues west to Parque Nacional Tierra del Fuego. The waterfront, its harbor protected by the nearby peninsula (site of the airport), is a good place to observe shorebirds.

Unlike most Argentine cities, Ushuaia has no central plaza. Most hotels and visitor services are on or within a few blocks of Av San Martín, the principal commercial street, one block north of Av Maipú. North of Av San Martín, streets rise very steeply, giving good views of the Beagle Channel.

Information

Tourist Offices The municipal Dirección de Turismo (☎ 32000) is at Av San Martín 660, between 25 de Mayo and Juana Fadul, with a branch at the airport and another at the port. They maintain a complete list of hotel accommodations and current prices and will assist in finding a room with private families; after closing time they post a list of available accommodations. They also have a message board, and the friendly, patient, and helpful staff usually includes an English speaker and, less frequently, a German, French or Italian speaker. Hours are weekdays 8:30 am to 8:30 pm, Sundays and holidays 9 am to 8 pm.

The Instituto Fueguino de Turismo (Infuetur, ☎ 23340) is on the ground floor of Hotel Albatros at Maipú and Lasserre. Included in the Instituto is an Oficina Antartica, with an extremely friendly staff, which sells postcards and an Antarctic Peninsula map (mostly in Spanish). There is also a modest display of artifacts from Nordenskjöld's ill-fated Swedish South Polar Expedition of 1901.

Foreign Consulates Chile has a consulate (☎ 22177) at Malvinas Argentinas 236, at the corner of Jainén. It's open 9 am to 1 pm weekdays. Germany maintains a consulate (☎ 22778) at Rosas 516.

Money All prices quoted in the Ushuaia section are in US dollars (US$). Banco de la Nación is at Av San Martín 190 near Rivadavia, while Banco del Sud is at Av Maipú 781. Banco del Territorio, at San Martín 396 at Roca, cashes traveler's checks for a 3% commission; it also has an ATM at San Martín 152. Banco de la Provincia de Santa Cruz, Lasserre 140, charges a fixed US$7 fee, no matter what the value of the check.

Banca Nazionale del Lavoro, Maipú 297 (corner of Godoy), has an ATM connected to the Cirrus system. Banco de Tierra del Fuego has one at San Martín 1052.

Post & Communications Correo Argentino is on Av San Martín, at the corner of Godoy. Ushuaia's postal code is 9410.

There are convenient places to make telephone calls *(locutorios)* at Av San Martín 133 and Av San Martín 957. Telefónica is on Roca between Deloquí and Av San Martín. The Dirección de Turismo has a very convenient line for collect and credit card calls to Brazil, Chile, France, Italy, Japan, Spain, Uruguay, and the US (AT&T, MCI, Sprint).

Ushuaia's area code is 0901.

Medical Services Ushuaia's Hospital Regional (☎ 22950, emergencies ☎ 107) is at Maipú and 12 de Octubre.

Museo Territorial Fin del Mundo

The city of Ushuaia is restoring the original facade of this unusual block construction, dating from 1903. Atypical of Magellanic architecture, the building once belonged to the family of early territorial governor Manuel Fernández Valdés. An informed, enthusiastic staff oversees exhibits on Fuegian natural history, aboriginal life, the early penal colonies (complete with a photographic rogues gallery), and replicas of an early general store and bank. There is also a bookstore and a good specialized library. On the waterfront at Av Maipú and Rivadavia, the museum (☎ 21863) is well worth the US$2 admission charge. It's open Monday to Saturday from 4 to 8 pm.

Murals

On Av Maipú along the waterfront, you'll see the striking mural of the Selknam/Ona 'Hain' initiation ceremony described by Lucas Bridges in his classic account, *The*

Uttermost Part of the Earth. Also along Av Maipú, between Don Bosco and Rosas, are some overtly political anti-nuclear, pro-environment murals.

Parque Nacional Tierra del Fuego
Just within the borders of Parque Nacional Tierra del Fuego lies **Glaciar Martial**, which hikers can reach via a magnificent walk that begins from the west end of Av San Martín. It passes the Parques Nacionales office and climbs the zigzag road (there are many hiker shortcuts) to the ski run 7.2 km northwest of town. Transportes Pasarela (☎ 21735), Fadul 40, runs five buses daily (US$5 return) to the Aerosilla del Glaciar, a chair lift that is open 10 am to 4:30 pm daily except Monday.

From the base of the Aerosilla (which costs US$5 and saves an hour's walk), the glacier is about a two-hour walk, offering awesome views of Ushuaia and the Beagle Channel. The weather is very changeable, so take warm, dry clothing and sturdy footwear.

All the travel agencies in Ushuaia arrange activities such as trekking, horseback riding, canoeing, mountain biking, and fishing in and around Parque Nacional Tierra del Fuego. See the Dirección de Turismo for a listing that rates these activities from *sin dificultad* (easy) to *pesado* (very difficult).

Organized Tours
Overland Trips Local operators offer tours to the principal attractions in and around Ushuaia, including Parque Nacional Tierra del Fuego. Trips to historic Estancia Harberton (US$30), east of Ushuaia, can be arranged with sufficient notice, but no one should arrive unannounced; admission to the estancia costs an additional US$6 and includes a visit to the Bridges family cemetery. There are also half-day tours of the city (US$15 including the museum), tours to Lapataia/Parque Nacional Tierra del Fuego (US$15), and excursions over Paso Garibaldi to Lago Kami/Fagnano (US$30 full-day) and Río Grande.

Cruises Popular boat trips, with destinations such as the sea lion colony at Isla de los Lobos, leave from the Muelle Turístico (tourist jetty) on Maipú between Lasserre and Roca. Trips cost about US$30 for a 2½-hour excursion; with an extension to Bahía Lapataia, they cost US$45. The most commonly seen species is the southern sea lion *(Otaria flavescens)*, whose thick mane will make you wonder why Spanish speakers call it *lobo marino* (sea wolf). Fur seals, nearly extinct because of commercial overexploitation during the past century, survive in much smaller numbers. Isla de Pájaros, also in the Beagle Channel, has many species of birds, including extensive cormorant colonies. Trips to Estancia Harberton and its *pingüinera* (penguin colony) cost US$55.

Places To Stay
In the summer high season, especially January and February, demand for accommodations in Ushuaia is very high and no one should arrive without reservations; if you must arrive without reservations, try to do so early in the day before everything fills up. Should you arrive without reservations and nothing is available, the 24-hour confitería at the Hotel del Glaciar (three km from downtown on the road to Glaciar Martial) is a good place to stay up drinking coffee. The tourist office does post a list of available accommodations outside the office after closing time.

Places to Stay – bottom end
The tourist office regularly arranges rooms in private homes, *casas familias*, which tend to be cheaper than hotels; because these are usually available only seasonally and change greatly from year to year, you should arrange to stay in one only through the tourist office. Prices are usually in the US$20–per-person range.

Places to Stay – middle
Midrange accommodations start around US$45/50 at *Hotel Maitén* (☎ 22745), 12 de Octubre 140, and *Hostería América* (☎ 23358), Gobernador Paz 1659.

Hospedaje Fernández, located at Onachaga 68 at Fitzroy (☎ 21192), is enthusiastically recommended. It has doubles at US$49.

Other possibilities in this price range include *Hotel César* (☎ 21460) at Av San Martín 753, which offers singles/doubles for US$50/60, and *Hostal Malvinas* (☎ 22626) at Deloquí 609, with rooms for US$60/70.

Places to Stay – top end

Waterfront hotels have the best views and highest prices, but the most exclusive of them are not particularly good values; the most reasonable choice is ACA's *Hotel Canal Beagle* (☎ 21117), Av Maipú 599 at 25 de Mayo, which charges US$70/80 singles/doubles. *Hotel Cabo de Hornos* (☎ 22187), Av San Martín at Rosas, costs US$69/79.

On the hillside at Magallanes and Fadul, *Hostal del Bosque* (☎ 21723) charges US$80/100. At *Hotel Ushuaia* (☎ 30671), Lasserre 933, rates are US$80/110, while at *Hotel Tolkeyén* (☎ 30532), on Estancia Río Pipo five km west of town on RN 3, rooms rent for US$90/100.

Badly overpriced *Hotel Albatros* (☎ 33446), Av Maipú 505 at Lasserre, charges US$120 with breakfast. For the same price, *Hotel del Glaciar* (☎ 30636), three km from downtown on the road to Glaciar Martial, is probably a better choice, but it's still hard to call it a good value.

Five-star *Las Hayas Resort Hotel* (☎ 30710), a bit less than three km from downtown on the road to Glaciar Martial, charges US$175/185 for singles/doubles 'surrounded by natural beauty, invading the hotel through its wide windows.' It sometimes lacks staff to provide all the services of a hotel in its category.

Places to Eat

Meals both cheap and good are scarce in Ushuaia. On the waterfront near the Muelle Turístico, *La Salchicha Austral* (☎ 24596) is among the most reasonable – and very convenient to the cruise ships, but *La Cocina*, on Av Maipú between Belgrano and Piedrabuena, is a phenomenal value by current Ushuaia standards, with excellent three-course meals like lomo a la champiñon (steak with mushrooms) and French fries for US$6.50. *Der Garten*, in the gallery alongside the tourist office on San Martín, has similarly priced weekday specials, as does *Los Amigos* (☎ 22473) at San Martín 150, which has a varied and interesting menu. *Pizzería El Turco* (☎ 23593), San Martín 1460, is also good and relatively inexpensive.

Café de la Esquina, at the corner of San Martín and 25 de Mayo, is Ushuaia's most popular confitería (a place specializing in coffee and desserts). At San Martín and Rosas, the long hours at the *Bidu Bar* (☎ 24605) make it a popular place; it has decent but not cheap meals. *Tante Sara*, at the corner of San Martín and Don Bosco, has outstanding ice cream and other desserts.

The US$12 tenedor libre ('all you can eat' special) at lively *Cafetería Ideal*, Av San Martín 393 at Roca, isn't really a bargain, but some travelers making it their only meal of the day find it a good choice. *Mi Viejo* (☎ 23565), Gobernador Campos 758, also has a tenedor libre special. *La Buena Esperanza*, at Maipú and 9 de Julio, has a handful of Chinese dishes.

At the pricier restaurants, reservations are essential for groups of any size. *Moustacchio* (☎ 23308), Av San Martín 298, has excellent food and service. *Tante Elvira* (☎ 21982, 21249), Av San Martín 234, also has a good reputation. *El Viejo Marino* (☎ 21911), Maipú 297, is a fairly expensive seafood restaurant.

Entertainment

Éxtasis, at Maipú and 9 de Julio, is a popular pub/dance club. *La Posada de los Pájaros* (☎ 30610), at the corner of Deloqui and Godoy, is a popular café featuring live music on weekends. *San Telmo Sur*, Godoy 53, showcases rock and pop, while *Gaudí*, at Godoy 136, offers musical and comedy performances.

Visitors should beware of some of the glitzier 'strip clubs' in Ushuaia, which are thinly veiled fronts for prostitution operations: Your first clue may be when a friendly 'hostess' asks you to buy her a drink, and her six-ounce beer 'costs' US$20.

Getting Around

The Airport Linked to town by a causeway, Aeropuerto Internacional Ushuaia is on the peninsula across from the waterfront. Cabs are moderately priced and there's also bus service along Av Maipú.

Car Rental rates for a Fiat Spazio start around US$30 per day plus US$0.30 per kilometer, plus at least US$15 insurance daily; rental companies include Avis/Tagle (☎ 22744), San Martín and Belgrano, and Localiza (☎ 30663) at Hotel Albatros. Rates go up to US$120 per day (with an additional charge for each kilometer) for a Toyota 4WD.

Southern Ocean & Subantarctic Islands

SOUTHERN OCEAN

Antarctica is surrounded and isolated by the southern portions of the Atlantic, Indian and Pacific oceans. These are separated from the Southern Ocean by a surface oceanographic phenomenon called the Antarctic Convergence. Although for many people this is the least interesting – and least comfortable – part of their trip to Antarctica, the Southern Ocean plays important biological and climatic roles for the continent in particular and the Earth in general.

There is a psychological benefit to the Southern Ocean as well: Sailing over it to reach Antarctica makes clear the continent's remoteness and immensity. The Southern Ocean gives one time to prepare for Antarctica, to anticipate it. Antarctica is unveiled to the sea traveler slowly, just as it was to human knowledge – the first astonishing iceberg, then many icebergs, then an island, and finally, the continent itself looming on the horizon.

First, of course, there is the wide open sea. Most visitors to Antarctica cross the Drake Passage, the narrow stretch of water separating South America from the Antarctic Peninsula. You may hear a lot about the 'Roaring Forties,' but Tierra del Fuego is located at about 55°S, so in fact you will be passing through only half of the 'Furious Fifties' and a small part of the so-called 'Screaming Sixties.' Generally, the passage is fairly quick, and if you are very fortunate, you will experience the quiet waters known as the 'Drake Lake.' Otherwise, prepare yourself for a 'Drake Shake.'

Sailing to Antarctica from Australia, New Zealand or South Africa naturally requires a longer voyage. With a longer voyage, there is a greater chance of encountering heavy weather, but there's also more time for activities such as bird-watching, star-gazing and observing the aurora australis.

No matter your point of embarkation, at some point on your voyage you will pass over the Antarctic Convergence, also called the Polar Front. The ocean south of the Convergence differs greatly from northern waters in salinity, density and temperature. A great mixing occurs where these two types of water meet at the Convergence, with nutrients from the sea floor being brought to the surface, making it a highly productive area for algae, krill and the other small creatures at the base of the Antarctic food web.

The exact location of the Convergence varies slightly throughout the year, and from year to year as well. Despite what you may read, there is very little sign of crossing the Convergence. The sea does not get rougher, and there is usually no visible change in the appearance of the sea. The primary indicator is a dip of 1.7° to 2.8°C in the water temperature, a change that the ship's instruments will detect, though you almost certainly will not! The engine room generally detects it before the bridge – and changes the flow of cooling water appropriately.

Another important feature of the Southern Ocean is the Antarctic Circumpolar Current. This is the world's biggest ocean current, flowing eastward at the rate of 153 million cubic meters per second, about a thousand times the Amazon River's flow.

SUBANTARCTIC ISLANDS

These tiny specks of land include the most remote islands in the world. Ecologically, they are extremely important – completely out of proportion to their size – for a large number of seabird, penguin and seal species, because they are often the only breeding places for many hundreds of kilometers in the vast ocean surrounding Antarctica.

Although many people consider a landing on the actual continent an integral

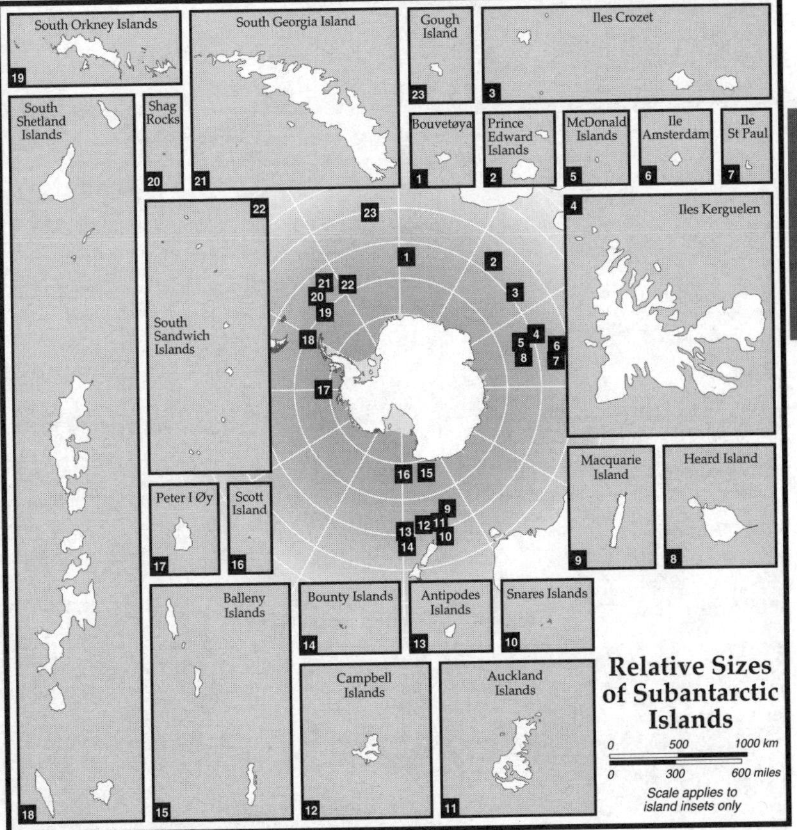

part of their visit to Antarctica, the subantarctic and Southern Ocean islands are in many ways much more interesting than large sections of the continental coast. Most of them, for instance, have more wildlife than does Antarctica. While Antarctic tour operators usually make every effort to land passengers on the continent, most of these islands are properly thought of as being part of the Antarctic as well.

No Antarctic voyage, even a circumnavigation, will visit all of the subantarctic and Southern Ocean islands – there are simply too many of them. But nearly every cruise will visit at least one of the following island groups, and there are even trips that visit *only* islands (see Getting There & Away). Cruises departing from South America or the Falkland Islands nearly always make a stop at one or more of the South Shetland Islands, while voyages sailing from Australia, New Zealand or South Africa will often stop at, respectively, Macquarie Island or Heard Island; New Zealand's subantarctic islands; or the Prince Edward Islands. Tristan da Cunha and Gough Island are usually visited on 'repositioning' cruises, when the Antarctic ships sail to or from the Northern Hemisphere, where they ply Arctic waters during the austral

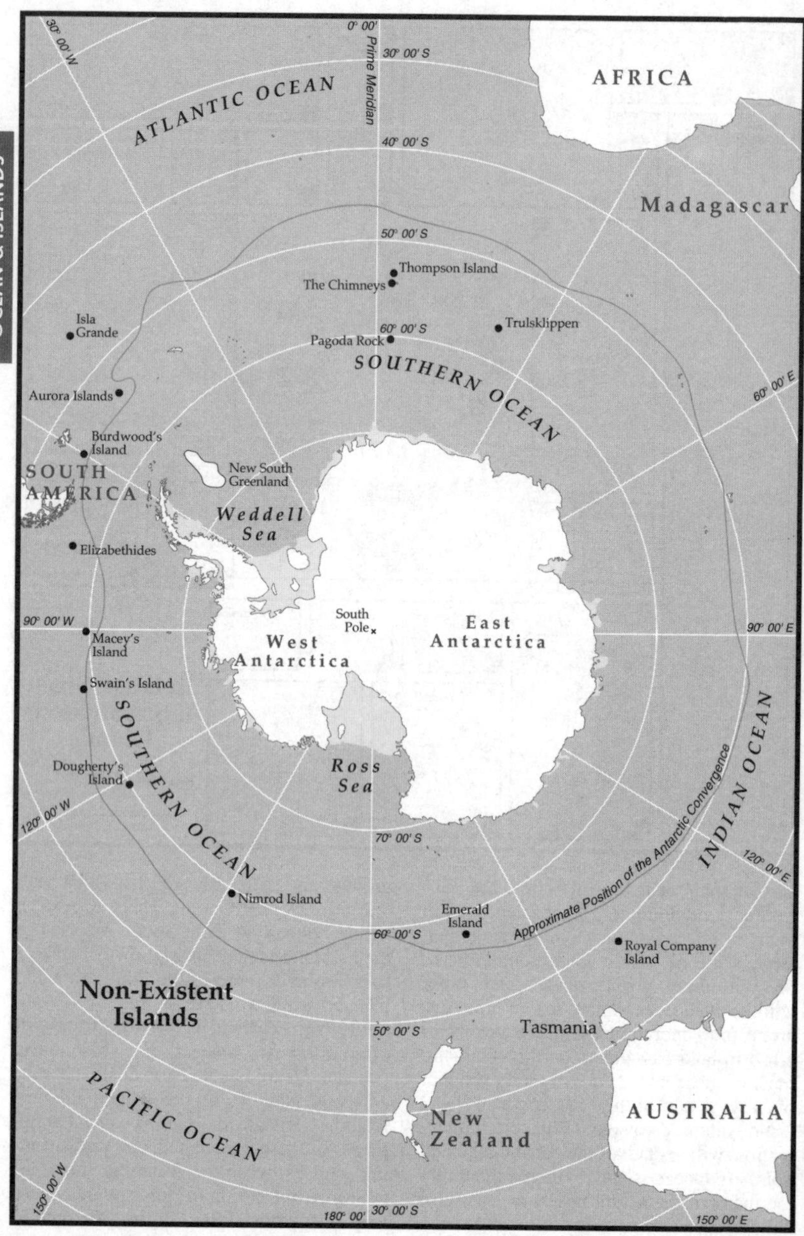

ATLANTIC OCEAN
AFRICA
Madagascar
Prime Meridian
0° 00'
30° 00' S
40° 00' S
50° 00' S
60° 00' S
70° 00' S
30° 00' W
60° 00' E
90° 00' W
90° 00' E
120° 00' W
120° 00' E
150° 00' W
150° 00' E
180° 00'
Thompson Island
The Chimneys
Trulsklippen
Pagoda Rock
Isla Grande
Aurora Islands
Burdwood's Island
SOUTH AMERICA
New South Greenland
Weddell Sea
Elizabethides
SOUTHERN OCEAN
South Pole
East Antarctica
West Antarctica
Macey's Island
Swain's Island
Ross Sea
Dougherty's Island
INDIAN OCEAN
Approximate Position of the Antarctic Convergence
Nimrod Island
Emerald Island
Royal Company Island
Non-Existent Islands
Tasmania
PACIFIC OCEAN
New Zealand
AUSTRALIA

Non-Existent Antarctic Islands

Along with the 19 groups of isolated oceanic islands surrounding Antarctica – known as the peri-Antarctic islands – there are reports of a curious assortment of 15 non-existent but putatively similar, far southern islands: Aurora Islands, Burdwood's Island, The Chimneys, Dougherty's Island, Elizabethides, Emerald Island, Isla Grande, Macey's Island, New South Greenland, Nimrod Island, Pagoda Rock, Royal Company Island, Swain's Island, Thompson Island and Trulsklippen. These have all been recorded in the Southern Ocean or extreme southern limits of the adjoining oceans and most have appeared on official charts. Several of these islands have been seen more than once and three may have once existed but been submerged following volcanic explosions.

Besides volcanoes, there are several reasons for these islands' supposed existence. Many may be explained by icebergs carrying rocks and moraine sighted in dirty weather. A captain, rightly erring for safety, would report these (dirty ice can convincingly look like an island – especially when extensive). Some sightings, however, were more likely the result of a bit too much rum. A few may be deliberate hoaxes: Sealers always tried to keep secret the locations of good sealing discoveries, especially new islands, in order to reduce the competition for a scarce resource. Some of them may well have deliberately led others on wild goose chases. One, New South Greenland, was probably added to embellish a book by an author who was known as 'the greatest liar in the Pacific.'

The problem with all these non-existent islands is getting rid of them. If there was a possibility of a supposedly sighted island being a hazard to navigation, the British Admiralty and other maritime authorities were very reluctant to expunge it from the charts. It usually took a substantial hydrographic survey before this was done (although the satellite age has now simplified this). The persistence of non-existent islands is phenomenal: Swains Island, ordered to be expunged from the charts in 1920, can still be found in a 1995 comprehensive world atlas produced by a well-known publisher. Some non-existent islands have even appeared in novels – there is much that can be made of writing with such a theme. ■

– **Robert Headland**, archivist and curator at the Scott Polar Research Institute in Cambridge, England

winter. The most rarely visited islands are Bouvetøya, Peter I Øy and Scott Island.

In the following pages, the subantarctic and Southern Ocean islands are presented in order, traveling eastwards from the Prime Meridian.

Bouvetøya

Bouvetøya (54°42'S, 03°37'E) is the most isolated island on earth. Not counting its tiny off-lying neighbor to the southwest, Larsøya, the nearest land is more than 1600 km away. Another island sighted by 19th century sealers, Thompson Island to Bouvetøya's northeast, is believed to have been destroyed during a volcanic explosion in 1895 or 1896. Sometime between 1955 and 1958, a low-lying shelf of lava appeared on Bouvetøya's west coast, providing the only bird nesting site of any size on the island.

Bouvetøya covers about 54 sq km. The highest point is Olavtoppen (780m); it and another high peak surround the ice-filled crater of an inactive volcano known as the Wilhelm II plateau. Glaciers cover 93% of the island and prevent landings on the south and east coasts, while steep cliffs as high as 490m block access to the north, west and southwest. Numerous offshore rocks make navigation hazardous. Bouvetøya's weather is nearly always cloudy or foggy. The mean temperature is -1°C; in summer, the average high is 2.2°C.

The island is named after French navigator Jean-Baptiste Charles de Lozier Bouvet, who, sailing in *Aigle*, first sighted it on January 1, 1739, but was unable to get a good fix to determine its position. In 1808, British whaling captains James Lindsay and Thomas Hopper, sailing in *Swan* and *Otter*, respectively, resighted it and proved that it was an island, but Bouvetøya's precise position was only pinned down 90 years later by a German expedition.

The first landing was made by an American sealing expedition led by Benjamin Morrell in *Wasp*, who came ashore December 8, 1822, and took 172 fur seal skins, encouraging other sealers, who visited sporadically during the 19th century. Two British sealing ships, *Sprightly* and *Lively*, rediscovered Bouvetøya on December 10, 1825, and named it Liverpool Island, taking possession in the name of the British crown.

Science, in the form of a Norwegian oceanographic expedition, first visited Bouvetøya in 1927. The island was claimed for Norway on December 1 of that year, and on January 23, 1928, it was formally annexed by Norwegian royal proclamation. (The British Parliament wisely declined to get upset about such an unpromising dot of territory and renounced all claim to Bouvetøya later in 1928.) In 1971, the Norwegian government made the island a nature reserve.

The island has only rarely been visited, so its history is brief. Two events, however, are rather mysterious: first, a sunken lifeboat and assorted supplies were discovered on the island in 1964, but their origin could not be determined. Then, on September 22, 1979, a thermonuclear bomb test very probably occurred to the west of Bouvetøya. Though no country ever publicly admitted to setting off a nuclear device there, an orbiting satellite detected a very brief, intense burst of light, and magnetic, seismographic and ionospheric evidence all point to a nuclear blast. Personnel at Australian Antarctic stations later detected radiation and radioactive debris.

Prince Edward Islands

Bleak and barren in winter but lush and green in summer, the Prince Edward Islands (46°60' to 46°97'S, 37°58' to 38°02'E) consist of Prince Edward Island and the larger Marion Island, 22 km to the southwest. The islands cover a total area of 316 sq km and are part of South Africa's Province of Cape of Good Hope. Domelike Marion is dotted by more than 100 small hills and many small lakes; Prince Edward is more vertical, with dramatic cliffs towering up to 490m high on the southwest coast. The islands' highest point, on Marion, is State President Swart Peak (1230m). The weather is depressingly constant: low temperatures throughout the year, extremely strong westerly winds, abundant snow and rain, and skies usually at least three-quarters covered by clouds.

The Prince Edward Islands were declared Special Nature Reserves by the South African government in 1995. Even scientific research on Prince Edward Island is severely restricted; a group of not more than four people is permitted to land only once every three to five years, staying no more than two or three days maximum.

The islands were first sighted by Dutchman Barent Barentszoon Lam (or, possibly, Ham) sailing in *Maerseveen* on March 4, 1663, who named the northerly island Dina, and the more southerly Maerseveen. But a subsequent Dutch expedition couldn't find the islands in the latitude reported (41°S), and they were all but forgotten.

Frenchman Marc Macé Marion du Fresne, sailing in *Mascarin*, rediscovered them on January 13, 1772. Not realizing at first that they were islands, however, he called the larger one Terre de l'Espérance, before changing it to Ile de l'Espérance; the smaller one he called Ile de la Caverne because of a large cave he saw while circumnavigating it. He also saw tiny white spots dotting Ile de la Caverne, which he somehow mistook for sheep (they were nesting albatrosses). However, a collision with his accompanying ship *Marquis de Castries* prevented Marion du Fresne from making a landing to investigate. Sailing further east, he discovered Iles Crozet (see below).

The ubiquitous British Capt James Cook searched for Ile de l'Espérance and Ile de la Caverne early in 1775, but was unable to find them. Meeting one of the few returning survivors of Marion du Fresne's expedition (which had been attacked by Maoris in New Zealand) in Cape Town, Cook obtained a chart of the islands' location. On December 12, 1776, Cook spotted the islands – and noting that the chart gave them no name, took it upon himself to name them, calling them the Prince Edward Islands after the fourth son of the reigning British monarch. Unknowingly causing considerable confusion to latter-day scholars, Cook gave the name Marion and Crozet Islands to the islands that Marion du Fresne had found later on his voyage, the present-day Iles Crozet. Nineteenth-century sealers further confused the issue by transferring the appellation Marion Island back to the island now known by that name.

French sealers may have made the first landing, in about 1799, though it is not certain, and sealing continued throughout the 19th century and well into the 20th. As did many subantarctic islands, the Prince Edwards saw their share of shipwrecks, and groups of hapless sailors were stranded for months at a time before being rescued, often by other sealing voyages.

Despite the islands' discovery by the Dutch (and the French), the British government felt it had enough proprietary rights over them to grant one William Newton a 21-year lease in 1908 to exploit guano deposits believed to lie on the islands, but he never used the concession. In 1926, the islands, along with the Heard and McDonald Islands, were leased for 10 years by the British government to the Kerguelen Sealing and Whaling Co of Cape Town, which was granted exclusive rights to seals, whales, guano and minerals. The company operated annually in those areas until 1930.

If the French had any inclination to challenge these tacit British claims of sovereignty over the islands, their opportunity vanished in 1947, when a secret South African naval expedition code-named 'Operation Snoektown' raised the Union of South Africa's flag at Marion Island on December 29, 1947, and at Prince Edward Island on January 4, 1948. A permanent meteorological, or 'met,' station was also established at Transvaal Cove on Marion's northeast coast. On January 12, 1948, the South African government issued a proclamation confirming that the British Crown's rights over the islands would henceforth be controlled by His Majesty's Government in South Africa rather than His Majesty's Government in London.

The met station, operated continuously since 1947 (despite a fire that destroyed the main living quarters and communications facilities in 1966), gradually expanded its scientific program to include biology. Currently as many as 17 people winter there; during summer, the population swells to about 50. A volcanic eruption occurred in December 1980 but did not damage the scientific station. A hydroelectric station was built to supply power in 1981-82, but it has since been declared unworkable and removed. The possibility of constructing a landing strip was investigated in 1987, but for environmental reasons, the project was not undertaken.

Introduced species have wreaked havoc on Marion's indigenous flora and fauna, just as they have on other subantarctic islands. The diamond-backed moth *(Plutella xylostella)*, for example, introduced itself to the island in 1986; it has badly damaged the Kerguelen cabbage. Mice, inadvertently introduced by early 19th century sealers, have also damaged plant and insect life. Far more damage, however, has been wrought by descendants of the five house cats brought to the meteorological station in 1949 to control rodents. By 1977, they had multiplied to an estimated 3400 animals and were ravaging the local bird population. The feline panleucopaenia virus, introduced in '77, brought a massive but temporary drop in the feral cat population; other control measures, including shooting, followed, and the cats have now been completely exterminated. As a result, the breeding success of burrowing petrels has increased rapidly.

Fur seals and elephant seals breed on the islands, as do hundreds of thousands of penguins (kings, gentoos, rockhopper and macaronis), hundreds of thousands of petrels and thousands of albatrosses.

Iles Crozet

Iles Crozet (45°95' to 46°50'S, 50°33' to 52°58'E) are divided into two groups, L'Occidental (Ile aux Cochons, Îlots des Apôtres, Ile des Pingouins and the reefs Brisants de l'Héroine) and L'Oriental (Ile de l'Est and Ile de la Possession, the largest of the Crozets), about 100 km east. The islands cover a total of 325 sq km. The highest point, Pic Marion-Dufresne on Ile de l'Est, has an elevation of 1090m; there are no glaciers. The islands are part of France's Terres Australes et Antarctiques Françaises and have been a national park since 1938. The Crozet's weather is generally cold, wet, windy and cloudy, but the winters are not severe.

Frenchman Marc Macé Marion du Fresne, sailing in *Mascarin*, discovered the islands on January 23, 1772. He went ashore the next day and took possession of them for France (on Ile de la Possession), naming them for his second-in-command, Jules Marie Crozet.

The first sealers arrived in 1804, taking the fur seal skins directly to Canton for sale and processing. Just two years later, a group of 14 wretched, stranded sealers was rescued from the Crozets by *Eliza*, sailing from Nantucket. Unscrupulous captains occasionally abandoned men to uncertain fates on the subantarctic islands, increasing their voyage's profitability. Relentless slaughter soon took its toll on the once-teeming beaches, however, and by 1835 the American sealing ship *Tampico* reported that fur seals were rare in the Crozets.

The islands' first recorded shipwreck was the British sealer *Princess of Wales*, which came to grief in 1821; the company was not rescued until 21 months later. After they wrecked on Ile de l'Est in 1825, the crew of the French sealer *Aventure* spent 17 months as castaways. The most inventive of the stranded seamen were the crew of the French ship *Tamaris*, which sank off Ile aux Cochons on March 9, 1887. During their seven-month unplanned sojourn on the island, they attached a message to a giant petrel, which was recovered seven months later near Fremantle, Western Australia, some 6500 km away. *Tamaris*' crew then set out for Ile de la Possession, but something happened en route, and they vanished without a trace.

Whaling in the vicinity soon replaced sealing as the islands' primary economic activity, and in 1841 12 whaling expeditions from the United States alone were operating in the waters around Iles Crozet. During the 1843-44 season, the armada of American whaling ships in the Crozets, as recorded by one sealer, grew to 18: *Aeronaut*, *Arab*, *Cicero*, *Dragon*, *Fenelon*, *France*, *Halcyon*, *Herald*, *John and Elizabeth*, *Majestic*, *Milwood*, *Neptune*, *Popmunnet*, *Romulus*, *Roscoe*, *Stonington*, *Superior* and *Tenedos*.

After several visits to the island in the 20th century to reassert its territorial sovereignty, France moved to consolidate its position on its subantarctic islands. In 1955, French law established the Terres Australes et Antarctiques Françaises, which includes Ile Saint-Paul, Ile Amsterdam, Iles Kerguelen, Iles Crozet and Terre Adélie in Antarctica. In 1978, concerned about fishing by countries including Taiwan and the Soviet Union, France declared a 370-km exclusive economic zone around each of the four archipelagos, patrolled by French naval vessels that arrested foreign ships for illegal fishing.

A temporary scientific camp was set up on Ile de la Possession in 1961, and in the 1963-64 austral summer, a station was established at Port-Alfred on the island's northeast coast, with an aerial cableway running from the beach to the station site. Now known as Alfred-Faure, for its first leader, the base houses 35 people over the winter.

As on the other subantarctic islands

where they were introduced by sealers and whalers, foreign species including cats, rats, rabbits and mice have damaged some of the islands' fragile ecosystems. Introduced pigs gave Ile aux Cochons its name, but they caused so much damage that they became extinct, as did the goats landed on Ile de la Possession.

The Crozets are noted for their birdlife, and half of the world's king penguins breed here.

Iles Kerguelen

Part of France's Terres Australes et Antarctiques Françaises, Iles Kerguelen (48°58' to 49°73'S, 68°72' to 70°58'E) consists of one major island, Grande Terre (sometimes called Ile Kerguelen), and about 300 tiny islets and rocks. The archipelago has a total land area of 7215 sq km, extending 195 km from Îlot du Rendez-Vous in the north to Rochers du Salamanca in the south, and 145 km from Iles de la Fortune in the west to the eastern tip of Péninsule Courbet on Grand Terre. A submarine shelf at a depth of 200m extends for many kilometers off Grand Terre's northern coast, evidence that the Iles once formed a much larger landmass.

Grand Terre is heavily serrated by fjords along its northeast and southeast coasts, providing excellent anchorages, and no point on the island is further than 21 km from the coast. Kerguelen is sculpted by glacier action, with deep valleys and lakes carved out of the high mountains and plateaus, and travel in the interior is hindered by many streams and torrents. The impressive Calotte Glaciaire Cook icecap, in the island's west, covers 10% of the island and is the remnant of the ice sheet that once covered the whole of Grande Terre. The island's highest point is Grand Ross (1850m), first climbed in 1975. Kerguelen has familiarly subantarctic weather: rainy, cloudy, cold and windy, with the prevailing westerlies frequently rising to gale force.

Sailing in *Fortune* in 1772, French Captain Yves Joseph de Kerguélen-Trémarac sighted the archipelago for the first time on February 12, calling it La France Australe because he didn't realize he was looking at islands. Two days later, François Alesno, Comte de Saint-Allouarn, the commander of the accompanying ship *Gros-Ventre*, sent a boat ashore to claim the territory in the name of King Louis XV. The two ships then separated, and Alesno died soon after his arrival at Mauritius.

With no one to challenge him upon his return to France, Kerguélen told wildly optimistic tales – if not outright lies – about his discovery. The lands, he boasted, 'appear to form the central mass of the Antarctic continent,' adding that they were perfectly suited to agriculture and promised abundant minerals and even precious gems. 'If men of a different species are not discovered,' he said, 'at least there will be people living in a state of nature.'

Understandably impressed, the French monarch dispatched Kerguélen on a second voyage in 1773, with three ships, *Rolland*, *Oiseau* and *Dauphine*, and 700 men, in order to colonize 'La France Australe.' A second landing was made, in January 1774, and this time there was no hiding from the reality that Kerguélen's discovery was far from a southern motherland. Upon his second homecoming, a French court martial sentenced Kerguélen to 20 years in prison (later reduced to six) and dismissed him from the navy.

When British Captain James Cook landed on Christmas Eve 1776, one of his men found a bottle containing a parchment inscribed in Latin telling of Kerguélen's visits. Cook, however, was much more sanguine about the islands, calling them the Isles of Desolation.

The first sealers, from the US, arrived in 1791, and remained for 15 months, killing the thick-furred creatures on their breeding beaches. (The first Kerguelen shipwreck occurred just two years later, stranding *Eleanora*'s crew for seven months.) By 1804-05, eight British sealing ships were landing gangs in the Iles. Repeating the pattern of slaughter they practiced on other islands, the sealers soon wiped out the giant colonies almost completely; by 1817, the

British ship *Eagle* was able to find just four seals (which, naturally, they killed).

With the fur seals gone (to another island, the sealers always seemed to believe; the thought of extinction appeared not to dawn on them), the sealers turned their attention to elephant seals, whose blubber was rendered into a valuable oil. In 1835-40, the British sealing ship *George Howe* visited Iles Kerguelen, taking 3000 barrels of elephant seal oil, while the American *Columbia* took 3700 barrels in 1838-40. From 1845-75, American sealers had a near-monopoly on the Kerguelens' elephant seal trade.

Unlike other subantarctic islands, the Kerguelens somehow appear to have induced labor in the occasional sealer's wife who visited their waters. On Christmas Day, 1852, the wife of Henry S Williams, captain of *Franklin* (part of a fleet of seven American whaling and sealing ships), gave birth to a daughter in the islands. Likewise, the wife of Tasmanian sealer James William Robinson, commander of *Offley*, gave birth to James Kerguelen Robinson in 1859.

Death was far more common, however, and at Anse Betsy on the north coast of Péninsule Courbet, a lonely cemetery is the final resting place for more than a dozen sealers and whalers.

In 1874, three separate expeditions, sent by the US, Britain and Germany, landed on Kerguelen to observe the December 9 transit of Venus, a phenomena in which the planet moves across the face of the sun. This rare opportunity allowed astronomers to gather data used to calculate the distance between the earth and the sun; since the accuracy of the measurement depended on a variety of sightings, many countries participated in making observations from various parts of the world. (The next two Transits of Venus will occur in 2004 and 2012.)

In 1877, a British company tried to develop a coal-mining operation on Kerguelen, but the coal was of poor quality and the attempt was abandoned.

France formally annexed Iles Kerguelen in 1893, and in that same year the French government granted an exclusive 50-year lease to the Frères Bossière, who in 1909 established a sealing and whaling station on Grand Terre's southeast coast. It operated until 1914, and again from 1920-29; another sealing and whaling station ran on the island from 1951 to 1956. The French reestablished elephant seal harvesting at Port-aux-Français from 1956 to 1960.

German Erich von Drygalski's *Gauss* expedition landed a scientific party on Grande Terre from 1902 to 1903. Although an outbreak of the deficiency disease beriberi killed several members, extensive biological and survey work was done.

During WWII, Kerguelen's myriad fjords provided valuable hiding places, and Allied powers rightfully fretted about the possibility of the Germans or Japanese using them as a strategic submarine or cruiser base. In fact, in December 1940 and January 1941, the German *Atlantis* (also known as 'raider C') stopped at Kerguelen, where a seaman was buried ashore, and another German ship, *Pinguin* ('raider F'), was resupplied from an anchorage in the Iles. In 1941, HMAS *Australia* cruised to Kerguelen and laid mines at four places in the archipelago; this action helped force the Germans to abandon their plans to establish a meteorological station on Kerguelen, but the mined waters remain dangerous places to anchor to this day.

France set up a temporary scientific station at Port-aux-Français, on Golfe Morbihan on the island's east coast, in 1949-50. The station has been permanently occupied since 1951, and can accommodate 80 expeditioners in winter and 120 in summer. Since 1994, the French National Center for Space Studies has operated a ground station for satellite tracking here.

Formerly administered as a dependency of Madagascar, Iles Kerguelen were incorporated into the Terres Australes and Antarctiques Françaises in 1955.

Rabbits, introduced in 1874 by the British Transit of Venus Expedition, have ravaged Grand Terre's native vegetation, but the namesake Kerguelen cabbage (once prized by sailors as an anti-scorbutic) and tussock grasses are widespread. In 1955, myxomytosis was introduced in an attempt to control the rabbits; after a large decrease in their population, they quickly recovered.

Other introduced animals have also caused severe damage to endemic species. Rats devour the eggs and chicks of petrels. Cats were introduced by early 19th century sailors and again in the 1950s, when they began preying on petrel colonies. An eradication program was begun in 1972, but so far it has not succeeded in eliminating them. Dogs, mink, reindeer, mules, ponies, pigs and cattle have all also lived on Grand Terre at one time, and several hundred sheep from a failed wool-raising operation remain today. Trout were introduced in 1958.

Heard & McDonald Islands

Heard and McDonald islands (52°97' to 53°20'S, 73°25' to 73°83'E), an external territory of Australia, consists of the main volcanic island of Heard, the tiny Shag Islands lying 11 km north and the three small McDonald Islands (Flat and McDonald Islands and Meyer Rock) 43 km west. Heard Island is a roughly circular active volcano, called Big Ben, with the 10-km-long Laurens Peninsula extending to the northwest and the 10-km-long Spit Point extending southeast. The island, with an area of 390 sq km, is 80% covered by glacier. Big Ben erupted in 1910, 1950, 1985 and, most recently, in 1992; its summit, and the island's highest point, is Mawson Peak (2745m), first climbed in 1965. The volcano constantly emits steam, and its upper slopes are nearly always shrouded in low cloud.

The climate, as on most of the other subantarctic islands, is cold, wet and windy. In fact, winds blow almost continuously, with frequent gales. The mean annual temperature is +1°C.

The date of the islands' first sighting is unknown; Capt James Cook noted 'signs of land' near their position in February 1773. Heard Island was possibly sighted in 1833

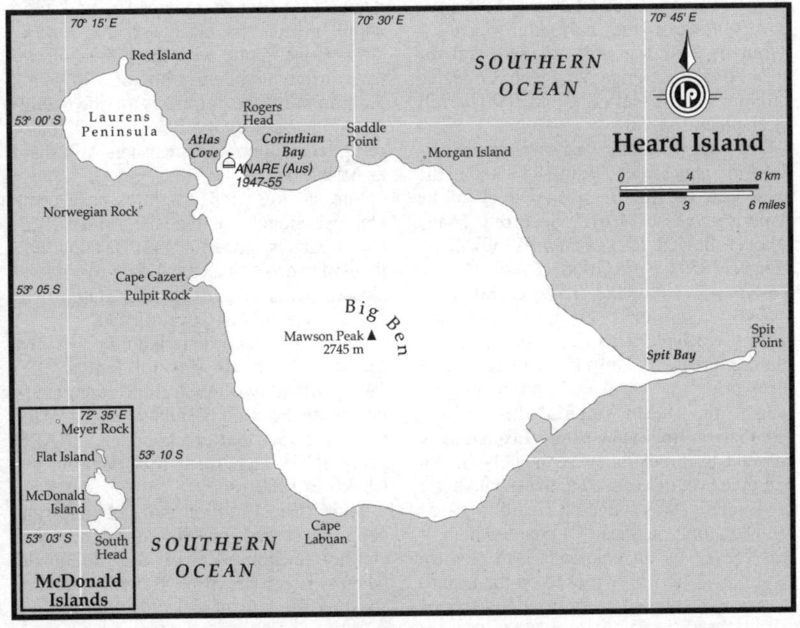

by Briton Peter Kemp, sailing in *Magnet*, and again, possibly, in 1848 by American Thomas Long, master of *Charles Carroll*.

John J Heard, captain of the American *Oriental*, definitely discovered the island that bears his name on November 25, 1853. Two months later, Briton William McDonald, sailing in *Samarang*, rediscovered Heard and discovered the McDonalds.

The islands were thrice rediscovered during the month of December 1854, by three British ships, *Earl of Eglinton*, *Herald of the Morning* and *Lincluden Castle*, each of which thought it was the first to see the islands, and each of which renamed them. The same thing happened again in 1857, when German Capt Johann Meyer, in *La Rochelle*, named them Kónig Max-Inseln for the King of Bavaria.

American Erasmus Darwin Rogers, sailing in *Corinthian*, made the first recorded landing on Heard in January 1855, although there is dubious evidence that fur sealers had been working on the island before this. Reluctant to give competing companies any evidence of their discovery, however, they may simply have left it out of their logbooks. Rogers and the crews of six accompanying ships collected full loads of fur seal skins and 3000 barrels of elephant seal oil.

The first wintering party was landed by the American sealer *Zoe* in 1856, and in the same year, the first Heard shipwreck, of the American vessel *Alfred*, occurred. Many others followed: *RB Coleman* (1859), *Mary Powell* (1859), *Exile* (1860), *Pacific* (1864), *ER Sawyer* (1866) and *Trinity* (1880).

Two exceptional artifacts from the sealing era have been found on Heard. A blubber press, the only known example in the world, was excavated and is now on loan to the Queen Victoria Museum and Art Gallery in Launceston, Tasmania. A carved basalt rock, likewise the only known example ever discovered in the subantarctic or Antarctic, was found on Heard in 1985-86. Depicting the face of a bearded man, it was carved by an unknown 19th century sealer, possibly shipwrecked on the island. It is now displayed at the headquarters of the Australian Antarctic Division in Kingston, Tasmania.

In 1908, Heard and McDonald islands were annexed by the British Government; this sovereignty was transferred to the Australian Government on December 26, 1947. On this date also, the first of the Australian National Antarctic Research Expeditions (ANARE), led by Stuart Campbell, established a base at Atlas Cove on Heard's northwest coast, using a WWII naval landing craft that was driven up onto the beach and unloaded through bow doors. An aircraft used for aerial surveys of the island was destroyed by a storm after making a single flight. The wintering party's experiences are chronicled in Arthur Scholes' *Fourteen Men: The Story of the Antarctic Expedition to Heard Island* (1952).

A group from the ANARE station completed the first journey on foot around the island in 1951. The station closed in 1955, transferring personnel and material to Mawson station on Antarctica, but collapsing early ANARE huts, dog pens, fuel drums, abandoned machinery and food supplies litter the black volcanic sand at Atlas Cove, along with the graves of two expedition members who died in 1952. Additionally, the remnants of the Admiralty Hut, built by the British in 1929 as a refuge for shipwrecked mariners, still stand at Atlas Cove.

Summer research programs have operated occasionally on the island since 1955, and a party wintered at Spit Bay in 1992, the first to do so since the Atlas Cove station closed. An automatic weather station was established at Atlas Cove in 1990.

The first recorded landing on the McDonald Islands was on January 27, 1970, when two Australian researchers landed on the main island by helicopter for a stay of less than an hour; an ANARE party of six men spent four days on the islands in 1980.

More than a million pairs of macaroni penguins breed on Heard Island, and another million pairs on the McDonald Islands. Long Beach on Heard's southern coast is the site of possibly the world's largest colony of macaronis. There are also approximately 1000 Heard Island sheathbills, a subspecies, in the islands. The rarest bird in the islands is the endemic Heard shag *(Phalacrocorax nivalis)*, of which fewer than 100 breeding pairs exist.

Heard and McDonald Islands are highly unusual in that no known introduced species are now present; for this reason, extreme care must be taken when visiting, and anyone going ashore must thoroughly clean footwear and clothing. The Australian government permits a total of 400 people to land at Heard and McDonalds Islands each year; no more than 60 are allowed ashore at Atlas Cove at one time, and no more than 15 are allowed ashore in other areas of the islands.

Tourist visits to the islands are extremely rare; through the 1993-94 season, only two small parties had made it ashore, thanks to the islands' notoriously bad weather and the hazards of landing. Any landing on the islands requires a permit, which can be obtained from the Australian Antarctic Division (see Hobart in the Gateways chapter).

Ile Amsterdam

An oval-shaped volcanic island, Ile Amsterdam (37°83'S, 77°52'E) is part of France's Terres Australes et Antarctiques Françaises, like its neighbor Ile St Paul, 89 km to the south. All of Amsterdam's 85 sq km are unglaciated. The two highest points, Mont de la Dives (867m) and La Grande Marmite (730m), are part of the now-collapsed rim of the volcano that formed the island; the volcano's floor now forms a plateau about 600m high. Lava flows radiate from this plateau, spilling down to the sea where they end in cliffs above narrow shingle beaches. These headlands are generally less than 30m high, except on the west coast, where they tower to heights of 700m.

Weather on Ile Amsterdam is comparitively warm, windy, wet and humid. June, the coolest month, averages 10°C, while January and February, the warmest, average 15°C.

Juan Sebastián de Elcano, the Basque who completed the voyage of the great Portuguese navigator Fernão de Magalhães (Ferdinand Magellan) after Magellan was killed, discovered the Ile on March 18, 1522, during the first ever circumnavigation of the earth. But Elcano did not give the island a name, a task left for Dutchman Anthonie van Diemen, sailing in *Nieuw Amsterdam* in 1633. The first landing was made by a three-ship Dutch survey expedition in 1696.

Sealers, unusually, did not arrive on the island until almost two centuries after its discovery. *Nootka*, a British ship, started Ile Amsterdam's Fur Rush, a process that was repeated on almost every other subantarctic island. *Nootka* landed parties on Iles Amsterdam and St Paul for 17 months in 1791-92 and took 15,000 fur seal skins. An American sealer, *Flora*, took 13,415 seals in 1792, while another American ship, *Mary*, took 44,517 seals in 1800.

Shipwrecks occurred on a fairly regular basis throughout the 19th century: *Lady Munro* (1833), *George* (1839), *Meridian* (1853), *Tuscany* (1855), *Vellore* (1865) and *Fernand* (1876) are among those recorded.

In 1870-71, a Frenchman, along with his wife, children and four employees, inhabited the island for seven months in an abortive attempt to raise cattle. Three years later, Capt Coffin of the ship *Annie Battles* and two of his crewmen were rescued from Ile Amsterdam after being abandoned there during a mutiny. Also in 1874, on December 9, a French expedition observed the Transit of Venus from the island.

France has operated a permanent scientific station on the island's north coast since 1949, when 10 men led by Paul Martin de Viviès wintered there. Now called Martin-de-Viviès for its first leader, the station accommodates 30 people in winter, more in summer.

Ile Amsterdam is one of the few subantarctic islands with trees *(Phylica arborea)* growing on it. An East India Company vessel visiting in 1770 described the island as having much tree cover, while a French naval expedition in 1792 noted a forest fire. In 1825-26, two Tasmanian sealers started a fire that lasted several months, and in 1833 the survivors of the wreck of the American ship *Lady Munro* caused another conflagration that destroyed much of the island's forest. Today, semi-wild descendants of introduced cattle are browsing on young saplings and the species is disappearing.

Among the island's bird species is the unusual long-crested rockhopper penguin, which also lives on Ile St Paul. Since 1948, the island's rock lobsters have been commercially harvested.

Ile St Paul

Ile St Paul (38°72'S, 77°53'E) is a volcanic cone, the eastern third of which has either been blown away by an eruption or eroded by wave action, leaving an unglaciated island shaped roughly like a right triangle, with its hypotenuse coast running from northwest to southeast. The volcanic crater has been breached by the sea, which enters to form Bassin du Cratère. The inner walls of the crater, and the island's eastern coastline, are steep cliffs up to 200m high; the western and southern slopes of the volcano are much less steep and end in 30m high seacliffs. These are generally unclimbable, making landings on the island from these approaches very difficult. Ile St Paul covers seven sq km; its highest point is Crête de la Novara (264m).

Dutchman Haevik Klaaszoon van Hillegom, sailing in *Zeewolf*, discovered Ile St Paul on April 19, 1618, but it was later found marked as 'S Paulo' on an earlier Portuguese chart, from 1559. The first landing was made by the Dutch in 1696.

Sealers first arrived, from Britain, in 1789, and the usual pattern of slaughter of the fur-bearing creatures followed, quickly wiping out most of the population. There are at least three recorded shipwrecks: *Fox* (1810), *Napoléon III* (1853) and *Holt Hill* (1889).

A solitary Polish settler, Józef Kosciuszko, lived on St Paul between 1819 and 1830; for several years of that time, the island was apparently without other human inhabitants. Fishermen from Réunion lived on the island periodically during the mid-19th century, with their settlement reaching a peak population of 45 in 1845. In 1871, after the British troop transport ship HMS *Megaera* sprang a leak and beached at Ile St Paul, 500 men were forced to set up a tent camp, where they remained for three months. A French expedition landed three years later to observe the Transit of Venus.

Abundant (and tasty) rock lobsters thrive in Ile St Paul's waters, and from 1928 to 1931 a French fishing company, La Langouste Française, operated a lobster-fishing enterprise on the island. As many as 100 men spent the summers ashore, fishing and canning. But four of the seven winterers died in 1930, and the next year, 30 more men died of beriberi, so the settlement was abandoned. Today, a ship-based lobster fishery operates around Ile Amsterdam and Ile St Paul.

In 1955, the island was formally incorporated with Ile Amsterdam, Iles Kerguelen, Iles Crozet and Terre Adélie in Antarctica as the Terres Australes et Antarctiques Françaises.

Among Ile St Paul's bird species is the unusual long-crested rockhopper penguin, also found on Ile Amsterdam.

Macquarie Island

Australian Antarctic explorer Douglas Mawson, who first visited it in 1911, called Macquarie Island 'one of the wonder spots of the world.' Roughly halfway between Tasmania (1467 km to the northwest) and the Antarctic continent (1296 km south), Macquarie (54°62'S, 158°97'E) is a good transition point between the two. The island's leading attractions are its residents: 100,000 seals, mainly the blubbery elephant seals, and four million penguins, including about 850,000 breeding pairs of the royal penguins, which breed nowhere else.

Rising in steep cliffs from the sea to a plateau 240 to 345m high, Macquarie is 34 km long and between 2.5 and five km wide; its total area is 128 sq km. The highest point, at 433m, is Mt Hamilton, named for an early father-son team of naturalists.

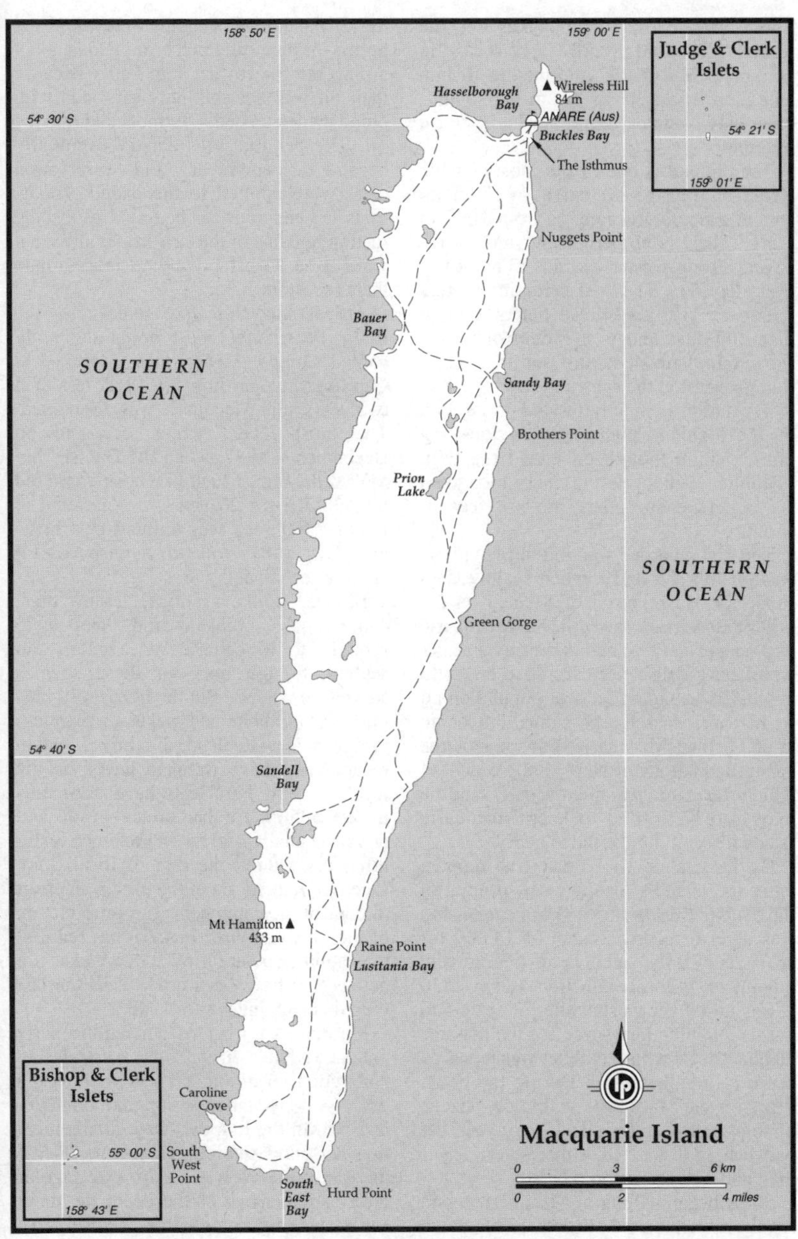
158° 50' E
159° 00' E
Judge & Clerk Islets
54° 21' S
159° 01' E
Hasselborough Bay
Wireless Hill 84 m
ANARE (Aus)
Buckles Bay
The Isthmus
54° 30' S
Nuggets Point
Bauer Bay
SOUTHERN OCEAN
Sandy Bay
Brothers Point
Prion Lake
SOUTHERN OCEAN
Green Gorge
54° 40' S
Sandell Bay
Mt Hamilton 433 m
Raine Point
Lusitania Bay
Bishop & Clerk Islets
55° 00' S
158° 43' E
Caroline Cove
South West Point
South East Bay
Hurd Point
Macquarie Island
0 3 6 km
0 2 4 miles

There are several small lakes on the plateau. The Judge and Clerk rocks lie 16 km to Macquarie's north; the Bishop and Clerk rocks lie 28 km to the south – obviously some cartographer had a sense of humor.

The climate is one of the most equable (least-changing) on earth, with mean annual temperatures ranging from 3.3°C to 7.2°C. There is no permanent snow or ice cover. Strong westerly winds blow nearly every day. The 91 cm of precipitation that falls each year are spread out over more than 300 days and in a variety of forms: snow, rain, hail, sleet, mist and fog, sometimes several in the same day.

Vegetation is mainly tussock grass and, on the highland plateau, peaty 'quaking bogs,' which though covered by a thin, floating mat of vegetation can be more than six meters deep. There are no trees or shrubs.

The first recorded sighting of Macquarie was on July 11, 1810, when sealing Capt Frederick Hasselburgh of Sydney on the brig *Perseverance* raised it, but Macquarie was conceivably visited earlier by a sealer who kept his discovery secret so he could exploit its abundant fur seal population all by himself. Hasselburgh named the island after Lachlan Macquarie, governor of the Australian colony of New South Wales (of which Tasmania was then a part), and he may also have tried to keep Macquarie Island a secret, but he failed badly.

By December 1810, just five months later, the island's location was printed in the *Sydney Gazette*. By 1812, a single ship was able to record a catch of 14,000 fur seals. Naturally, such heavy harvesting quickly led to local extinction, and by 1830 it was no longer worthwhile for sealers to bother stopping here, even for the massive elephant seals whose blubber was rendered down to a valuable oil. During the boom years for the Macquarie seal trade, dozens of ships called at the island every year, but between 1830 and 1874 there were fewer than half a dozen recorded visits.

Ships began calling at Macquarie again regularly in the mid- to late-1870s when the king and royal penguins were killed and boiled for their oil. Each bird yielded about a pint, but the royals were better because their oil was not as highly saturated with blood, which tended to ferment and ruin the oil. The penguin-oil industry eventually became uneconomical – and conservation rules were applied to the island. Today, seals and penguins can be found amidst the rusting remains of the cast-iron boilers that were used so effectively to exterminate their ancestors.

At least nine ships have wrecked on the rocky coast, the oldest being the aptly named *Campbell Macquarie*, wrecked at Caroline Cove on June 10, 1812, less than two years after Macquarie was discovered. The most recent wreck occurred on December 3, 1987, when the Danish ship MV *Nella Dan*, which had been chartered by ANARE for 26 years, ran aground at Buckles Bay; she was scuttled on Christmas Eve 1987, following unsuccessful attempts at salvaging her.

Horses, donkeys, dogs, goats, pigs, cattle, ducks, chickens and sheep were brought to Macquarie by whalers and sealers, though none of these species survive here today. But the introduced rats, mice, cats, rabbits and wekas (a flightless bird from New Zealand) did thrive – and in recent years have wreaked havoc on the local ecology. Feral cats have been estimated to kill more than 60,000 prions and petrels annually, and rabbit grazing has significantly altered the mix of local flora. Licensed rangers shoot the cats in an effort to control their numbers, and introduction of the myxoma virus in 1978 has reduced the rabbit population by 93%. Wekas are believed to have been eradicated; the last recorded sighting was in 1988.

Mawson, who landed a scientific party on the island during his Australasian Antarctic Expedition of 1911-1914, used a wireless relay station set up here on Wireless Hill in the first two-way communication with the Antarctic continent. One of the transmissions was a grim exchange of information: news of the death of Mawson's sledging companions, Lt Belgrave

Ninnis and Xavier Mertz, was sent from Commonwealth Bay to Macquarie, while word of Capt Scott's death was sent to the Australian explorers in Antarctica.

Other expedition leaders who stopped at Macquarie include Bellingshausen (who traded one of the sealers three bottles of rum for two albatrosses, a live parrot and two dead ones), Wilkes, Scott and Shackleton.

In 1948, a scientific station was established by ANARE at the isthmus on the site occupied by Mawson's men in 1911. About 15 to 20 people winter at the ANARE station; the number climbs to 40 during the summer. Researchers here study biology, meteorology, geology, oceanography and atmospheric physics. The first woman to winter at an ANARE station, Zoe Gardner, was the station doctor at Macquarie in 1976.

The first tourists to visit Macquarie were four men carried by the New Zealand sealing ship *Gratitude* in 1891. Today, Macquarie is Australian territory, specifically a Tasmanian State Reserve, and permits to land must be obtained in advance through the Tasmanian Parks and Wildlife Service (TASPAWS), 134 Macquarie St, Hobart (☎ 61-3-6233-6203; fax 61-3-6233-3477). Ships or yachts that arrive unannounced are not allowed to put people ashore. There is a landing fee of US$100 per person, though most visitors are unaware of it, since it is included in the price of their cruise. Part of this fee pays for the color brochure distributed to visitors.

TASPAWS rangers oversee visits to the island. Boardwalks have been constructed in several places to prevent erosion, and regulations govern how many people can come ashore at one time. At Sandy Bay, site of a royal penguin rookery, for instance, no more than 60 people may be landed simultaneously. At Lusitania Bay, home of a massive king penguin colony, no visitors are permitted on the beach, and Zodiacs must remain at least 200m offshore. All visitors to the island must be off by 7 pm, and no food or drink can be brought ashore. Just as in Antarctica, nothing – not even a pebble – should be removed from the island.

Balleny Islands

These islands, 95% covered in ice and straddling the Antarctic Circle, are the tops of volcanoes rising from ocean depths of three km. Rarely visited by either tourists or scientists, the Ballenys (66°25' to 67°58'S, 162°50' to 165°00'E) are the

northernmost territory of New Zealand's Ross Dependency. Stretching some 195 km from north to south are Young, Row, Borradaile, Buckle and Sabrina islands, The Monolith and Sturge Island, where the group reaches its highest point at 1524m Brown Peak.

Largely unlandable because of their steep basaltic cliffs, the Ballenys have been visited only a handful of times throughout recorded history. Without large beaches to attract seals, they were ignored by sealers, who regarded them as little more than a hazard to navigation. English whaling captains John Balleny in the schooner *Eliza Scott* and Thomas Freeman in the cutter *Sabrina* were the first to record visits here. Freeman went ashore – or at least stepped into waist-deep water and collected some pebbles – probably on Sabrina Island, on February 9, 1839. This 'landing' was the first ever south of the Antarctic Circle. Unfortunately, *Sabrina* later became separated from *Eliza Scott* and was never heard from again, which helps to explain how the islands came to be called the Ballenys and not the Freemans.

Because of the archipelago's isolation, Sabrina Island was designated in 1969 as the fourth Specially Protected Area under the Antarctic Treaty system; no landings can be made there without special permission. About 500 Adélies nest there each year, as well as the occasional chinstrap or macaroni penguin and numerous species of seabirds.

The first tourist landing was made in the Ballenys in 1968, though they are not often visited. An automatic weather station set up by the US Antarctic Research Program on Brown Peak is rechecked annually by helicopter for maintenance such as changing of batteries. The mountain, however, remains unclimbed.

Australian physicist Louis Bernacchi, who sailed past one of the Ballenys in 1899 while taking part in Borchgrevink's *Antarctic* expedition, was moved by its bleak aspect to write: 'I can imagine no greater punishment than to be 'left alone to live forgotten and die forlorn' on that desolate shore.'

New Zealand's Subantarctic Islands

New Zealand maintains five subantarctic island groups as National Nature Reserves: the Antipodes, Auckland, Bounty, Campbell and Snares groups. All are managed by the NZ Dept of Conservation, PO Box 743, Invercargill (☎ 64-3-214-4589). Entry is by permit only, and permits are issued only if the group is accompanied by a Dept of Conservation representative. To prevent the accidental introduction of non-native species such as rats, which could wipe out local bird and insect populations, no landings are allowed in the Antipodes or Snares groups, or on pristine islands of the Aucklands and Campbells. There is a NZ$200 per person fee charged for landing, good for all of the islands on the same trip, which includes a handsome four-color guidebook. For those who cannot afford the time or the fare to visit the islands, some idea of their environment can be gleaned from watching the 'Roaring Forties Experience' audiovisual at the Southland Museum & Art Gallery in Invercargill, New Zealand.

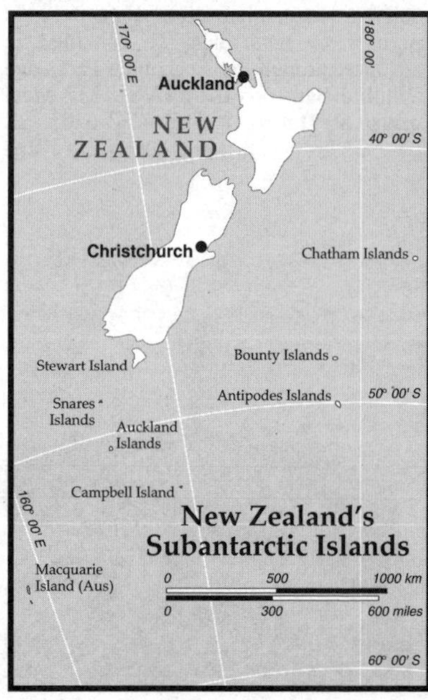

Antipodes Islands The Antipodes group (49°41'S, 178°45'E) consists of the namesake main island, with the two Windward Islands lying appropriately to the west and Leeward Island to the east, and Bollons Island to the northeast. They were named 'the Penantipodes' on March 26, 1800, by their discoverer, Capt Henry Waterhouse of HMS *Reliance*, for being almost directly opposite the globe from London.

Sealing began in the Antipodes Islands in 1804, when a group landed by the American ship *Union* was stranded ashore for a year after the ship dropped them off and went on to Fiji, where it was wrecked and its crew massacred. The castaways made profitable use of their time, killing 60,000 fur seals before being rescued by another American ship, *Favorite*, in 1806. The Antipodes fur seal trade reached its peak in the season of 1814-15, when 400,000 animals were killed. One especially galling mistake was made in that season by the British sealer *Pegasus*, which took 100,000 skins to London. Upon arrival, it was found that the skins had rotted during the voyage due to insufficient salting, and the once-valuable cargo was sold for fertilizer.

No landings can be made in the Antipodes, but there would be little room for people ashore anyway, as the islands are almost completely covered with the burrows and nests of seabirds. Along with the Bounty Islands, the Antipodes are the only home of the world's estimated 200,000 pairs of erect-crested penguins. Also endemic to the islands is the Antipodes parakeet, which is found with, but does not breed with, the red-crowned parakeet (similar to the New Zealand species of this parakeet). In the short grass at the top of the islands, wandering albatross nest. The Antipodes' only introduced species are sheep and mice.

Auckland Islands The Aucklands (50°48' to 50°93'S, 165°87' to 166°33'E), at 627 sq km the largest of New Zealand's subantarctic island groups, consists of four main islands. Southernmost Adams Island was declared a nature reserve in 1910 in recognition of its pristine state with no introduced species. Between Adams and the main island, Auckland Island, lies the superb three-armed natural anchorage of Carnley Harbor, once known as Sarah's Bosom after an early visitor, the British whaling ship *Sarah*, which stopped in 1807. The islands' highest point is Mount Dick (668m) on Adams Island.

Deep fjords serrate Auckland Island's east coast, while the windward west side features steep cliffs up to 300m high. At times the powerful westerlies striking the cliffs turn cascades there into 'reversible' waterfalls, actually blowing the water that has fallen partway down the cliffs back up onto the plateau, where the process is repeated as long as the wind keeps up. Disappointment Island lies to the west of Auckland Island, while Enderby Island, with its striking cliffs of columnar basalt, lies to its northeast.

The group was discovered on August 18, 1806, by Capt Abraham Bristow, of the whaler *Ocean,* who named them for his friend Lord Auckland, but like other New Zealand subantarctic islands, the early Maori may have known about it.

An odd near-meeting occurred in 1840 in a natural harbor on Auckland Island's northeast tip: Charles Wilkes' US Exploring Expedition ship *Porpoise* landed on March 10 and set up a sign for anyone who might follow. Two posts were set in the ground on a prominent spot, and a message painted on boards was nailed to them. Incredibly, Frenchman Jules-Sébastien-César Dumont d'Urville came ashore just two days later and added to the sign a message of his own. Both were found eight months later by British explorer James Clark Ross, who must have been annoyed to find such a visible reminder that the section of Antarctica that he considered 'his' had been blithely tread upon by foreign interlopers. Still, the harbor came to bear Ross' – not Wilkes' or d'Urville's – name.

A group of Maori – with a group of Moriori as their slaves – moved to Port Ross in 1842, after finding it convenient to leave the Chatham Islands (located 770 km east of Christchurch). The aboriginals greeted Charles Enderby, of the famous London whaling firm Samuel Enderby & Son, when he arrived in 1849 to set up a colony he called Hardwicke, hoping to duplicate the success of the Falkland Islands colony, which thrived on whaling and ship refitting. Perhaps he should have called it Hardworke instead. Though its peak population of nearly 300 people struggled mightily, the colony survived just three years; crops failed, whale catches were minimal and few ships called in needing overhaul.

By 1852, the last colonists had departed, leaving behind a forlorn ghost town at Erebus Cove on Port Ross' northern shore. Two buildings stand there today, though neither is contemporary to the colony; one is a former depot for castaways, the other a boatshed now rather grandiosely called the Erebus Cove Museum, which contains island relics. Starting from just south of Erebus Stream, 10 minutes' walk up from the beach brings you to Hardwicke's cemetery, where half of the graves are of shipwrecked sailors. Further to the east lie the settlement's overgrown cobblestone paths, and at Davis Bay (directly south of Davis Island) are the glass-strewn ruins of the colony's house sites. Souveniring is forbidden.

The Maori themselves left soon after the Hardwickers did. Interestingly, there was no sign at their departure of the Moriori, who may have been eaten. By 1856 the islands were uninhabited again.

At least nine ships have wrecked on the Aucklands, including, most famously, *General Grant* in 1866. London-bound from Melbourne and the Australian goldfields, the American-flagged treasure ship was driven into a huge cavern on Auckland Island's west coast, ironically, not by a storm, but by very light winds which prevented her from making steerage way. When a rising tide and the cavern's roof forced the mainmast down through the hull, the 83 people aboard *General Grant* abandoned ship; only 15 survived, but most of them lived the 18 months it took them to be rescued. Also lost in the wreck: at least 70 kg of gold, according to official records; rumor made the haul as large as eight metric tons. Despite at least 18 salvage attempts, however, no trace of *General Grant* or the gold has ever been found.

Many other ships were lost during the years when the Great Circle Route was used to sail from Australia to New Zealand. So high was the danger of a ship coming to grief here that the New Zealand government set up castaway huts containing food, clothing, blankets and weapons (for procuring food) at various prominent places. 'Finger posts' – poles supporting wooden hands with pointing fingers – were placed on headlands to show the way. Pigs, rabbits, goats and other food animals were also released on the islands to provide emergency food sources for shipwrecked sailors. Since castaways sometimes spent up to two years waiting to be rescued, such measures saved many lives over the years. The oldest remaining such castaway depot, the Stella Hut at Sandy Bay on Enderby Island, dates to 1880. New Zealand maintained a program of annual cruises in search of castaways in all of the five subantarctic island groups until 1927, when it was considered that widespread radio technology had rendered them unnecessary.

Pastoral leases were set up in the Aucklands in 1894, but the 2020 sheep landed did not thrive and the last lease was forfeited in 1910. Wild cattle, descendants of an early rancher's herd, have been removed from Enderby, while introduced goats are being removed from Auckland Island. Feral cats, mice and rabbits, however, are on the island to stay.

During WWII, the secret Cape Expeditions set up coast-watching stations on the islands to watch Ross and Carnley harbors to ensure that enemy ships weren't using the islands as a staging post for an invasion. Despite their bleak daily treks to observation areas (the stations were well inland to avoid detection), the coast watchers never saw a single enemy vessel, and one of them, Alan W Eden wrote a book in 1955 about his experiences with the revealing title, *Islands of Despair*.

Among the twisted trunks of Enderby Island's red-flowering southern rata tree *(Metrosideros umbellata)* hides the elusive and solitary-nesting yellow-eyed penguin. Rarest of the 17 species of penguin, the yellow-eyed numbers only about 5000 animals and prefers not to congregate in large colonies like most other penguins. More breed on Enderby than anywhere else.

The Hooker's sea lion, the world's rarest sea lion with about 6000 animals, breeds at Enderby Island's Sandy Bay – one of only three places in the world where it does. But Sandy Bay has illustrated the sea lions' fragility: Rabbit burrows behind the beach once killed one of every 10 pups born each year after they crawled in and got stuck. Unfortunately, 70 to 100 adults are still killed each year in squid trawlers' nets.

The Aucklands are also the home of the world's largest breeding population of wandering albatrosses, as well as some 50,000 white-capped mollymawks.

Bounty Islands The Bountys (47°45'S, 170°02'E) are a sprinkling of some 22 islets, the largest of which is not more than a kilometer across. Discovered on September 9, 1788, by the infamous Capt William Bligh of mutiny fame, they were named for his ship, *Bounty*.

Here, too, the onslaught of sealers arrived soon after the islands' discovery, and by 1831, when British whaler-explorer John Biscoe visited, the Bountys' fur seals had nearly been exterminated.

British captain George Palmer, in HMS *Rosario*, landed and took formal possession of the islands in the name of Queen Victoria in 1870.

The erect-crested penguin breeds only here and on the Antipodes Islands. The Bountys are also home to 76,000 pairs of Salvin's albatrosses, a type of shy or white-capped albatross.

Campbell Islands Most southerly of the five New Zealand subantarctic island groups and of volcanic origin, Campbell Island (52°55'S, 169°15'E) covers 114 sq km and consist of a large main isle and two tiny accompaniments: Dent to the west and Jacquemart to the south. The highest point is Mt Honey (569m).

Campbell Island was discovered on January 4, 1810, and named for the owner of his sealing company by captain Frederick Hasselburgh in the ship *Perseverance*, for which Perseverence Harbour is named. Sadly, Hasselburgh drowned in that very harbor exactly 10 months later, and, in an ironic twist of fate, *Perseverance* itself was wrecked in the same place 18 years after that. Hasselburgh was able to keep his discovery a secret for nearly a year, enabling him to profit from the island's seal-rich beaches. But as on all the other subantarctic islands, the sealing 'gold-rush' eventually swept over Campbell, too, and by the 1820s the local population had effectively been exterminated.

Shipwrecks occurred here at a frequency only slightly less alarming than at the Auckland Islands; in 1839, for example, a party of three men and one woman were rescued after being marooned here for 27 months.

Pastoral enterprises, however, fared more successfully on Campbell than they did on Auckland. A lease was set up in 1895, and a rancher built a homestead at Tucker Cove on Perseverance Harbour. Wool-raising continued until 1931, when the island was abandoned to the 4000 remaining sheep. After the island became a nature reserve in 1954, a control program was begun to limit the destruction of native vegetation. Though the last sheep were shot in 1990, the Tucker Cove homesite is still visible.

The secret wartime 'Cape Expeditions' set up a coast-watching station in 1941 to keep Perseverance Harbour under surveillance and detect any enemy ships endeavoring to use it as a base. Although no unauthorized vessel was ever spotted, the coast-watchers performed valuable surveys on the island and maintained meteorological records. After the war, this work was continued. But because the coast-watch station was built 800m inland to avoid detection, the scientific station was moved in 1957 to Beeman Point on Perseverance Harbour. In 1992, the station's five members were on a snorkeling trip at Northwest Bay when a shark attacked, tearing off one man's arm. The station closed in October 1995, replaced, after 54 years of service, by automatic instrumentation.

From the landing dock at the station, a boardwalk leads about five km up to the Col-Lyall Saddle, where a large colony of royal albatrosses nest.

Campbell Island is also the home of the world's 'loneliest tree,' according to *The Guinness Book of World Records*. A single six-meter-tall Sitka spruce, planted in 1902 by New Zealand's governor, is the only tree for hundreds of kilometers.

Snares Islands The Snares (48°01'S, 166°36'E) consist of the Western Chain (Rima, Wha, Toru, Rua and Tahi) and Northeast Island and its accessories, Alert Stack, Broughton Island and Daption Rocks. The Snares were named for their unpleasant habit of 'snaring' ships eastbound on the Great Circle route from Australia to Cape Horn; a smaller group of nearly unchartable rocks called The Traps were once equally deadly.

In a rare coincidence, the Snares were discovered independently – on the same day, November 23, 1791 – by two different ship masters, Capt George Vancouver of *Discovery*, and Lt Broughton of *Chatham*. Vancouver called the islands the Snares, a name that stuck, while Broughton called them Knight's Islands, which did not.

Literally millions of seabirds breed in the Snares group, underlining subantarctic islands' importance as the only solid land for hundreds of kilometers around. Nearly three million pairs of sooty shearwaters alone shelter in burrows, where they hide from predators. Taking off at dawn on hunting flights and returning home before sundown, the clouds of birds are an awesome sight. The Snares are the only home of the Snares crested penguin, though little is known about the bird's life cycle. Because of the Snares' abundance of wildlife, no landings are permitted on any of the islands.

Scott Island

Remote, barren and rarely visited, Scott Island (67°40'S, 179°92'E) is the remains of a volcanic crater, with an isolated offshore stack, the 63m Haggit's Pillar, about 800m west. Covering a mere 40 hectares, Scott Island is about 370m long and 180m wide, with its long axis running north and south. The northern coast ends in cliffs 50m high, while the southern coast is barely above sea level. The island is entirely covered in snow and ice during the winter, but in summer large areas of bare rock are exposed.

Its location and extremely tiny size enabled Scott Island to evade detection until 1902, when it was found by British Capt William Colbeck, sailing in *Morning*, on Christmas Day. Colbeck, who was carrying stores to Robert F Scott in McMurdo Sound, sent a party ashore and claimed the island for Britain, calling it Markham Island after Sir Clements Markham, President of the Royal Geographical Society and the architect of Scott's Discovery expedition. (The island's name was later changed to memorialize Scott.)

Tourists were first landed on the island in 1982.

Peter I Øy

Surrounded by thick pack ice nearly all year round, Peter the First Øy's (68°85'S, 90°62'W) 158 sq km are 95% glacierized. The highest point, 1640m Lars Christensentoppen, is an extinct volcano. Glaciers extend tongues into the sea nearly all around the island, but in a few places, narrow, rocky beaches are exposed. To the east of the island lie two flat-topped, ice-free columns, the Tvistein Pillars.

Peter I Øy was discovered on January 21, 1821, by the Russian Fabian von Bellingshausen, who named it for czar Peter the Great, founder of the Russian Navy. It was the first land discovered south of the Antarctic Circle and thus the most southerly land known at the time.

Due to the island's extreme inaccessibility, the first landing on Peter I Øy took place more than a century after its discovery, when Norwegian Ola Olstad, leading the *Norvegia* expedition, went ashore February 2, 1929, and claimed it for Norway. It was formally annexed by Norwegian Royal Proclamation in 1933.

Beginning in 1980, several tourist ships have succeeded in landing passengers on the island.

South Shetland Islands

This major group of islands at the northern end of the Antarctic Peninsula (61°00' to 63°37'S, 53°83' to 62°83'W) is one of the continent's most-visited areas, thanks to its spectacular scenery, abundant wildlife and proximity to Tierra del Fuego, which lies 1000 km to the north across the Drake Passage. The 540-km-long chain consists of four main island groups. From northeast to southwest, they are: Clarence and Elephant islands; King George and Nelson islands; Robert, Greenwich, Livingston, Snow and Deception islands; and Smith and Low islands. There also 150-odd islets and rocks, many with interesting or picturesque names: Potmess Island, Hole Rock, Stump Rock, Sea Leopard Patch, Square End Island, The Watchkeeper, Desolation Island, Pig Rock, Salient Rock, Cone Rock, Conical Rock, The Pointers and Sewing-Machine Needles. The South Shetlands, which are about 80% glacierized, cover an area of 3688 sq km, and the highest point is Mt Foster (2105m) on Smith Island.

William Smith, sailing in the British ship *Williams*, was blown off course while rounding Cape Horn for Valparaiso, Chile, and discovered the islands on February 19, 1819, but he made no landing. Sailing eastward on his return voyage from Chile, he headed south again, but this time was too far west and missed the islands. But he returned later in the year and landed on King George Island on October 16, taking possession of them in the name of King George III.

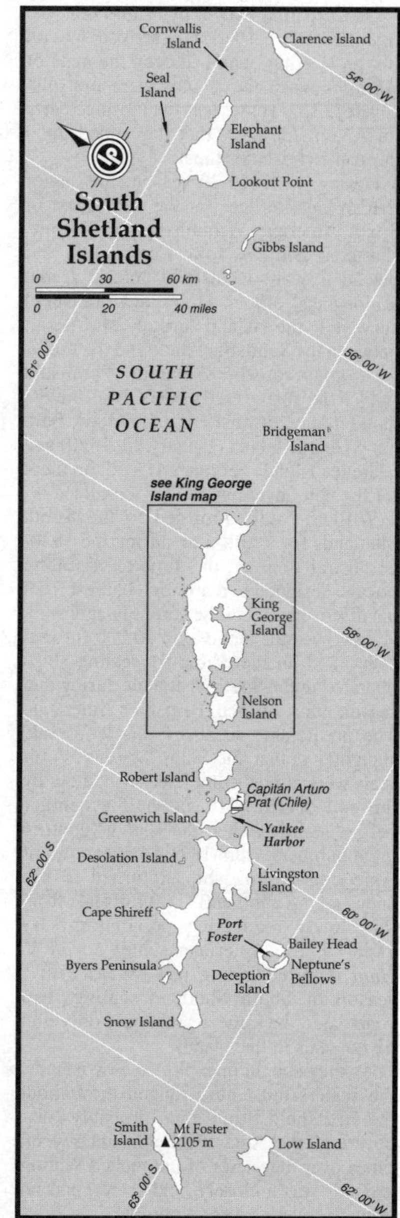

On Christmas Day of that same year, the first British sealing ship arrived – with Joseph Herring, who had been the mate of *Williams* when the islands were first discovered. This vessel was the advance party for a veritable navy that descended upon the seal-rich islands the next year.

During the 1819-20 season, the senior British naval officer for the west coast of South America, William Henry Shirreff, chartered *Williams* from Capt Smith, and placed Edward Bransfield aboard as the senior naval officer. Smith and Bransfield surveyed the island group; the strait between the South Shetlands and the northwest coast of the Antarctic Peninsula (which he discovered) bears Bransfield's name today. Bransfield landed on both King George Island (January 22, 1820) and Clarence Island (February 4) to claim them for the new sovereign, King George IV.

William Smith returned to the South Shetlands for a fifth time during the 1820-21 austral summer, this time on a sealing voyage designed to reap a rich harvest from his discovery, a goal he certainly achieved. His two vessels alone took 60,000 fur seal skins, and an incredible 91 sealing ships operated in the South Shetlands during that season, most of them British or American. The predictable result of this wholesale slaughter is that the South Shetlands' fur seals were almost completely wiped out by the end of 1821. It was half a century before sealers visited the islands again in great numbers; from 1871-74, a handful of American sealing ships returned to kill anew, taking another 33,000 fur seals from the slowly recovering populations. By 1888-89, the American sealer *Sarah W Hunt* reported taking just 39 skins in a season of South Shetland sealing; two years later, the same vessel could only find 41 fur seals in the islands.

As they sought unexploited new islands, the sealers must have ranged throughout the Bransfield Strait area, probably 'discovering' the Antarctic Peninsula several times over, but news of untouched sealing grounds was a closely held secret, and no such discoveries were reported.

Death visited the sealers as well as the seals: with such a large number of vessels operating in such treacherous waters, predictably there were also a large number of wrecks. Six ships – *San Telmo*, *Ann*, *Clothier*, *Lady Troubridge*, *Cora* and *Venus* – foundered in just three years, 1819-21. The 1819 loss of *San Telmo*, in fact, is the worst disaster in Antarctic history, killing 644 people. Over the succeeding decades, other ships joined them in the depths, including *Richard Henry* (1845), *Catherine* (1847), *Lion* (1854), *Graham* (1924) and *Professor Gruvel* (1927).

In 1944, despite having its hands full with war in Europe, the British government moved to underscore its sovereignty over the islands. Through the Falkland Islands Dependencies Government, it established permanent stations and issued postage stamps for four of the Dependencies (South Shetlands; South Orkneys; South Georgia; and Graham Land, or the Antarctic Peninsula), a show of ownership that Argentina and Chile naturally protested, since each had made rival claims over the territory.

Antarctic tourism made some of its earliest appearances in the South Shetlands, given their proximity to South America's southern tip. The first Antarctic tourist flight, by LAN Chile in 1956, flew over the South Shetlands and the Antarctic Peninsula, and two of the earliest tourist cruises to Antarctica, by the Argentine ship *Les Eclaireurs*, reached the South Shetlands in January and February 1958. In 1959, the Argentine ship Yapeyú and the Chilean vessel *Navarino* both took passengers to the South Shetlands. In 1961, 21 passengers were stranded for three days on Half Moon Island in the South Shetlands when the landing craft from their chartered vessel *Lapataia* was damaged. And in one of the largest mass visits ever to the Antarctic, the Spanish cruise ship *Cabo San Roque* carried 900 passengers to the South Shetlands and the Peninsula in 1973; the ship visited again in 1974 and 1975, but no landings were made.

Among the attractions of the South Shetlands are several islands with distinct individual histories. **Elephant Island**, at the archipelago's northeastern end, is notorious as the temporary, privation-filled home for 105 days of 22 members of the crew of Ernest Shackleton's *Endurance*, stranded there after their ship was crushed in Weddell Sea pack ice in 1915. Elephant and Clarence islands also have very old moss colonies, with some dated at more than 2000 years old having peat nearly three meters deep. **Greenwich Island's** Yankee Harbor was another important anchorage for the sealing fleets as early as 1820. Somewhat confusingly, the caldera harbor on Deception Island (see below) was sometimes also known as Yankee Harbor. Hannah Point, on the southern coast of **Livingston Island**, is another extremely popular stop, with a large chinstrap penguin colony. Hannah Point is named after the British sealer *Hannah* of Liverpool, which wrecked there on Christmas Day, 1820. Crescent-shaped **Half Moon Island**, just two km long and lying in the entrance of Moon Bay on the east side of Livingston Island, has a small Argentine base called Teniente Camára, in addition to its own large chinstrap colony.

The following two islands, Deception and King George, are even more noteworthy.

Deception Island Easily recognized on any map by its broken-ring shape, Deception Island's collapsed volcanic cone provides one of the safest natural harbors anywhere in the world – despite periodic eruptions. Entering through the narrow channel at Neptune's Bellows, ships glide into relatively calm waters in the enormous volcano's sea-breached caldera, which is surrounded by sloping snow-covered walls towering to 580m.

Early sealers used Deception's harbor, 12 km wide and known as Port Foster, as a base for operations. From the break in the caldera wall at **Neptune's Window**, American sealer Nathaniel Palmer, who first explored the island, is thought to have seen the Antarctic Peninsula in 1820.

In 1906, a Norwegian-Chilean whaling company began using an area on the north side of the caldera, which later became known as **Whalers Bay**, as a site for a factory ship. In the next season, they were joined by two Norwegian whaling companies and another from Newfoundland, all of which operated factory ships at Deception Island.

Britain, which had formally claimed the island in 1908 as part of the Falkland Islands Dependencies, gave a 21-year lease to Hektor, a Norwegian whaling company, in 1911. By 1914-15, there were 13 floating factories and a shore station operating at Whalers Bay on Deception; the shore station closed in 1931. Today at Whalers Bay, where the beach is more than 300m wide in places, several crude wooden huts stand disintegrating and wooden whaling boats lie buried to their gunwales in black volcanic sand.

Australian Hubert Wilkins made the first powered flight in Antarctica on November 16, 1928, taking off from within Deception's caldera in his Lockheed Vega monoplane *Los Angeles* and flying for 20 minutes. A month later, on December 20, Wilkins and his pilot, Carl Ben Eielson, took off from the same crude Deception Island runway in his other Vega, *San Francisco*, and flew 2100 km to about 71°20'S along the Antarctic Peninsula.

Wilkins then prepared to return home, but decided to remain long enough to accept the hospitality of the Norwegian whalers who had been so helpful to his aviation efforts. New Years' Day at the whaling station, as recounted in Lowell Thomas' biography of Wilkins, was celebrated with enormous exuberance in games, songs, eating, drinking and much gunfire. Two drunk whalers climbed atop a pair of big sperm whales lying on the flensing plan awaiting processing. The whales had been cooking themselves from the heat of the blood inside their thick insulating blubber and were swollen with gas. One whaler thrust his long knife into this veritable whale-balloon, which promptly exploded, hurling both men into the harbor, where they had to be rescued by some of the few sober observers. Meanwhile, two other whalers had decided to ignite the explosives barge that was moored to the beach. Containing 65 metric tons of black powder and other combustibles. Taking a 22-kg keg of powder, they began laying a trail to the barge. One of the pair got impatient, and lit the powder trail, which burned up to the half-empty keg that had been dropped by the other man. The keg exploded, blowing both some distance and burning off all their hair. Flames had ignited in the other direction, too, and were still burning steadily toward the barge. Fortunately, the fire trail stopped on the gangplank to the barge, or everything at the whaling station would probably have been destroyed.

The volcano that formed Deception is not extinct – far from it, in fact. Eruptions have occurred several times this century, as recently as 1991-92. During the 1920-21 whaling season, water in the harbor boiled and removed the paint from ships' hulls, and in 1930, the floor of the harbor dropped five meters during an earthquake. In 1967, two volcanic eruptions forced the evacuation of the Argentine, British and Chilean stations at Deception, and the Chilean station was destroyed. More eruptions occurred in 1969, forcing another round of evacuations and damaging the British station, and there were further eruptions in 1970.

There's a positive side to all this volcanic activity, however. **Pendulum Cove**, which takes its name from pendulum and magnetic experiments performed there by the British in the early 19th century, is one of the top-10 sites in all of Antarctica for tourist visits. The reason: you can doff your parka and go bathing in the thermally heated waters there. You can't really swim, however, and most people who take a dip do it mainly to be able to tell people about it later. But be forewarned: moving even a meter from the warm water can lead to a real shock – you may either scald yourself or hit a patch of frigid unheated water!

Deception's strategic location and superb harbor have made it a heavily contested piece of real estate. During WWII, a British naval operation in 1941 destroyed coal and fuel oil depots at the whaling station to thwart German raiders. In 1942, Argentina sent its naval vessel *Primero de Mayo* to the island to take formal possession of all territory south of 60°S between 25°W and 68°34'W. The ship repeated the ceremony at two other island groups and left behind copper cylinders containing official documents at each of them that claimed the islands for Argentina. In January 1943, Britain dispatched HMS *Carnarvon Castle* to the Deception Island site, where it removed evidence of the Argentine visit, hoisted the Union Jack and promptly returned the copper cylinder and its contents to Argentina, through the British Ambassador in Buenos Aires. Two months later, *Primero de Mayo* was back, removing the British emblems and repainting the Argentine flag. At the end of 1943, the British once again removed Argentina's marks and probably thought it was putting an end to all the territorial squabbling when it established a permanent meteorological station (Base B) at Deception.

The bickering continued, however, and the Argentines, built their own base (Decepción) in 1948. In 1952, the Argentines and Chileans each built refuge huts on Britain's airstrip (formerly Wilkins') near Whalers Bay. The British navy removed the huts the next year and deported two Argentines to South Georgia. In 1953-54, a detachment of British Royal Marines arrived to keep the peace and spent four months on Deception. In 1955, Chile formalized its presence on Deception, building a new station, 'Presidente Pedro Aguirre Cerda,' at Pendulum Cove. In 1957, an Argentine navy ship speeding through Neptune's Bellows into the harbor caused the wreck of a Scottish whaling ship, *Southern Hunter*, which tried to avoid a collision. In 1961, Argentina sent its president, Arturo Frondizi, to show the country's official interest in the island. Today all three countries claim the island as their own and maintain bases on Deception; and official posturing aside, they manage to get along pretty well.

Chinstrap penguins are the most common birds on Deception Island, with several rookeries exceeding 50,000 breeding pairs. The rookeries are found along the exterior coast at points on the east at **Baily Head** (officially gazetted as Rancho Point, though nobody ever calls it that) and **Macaroni Point** and on the southwest at **Vapour Col**. Aside from the occasional whale or seal, few marine animals venture into Port Foster, since numerous volcanic vents heat the water inside Deception's caldera, making it several degrees warmer than the sea around the island.

Entering Port Foster through the narrow opening of **Neptune's Bellows**, you will notice the striking colors of the rock faces that rise on either side. These cliffs, as the British Royal Navy's venerable *Antarctic Pilot* puts it, 'present a curious and not unpleasing appearance.' Ships should stay on the right-hand, or north, side of the channel while navigating the Bellows, as **Ravn Rock** – covered by just 2.5m of water – lies dead center in the entrance.

King George Island Sometimes called Antarctica's 'unofficial capital,' thanks to the large number – eight – of national winter stations crowded onto it, King George Island is the largest of the South Shetlands and the first stop in the Antarctic for many tourists. Less than 10% of the island's 1295 sq km are ice-free, yet it supports facilities constructed by Argentina, Brazil, Chile, China, South Korea, Poland, Russia and Uruguay, along with nearly 13 km of gravel roads. There are also Ecuadorian, German, Peruvian and US summer bases. The stations, often within walking distance of one another, are here largely because King George Island is so accessible to the rest of the world – and thus an easy place to build a scientific base, perform significant scientific research and thus earn the status of a consultative party, or full member, of the Antarctic Treaty.

Before the island's scientific station-building boom began, however, the whalers set up operations at Admiralty Bay on the southern coast in 1906. Two years later, the whaling supply vessel *Telefon* ran aground on Telefon Rocks, at the entrance to Admiralty Bay, and was abandoned. In 1909, the ship was salvaged and towed to Telefon Bay at Deception Island, where it was repaired.

The British were first to build a base on King George Island, in 1946-47, on Admiralty Bay, but it was closed in 1961. The following season, the Argentines built a refuge hut on Admiralty Bay, and another at Potter Cove, called **Teniente Jubany**, now a permanent wintering base.

Russia set up its **Bellingshausen station** on the nearly ice-free Fildes Peninsula at the island's southwestern tip, in 1968. Bellingshausen has gained a reputation in recent years as a popular trading post, with station members often willing to swap or sell (very cheaply) items such as pins, flags, articles of clothing and trinkets.

The building boom continued with Chile's establishment of **Presidente Eduardo Frei Montalva station** in 1969. Ten years later, Chile built Teniente Rodolfo Marsh Martin station less than a kilometer across the Fildes Peninsula from Montalva station, which it incorporated. (Thus, the station's name appears either as Frei or Marsh on various charts; presently, Frei is in use.) Marsh station includes a gravel runway, on which wheeled Hercules aircraft began landing in 1980, and several of the station's international neighbors, including China, have flown personnel in to their own stations using this airstrip. In 1982, Chile held an international conference on Antarctic resources policy at Marsh, with delegates from 12 countries attending. Chilean military ruler Augusto Pinochet visited the station in 1984 and officially opened its 'married quarters.'

Chilean airlines made six tourist flights to the station in 1983-84, and passengers were accommodated in a converted military barracks called Hotel Estrella Polar (Polar Star Hotel) with 80 beds. During the 1992-93 season, however, the Chileans halted the practice of carrying passengers

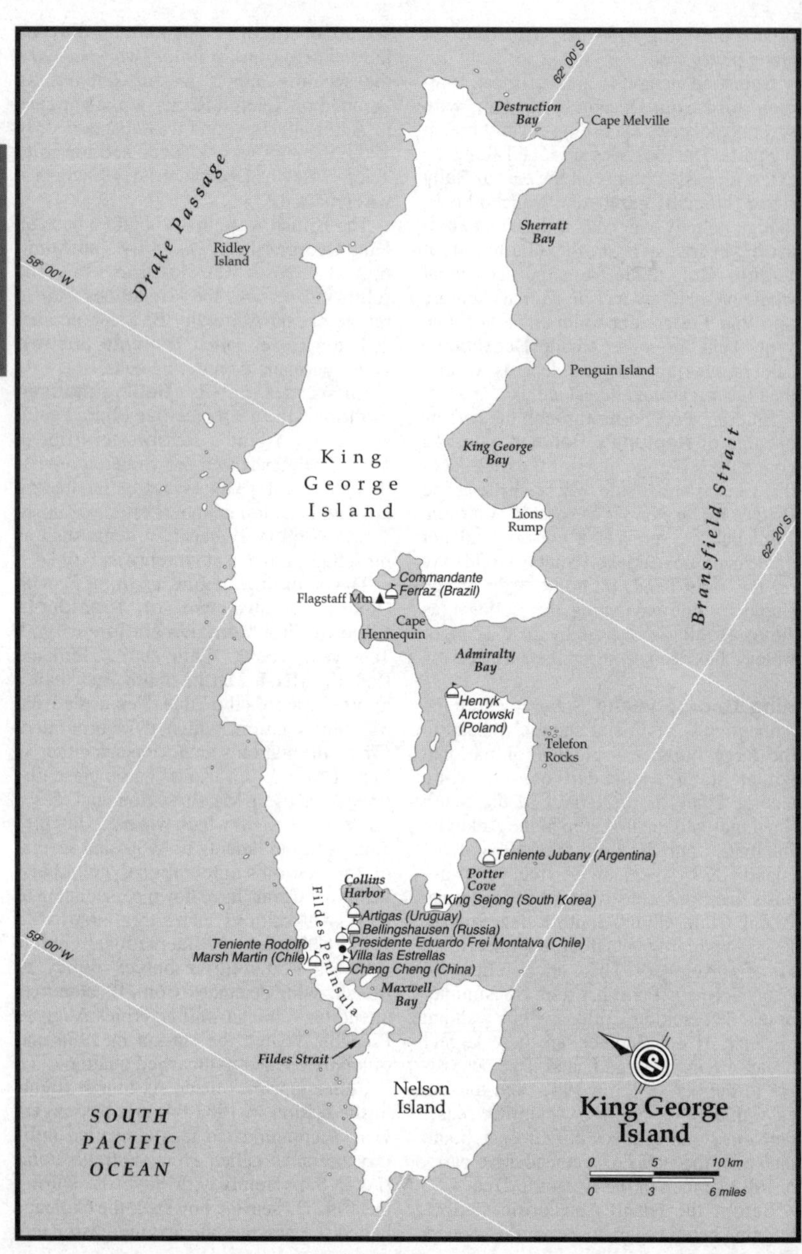
62° 00' S
Destruction Bay
Cape Melville
Drake Passage
Sherratt Bay
Ridley Island
58° 00' W
Penguin Island
King George Bay
Bransfield Strait
King George Island
Lions Rump
62° 20' S
Commandante Ferraz (Brazil)
Flagstaff Mtn
Cape Hennequin
Admiralty Bay
Henryk Arctowski (Poland)
Telefon Rocks
Teniente Jubany (Argentina)
Potter Cove
Collins Harbor
King Sejong (South Korea)
Fildes Peninsula
Artigas (Uruguay)
Bellingshausen (Russia)
Presidente Eduardo Frei Montalva (Chile)
59° 00' W
Teniente Rodolfo Marsh Martin (Chile)
Villa las Estrellas
Chang Cheng (China)
Maxwell Bay
Fildes Strait
Nelson Island
SOUTH PACIFIC OCEAN
King George Island
0 5 10 km
0 3 6 miles

JEFF RUBIN

Sunset on the Antarctic Peninsula: in the long summer twilight, sunsets last for hours

JEFF RUBIN

Penguins waddling single file

GREG WILES

US Geological Survey research team's polar pyramid tent during a blizzard

JEFF RUBIN

Icebreaker *Kapitan Khlebnikov* pushing through heavy pack ice in the northern Ross Sea

on official flights, and the Hotel Estrella Polar no longer accommodates guests, other than a DV (distinguished visitor – see glossary) or two. As part of Chile's policy of trying to incorporate its claimed Territorio Chileno Antártico into the rest of the country as much as possible, the government has encouraged families to live at Marsh station, and the first of several children was born there in 1984. Families are housed in an apartment complex around Villa Las Estrellas, with a bank, post office, supermarket, school and even a lottery-ticket office. Today Marsh accommodates about 80 to 90 summer personnel, and 30 in the winter. Parties of children from the station sometimes greet tourists upon landing.

Poland's **Henryk Arctowski station** opened in 1977 and since then has earned a reputation as being one of the most welcoming scientific stations in the Antarctic. A handsome and well-illustrated 24-page color brochure (in English) sold in a makeshift shop in the mess provides a brief history and proudly declares that 'visitors are honoured at Arctowski.' This is truer here than perhaps anywhere else on the continent. Women visitors, for example, were once presented with small bouquets of flowers grown in the station greenhouse, but the practice had to be discontinued because growing of non-food plants now requires special permission under environmental protection provisions of the Antarctic Treaty.

Arctowski's legendary hospitality may have sown the seeds of its own destruction, however: during the summer of 1992-93, the station played host to 33 tourist ships, sometimes at the rate of three ships a day, and station personnel were understandably less than enthusiastic about the invading hordes. More than 15,000 tourists have visited Arctowski, making it among the most-visited tourist attractions in Antarctica.

Thanks to all that traffic, unfortunately, sad evidence of humans' negative effects on Antarctica can be found at Arctowski station. Whalebones, relics of the whaling industry that operated there long before the station opened, were once so numerous on the black pebble beach that it appeared white with the sun-bleached bones, and walking was even difficult in places. The bones are noticeably absent today, however, taken by hundreds of selfish visitors – many of them scientists from Poland as well as other countries.

The United States has operated the small **Peter J Lenie field station** near Poland's Arctowski since 1985; it's more informally known as 'Copacabana.' Researchers from Copa sometimes visit Arctowski when cruise ships are in, joining in the social occasion.

In 1984, three stations opened on King George Island: Brazil's **Commandante Ferraz** on Admiralty Bay, and Uruguay's **Artigas** and China's **Chang Cheng** (The Great Wall of China), both on the Fildes Peninsula. One of Antarctica's oddest ceremonies was performed at the latter in 1987-88, when the Chinese introduced hundreds of domestic pigeons in a 'Dove of Peace' ritual, but nearly all of the birds died on the first day.

South Korea set up **King Sejong station** at Marian Cove close to Maxwell Bay in 1987, and Peru established its **Machu Picchu station** on Admiralty Bay in 1988-89. Italy also set up a small hut on the island in 1977, which was later removed unilaterally by the Argentines, and Ecuador established a summer-only facility in 1987-88.

Tourism to King George Island, like anywhere else in Antarctica, is not without its hazards. In 1972, *Lindblad Explorer*, the first passenger ship built specifically for polar cruising, ran aground in Admiralty Bay. The 90 passengers were rescued by a Chilean naval vessel, and a German tugboat towed the ship off the rocks 18 days later.

South Orkney Islands

Four major islands (Coronation, the largest, and Signy, Powell & Laurie islands) make up the South Orkneys (60°50' to 60°83'S, 44°25' to 46°25'W), accompanied by several minor islands and rocks, as well as the Inaccessible Islands 29 km west. The group covers a total of 622 sq km, and 85% is glacierized. The highest point, Mount Nivea (1265m) was first scaled in 1955-56. The weather is cold, windy (westerlies) and overcast, and on average the sun shines for less than two hours a day.

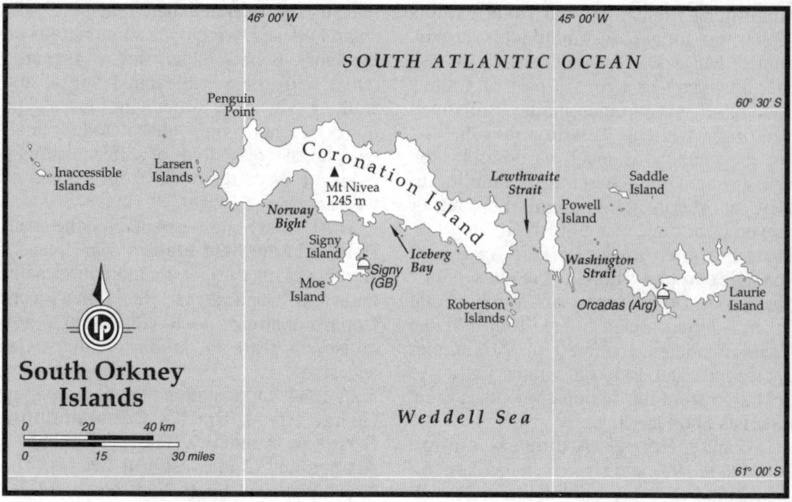

The South Orkneys were discovered jointly by American sealer Nathaniel Brown Palmer, sailing in *James Monroe*, and British sealer George Powell, in *Dove*, on December 6, 1821. Powell named the islands Powell's Group and took possession for the British crown the next day on Coronation Island. On December 12, British sealer Michael McLeod, sailing in *Beaufoy*, independently discovered the group. British sealer James Weddell, who visited in *Jane* in February 1822, gave the islands their present-day name in recognition of their position at the same latitude in the south that Britain's Orkney Islands occupy in the north.

Sealing continued on in its usual course – that is, until nearly every last animal had been hunted down. As late as 1936, a visitor to the South Orkneys found just one solitary fur seal.

In 1903, William Spiers Bruce, leader of the Scottish National Antarctic Expedition, wintered in the South Orkneys on mountainous Laurie Island, where a meteorological station was set up on April 1. When the expedition departed in February 1904, the met station was turned over to Argentina's Oficina Meteorologica, which has operated it ever since. The oldest continuous research facility in Antarctica, the station was named **Orcadas** in 1951.

Britain declared the islands part of its Falkland Islands Dependencies in 1908, a territorial claim challenged by Argentina in 1925.

Whaling began in January 1912, when a Norwegian company deployed the factory ship *Falkland* at Powell Island. A Norwegian-Chilean enterprise, Sociedad Ballenera de Magallanes, sent a factory ship to low-lying Signy Island in 1911-12, and floating factory ships visited the archipelago until 1914-15. *Tioga*, the first ship to undertake open-ocean whaling in Antarctica, was wrecked at Signy in 1913. Whaling reopened in the South Orkneys in 1920-21, when a Norwegian company operated a station on Signy Island, and floating factories operated here from 1920 to 1930; about 3500 whales were caught in that decade. The shore station at Signy took the *skrotts*, or stripped carcasses, cast off by the floating factories and extracted any remaining oil as well as the 'guano,' or meat and bone meal made from the whale remains after oil extraction.

Tourists first visited the South Orkneys on an Argentine naval voyage to relieve the Laurie Island meteorological station in 1933, making it one of the earliest Antarctic regions to receive tourists.

Britain established a met station (**'Base H'**) on Signy Island in 1946-47, a move that undoubtedly concerned Argentina, with its territorial claim on the South Orkneys. Over the years, Signy gradually expanded its program to include biological studies. In 1995, a single-story accommodation building was erected of prefab wooden panels on concrete pylons. Signy operated as a permanently staffed research base until 1995; from 1996 it will operate on a summer-only program.

Shag Rocks

Comprising six isolated, guano-covered rocks, along with Black Rock and another low-lying rock 20 km to the southeast, the group known as Shag Rocks (55°55'S, 42°03'W) is the smallest of the subantarctic islands and part of Britain's South Georgia and South Sandwich Islands territory. Covering 20 hectares, Shag Rocks are located 240 km west of South Georgia. They rise straight out of the sea, reaching a peak elevation of 71m, and landings are almost impossible.

Mislocated by their discoverer, the Spaniard Joseph de la Llana sailing in *Aurora* in 1762, the rocks were originally named the Aurora Islands. In 1819, American sealer James Sheffield in *Hersilia*, searching for the Auroras, found Shag Rocks. The first landing was made only in 1956, when an Argentine geologist was lowered by helicopter and spent a few hours collecting samples. The first tourists landed on Shag Rocks only in 1991.

Wildlife on Shag Rocks includes prions, wandering albatrosses and the eponymous shags.

South Georgia Island

Crescent-shaped South Georgia (53°50' to 55°00'S, 35°50' to 38°67'W), 170 km long and 40 km wide at its broadest, was one of the first gateways to Antarctica and the center for the huge Southern Ocean whaling industry from 1904 to 1966. Several important expeditions to Antarctica called in at the whaling stations en route to or from Antarctica, notably those of Ernest Shackleton and Robert Scott.

With its sharp, heavily glaciated peaks, South Georgia presents a rugged appearance. The Allardyce Range forms the island's spine; its highest point is Mt Paget (2934m), first ascended in 1964. Glaciers cover 57% of the island, which covers an area of 3755 sq km. The northeast coast, with many fjords, is protected by the mountains from the prevailing westerlies; this is where all of the whaling stations were built. Bird Island and the Willis Islands lie off South Georgia's northwest tip, Annenkov Island lies off the southwest coast, and Cooper Island off the east coast. The outlying Clerke Rocks are 72 km southeast of the island. South Georgia's weather is cold, cloudy and windy, with little variation between summer and winter.

London-born merchant Antoine de la Roché probably was the first to sight the island. In April 1675, as he was sailing from Lima to England, his ship was blown south as he rounded Cape Horn and caught a glimpse of South Georgia's ice-covered mountains. The island was seen again in 1756 by Spaniard Gregorio Jerez, sailing in *Léon*, who called it 'Isla de San Pedro.'

Capt James Cook made the first landing, on January 17, 1775, when he named it the Isle of Georgia after King George III and claimed it in the name of His Majesty. Cook called it 'savage and horrible . . . the wild rocks raised their lofty summits until they were lost in the clouds, and the valleys lay covered with everlasting snow. Not a tree was to be seen nor a shrub even big enough to make a tooth-pick.'

When Cook's account of South Georgia was published in 1777, his descriptions of fur seals there set off a stampede of British

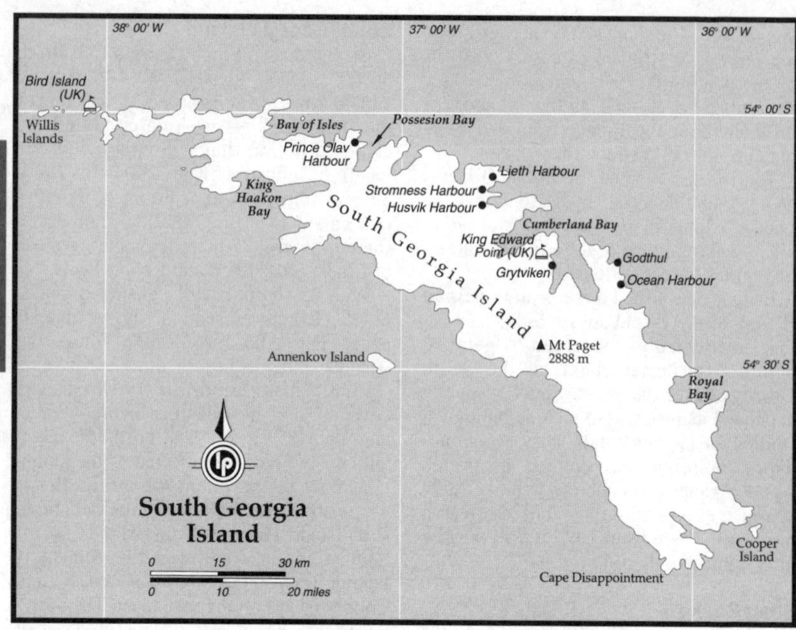

sealers, who arrived beginning in 1786. American sealers followed shortly after, and within five years there were more than a hundred ships in the Southern Ocean taking fur seal skins and elephant seal oil. The British sealer *Ann*, for example, took 3000 barrels of elephant seal oil and 50,000 fur seal skins from South Georgia in 1792-93. In that same season, an American sealer hit upon the idea of taking his fur seals skins from the Southern Ocean to the market in China, circumnavigating the globe in the process. In the next season, eight British sealing ships were working in South Georgian waters; one of them, *Mary*, took 5000 fur seals, which one can reasonably assume was an average harvest.

South Georgia's rock-laden waters proved treacherous for ships, a number of which wrecked or sank near the island. These include: *Sally* (1796), *Regulator* (1799), *Canada* (c1800), *Earl Spencer* (c1801), *Admiral Colpoys* (1817), *Hope* (1829), *Fridtjof Nansen* (1906) and *Ernesto Tornquist* (1950).

An amazing 57,000 fur seal skins were taken in 1800-02 by American sealer Edmund Fanning, in what was probably the most profitable sealing voyage ever made to South Georgia. There were 16 other British and US sealers working at South Georgia that season. But by 1831, the damage was done: The American ship *Pacific*, landing a sealing gang for eight months, found that fur seals were scarce. As late as 1909, when the American ship *Daisy* stayed for five months in what was probably the last fur-sealing visit to South Georgia, only 170 fur seals could be found.

Elephant seals likewise were slaughtered by the thousands for their oil, which was rendered from the animals' thick layer of blubber. One large elephant seal yielded one 170-liter barrel of oil (though a big bull could well produce double that), so the 15,000 barrels taken in 1877-78 by the American sealer *Trinity* shows the huge number of seals that could be exterminated in a single year by just one ship. By 1885-86, the American *Express* secured just two elephant seals and 123 'sea leopards' (probably Weddell seals), which together produced a mere 60 barrels of oil.

Science intruded briefly on this frenzy of commercial activity in 1882-83, when the German International Polar Year Expedition, part of a 12-country effort to make scientific observations in the polar regions, set up a station at Royal Bay on the southeast coast. They studied there for 13 months, and ruins of their hut remain at Royal Bay today.

Whaling began in 1904, when the Buenos Aires-based Compañía Argentina de Pesca, a Norwegian company based in Buenos Aires, established the first Antarctic whaling station at Grytviken (see the sidebar on Grytviken, below). Using only one whale-catching ship, the Compañía took 183 whales in its first year. This modest start presaged an enormous industry that generated millions of dollars for its primarily Norwegian owners, and also marked the beginning of South Georgia's permanent occupation.

Eventually seven shore stations were built on South Georgia – at Grytviken, Godthul, Ocean Harbour, Leith Harbour, Husvik Harbour, Stromness Harbour, and Prince Olav Harbour. Grytviken was the first and longest-lived, operating until 1965. Godthul ran from 1908 to 1917 and from 1922 to 1929. Ocean Harbour, opened in 1909, closed in 1920. Leith Harbour opened in 1909, closed for a year in 1933 and during WWII and closed for good in 1964. Husvik Harbour operated from 1910 to 1931, again from 1945 to 1947, and again from 1957 to 1960, missing the 1957-58 season. Stromness Harbour operated from 1912 to 1931, then became a repair yard until it closed in 1961. Prince Olav Harbour operated from 1917 to 1931.

Considering the whaling catch during just two of South Georgia's peak seasons, it's easy to understand why whales are so scarce today. In the 1925-26 season, there were five shore stations, one factory ship and 23 whale-catching ships. In that season, 1855 blue whales, 5709 fin whales, 236 humpbacks, 13 sei whales and 12 sperm whales were caught. The total catch made it a record year: 7825 whales, which produced 404,457 barrels of whale oil. During the 1926-27 season, the same number of catcher ships took 3689 blue whales (a record), 1144 fin whales, no humpbacks, 365 sei whales and 17 sperm whales. The total catch was 'only' 5215 whales, but they produced a then-record 417,292 barrels of whale oil. Of the total Antarctic whale catch, however, land stations took only 10%.

The fortuitous intervention of the global economic Depression beginning in 1929 – combined with a barely nascent realization that controls on whaling were needed – put the brakes on the booming business of whale-hunting. By the 1931-32 season the economic crisis, as well as severe overproduction the season before, forced three stations (Husvik, Prince Olav and Stromness) to close for good; Husvik reopened for the season of 1945-46. (Leith closed only for the 1932-33 season, and Grytviken never closed.)

By 1961-62, the Norwegian companies which once dominated the trade (a 1909 census at Grytviken found that 93% of the 720 whalers were Scandinavian) could no longer make a satisfactory profit. The Japanese took over the South Georgia whaling operations the next season, but they also soon found it unprofitable and closed the last shore station, Grytviken, in 1965.

South Georgia's whale catch from 1904 to 1966 included 41,515 blue whales; 87,555 fin whales; 26,754 humpbacks; 15,128 sei whales; and 3716 sperm whales. The total kill: 175,250 animals. One of them, a female blue whale landed at Grytviken in 1911-1912, was measured at just over 33.5m long – the largest animal ever recorded.

Elephant seals were also killed again during the whaling era; their oil was mixed with inferior-quality whale oil to improve it. Grytviken was able to remain open

Grytviken Whaling Station

Grytviken means 'Pot Cove' and is named for the sealers' trypots which were discovered there. As a 'bay within a bay' it is the best harbor in South Georgia and was chosen by the Norwegian Captain CA Larsen as the site of the first whaling station in Antarctic waters. Larsen arrived with a small fleet of ships on November 16, 1904, to build the factory, and whaling started five weeks later. Although the company was Argentine-owned, the whalers were mostly Norwegians. Whaling continued at Grytviken without a break until 1962. It was then leased to a Japanese company between 1963 and 1965. Huge profits were made at first but Grytviken was eventually forced to close because whales had become so rare.

During Grytviken's first years, only the blubber from the whale was utilized. Later meat, bones and viscera were cooked to extract the oil, leaving bone- and meat-meal as important by-products. Elephant seal oil was also produced from bull elephant seals, which were shot and flensed on the beaches around South Georgia. High quality seal oil was an important contribution to the economy of Grytviken.

Life for the station workers was arduous. The 'season' ran from October to March and the men worked 12-hour days. There were as many as 300 men working during the heyday of the industry. A few stayed over winter to maintain the boats and factory. Transport ships brought down coal and fuel oil, stores and food for the workers and took away the oil and other products.

Attitudes to whaling were very different a generation ago and whaling was a highly respectable profession among Norwegians. Through the development of its whaling industry, Norway became a leading industrialized nation with special skills in shipbuilding and oil technology. Whaling is an example of human folly, but Grytviken is also an example of human endeavor – what else to call a factory complex built in a desolate, inhospitable corner of the world, 16,000 km from home?

Warning: Many parts of the whaling station are unsafe. Do not enter buildings that are boarded up and marked as off limits. Fire is a serious hazard in wooden structures. Do not smoke in the whaling station.

Visitors' Trail (Read in conjunction with the map) Start at the flensing plan, the large open space between the two main jetties. Whale carcasses were brought to the iron-plated whale slip at the base of the plan and hauled onto the plan by the whale winch. (The 40,815-kg electric winch has been removed from the top of the plan.) The blubber was slit by flensers armed with hockey-stick–shaped flensing knives. Strips of blubber were ripped off the carcass, like the skin from a banana, by cables attached to steam winches, which you can still see.

The blubber went to the blubber cookery, the large building on the right of the plan. It was minced and fed into huge pressure cookers. Each cooker held about 24 metric tones of blubber which was cooked for approximately five hours to drive out the oil. The oil was piped to the separator house for purification by centrifuging. The separator house, and the generator house behind it, have been destroyed by fire but you can still see the separators in the ruins. Finally, the oil was pumped into tanks behind the station. If there was a good supply of whales, about 25 fin whales, each 18 m long, could be processed in 24 hours. They would yield 1000 barrels or 160 tons of oil.

When the whale had been flensed, the meat, tongue and guts were cut off by the lemmers, drawn up the steep ramp on the left of the plan to the meat cookery, and dropped into rotating cookers. The head and backbone were dragged up another ramp at the back of the plan to the bone cookery, where they were sawn up with large steam saws and also cooked. After oil extraction, the remains of the meat and bone were dried and turned into meal, known as 'guano,' for sale as animal feed and fertilizer. In later years meat extract was made by treatment with sulphuric acid in a plant next to the blubber cookery. Meat extract was used in dried soups and other prepared foods.

From the plan, walk along the shore past the boiler house and guano store to the slipway where *Petrel* lies. Built in 1928, she was used for whaling until 1956 and was then converted for sealing. The catwalk connecting the bridge to the gun platform has been removed and the present gun is a recent addition. This area contains the engineering shops, foundry and smithy, which enabled the whalers to repair their boats. Farther along the trail is the piggery, the meat freezer and, on the hillside, the hydroelectric power plant. On the shore is the burnt-out remains of the wooden barque *Louise*, a sailing ship built at Freeport, Maine, in 1869. She came to Grytviken in 1904 as a supply ship and remained as a coaling hulk. At the end of the trail is the cemetery (see below).

Walking back, turn left at *Petrel*, follow the road around the back of the station and turn up the stream to the Whalers' Church (see below). Note the remains of the ski jump on the hill behind the church and the football (soccer) pitch on the left. Returning from the church, call in at the Museum (see below).

Whalers' Cemetery & Shackleton's Grave This is the resting place mainly of whalers, but there are a few graves of 19th century sealers. The most recent grave is that of Felix Artuso, an Argentine sailor. At the back is the grave of Ernest Shackleton, who died on board his expedition ship *Quest* in King Edward Cove on January 5, 1922. The granite stone bears the nine-pointed star which Shackleton used as his personal symbol. On the reverse of the stone is one of Shackleton's favorite quotations, from the poet Robert Browning: 'I hold that a man should strive to the uttermost for his life's set prize.' The cross on the hillside above commemorates Walter Slossarczyk of the *Deutschland* expedition. (There is a rough path to this cross, which is a good point for taking photographs of the whaling station and King Edward Cove.)

Whalers' Church This is a typical Norwegian church and is the only building at Grytviken that retains its original function. It was consecrated on Christmas Day 1913. Inside there are memorials to Carl Anton Larsen and Ernest Shackleton, whose funeral service was held here. There are also two bells that visitors are invited to ring. The church's wooden structure has deteriorated over the years and storm damage to the roof in 1994 prompted a major program of restoration.

The first pastor, Kristen Loken, had to admit that 'religious life among the whalers left much to be desired.' The church has been used for a few baptisms and marriages. The first baptism was on Christmas Day 1913, and 13 births have been registered on South Georgia. There have also been three marriages, but the church was used more often for funerals. Twelve men died of typhus brought by ship in 1912.

South Georgia Whaling Museum The Museum is housed in the former manager's house. It was founded to preserve something of this historic site and to interpret the remains of the Antarctic whaling industry. It was opened by the South Georgia Museum Trust in 1992 and is supported by the South Georgia government. Material has been collected from Grytviken and other South Georgia whaling stations. Exhibits illustrate the social and working lives of the whalers and displays on the history of the island and its wildlife are being installed. There is also a continuing program of cleaning up and preventing further damage to the whaling station.

The Museum has a shop where you can buy T-shirts, sweatshirts, patches, woolly hats and other souvenirs, as well as postcards, side sets and books. American dollars, British pounds and German deutsche marks are accepted, but credit cards are not. ■

– **Robert Burton**, Director of the South Georgia Whaling Museum

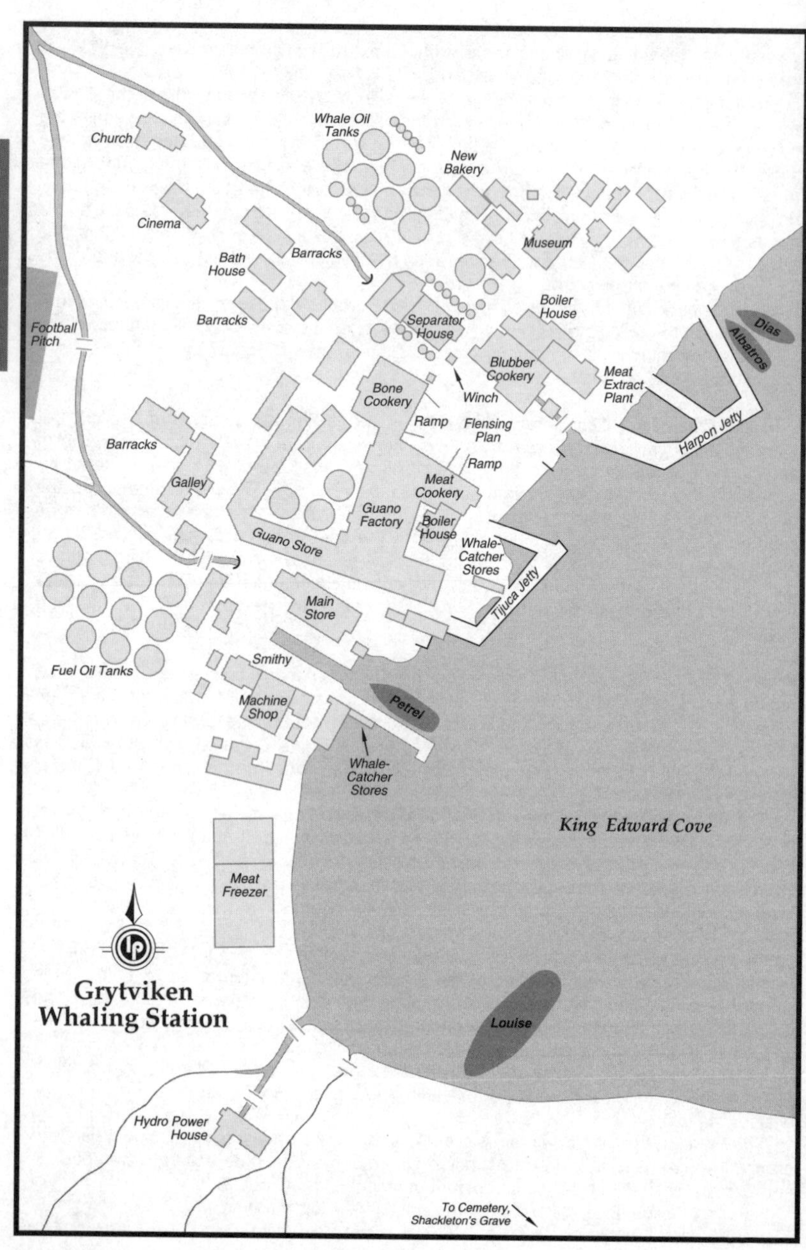
Grytviken
Whaling Station
Church
Whale Oil
Tanks
New
Bakery
Cinema
Museum
Bath
House
Barracks
Barracks
Boiler
House
Separator
House
Dias
Albatros
Football
Pitch
Blubber
Cookery
Meat
Extract
Plant
Bone
Cookery
Winch
Ramp
Flensing
Plan
Harpon Jetty
Barracks
Ramp
Galley
Meat
Cookery
Guano
Factory
Boiler
House
Guano Store
Whale-
Catcher
Stores
Tijuca Jetty
Main
Store
Smithy
Fuel Oil Tanks
Machine
Shop
Petrel
Whale-
Catcher
Stores
King Edward Cove
Meat
Freezer
Louise
Hydro Power
House
To Cemetery,
Shackleton's Grave

longer than the other South Georgia whaling stations in part because it processed elephant seals. From 1905 to 1964, another 498,870 seals (most of them elephant seals) were killed at South Georgia for their oil.

Ernest H Shackleton achieved one of the greatest of his many accomplishments on South Georgia, making the first major crossing of its 1800m range as the final lap in his rescue of the crew of his doomed *Endurance*. Shackleton returned to South Georgia again in January 1922, aboard *Quest*. Although he hoped to cross the Antarctic continent, at 47, Shackleton's health was failing him, and he died of a heart attack in his cabin aboard *Quest* at Grytviken on January 5. Even as his body was en route home to Britain, his widow, Lady Shackleton, decided that Shackleton should be buried at South Georgia, and he rests today in the whaler's cemetery at Grytviken.

In 1908, the British government consolidated earlier claims of sovereignty into a territory called Dependencies of the Falkland Islands, which includes South Georgia, as well as the South Orkneys, the South Shetlands, the South Sandwich Islands and Graham Land on the Antarctic Peninsula. A magistrate has resided there continuously from 1909 (except briefly during the war in 1982).

In 1949-50, the Falkland Islands Dependency Survey established a new base at King Edward Point on South Georgia's northeast coast. This station assumed responsibility for meteorological observations which had been made since 1905 and continued throughout the whaling era. In the 1962-63 season, a large hospital and residential building, 'Shackleton House,' was built at King Edward Point, but today there are no scientists working at the station; all are located in field camps.

War intruded on South Georgia in 1982. On March 25, the Argentine naval vessel *Bahía Paraíso*, which was later to become infamous for spilling fuel at Anvers Island, arrived at Leith Harbour and set up a garrison in a clear challenge to Britain's claim of territorial sovereignty over South Georgia. On April 3, *Bahía Paraíso*, *Guerrico* and their accompanying helicopters landed 200 Argentine forces at King Edward Point, which was defended by a small force of 22 Royal Marines. After a two-hour battle, the station was taken by the Argentines, and the Marines and scientists were taken prisoner and moved to Argentina. (Fifteen British researchers at four field stations on South Georgia were later relieved by the Royal Navy.) In response to the Argentine aggression, London dispatched six Royal Navy ships, including the nuclear submarine HMS *Conquerer* for reconnaissance, which retook the station on April 25, and another Argentine garrison at Leith Harbor the next day. An Argentine submarine, *Santa Fé*, was sunk; 185 Argentines were taken prisoner and later released in Uruguay. During the Falklands war, the Royal Navy used South Georgia as a base; several dozen British troops – the exact number is a secret – are still stationed at the garrison at King Edward Point today.

South Georgia's wildlife is varied and abundant, despite the incredible slaughter of just a century ago. During the 1960s and 1970s, the Antarctic fur seal population increased about 15% annually. Now found mainly on the northwest side of the island, they are so numerous that they present a hazard to Zodiacs trying to land there. More than five million pairs of macaroni penguins nest on the island, and there is a huge king penguin colony at St Andrews Bay and another at Salisbury Plain. First introduced by whalers in 1911, South Georgia's 2000 reindeer are confined by glaciers to two valleys.

South Sandwich Islands

The 11 islands of the South Sandwich group (56°30' to 59°47'S, 26°23' to 28°18'W) are spread out over a rough arc running north to south: Zavodovski, Leskov (the archipelago's smallest), Visokoi, Candlemas, Vindication, Saunders, Montagu (the largest), Bristol, Bellingshausen, Cook and Southern Thule islands.

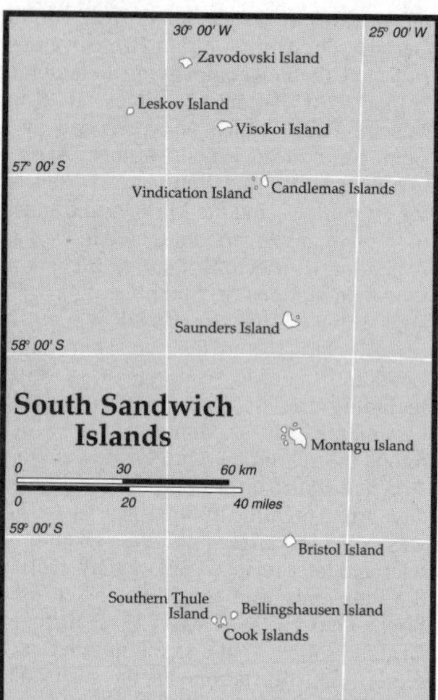

The islands (somtimes called the South Sandwiches) are 80% glacierized and cover an area of 310 sq km. The highest point is Mt Belinda (1375m) on Montagu Island.

Volcanoes formed all of the South Sandwich Islands a relatively short time ago, and volcanic activity has been recorded in this century on all of the islands except Cook, Montagu and Vindication. Indeed, in 1908, Norwegian whaling captain Carl Anton Larsen was almost asphyxiated by volcanic fumes on Zavodovski Island. In 1962, the South African research ship *RSA*, beset by ice, was freed by shock waves believed caused by a volcanic eruption in the South Sandwich Islands, and there is a submarine volcanic cone 25m beneath the surface about 35 km off the northwestern end of the island chain. The features of Candlemas Island, in recognition of its underworld-like landscape, were appropriately named – Chimaera Flats, Gorgon Pool, Lucifer Hill, Sarcophagus Point – by the British Antarctic Survey.

Although they are more northerly than either the South Shetlands or the South Orkneys, the South Sandwich Islands have a much colder climate, thanks to a cold ocean current originating in the Weddell Sea. The sky is almost constantly cloud-covered.

The eight most southerly islands in the group were discovered on January 30, 1775, by British Capt James Cook, sailing in HMS *Resolution*. The three northernmost were first sighted by Russian explorer Fabian von Bellingshausen in 1819. Bellingshausen landed on Zavodovski Island and named it for Lt Ivan Zavodovski, captain of his flagship *Vostok*, on Christmas Eve 1819. Sealers made the first landing, in 1818.

The islands are claimed by the British as part of South Georgia and South Sandwich Islands territory, but they are also claimed by Argentina as part of its Islas del Atlántico Sur. These conflicting claims have occasionally threatened to erupt into violence. In 1976, Argentina established a 50-member naval station on Thule and occupied it for the summer without authorization from the British government. The next season the station, known as 'Corbeta Uruguay station,' opened for the winter. It remained active until June 20, 1982, when it was closed and its remaining personnnel removed by the British Navy for its role as a staging point in the attack on South Georgia. The following January, the station was destroyed (except for one refuge hut) by British forces after they discovered an Argentine flag flying there.

Tourists were first landed on the islands in 1982. Among the islands' attractions are the five million pairs of chinstrap penguins that breed there. Although many of the Antarctic tour companies' brochures claim that more than 12 million chinstraps breed on Zavodovski Island alone, this is a vast exaggeration (spread, innocently enough, by overzealous marketing writers). In fact, biologists say there are about 500,000 breeding pairs on Zavodovski – or about a million birds – which still makes it one of the largest penguin colonies in the world, and a very impressive sight indeed.

Tristan da Cunha Group

Located midway between South Africa and Brazil (37°02' to 37°24'S, 12°12' to 12°42'W), the volcanic islands of the Tristan da Cunha group are actually astride the border between the subantarctic and subtropical climatic zones. But the Tristan da Cunha group is often included on the itineraries of ships visiting the Antarctic, in part because of the millions of seabirds that nest in the islands.

The northernmost of the group, Tristan Island, is also the largest, being roughly circular and covering an area of 98 sq km. It has a steep volcanic cone that rises to 2060m, the group's highest point, and is the only inhabited island in the group. A small settlement, Edinburgh, is home to about 300 Tristanians. Inaccessible Island is about 40 km to the west-southwest and its neighbor, Nightingale Island, is about 38 km to the south-southwest; they lie nearly 23 km apart. Appropriately named Inaccessible Island covers about 18 sq km and is almost completely ringed with vertical cliffs. Nightingale, covering less than 260 hectares, is the most densely populated with bird life. Nightingale also has two tiny off-lying islands, Middle and Stoltenhoff.

Portuguese Admiral Tristão d'Acunha, sailing in *Santiago*, discovered the islands in 1506 while traveling in company with 13 other ships. The first recorded landing was made by Dutchman Claes Gerritszoon Bierenbroodspot, sailing in *Heemstede*, on February 7, 1643.

Austrian Guilleme Bolts, sailing in *Joseph et Thérèse*, landed on Tristan da Cunha in 1775 and took possession for the Emperor of Austria, Joseph II, in what was to be the only claim in Antarctic history made by the Austro-Hungarian Empire.

The usual sad refrain of 'discovery, exploitation, extinction' was repeated once more on Tristan da Cunha: the first sealers, Americans sailing in *Industry*, visited for eight months in 1790-91, industriously taking 5600 fur seal skins, and by 1801-02, sealers sailing from the Cape Colony in *Phiamingi* reported that fur seals were very rare. In several weeks, they were able to take fewer than 10 skins.

Three Americans landed by the sealing ship *Baltic* in 1810-12 established the first known settlement on Tristan. The trio took personal possession of the island group in 1811 and began killing fur seals, hoping to sell the skins to passing vessels. After two of the men drowned in 1812, the lonely survivor continued working and when a British naval vessel stopped in March 1813, two new settlers joined him.

During the 1812-15 war between Britain and the US, the islands were used by American naval ships and privateers as a staging point for raids on British vessels. In one such gunbattle, USS *Hornet* sank HMS *Penguin* off the islands' shores. British forces – partly thanks to this unhappy state of affairs and partly to prevent a rescue of Napoleon Bonaparte exiled on St Helena in 1815 – set up a garrison and took formal possession of Tristan da Cunha in 1816.

After the garrison was withdrawn in 1817, three men, a woman and two children, all British, were left on the island, along with horses and cattle. One of the men was Cpl William Glass of Scotland, who is recognized as the founder of the present settlement.

Shipwrecked sailors added to the tiny community, and by 1826 the island's population was 14: Glass, his wife, their seven children, and five other men. The population began to rise fairly quickly after the bachelors negotiated with a ship captain to procure wives for them from the British colony of St Helena 2100 km to the northeast. The little settlement thrived as a convenient mid-ocean filling station for ships, which called in for water, meat and vegetables. Later, however, the traffic decreased as whaling came to an end and the Suez Canal opened in 1869, eliminating the need to sail around Africa to reach India and the Far East.

The settlement also rescued dozens of mariners whose ships foundered or burned offshore. During the 19th century alone, an eye-opening number of ships came to grief near Tristan da Cunha: HMS *Julia* (1817),

Sarah (1820), *Blenden Hall* (1821), *Nassau* (1825), *Emily* (1836), *Joseph Somes* (1856), *Sir Ralph Abercrombie* (1868), *Bogata* (1869), *Beacon Light* (1871), *Czarina* (1872), *Olympia* (1872), *Mabel Clark* (1878), *Edward Vittery* (1881), *Henry B Paul* (1882), *Shakespeare* (1882), *Italia* (1892), *Allan Shaw* (1893), *Helen S Lea* (1897) and *Glenhuntley* (1898).

So many times did the islanders come to the aid of such sailors that the British government sent provisions in 1858 and a new lifeboat and other rescue equipment in 1884 in recognition and thanks. In 1879-80, a British naval voyage dropped off presents sent by US President Rutherford B Hayes, in gratitude for the Tristanians' role in saving the crew of *Mabel Clark* two years before.

Perhaps the most interesting of the islands' many wrecks was that of the American ship *Lark* during a hurricane in 1864. The crew managed to get ashore with £35,000 in gold and currency, a considerable fortune at the time. This treasure was left on the island after the survivors were rescued. *Lark*'s captain died of smallpox on the voyage home, but the first mate later returned and picked up the stash.

To prevent overpopulation, a British naval expedition removed 45 of Edinburgh's settlers in 1857, leaving a total of 28 people. Ironically, fate took its own cruel measure 27 years later, when 15 of the adult male population drowned while rowing a small boat out to try to hail a passing ship in 1884, leaving only three grown men on the island.

Annual voyages to bring mail and provisions to the island were instituted by the British Colonial Office in 1927, and in 1938 British Letters Patent defined the Tristan da Cunha group and Gough Island as Dependencies of St Helena.

During WWII, the British navy established a meteorological and radio station on the island, primarily to prevent Nazi ships from using the island as a watering place. The detachment was withdrawn in 1946 and the South African Weather Bureau took over responsibility for the met station.

A volcanic eruption in 1961, after more than two months of seismic activity, forced the evacuation of Edinburgh on October 10. Two fishing boats took the entire population (289 people) to Nightingale Island. The next day, they sailed for Cape Town, and later, to England, where they remained, before returning home in November, 1963.

Edinburgh's population today is 300. Employment consists of either a Government job or working for Tristan Investments Ltd, a subsidiary of the South Atlantic Islands Development Corp, which runs a plant processing the local catch of rock lobster (crayfish), exported to France, Japan and the US. Other exports include postage stamps and handicrafts.

The islanders' somewhat unusual speech is characterized by slow enunciation; their accent is thought to resemble that of English spoken in parts of Britain during the early 19th century. Some unusual words used on the island include cappie (hood) and gansey (pullover), and the island's cultivated land is called Potato Patches.

Gough Island

Oblong Gough Island (40°32'S, 09°95'W), part of Britain's Dependencies of St Helena, rises steeply out of the Southern Ocean 340 km southeast of Tristan da Cunha. The island covers 65 sq km, with several pillars and rocks lying offshore. Gough's coasts are nearly all steep cliffs, especially on the windward western side, where they stand nearly 460m high. Edinburgh Peak, the highest point, has an elevation of 910m. There are no glaciers on the island. With more than three meters of rainfall each year, and an average annual temperature of 11.7°C, a lush carpet of mosses, tussock grasses and ferns covers its slopes.

Gough was probably first sighted in 1505 by the Portuguese sailor Gonçalo Alvarez when he was blown south while rounding the Cape of Good Hope. For this reason, the island is infrequently referred to as Gonzalo Alvarez. The Dutchman January Jakobszoon van Amsterdam examined Gough and the Tristan da Cunha group in 1655-56. The first landing on Gough was probably made when Antoine de la Roché, a London-born merchant, came ashore in May 1675, a month after he discovered South Georgia. Such mid-ocean discoveries were not always shared, however, especially with rival seafaring nations. British Capt Charles Gough, sailing in *Richmond*, rediscovered the island on March 3, 1732, and named it for himself, though he made no landing.

The first sealers arrived in 1804, and the island's resources continued to be exploited throughout the 19th century. In 1881, for example, parties who landed from Cape Town reported taking eight tons of guano, 4000 penguin eggs and 151 fur seal skins. Among the more optimistic expeditions to Gough Island was a group from Cape Town, which spent four months in 1919 prospecting (unsuccessfully) for diamonds.

Shortly after British Letters Patent defined Gough Island as a dependency of St Helena in 1938, a formal territorial claim was made during a British naval visit to the island by HMS *Milford*.

During WWII, the Germans sent *Stier*, also known as 'Raider J,' to investigate Gough as a potential base of operations and prison camp. The British quickly dispatched HMS *Hawkins* to ensure that the Germans were not able to establish a beachhead on the island.

In 1955-56, a comprehensive examination of the island was made by British scientists. In May 1956, the British scientific station was transferred to the South African Weather Bureau, which continues meteorological observations there today.

The first tourist landing on Gough was made in 1970, and the island was declared a Wildlife Reserve in 1976. In late 1995, Gough was declared a World Heritage Site, the first Southern Ocean or subantarctic island so designated, after a comprehensive management plan was adopted for the island. Among the species breeding here is the unusual long-crested rockhopper penguin, and two endemic birds, the Gough bunting and the Gough flightless moorhen. The island is also one of the most northerly habitats for both the elephant seal and the wandering albatross.

Falkland Islands

Although they are not subantarctic islands, the Falklands (51°0' to 52°30'S, 57°30' to 62°0'W) are a popular addition to the itinerary of many Antarctic voyages. Surrounded by the South Atlantic and centuries of controversy, the Falklands lie 490 km east of the Patagonian mainland. Consisting of two main islands, East and West Falkland, and several hundred smaller ones, they support a permanent population of about 2000 people, most of whom live in the capital of Stanley (see Antarctic Gateways chapter). The remaining Falklanders live on widely dispersed sheep stations.

Every part of the Falklands outside Stanley is 'camp,' including those parts of East Falkland accessible by road from Stanley, all of West Falkland, and the numerous smaller offshore islands, only a few of which are inhabited. Nearly everyone in camp is engaged in sheep ranching, though a few work in tourism and minor cottage industries.

Since the advent of the large sheep stations in the late 19th century, rural settlement in the Falklands has consisted of tiny hamlets, really company towns, near sheltered harbors where coastal shipping could collect the wool clip. In fact, these settlements were the models for the sheep estancias of Patagonia, many of which were founded by Falklands emigrants. On nearly all of them, shepherds lived in 'outside houses' that still dot the countryside. Since the agrarian reform of the late 1970s and 1980s, this pattern of residence has not changed greatly despite the creation of many new farms.

Many of the Islands' best wildlife sites are on smaller offshore islands such as Sea Lion Island and Pebble Island, where there are comfortable but fairly costly tourist lodges. (These are described in detail below.) Some of the most interesting islands have few or no visitor facilities and very difficult access, but it is worthwhile

OCEAN & ISLANDS

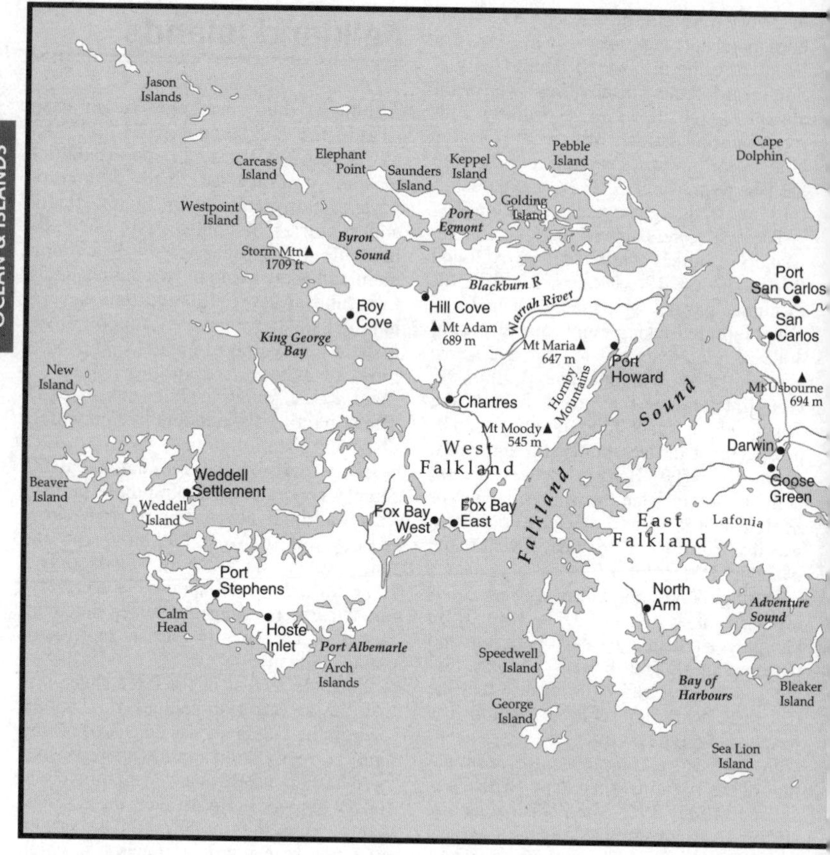

asking at the Tourist Board about them when you arrive in the Falklands.

History

Although there is some evidence that Patagonian Indians may have reached the Falklands in rudimentary canoes, the Islands were uninhabited when Europeans began to frequent the area in the late 17th century. Their Spanish name, Islas Malvinas, derives from early French navigators from the Channel port of St Malo, who called the islands 'Les Malouines' after their home port.

No European power established a settlement until 1764, when the French built a garrison at Port Louis on East Falkland, disregarding Spanish claims under the papal Treaty of Tordesillas that divided the New World between Spain and Portugal. Unknown to either France or Spain, Britain soon planted a West Falkland outpost at Port Egmont, on Saunders Island. Spain, meanwhile, discovered and then supplanted the French colony after an amicable settlement between the two European states. The Spanish forces then detected and expelled the British in 1767. Under threat of war, Spain restored Port Egmont to the British, who only a few years later abandoned the

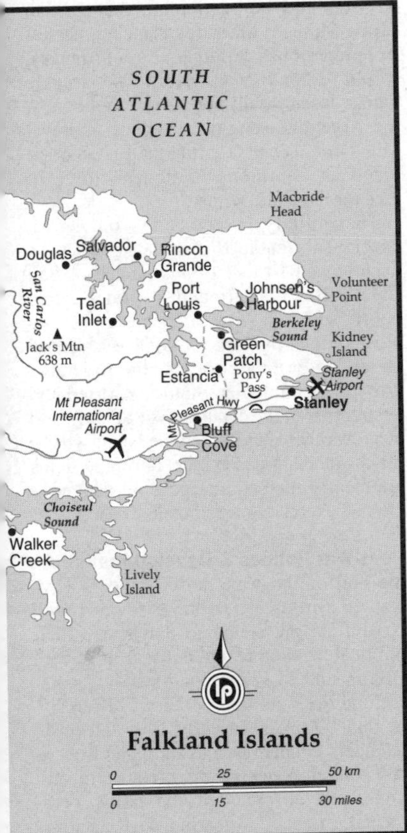

area – without, however, renouncing their territorial claims.

For the rest of the 18th century, Spain maintained the Islands as one of the world's most secure penal colonies. After it abandoned them in the early 1800s, only maverick whalers and sealers visited, until the United Provinces of the River Plate sent a military governor in the early 1820s to assert its claim as successor to Spain. Later, a naturalized Buenos Aires entrepreneur named Louis Vernet initiated a project to monitor uncontrolled sealers and exploit local fur seal populations in a sustainable manner, as well as tame the numerous wild cattle and horses that had multiplied on the abundant pastures since the Spaniards' departure.

Vernet's seizure of three American sealers triggered reprisals from a hotheaded US naval officer, who vandalized the Port Louis settlement beyond restoration in 1831. After Vernet's departure, Buenos Aires kept a token force there until early 1833, when it was expelled by British forces. Vernet pursued his claims for property damages in British courts for nearly 30 years, with little success, but Argentina has since asserted its territorial claim to the Islands by diplomacy and, in 1982, by force.

Under the British, the Falklands languished until the mid-19th century, when sheep began to replace cattle, and wool became an important export commodity. Founded by Samuel Lafone, an Englishman from Montevideo, the Falkland Islands Company became the Islands' largest landholder, but other immigrant entrepreneurs occupied all available pastoral lands in extensive holdings by the 1870s.

The steady arrival of English and Scottish immigrants augmented the early population, which was a mix of stranded mariners and holdover gauchos from the Vernet era. Roughly half resided in the new capital and port of Stanley, founded in 1844, while the remainder became resident laborers on large sheep stations resembling those in Australia. The population has never exceeded its 1931 maximum of 2400.

Most of the original landowners lived and worked in the Falklands, but in time they or their descendants returned to Britain and ran their businesses as absentees. For nearly a century the Falkland Islands Company, owner of nearly half the land and livestock, dominated the local economy.

Until the late 1970s, when local government began to encourage the sale and subdivision of large landholdings to slow high rates of emigration, little changed in the Islands' only industry. Since then, nearly every unit has been sold to local family farmers. Beginning in 1982, change became even more rapid with the Falklands War and the subsequent expansion of long-distance, deep-sea fishing in the surrounding South Atlantic. There is speculation, but still no firm evidence, of offshore petroleum in Falklands waters.

The Falklands War Although Argentina had persistently affirmed its claim to the Falklands since 1833, successive British governments never publicly acknowledged their seriousness until the late 1960s. By then, the Foreign & Commonwealth Office and the military government of General Juan Carlos Onganía had reached a communications agreement giving Argentina a significant voice in matters affecting Falklands transportation, fuel supplies, shipping, and even immigration, beginning in 1971.

Islanders (sometimes called 'Kelpers') and their supporters in Britain saw the Argentine presence as an ominous development. Only a few years earlier, right-wing guerrillas had hijacked an Aerolíneas Argentinas jet, which crash-landed on the Stanley racecourse (the Islands had no airport at the time); afterward, the guerrillas briefly occupied parts of town. Concerned about Argentina's chronic political instability, Falklanders suspected the FCO of secretly arranging transfer of the Islands to Argentina, and they may well have been correct.

This process dragged on for more than a decade, during which Argentina's brutal Dirty War after 1976 gave Falklanders good reason to fear increasing Argentine presence. What was too fast for the Islanders was too slow for the Argentines, especially for the desperate military government of General Leopoldo Galtieri, which invaded the almost undefended Islands on April 2, 1982.

Galtieri's disintegrating government had come under increasing pressure from Argentines fed up with the corruption, economic chaos and totalitarian ruthlessness of the Proceso, but his seizure of the Malvinas briefly united a divided country and made him an ephemeral hero. Galtieri and his advisers did not anticipate that British Prime Minister Margaret Thatcher, herself in precarious political circumstances, would respond so decisively. In a struggle whose loser would not survive politically, the Argentine sought diplomatic approval of his *fait accompli*, while the Briton organized an enormous naval task force to recover the lost territory.

The military outcome was one-sided, despite substantial British naval losses, as experienced British troops landed at San Carlos Bay and routed ill-trained and poorly supplied Argentine conscripts. The most serious fighting took place at Goose Green, on East Falkland, but the Argentine army's surrender at Stanley averted the destruction of the capital. Near Stanley, and at a few other sites around the Islands, there remain unexploded mines, but mine fields are clearly marked and pose no danger to anyone exercising reasonable caution.

Post-War Politics & Development Since the end of the war, most Islanders have wanted little or nothing to do with Argentina, preferring to emphasize their political, economic and cultural links with Britain and to renew long-standing commercial ties with the southern Chilean city of Punta Arenas. In early 1995, however, Islanders Graham Bound and Janet Robertson toured Argentina as private citizens, under the auspices of the non-governmental Consejo Argentino de Relaciones Internacionales (Argentine International Relations Council), to establish dialogue and explain recent developments on the Islands to the Argentine public. While many Islanders opposed the visit, Argentine audiences generally treated the visitors cordially and respectfully.

Official Argentina, at the same time, continues to send mixed messages to the Islanders. President Carlos Menem has repeatedly renounced the use of force to support his country's claim to the Malvinas, yet he has also bragged that the Islands will once again be Argentine by the turn of the century. Foreign minister Guido di Tella, meanwhile, has carried out an ineffective policy of buttering up the Islanders by sending Christmas cards, gifts like children's videos and even Queen's birthday greetings, while simultaneously proposing indemnities of US$100,000 or more per Islander should they vote to accept Argentine sovereignty in a referendum. Nearly all Falklanders angrily dismiss di Tella's efforts to purchase their allegiance as insulting and patronizing, but many have no objection to a strictly economic relationship with their larger neighbor.

Geography & Climate

The Falklands' total land area is 12,173 sq km, about the same as that of Northern Ireland or the US state of Connecticut. There are two main islands, East and West Falkland, separated by the Falkland Sound; of the many smaller islands, only a handful are large enough for human habitation.

Except for the low-lying southern half of East Falkland, known as Lafonia, the terrain is generally hilly to mountainous, although the highest peaks do not exceed 700m. Among the most interesting geological features are the 'stone runs' of quartzite boulders that descend from many of the ridges and peaks on East and West Falkland. The numerous bays, inlets, estuaries and beaches present an often spectacular coastline, with abundant, accessible and remarkably tame wildlife.

Because the settlements are so far apart, often separated by water, and the Islands' road network is so limited, light aircraft is the easiest way to visit areas beyond the immediate Stanley to Goose Green area. In some areas, riding is still a common means of travel, but the Land Rover and the motorcycle have for the most part supplanted the horse. For adventurous travelers, walking is feasible, but trekkers must be prepared for changeable and sometimes inclement weather.

Despite a reputation for dismal weather, the Islands' oceanic climate is temperate, but with frequent high winds. Maximum temperatures rarely reach 24°C, while even on the coldest winter days the temperature usually rises above freezing at some time during the day. The average annual rainfall at Stanley, one of the Islands' most humid areas, is only about 600 mm.

Flora & Fauna

Grasslands and prostrate shrubs dominate the Falklands flora; there are no native trees. At the time of European discovery, extensive stands of the native tussock grass *Parodiochloa flabellata* dominated the coastline and provided nutritious fodder for livestock, but it proved highly vulnerable to overgrazing and fire. Today, very little tussock remains on East or West Falkland, although well-managed farms on offshore islands have preserved significant areas of it. Most of the native pasture is rank white grass *(Cortaderia pilosa)*, which supports only about one sheep per four or five acres.

Most visitors will find the Falklands' fauna more varied and interesting, and remarkably tame and accessible. The Islands' beaches, headlands and offshore waters support the largest and finest concentrations of South Atlantic wildlife north of South Georgia and Antarctica. The Magellanic penguin, the only species that visits the South American continent, is common, but four other species breed regularly in the Falklands: the rockhopper, the closely related macaroni, the gentoo and the king. Four other species have been recorded, but do not breed here.

Many other birds, equally interesting and uncommon, breed in the Falklands. Undoubtedly the most beautiful is the black-browed albatross, but there are also caracaras, cormorants, gulls, hawks, peregrine falcons, oystercatchers, snowy sheathbills, sheldgeese, steamer ducks and swans – among others. Most are present in very large and impressive breeding colonies and are easy to photograph.

Elephant seals, southern sea lions and southern fur seals breed on the beaches, while six species of dolphins have been observed offshore. Killer whales are common, but the larger species of South Atlantic whales are rarely seen.

While the Falklands have no formally designated national parks, there are many outstanding wildlife sites. Over the past decade, local government has encouraged nature-oriented tourism, constructing small lodges near some of the best areas, but there are also less-structured opportunities away from these places. Hiking and trekking possibilities are excellent.

Government

In international politics, the Falklands remain a colonial anachronism, administered by a governor appointed by the FCO in London, but in local affairs the eight-member, elected Legislative Council (Legco) exercises power over most internal matters. The British government controls defense and international relations. Four of the eight members come from Stanley, while the remainder represent camp. Selected Legco members advise the governor as part of his Executive Council (Exco), which also includes the Chief Executive and the Financial Secretary.

Economy

From the mid-19th century, the Falklands' economy has depended almost exclusively on the export of wool. Since 1986, however, fishing has eclipsed agriculture as a revenue producer under a licensing scheme established by the local government with the approval of the FCO. Asian and European fleets seeking both squid and fin fish have brought as much as £25 million per year into the Islands, most of which has gone to fund overdue improvements in public services, such as roads, telephones and medical care. Tourist traffic is numerically small, but facilities in Stanley and at some wildlife sites are more than adequate and often excellent. Local government began permitting offshore seismic surveys for oil in 1993, and it is considering issuing licenses for offshore petroleum exploration, a subject that generates great ambivalence among Islanders because of the potential environmental impact. Among the postulants for exploration licenses is the former Argentine state oil company YPF, as a partner of British Petroleum (BP).

Most of the population of Stanley works for the local government (FIG) or for the Falkland Islands Company (FIC), which has been the major landowner and economic power in the Islands for more than a century. FIC has sold all its pastoral property to the government for subdivision and sale to local people, but it continues to provide shipping and other commercial services for ranchers and other residents of the Islands. In camp, nearly everyone is involved in wool-growing on relatively small, widely dispersed family owned units.

Population & People

According to the 1991 census, the population of the Falklands is 2050, of whom about three-quarters live in Stanley. About 60% of the population is native-born, some tracing their ancestry back six or more generations, while the great majority of the remainder are immigrants or temporary residents from the United Kingdom. Islanders' surnames indicate that their origins can be traced to a variety of European backgrounds, but English is both the official language and the language of preference, though a few people speak and understand Spanish. There are a few immigrants from South America, nearly all of them Chilean.

Because of the Islands' isolation and small population, Falkland Islanders are traditionally versatile and adaptable. Almost every male, for example, is an expert mechanic, while lack of spare parts has encouraged many to become improvisational machinists. This adaptability has also been a virtue for individuals who rely on seasonal labor like sheep shearing and peat cutting, both of which are well paid. Many camp women also perform a variety of tasks, including shearing. Recently, however, these jobs are less gender segregated than they once were.

The Islands' history of colonial rule and the paternalistic social system of the large sheep stations and other workplaces left an unfortunate legacy of public timidity in the face of authority, even when private opinions are very strong. At the same time,

Falkland Islanders are extraordinarily hospitable, often welcoming visitors into their homes for 'smoko,' the traditional mid-morning tea or coffee break, or for a drink. This is especially true in camp, where visitors of any kind can be infrequent. When visiting people in camp, it is customary to bring a small gift – rum is a special favorite. Stanley's several pubs are popular meeting places.

Maps

Excellent topographic maps, prepared by the Directorate of Overseas Surveys, are available from the Secretariat in Stanley for about £2 each. There is a two-sheet, 1:250,000 map of the entire Islands that is suitable for most purposes, but for more detail, obtain the 1:50,000 sheets. For maritime charts, contact the Customs & Immigration Department (☎ 27340) on Ross Rd in Stanley.

Tourist Offices

The local tourist office is the Falklands Islands Tourist Board (☎ 500-25115, fax 22619) in Stanley, but the Islands also have representation in the UK, Europe and the Americas.

United Kingdom
: Falkland House, 14 Broadway, Westminster, London SW1H 0BH (☎ 44-171-222-2542, fax 222-2375)

Germany
: HS Travel & Consulting, PO Box 1447, 64529 Moerfelden (☎ /fax 49-61-05-1304)

USA
: Leo Le Bon & Associates, 190 Montrose Ave, Berkeley, CA 94707 (☎ /fax 1-510-525-8846)

Chile
: Broom Travel, Roca 924, Punta Arenas (☎ 56-61-22-8312)

Visas

All nationalities, including British citizens, must carry valid passports. For non-Britons, visa requirements are generally the same as those for foreigners visiting the UK, except that Argentines must obtain a visa in advance (not easily accomplished). For more details, inquire at the Islands' UK representative at Falkland House (☎ 222-2542), 14 Broadway, Westminster, London SW1H 0BH. In Punta Arenas, Chile, contact Aerovías DAP (☎ 22-3340, fax 22-1693) at O'Higgins 891, which operates flights to the Islands, or British consul John Rees (☎ 22-8312) at Roca 924.

Customs

Customs regulations are few except for limits on importation of alcohol and tobacco, which are heavily taxed but readily available locally.

Money

The legal currency is the Falkland Islands pound (£), on a par with sterling. Sterling notes and coins circulate alongside local currency, but Falklands currency is not legal tender in the UK, nor on Ascension Island, where flights to and from the UK make a brief refueling stop. Ascension/St Helena bank notes and coins are not legal tender in either the Falklands or the UK.

Credit cards are not widely used in the Islands, but traveler's checks are readily accepted with a minimum of bureaucracy. Britons with guarantee cards from Barclays, Lloyds, Midland and National Westminster Banks can cash personal checks up to £50 at Stanley's Standard Chartered Bank.

Post & Telecommunications

Postal services are very dependable. There are two airmail services weekly to and from the UK, but parcels larger than about half a kilogram arrive or depart by sea four to five times yearly. The Government Air Service delivers the post to outer settlements and islands

Cable and Wireless PLC operates both local and long-distance telephone services; all local numbers have five digits. The Falklands' international country code is 500, valid for numbers in Stanley and in camp.

Local calls cost 5p per minute, calls to the UK 15p for six seconds and calls to the rest of the world 18p per six seconds. Operator-assisted calls cost the same but have a three-minute minimum. Collect calls are possible only locally and to the UK.

Books

Many books have been written since the 1982 war, but the most readily available general account is the third edition of Ian Strange's *The Falkland Islands* (David & Charles, 1983), which deals with the geography, history and natural history of the Islands. More recent are Paul Morrison's *The Falkland Islands* (Aston Publications, 1990) and Tony Chater's *The Falklands* (Penna Press, 1993).

Visitors interested in wildlife should acquire Robin Woods' *Falkland Islands Birds*, which is a suitable field guide with excellent photographs. More detailed but unsuitable for field use is his *The Birds of the Falkland Islands*. Ian Strange's *Field Guide to the Wildlife of the Falkland Islands and South Georgia* is also worth a look, along with TH Davies and JH McAdam's *Wild Flowers of the Falkland Islands*.

Media

Radio is the most important communications medium in the Falklands. The Falkland Islands Broadcasting Service (FIBS) produces local programming and also carries news from the BBC and programs from the British Forces Broadcasting Service (BFBS). Do not miss the nightly public announcements, to which local people listen religiously; they're part of the local news program. The Falklands may be the only place in the world where the purchase of air time is within anybody's reach. Frequencies are 550 kHz on the AM band and 96.5 MHz on the FM band.

Television is available at least 10 hours daily from the BFBS station at Mt Pleasant airport; programs are taped and flown in from the UK on a regular basis. The only print media are the weekly newspapers *Penguin News* and *Teaberry Express*, both available from shops in Stanley.

Time

The Falklands are four hours behind GMT. In summer, Stanley adjusts its clocks to daylight saving time, but camp remains on standard time.

Electricity

Electric current operates on 220/240 V, 50 cycles. Plugs are identical to those in the UK.

Useful Organizations

Based in both the UK and Stanley, Falklands Conservation is a nonprofit organization promoting wildlife conservation research as well as the preservation of wrecks and historic sites in the Islands. Membership, which costs £15 per year and includes its annual newsletter, is available from Falklands Conservation (☎ 181-346-5011), 1 Princes Rd, Finchley, London N3 2DA, England. Its local representative (☎ 22247, fax 22288) is at the Beauchene Complex on John St between Philomel and Dean Sts in Stanley.

The Falkland Islands Association (☎ 171-222-0028), 2 Greycoat Place, Westminster, London SW1P 1SD, is a political lobbying group that publishes a quarterly newsletter on the Falklands with much useful information.

Dangers & Annoyances

Near Stanley and in a few camp locations on both East and West Falkland, there remain unexploded plastic land mines, but mine fields are clearly marked and, in the 10 years since the Falklands War, no civilian has been injured. *Never* even consider entering one of these fields – the mines will bear the weight of a penguin or even a sheep, but not of a human. Report any suspicious object to the Explosive Ordinance Disposal (EOD, ☎ 22229) opposite the Stanley police station, which distributes free mine field maps (which, incidentally, are handy for walks in the Stanley area).

Trekking in camp is safe for anyone with confidence in his or her abilities, but it's better not to trek alone. The camp is so thinly populated that the consequences of an accident, however unlikely, could be very serious. Walkers in camp should be aware that so-called soft camp, covered by white grass, is boggy despite its firm appearance. There is no quicksand, but step carefully.

Cultural Events & Holidays

No visitor should miss the annual summer sports meetings, which consist of horse racing, bull riding and similar competitions. These take place in Stanley between Christmas and New Year's, and on West Falkland at the end of the shearing season, usually in late February. The West Falkland sports rotate yearly among the settlements.

The sports meetings have been a tradition since the advent of sheep farming in the 19th century. In a land where most people lived a very isolated existence, they provided a regular opportunity to get together and share news, meet new people and participate in friendly competitions such as horse racing, bull riding and sheepdog trials.

The rotating camp sports meeting on West Falkland carries on this tradition best, hosting 'two-nighters,' during which Islanders party till they drop, go to sleep for a few hours, and get up and start all over again. Independent visitors should not feel shy about showing up at one of these events, although it is best to arrange for accommodations in advance – this will usually mean floor space for your sleeping bag.

Accommodations

Accommodations are limited and improvised in some areas, but are still reasonably good everywhere. Stanley has several B&Bs and two hotels. Several farms have converted surplus buildings into lodges, some very comfortable, to accommodate tourists, but there are also self-catering cottages. A few have caravans or surplus Portakabin shelters obtained from the British military. These shelters are modular shell units similar to cargo containers but with doors and windows. They can be outfitted with beds or more elaborate furnishings, and sometimes plumbing and electricity.

In areas not frequented by tourists, Islanders often welcome houseguests; in addition, many farms have 'outside houses' or shanties that visitors may use with permission. Some outside houses, traditionally used by shepherds on distant parts of a farm, are very comfortable if a bit old, while others are very run-down. Camping is possible only with permission.

Getting Around

Transportation outside the Stanley/Mt Pleasant area is not cheap, since roads are few and the only regular public transportation is the Falkland Islands Government Air Service (FIGAS), an on-demand service that flies 10-passenger Norman-Britten Islander aircraft to grass airstrips throughout the Islands. The approximate charges of £1 per minute would make the fare to Carcass Island, off West Falkland, about £145 roundtrip. The baggage limitation of 13.5 kg per passenger is strictly enforced for safety reasons.

Rental vehicles are available in Stanley, while lodges at Pebble Island, Sea Lion Island, Port Howard, and San Carlos have comfortable County Land Rovers available with drivers/guides for guests. Visitors may use their own state or national driver's licenses in the Falklands for up to 12 months.

EAST FALKLAND

East Falkland has the Islands' most extensive road network, consisting of a good highway to Mt Pleasant international airport and Goose Green. From Pony's Pass on the Mt Pleasant Hwy, there is also a good track north to the Estancia (a farm west of Stanley) and Port Louis, and also one west toward Douglas and Port San Carlos. There's also a Rover track from Darwin north toward San Carlos (which is different from Port San Carlos). Most other tracks are usable for 4WDs only, so FIGAS is still the quickest and most reliable means of transport.

Salvador

Originally founded by Andrés Pitaluga, a Gibraltarian who arrived in the Islands via South America in the 1830s, Salvador is one of East Falkland's oldest owner-occupied sheep farms. On the station's north coast are colonies of five different species of penguins and other shorebirds

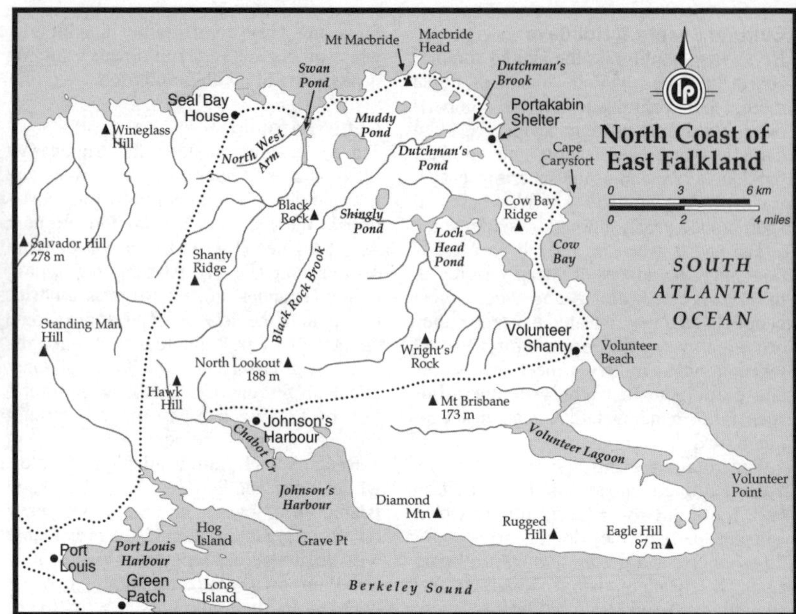

and waterfowl, while Centre Island in Port Salvador (also known as Salvador Water) has breeding populations of elephant seals and sea lions. Trekking along the north coast is possible with permission.

Owner Rob Pitaluga of *Salvador Lodge* (☎ 31199) offers self-catering accommodations (they provide the bedding, you provide and cook your own food) for £10 per person per night, £5 for children under 12.

Trekking the Northeast Coast

If you can do only one trek in the islands, this is the one. From Seal Bay to Volunteer Point on the north coast of East Falkland, a mixture of broad, sandy beaches and rugged headlands, a trekker always has penguins in view.

Port Louis to Seal Bay Port Louis is the starting point, reached by car – ask around town for a vehicle – or on foot from Stanley in one very long day. You will need permission from station manager Michael Morrison at Port Louis (☎ 31004) and owner George Smith of Johnson's Harbour (☎ 31399).

Port Louis is the Falklands' oldest settlement, dating from the French foundation of the colony by Louis de Bougainville in 1764. One of the oldest buildings in the colony is the ivy-covered 19th-century farmhouse, still occupied by farm employees, but there are also ruins of the French governor's house and fortress and Louis Vernet's settlement scattered nearby. Visit the grave of Matthew Brisbane, Vernet's lieutenant, who was murdered by gauchos after British naval officer JJ Onslow left him in charge of the settlement in early 1833.

From Port Louis, Seal Bay is a six- to eight-hour walk, depending on weather – with luck, the wind will be at your back. A Land Rover track follows a fence line almost all the way; be sure to close gates whenever you pass through them. Since much of the hiking is through soft white grass camp, choose your route to avoid sinking in.

Ask Michael Morrison's permission to stay or camp at Seal Bay House, which has a peat-burning Rayburn stove, before beginning the hike along the coast proper. Here, in the solitude of the north coast, you can get an idea of what it was to be a shepherd in the 19th century.

Seal Bay to Dutchman's Brook After leaving Seal Bay House, carry as much fresh water as possible, since penguins have fouled most of the watercourses along the way. Follow the arc of the coast eastward, past several colonies of rockhopper penguins and king cormorants, to the sea lion colony at Macbride Head. En route, there are also thousands of burrows of Magellanic penguins and occasional macaronis and gentoos.

Although the 1:250,000 map of East Falkland indicates a large inlet at Swan Pond, there is a broad, sandy beach there that only requires wading one shallow creek. The best campsite is Dutchman's Brook, where there is a Portakabin shelter but no dependable source of fresh water.

Dutchman's Brook to Volunteer Shanty About 1½ hours south of Dutchman's Brook, in a patch of white grass along a fence line near a colony of gentoo penguins, a tiny spring is the only likely source of fresh water until Volunteer Shanty, another four hours south. On the way, you will see many more penguins, elephant seals, nesting turkey vultures, upland and kelp geese, and many other birds. Volunteer Shanty is in fact a well-maintained outside house, but George Smith no longer permits non-farm personnel to use it. You can, however, camp nearby, collect fresh water from the tap, and use its very tidy outhouse.

Volunteer Shanty to Johnson's Harbour Volunteer Beach has the largest concentration of the photogenic king penguins in the Falklands, where the species is at the northern limit of its range. This colony has grown steadily over the past two decades and now contains about 150 breeding pairs. At Volunteer Point, several hours' walk from the shanty, an offshore breeding colony of southern fur seals is visible through binoculars. Return along Volunteer Lagoon to see more birds and elephant seals.

From Volunteer Beach, the settlement at Johnson's Harbour is an easy four- to five-hour walk along Mt Brisbane. If you are trekking back to Stanley, the small store at Johnson's Harbour may provide some supplies. FIGAS now stops at Johnson's Harbour only for emergencies.

AD (Tony) Smith (☎ 21027) runs full-day excursions to Volunteer Beach from Stanley, as does Mel Lloyd's Falcon Tours (☎ 32220). Mike Rendell at Malvina House Hotel (☎ 21084), 8 Ross Rd West in Stanley, arranges overnight excursions for a maximum of five people.

OCEAN & ISLANDS

San Carlos

British forces in the 1982 conflict first came ashore at San Carlos settlement, at the south end of San Carlos Water on the Falkland Sound side of East Falkland; there is a small military cemetery nearby. Until 1983, when it was subdivided and sold to half a dozen local families, San Carlos was a traditional large sheep station – the isolated 'big house,' with its lengthy approach, will give you some idea how farm owners and managers distanced themselves from laborers.

There is fishing on the San Carlos River, north of the settlement, while the comfortable *Blue Beach Lodge*, operated by William and Lynda Anderson, charges £49 for full board, with discounts for children. Self-catering accommodations are available at Robin and Mandy Goodwin's *Waimea Fishing Lodge* (☎ 32220) for £15 per person.

Across San Carlos Water, on Ajax Bay, are the fascinating ruins of the **Ajax Bay Refrigeration Plant,** a Colonial Development Corporation (CDC) boondoggle of the 1950s that failed when farmers did not provide it with sufficient high-quality mutton from flocks raised primarily for wool. After its abandonment, prefab houses that were imported for laborers were

Aurora Australis

Mysterious, beautiful, wonderful – colored profusion in visual chaos – ribbons of light snake across the night sky – batteries of celestial searchlights zero in on the magnetic zenith, waltzing to the music of the celestial spheres, forming an ever-changing crown in the heavens. Successive bands of increased light intensity move upwards, highlighting the display and flaming heavenwards – patches of light pulsate rhythmically; in another region of the night sky, other patches of light pulsate, out of phase – such is the aurora australis or southern lights at the height of a display.

FR Bond, 'Background to Aurora Australis'

The aurora is the collective name given to photons (light) emitted by atoms, molecules and ions that have been excited by energetic charged particles (principally electrons) traveling along magnetic field lines into the Earth's upper atmosphere. The aurora results from the interaction of the solar wind with the Earth's magnetic field.

The colors in the aurora result from photons of specific energy level transitions in the excited atoms, molecules and ions of the upper atmosphere returning to their lowest energy state. There are hundreds of individual colors in an auroral display, but three are dominant in the visible spectrum. The brightest auroral line is generally a green line emitted by excited oxygen atoms. A red diffuse glow results from another oxygen atom transition. A purple color results from a transition in a nitrogen molecular ion. The mixture of the major green, red and purple emissions may combine to give an aurora a general whitish appearance.

Most commonly, auroral glows form a band aligned in a magnetic east-west direction. If sufficient numbers of energetic electrons are impacting the upper atmosphere, bands may have shimmering rays extending upwards from them. These rays define magnetic field lines along which the auroral electrons travel into the atmosphere. The twisting of auroral rays and bands results from dynamic interaction of electric currents and magnetic fields in the upper atmosphere.

In active displays, multiple bands may be visible. These may break into small arcs. If

dismantled and moved to Stanley, where they can be seen on Ross Rd West. Gentoo penguins occasionally wander through the ruins, which served as a military field hospital during the 1982 conflict. Take a flashlight if you plan to explore the ruins, which are about a four-hour walk around the south end of San Carlos Water.

Darwin & Goose Green

Darwin, at the narrow isthmus that separates the southern peninsula of Lafonia from the northern half of East Falkland, was the site of Samuel Lafone's saladero, where the Montevideo merchant's local agents slaughtered feral cattle and processed their hides; later it became the center of the Falkland Islands Company's camp operations and, with nearby Goose Green, the largest settlement in the Falklands outside Stanley.

Built across Bodie Creek in 1926 to improve communications between Goose Green and Darwin, the world's southernmost suspension bridge is an unexpected sight. The heaviest ground fighting of the Falklands war took place at Goose Green, where there are several military landmarks, including an Argentine military cemetery and a memorial to British Col H Jones.

Sea Lion Island

The most southerly inhabited island in the Falklands is little more than a kilometer across at its widest point, but still has more wildlife in a smaller area than almost

rapid horizontal motion of the auroral form is apparent, the form may appear more purplish on its leading edge and greenish on its trailing edge. This results from a small delay (less than a second) between the peak intensity of the nitrogen molecular ion emission and the green oxygen atom emission. The active phase of an auroral display will last on the order of 15 to 40 minutes and may recur in two to three hours. Auroral band features may persist much longer. A red dominated auroral glow will be very diffuse. It will fluctuate slowly in location and intensity (on time scales of half a minute or so). This results from a significant time delay in the emission of light by the atomic oxygen state, which smooths out any rapid variation in which the auroral electrons are impacting on the atmosphere.

If an auroral band has an easily discernible lower border, this will generally be at around 100 to 110 km in altitude. Auroral rays may extend above the lower border for hundreds of kilometers. If the lower border has a pinkish edge (resulting from an emission of molecular nitrogen), the altitude may be around 90 to 100 km. A diffuse red aurora occurs above 250 km.

During an active auroral display, the intensity variations will be rapid and spectacular. A most dramatic variation is an increase in brightness moving up the auroral display. Faster electrons reach the atmosphere first and deposit their energy low in the atmosphere. These are followed by lower energy electrons, which are stopped at progressively higher altitudes giving an enhanced brightness moving upwards from the lower border. These variations may occur in rapid succession.

The global distribution of auroral activity is an oval around the magnetic poles in both hemispheres. As the level of magnetic disturbance of the Earth's magnetic field increases, the oval of auroral activity expands equatorward. The auroral oval in the Southern Hemisphere, the aurora australis, is linked by means of magnetic field lines to the auroral oval in the Northern Hemisphere, the aurora borealis. ■

–**Dr Gary Burns,** Senior Research Scientist with the Australian Antarctic Division, & **Dr Ray Morris**, Program Manager of the Atmospheric and Space Physics group at the Australian Antarctic Division

anywhere in the Islands, including all five species of Falklands penguins, enormous colonies of cormorants, giant petrels and the remarkably tame and charming predator known locally as the 'Johnny Rook,' more properly the striated caracara *(Phalcoboenus australis)*. Hundreds of elephant seals haul up to breed on its sandy beaches every spring, while sea lions line the narrow gravel beaches below the southern bluffs and lurk among the towering tussock grass.

For most of its history, Sea Lion's isolation and difficult access undoubtedly contributed to the continuing abundance of wildlife, but much of the credit has to go to Terry and Doreen Clifton, who farmed Sea Lion Island since the mid-1970s before selling it in the early 1990s – the Cliftons developed their 930-hectare farm with the idea that wildlife, habitat and livestock were compatible uses. Sea Lion Island is one of few working farms in the Falklands with any substantial cover of native tussock, which once covered the coastal fringe of both East and West Falkland and many offshore islands before careless fires and overgrazing nearly eliminated it.

Through improved fencing and other conscientious management decisions, the Cliftons made the island both a successful sheep station and a popular tourist site, mostly for day trips from Stanley and the military base at Mt Pleasant. Since 1986 the modern *Sea Lion Lodge* (☎ 32004), operated by Dave and Pat Grey, has offered twin-bedded rooms with full board for £51 per person, including access to a County Land Rover for visiting wildlife sites, although almost anyone can walk the length of the island in a few hours. To see the island in its entirety, allow at least two full days.

WEST FALKLAND

Nearly as large as East Falkland, West Falkland's only proper road runs from Port Howard on Falkland Sound to Chartres on King George Bay, but a system of rough tracks is also suitable for Land Rovers and motorcycles. Although offshore Saunders Island was the site of the first British garrison in 1765, West Falkland was settled permanently only in the late 1860s, when pioneer sheep farmer JL Waldron founded Port Howard. In short order, British entrepreneurs established stations at Hill Cove, Fox Bay, Port Stephens, Roy Cove, Chartres and many smaller offshore islands. One of the most interesting experiments was the founding of a mission for Indians from Tierra del Fuego on Keppel Island.

West Falkland, as well as adjacent offshore islands, has outstanding wildlife sites and good trekking in its interior, which is generally more mountainous than East Falkland. Only a few of these sites have formal tourist infrastructure, but independent travelers should look into visiting all parts of the island. Ask local farm owners for permission to walk across their properties.

Port Howard

West Falkland's oldest farm is one of very few large sheep stations to survive the major agrarian reform of the past decade. For more than a century it belonged to JL Waldron Ltd, but in 1987 it was sold to local managers Robin and Rodney Lee, who have kept the farm and settlement intact rather than subdividing it. About 40 people live on the 81,000-hectare station, which has 42,000 sheep, 800 cattle and its own dairy, grocery, abattoir, social club and other amenities. Unusual for the Falklands, employees have been given the opportunity to purchase their houses, and at least one has chosen to retire here rather than move to Stanley. Port Howard will be the West Falkland terminus of the anticipated ferry across Falkland Sound.

Port Howard is a very scenic settlement at the foot of 647m Mt Maria, at the north end of the Hornby range. Although there is wildlife, most of it is distant from the settlement, the immediate surroundings of which offer opportunities for hiking, horseback riding and fishing. It is also possible to view summer shearing and other camp activities, and there is a small museum of artifacts from the 1982 war, when Argentine forces occupied the settlement.

Port Howard Lodge (☎ 42150) is the former manager's house, a classic of its era with a beautiful conservatory that feels like the tropics when the sun comes out – see also the antique West Falkland telephone exchange, which no longer functions. Accommodations cost £48 per person with full board, but make arrangements in advance to lodge at the farm's cookhouse for a fraction of the cost.

From Port Howard it is possible to hike up the valley of the Warrah River, a good trout stream, and past the Turkey Rocks to the Blackburn River and Hill Cove settlement, another pioneer 19th-century farm. Where the track is unclear, look for the remains of the old telephone lines. Ask permission to cross property boundaries, and remember to close gates. There are other, longer hikes south toward Chartres, Fox Bay and Port Stephens.

Pebble Island

Elongated Pebble, off the north coast of West Falkland, has varied topography, a good sampling of wildlife and extensive wetlands. *Pebble Island Hotel* (☎ 41093) charges £48 per person for room with full board, but ask about self-catering cottages at the settlement and *Marble Mountain Shanty* at the west end of the island, both of which charge £15 per night.

Keppel Island

In 1853, the South American Missionary Society established an outpost on Keppel Island to catechize Yahgan Indians from Tierra del Fuego and teach them to become potato farmers instead of hunters and gatherers. The mission was controversial because the government suspected that Indians had been brought against their will, but it lasted until 1898, despite the Indians' susceptibility to disease – contrast the unmarked but discernable Yahgan graves with the marked ones of the mission personnel. One Falklands governor attributed numerous Yahgan deaths from tuberculosis to their

> delicacy of constitution . . . developed owing to the warm clothing which they are for the sake of decency required to adopt after having been for 15 or 20 years roaming about in their canoes in a very cold climate without clothing of any kind.

It's likely that hard physical labor, change of diet, European-introduced diseases and harsh living conditions in their small, damp stone houses played a greater role in the Yahgans' demise than any inherent delicacy of constitution. The mission was undoubtedly prosperous, though, bringing in an annual income of nearly £1,000 from its herds of cattle, flocks of sheep and gardens by 1877.

Although Keppel is now exclusively a sheep farm, there remain several interesting ruins. The former chapel is now a wool shed, while the stone walls of the Yahgan dwellings remain in fairly good condition. The mission bailiff's house stands intact, though in poor repair. Keppel is also a good place to see penguins. Visitors interested in exploring the island should contact LR Fell (☎ 41001), the owner of Keppel.

Saunders Island

Only a few kilometers west of Keppel, Port Egmont on Saunders Island was the site of the first British garrison on the Falklands, built in 1765. In 1767, after France ceded its colony to Spain, Spanish forces dislodged the British from Saunders and nearly precipitated a general war between the two countries. After the British left voluntarily in 1774, the Spaniards razed the settlement, including its impressive blockhouse, leaving the still remaining jetties, extensive foundations and some of the buildings' walls, plus the garden terraces built by the British marines. One British sailor left a memoir indicating how well developed the settlement was:

> The glory of our colony was the gardens, which we cultivated with the greatest care, as being fully convinced how much the comforts of our situation depended on our being supplied with vegetables . . . We were plentifully supplied with potatoes, cabbages, broccoli, carrots, borecole, spinach, parsley, lettuce, English celery, mustard, cresses and some few, but very fine cauliflowers.

Saunders Island continued to be controversial into the late 1980s because the property was passed by inheritance into the hands of Argentine descendants of the Scottish pioneer sheep farmer John Hamilton, who also had extensive properties near Río Gallegos in Santa Cruz province. For years, Islanders agitated for the farm's expropriation, but the owners finally consented to sell the Island to its local managers in 1987.

In addition to historical resources, Saunders Island has an excellent sample of Falklands wildlife and offers good trekking, especially out the north side of Brett Harbour to The Neck. About four hours' walk from the settlement, this sand-pit beach connects Saunders Island to Elephant Point peninsula, once a separate island. The Neck has a Portakabin shelter near a large colony of black-browed albatrosses and rockhopper penguins, as well as a few king penguins. Farther on, toward Elephant Point proper, are thousands of Magellanic penguins, breeding kelp gulls, skuas and a colony of elephant seals in a very scenic area. From The Neck, Elephant Point is about a four-hour walk one way.

David and Suzan Pole-Evans on Saunders (☎ 41298) rent a comfortable self-catering cottage in the settlement for £10 per person per night, as well as the Portakabin at The Neck, which sleeps six (bedding supplied) and has a gas stove and a chemical toilet outside. Fresh milk and eggs are usually available in the settlement, but otherwise visitors should bring their own food. Depending on the farm workload, transportation to The Neck is available for £10 per person.

Carcass Island

Despite its name, Carcass is a small, scenic island west of Saunders with a good variety of wildlife. It is a popular weekend and holiday vacation spot for Stanleyites. A couple of self-catering cottages in the settlement rent for £15/25 single/double, plus £5 per additional person; for details, contact Rob McGill on Carcass Island (☎ 41106).

Port Stephens

Unquestionably the most scenic part of the Falklands, Port Stephens' rugged headlands are open to the blustery South Atlantic and are battered by storms out of the Antarctic. Thousands upon thousands of rockhopper penguins, cormorants and other seabirds breed on the exposed coast, only a short distance from the settlement's sheltered harbor, until recently the center of one of the FIC's largest stations. Like many other settlements, Port Stephens has no formal tourist facilities, but it is well worth a visit.

Less than an hour's walk from the settlement, Wood Cove and Stephens Peak are excellent places to see gentoo and rockhopper penguins and other local birds. The peak of Calm Head, about a two hours' walk, has excellent views of the jagged shoreline and the powerful open South Atlantic.

One interesting longer trek goes from the settlement to the abandoned sealing station at Port Albemarle and huge gentoo penguin colonies near the Arch Islands. Hoste Inlet, where there is a habitable outside house, is about a five-hour walk in good weather, while the sealing station, another post-WWII Colonial Development Corporation blunder, is four hours farther. Like the Ajax Bay freezer, the sealing station is a monument to bureaucratic ineptitude, but photographers and aficionados of industrial archaeology will find its derelict power station, boilers, rail track, water tanks, jetty and Nissen huts surrealistically intriguing. There is a habitable shanty with a functional Rayburn stove nearby, but unfortunately squaddies from the radar station on Mt Alice have vandalized the larger outside house.

The massive penguin colonies are an hour's walk beyond the sealing station. The Arch Islands, inaccessible except by boat, take their name from the opening that the ocean has eroded in the largest of the group – and it is large enough to allow a good-sized vessel to pass through it.

Visitors interested in exploring Port Stephens and trekking in the vicinity should contact Peter or Anne Robertson (☎ 42307) at the settlement, or Leon and Pam Berntsen (☎ 42309) at Albemarle Station.

Weddell Island

Scottish pioneer John Hamilton, also a major landholder in Argentine Patagonia, acquired this western offshore island and others nearby to experiment on various agricultural improvement projects, including the replanting of tussock grass, forest plantations, the importation of Highland cattle and Shetland ponies, and the well-meaning but perhaps misguided introduction of exotic wildlife like guanacos (still present on Staats Island), Patagonian foxes (common on Weddell proper) and otters (apparently extinct). Saunders still hosts abundant local wildlife, including gentoo and Magellanic penguins, great skuas, night herons, giant petrels and striated caracaras.

Unfortunately, Hamilton's original farmhouse, which had spectacular interior woodwork, burned to the ground a few years ago, but farm owners John and Steph Ferguson (☎ 42398) still welcome guests at *Seaview Cottage* or *Hamilton Cottage* for £15 per person per night (self-catering) or £30 per person per night with full board.

New Island

The Falklands' most westerly inhabited island is almost inaccessible (unless the new grass airstrip has been finished), but it has great historic interest, having been a refuge for whalers from Britain and North America from the late 18th century well into the 19th, despite the objections of Spanish and British authorities. There remain ruins of a shore-based, turn-of-the-century Norwegian whaling factory that failed because there simply were not enough whales.

On the precipitous western coast are gigantic colonies of rockhopper penguins and black-browed albatrosses and a large rookery of southern fur seals. Facilities are few, but potential visitors should contact Tony or Annie Chater (☎ 21399), or Ian or María Strange (☎ 21185) in Stanley.

Antarctic Peninsula & Weddell Sea

With its hundreds of tiny offshore islands, the Antarctic Peninsula is one of the richest breeding grounds for seabirds, seals and penguins. During the 19th century, it was extensively explored, not just by scientific expeditions but, in fact, primarily by sealers from the US, Britain, the Cape Colony, New South Wales and New Zealand. The following sites – which include the main stopovers on most tourist cruises to the Antarctic Peninsula – are listed in order from north to south.

JOINVILLE ISLAND

The largest of the three islands at the tip of the Antarctic Peninsula, Joinville was discovered in 1838 by French explorer Jules-Sebastien-César Dumont d'Urville. He named it for a French nobleman, François Ferdinand Phillipe Louis Marie, Prince de Joinville, the third son of the Duc d'Orléans.

Joinville Island's northerly neighbor, **D'Urville Island**, was charted by Swedish explorer Otto Nordenskjöld in 1902 and named for his predecessor, Dumont d'Urville.

DUNDEE ISLAND

Immediately south of Joinville Island is Dundee Island, where the millionaire American aviator Lincoln Ellsworth took off on the first trans-Antarctic flight on November 22, 1935. With his quiet, pipe-smoking co-pilot, Herbert Hollick-Kenyon, Ellsworth flew – in five hops over a two-week period – across the continent to the Bay of Whales on the Ross Ice Shelf.

Dundee Island was discovered in 1893 by British whaling captain Thomas Robertson, who named it for his home port of Dundee, Scotland.

PAULET ISLAND

This circular volcanic island almost two km in diameter, which lies five km south-east of Dundee Island, is one of the most-visited sites in all of Antarctica. Hundreds of thousands of Adélie penguins breed here, and the huge number of these small birds on their nests is indeed a sight (and smell!). Paulet was discovered by Briton James Clark Ross' expedition of 1839-43 and named for the Right Honorable Lord George Paulet, a captain in the Royal Navy.

On February 12, 1903, Swedish explorer Otto Nordenskjöld's ship *Antarctic*, which had been crushed by the Weddell Sea pack ice for weeks, finally sank 40 km east of Paulet, and the men sledged for 14 days to reach it. Later, the island's Adélies provided meat and thousands of eggs for food.

HOPE BAY

Hope Bay, on the tip of the Antarctic Peninsula, is home to the largest colony of Adélie penguins in the world. Thousands of them breed here every year.

Hope Bay is also where three members of Nordenskjöld's ill-fated Swedish Antarctic expedition were forced to spend a desperate winter in 1903, surviving mainly on a diet of seal meat. Nordenskjöld named the bay after these three men. The Argentines at Esperanza station rebuilt the Swedish trio's rude stone hut in 1966-67, and its ruins can be seen here today.

Esperanza

Built by Argentina in 1952, Esperanza can accommodate 42 winterers and more than 50 people during the summer.

Argentina has frequently sent women and children to its Esperanza station at Hope Bay as part of its efforts to establish 'sovereignty' over the territory, which it claims as its own despite rival claims by the British and the Chileans. One of these women, Silvia Morello de Palma, was married to Army Captain Jorge de Palma, Esperanza's station leader, and on January 7, 1978, she

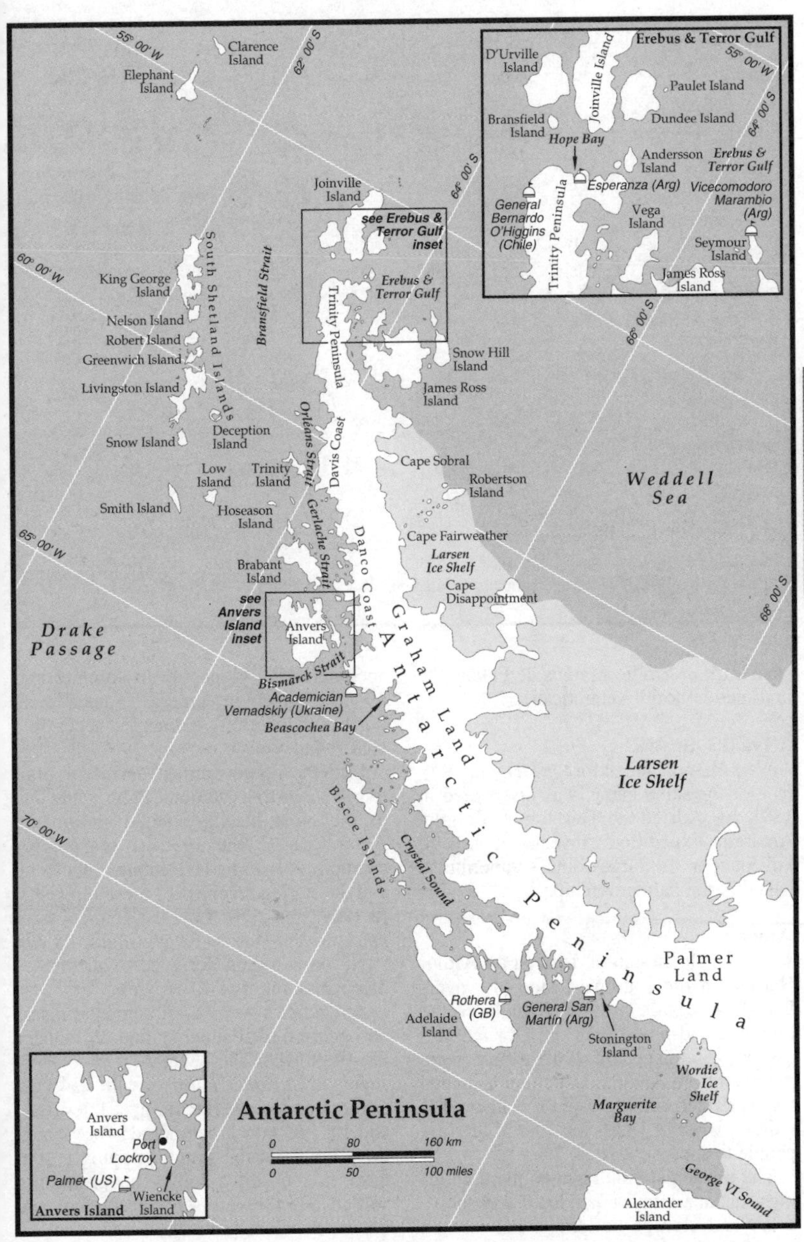
Antarctic Peninsula
Erebus & Terror Gulf
D'Urville Island
Joinville Island
Paulet Island
Bransfield Island
Dundee Island
Hope Bay
Andersson Island
Erebus & Terror Gulf
Esperanza (Arg)
Vicecomodoro Marambio (Arg)
General Bernardo O'Higgins (Chile)
Trinity Peninsula
Vega Island
Seymour Island
James Ross Island
55° 00' W
64° 00' S
Clarence Island
Elephant Island
62° 00' S
Joinville Island
see Erebus & Terror Gulf inset
Erebus & Terror Gulf
South Shetland Islands
Bransfield Strait
King George Island
Nelson Island
Robert Island
Greenwich Island
Livingston Island
Deception Island
Snow Island
Low Island
Trinity Island
Smith Island
Hoseason Island
Brabant Island
Trinity Peninsula
Snow Hill Island
James Ross Island
Orléans Strait
Davis Coast
Gerlache Strait
Danco Coast
Cape Sobral
Robertson Island
Cape Fairweather
Larsen Ice Shelf
Cape Disappointment
Weddell Sea
66° 00' S
68° 00' S
60° 00' W
65° 00' W
70° 00' W
Drake Passage
see Anvers Island inset
Anvers Island
Bismarck Strait
Academician Vernadskiy (Ukraine)
Beascochea Bay
Graham Land
Antarctic Peninsula
Larsen Ice Shelf
Biscoe Islands
Crystal Sound
Palmer Land
Rothera (GB)
General San Martín (Arg)
Adelaide Island
Stonington Island
Wordie Ice Shelf
Marguerite Bay
George VI Sound
Alexander Island
Anvers Island
Port Lockroy
Palmer (US)
Wiencke Island
0 80 160 km
0 50 100 miles
PENINSULA

Top Ten Most Visited Sites in the Antarctic Peninsula Region 1989-1996

Location	1989-90	1990-91	1991-92	1992-93	1993-94	1994-95	1995-96	total
Whalers Bay, Deception Island	1682*	1496	2899	1711	3480	5241*	5033	21,542*
Half Moon Island	1191	1011	2984*	1585	2961	3017	5221*	17,970
Port Lockroy, Wiencke Island	796	1067	2615	2139*	4274*	1769	3851	16,511
Cuverville Island	883	936	2565	1589	2174	3367	4343	15,857
Pendulum Cove, Deception Island	587	1215	2011	1936	3159	2803	3492	15,203
Petermann Island	761	1084	1376	1376	2828	3406	3504	14,335
Argentina's Almirante Brown Station, Paradise Harbor	1191	1471	2899	1659	3513	1307	2244	14,284
Chile's Gonzalez Videla Station, Paradise Harbor	1038	1965*	2398	1671	3248	1559	2384	14,263
Hannah Point, Livingston Island	419	192	1632	1542	2740	4010	3048	13,583
Poland's Arctowski Station, King George Island	930	601	1509	598	3031	2445	1724	11,838

* Antarctica's most visited tourist site in that season
Source: Office of Polar Programs, US National Science Foundation

gave birth to Emilio Marcos de Palma, the first 'native-born' Antarctican.

ANVERS ISLAND

Anvers Island, named for the Belgian province of the same name, was discovered in 1898 by Adrien de Gerlache's Belgian Antarctic Expedition. Anvers, which is 70 km long, is the largest and southernmost island in the Palmer Archipelago.

Palmer

The US Palmer station, located on Arthur Harbor on the southwest side of Anvers Island, was built in 1968. It replaced the prefabricated wood huts of 'Old Palmer' station, established in 1965, which were removed from Antarctica. Palmer is named for American sealing captain Nathaniel B Palmer, who, in 1820, was one of the first people to spot Antarctica.

The present station has two main buildings, an aquarium, a boathouse, workshops, a lab and storage buildings. Palmer can accommodate 44 people in summer and about a dozen in winter. Thanks to its northerly location, Palmer is accessible year round.

Until the US government decided to limit tourist visits to its stations, Palmer was one of the most heavily visited stations in Antarctica. In the 1990-91 season, for example, Palmer had 60 summer members, and the station received 12 tour-ship visits. In 1969, about 70 American tourists were marooned at Palmer for the night – a real strain on a station designed to accommodate a maximum of 40 people!

Antarctica's worst environmental disaster occurred off Palmer station on January 28, 1989, when the 131m Argentine Navy supply ship *Bahía Paraíso*, with 234 passengers and crew (including 81 tourists) aboard, ran into a submerged rock about three km from the station, ripping a 10m gash in the ship's hull. The grounding spilled 645,000 liters of diesel fuel and other petroleum products, creating an oil slick that covered a 27 sq km area. Although no one was injured and two other nearby cruise ships picked up the passengers, the oil spill heavily damaged the marine environment. It also disrupted or destroyed research that in some cases went back for two decades.

WIENCKE ISLAND

Wiencke Island was named by Belgian explorer Adrien de Gerlache in 1897-99 for Auguste-Karl Wiencke, a young seaman who fell overboard and drowned while trying to clear *Belgica*'s clogged scuppers.

Port Lockroy

Port Lockroy is an 800m-long harbor on the western coast of Wiencke Island, discovered by Jean-Baptiste Charcot's *Français* expedition of 1903-05 and named for Edouard Lockroy, the vice president of France's Chamber of Deputies, who helped Charcot secure government funding for his expedition.

After the Argentine navy ship *Primero de Mayo* left a cylinder at Port Lockroy in 1943 claiming it and all territory between 25°W and 68°34'W, south of 60°S, the British government decided to take action to uphold its own rival claim to the territory. In 1943-44, in an operation code-named 'Tabarin' (after a bawdy Parisian nightclub), Britain removed the Argentine emblems and established its own permanent meteorological station ('Base A') at Port Lockroy. The base was staffed until 1962; the normal occupancy was four to nine people, comprising a meteorologist, ionosphericist, biologist, surveyor, mechanic, radio operator and handyman. The usual tour of duty in the Antarctic for most personnel was 2.5 years.

Port Lockroy's original station hut, Bransfield House, was beautifully restored by the United Kingdom branch of the Antarctic Heritage Trust in 1996. Visual displays of the station's history hang on the interior walls of Bransfield House, and it is planned for two AHT staff members to live at Port Lockroy during the austral summer to act as tour guides for visiting shore parties. These staff members will also run a small souvenir shop and post office.

Tourist vessels that wish to visit the station must seek permission from the British Antarctic Survey well in advance; unscheduled visits will not be accepted. Smoking is not permitted inside or within 10m of any building; no more than 10 people are allowed inside any building simultaneously; and collection of any artifact or natural history specimen is forbidden.

Port Lockroy is a popular stopover, with its gentoo penguins and blue-eyed shags. As a reminder of the whaling floating factories that operated here earlier this century, whalebones litter the rocky beach. Some have even been arranged into a rough skeleton, showing the animal's large size.

CUVERVILLE & RONGÉ ISLANDS

Cuverville Island, discovered by Belgian explorer Adrien de Gerlache in 1897-99, and named for JMA Cavalier de Cuverville, a vice-admiral in the French Navy, is a popular stopover often made in conjunction with Rongé Island, which de Gerlache named for Madame de Rongé, a wealthy contributor to the expedition. Cuverville and Rongé islands both have a large colony of gentoo penguins. The channel between the islands was recently the site of some unorthodox activities by the staff of one tour operator, who went water-skiing behind a Zodiac.

LEMAIRE CHANNEL

This narrow channel running between the mountains of Booth Island and the Peninsula is so photogenic that its nickname is 'Kodak Gap.' Steep cliffs line both sides of the Lemaire Channel, and it is only until you are nearly inside the passage that the way through can be seen. Unfortunately, ice sometimes blocks the path, so ships are forced to retreat and sail outside Booth Island. At the northern end of the Lemaire Channel are two tall, rounded and often snowcapped peaks, informally known as **Una's Tits**. They're quite picturesque.

The Lemaire Channel was discovered by

a German expedition in 1873-74, but it was not navigated for another 25 years, when Adrien de Gerlache's *Belgica* sailed through in December 1898. In a rather odd choice of commemoration, de Gerlache named the channel for the Belgian explorer Charles Lemaire, who explored parts of the Congo.

NEKO HARBOR

Neko Harbor was discovered by Adrien de Gerlache's Belgian Antarctic Expedition of 1897-99, but it takes its name from a Norwegian floating factory whaling ship, *Neko*, which operated in the area for many seasons in 1911-12 and 1923-24. Many passengers are especially glad to land at Neko Harbor, if only because it is on the Antarctic continent itself, and they can thus officially 'bag' the continent.

PARADISE HARBOR

Paradise Harbor (often incorrectly called Paradise Bay) is described in Antarctic tour brochures as 'the most aptly named place in the world.' While that may be overstating the case – many more people would probably consider 'paradise' to be a sun-drenched tropical island – the harbor, with its majestic icebergs and reflections of the surrounding mountains, is undeniably beautiful.

This is a favorite place for 'Zodiac cruising,' in which no landings are made and you simply motor around the sculpted pieces of floating ice that frequently calve from the glacier at the harbor's head.

Waterboat Point The Argentine station **Almirante Brown,** now abandoned, was destroyed by a fire on April 12, 1984, set by the station's physician/leader, who did not want to return home. Today, thanks to the station's proximity to Paradise Harbor, Almirante Brown is one of the most-visited sites in Antarctica. In 1921, two British researchers, TW Bagshawe and MC Lester, spent the winter here in a rough shelter partially constructed from an upturned whaler's water boat.

Icebergs

The Antarctic ice sheet is the iceberg 'factory' of the Southern Ocean. The total volume of ice calved from the ice sheet each year is about 2300 cubic km, and it has been estimated that there are about 300,000 icebergs in the Southern Ocean at any one time. Individual icebergs range in dimensions from a few meters (these are often called 'growlers') to tens of meters ('bergy bits') to kilometers.

From time to time, particularly large icebergs break off the Antarctic ice sheet. These can be tens of kilometers to even a hundred kilometers long. At any one time there might be four or five gigantic icebergs in excess of 50 km in length in the Southern Ocean, usually close to the Antarctic coast. It has been estimated that as much as 70% of the total volume of ice discharged from the Antarctic Ice Sheet is accounted for by the icebergs of greater than a kilometer in length.

These larger icebergs are tabular in shape and form by calving from the large Antarctic ice shelves (the Ross, Filchner or Amery ice shelves, for example). Typically, these icebergs are about 30 to 40m high (above sea level) and as much as 300m deep. After erosion from wind and waves, and melting from the warmer sea temperatures away from the Antarctic coast, the tabular icebergs become unstable and roll over to form jagged irregular icebergs, sometimes with spikes towering up to 60m into the air and with even greater protrusions deep under the ocean surface. Ultimately, icebergs melt completely as they drift to more northerly, warmer water. ■

–**Dr Jo Jacka,** glaciologist, Antarctic Cooperative Research Centre and the Australian Antarctic Division

PETERMANN ISLAND

Petermann Island, home to the southernmost gentoo penguin colony in the world, is another of the Antarctic's most-visited spots. Just under 2 km long, the island was discovered by a German expedition in 1873-74 and named for August Petermann, the noted German geographer. The French Antarctic Expedition of 1908-1910, led by Jean-Baptiste Charcot, wintered at Petermann Island.

BEASCOCHEA BAY

Discovered by the Belgian Antarctic Expedition of 1897-99, and more completely mapped by Jean-Baptiste Charcot's *Français* expedition of 1903-05, this bay is named for Commander Beascochea of the Argentine Navy.

CRYSTAL SOUND

This island-dotted sound was named by the British because many of the geographical features in the sound, including several islands, commemorate scientists who studied the structure of ice crystals.

STONINGTON ISLAND

Stonington Island, named for Stonington, CT, the home port of American sealing captain Nathaniel Brown Palmer's sloop *Hero*, was the site of East Base during Richard Byrd's third Antarctic expedition, the United States Antarctic Service Expedition of 1939-41. The US government recently funded a conservation program at East Base, and a small display of artifacts was set up in one of the base buildings. In 1945-46, the British government set up its 'Base E' here.

In 1947-48, a private American expedition, the Ronne Antarctic Research Expedition, occupied East Base. Included in the group were the first women to winter in Antarctica, Edith Ronne and Jennie Darlington, who accompanied their husbands. Unfortunately, their husbands quarreled, so out of loyalty, the women also did not speak to one another. It must have been a long year: Mrs Ronne later said she 'wouldn't have missed it for a million dollars, and wouldn't go back for two million.'

MARGUERITE BAY

Few Antarctic tour ships make it as far south as this extensive bay on the west side of the Antarctic Peninsula. Well below the Antarctic Circle, Marguerite Bay was discovered by Jean-Baptiste Charcot on his *Pourquoi Pas?* expedition in 1909 and named for his wife.

WEDDELL SEA

The Weddell Sea is one of the least-visited parts of Antarctica, since its extremely heavy pack ice rarely allows ships to penetrate to any great distance. The Weddell Sea's primary attractions are its emperor penguin rookeries and the Ronne and Filchner Ice Shelves.

British sealer James Weddell, sailing in the brig *Jane*, discovered the sea in February 1823 and named it 'King George IV Sea' for the British sovereign. German Antarctic historian Karl Fricker proposed the name Weddell Sea in 1900, and it has since become the accepted name.

Snow Hill Island

This descriptively named 395m-high island was discovered by James Clark Ross in 1843, who called it simply 'Snow Hill' because he was uncertain of its connection with the mainland. Otto Nordenskjöld, who set up a winter base here in February 1902, determined its insular nature.

Seymour Island

Seymour was discovered by James Clark Ross in 1843, who named it Cape Seymour after British Rear Admiral George Seymour. Norwegian whaling captain Carl Anton Larsen determined that Seymour was an island, not a cape, in 1892-93.

In December 1902, Swedish explorer Otto Nordenskjöld, who was wintering at Snow Hill Island directly to the south, made some striking fossil discoveries here, including the bones of a giant penguin, bolstering earlier fossil finds made by Capt Larsen on the island in 1893.

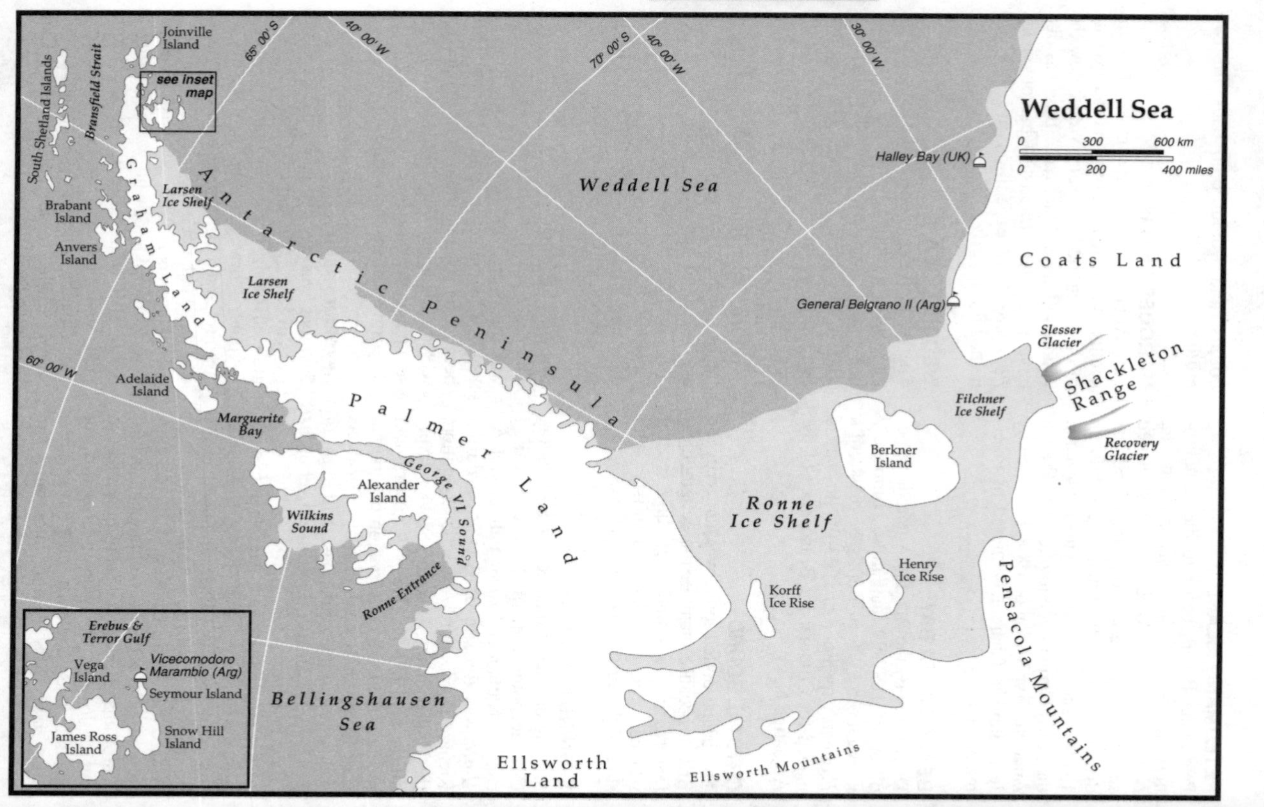
Weddell Sea
0 300 600 km
0 200 400 miles
Joinville Island
see inset map
65° 00' S
40° 00' W
70° 00' S
40° 00' W
30° 00' W
60° 00' W
South Shetland Islands
Bransfield Strait
Brabant Island
Anvers Island
Graham Land
Larsen Ice Shelf
Larsen Ice Shelf
Antarctic Peninsula
Weddell Sea
Halley Bay (UK)
Coats Land
General Belgrano II (Arg)
Slesser Glacier
Shackleton Range
Recovery Glacier
Filchner Ice Shelf
Berkner Island
Adelaide Island
Marguerite Bay
Palmer Land
George VI Sound
Alexander Island
Wilkins Sound
Ronne Entrance
Ronne Ice Shelf
Henry Ice Rise
Korff Ice Rise
Pensacola Mountains
Erebus & Terror Gulf
Vega Island
Vicecomodoro Marambio (Arg)
Seymour Island
James Ross Island
Snow Hill Island
Bellingshausen Sea
Ellsworth Land
Ellsworth Mountains

Argentina's **Vicecomodoro Marambio** station, built here in 1969-70, boasts one of only three functioning hard-rock airstrips in the Antarctic. The station accommodates 42 winterers and more than 100 people in summer.

Ronne Ice Shelf

This large ice shelf, together with its eastern neighbor, the Filchner Ice Shelf, forms the southern coast of the Weddell Sea. It was discovered by American naval commander Finn Ronne, leader of the private Ronne Antarctic Research Expedition (RARE) of 1947-48, and named for his wife, Edith, who had accompanied the expedition at the last minute and who spent a difficult year at the expedition's base on Stonington Island. Although there was one other woman on the expedition, Jennie Darlington, a disagreement between their husbands caused the women not to speak to one another for practically the whole time.

Filchner Ice Shelf

German explorer Wilhelm Filchner, who discovered this ice shelf in January 1912, named it after his emperor, Kaiser Wilhelm, who promptly decided that the honor should go to Filchner. Berkner Island separates the Filchner Ice Shelf from the Ronne Ice Shelf.

General Belgrano II Argentina's Belgrano II station was built in 1979 and can accommodate about 18 people year-round. The base's predecessor, General Belgrano station, was built as a meteorological center by the Argentine Army in 1954-55. In 1969-70, it became a scientific station. The original Belgrano station was abandoned in January 1980, having been nearly destroyed by the ice shelf's crushing pressure.

Halley Bay

This British station, built in 1956 on stilts over the Brunt Ice Shelf in the Weddell Sea, is where British scientists first measured the ozone depletion in the Antarctic stratosphere in 1985. Their discovery that this critical protection from ultraviolet radiation had been decreasing from 1975 to 1985 made headlines around the world and spurred the international agreement on banning chlorofluorocarbons (CFCs). Halley has been rebuilt four times (in 1966, 1972, 1982 and 1989) after sinking into the ice.

Ross Sea

Sometimes called the 'Gateway to Antarctica,' the Ross Sea was the path by which explorers of the Heroic Era penetrated the continent. James Clark Ross, for whom the sea is named, pushed through the Ross Sea pack ice, the first to reach the Ross Ice Shelf, in February 1842. Thanks to that often-heavy pack ice, the Ross Sea has been little-visited by tourists – despite its fascinating historic huts – until the last decade.

The first two tourist cruises to the Ross Sea, on the American-chartered Danish ship *Magga Dan* (also the first tour ship to cross the Antarctic Circle), were in 1968. Unfortunately, *Magga Dan* ran aground off Hut Point but was freed two days later with assistance from the US Coast Guard. *Lindblad Explorer* visited the Ross Sea in 1974, '79, '81 and '82, the only tourist vessel to do so during that period. By 1983, other ships began visiting the area on an infrequent basis, and in 1992 annual tourist cruises began, with two and sometimes three ships visiting in the same season. Even today, however, the Ross Sea gets nowhere near the traffic that the Antarctic Peninsula does.

What makes the Ross Sea special are its historic huts, the Dry Valleys, and the awe-inspiring Ross Ice Shelf. Nowhere else in Antarctica is there a richer historical heritage – and, if not for the fact that the Ross Ice Shelf periodically calves off great sections of itself as icebergs, there would be even more history for visitors to examine firsthand. Amundsen's base at Framheim in the Bay of Whales, plus all five of Richard E Byrd's Little America stations, covered over by drifting snows, have long since gone out to sea inside giant tabular icebergs.

Only by stepping inside the historic explorers' huts can you get a feel for what it must have been like on the early expeditions. In the B&W photos of the era, the men crowd around a table or pack together in groups of bunks. When you step inside, say, Scott's hut at Cape Evans, you suddenly realize: Those men did not crowd together so the photographer could get a good picture – this was how they lived every day. Another thing you notice is the often quite rough construction of the shelves and bunks inside. No one cared what happened to the huts beyond their expected two- or three-year lifespan, so they built them in a hurry, not bothering to square off corners or sand rough edges.

Today, the huts are all locked, and a representative of New Zealand's Antarctic Heritage Trust (see Useful Organizations in Facts for the Visitor), which maintains and conserves the huts, will monitor your visit. The AHT representatives are not policemen, however, but caretakers. They are also very good guides, thanks to their familiarity with the huts through restoration and conservation work, so they can point out things that visitors would otherwise miss. One good suggestion if the guides don't remember it themselves (though they probably will): Keep backpacks, life jackets, fire extinguishers and other gear at least 10m from all huts so they don't spoil your photos with their modern look.

David Harrowfield's handsome book *Icy Heritage: Historic Sites of the Ross Sea Region*, available from Antarctic Heritage Trust, is fascinating reading for any visitor to the Ross Sea. It gives the details of 34 sites and includes dozens of photographs, many of them in color and many published for the first time. The Trust representative on your ship will also distribute a collection of colored-paper brochures about each hut, a valuable source of information.

CAPE ADARE

This northernmost headland at the entrance to the Ross Sea was named for Viscount Adare, the Member of Parliament for Glamorganshire, by his friend British explorer James Clark Ross, who discovered

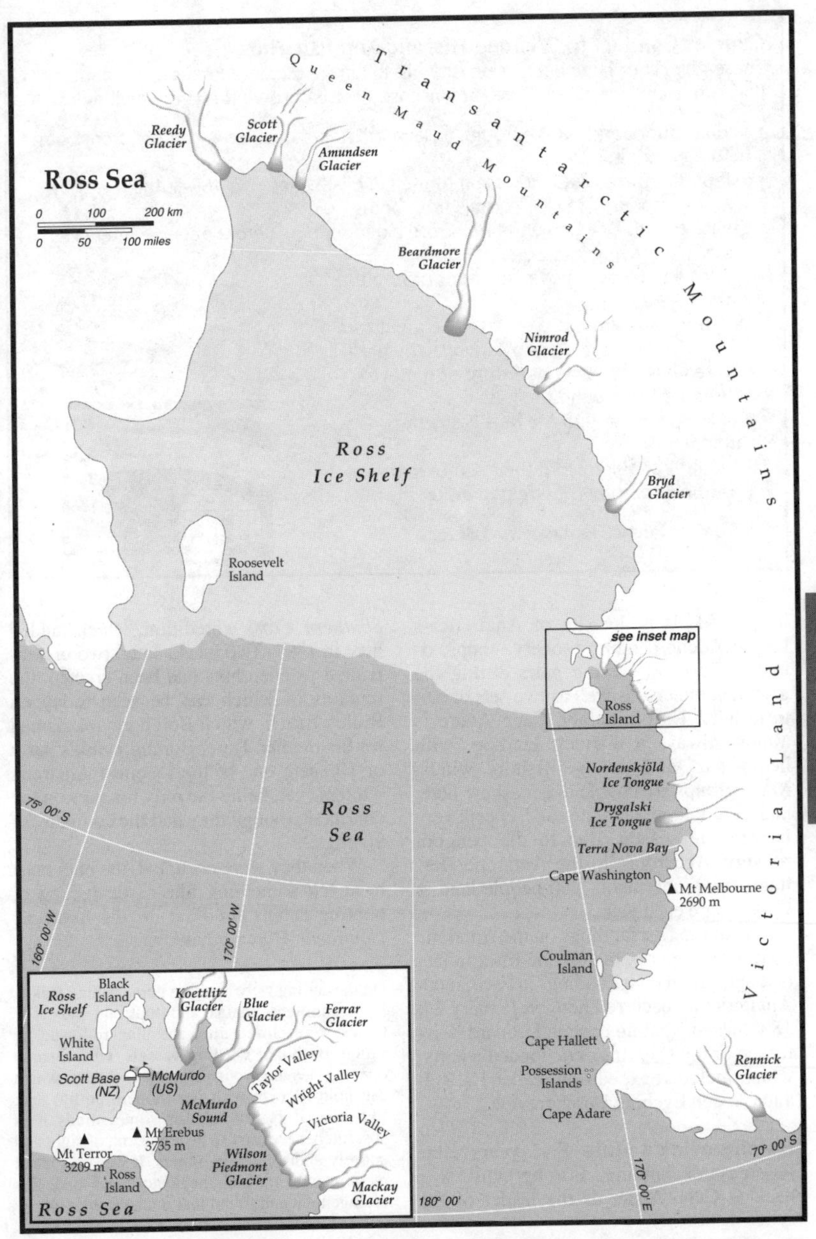
Ross Sea
0 100 200 km
0 50 100 miles
Transantarctic Mountains
Queen Maud Mountains
Reedy Glacier
Scott Glacier
Amundsen Glacier
Beardmore Glacier
Nimrod Glacier
Ross Ice Shelf
Bryd Glacier
Roosevelt Island
see inset map
Ross Island
Victoria Land
Nordenskjöld Ice Tongue
Drygalski Ice Tongue
Terra Nova Bay
Cape Washington
Mt Melbourne 2690 m
Ross Sea
75° 00' S
160° 00' W
170° 00' W
Coulman Island
Cape Hallett
Possession Islands
Cape Adare
Rennick Glacier
70° 00' S
170° 00' E
180° 00'
Ross Ice Shelf
Black Island
White Island
Koettlitz Glacier
Blue Glacier
Ferrar Glacier
Taylor Valley
Wright Valley
Victoria Valley
Scott Base (NZ)
McMurdo (US)
McMurdo Sound
Mt Erebus 3735 m
Mt Terror 3209 m
Ross Island
Wilson Piedmont Glacier
Mackay Glacier
Ross Sea

Code of Conduct for Visiting Historic Antarctic Huts

These guidelines have been established to minimize the deterioration and damage that can result from the intrusion of visitors. Please observe this code at all times.

- Reduce floor abrasion. Thoroughly clean grit and scoria, ice and snow, from boots before entering.
- Salt particles accelerate corrosion of metal objects. Remove any clothing wet by seawater, and any sea ice crystals from boots.
- Create an airlock when entering. Close exterior doors before opening interior doors and moving into huts.
- Do not handle or remove any items or furniture in the huts.
- When moving around the sites, take great care not to tread on any items. Many may be partially covered by snow. Do not disturb or remove anything from around the huts.
- Smoking in or around the huts is strictly forbidden.
- All visitors should record their names in the book.
- Flash photography *is* permitted inside the huts.

–from Antarctic Heritage Trust ■

it in 1841. It is the site of Antarctica's largest Adélie penguin rookery – approximately 250,000 nesting pairs during the austral summer – as well as two sets of historic huts. Unfortunately, Cape Adare is almost always a difficult landing, with heavy surf and strong offshore winds. Many groups are unable to get ashore here, and helicopters cannot be used, except very late in the season, due to the penguin rookery. According to the Antarctic Heritage Trust, only about 200 people land at Cape Adare each year.

One of the first landings on the Antarctic continent – approximately the fifth, in fact (see sidebar on First Landings in Facts about Antarctica) – occurred here on January 24, 1895, when whaling captain Leonard Kristensen of the ship *Antarctic* landed a party, which included expedition leader HJ Bull and Carsten Egeberg Borchgrevink.

Borchgrevink's Huts Five years after Kristensen's landing, Borchgrevink was back at Cape Adare as the leader of the *Southern Cross* expedition, which landed here in 1899. Two weeks later, two prefabricated wooden huts had been erected, the remains of which can be seen today on Ridley Beach, which Borchgrevink named for his mother. Here, Borchgrevink's party of 10 spent one of the loneliest Antarctic winters ever, being the only humans on the continent, though they had the company of 90 dogs.

When they were occupied, the huts must have felt something like rustic fishing or hunting cabins. In *First on the Antarctic Continent*, Borchgrevink wrote:

> On the ceiling were hanging guns, fishing tackle, knives, mittens, chains, and odds and ends. The bunks were closed after the plan followed by sailors on board whaling vessels, with a small opening, leaving yourself in an enclosure which can hold its own with our modern coffin; and, like this, it is private; for some minds it is absolutely necessary to be alone, out of sight and entirely undisturbed by others. It was by special recommendation from the doctor that I made this arrangement and found that it answered well.

Borchgrevink's huts have outlasted the 'Northern Party' Huts (see below), even though they are 12 years older, because they were built with much sturdier materials. The heavy construction, of interlocking boards of Norwegian spruce, has proved fairly durable against Cape Adare's strong winds.

The accommodation hut, which housed all 10 men, was 5.5m by 6.5m in size. Upon entering, an office/storeroom is directly to your left and a darkroom to the right; both were once lined with furs for insulation. Continuing inside, a stove stands to the left, a table and chairs are on the left past the stove, and five double-tiered coffin/bunks line the remaining wall space. Borchgrevink's was in the back left corner, on top. The hut had papier-mâché insulation and a single double-paned window. Despite Borchgrevink's careful planning, the huts were not, apparently, comfortable homes. Australian physicist Louis Bernacchi wrote of leaving Cape Adare: 'May I never pass such another 12 months in similar surroundings and conditions.'

The stores hut, standing adjacent to the west, is now roofless. It contains boxes of ammunition that Borchgrevink brought in case the expedition encountered large predators such as polar bears. (Remember, he was the first to winter on the continent.) Among the expedition's other provisions was nearly a ton of Irish butter. Coal briquettes and stores barrels litter the ground outside this hut.

Today, the huts are completely surrounded by an Adélie colony, and care must be taken to avoid disturbing the penguins when visiting the site. The Antarctic Heritage Trust, which is working to conserve the huts, reroofed the accommodation hut during the 1989-90 season and installed support braces extending down to the ground.

Only four people (including the AHT representative, who will accompany your cruise or come over from Scott Base) are permitted inside the Cape Adare huts at one time to limit the possibility of damage; in any case, there is not much room inside.

Hanson's Grave The expedition's biologist Norwegian Nikolai Hanson died on October 14, 1899, probably of an intestinal disorder. His deathbed wish was to be buried on the ridge above Ridley Beach, so his expedition mates built a coffin and dynamited a grave up on the stone ridge, the first known human burial on Antarctica. Dragging Hanson's heavily laden coffin up the steep incline required a major effort.

When *Southern Cross* returned, a graveside memorial was held and an iron cross and brass plaque were attached to a boulder on the site. Later, when Campbell's men used the ridge as a lookout for *Terra Nova*, one of them spelled out Hanson's name with white quartz pebbles, and visitors to the site in 1982 restored the inscriptions.

The climb up the 350-m ridge is very strenuous, and the 1.5-km-long return trip to the grave can take well over two hours – even in good weather and with little ice. Wind, loose rock, ice and drifting snow can make it impossible. Only very fit and agile people should attempt the climb, and many expedition leaders discourage it altogether in the interests of safety and time.

Access to the grave is by a rough trail at the north end of Ridley Beach. You will sight a large greenish boulder at the top; keep going but head slightly to the right; the iron cross will come into view atop the boulder.

'Northern Party' Huts Almost nothing remains of the hut built by Victor Campbell, of Scott's *Terra Nova* expedition of 1911-14; Cape Adare's raging winds have pretty well wrecked it. Its ruins lie east of Borchgrevink's Huts. The prefabricated building, originally standing 6.4m by 6.1m, once housed six men.

POSSESSION ISLANDS

The group's two main islands, Foyn and Possession, were discovered by James Clark Ross. After pushing his ships *Erebus* and *Terror* through the Ross Sea pack ice to open water, Ross was surprised to sight land on January 10, 1841. To Ross, this was an unexpected development, because he had been hoping to sail west from the Ross Sea to the area where the South Magnetic Pole was calculated to lie. In that era, the pole was in fact well inland.

Despite his disappointment, Ross landed a boat two days later on Possession Island and claimed the new territory in the name of Queen Victoria. It was, declared the expedition's 24-year-old naturalist Joseph Dalton Hooker, 'surely the whitest if not the brightest jewel in her crown.' A handsome engraving of the event shows penguins lined up even on the highest ridge of the island, and indeed the Adélies that nest on both islands today climb right to the top of the small hill on Possession.

In 1895, Carsten Borchgrevink found a lichen here, the first plant to be discovered in Antarctica.

A century later, in February 1995, a small modern wreck of unknown origin was discovered on the western side of Possession Island.

CAPE HALLETT

Cape Hallett was discovered by James Clark Ross in 1841 and named for Thomas Hallett, the purser on *Erebus*. A scientific station, jointly run by the US and New Zealand, was built in January and February 1957 as part of the International Geophysical Year. Some 8000 Adélie penguins were moved to another part of the cape to make way for the base, which accommodated 11 Americans and three New Zealanders for the winter. The station was operated year round until 1964, when it became a summer-only station after fire destroyed the main science building.

Cape Hallett station was closed in 1973, and since the late 1970s the disused buildings have gradually been removed to allow the Adélies to reclaim their space. Most if not all of the remaining buildings and the large fuel tank are to be removed in 1997.

Cape Hallett can usually only be visited by Zodiac; helicopter landings are not permitted while the penguins occupy their rookery.

MOUNT MELBOURNE

Surmounting the coast above Cape Washington (which, like so many other features in the Ross Sea region, was discovered in 1841 by James Clark Ross, who named it for a secretary of the Royal Geographical Society), this 2733-m cone is the only known volcano on the Antarctic continent itself. All the others – including Mt Erebus, Mt Siple and Deception Island – are on offlying islands. Like the Australian city of the same name, the volcano commemorates Lord Melbourne, the British Prime Minister of Ross' day.

TERRA NOVA BAY

This 65-km-long bay, discovered by Scott's *Discovery* expedition and named for the relief ship *Terra Nova*, is surrounded by the Society Ranges.

Germany operates the summer station Gondwana here, while Italy operates the summer station Baia Terra Nova, said to have Antarctica's best espresso.

DRYGALSKI ICE TONGUE

Discovered by Robert Scott in 1902 and named for German explorer Erich von Drygalski, this ice tongue is the seaward extension of the David Glacier. It ranges from 14 to 24 km wide and is nearly 50 km long.

FRANKLIN ISLAND

The ubiquitous James Clark Ross landed on this 11-km-long island on January 27, 1841, claiming the Victoria Land coast for Queen Victoria. He named the island itself for John Franklin, the Governor of Van Diemen's Land (Tasmania) who had shown the expedition considerable hospitality when it called in at Hobart in 1840 on the way south. Affixed to only this tiny island in the Antarctic, Franklin's name is writ much larger in the history of the Arctic, where major discoveries were made by explorers searching for his missing ships, *Erebus* and *Terror*, the same ships Ross used to explore this area.

Franklin Island is home to a large Adélie penguin rookery.

NORDENSKJÖLD ICE TONGUE

Discovered by Robert Scott's National Antarctic Expedition of 1901-04, this ice tongue is named for Swedish explorer Otto Nordenskjöld. It is the seaward extension of the Mawson Glacier.

DRY VALLEYS

The Dry Valleys are some of the most unusual places on Earth, in no small part because no rain has fallen there for at least two million years. They are magnificent spaces: huge, desolate and beautiful. As in other parts of Antarctica, it can be hard to maintain a sense of the Dry Valleys' scale. What appears to be a nearby mountainside or glacier could in fact be several hours' walking distance.

From north to south, the three main Dry Valleys are Victoria, Wright and Taylor. Covering 3000 sq km, the Dry Valleys have no snow or ice; none can persist there because the air is so dry. Such ice-free areas in Antarctica are called *oases*. The conditions required for an oasis are a retreating or thinning ice sheet and a large area of exposed rock from which snow ablates, due to the solar radiation absorbed by the rock. Although these valleys are the most prominent of the Antarctic oases, there are at least 20 others, including the Bunger, Larsemann and Vestfold Hills of East Antarctica. The Dry Valleys were formed when the terrain uplifted at a faster rate than glaciers could cut their way down through them. Eventually, the glaciers were stopped by high necks at the head of each valley.

Robert Scott accidentally discovered the first of the Dry Valleys in December 1903, naming it for geologist Griffith Taylor. Scott and two others had sledged up the Ferrar Glacier to the East Antarctic Ice Sheet. During their return, they became lost in thick cloud and descended the wrong valley. Because they were equipped for sledging, not hiking, they were forced to turn back after a brief exploration. In *The Voyage of the Discovery*, Scott wrote:

> I cannot but think that this valley is a very wonderful place. We have seen today all the indications of colossal ice action and considerable water action, and yet neither of these agents is now at work. It is worthy of record, too, that we have seen no living thing, not even a moss or a lichen; all that we did find, far inland amongst the moraine heaps, was the skeleton of a Weddell seal, and how that came there is beyond guessing. It is certainly a valley of the dead; even the great glacier which once pushed through it has withered away.

Although the valleys do indeed appear lifeless, in fact they harbor some of the most curious organisms on the planet. In 1978, American biologists discovered algae, bacteria and fungi growing *inside* the rocks of the Dry Valleys. This 'endolithic' vegetation actually grows in the air spaces in porous rocks; light, carbon dioxide and moisture penetrate the rock, but the rock protects the organisms against excessive drying and harmful radiation. Some of these plants are believed to be up to 200,000 years old.

Another reason the valleys appear so otherworldly are the bizarre, sculptured forms of the rocks. These are called ventifacts, and they are highly polished on their windward surface. Others are carved by the wind into pocked boulders or thin, delicate wafers. Others fit into your hand so well that they resemble smoothly ground primitive tools. Although they feel good to pick up, the ventifacts should not be removed. As one scientist familiar with the Dry Valleys puts it: 'You either understand the ethics of such a place, or you don't.'

Mummified seals, as recorded by Scott, are not uncommon in the Dry Valleys, though most appear to be crabeaters, not Weddells. They have been found as far as 40 km inland, a remarkable journey for an animal as awkward as seals are on land. Given the number of seals, however, it is not hard to believe that one or two per year might wander into the valleys and get mixed up about which way is back to the sea. The occasional carcass of a disoriented Adélie penguin has also been found in the Dry Valleys, as far as 50 km from the sea. The remains of both creatures are effectively freeze-dried by the extreme aridity of the valleys, and they are then eroded by the scouring wind just like the ventifacts.

Scientists believe the Dry Valleys are the nearest equivalent on earth to the terrain of Mars. For this reason, NASA performed extensive research here before launching the Viking probe to Mars.

In addition to Victoria, Wright and Taylor valleys, there are several smaller valleys that are also part of the region. Interestingly, the Americans call them the 'McMurdo Dry Valleys,' while the British prefer the 'Victoria Land Dry Valleys.' Most people just call them plain old 'Dry Valleys.' Tourists generally fly by helicopter into Taylor Valley, the most accessible from the Ross Sea; large sections of the others are protected areas under the Antarctic Treaty.

ROSS ISLAND

Both the New Zealand Antarctic Programme and the United States Antarctic Research Program have their principal bases on Ross Island. As part of New Zealand's territorial claim of the Ross Dependency, Ross Island is – as the joke goes – the only island in New Zealand that doesn't have sheep on it.

Scott Base

New Zealand's Scott base is located on Pram Point, on the southeast side of Hut Point Peninsula. Pram Point was so named by Scott's Discovery expedition because getting from there to the Ross Ice Shelf in summer requires a pram, or small boat.

Scott base, an attractive collection of lime-green buildings, looks trim and tidy compared to McMurdo's 'urban sprawl.' It accommodates 11 winterers and as many as 70 people in the summer.

Tourist visits can easily overwhelm a smaller Antarctic station like Scott base, where the entire staff must dedicate itself to accommodating a tourist ship visit. Still, the New Zealanders are very friendly and welcoming, and they appear eager to offer a counterpoint to their larger neighbor, McMurdo.

Although there are no mail facilities at Scott base, phone calls can be made using public telephone booths in the foyer of the Command Centre. You can use phone cards purchased in the base shop, or call collect or with a credit card. Calls must be short so that all visitors have an opportunity to call. The Scott Base shop accepts NZ and US currencies, as well as Visa, Mastercard and American Express.

McMurdo Station

The US McMurdo station is Antarctica's largest station, accommodating as many as 1200 people during the summer and 200 in winter. The station covers nearly 4 sq km between Hut Point and Observation Hill and has more than a hundred buildings. The structures are built on short stilts, and water, sewer, telephone and power lines all run aboveground.

Although the sprawling station can be a shocking sight at first, after Antarctica's clean white icebergs and bare mountains and few signs of human life, the US government has actually made enormous strides in decreasing McMurdo's environmental impact, especially when compared to even a few years ago. Before 1990, the station's accumulated trash – including junked vehicles, empty fuel barrels and scrap metal – was hauled out onto the sea ice each spring before the annual breakup. Today, this practice is a thing of the past. In fact, rubbish throughout the station is now separated into such recyclable categories as aluminum, clothing, construction debris, food waste, hazardous waste, heavy metals, light metals, magazines, newspapers, packaging, plastics, white paper and wood. Still, in the summer when the station's dusty ground mixes with meltwater, the station resembles a mining town of the Old West

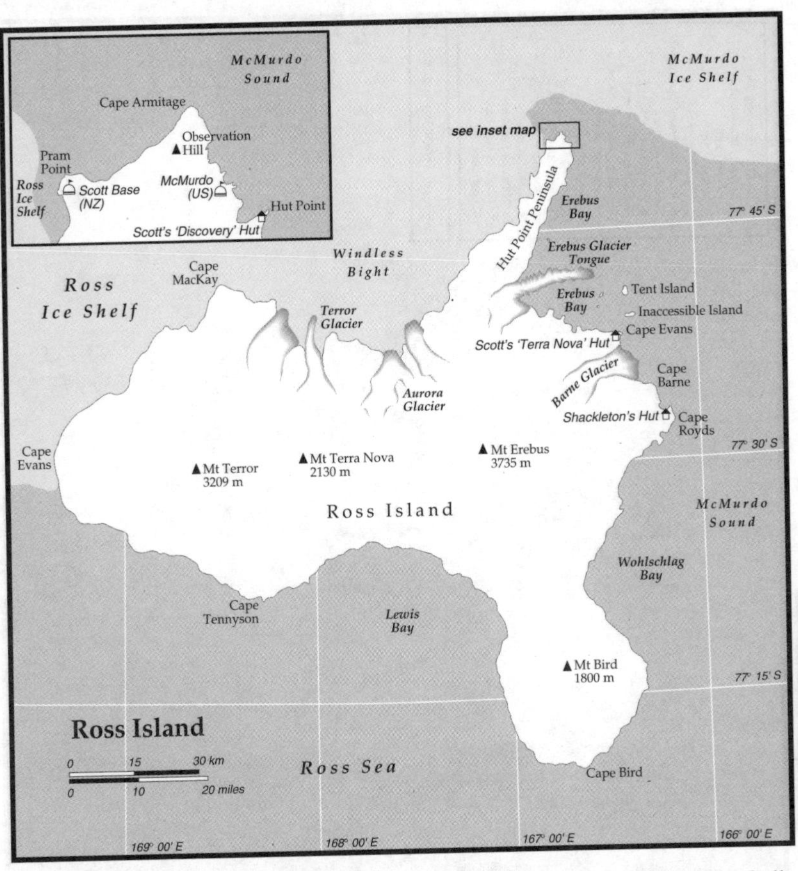

and some residents unflatteringly refer to it as 'McMudhole.'

McMurdo was established in January 1956. The station takes its name from McMurdo Sound, which James Clark Ross named after Lt Archibald McMurdo of the ship *Terror* in 1841. McMurdo station was originally going to be situated at Cape Evans, but the death of a tractor driver whose Caterpillar D8 fell through the sea ice caused the station's builders to reconsider their choice, and they put McMurdo at Hut Point instead. McMurdo was big right from the start: Ninety-three men wintered over in its first year.

Today, McMurdo is both a logistics facility as well as Antarctica's premier scientific base. Researchers are flown from McMurdo to nearby field camps via helicopter and to remote field camps and the South Pole via ski-equipped LC-130 Hercules aircraft.

'You will find,' says a welcoming handbook issued to all new residents, 'that McMurdo Station resembles an urban center in its population diversity and hectic pace.' Nicknamed MacTown (or to some of its denizens, just 'Town'), McMurdo does have the feeling of a bustling village – with all of the problems and benefits of a small

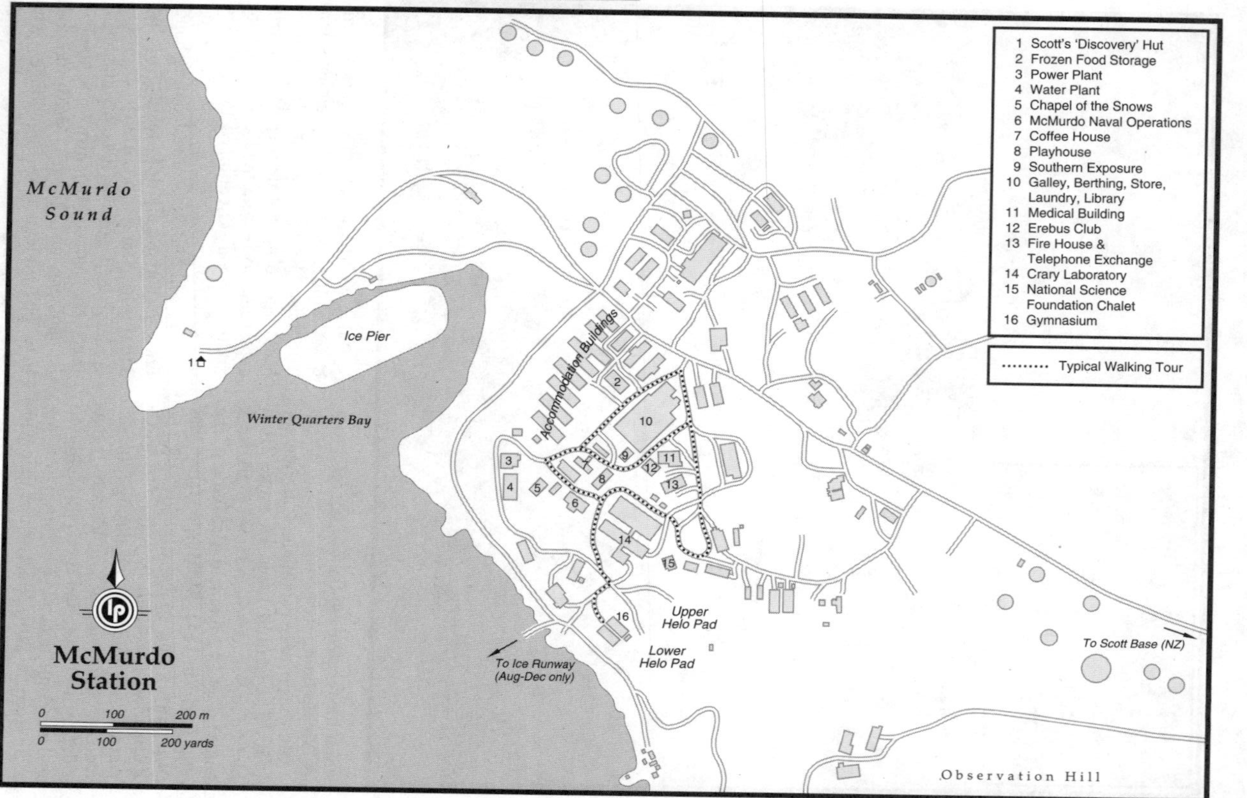
1 Scott's 'Discovery' Hut
2 Frozen Food Storage
3 Power Plant
4 Water Plant
5 Chapel of the Snows
6 McMurdo Naval Operations
7 Coffee House
8 Playhouse
9 Southern Exposure
10 Galley, Berthing, Store, Laundry, Library
11 Medical Building
12 Erebus Club
13 Fire House & Telephone Exchange
14 Crary Laboratory
15 National Science Foundation Chalet
16 Gymnasium
Typical Walking Tour
McMurdo Sound
Ice Pier
Winter Quarters Bay
Accommodation Buildings
Upper Helo Pad
Lower Helo Pad
To Ice Runway (Aug-Dec only)
To Scott Base (NZ)
Observation Hill
McMurdo Station
0 100 200 m
0 100 200 yards

town. The oldest section of the station is called 'Downtown McMurdo' or 'the historic district.' Nearly 80 vehicles (excluding heavy equipment) roll through its streets, though not very quickly: The station speed limit is 30 km/h.

Compared to the modest facilities at other Antarctic stations, McMurdo is almost overwhelming. It has its own hospital, church, fleet post office (FPO), library, video store, (free) barbershop, two clubs (the Erebus Club and the no-smoking Southern Exposure), coffeehouse, shuttle bus, seawater reverse osmosis desalination plant, video teleconferencing facilities, diving recompression chamber, Ice Pier, fuel tank farm and hydroponics greenhouse (whose crops include lettuce, tomatoes and green peppers).

McMurdo once also boasted the continent's only large nuclear power plant, a 1.8 megawatt experimental reactor known colloquially as 'Nukey Poo.' It was deployed on Observation Hill in December 1961 and went on-line in March 1962. Unfortunately, the reactor experienced numerous problems, and, faced with a large repair bill, the US Government decided to shut it down in 1973. Eventually, some 11,000 tons of radioactively contaminated soil and rock were removed from the site.

Housing is allocated through a points system, in which position and previous months on The Ice determine your berth. Scientists and others 'moving frequently between the field and town' will probably bunk down in one of the large dormitories overlooking the helicopter pad, two of which are picturesquely named 'The Hotel California' and 'The Mammoth Mountain Inn.' The newer dorms overlook the Ice Pier.

The station's six-page newspaper, the *Antarctic Sun Times*, is published weekly during the summer by US Navy and civilian personnel and includes a popular 'Around the Continent' section. There's also 'The Scroll' – a televised list of the day's activities, announcements, weather information, movie schedules and other station news – that can be viewed on one of the several dozen televisions scattered around McMurdo's lounges and offices. Other media include Radio McMurdo (104.5 on your FM dial), and two TV broadcast channels, 8 and 13.

Recreation opportunities for station personnel abound: McMurdo offers aerobics, basketball, bingo, bowling, chili cook-offs, country dancing, darts, soccer, softball, table tennis, tae kwon do, volleyball, and in good weather, bicycle rental (US$5 a day). For golfers, there's the McMurdo Open tournament; for runners, there are several races: the five-km Run Across Ross Island; the McMurdo Midsummer Midnight Mile; and the 7.25-km Scott's Hut race.

There are Sunday Science Lectures, computer classes, cardio-pulmonary rescue (CPR) training, Alcoholics Anonymous meetings, Town Choir rehearsals, the Ross Island Drama Festival, the Ross Island Art Show, the Icestock rock and comedy festival, and even occasional tours of Scott's Discovery Hut, as well as trips to nearby ice caves. Station residents occasionally have the opportunity to go on a very special vacation from McMurdo by taking a space-available flight to South Pole station, a unique reward known locally as a 'sleigh ride.'

McMurdo is served by three different airport facilities, each operating at different times of the year. In the spring, a landing field is laid out on the annual sea ice of McMurdo Sound for use by wheeled aircraft flights in October, November and early December. Later in December, as the summer temperatures weaken the sea ice, flight operations shift to **Williams Field**, a skiway laid out on the Ross Ice Shelf. Also known as Willy Field or just plain 'Willy,' this airfield was named for Richard T Williams, who died during Operation Deep Freeze I (1955-56) when his 30-ton tractor broke through sea ice 6.5 km off Cape Royds. Williams Field is located 16 km from the station, and, this being McMurdo, there is an airport bus to transport the large number of new arrivals to the station! Huge TerraBus vehicles carry passengers over a snow road called 'Antarctic 1' to the station. A new airfield, the Pegasus blue ice runway about 45 minutes' drive from McMurdo, was completed in 1992 and can be used nearly year round, except for the height of the summer, when warm temperatures cause pitting and melting of the blue ice surface.

About 250 flights from Christchurch land at McMurdo each year, using C130 Hercules, C5 Galaxies, C141 Starlifters and LC-130 ski-equipped Hercules. While most of them occur between early October and late February, some additional flights take place in late August, during the latter part of the austral winter, in an operation called 'Winfly,' or Winter Fly-In. Until recently, midwinter airdrops of mail and supplies were made in June, but funding for the flight was cut for the 1996 season. (LC-130s, the workhorses of the US Antarctic Program, cost about US$3500 per hour to operate.)

Tourists, of course, will only glimpse a tiny slice of the station's busy life, including **Chapel of the Snows**, a church with a unique penguin-motif stained-glass window.

Crary Lab This science laboratory, completed in 1991, is named for Albert P Crary, a geophysicist and glaciologist who was the first man to visit both the North and South Poles. The 4300 sq meter structure houses workspace for biological studies, earth science and atmospheric science. The lab's equipment is state-of-the-art, with facilities as good as or better than those found at major research universities. It's a bit disconcerting to go straight from a penguin rookery to a place where scientists have digital card keys to their offices, but this is the 'Big City,' after all! The Crary Lab also boasts a darkroom, freezers for processing ice cores, an electronics workshop, a library, a seismic observatory that monitors Mt Erebus (it's a volcano after all!) and three large aquaria filled with McMurdo Sound marine life, a sight often shown to tourists. The street in front of the Crary Lab is called Beeker St. Although 'beaker' is a nickname for scientists, the spelling on the street sign leads one to believe that it's a clever pun on Bleecker St in New York City's Greenwich Village.

Ship's Store No, this isn't on a ship, but since the Navy runs it (or did until recently), this is the ship's store nevertheless. They sell postcards, calendars, batteries, ceramic sculptures, T-shirts, sweatshirts and other souvenirs. Liquor and cigarette prices are quite reasonable, at least compared to those aboard ship, but the clerks might not sell these items to you, as that depletes the station stock. Prices, of course, are in US dollars. Note also that the US Antarctic Program does not carry tourist mail on its ships or aircraft, so you can't send letters or postcards from McMurdo.

Beginning with the 1996-97 season, the US Antarctic Program will begin a transition away from selling souvenirs at its stations. Instead, t-shirts and other items will be sold through a catalog, a change made to save the expense of shipping the souvenirs to Antarctica and storing them at the stations. Eventually, program administrators hope to sell only smaller articles such as postcards and pins at the stations.

Scott's *Discovery* Hut

Robert Scott's National Antarctic Expedition built this hut in February 1902. The prefabricated building, purchased in Australia, is of a type still found in rural Australia, with a wide overhanging veranda on three sides. Despite the building's expense and the effort required to erect it, Scott's men never used it for accommodations, since it was difficult to heat efficiently. The expedition members instead used it for storage, repair work and as an entertainment center, when it was called 'The Royal Terror Theatre.'

In fact, the *Discovery* Hut was used more heavily by nearly every expedition that came after it than it ever was by the *Discovery* expedition itself. Shackleton's *Nimrod* expedition, based at Cape Royds, found the hut to be a convenient *en route* shelter during sledge trips to and from the Ross Ice Shelf in 1908. Scott's second (and last) expedition on *Terra Nova* also made use of the hut in 1911 for the same purpose. The Ross Sea party of Shackleton's ill-fated Imperial Trans-Antarctic Expedition probably benefited the most from the hut. While Shackleton's *Endurance* was being crushed and sunk by the Weddell Sea ice, the Ross Sea party holed up in the hut in 1915 and, later, in 1916. The resources they were able to use from the hut included food, cigars, Crème de Menthe, sleeping bags and a pair of long underwear. The blackened interior of the hut is due to the smoky blubber stove used by the Ross Sea party to stay warm.

Probably because it is the closest to McMurdo station and has received the most visitors (and souveniring) over the years, the *Discovery* Hut is the least interesting of the three Ross Island historic sites. The Antarctic Heritage Trust estimates that 1000 people visit the hut each year.

There are few artifacts in the rather dingy interior, which smells strongly of burnt seal blubber. Stores line the right-hand wall as you enter; a central area is occupied by a stove, piles of provisions and a sleeping platform. Much of the hut feels empty. A square hole in the floor was used for pendulum experiments. A mummified seal lies on the open southern veranda, its back covered in liquefying blubber. If anything, the hut sharply conveys the hardships that were endured by the early explorers. Despite its present decrepitude, if it were the only shelter for thousands of kilometers, this hut would quickly become home, albeit a rough one.

For conservation purposes, only eight people are permitted inside the hut at one time. Make sure you sign the visitor's book, which helps Antarctic Heritage Trust maintain its records.

Vince's Cross

About 100m from the *Discovery* Hut, an oak cross stands as a memorial to Able Seaman George T Vince, who fell to his death over an ice cliff into McMurdo Sound on March 11, 1902.

Observation Hill

The 3.5m tall cross that surmounts this 230m volcanic cone was raised in memory of the five men who perished on the return from the South Pole: Edgar Evans, Laurence Oates, Edward Wilson, Robert Scott and Henry Bowers. Its fading inscription is the closing line from Tennyson's poem *Ulysses* – 'To strive, to seek, to find, and not to yield.' The cross, erected on January 20, 1913, has been blown over by storms at least twice. At the last re-erection, in January 1994, it was placed in a new concrete base.

Cape Evans

In stark contrast to the *Discovery* Hut, Scott's Hut from the *Terra Nova* expedition is filled with an incredible feeling of history. Erected in January 1911 at the place Scott named Cape Evans after his second in command, Edward Evans, the prefabricated hut is 14.6m long and 7.3m wide. It accommodated 25 men in fairly crowded conditions. It must have been chilly inside, though the hut did boast insulation made of seaweed sewn into jute bags.

This is the real thing, what you came for, the reason you paid thousands of dollars and suffered through long days of seasickness. Here, dog skeletons bleach on the sand in the Antarctic sun, chiding *memento morii* of Scott's death march from the Pole. Inside the hut, unquiet ghosts glide soundlessly through memories of sledging pennants, the rustle of pony harnesses and a sighing wind. It is an absolutely amazing and eerie feeling to stand at the head of the wardroom table and recall the famous photo of Scott's final birthday party, with the men gathered around the huge meal spread out before them, with their banners hung behind them. You definitely feel their ghostly presence! According to the Antarctic Heritage Trust, about 900 people land at Cape Evans each year.

Located on the beach at what Scott called Home Bay, the hut stands close to

… McMurdo Sound. A long, …ing (which housed the latrines, …arate facilities for officers and …ands along the seaward side of the hu…

Entering the hut, you pass through an outer porch area leading off to the left to the stables on the hut's beachfront side. Still in the porch to this day are a box of penguin eggs, big piles of suppurating seal blubber, lots of shovels and implements hanging on the walls, and geologist Griffith Taylor's bicycle.

Inside the hut proper, your eyes will take a while to adjust to the half light. Just stand there quietly for a moment and take it all in. You are standing in what the expedition called the mess deck. Scott, in keeping with Royal Navy practice, segregated expedition members into officers and men. In the mess deck lived PO Evans, Crean, Keohane, Ford, Anton, Dmitri, Clissold, Lashly and Hooper. Here also is the galley, including a stove, to the right as you enter.

Continuing further into the hut, past what was once a dividing wall made out of packing cases, you are in the wardroom. Straight in back is the darkroom; to the right is the laboratory, along with Wright's and Simpson's bunks. To the left of the Wardroom table from front to back of their alcove were: Bowers (top bunk) and Cherry-Garrard; Oates (with no bunk beneath); and Mears (top) and Atkinson. To the right of the wardroom table were (front of hut to back): Gran (top bunk) and Taylor; a small geology lab; Debenham; and Nelson (top bunk) and Day.

The back left corner of the hut is the *sanctum sanctorum*. Scott's bunk, to the left, is separated from Wilson's and Evans' bunks by a work table, covered with an open book and a fading stuffed emperor penguin.

Throughout the hut, there are lots of provisions and photographic supplies. There's a strong, not unpleasant musty smell, like that of dusty old books and pony straw. Boxes hold candles that could be used today without problem. Many brands are still familiar, with labels that are hardly changed even now.

Only 12 people are permitted inside the Cape Evans hut at one time, and only 40 people are allowed ashore at once.

Other Sites at Cape Evans

Cross on Wind Vane Hill After Scott's Last Expedition, 10 members of the Ross Sea Party of Shackleton's Imperial Trans Antarctic Expedition were stranded here in May 1915, when their ship *Aurora* was blown from its moorings. The men passed a very difficult 20 months before *Aurora* was able to return. During that time, three of the members perished while returning from a trip laying depots for the Weddell Sea party, which they were expecting to arrive from across the continent. The Rev Arnold Spencer-Smith died of scurvy on March 9, 1916, and two others, Aeneas Mackintosh and VG Hayward, vanished in a blizzard while walking on thin sea ice on May 8, 1916.

Greenpeace Base Plaque The environmental organization had a year-round base at Cape Evans for four years. It was dismantled and every scrap was removed in 1991-92. A rather difficult-to-find plaque is now all that marks the site. Walk north up the beach to find it.

Cape Royds

Besides being the home of Shackleton's *Nimrod* expedition, Cape Royds is also the most southerly recorded penguin rookery in the world, filled with 3500 pairs of Adélies. The cape was named by Robert Scott for *Discovery*'s meteorologist, Charles Royds, and the small pond in front of the hut is called Pony Lake, because the expedition kept its ponies tethered nearby.

Shackleton erected his hut here in February 1908. Unlike the class-minded Scott, he imposed no division between officers and men at Cape Royds, though as 'The Boss' he did invoke executive privilege to give himself a private room (near the hut's

Shackleton's *Nimrod* expedition hut on Cape Royds

front door). Fifteen men lived in the hut, which is much smaller than Scott's at Cape Evans.

The feeling inside is still very ghostly, though perhaps not quite as eerie as Cape Evans, with its lingering sense of tragedy. All of Shackleton's men, after all, left here alive. In fact, when members of the *Terra Nova* expedition visited in 1911, they found socks hanging to dry and a meal still on the table. Members of Shackleton's Ross Sea party also stopped by, collecting tobacco and soap among other items.

Although the hut has been cleaned up since then (snow filled it during one long interval between visits), there's still a strong historical presence about the place. If you're tall, you'll need to duck slightly as you step inside the hut so that you don't hit your head on the acetylene generator over the entryway; it once powered the hut's lamps.

Cape Royds is the least-visited of the Ross Island historic huts; the Antarctic Heritage Trust estimates that 700 people land here each year.

A freeze-dried buckwheat pancake still lies in a cast-iron skillet on top of the large stove at the back of the hut, beside a tea kettle and a large cooking pot. Colored glass medicine bottles still line several shelves, and large photographs of King Edward VII and Queen Alexandra dominate the hut's right-hand wall. One of the few surviving bunks, to the left toward the back, has its fur sleeping bag laid out on top of it. Lots of tins of unappetizing-sounding food items like Irish brawn (head cheese), boiled mutton, 'Army Rations.' 'Aberdeen marrow fat,' 'lunch tongue' and 'pea powder' lay on the floor next to the walls, along with still-bright red tins of Price's Motor Lubricant. The dining table, which was lifted up from the floor each night to

allow for extra space, is now gone; it may have been burned up by one of successive parties who ran out of fuel. A bench piled with mitts and shoes stands on the right.

Ask your AHT guide to point out Shackleton's signature in his tiny bunk room. It's upside down on a packing crate marked 'Not for Voyage' that Shackleton made into a headboard for his bunk.

Outside the hut, the remnants of the pony stables, and the garage built for the Arrol-Johnson motor car (Antarctica's first) are tumbling into ruin. Pony oats spill from feed bags onto the ground, while one of the car's wheels leans up against a line of provision boxes, its wooden spokes scoured by the wind. Two wooden doghouses likewise are being eroded.

On the hut's southern side, its wood has weathered a handsome bleached grey color. Nail heads that were once pounded flush now stick out a centimeter or more. Boxes of rusting food tins stand against the side and back. Although rust has completely destroyed any labels, one wooden carton is literally spilling its beans.

Cables running over the hut lash it to the ground, and the AHT attached rubber sheathing to the roof in 1990 for further protection. For conservation reasons, only eight people are permitted inside Shackleton's Hut at one time, and only 40 people are allowed ashore at once.

Mts Erebus & Terror

Mt Erebus, the world's most southerly volcano, is 3795m high. Its lazily drifting plume of steam is a familiar sight in the Ross Sea, and gives a good indication of wind speeds at altitude. Mt Erebus was first climbed by a party from Shackleton's *Nimrod* expedition in 1908.

Modern-day visitors will relate to the awe of Erebus expressed by Joseph Hooker, the young botanist on James Clark Ross' expedition, in a letter to his father written in 1841:

> To see the dark cloud of smoke, tinged with flame, rising from the volcano in a perfectly unbroken column, one side jet black, the other giving back the colours of the sun, sometimes turning off at a right angle by some current of wind, and stretching many miles to leeward . . . was a sight so surpassing everything that can be imagined, and so heightened by the consciousness that we had penetrated into regions far beyond what was ever deemed practicable, that it really caused a feeling of awe to steal over us at the consideration of our own comparative insignificance and helplessness, and at the same time, an indescribable feeling of the greatness of the Creator in the works of His hand.

All 257 people aboard Air New Zealand Flight 901 were killed when their DC-10 slammed into Mt Erebus on November 28, 1979. The crash site has been declared a tomb by the Antarctic Treaty members.

Mt Terror, an extinct volcano, rises to an elevation of 3261m; it is separated from Mt Erebus by Mt Terra Nova.

ROSS ICE SHELF

Covering 520,000 sq km, an area roughly the size of France, the Ross Ice Shelf was discovered by James Clark Ross on January 28, 1841, who called it the Victoria Barrier in honor of Queen Victoria. Since then it has variously been called the Barrier, the Great Barrier, the Great Ice

Barrier, the Great Southern Barrier, the Ice Barrier, the Icy Barrier, the Ross Barrier, the Ross Ice Barrier, and, these days, the Ross Ice Shelf.

Its mean ice thickness is 335 to 700m, but where glaciers and ice streams meet it, the shelf is up to 1000m thick. At the ice front facing the Ross Sea, however, it is less than 100m thick. Still, it is rather hard to believe that the whole shelf is actually *floating*.

The Ross Ice Shelf moves at a velocity of up to 1100m per year, and calves an estimated 150 cubic km of icebergs annually, out of its total of 23,000 cubic km of ice. In late September to early October 1987, an enormous berg, measuring 155 km by 35 km and later named B-9, calved from the eastern side of the Ice Shelf.

Over the years, the Ross Ice Shelf has inspired many awestruck responses from those who gazed upon its immensity. The blacksmith aboard *Erebus* in 1841 was uncharacteristically moved to write a couplet: 'Awful and sublime, magnificent and rare/ No other Earthly object with the Barrier can compare.' Ross himself called it 'a mighty and wonderful object far beyond anything we could have thought or conceived.'

'At 2:30 pm we came in sight of the Great Ice Barrier,' Roald Amundsen recorded on January 11, 1911. 'Slowly it rose up out of the sea until we were face to face with it in all its imposing majesty. It is difficult with the help of the pen to give any idea of the impression this mighty wall of ice makes on the observer who is confronted with it for the first time. It is altogether a thing which can hardly be described . . .'

Louis Bernacchi, the Australian physicist on Borchgrevink's *Southern Cross* expedition, climbed to the top of the Ross Ice Shelf in 1900 with William Colbeck, the British surveyor. 'Nothing was visible,' Bernacchi later wrote, 'but the great ice-cap stretching away for hundreds of miles to the south and west. Unless one has actually seen it, it is impossible to conceive the stupendous extent of this ice-cap, its consistency, utter barrenness, and stillness, which sends an indefinable sense of dread to the heart.'

Borchgrevink himself found the Barrier to be much smaller than it appeared when Ross discovered it. In fact, at a place located at about 164°W (Scott later called it 'Discovery Inlet,' after his ship), the ice shelf was only 4.5m or so above the water. Here, in 1900, Borchgrevink landed stores, sledges and dogs and with two members of his expedition, William Colbeck and Per Savio, pushed south to 78°50'S, at the time the furthest south ever reached.

East Antarctica

East Antarctica derives its name from the fact that nearly all of it lies in the Eastern Hemisphere. It is sometimes called Greater Antarctica, since it is the larger half of the continent, but the name East Antarctica, coined by Antarctic historian Edwin S Balch in 1904, is preferred. East Antarctica is a high plateau covered by a thick and enormous ice sheet, divided from West Antarctica by the Transantarctic Mountains.

In tourist brochures, East Antarctica is often called Antarctica's 'Far Side' (and these same brochures urge you to 'get away' from the 'crowded' Antarctic Peninsula!). Thanks to its isolation and the long voyages required to reach it, the region has been all but unvisited by tourists until very recently, with the first tour ships calling at the three Australian stations only during the 1992-93 season.

For tourists, one of the primary attractions of East Antarctica is the numerous emperor penguin rookeries. The largest species of penguin, they are the only animals to breed during the long Antarctic night, and the sight of one of their rookeries, with the tall, dignified-looking adult birds and their downy silver-and-black chicks, is one of Antarctica's most stunning.

East Antarctica includes the regions claimed by Norway, Australia and France. Much of the Norwegian claim (which is called Dronning Maud Land and extends from 20°W to 45°E) was explored by Norwegian whalers. During the 1930-31 whaling season alone, about 265 whaling ships, most of them Norwegian, worked the Southern Ocean in the area between 20°W to 50°E. Although exploration was only their second line of work, these whalers discovered much of the Dronning (Queen) Maud Land coast, naming sections of it for members of the Norwegian royal family, including Kronprinsesse Martha Kyst (Crown Princess Martha Coast), Prinsesse Astrid Kyst (Princess Astrid Coast) and Prinsesse Ragnhild Kyst (Princess Ragnhild Coast).

Australia's claim, called the Australian Antarctic Territory (or AAT), extends from 45°E to 160°E, except for the thin slice of France's Terre Adélie. It was explored by Australians including Douglas Mawson, George Hubert Wilkins and Phillip Law. Reflecting its other varied discoverers, the region includes Enderby Land, Kemp Land, MacRobertson Land, Princess Elizabeth Land, Wilhelm II Land, Queen Mary Land, Wilkes Land and George V Land.

Terre Adélie, France's Antarctic claim, extends from 136°E to 142°E and is wholly within Australia's claim. This section of the coast is easily distinguished on maps by the sudden appearance of French names: Cap Bienvenue, Glacier du Commandant Charcot, Glacier du Français.

The principal sights of interest that have a describable human history are spread out rather sparsely along the thousands of kilometers of East Antarctica's coast. But the coast itself, with its enormous white grounded bergs and massive iceberg tongues, is magnificent. Below are some of the coast's main features, beginning at the western end.

GEORG VON NEUMAYER STATION

This German station, located on the Ekström Ice Shelf, is operated year round. Nine people generally winter over. The first Neumayer station was built in 1981 and named for one of the promoters of the First International Polar Year, 1882-83. In December 1990 Neumayer was staffed by the first all-female group to winter on Antarctica, which consisted of two meteorologists, two geophysicists, two engineers, a radio operator, a cook, and a medical doctor who also served as the station leader. The group spent 14 months on The Ice, including nine months in complete

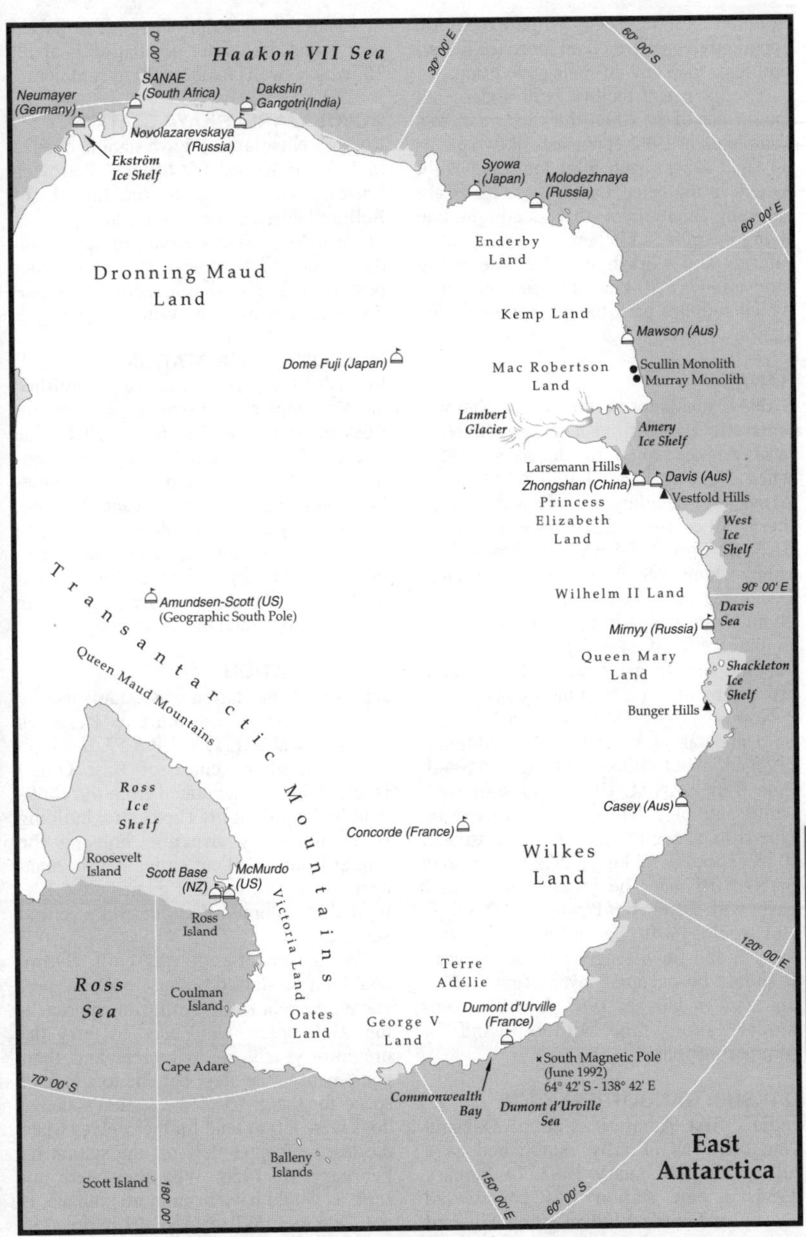
Haakon VII Sea
0° 00'
30° 00' E
60° 00' S
Neumayer (Germany)
SANAE (South Africa)
Dakshin Gangotri(India)
Novolazarevskaya (Russia)
Ekström Ice Shelf
Syowa (Japan)
Molodezhnaya (Russia)
60° 00' E
Enderby Land
Dronning Maud Land
Kemp Land
Mawson (Aus)
Dome Fuji (Japan)
Mac Robertson Land
Scullin Monolith
Murray Monolith
Lambert Glacier
Amery Ice Shelf
Larsemann Hills
Davis (Aus)
Zhongshan (China)
Vestfold Hills
Princess Elizabeth Land
West Ice Shelf
90° 00' E
Wilhelm II Land
Amundsen-Scott (US)
(Geographic South Pole)
Transantarctic Mountains
Davis Sea
Mirnyy (Russia)
Queen Maud Mountains
Queen Mary Land
Shackleton Ice Shelf
Bunger Hills
Ross Ice Shelf
Casey (Aus)
Concorde (France)
Wilkes Land
Roosevelt Island
Scott Base (NZ)
McMurdo (US)
Victoria Land
Ross Island
120° 00' E
Terre Adélie
Ross Sea
Coulman Island
Dumont d'Urville (France)
Oates Land
George V Land
Cape Adare
South Magnetic Pole
(June 1992)
64° 42' S - 138° 42' E
70° 00' S
Commonwealth Bay
Dumont d'Urville Sea
Balleny Islands
East Antarctica
Scott Island
180° 00'
150° 00' E
60° 00' S

isolation. Not surprisingly, the expedition apparently experienced no more (or fewer) problems than any all-male expedition.

A replacement facility, built underneath the surface of the 200m-thick ice shelf, was completed in 1992. It consists of two parallel steel tubes, each 90m long and eight meters in diameter. Inside these tubes are shipping containers that accommodate living quarters, a kitchen, a hospital, laboratories and workshops. One interesting innovation is a 20-kilowatt wind generator, which supplies part, though not all, of the station's power.

SANAE

SANAE stands for South African National Antarctic Expedition. The first SANAE base was occupied in December 1959, when Norway handed it over to South Africa after deciding its work was finished there. Since then, there have also been SANAE II and SANAE III bases. The latter, which was closed for wintering in December 1994, had over the years sunk about 14m beneath the surface of the Fimbul Ice Shelf on which it was built and become unsafe as it was slowly being crushed by the weight of the ice above.

Now a SANAE IV is being constructed on a nunatak at Velseskarvet in Ahlmannryggen, about 200 km towards the South Pole from SANAE III. A handsome red, white and blue building constructed on blue stilts above the ice-free rock surface, it is expected to last much longer than SANAE III did. The location of the new base will allow field research (biology and geology) to be more easily conducted, and for a longer part of the year. It should be occupied by its first wintering team in January 1997. It will accommodate about nine winterers and 70 summer personnel.

DAKSHIN GANGOTRI STATION

India's first Antarctic station, Dakshin Gangotri was initially established as a refuge hut in January 1982. In January 1984, a new station was constructed nearby, and the first Indian group wintered in Antarctica. Dakshin Gangotri is staffed year round; its winter population is about 15, which swells to about 40 in summer.

NOVOLAZAREVSKAYA STATION

Russia's Novolazarevskaya station, opened in 1961, is named for Mikhail Petrovich Lazarev, the second-in-command of Bellingshausen's expedition and captain of *Mirnyy*. Novolazarevskaya can accommodate about 57 winterers and 60 summer personnel. The station leader's accommodation is known as 'the White House.'

MOLODEZHNAYA STATION

Russia's Molodezhnaya station, established in 1962, replaced Mirnyy as the premier Russian station on The Ice in 1970. The research focus at Molodezhnaya is meteorology. A compacted snow runway allows intercontinental aircraft to reach the base, and as many as 130 people winter here. In summer, the station can accommodate as many as 390 people. Molodezhnaya takes its name from the *molodezh*, or young people, who helped to construct it.

SYOWA STATION

Japan's Syowa station was established by the first Japanese Antarctic Research Expedition (JARE 1) in 1956-57. It is built on the northern coast of East Ongul Island, which is separated from the continent by Ongul Strait. The central building is a three-story structure housing the dining room, medical suite, station manager's quarters, bar and games area. It is topped by a domed skylight over a central stairway.

The season after it was built, Syowa could not be staffed because pack ice prevented the relief ship *Soya* from approaching. Helicopters were used to ferry the previous year's overwinterers and their equipment to the ship, but due to a lack of space for them, 15 of the station's sledge dogs were left to fend for themselves when the last helicopter flew off the station on February 11, 1958. Why they were not shot, as would have been more humane, is not clear now. When JARE III returned in

January 1959, just two of the dogs, Taro and Jiro, were alive. They became famous in Japan, and a film made about their story, Koreyoshi Kurahara's *Antarctica*, was the country's biggest movie in 1984.

Among the research that has been done in recent years at Syowa is a fascinating study of the microclimates that exist in Antarctic moss beds.

MAWSON STATION

Australia's Mawson station was established in February 1954. Named for Douglas Mawson, it is the oldest continuously occupied station on the continent. Mawson is approached through Iceberg Alley, a channel lined with huge tabular icebergs that have run aground on underwater banks. Horseshoe Harbour, a sanctuary for ships from the restless Southern Ocean, is the best natural harbor for thousands of kilometers of Antarctic coastline, protected as it is by two projecting arms of land.

Mawson's high-latitude location makes it a good place for studying cosmic rays. This research is done in an underground vault in solid rock, 20m below the surface. The station was also the principal home of Australia's much-loved Antarctic huskies, before the Antarctic Treaty's Protocol on Environmental Protection forced their removal. Many of the dogs now live in northern Minnesota in the US.

As at the other two Australian stations in Antarctica, a massive construction program has modernized the station buildings during the past decade. Each structure is color-coded and vividly visible against the white Antarctic snows. The large living quarters building at Mawson, like its counterparts at Davis and Casey stations, is known as the 'Red Shed.'

The longest golf drive on earth (the lunar golf drive record is admittedly longer) was made at Mawson in 1956, when Norwegian dogsled driver Nils Lied whacked a black-painted golf ball 4000m across new and extremely smooth sea ice. 'For once, I made a good hit,' Lied later told Tim Bowden, author of *Antarctica and Back in Sixty Days*. 'It was a beauty! . . . So we saddled up Oscar, my lead dog, with a sledge behind him. We knew if any dog could sniff the ball out, Oscar would. And he did.'

SCULLIN MONOLITH

Scullin Monolith, 180 km east of Mawson, is known for its remarkable bird life. It is home to the world's highest concentration of breeding Antarctic petrels – about 157,000 pairs nest here – as well as an extensive Adélie penguin rookery.

The crescent-shaped monolith was named by Douglas Mawson, who discovered it on his BANZARE expedition in 1931, for James H Scullin, the Australian prime minister. At about the same time, a group of Norwegian whalers charted the feature, and named it for Norwegian whaling captain Klarius Mikkelsen. A compromise was later reached, and the names are thus: The highest point on Scullin Monolith is 420m Mikkelsen Peak.

AMERY ICE SHELF

The Amery Ice Shelf is the seaward extension of the Lambert Glacier, which, at up to 65 km wide and 400 km long, is the world's largest glacier. The Lambert drains approximately 8% of the Antarctic ice sheet out into Prydz Bay. It was named for Bruce Lambert, Australia's director of National Mapping, in 1957, but it was originally called Baker Three Glacier for the photo reconnaissance air crew who discovered it during Operation 'Highjump' in 1946-47.

West of the Lambert Glacier is Fram Bank, a frequent stopping place for huge tabular bergs that become grounded on the shallow bottom.

DAVIS STATION

Australia's Davis station opened for the IGY in January 1957. Located on the edge of the Vestfold Hills (see below), Davis is named for John King Davis, the master of ships used on expeditions led by Ernest Shackleton and Douglas Mawson. During its first years, Davis accommodated very small wintering parties: In some cases, just four or five men stayed through the long

The Origins of ANARE

The Australian National Antarctic Research Expedition (ANARE) was established in 1947, partly as a result of the urging of Douglas Mawson that Australia send another expedition to Antarctica. The word 'Expedition' was later changed to the plural, 'Expeditions,' to reflect the ongoing nature of ANARE's work.

During its first season, ANARE sent the naval vessel *HMALST 3501* to establish bases on Heard Island (in December 1947) and on Macquarie Island (in March 1948). Meanwhile, another ship, HMAS *Wyatt Earp*, which had sailed to Antarctica four times with American aviator Lincoln Ellsworth, was dispatched to find a site suitable for a permanent Australian Antarctic base. Bad ice conditions and the lateness of the season, however, prevented *Wyatt Earp* from reaching the Antarctic coast.

Wyatt Earp had proved quite unsuitable for our purposes, and in the absence of any other vessel, further efforts in Antarctic waters were not possible, so I concentrated on building up the scientific programs at our island stations. Then, in 1952, I learned that the Lauritzen shipping line in Denmark had built a polar ship, *Kista Dan*, for work in Greenland, and I was able to interest them in chartering it to us during the Northern Hemisphere winter. I explained this to the Australian government and obtained approval to mount an expedition in 1954 to establish an Antarctic station. My book *Antarctic Odyssey* describes this in greater detail.

Aerial photographs of the Antarctic coast taken by the US Operation Highjump helped me to select a suitable site for the station. The area appeared as a horseshoe-shaped expanse of rock attached to the fringe of the continental ice. Mawson station, established in February 1954, was built in the head of the horseshoe. The two arms of the horseshoe circled around to the entrance, where the water was deep enough to allow a ship to enter and stand with hawsers running to the shore in various directions.

It was an exciting moment for me as we raised the Australian flag over the site. I had been brought up on the stories of Scott and Shackleton and other explorers – and here I

polar night. In January 1965, Davis was closed temporarily to allow Australia to concentrate its efforts on the building of Casey station (see below). It reopened in February 1969 and has been operated continuously since then.

Compared to its two Australian sister stations, Casey and Mawson, Davis' climate is relatively mild, a fact that has earned it the nickname 'Riviera of the South.'

VESTFOLD HILLS

The Vestfold Hills, which cover about 400 sq km, are a unique area of ice-free rock (technically, an *oasis*). These hills, 25 km across with a maximum elevation of 159m, are especially beautiful when viewed from the air, revealing long, black volcanic dikes striping the bare rock.

The first woman to set foot in Antarctica, Caroline Mikkelsen, came ashore here on February 20, 1935, with her husband, Klarius Mikkelsen, the captain of the Norwegian whaling ship *Thorshavn*. The Mikkelsens named the Vestfolds for their home county in Norway, Vestfold.

The Vestfolds are biologically unique because they are dotted with a series of remarkable lakes, both freshwater and saline. Some of the hypersaline lakes are more than 13 times as salty as seawater, and have freezing points as low as -17.5°C. In winter, when the ice on these lakes acts as a lid trapping the solar energy absorbed by the saline water, the temperature at the bottom of the lakes can reach 35°C.

Life in these lakes is highly specialized – and rare. In Deep Lake, for instance, only two species have been found, an alga and a bacterium. Because no burrowing animals disturb the lake-bottom sediment, cores

found myself in a similar position, on virgin territory, raising a flag and claiming the land in the name of the English sovereign.

Today, Mawson is the oldest permanently occupied station in Antarctica. It is fascinating for me to look back and remember Mawson as it was when I first walked to the rocky area, with our airplane waiting on the frozen sea offshore. Over the years, I photographed the gradual development of the station from a fixed point in the rock area, chronicling the steady development of the number of buildings and the total space occupied by the station.

When the International Geophysical Year (1957-58) was mooted, I approached my government again, suggesting a second station on a rocky expanse of land known as the Vestfold Hills, where Lincoln Ellsworth had once landed. I established Davis station (about 550 km east of Mawson) in January 1957.

At the end of the IGY, the US Antarctic organization, in order to cut back its extensive program, had decided to close its Wilkes station (about 1300 km east of Davis). Several US scientists approached me, suggesting that because of its value as a scientific observatory, it would be fine if Australia could agree to take it over and continue its programs. I was able to persuade my government to accept this offer. For several years, Wilkes was run as a joint US-Australian station, before finally coming under total Australian control. About 10 years later, Wilkes station, which had deteriorated badly, was evacuated, and a new station that we had built nearby – Casey – was opened.

'Hit and run' landings from ships were also made at numerous points along unknown coasts, while men from ANARE stations made long inland traverses. Memorable exploits include a 700-km dogsled journey from Enderby Land to Mawson in 1958, a 2900-km tractor train journey from Wilkes to Vostok and back in 1962-63, and a four-man winter occupation of a camp on the Amery Ice Shelf for glaciological research in 1967. ■

–Phillip G Law, leader of ANARE from 1949 to 1966. In 1987, Australia established Law Base, named in his honor.

taken here provide an unparalleled record going back as far as 5000 years ago.

At nearby Marine Plain, fossils of whales and dolphins have been found. The area is protected as a site of special scientific interest (SSSI).

LARSEMANN HILLS

The Larsemann Hills, eleven rocky peninsulas discovered by Norwegian whaling captain Klarius Mikkelson in 1935, are an ice-free oasis extending for about 15 km from the Daålk Glacier. The Larsemanns, which reach a maximum elevation of 160m, contain about 200 lakes, including some with water that is among the freshest in the world.

Three scientific stations are located in the Larsemann Hills: China's Zhongshan station runs year round, while Russia's Progress base and Australia's Law base (named for Phillip Law) and are summer-only facilities.

MIRNYY STATION

Russia's Mirnyy station, opened in 1956, was Russia's first on the Antarctic continent. Its 200-meter-long main street was once officially called Lenin Street, though what it might have been referred to as locally is an interesting thought.

BUNGER HILLS

Named for US Navy pilot David Bunger, who landed a seaplane on an unfrozen lake here in February 1947 while on a photographic mission for Operation 'Highjump,' the 780 sq km Bunger Hills caused a sensation when their discovery was announced. Newspaper headlines screamed about an 'Antarctic Shangri-La,' which may help explain some of the science fiction movies about Antarctica having a tropical region inhabited by dinosaurs.

Dotted with numerous meltwater ponds, the Bunger Hills are bisected by Algae Lake, which runs east-west. The hills, which reach a maximum elevation of 180m, are surrounded on all sides by walls of ice rising nearly 120m high.

CASEY STATION

Australia's Casey Station was established in February 1959, when Australia took over responsibility for the US' Wilkes station, which was built in 1957 for the IGY and named for Lt Charles Wilkes, leader of the United States Exploring Expedition.

Ten years later, when its main building was covered by snow, Australia replaced Wilkes with Casey station, three km to the south across the bay. Casey was a radical innovation in Antarctic design: It was built on stilts to allow snow to blow beneath it, with a long tunnel on the windward side that connected all the buildings. The buildings had been built separately as a safety measure in case of fire. Casey was at first known as 'Repstat,' or 'Replacement Station,' but upon its opening, 'Repstat's' name was changed to Casey, in honor of Australia's governor-general, Richard Casey.

Casey itself had to be replaced in the late 1980s when corrosion threatened to destroy its metal supports. The new station, also called Casey, was built a kilometer away and completed in December 1988. The 'old' Casey was dismantled during the 1991-92 and 1992-93 summer seasons and returned to Australia. About 17 people overwinter at Casey, which can accommodate up to 70 people in summer.

The first flight from Australia to land in Australia's claimed territory in Antarctica was made by electronics mogul and *Australian Geographic* magazine publisher Dick Smith and copilot Giles Kershaw (cofounder of Adventure Network International) in November 1988, when the pair flew from Hobart to Casey. They went on to the South Pole and proceeded to make the first global circumnavigation flight via both poles.

Casey has long been a leading center for glaciological research, with several long inland traverses made and a deep ice-drilling program that penetrated nearly 1200m of ice to the underlying bedrock. The station is also located near extensive moss beds, which have been intensively studied for more than two decades.

A large emperor penguin colony was sighted among the grounded icebergs of Peterson Bank, offshore of Casey, in late 1994. Despite more than 40 years of operations, including helicopter flights over the bank during station resupply visits, the bank is so large that the penguins remained undiscovered.

COMMONWEALTH BAY

Australian geologist Douglas Mawson's Australasian Antarctic Expedition (AAE) used Cape Denison on Commonwealth Bay as its base from 1912 to 1914. Comprising 31 men, most of them Australians and New Zealanders, the expedition left Hobart on December 2, 1911, in *Aurora*. Arriving at the continent, they were forced further west than they intended, and seeking along the coast for a suitable landing place, they arrived at Commonwealth Bay, which Mawson named after the Commonwealth of Australia. He named Cape Denison after one of the expedition's main supporters, Hugh Denison, and the Cape's two points of attachment to the mainland he called Land's End and John O'Groats, signaling his Anglophilia.

The same furious katabatic winds that caused Mawson to call this region the 'Home of the Blizzard' can make a landing impossible here, but you can't go inside the huts anyway, since they have become filled with snow and ice (and, in fact, without the support provided by the ice, the huts would probably have been blown away by now). Because of these violent winds, conservation of Mawson's huts is much more difficult that it is for the historic buildings elsewhere in Antarctica, on Ross Island, for instance.

No more than 20 people are allowed to come ashore at one time here. Visitors to the Hut are asked not to climb on structures and must not take any materials of any kind from the site.

WARNING: Explosives left over from the expedition lie approximately 50m southwest (or inland) of the Main Hut. Keep away from the area.

Main Hut Mawson originally intended to have two separate huts, one housing 12 men, the other six. But it was decided instead to join the two, creating one accommodations area and a workshop. The larger building, about 53 sq meters in size, was surrounded on three sides by a veranda that held stores, food and biological supplies. A central dining table was surrounded by Mawson's room, a photographic darkroom and the cook's table and stove. Bunks were placed along the perimeter of the room, and four unfortunate men had to sleep next to the bacteriological research area.

The smaller workshop of roughly 30 sq meters was connected by a door on the north side of the larger building. The workshop contained generators, biology and geology labs, a mechanics' bench, a lathe, a sewing machine and a wireless operating bench, along with another stove. Dogs were housed in kennels on the east veranda, while the west veranda contained a meat cellar, a roof door for winter entrance and a latrine. The entrance to the whole hut complex was through a 'cold porch' on the west veranda, with the door facing north to avoid the furious winds coming from the south.

Lighting consisted of acetylene lamps and skylights, four in the accommodations area, two in the workshop. Winter snowdrifts kept the quarters at a frosty 4–10°C.

Magnetograph House & Magnetic Absolute Hut Cape Denison's location close to the South Magnetic Pole makes it an ideal place for observing the earth's magnetic field; these huts located NE of the Main Hut are where this work was conducted. The magnetograph house, the best-preserved building at Cape Denison, was bought by the expedition from Risby Bros Timber Merchants in Hobart. A stone wall was built outside the magnetograph house to protect it from the wind, which probably helps explain its good condition.

Transit Hut Located just east of the Main Hut, this building was used as shelter while taking sights from stars to determine the exact position of Cape Denison.

Memorial Cross Erected by the expedition in the spring of 1913, this memorial honors Mertz and Ninnis, who perished on the Far Eastern Journey with Mawson, an ordeal from which Mawson himself barely escaped with his life.

Areas where artifacts (building materials, domestic and scientific equipment, food, packaging, clothing and other historic rubbish) are scattered on the ground between the Main Hut and the Boat Harbor are off-limits and should be avoided.

Two ANARE huts are located at Cape Denison: the Sørenson Hut (1986), located to the east of Mawson's Hut, and the Granholm Hut (1978), located to the northwest.

From January 1995 to January 1996, an Australian couple named Don and Margie McIntyre wintered at Cape Denison, the first to do so since Mawson. They lived in a 2.4m by 3.7m cabin they built near Mawson's Hut at Commonwealth Bay (see the sidebar Expedition Ice-Bound on the following page).

DUMONT D'URVILLE STATION

France's Dumont d'Urville station, named for French explorer Jules-Sébastien-César Dumont d'Urville, is located on Pétrel Island in the Géologie Archipelago. It was built in 1956 to replace the French Port Martin station, which burned down on the night of January 24, 1952, without injury to anyone.

Colloquially known as 'Du-d'U' ('doodoo'), the station sensibly allows only 30 to 40 people to come ashore at one time. Ice and/or strong katabatic winds may well prevent a landing here, either by

Expedition Ice-Bound: A Year at Commonwealth Bay

In 1911-14, Douglas Mawson spent two winters at Cape Denison in Commonwealth Bay, one of the most inhospitable spots on earth. He had come well equipped and with a number of companions. Though tragedy struck during a foray onto the Antarctic icecap, Mawson and the rest of his men fared well in the relative comfort of their hut. Could a privately funded and much-smaller expedition winter as successfully?

That was the question in Don's mind after he returned from a voyage to Cape Denison early in 1993. We decided to find out, launching what we called Expedition Ice-Bound in February 1994.

Living for a year at the windiest place on the planet would be more than just a simple camping trip. Among other preparations, it required nearly 10 months of negotiations with the Australian Antarctic Division. We submitted a full report on our proposed activities to the Division's policy section, and we sought in every way to meet the same criteria that official government activities must meet. We assessed all impacts on flora, fauna, ecological processes, ice, air, water and the heritage qualities of Cape Denison, along with the waste-handling methods we would use while living there.

On January 15, 1995, we reached Commonwealth Bay in our 18m expedition support vessel, *Spirit of Sydney*. On board were 4.5 tons of equipment, including two years of food and fuel and a prefab 2.4m by 3.6m box, which was to be our home. Before the month was out, the yacht's five-member crew had sailed home and we were left alone in the world's last great wilderness.

Only days later, the wind worked itself up into a screaming fury and the first blizzard struck. The roar of the wind would rise to a howling climax in a gust and there was no way we could hide from the sound. It filled our world, needling us second by second, worrying, tormenting, wearing us down. All we could do was sit there and wonder how long the hut, which we called Gadget Hut (after one of the huskies on Mawson's expedition), could stand the punishment. Battered by winds that exceeded 240 km/h and gripped by temperatures as low as -38°C, our tiny hut shook and creaked and grew a lining of frost as thick as that found in any home freezer. At times, the interior temperature dropped to -18°C and our breath froze to our sleeping bags.

We had come in search of adventure. We were alone together without any possibility of rescue, yet we were able to share our experience with thousands of schoolchildren around the world on a daily basis, thanks to our sponsor, COMSAT, who provided a satellite telephone system. (Despite this connection to the outside world, we sometimes found ourselves feeling depressed on Sunday nights when we would leave the telephone on and no one would call!) We also spent time writing, observing wildlife, recording weather data, and in Margie's case,

DON McINTYRE

Gadget Hut

hand-sewing 86 teddy bears to be auctioned for charity.

There were dangers, difficulties and disappointments. On two occasions, we nearly died from carbon monoxide poisoning when our roof ventilators iced up. Whenever we cooked or turned on the heater, the ice on the walls and ceiling melted, creating rain inside the hut. We had to cover the bed every day to catch the meltwater, and pools of water puddled the floor. When we opened what we thought was our last can of potatoes, which we had been hoarding, we were crest-fallen to discover that they were in fact asparagus.

DON McINTYRE

Holiday celebrations broke the monotony of the long, cold winter.

As autumn gave way to lifeless winter, the psychological pressure increased. For three months, we lived in almost complete darkness, and for 21 days we didn't see the sun at all. Margie suffered bouts of profound despondency, particularly when we were confined indoors for long periods; she cried for six months, from March until October, and felt sorry for Don when she couldn't stop the crying. Once, we were stuck inside for 20 days in a row. We'll never forget the roar of the wind – it will stay with us forever. We had to shout just to talk to each other in bed.

With the arrival of spring came life – killer whales, seals and penguins – and days of never-ending sunshine. Occasionally, we had such brilliant days that the stunning panoramas outside inspired moods close to euphoria. We would sit for hours watching the penguins and seals, who became our friends. At night, we were impressed by the aurora, with its green and yellow 'waterfall' effects. On Christmas, we were visited by a US helicopter – the first people we had seen in 12 months!

Our adventure cost us around A$600,000, including the purchase of *Spirit of Sydney*. You could say that our hut was the most expensive – and smallest – hotel room in the world. But we were privileged to be staying at the most remote and beautiful place in the world.

We found that we are two sides of the same coin; we have our differences, but we make a formidible unit. Don is 41 and Margie is 35; we have been married for 12 years. We didn't have a single fight all year – except for what we'd term two 'debates.' That's pretty incredible, considering that we were never more than 100m apart for a whole year. We really had to support each other to survive, which meant that we had to become closer. Yet our differences came to an extraordinary climax at the end of our stay, when Don pleaded with Margie to let him stay on for another year, completely alone. It was another testing time for our relationship, which survived stronger than ever. (Don came home with Margie.)

We are now seeking couples worldwide to spend 1997, 1998, 1999 or 2000 in our hut. By means of satellite technology, we hope to create a dynamic and adventurous education program with live video-conferencing from what is presently the only private year-round base in Antarctica. ■

–Don & Margie McIntyre, authors of *Two Below Zero: A Year in Antarctica*

Zodiac or helicopter. About 30 winterers are accommodated at Dumont d'Urville, and as many as 67 people live at the station during the summer.

Dumont d'Urville became the focus of international attention in 1983, when the French government began construction of a 1000m hard rock airstrip. Unfortunately, five islands were dynamited to level them and to provide material to fill in the water separating them. Greenpeace made headlines around the world when it visited the runway construction site during the 1983-84 season and obtained photos of dead penguins killed by flying rock shrapnel. The airstrip was completed in early 1993 and was due to be used for test flights the next season. However, in January 1994, the nearby Astrolabe Glacier calved, causing an enormous wave that damaged the runway and an aircraft hangar. The French government subsequently decided not to repair the airstrip.

South Pole

'Great God! This is an awful place!' British explorer Robert Falcon Scott famously wrote in his diary on the day in 1912 that he reached the South Pole – only to discover that his Norwegian rival, Roald Amundsen, had arrived 34 days before him. Scott's exclamation reflected not just his anguish over losing the great polar race he had labored for a decade to win, but also his awe of the near-mythical spot itself. He had good reason to marvel.

Almost nothing lives here – the two exceptions are a species of algae and a species of bacteria, which were probably blown in from somewhere else, as there are no indigenous species at the Pole. Only four other animal species have ever visited: humans, sledge dogs, hamsters (experiment subjects) and a few, presumably very lost skuas, which may have followed the vapor trails of aircraft resupplying the station here.

Just eight years ago, the South Pole (known to its denizens simply as 'Pole') was still accessible only to the US government and a few other national expeditions that made long traverses from the coast. A few adventurers launched private expeditions at a cost of hundreds of thousands of dollars – and their safe return was doubtful. Now, anyone with a reasonably thick wallet can visit this remote redoubt in the high Antarctic desert. Still, in recent years, fewer than 40 tourists annually have reached the Farthest South.

Coping with Isolation

Although it's rarely a problem for tourists, Antarctica's remoteness can be difficult to handle for many winterers, and several mental-health coping mechanisms are common. To relieve the boredom of the polar winter, expeditioners sometimes shave their head or pierce their ears or nose, knowing they can revert back to their 'old selves' before returning home. Sometimes whole research bases indulge in a kind of collective 'cultism,' in which a particular song or movie is replayed over and over, with station members memorizing the entire dialogue and playing particular roles. A film version of Jane Austen's *Pride and Prejudice* assumed bizarre importance for a wintering party at one subantarctic island, for instance, while another group at a continental station became fairly infatuated with a ZZ Top music video. For obvious reasons, drag enjoys a long history in Antarctica, from Scott's *Discovery* expedition's Royal Terror Theatre to Australian stations' four-decade tradition of performing bawdy versions of *Cinderella*. ■

GEOGRAPHY

Unlike its northern conjugate, which sits in the middle of the Arctic Ocean, the South Pole lies amid a mind-bending wasteland of monotonously flat snow-covered ice called the polar plateau. The Pole itself is among the most isolated spots on earth, surrounded by thousands of square kilometers unrelieved by a single feature to interest the eye. In every direction you look, there is only unbroken horizon.

CLIMATE

Temperatures on the Polar Plateau range from -82°C to -14°C; the mean temperature – and boy, *is* it mean – is -49°C. Winter windchills can plummet to -100°C. The elevation is 2835m above sea level, but the cold and polar location make the air pressure the equivalent of 3230m; first-timers are often exhausted after even gentle exercise until they become acclimated.

Snowfall is less than 21 cm annually, and the average wind speed is just 19 km/h, a summer breeze compared to the infamous 320 km/h katabatic winds found on the coast. The extreme cold and lack of humidity (0.03%) combine to make this the world's driest desert.

The sun ends a spectacular weeks-long sunset and dips below the horizon on March 22 (though twilight lingers for another three weeks). Then the potentially depression-inducing unbroken darkness sets in, lightened only by the surreal sky show of the aurora australis. On September 22, the pale, deprived winterers rejoice at sunrise. All year round, however, South Polarites can fall victim to a peculiar form of polar pathology: 'Big Eye,' a period of disorientation and sleeplessness caused by the lack of a regular light-dark cycle.

The disintegration of the ozone layer – the notorious 'ozone hole' – allows powerful ultraviolet rays to penetrate the atmosphere, causing severe sunburn to unprotected skin (though it will be frozen long before it is sunburned).

HISTORY

Robert F Scott's *Discovery* expedition of 1901-04 was the first to set off with the explicit goal of reaching the Pole – and to have a reasonable chance of doing so. After an initial push to the south with a large supporting party, Scott and two fellow Britons, Edward Wilson and Ernest Shackleton, set off on what they hoped would be the final push to the Pole. But the untrained men's attempts at driving their sled dogs were inefficient, and they failed miserably, reaching only 82°16.5'S. Though this was a record for furthest south, it was still more than 725 km from the mark.

Shackleton tried again in 1908. His *Nimrod* expedition was another close scrape with death, part of an emerging pattern for South Polar exploration that by this time was becoming all too familiar (and, in hindsight, completely unnecessary, with better planning). Shackleton and three compatriots – Eric Marshall, Jameson Adams and Frank Wild – trekked on foot to within about 160 km of the elusive destination before they calculated that their dwindling provisions would make suicide the price of reaching the Pole. Making a decision that would haunt him for the rest of his life, Shackleton ordered a retreat, telling his wife, Emily, later: 'I thought you'd rather have a live donkey than a dead lion.' They returned to base in extremely poor condition and with all their supplies exhausted.

It was generally believed that the next expedition to tackle the Pole, strengthened by knowledge gained from the previous attempts, would most likely reach it. Scott, therefore, felt justifiably confident when he set sail for the south again in 1910, on his *Terra Nova* expedition. Unfortunately, as had Shackleton before him, Scott drew the wrong conclusion from his earlier ill-fated experiments with dogsledging. He tried several methods of travel – including motor sledges, ponies and dogs – but eventually selected man-hauling. This brutal exercise – walking or skiing while pulling sledges heavily laden with supplies – is among the most strenuous activities known to humans.

Once again, it was a race with death. Scott and his four companions arrived at the Pole to find, in his words, that they had done so 'without the reward of priority.' Amundsen's green tent, topped with the Norwegian flag, made that painfully clear. The grim photo Scott and his men snapped of themselves tells it all: Complete, hollow-eyed despair darkens their faces. Some now wonder if they didn't deliberately martyr themselves on their desperate return journey, preferring the converse of Shackleton's simple equation.

Certainly one of the men did just that, sacrificing himself in the hope that his three remaining companions might live. On the morning of his 32nd birthday, his feet badly frostbitten, Capt Lawrence 'Titus' Oates had hoped not to wake. When he found that he had lived through the night, he walked out into a raging blizzard, excusing himself to his companions with the courtly exit line: 'I am just going outside and may be some time.' They never saw him again. Meanwhile, their own fate was sealed. Just two days later, another severe blizzard pinned them down in their tent – only 18 km from a major cache of supplies they called One Ton Depot. They remained trapped there for 10 days, their supplies gradually dwindling to a single sputtering lamp. By its light, Scott, who may or may not have been the last to die, scrawled his immortal words: 'It seems a pity, but I do not think I can write more . . . For God's sake, look after our people.'

A search party found their bodies the following August. The polar party's bodies, buried in their tent beneath a snow cairn by the search party, probably reached the Ross Sea in about 1980, give or take several years. Because of the accumulated snowfall on the icecap as it advanced toward the sea, Scott – along with Wilson and Bowers and their tent – would have reached the sea through the *bottom* of the Ross Ice Shelf, making it extremely unlikely that they would be spotted by human eyes. All in all, a fitting grave.

Roald Amundsen, Scott's rival, was a polar technician. His approach was slow, methodical, proven (though he made one false start, trying to leave his coastal base too early in the season, and was forced to retreat with severe frostbite). He carried spare food, extra fuel and backups for all essential equipment. Most importantly, he brought dogs to do the heavy pulling, saving the men's strength. He also coldly calculated the worn-out dogs as food for the others. Amundsen had a different problem from Scott: He actually wanted to reach the North Pole, and his expedition left Norway with that stated intention. But after American Robert Peary announced that he had attained the North Pole on April 6, 1910, Amundsen secretly turned his ambition 180°. He remarked upon this ultimate of ironies in his diary, published as *The South Pole*, on reaching the South Pole on December 14, 1911:

Amundsen: slow and methodical

> The goal was reached, the journey ended. I cannot say – though I know it would sound much more effective – that the object of my life was attained. That would be romancing rather too bare-facedly. I had better be honest and admit straight out that I have never known any man to be placed in such a diametrically opposite position to the goal of his desires as I was at that moment. The regions around the North Pole – well, yes, the North Pole itself – had attracted me from childhood, and here I was at the South Pole. Can anything more topsy-turvy be imagined?

By contrast to the Britons' desperate race against starvation, the Norwegians' return trip from 90°S was little more than a bracing ski outing. After three days spent at the Pole making weather observations and precisely calculating their position, they headed north, reaching their base on the coast 'all hale and hearty.' Amundsen's polar camp, by the way, also remains buried under the annual accumulations of snow, and by now should be

Farthest South

Claims to have reached the North Pole were made in 1908 by Frederick Cook and in 1909 by Robert Peary. Though both claims are contentious, their presumed authenticity served to divert attention to attaining the South Pole. The following notes describe successive penetrations leading up to Roald Amundsen's attainment of the Pole in December 1911, as well as subsequent landmark voyages.

1603 Gabriel de Castilla (Spain), with a ship's company, probably penetrated the Southern Ocean south of Drake Passage. Subsequently several Spanish and other merchant vessels reported being blown south of 60°S rounding Cape Horn in severe weather.

1774 James Cook (UK), with companies aboard HMS *Resolution* and HMS *Adventure*, crossed the Antarctic Circle (66.55°S) off Enderby Land, on January 17, and 13 days later he reached a farthest south of 71.17°S off Marie Byrd Land.

1842 James Clark Ross (UK), with companies aboard HMS *Erebus* and HMS *Terror*, reached 78.17°S in the Ross Sea, on February 23. The volcanoes bearing the names of his ships were discovered.

1900 Hugh Evans (UK) and three others from the ship *Southern Cross* sledged to 78.83°S on the Ross Ice Shelf, on February 23. This was the first southern penetration by land.

1902 Robert Scott (UK) and two others sledged to 82.28°S, near the foot of the Beardmore Glacier, on December 30.

1909 Ernest Shackleton (UK) and three others sledged up the Beardmore Glacier to 88.38°S on January 9. This was approximately 180 km from the South Pole – but insufficient supplies necessitated their return.

about 12m down. In 1993, a Norwegian group came to the Pole with hopes of recovering the tent, Norwegian flag and sledge for display at the 1994 Winter Olympics in Lillehammer, but had to give up when one of its members fell 40 meters down a crevasse and was killed during a skiing journey near the coast. (Just the sort of accident that the governments operating in Antarctica fear they will be called upon to rescue, cutting into their already tight budgets and limited summer research season.) Unlike Scott, who left behind two huts as well as his ship *Discovery*, now a museum in Dundee, Scotland, Amundsen left huts at his camp on the Ross Ice Shelf at the Bay of Whales, long since gone as the ice shelf calved and floated out to sea.

American Richard Evelyn Byrd, the next to claim to have seen the Pole, reported flying over with three other men on November 29, 1929. Byrd pretty well summed up the quixotic quality of all quests, polar and otherwise: 'One gets there, and that is about all there is for the telling. It is the effort to get there that counts.' He dropped a rock wrapped in the American flag out the window of his Ford Trimotor plane and flew back to his camp at Little America. Although the navigation of Byrd's flight has been questioned by some authorities, the point is actually moot, for Byrd himself was among the six men in two aircraft who definitely flew over 90°S on February 15, 1947.

On neither of his flights did Byrd land, however, meaning that after Amundsen and Scott, the Pole lay untouched for another 44 years. During that interval, two world

1911 Roald Amundsen (Norway) and four others dog-sledged to 90°S on December 14.

1912 Robert Scott and four others sledged to 90°S on January 17. They arrived 33 days after the Norwegians had departed and all perished during the return journey. Their bodies and notes were found in August 1912.

1929 Richard Byrd (US), with an aircraft crew, claimed to have flown over the South Pole from the Ross Ice Shelf on November 29, but the navigation has been questioned. On February 15, 1947, he definitely flew over it, with crew aboard two aircraft from 'Little America IV' station on the Ross Ice Shelf.

1956 John Torbert (US) and six others flew across Antarctica via the South Pole (Ross Island to Weddell Sea and back, without landing) on January 13. On October 31, Conrad Shinn (US), with an aircraft crew, landed at the South Pole. A permanent station was established and sustained by aircraft. Subsequently, aircraft have routinely landed at the South Pole, as many as several a week during recent summers.

1958 Vivian Fuchs (British Commonwealth), with an expeditionary party, reached the South Pole by motor vehicles and dog sledges on January 20, and continued across Antarctica (Weddell Sea to Ross Sea).

Subsequently, several expeditions have crossed the Antarctic through the South Pole by surface, and many have made one-way surface journeys to the Pole, departing by aircraft. Most adventurers' South Pole journeys during the past decade have used aircraft and many started well inland, far from any place that a ship could reach. ■

–**Robert Headland**, archivist and curator at the Scott Polar Research Institute in Cambridge, England

wars raged, and a third appeared imminent, when an American ski-equipped plane set down on the ice on October 31, 1956, the first aircraft landing at the Pole. Pilot Conrad 'Gus' Shinn set down his Navy R4D (the military version of a DC-3) named *Que Sera Sera* with Admiral George Dufek and five other US Navy men who surveyed the area for a permanent scientific base. Construction began the next month, and the first South Pole station was completed by February 1957. It has operated ever since.

Three modified Ferguson farm tractors, outfitted with rubber tracks, were the next vehicles to reach the Pole overland, on January 2, 1958, led by New Zealander Edmund Hillary of Mt Everest fame. Hillary's team was laying depots for the first successful crossing of the continent, by British explorer Vivian Fuchs' Commonwealth Trans-Antarctic expedition.

Women were notably absent from these exploration heroics. In fact, most governments operating in Antarctica had an all-but-official ban on women in Antarctica for decades. This is perhaps better understood today when we recall that expeditions were often staffed by members of the military – a group that was all-male at that time. Still, Antarctic sexism was often justified by lame rationalizations about physical strength, sexual frustrations and even the difficulty of providing separate toilet facilities, but in fact, the influence of the male expedition members' wives back home had as much as anything else to do with the policy. In 1969, the first women joined the US Antarctic program, and the first women to reach the Pole arrived by US Navy aircraft on November 11, 1969. The six of them – not wishing for one to later claim she had been first out of the aircraft – linked arms and walked out of the back of the plane together. They spent a few hours visiting the station before flying back to McMurdo. Another two years passed before the first woman actually spent a 'night' at the Pole, in December 1971. She was Louise Hutchinson, a reporter for the *Chicago Tribune*, and she only got to stay because weather delayed her flight out. But two years later, two American women, Nan Scott and Donna Muchmore, became the first women to work at the Pole. By 1979, the Pole station had a female physician, Dr Michele Eileen Raney, the first woman to winter at 90°S. On January 6, 1995, Norwegian Liv Arnesen arrived at the Pole after skiing unaccompanied from the edge of the continent in 50 days, the first female to accomplish that feat.

Tourists first arrived at the South Pole in 1968, when a chartered Convair flew over both poles from November 22 to December 3 in a fund-raising effort for a Boston museum. The south polar leg left Christchurch, landed at McMurdo Sound for a few hours' look at both Scott's Hut and McMurdo Station, then flew over the Pole at a low altitude and on to Argentina. The first tourist flight to land at the Pole was on January 11, 1988, when a DHC-6 Twin Otter operated by Adventure Network International, also known as 'Antarctic Airways' (see Getting There & Away), brought the first paying passengers to 90°S – for a cool $15,000 each.

THINGS TO SEE

Ceremonial Pole

If you only spend a few hours at the Pole (as most tourist flights do), you'll be sure to stop here, close to the station and within the 'turnaround' (taxiway) of the ice runway. The red-and-white-striped 'barber' pole, capped by a metallic chromium globe, is surrounded by the flags of the original 12 Antarctic Treaty signatories, so it offers the perfect photo-op. But it's not the real thing – it's just for show.

Geographic Pole

Because the 2850m-thick ice at the Pole moves about 10m per year in the direction of 43°W, the Geographic Pole marker has to be moved each austral summer. At this rate of movement, the ground you are standing on here will drop into the Southern Ocean in about 120,000 years. The 'new' South Pole is recalculated every year using a combination of old-fashioned science (the shadow tip method) and the latest technology (global positioning satellites). The marker is about four meters long, but two-thirds of it gets pounded into the ice with a special Day-Glo orange mallet during the brief annual Pole-moving ceremony, after which the South Polar denizens rush back indoors for medicinal hot chocolate. The long line of markers stretching off into the distance marks the former South Poles; due to the snow buildup, they appear to be sinking into the ground. The American flag is conspicuously planted about a meter from the Pole marker.

You may hear about three other Poles while you are in Antarctica:

- The South Magnetic Pole (65°S, 139°E), off the coast near Commonwealth Bay, is where a magnetic compass needle will try to point straight down. Its position moves about 10 to 15 km a year presently in a north to northwesterly direction. The South Magnetic Pole, then on land, was first reached in 1909 by Douglas Mawson, Edgeworth David and Alistair Mackay.
- The South Geomagnetic Pole (78°S, 107°E) is where the flux in the Earth's electromagnetic field is manifested. Russia's Vostok station occupies this pole.
- The Pole of Maximum Inaccessibility (84°S, 65°E) is the point furthest from any Antarctic coast.

AMUNDSEN-SCOTT SOUTH POLE STATION

The Dome

The Dome, as it's universally known, was built in 1971-75. Standing 50m in diameter at its base and 15m high, the silver-grey aluminum geodesic dome covers three structures, each two stories high, that provide accommodations, dining, laboratory and recreation facilities. A line of steel arches runs off to the left and right of the Dome's entryway; the arches house the garage complex, gymnasium, carpenter shop, power plant, biomedical facility and main fuel storage. Sub-ice utility corridors, called utilidors, carry glycol heat-circulation pipes and water, sewage, phone, computer and electric lines between facilities.

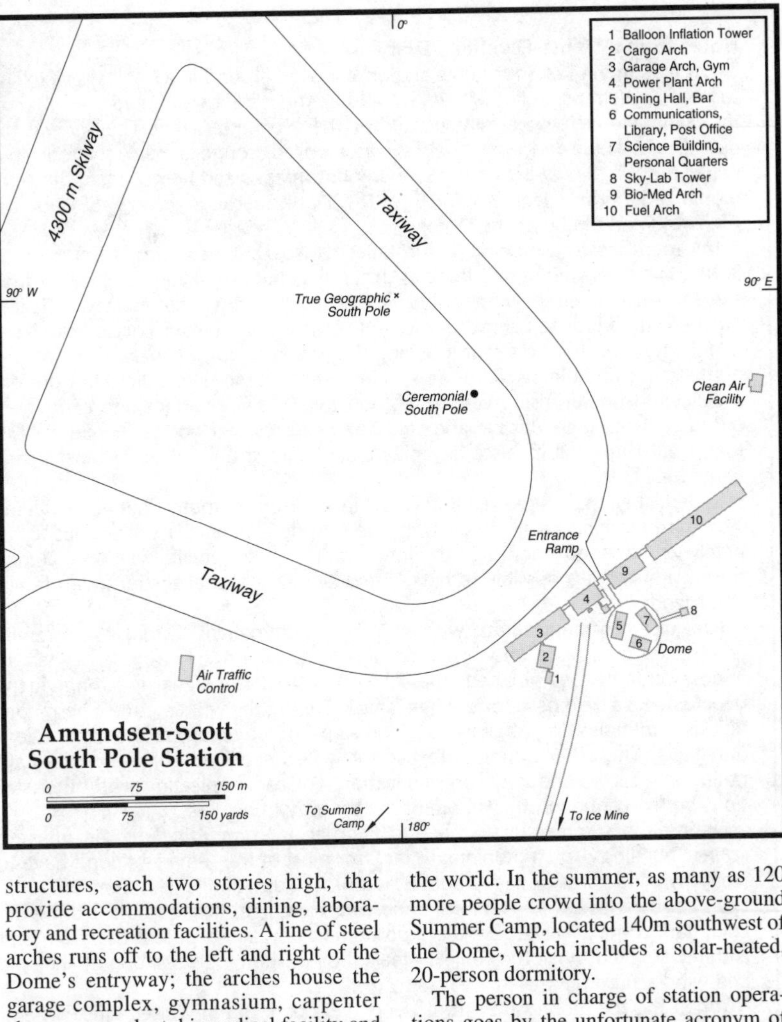

Twenty-eight people inhabit the Dome during winter, and from mid-February to late October no flights can make it in, so they are physically cut off from the rest of the world. In the summer, as many as 120 more people crowd into the above-ground Summer Camp, located 140m southwest of the Dome, which includes a solar-heated, 20-person dormitory.

The person in charge of station operations goes by the unfortunate acronym of SPAM: South Pole Area Manager. Equal in stature is the Chief Scientist, who is in charge of scientific personnel. Above both of these members ranks the National Science Foundation Representative, the senior US Government official at the station – a person you could call the top dog at the bottom of the world.

Notes from a Dome-Dweller's Diary

Upon first arriving at South Pole station, I looked around in awe. It was exciting to have finally made it to 90°S. As we gathered our things and made our way off the plane, we were cheerfully greeted by the overwinter crew. The sky was the purest crystal blue and snow bright white. I looked around and saw the few landmarks that I had only previously seen in photographs and home video: the ceremonial Pole, the Clean Air Facility, the Dark Sector buildings, Skylab, the Archways and of course the Dome.

My room inside the Dome is the tiniest of spaces, measuring 1.8m wide by 3.2m long. Some might find this claustrophobic, but I think it quite cozy. I added some much-needed shelving for books, CDs, stereo, humidifier and space heater. The bed was a little too short for me, so I constructed an extension so I can sleep at a diagonal without my feet touching the very cold outside wall.

The galley and dining room are also inside the Dome. The galley staff put out a delicious and surprising variety of food for both vegetarians and carnivores. Because of the high altitude and cold temperatures, our bodies require a lot of fuel: I eat three full meals a day plus many snacks, but I have still lost nearly seven kg.

I spend my spare time reading, playing pool or computer games, watching videos and writing email. News from the outside is definitely sparse, but fortunately we have some access to the Internet during our satellite windows. During these windows, it's possible to have interactive talk or chat sessions with family and friends.

For voice communications, we have several alternatives. During the summer, amateur or ham radio phone patches are possible and very popular. When an announcement goes out over the PA system that the signal is strong, many people make a mad dash for the ham shack. During the winter, atmospheric conditions sometimes do not allow for good signal propagation, so the ham radio is unreliable. The other option is to use the ATS-3 satellite, which, like the ham radio, only allows one-way communication. For communicating with other stations on the continent, the HF radios are the way to go.

During the summer (November to February), 'commuting' to the outlying science buildings isn't a problem. In fact, for most of the summer, I don't have to wear my wind pants or heavy boots. As long as I don't linger outdoors too long, I can get by with Levis (with long underwear) and light hiking boots. During the cold, dark winter, I make sure that I don't have any skin exposed. Even skin that is thinly covered by clothes quickly feels the hot, burning sensation of the cold and wind attacking.

When the full moon isn't out, it's very, very dark out in winter. Once when I was leaving work, I couldn't see anything. There were no lights coming from the Dome or from the Clean Air Facility. I could only see two small lights coming from the AMANDA building, which is about 800m away from the Dome. It was so dark I couldn't see my own hand in front of my face. I might as well have been walking with my eyes closed. It took my eyes at least three minutes to adjust enough so that I could see even very faint outlines of nearby buildings.

My first full-fledged Antarctic storm was great: winds were blowing 37 km/h with 56 km/h gusts. Snow was blowing everywhere, and visibility was incredibly low. You had to lean into the wind in order not to be blown over. I had to wear my goggles or else my eyelashes would freeze together in a matter of seconds. It was exhilarating! This is what I had thought the South Pole was going to be like. I've never felt more alive.

The auroral displays have been awesome. Sometimes they stretch from one horizon to the other. Their color is hard to describe. It's an eerie green, sometimes with just a hint of red or pink. The auroras are very active when directly overhead. They twist, turn and oscillate and give us a delightful show. When the auroras aren't out and it's clear outside, the sky is filled with stars.

According to Nancy, our cook, consumption of chocolate has increased tremendously since sunset. Apparently, without sunlight our bodies are deprived of stimuli – and to counterbalance this, we crave chocolate. The chocolate triggers a chemical in our brain that replaces the lost stimulus. My particular desire is for a chocolate shake!

Also, with no sun around for a visual cue, some people have a very hard time sleeping. They either can sleep for only a few hours each night or they sleep for 20 or more hours at a time. Some of the overwinter crew routinely spend time in the greenhouse underneath sodium lamps to adjust their internal clocks.

One day, it was announced that the temperature was steadying at around -101°F (-73.9°C). So a group of us – 15 men and four women – gained our exclusive membership to the 300 Club. We crowded into the sauna – cranked up to 200°F (93°C) – and began to work up a sweat. About 15 minutes later, we burst through the door, down the hallway and out of the Dome – a sheer drop of 300°F. I wore nothing but socks, tennis shoes and a neck gaitor over my nose and mouth so my lungs wouldn't get frostbitten while I ran. Someone was taking pictures – I could see the flash going off but not much else, thanks to all the steam coming from our bodies. Once outside, I ran up the slight snow incline to the surface. Some people stopped there, took a few photos and returned to the sauna. A few of us continued on. I stopped halfway across the taxiway because I couldn't run any farther, but six people made it to the Ceremonial Pole, and one person made it all the way to the Geographic Pole. Then it's a mad dash back inside. I'm glad I did it, though I did get a touch of frostbite on my thumbs (of all places) – nothing serious. Better my thumbs than somewhere more important!

After months of darkness I find myself thinking about what it will be like to see the sun rise above the horizon again. Will I be overjoyed to know that soon a plane will come and take me away? Or will I feel sad knowing that my year at Pole will be coming to an end? Right now, in order to cope with the darkness and isolation, I find it best to concentrate on day-to-day matters. Thinking about what will happen four or five months from now somehow makes those things seems like an eternity away. ■

–**Ricardo Ramos, LtJG, NOAA**, 1995/96 Officer-In-Charge of the Clean Air Facility and Station Science Leader at Amundsen-Scott South Pole station. He sent this article by email from the Pole.

Walking down the ramp into the Dome through the huge garage-like doors, you can't help notice the sign above your head: 'The United States of America Welcomes You to Amundsen-Scott South Pole Station.' This causes many people to ask: 'No one owns the South Pole, do they?' The answer, of course, is No. But Amundsen-Scott South Pole Station is, among other things, an aluminum-and-concrete lesson in Antarctic *realpolitik*. While no certain ownership of Antarctica exists, and the Antarctic Treaty agreed to set aside the territorial claims made by seven countries, the stark reality is that some countries are 'more equal' than others in Antarctic politics. Before its collapse, the Soviet Union, for example, maintained a ring of research bases that encircled the continent, while the US' Pole station sits astride all the lines of longitude, neatly occupying all time zones – and six of the seven Antarctic claims – at once. (Amundsen-Scott station, by the way, uses New Zealand time since resupply flights to the Pole and McMurdo station originate in Christchurch and this simplifies logistics.)

In the recent past, private expeditions arriving at the Pole were greeted by the Americans with a decidedly chilly welcome, one that had nothing to do with the subzero temperatures. Not that the scientists, technicians and support staff at Amundsen-Scott disliked visitors; in fact, just the reverse was true. But thanks to the official US government prohibition of support to non-governmental activities in Antarctica (the reasoning was that scientists would be disrupted by tourists and the inevitable accidents would require costly search-and-rescue), the station staff were told to have no contact with visitors. Now, thankfully, a more enlightened policy now operates, and a warm welcome is offered by the South Polarites.

The Dome has had a hard life under harsh conditions, and parts of the under-ice complex are safety hazards. Occasional power brownouts and fuel leaks also threaten station security, as does drifting snow, which will eventually crush the Dome. Because of all these problems, the US government is studying a plan to replace the aging structure with a new above-ground facility. Three separate horseshoe-shaped modules would be connected by flexible walkways and raised on stilts to prevent the destructive snow buildup. The stilts could be jacked up as snow accumulated underneath and eventually rose to the level of the buildings. Being on the surface, the new station would also prevent the claustrophobic 'cabin fever' induced by living underground. Plans call for it to accommodate 110 people and require 80 construction workers and ten years to build at a cost of US$180 million; included in the design are a sound-proof practice room for the pickup rock bands popular among Polarites, and a 280-sq-meter greenhouse fertilized by treated sewage. The proposed rebuilding program would use annual tractor trains to bring tons of construction materials overland from McMurdo – in just 20 days, quite a change from Scott's ordeal. The old Dome would then be taken apart piece by piece and taken back to the US for disposal or re-erection, perhaps as the centerpiece of a national Antarctic museum. Given the current budget-slashing mood of the US Congress, however, funding for a replacement facility at the Pole seems parlous at best.

Life Under the Dome South Polar living is difficult. As one recent SPAM told the *Antarctica Sun Times* weekly newspaper at McMurdo station: 'We use the psychological tests to weed out the sane.' It takes some people two or three weeks simply to adjust to the Pole's altitude, as the body strives to produce more red blood cells to handle the oxygen-thin air. Extreme cold limits the time one can spend outdoors, and the darkness and even more extreme cold of the polar winter can be very hazardous to human life. (Station members, however, routinely go outside the Dome even on the coldest and darkest days. Flag lines –

bamboo poles with small flags attached to the top and spaced every two meters – guide the way from the Dome to outlying buildings.) During the summer, when much of the station's water has to be made by melting snow, showers are limited to two minutes' running water and can be taken only twice a week. Fire is an omnipresent danger in the thin, dry atmosphere. That same dry air cracks skin, lips and the inside of nostrils, so petroleum jelly must be used to keep the skin moist.

The isolation can be overwhelming – wintering at the Pole is in some ways similar to being an astronaut, albeit one who has a bit more room to walk around and can use email. The South Pole's isolation has recently been made a little worse, thanks to budget-cutting that eliminated the Pole's annual midwinter airdrop from a C-141 cargo plane. This operation, usually staged in June by the light of a full moon to enable ground spotters to find the parachuted crates, delivered nearly 30,000 kg of mail, spare parts and fresh fruits and vegetables to the lonely Polarites, who looked forward to it like Christmas for weeks. Eliminating the drop, however, trimmed a small sum from the US Antarctic program's US$195 million budget.

Recreation opportunities on the barren polar plateau are obviously limited, but inventive South Polarites have come up with improvisations such as volleybag, a version of volleyball that uses a beanbag instead. On Christmas Eve, the 4.4 km 'Race Around the World' circles the Pole in -23°C temperatures, challenging runners, joggers, walkers, skiers and even snowmobilers; the 1995 winner (on foot) had an impressive time of 13:55.

Then there's the unique membership known as the 300° Club: To join, you simply wait until the temperature drops below -100°F (-73°C) – which happens only during the deepest cold of winter, steam in a 200°F (93°C) sauna until you begin to sweat, then streak stark naked (shoes, however, are highly recommended) about 100m out of the Dome and up to the snow surface. Some members push on even further, going about 100m out of the Dome and around the Ceremonial Pole. Though some people claim that the rime of flash-frozen sweat actually acts as insulation, if you fall, the feeling of the ice against your reddened skin is similar to that of burning and as rough as falling on granite. Induction into the 300° Club requires photographic documentation – and yes, there are female members.

Science Facilities

Most, if not all, of the scientific facilities at the Pole will be off-limits to visitors, in order to prevent disruption to the research. Time is at a premium for most of the scientists working here, since if they are unable to complete their work in the time allotted, they may not be able to win a grant to return to Antarctica. Other laboratories at the Pole station are off-limits because their delicate instrumentation could be contaminated or decalibrated by the presence of unauthorized visitors. Still, it's interesting to know what work is being done.

Chief among the research being done at the South Pole is work on the notorious 'ozone hole,' the thinning of the atmosphere's ozone layer, caused by halocarbons and other manmade chemicals (see Antarctic Science chapter).

Scientists at the Pole's Clean Air Facility, located 450m upwind of the station, study some of the purest air on earth in hopes of learning about pollution and how it is spread around the globe.

The South Pole is also a world center for astronomy, thanks to its high altitude and thin, dry atmosphere. (The centrifugal force of the earth's rotation flattens out the atmosphere at both poles, and the extreme cold freezes water vapor out of the air.) The astronomical instruments are located about a kilometer from the Dome in the so-called 'Dark Sector,' where extraneous light, heat and electromagnetic radiation are prohibited, so as not to disturb the experiments. Noise and other earth-shaking activity, meanwhile, are banned in the 'Quiet Sector,' where seismological studies are done.

Because their highly technical work may appear dull to the uninitiated, scientists sometimes like to jazz up the names of their experiments for the general public (and their funding governments). So the astronomers at the South Pole's CARA, the Center for Astrophysical Research in Antarctica, use telescopes with cool-sounding names. SPIREX, the South Polar Infrared Explorer, seeks infrared radiation from deep space that signals young galaxies. COBRA, the Cosmic Microwave Background Anistopy experiment, looks for small variations in the temperature of microwave radiation dating back to just one million years after the Big Bang; this may reveal mysteries about the structure of the universe. AMANDA, the Antarctic Muon and Neutrino Detector Array, is a collection of 200m-long strings of instruments lowered into holes drilled up to 2180m down into the ice with hot water. AMANDA looks for the ultra-high-energy subatomic particles called neutrinos that pass through the earth and interact with atoms in the ice, which is perfectly transparent at that depth. Scientists believe that neutrinos will shed light on the power sources of galaxies and the workings of supernovae, the massive explosions of stars. Finally, AST/RO, the Antarctic Submillimeter Telescope and Remote Observatory, surveys emissions of carbon atoms from the large clouds of gas and dust that lie between stars. Researchers hope to learn more about how the collapse of these dust clouds gives birth to stars.

All of these instruments detect radiation not visible to the human eye. There are, of course, at the Pole several telescopes in the visible range of light (including SPOT, the South Polar Optical Telescope) that take advantage of the thinner atmosphere to peer far into the star-filled blackness of the polar night.

The astrophysicists are no less creative in their naming, so they use GASP (Gamma-Ray Astrophysics at the South Pole) and SPASE (South Pole Air Shower Experiment) to search for sources of gamma radiation out in the universe.

PLACES TO STAY

Most tourist visitors to the Pole remain for fewer than 24 hours, so there's no need for accommodations. Because there is no room under the Dome for extra people, visitors are expected to be completely self-sufficient. So Adventure Network International, currently the sole tour operator offering Polar visits, carries a full complement of emergency equipment and food to enable their clients to camp at the Pole for several days if necessary. But the accommodations at ANI's Patriot Hills base camp are much more comfortable, so they prefer to take people to the Pole on day trips only. Of course, if clients actually want to sleep in tents at the Pole, ANI can arrange it.

THINGS TO BUY

You can expect to be invited inside the Dome for a visit to the mess hall, possibly to some accommodation facilities, and to the station's 'gift shop.' They carry a\ widely varying stock of T-shirts, sweatshirts, baseball caps, souvenir water bottles, postcards, stamps, envelopes, pins and other little trinkets to commemorate your visit to 90°S, all of them, of course, originating somewhere else (probably Taiwan).

Beginning with the 1996-97 season, the US Antarctic Program will begin a transition away from selling souvenirs at its stations. Instead, t-shirts and other items will be sold through a catalog, a change made to save the expense of shipping the souvenirs to Antarctica and storing them at the stations. Eventually, program administrators hope to sell only smaller articles such as postcards and pins at the stations.

But a more unique souvenir can be obtained simply by using an ice ax to take a chip off the world's largest block of ice, the polar plateau. Some Antarcticans are fond of sipping their old Scotch on *very* old rocks.

Appendix: The Antarctic Treaty

The Antarctic Treaty was made on December 1, 1959, and came into force June 23, 1961.

TEXT OF THE ANTARCTIC TREATY

The Governments of Argentina, Australia, Belgium, Chile, the French Republic, Japan, New Zealand, Norway, the Union of South Africa, the Union of Soviet Socialist Republics, the United Kingdom of Great Britain and Northern Ireland, and the United States of America,

Recognizing that it is in the interest of all mankind that Antarctica shall continue for ever to be used exclusively for peaceful purposes and shall not become the scene or object of international discord;

Acknowledging the substantial contributions to scientific knowledge resulting from international cooperation in scientific investigation in Antarctica;

Convinced that the establishment of a firm foundation for the continuation and development of such cooperation on the basis of freedom of scientific investigation in Antarctica as applied during the International Geophysical Year accords with the interests of science and the progress of all mankind;

Convinced also that a treaty ensuring the use of Antarctica for peaceful purposes only and the continuance of international harmony in Antarctica will further the purposes and principles embodied in the Charter of the United Nations;

Have agreed as follows:

ARTICLE I

1. Antarctica shall be used for peaceful purposes only. There shall be prohibited, inter alia, any measure of a military nature, such as the establishment of military bases and fortifications, the carrying out of military manoeuvres, as well as the testing of any type of weapon.

2. The present Treaty shall not prevent the use of military personnel or equipment for scientific research or for any other peaceful purpose.

ARTICLE II

Freedom of scientific investigation in Antarctica and cooperation toward that end, as applied during the International Geophysical Year, shall continue, subject to the provisions of the present Treaty.

ARTICLE III

1. In order to promote international cooperation in scientific investigation in Antarctica, as provided for in Article II of the present Treaty, the Contracting Parties agree that, to the greatest extent feasible and practicable:

(a) information regarding plans for scientific programs in Antarctica shall be exchanged to permit maximum economy of and efficiency of operations;

(b) scientific personnel shall be exchanged in Antarctica between expeditions and stations;

(c) scientific observations and results from Antarctica shall be exchanged and made freely available.

ARTICLE IV

1. Nothing contained in the present Treaty shall be interpreted as:

(a) a renunciation by any Contracting Party of previously asserted rights of or claims to territorial sovereignty in Antarctica;

(b) a renunciation or diminution by any Contracting Party of any basis of claim to territorial sovereignty in Antarctica which it may have whether as a result of its activities or those of its nationals in Antarctica, or otherwise;

(c) prejudicing the position of any Contracting Party as regards its recognition or non-recognition of any other State's rights of or claim or basis of claim to territorial sovereignty in Antarctica.

2. No acts or activities taking place while the present Treaty is in force shall constitute a basis for asserting, supporting or denying a claim to territorial sovereignty in Antarctica or create any rights of sovereignty in Antarctica. No new claim, or enlargement of an existing claim, to territorial sovereignty in Antarctica shall be asserted while the present Treaty is in force.

ARTICLE V

1. Any nuclear explosions in Antarctica and the disposal there of radioactive waste material shall be prohibited.

2. In the event of the conclusion of international agreements concerning the use of nuclear energy, including nuclear explosions and the disposal of radioactive waste material, to which all of the Contracting Parties whose representatives are entitled to participate in the meetings provided for under Article IX are parties, the rules established under such agreements shall apply in Antarctica.

ARTICLE VI

The provisions of the present Treaty shall apply to the area south of 60 deg.South Latitude, including all ice shelves, but nothing in the present Treaty shall prejudice or in any way affect the rights, or the exercise of the rights, of any State under international law with regard to the high seas within that area.

ARTICLE VII

1. In order to promote the objectives and ensure the observance of the provisions of the present Treaty, each Contracting Party whose representatives are entitled to participate in the meetings referred to in Article IX of the Treaty shall have the right to designate observers to carry out any inspection provided for by the present Article. Observers shall be nationals of the Contracting Parties which designate them. The names of observers shall be communicated to every other Contracting Party having the right to designate observers, and like notice shall be given of the termination of their appointment.

2. Each observer designated in accordance with the provisions of paragraph 1 of this Article shall have complete freedom of access at any time to any or all areas of Antarctica.

3. All areas of Antarctica, including all stations, installations and equipment within those areas, and all ships and aircraft at points of discharging or embarking cargoes or personnel in Antarctica, shall be open at all times to inspection by any observers designated in accordance with paragraph 1 of this Article.

4. Aerial observation may be carried out at any time over any or all areas of Antarctica by any of the Contracting Parties having the right to designate observers.

5. Each Contracting Party shall, at the time when the present Treaty enters into force for it, inform the other Contracting Parties, and thereafter shall give them notice in advance, of

(a) all expeditions to and within Antarctica, on the part of its ships or nationals, and all expeditions to Antarctica organized in or proceeding from its territory;

(b) all stations in Antarctica occupied by its nationals; and

(c) any military personnel or equipment intended to be introduced by it into Antarctica subject to the conditions prescribed in paragraph 2 of Article I of the present Treaty.

ARTICLE VIII

1. In order to facilitate the exercise of their functions under the present Treaty, and

without prejudice to the respective positions of the Contracting Parties relating to jurisdiction over all other persons in Antarctica, observers designated under paragraph 1 of Article VII and scientific personnel exchanged under sub-paragraph 1(b) of Article III of the Treaty, and members of the staffs accompanying any such persons, shall be subject only to the jurisdiction of the Contracting Party of which they are nationals in respect of all acts or omissions occurring while they are in Antarctica for the purpose of exercising their functions.

2. Without prejudice to the provisions of paragraph 1 of this Article, and pending the adoption of measures in pursuance of subparagraph 1(e) of Article IX, the Contracting Parties concerned in any case of dispute with regard to the exercise of jurisdiction in Antarctica shall immediately consult together with a view to reaching a mutually acceptable solution.

ARTICLE IX

1. Representatives of the Contracting Parties named in the preamble to the present Treaty shall meet at the City of Canberra within two months after the date of entry into force of the Treaty, and thereafter at suitable intervals and places, for the purpose of exchanging information, consulting together on matters of common interest pertaining to Antarctica, and formulating and considering, and recommending to their Governments, measures in furtherance of the principles and objectives of the Treaty, including measures regarding:

(a) use of Antarctica for peaceful purposes only;

(b) facilitation of scientific research in Antarctica;

(c) facilitation of international scientific cooperation in Antarctica;

(d) facilitation of the exercise of the rights of inspection provided for in Article VII of the Treaty;

(e) questions relating to the exercise of jurisdiction in Antarctica;

(f) preservation and conservation of living resources in Antarctica.

2. Each Contracting Party which has become a party to the present Treaty by accession under Article XIII shall be entitled to appoint representatives to participate in the meetings referred to in paragraph 1 of the present Article, during such times as that Contracting Party demonstrates its interest in Antarctica by conducting substantial research activity there, such as the establishment of a scientific station or the despatch of a scientific expedition.

3. Reports from the observers referred to in Article VII of the present Treaty shall be transmitted to the representatives of the Contracting Parties participating in the meetings referred to in paragraph 1 of the present Article.

4. The measures referred to in paragraph 1 of this Article shall become effective when approved by all the Contracting Parties whose representatives were entitled to participate in the meetings held to consider those measures.

5. Any or all of the rights established in the present Treaty may be exercised as from the date of entry into force of the Treaty whether or not any measures facilitating the exercise of such rights have been proposed, considered or approved as provided in this Article.

ARTICLE X

Each of the Contracting Parties undertakes to exert appropriate efforts, consistent with the Charter of the United Nations, to the end that no one engages in any activity in Antarctica contrary to the principles or purposes of the present Treaty.

ARTICLE XI

1. If any dispute arises between two or more of the Contracting Parties concerning the interpretation or application of the

present Treaty, those Contracting Parties shall consult among themselves with a view to having the dispute resolved by negotiation, inquiry, mediation, conciliation, arbitration, judicial settlement or other peaceful means of their own choice.

2. Any dispute of this character not so resolved shall, with the consent, in each case, of all parties to the dispute, be referred to the International Court of Justice for settlement; but failure to reach agreement on reference to the International Court shall not absolve parties to the dispute from the responsibility of continuing to seek to resolve it by any of the various peaceful means referred to in paragraph 1 of this Article.

ARTICLE XII

1.–(a) The present Treaty may be modified or amended at any time by unanimous agreement of the Contracting Parties whose representatives are entitled to participate in the meetings provided for under Article IX. Any such modification or amendment shall enter into force when the depositary Government has received notice from all such Contracting Parties that they have ratified it.

(b) Such modification or amendment shall thereafter enter into force as to any other Contracting Party when notice of ratification by it has been received by the depositary Government. Any such Contracting Party from which no notice of ratification is received within a period of two years from the date of entry into force of the modification or amendment in accordance with the provision of subparagraph 1(a) of this Article shall be deemed to have withdrawn from the present Treaty on the date of the expiration of such period.

2.–(a) If after the expiration of thirty years from the date of entry into force of the present Treaty, any of the Contracting Parties whose representatives are entitled to participate in the meetings provided for under Article IX so requests by a communication addressed to the depositary Government, a Conference of all the Contracting Parties shall be held as soon as practicable to review the operation of the Treaty.

(b) Any modification or amendment to the present Treaty which is approved at such a Conference by a majority of the Contracting Parties there represented, including a majority of those whose representatives are entitled to participate in the meetings provided for under Article IX, shall be communicated by the depositary Government to all Contracting Parties immediately after the termination of the Conference and shall enter into force in accordance with the provisions of paragraph 1 of the present Article.

(c) If any such modification or amendment has not entered into force in accordance with the provisions of subparagraph 1(a) of this Article within a period of two years after the date of its communication to all the Contracting Parties,any Contracting Party may at any time after the expiration of that period give notice to the depositary Government of its withdrawal from the present Treaty; and such withdrawal shall take effect two years after the receipt of the notice by the depositary Government.

ARTICLE XIII

1. The present Treaty shall be subject to ratification by the signatory States. It shall be open for accession by any State which is a Member of the United Nations, or by any other State which may be invited to accede to the Treaty with the consent of all the Contracting Parties whose representatives are entitled to participate in the meetings provided for under Article IX of the Treaty.

2. Ratification of or accession to the present Treaty shall be effected by each State in accordance with its constitutional processes.

3. Instruments of ratification and instruments of accession shall be deposited with the Government of the United States of America, hereby designated as the depositary Government.

4. The depositary Government shall inform all signatory and acceding States of the date of each deposit of an instrument of ratification or accession, and the date of entry into force of the Treaty and of any modification or amendment thereto.

5. Upon the deposit of instruments of ratification by all the signatory States, the present Treaty shall enter into force for those States and for States which have deposited instruments of accession. Thereafter the Treaty shall enter into force for any acceding State upon the deposit of its instruments of accession.

6. The present Treaty shall be registered by the depositary Government pursuant to Article 102 of the Charter of the United Nations.

ARTICLE XIV

The present Treaty, done in the English, French, Russian and Spanish languages, each version being equally authentic, shall be deposited in the archives of the Government of the United States of America, which shall transmit duly certified copies thereof to the Governments of the signatory and acceding States.

In witness thereof, the undersigned Plenipotentiaries, duly authorized, have signed the present Treaty.

Done at Washington this first day of December, one thousand nine hundred and fifty-nine.

Antarctic Treaty Parties

Country, Date Ratified or Acceded to Treaty
Argentina, June 23, 1961
Australia, June 23, 1961
Austria, August 25, 1987
Belgium, July 26, 1960
Brazil, May 16, 1975
Bulgaria, September 11, 1978
Canada, May 4, 1988
Chile, June 23, 1961
China, June 8, 1983
Colombia, January 31, 1989
Cuba, August 16, 1984
Czech Republic, June 14, 1962[1]
Dem People's Rep of Korea, January 21, 1987
Denmark, May 20, 1965
Ecuador, September 15, 1987
Finland, May 15, 1984
France, September 16, 1960
Germany, February 5, 1979 [2]
Greece, January 8, 1987
Guatemala, July 31, 1991
Hungary, January 27, 1984
India, August 19, 1983
Italy, March 18, 1981
Japan, August 4, 1960
Netherlands, March 30, 1967
New Zealand, November 1, 1960
Norway, August 24, 1960
Papua New Guinea, March 16, 1981
Peru, April 10, 1981
Poland, June 8, 1961
Rep of Korea, November 28, 1986
Romania, September 15, 1971
Russian Federation, November 2, 1960 [3]
Slovak Republic, June 14, 1962 [1]
South Africa, June 21, 1960
Spain, March 31, 1982
Sweden, April 24, 1984
Switzerland, November 15, 1990
Turkey, January 24, 1995
Ukraine, October 28, 1992 [4]
United Kingdom, May 31, 1960
United States, August 18, 1960
Uruguay, January 11, 1980

Notes:
1. The Czech and Slovak Republics inherited Czechoslovakia's obligations; Czechoslovakia ratified the Treaty on June 14, 1962.
2. The German Democratic Republic united with the Federal Republic of Germany on October 2, 1990; the GDR had acceded to the Treaty on November 19, 1974.
3. Following the dissolution of the USSR, Russia assumed the rights and obligations of being a party to the Treaty.
4. Ukraine has asserted that it has succeeded to the Treaty following the dissolution of the USSR.

Glossary

ablation The loss of snow or ice by melting or evaporation.
anchor ice Submerged ice which is attached to the sea bottom.
Antarctic 10 A man – or more often, a woman – who is described as being quite beautiful in Antarctica, but 'just a plane ride away from being ordinary.'
Antarctic Convergence The region where the colder Antarctic seas meet the warmer waters of the northern oceans; also called the Polar Front.
apple A small round red prefabricated hut used in Australian government field camps in Antarctica; by adding additional panels to make an apple hut larger, you get 'melons,' 'zucchinis' and 'cucumbers.'

bag drag (US) A designated time before leaving McMurdo station when station members' luggage is put on a pallet and weighed for loading onto departing aircraft.
banana belt A warmer part of Antarctica, especially the Antarctic Peninsula.
beachmaster A large dominant male seal who guards – and breeds with – a harem (qv) on a breeding beach.
beaker An American nickname for scientists.
bergy bit A piece of floating ice rising one to five meters out of the water.
Big Eye A period of sleeplessness caused most often by the 24-hour daylight of Antarctic summertime, but also by the 24-hour darkness of winter.
blat (British) To shoot, with either a camera or a gun.
blegs (British) Bits of dirt on transparencies or photos.
blinder (British) An astonishing act of foresight, a smart move.
blizz static Electric charge that builds up because of the dry atmosphere, high winds and blowing snow in a blizzard.
blow A blizzard.
boffin An Australian nickname for scientists.
BOLOW (Australian) Burnt-Out Left-Over Winterer.
bondu (British) An anonymous or featureless country.
bondu-bashing Travelling over bondu (qv), cross-country traveling.
brash ice The wreckage of larger pieces of ice.
bummock A submariner term for a stalactite-like ice formation hanging down from beneath pack ice; an underwater hummock (qv).

cairn A pyramid of stones or pieces of ice or cut snow raised as a marker.
calve The breaking off of an iceberg from a glacier or ice shelf.
camp Falkland Islands term for the countryside; all areas outside of Stanley.
chompers (British) Snacks.
collapso (British) Cheap wine.
crack Crevasse.
creche A group of penguin chicks attended by a small group of adults while most of the parents are out at sea hunting for food.

dieso (Australian) A mechanic.
donga (Australian) Individual bedroom at Antarctic station.
'doo (British) Skidoo; snowmobile.
DV Distinguished Visitor; bureaucratic parlance for politician or bureaucrat visiting The Ice through the auspices of a national research program.

ECW gear (US) Extreme Cold Weather gear.

fast ice Sea ice attached to the shore or between grounded bergs.
FID A British Antarctic worker (this term is still in use today, even though the Falkland Islands Dependencies Survey from which

the name derives was long ago replaced by the name British Antarctic Survey).
firn – *See* névé.
frazil ice Needle-shaped ice crystals forming a slush in the water.
freezer suit A windproof insulated jump-suit.
frost smoke Condensed water vapor that forms a mist over open water in cold weather.

gash (British) Rubbish, trash.
GPS Global Positioning System; a satellite-based system that uses triangulation to determine geographic location to within 10 meters.
grease ice Ice in a later stage of freezing than frazil ice; takes its name from the matte appearance it gives to the sea.
growler Small – and therefore difficult to see or pick up on radar – piece of ice awash with waves and thus a hazard to shipping.
guano (1) Bird excrement. (2) The remains of whale's meat and bone after oil extraction, which was dried and turned into meal.

Hägglunds A Swedish-made tracked vehicle used at many Antarctic stations.
harem A group of female seals jealously guarded on a breeding beach by a beach-master (qv).
helo American station lingo for helicopter (never 'chopper').
homer Home-brewed beer popular on Australian stations.
hoosh Thick hot stew made usually of pemmican (qv) crumbled dry sledging biscuits (qv), and boiled water, eaten on early expeditions.
house mouse A duty, rotated among members of South Pole Station, consisting of cleaning up common areas.
hummock An area where ice floes have rafted, or piled atop one another, often reaching heights of several yards.

IAATO International Association of Antarctica Tour Operators.
ice blink A lighter, brighter section on the underside of clouds, caused by light reflected up from ice below; used by early explorers to avoid the pack ice.
ice window The short summer season when the fast ice has broken out, allowing ships to near the Antarctic coast.
IGY The International Geophysical Year, which ran from July 1, 1957, to December 31, 1958.
INMARSAT International Maritime Satellite, used to make telephone calls and send faxes and email aboard ship.

jobbie (Australian) Seal feces.
jolly (Australian) A pleasure or sightseeing trip, often made by helicopter.

katabatic Gravity-driven wind caused by colder, heavier air rushing down from the polar plateau.
knot One nautical mile (1.15 statute miles or 1.85 km) per hour.
Kodachrome poisoning A phenomenon experienced by heavily-photographed Antarctic wildlife such as Adélie penguins; also known as Kodak poisoning or Kodak attack.

LARC Lighter Amphibious Resupply Cargo, a five-ton combination boat/truck used by Australia to service ships and bases; their drivers are known as LARCies.
lead A section of open water within pack ice between large floes.

mank (British) *v* To turn bad or deteriorate (said of weather).
manky (British) *adj* Bad or foul (said of weather).
me-pickie (Australian) A Photo of oneself.
moon dog A 'false moon,' or paraselena; an optical phenomenon caused by the refraction of moonlight by ice crystals suspended in the air; cf 'sun dog.'
moraine Rock debris moved and deposited by a glacier; lateral (at the sides); medial (at the center); or terminal (at the foot).

nelly A member of either of the two species of giant petrel.
NGO Non-governmental organization.
nilas Thin crust of floating ice that bends

with waves but does not break; the darker its appearance, the thinner the nilas is.
nunatak A mountain or large piece of rock sticking up through an ice sheet.
névé Literally, 'last year's snow.' Hard granular snow on the upper part of a glacier that hasn't yet turned to ice.

oasis An area of bare rock without ice or snow caused by a retreating or thinning ice sheet and ablation of any snow that does fall; examples include the Bunger Hills, Dry Valleys, Larsemann Hills and Vestfold Hills.
old ice Sea ice that is more than two years old; up to 10 feet thick.

pancake ice Discs of young ice, formed when waves jostle them against one another, rounding their edges.
pax Passengers.
pemmican Ground dried meat mixed with equal parts lard. This concentrated food was a primary ration on early expeditions.
polar pyramid A double-skinned pyramid-shaped tent used in field work in Antarctica.
polynya An area of open water within the pack ice that remains free of ice throughout the winter.

quad, quike A four-wheeled motorized vehicle.

Red Shed The nickname given to the large living quarters buildings on the three Australian scientific bases in Antarctica.
rotten ice Older ice that has severly weakened prior to melting.
RTA (Australian) *v* To Return To Australia supplies, materials or specimens.

sastrugi Furrows or irregularities formed on a snow surface by the wind.
SCAR Scientific Committee on Antarctic Research, originally the Special Committee on Antarctic Research.
scradge (British) Food.
shuga Spongy white ice lumps, formed from grease ice or slush.
skijouring Being pulled on skis by one or more dogs in harness; no longer possible in Antarctica since dogs were banned.
sledging biscuits Dry cracker-like food usually made from wheat.
slot A crevasse; to 'go slotting' is to practice crevasse rescue techniques, while 'to get slotted' is to fall into a crevasse unintentionally.
slushy (Australian) Kitchen hand, a rotating duty.
smoko (Australian, British) Tea break.
snow blindness A debilitatingly-painful inflammation of the eyes, with a resultant (but usually temporary) loss of sight; caused by the glare of sunlight reflected off ice or snow.
snow bridge The crust-like lid that often covers a crevasse; formed when windblown snow builds up on the leeward wall of the crevasse.
souvenir *v* To remove (steal) artifacts or natural history specimens; the term is usually used to refer to the theft of historic items from an early explorer's hut for a personal collection, an act performed mainly by staff from nearby scientific stations, as they were the only people who had access to these huts.
SPA Specially Protected Area; may not be entered without a permit.
SSSI Site of Special Scientific Interest; may not be entered without a permit.
starchy A thrush common to the Tristan da Cunha group.
sublimate *v* To pass from the solid state directly to vapor.
sundog 'False sun,' or more correctly, a parhelion; an optical phenomenon caused by the refraction of sunlight by tiny ice crystals, themselves known as 'diamond dust,' suspended in the air.
sun pillar Another solar phenomenon, this one a vertical shaft of light from the rising or setting sun, also caused by ice crystals in the atmosphere.

tabular berg Iceberg with straight sides and a flat top, indicating that it has calved relatively recently.

Terres Australes et Antarctiques France's subantarctic islands and territorial claim in Antarctica, Terre Adélie.

The Crud A flu-like illness that strikes the wintering-over crew of an Antarctic station when a new group arrives, caused by the weakening of the winterers' immune systems, which have not been stimulated by any germs for many months.

The Ice Antarctica.

tide crack A crack separating sea ice from the shore, caused by the rise and fall of the tide; these are often to wide to cross safely.

trypot or **tryworks** A cauldron for boiling down the blubber of whales, seals or penguins into oil.

ventile Windproof outer clothing.

wallow A muddy, noxious-smelling hollow made by seals, especially elephant seals.

water sky A dark section on the underside of clouds, indicating open water below; used by early explorers to help penetrate the pack ice.

whiteout A condition in which overcast sky descends to horizon, causing a blurring between ground and sky and eliminating all points of perspective; described by one pilot as being 'like flying in a bowl of milk.'

Winfly Winter Fly-In; flights made by the US Antarctic Program in mid-August to bring supplies and new personnel to McMurdo station to help prepare it for the summer season.

wobbler (British) A panic attack, as in 'to throw a wobbler.'

WYSSA (Australian) A message sent to or received from home, from code letters used in telex messages meaning All My Love Darling.

zodiac An inflatable rubber dinghy powered by an outboard engine and used for making shore landings.

NOTE: Several of these entries are taken from *A Dictionary of Antarctic English*, compiled by Australian Bernadette Hince.

Index

MAPS

TEXT

Map references are in **bold** type.

ANTARCTIC ACRONYMS

ANI – Adventure Network International
ATS – Antarctic Treaty System
ANARE – Australian National Antarctic Research Expeditions
CCAMLR – Convention for the Conservation of Antarctic Marine Living Resources
CCAS – Convention for the Conservation of Antarctic Seals
CRAMRA – Convention for the Regulation of Antarctic Mineral Resource Activities
IAATO – International Association of Antarctica Tour Operators
IGY – International Geophysical Year
IWC – International Whaling Commission
SCAR – Scientific Committee for Antarctic Research
SSSI – Site of Special Scientific Interest
SANAE – South African National Antarctic Expedition
SPA – Specially Protected Area

PLANET TALK

Lonely Planet's FREE quarterly newsletter

We love hearing from you and think you'd like to hear from us.
When... is the right time to see reindeer in Finland?
Where... can you hear the best palm-wine music in Ghana?
How... do you get from Asunción to Areguá by steam train?
What... is the best way to see India?

For the answer to these and many other questions read PLANET TALK.

Every issue is packed with up-to-date travel news and advice including:

- a letter from Lonely Planet founders Tony and Maureen Wheeler
- travel diary from a Lonely Planet author–find out what it's really like out on the road
- feature article on an important and topical travel issue
- a selection of recent letters from our readers
- the latest travel news from all over the world
- details on Lonely Planet's new and forthcoming releases

To join our mailing list contact any Lonely Planet office .

Also available: Lonely Planet T-shirts. 100% heavyweight cotton (S, M, L, XL)

LONELY PLANET ONLINE

Get the latest travel information before you leave or while you're on the road

Whether you've just begun planning your next trip, or you're chasing down specific info on currency regulations or visa requirements, check out the Lonely Planet World Wide Web site for up-to-the-minute travel information.

As well as travel profiles of your favorite destinations (including interactive maps and full-color photos), you'll find current reports from our army of researchers and other travelers, updates on health and visas, travel advisories, and the ecological and political issues you need to be aware of as you travel.

There's an online travelers' forum (the Thorn Tree) where you can share your experiences of life on the road, meet travel companions and ask other travelers for their recommendations and advice. We also have plenty of links to other Web sites useful to independent travelers.

With tens of thousands of visitors a month, the Lonely Planet Web site is one of the most popular on the Internet and has won a number of awards including GNN's Best of the Net travel award.

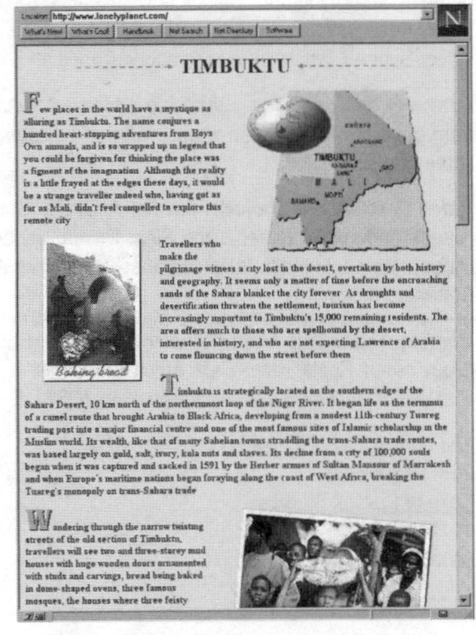

http://www.lonelyplanet.com

LONELY PLANET TRAVEL ATLASES

Lonely Planet has long been famous for the number and quality of its guidebook maps. Now we've gone one step further and in conjunction with Steinhart Katzir Publishers produced a handy companion series: Lonely Planet travel atlases–maps of a country produced in book form.

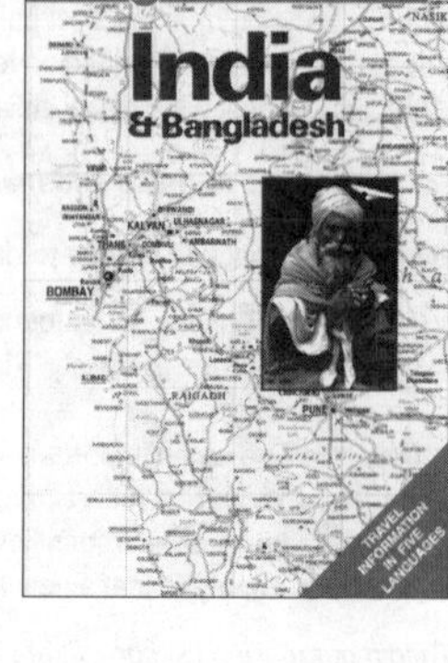

Unlike other maps, which look good but lead travelers astray, our travel atlases have been researched on the road by Lonely Planet's experienced team of writers. All details are carefully checked to ensure the atlas corresponds with the equivalent Lonely Planet guidebook.

The handy atlas format means no holes, wrinkles, torn sections or constant folding and unfolding. These atlases can survive long periods on the road, unlike cumbersome fold-out maps. The comprehensive index ensures easy reference.

- full-color throughout
- maps researched and checked by Lonely Planet authors
- place names correspond with Lonely Planet guidebooks –no confusing spelling differences
- legend and traveling information in English, French, German, Japanese and Spanish
- size: 230 x 160 mm

Available now:

Thailand; India & Bangladesh; Vietnam; Zimbabwe, Botswana & Namibia

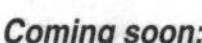

Coming soon:

Chile; Egypt; Israel; Laos; Turkey

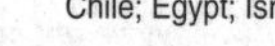

LONELY PLANET TV SERIES & VIDEOS

Lonely Planet travel guides have been brought to life on television screens around the world. Like our guides, the programs are based on the joy of independent travel, and look honestly at some of the most exciting, picturesque and frustrating places in the world. Each show is presented by one of three travelers from Australia, England or the USA and combines an innovative mixture of video, Super-8 film, atmospheric soundscapes and original music.

Videos of each episode–containing additional footage not shown on television–are available from good book and video shops, but the availability of individual videos varies with regional screening schedules.

Video destinations include: Alaska; Australia (Southeast); Brazil; Ecuador & the Galápagos Islands; Indonesia; Israel & the Sinai Desert; Japan; La Ruta Maya (Yucatán, Guatemala & Belize); Morocco; North India (Varanasi to the Himalaya); Pacific Islands; Vietnam; Zimbabwe, Botswana & Namibia.

Coming soon: The Arctic (Norway & Finland); Baja California; Chile & Easter Island; China (Southeast); Costa Rica; East Africa (Tanzania & Zanzibar); Great Barrier Reef (Australia); Jamaica; Papua New Guinea; the Rockies (USA); Syria & Jordan; Turkey.

The Lonely Planet TV series is produced by:
Pilot Productions
Duke of Sussex Studios
44 Uxbridge St
London W8 7TG UK

Lonely Planet videos are distributed by:
IVN Communications Inc
2246 Camino Ramon
California 94583, USA

107 Power Road, Chiswick
London W4 5PL UK

Music from the TV series is available on CD & cassette.
For ordering information contact your nearest Lonely Planet office.

LONELY PLANET JOURNEYS

JOURNEYS is a unique collection of travelers' tales–published by the company that understands travel better than anyone else. It is a series for anyone who has ever experienced–or dreamed of–the magical moment when they encountered a strange culture or saw a place for the first time. They are tales to read while you're planning a trip, while you're on the road or while you're in an armchair, in front of a fire.

JOURNEYS books will catch the spirit of a place, illuminate a culture, recount a crazy adventure, or introduce a fascinating way of life. They will always entertain, and always enrich the experience of travel.

ISLANDS IN THE CLOUDS

Travels in the Highlands of New Guinea

Isabella Tree

This is the fascinating account of a journey to the remote and beautiful Highlands of Papua New Guinea and Irian Jaya. The author travels with a PNG Highlander who introduces her to his intriguing and complex world. Islands in the Clouds is a thoughtful, moving book, full of insights into a region that is rarely noticed by the rest of the world.

'One of the most accomplished travel writers to appear on the horizon for many years . . . the dialogue is brilliant' **– Eric Newby**

LOST JAPAN

Alex Kerr

Lost Japan draws on the author's personal experiences of Japan over a period of 30 years. Alex Kerr takes his readers on a backstage tour: friendships with Kabuki actors, buying and selling art, studying calligraphy, exploring rarely visited temples and shrines . . . The Japanese edition of this book was awarded the 1994 Shincho Gakugei Literature Prize for the best work of non-fiction.

'This deeply personal witness to Japan's willful loss of its traditional culture is at the same time an immensely valuable evaluation of just what that culture was'

– Donald Richie of the Japan Times

THE GATES OF DAMASCUS

Lieve Joris

Translated by Sam Garrett

This best-selling book is a beautifully drawn portrait of day-to-day life in modern Syria. Through her intimate contact with local people, Lieve Joris draws us into the fascinating world that lies behind the gates of Damascus.

'A brilliant book . . . Not since Naguib Mahfouz has the everyday life of the modern Arab world been so intimately described' **– William Dalrymple**

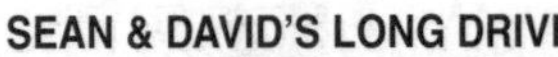

SEAN & DAVID'S LONG DRIVE

Sean Condon

Sean and David are young townies who have rarely strayed beyond city limits. One day, for no good reason, they set out to discover their homeland, and what follows is a wildly entertaining adventure that covers half of Australia. Sean Condon has written a hilarious, offbeat road book that mixes sharp insights with deadpan humor and outright lies.

'Funny, pithy, kitsch and surreal . . . This book will do for Australia what Chernobyl did for Kiev, but hey you'll laugh as the stereotypes go boom'

– Andrew Tuck, Time Out

LONELY PLANET PRODUCTS

Lonely Planet is known worldwide for publishing practical, reliable and no-nonsense travel information in our guides and on our web site. The Lonely Planet list covers just about every accessible part of the world. Currently there are eight series: *travel guides, shoestring guides, walking guides, city guides, phrasebooks, audio packs, travel atlases* and *Journeys*–a unique collection of travelers' tales.

EUROPE

Austria • Baltic States & Kaliningrad • Baltic States phrasebook • Britain • Central Europe on a shoestring • Central Europe phrasebook • Czech & Slovak Republics • Denmark • Dublin city guide • Eastern Europe on a shoestring • Eastern Europe phrasebook • Finland • France • Greece • Greek phrasebook • Hungary • Iceland, Greenland & the Faroe Islands • Ireland • Italy • Mediterranean Europe on a shoestring • Mediterranean Europe phrasebook • Paris city guide • Poland • Prague city guide • Russia, Ukraine & Belarus • Russian phrasebook • Scandinavian & Baltic Europe on a shoestring • Scandinavian Europe phrasebook • Slovenia • St Petersburg city guide • Switzerland • Trekking in Greece • Trekking in Spain • Ukrainian phrasebook • Vienna city guide • Walking in Switzerland • Western Europe on a shoestring • Western Europe phrasebook

NORTH AMERICA

Alaska • Backpacking in Alaska • Baja California • California & Nevada • Canada • Florida • Hawaii • Honolulu city guide • Los Angeles city guide • Mexico • Miami city guide • New England • New Orleans city guide • Pacific Northwest USA • Rocky Mountain States USA • San Francisco city guide • Southwest USA • USA phrasebook

CENTRAL AMERICA & THE CARIBBEAN

Central America on a shoestring • Costa Rica • Cuba • Eastern Caribbean • Guatemala, Belize & Yucatán: La Ruta Maya • Jamaica

SOUTH AMERICA

Antarctica • Argentina, Uruguay & Paraguay • Bolivia • Brazil • Brazilian phrasebook • Buenos Aires city guide • Chile & Easter Island • Colombia • Ecuador & the Galápagos Islands • Latin American Spanish phrasebook • Peru • Quechua phrasebook • Rio de Janeiro city guide • South America on a shoestring • Trekking in the Patagonian Andes • Venezuela

Travel Literature: Full Circle: A South American Journey

AFRICA

Arabic (Moroccan) phrasebook • Africa on a shoestring • Cape Town city guide • Central Africa • East Africa • Egypt & the Sudan • Ethiopian (Amharic) phrasebook • Kenya • Morocco • North Africa • South Africa, Lesotho & Swaziland • Swahili phrasebook • Trekking in East Africa • West Africa • Zimbabwe, Botswana & Namibia • Zimbabwe, Botswana & Namibia travel atlas

ISLANDS OF THE INDIAN OCEAN

Madagascar & Comoros • Maldives & Islands of the East Indian Ocean • Mauritius, Réunion & Seychelles

Also Available: Travel with Children • Traveller's Tales

MAIL ORDER

Lonely Planet products are distributed worldwide. They are also available by mail order from Lonely Planet, so if you have difficulty finding a title please write to us. North American and South American residents should write to Embarcadero West, 155 Filbert St, Suite 251, Oakland CA 94607, USA; European and African residents should write to 10 Barley Mow Passage, Chiswick, London W4 4PH; and residents of other countries to PO Box 617, Hawthorn, Victoria 3122, Australia.

NORTH-EAST ASIA

Beijing city guide • Cantonese phrasebook • Central Asia • China • Hong Kong city guide • Hong Kong, Macau & Canton • Japan • Japanese phrasebook • Japanese audio pack • Korea • Korean phrasebook • Mandarin phrasebook • Mongolia • Mongolian phrasebook • North-East Asia on a shoestring • Seoul city guide • Taiwan • Tibet • Tibet phrasebook • Tokyo city guide

Travel Literature: Lost Japan

MIDDLE EAST & CENTRAL ASIA

Arab Gulf States • Arabic (Egyptian) phrasebook • Central Asia • Iran • Israel • Istanbul city guide • Jordan & Syria • Middle East • Turkey • Turkish phrasebook • Trekking in Turkey • Yemen

Travel Literature: The Gates of Damascus

INDIAN SUBCONTINENT

Bengali phrasebook • Bangladesh • Delhi city guide • Hindi/Urdu phrasebook • India • India & Bangladesh travel atlas • Indian Himalaya • Karakoram Highway • Kashmir, Ladakh & Zanskar • Nepal • Nepali phrasebook • Pakistan • Rajasthan • Sri Lanka • Sri Lanka phrasebook • Trekking in the Indian Himalaya • Trekking in the Karakoram & Hindukush • Trekking in the Nepal Himalaya

Travel Literature: Shopping for Buddhas

SOUTH-EAST ASIA

Bali & Lombok • Bangkok city guide • Burmese phrasebook • Cambodia • Ho Chi Minh city guide • Indonesia • Indonesian phrasebook • Indonesian audio pack • Jakarta city guide • Java • Laos • Lao phrasebook • Malay phrasebook • Malaysia, Singapore & Brunei • Myanmar (Burma) • Philippines • Pilipino phrasebook • Singapore city guide • South-East Asia on a shoestring • Thailand • Thai phrasebook • Thailand travel atlas • Thai audio pack • Thai Hill Tribes phrasebook • Vietnam • Vietnamese phrasebook • Vietnam travel atlas

AUSTRALIA & THE PACIFIC

Australia • Australian phrasebook • Bushwalking in Australia • Bushwalking in Papua New Guinea • Fiji • Fijian phrasebook • Islands of Australia's Great Barrier Reef • Melbourne city guide • Micronesia • New Caledonia • New South Wales & the ACT • New Zealand • Northern Territory • Outback Australia • Papua New Guinea • Papua New Guinea phrasebook • Queensland • Rarotonga & the Cook Islands • Samoa • Solomon Islands • South Australia • Sydney city guide • Tahiti & French Polynesia • Tasmania • Tonga • Tramping in New Zealand • Vanuatu • Victoria • Western Australia

Travel Literature: Islands in the Clouds • Sean & David's Long Drive

THE LONELY PLANET STORY

Lonely Planet published its first book in 1973 in response to the numerous 'How did you do it?' questions Maureen and Tony Wheeler were asked after driving, bussing, hitching, sailing and railing their way from England to Australia.

Written at a kitchen table and hand collated, trimmed and stapled, Across Asia on the Cheap became an instant local best seller, inspiring thoughts of another book.

Eighteen months in South-East Asia resulted in their second guide, South-East Asia on a shoestring, which they put together in a backstreet Chinese hotel in Singapore in 1975. The 'yellow bible', as it quickly became known to backpackers around the world, soon became the guide to the region. It has sold well over half a million copies and is now in its 8th edition, still retaining its familiar yellow cover.

Today there are 200 titles, including travel guides, walking guides, language kits & phrasebooks, travel atlases and travel literature. The company is one of the largest travel publishers in the world. Although Lonely Planet initially specialized in guides to Asia, we now cover most regions of the world, including the Pacific, North America, South America, Africa, the Middle East and Europe.

The emphasis continues to be on travel for independent travelers. Tony and Maureen still travel for several months of each year and play an active part in the writing, updating and quality control of Lonely Planet's guides.

They have been joined by over 50 authors and 155 staff at our offices in Melbourne (Australia), Oakland (USA), London (UK) and Paris (France). Travelers themselves also make a valuable contribution to the guides through the feedback we receive in thousands of letters each year.

The people at Lonely Planet strongly believe that travelers can make a positive contribution to the countries they visit, both through their appreciation of the countries' culture, wildlife and natural features, and through the money they spend. In addition, the company makes a direct contribution to the countries and regions it covers. Since 1986 a percentage of the income from each book has been donated to ventures such as famine relief in Africa; aid projects in India; agricultural projects in Central America; Greenpeace's efforts to halt French nuclear testing in the Pacific; and Amnesty International.

'I hope we send the people out with the right attitude about travel. You realize when you travel that there are so many different perspectives about the world, so we hope these books will make people more interested in what they see. These are guidebooks, but you can't really guide people. All you can do is point them in the right direction.'

– Tony Wheeler

LONELY PLANET PUBLICATIONS

Australia
PO Box 617, Hawthorn 3122, Victoria
☎ (03) 9819 1877 fax (03) 9819 6459
e-mail talk2us@lonelyplanet.com.au

USA
Embarcadero West, 155 Filbert Street, Suite 251, Oakland, CA 94607
☎ (510) 893 8555, TOLL FREE (800) 275 8555
fax (510) 893 8563
e-mail info@lonelyplanet.com

UK
10 Barley Mow Passage, Chiswick, London W4 4PH
☎ (0181) 742 3161 fax (0181) 742 2772
e-mail 100413.3551@compuserve.com

France
71 bis rue du Cardinal Lemoine, 75005 Paris
☎ 1 44 32 06 20 fax 1 46 34 72 55
e-mail 100560.415@compuserve.com

World Wide Web: http://www.lonelyplanet.com